12e

American Government

Institutions & Policies

Brief Version

James Q. Wilson
University of California, Los Angeles, emeritus
Pepperdine University
Boston College

John J. Dilulio, Jr.
University of Pennsylvania

Meena Bose
Hofstra University

 CENGAGE
Learning·

Australia · Brazil · Japan · Korea · Mexico · Singapore · Spain · United Kingdom · United States

CENGAGE
Learning

American Government, Brief Version, twelfth Edition
James Q. Wilson, John J. DiIulio, Jr., Meena Bose

Product Team Manager: Carolyn Merrill

Content Developer:
Ohlinger Publishing Services

Associate Content Developer: Amy Bither

Product Assistant: Abigail Hess

Senior Media Developer: Laura Hildebrand

Marketing Manager: Valerie Hartman

Senior Content Project Manager:
Catherine G. DiMassa

Senior Art Director: Linda May

Print Buyer: Fola Orekoya

IP Analyst: Alex Ricciardi

IP Project Manager: Farah Fard

Production Service:
Integra Software Services Pvt. Ltd.

Compositor: Integra Software Services Pvt. Ltd.

Text Designer: Chris Miller Design

Cover Designer: Chris Miller Design

Cover Image: MLADEN ANTONOV/AFP/ Getty Images

For product information and technology assistance, contact us at
Cengage Learning Customer & Sales Support, 1-800-354-9706

For permission to use material from this text or product, submit all requests online at **www.cengage.com/permissions**. Further permissions questions can be emailed to **permissionrequest@cengage.com**.

Library of Congress Control Number: 2014943042

Student Edition:

ISBN-13: 978-1-305-10900-1

ISBN-10: 1-305-10900-7

Cengage Learning
20 Channel Center Street
Boston, MA 02210
USA

Cengage Learning is a leading provider of customized learning solutions with office locations around the globe, including Singapore, the United Kingdom, Australia, Mexico, Brazil and Japan. Locate your local office at **international.cengage.com/region**.

Cengage Learning products are represented in Canada by Nelson Education, Ltd.

For your course and learning solutions, visit **www.cengage.com**.

Purchase any of our products at your local college store or at our preferred online store **www.cengagebrain.com**.

Instructors: Please visit **login.cengage.com** and log in to access instructor-specific resources.

Printed in the United States of America
Print Number: 01   Print Year: 2014

Brief Contents

Contents

Preface

We wrote *American Government: Institutions and Policies, Brief Version* not only to explain to students how the federal government works, but also to clarify how its institutions have developed over time and describe their effects on public policy. Within this distinguishing framework, we explain the history of Congress, the presidency, the judiciary, and the bureaucracy because the politics we see today are different from those we would have seen a few decades ago. And, of course, change never stops: in another decade, federal politics may be very different from what they are today.

American Government: Institutions and Policies, Brief Version is written around certain key ideas that help students understand, not simply American government, but the reasons why the government in this country is different from those in other democracies. These ideas are the U.S. Constitution, America's adversarial political culture, and a commitment to freedom and limited government. This book is an attempt to explain and give the historical and practical reasons for these differences.

And as always, the book is thoroughly revised to excite students' interest about the latest in American politics and encourage critical thinking.

Special Features

- **Learning Objectives** open and close each chapter, serving as a road map to the book's key concepts and helping students assess their understanding.

- **Now and Then** chapter-opening vignettes offer attention-grabbing looks at a particular topic in the past and in the present, reinforcing the historical emphasis of the text and applying these experiences to the students' lives. These will help sensitize students to the still-unfolding saga of continuity and change.

- New **Constitutional Connections** features raise analytical issues from the constitutional debates that remain relevant today.

- **Landmark Cases** provide brief descriptions of important Supreme Court cases.

- **How We Compare** features show how other nations around the world structure their governments and policies in relation to the United States and ask students to think about the results of these differences.

- **How Things Work** boxes summarize key concepts and important facts that facilitate students' comprehension of the political process.

- **To Learn More** sections close each chapter with carefully selected Web resources and classic and contemporary suggested readings to further assist students in learning about American politics.

New to This Edition

Updates throughout the text reflect the latest scholarship and current events. The most current information available has been incorporated into the narrative, including the 2012 Supreme Court ruling upholding the health care law; the 2014 elections; budget battles and the sequestration of funds; ongoing debates about immigration, gay marriage, and other key issues in American politics; and foreign-policy decisions on Afghanistan, the Middle East, and North Korea. Many of the book's tables, figures, citations, and photographs are updated as well. The book has been streamlined and reorganized to introduce James Q. Wilson's politics of the policy process classification in Chapter 1, so that students may evaluate policy dynamics throughout the rest of the text.

Additionally, significant chapter-by-chapter changes have been made as follows:

- **Chapter 1:** *American Government's* classic politics of policymaking framework is now introduced in Chapter 1, along with a new feature titled Constitutional Connections.

- **Chapter 2:** This chapter includes an expanded discussion of the views of John Locke and Thomas Hobbes and how their philosophies influenced the Framers. The Constitutional Connections feature discusses women's rights and the Constitution.

- **Chapter 3:** The opening vignette looks at the Antifederalists' opposition to the Constitution on the grounds that it gave too much power to the national government and how that has played out today. The chapter includes a new discussion on federalism and health care reform, with a Constitutional Connections feature on States and Health Exchanges. The Landmark Cases: Federal-State Relations box has been greatly expanded.

- **Chapter 4:** The Constitutional Connections feature discusses the Supreme Court's "selective incorporation" process of applying the Bill of Rights to the states.

- **Chapter 5:** The opening vignette explores how civil rights have changed over the years and a new section on Race and Civil Rights opens the chapter. The chapter includes updated coverage of affirmative action, same-sex marriage (including the Supreme Court's 2012 Defense of Marriage Act [DOMA] ruling), and other gay rights issues. The Constitutional Connections feature examines the evolution of race as a "suspect classification" in American politics. Rev. Dr. Martin Luther King, Jr.'s "I Have a Dream" speech now appears in the appendix.

- **Chapter 6:** Updated public opinion statistics are included throughout the chapter. The Constitutional Connections feature examines how public opinion influences policy making. The chapter also includes expanded coverage of the role of electronic media in American politics.

- **Chapter 7:** The Constitutional Connections feature discusses how perspectives on political parties have evolved since the founding of the American republic.

- **Chapter 8:** The chapter is updated to include the 2012 elections. The Constitutional Connections feature looks at variations in state voting laws.

- **Chapter 9:** The chapter is updated to incorporate the 113th Congress. The Constitutional Connections feature discusses the Framers' expectations for the new Congress.

- **Chapter 10:** The chapter is updated to incorporate governance in the Obama administration. The Constitutional Connections feature discusses how the Framers viewed presidential power.

- **Chapter 11:** The Constitutional Connections feature discusses how, if at all, the federal bureaucracy fits into the constitutional system of checks and balances.

- **Chapter 12:** The Constitutional Connections feature discusses how Congress uses the "Exceptions" clause in the Constitution to restrict the appellate jurisdiction of the Supreme Court.

- **Chapter 13:** This new Domestic Policy chapter discusses Social Welfare Policy and Environmental Policy.

- **Chapter 14:** This chapter includes updated information about foreign-policy decisions on Afghanistan, the Middle East, and North Korea, as well as a new figure on the public's view of the United States as a world leader.

- **Chapter 15:** The closing chapter presents a portrait of the current political landscape and asks readers to consider the future of American government using the tools they have acquired. A new How We Compare feature looks at deficit spending in America and Europe.

Resources

STUDENTS Access your *American Government: Brief Version, 12e* resources by visiting www. cengagebrain.com/shop/isbn/9781305109001
If you purchased CourseReader access with your book, enter your access code and click "**Register**." You can also purchase the book's resources here separately through the "**Study Tools**" tab or access the free companion website through the "**Free Materials**" tab.

INSTRUCTORS Access your *American Government: Brief Version, 12e* resources via www.cengage. com/login.
Log in using your Cengage Learning single sign-on user name and password, or create a new instructor account by clicking on "**New Faculty User**" and following the instructions.

Instructor Companion Website for *American Government: Brief Version, 12e*
ISBN: 978-1-305-10902-5
This Instructor Companion Website is an all-in-one multimedia online resource for class preparation, presentation, and testing. Accessible through Cengage.com/login with your faculty account, you will find available for download: book-specific Microsoft® PowerPoint® presentations; a Test Bank compatible with multiple learning management systems; an Instructor's Manual; Microsoft® PowerPoint® Image Slides; and a JPEG Image Library.

The Test Bank, offered in Blackboard, Moodle, Desire2Learn, Canvas, and Angel formats, contains Learning Objective-specific multiple-choice and essay questions for each chapter. Import the test bank into your LMS to edit and manage questions, and to create tests.

The Instructor's Manual contains chapter-specific learning objectives, an outline, key terms with definitions, and a chapter summary. Additionally, the Instructor's Manual features a critical thinking question, lecture launching suggestion, and an in-class activity for each learning objective.

The Microsoft® PowerPoint® presentations are ready-to-use, visual outlines of each chapter. These presentations are easily customized for your lectures and offered along with chapter-specific Microsoft® PowerPoint® Image Slides and JPEG Image Libraries. Access the Instructor Companion Website at www.cengage.com/login.

Student Companion Website for *American Government: Brief Version, 12e*
ISBN: 978-1-305-10903-2
This free companion website for *American Government: Brief Version, 12e* is accessible through cengagebrain. com and allows students access to chapter-specific interactive learning tools including flashcards, glossaries, and more.

Cognero for *American Government: Brief Version, 12e* — for instructors only
ISBN: 978-1-305-10906-3
Cengage Learning Testing Powered by Cognero is a flexible, online system that allows you to author, edit, and manage test bank content from multiple Cengage Learning solutions, create multiple test versions in an instant, and deliver tests from your LMS, your classroom, or wherever you want. The test bank for *American Government: Brief Version, 12e* contains Learning Objective-specific multiple-choice and essay questions for each chapter.

 **CourseReader for American Government**
CourseReader 0-30 Instant Access Code: 978-1-111-47997-8
CourseReader 0-30 Printed Access Code: 978-1-111-47995-4
CourseReader: American Government allows instructors to create your reader, your way, in just minutes. This affordable, fully customizable online reader provides access to thousands of permissions-cleared

readings, articles, primary sources, and audio and video selections from the regularly-updated Gale research library database. This easy-to-use solution allows you to search for and select just the material you want for your courses. Each selection opens with a descriptive introduction to provide context, and concludes with critical-thinking and multiple-choice questions to reinforce key points. CourseReader is loaded with convenient tools like highlighting, printing, note-taking, and downloadable PDFs and MP3 audio files for each reading. CourseReader is the perfect complement to any Political Science course. It can be bundled with your current textbook, sold alone, or integrated into your learning management system. CourseReader 0-30 allows access to up to 30 selections in the reader. Instructors can contact your Cengage learning consultant for details. Students should only purchase CourseReader if assigned by their instructor.

Election 2014 Supplement
ISBN: 978-1-305-50018-1
Written by John Clark and Brian Schaffner, this booklet addresses the 2014 congressional and gubernatorial races, with real-time analysis and references.

Acknowledgments

A number of scholars reviewed the book. They include:

Dr. Robert Carroll, East West University
Albert Cover, Stony Brook University
Nicholas Damask, Scottsdale Community College
Virgil H. Davis, Pellissippi State Community College

Jenna P. Duke, Lehigh Carbon Community College
Ethan Fishman, University of South Alabama
Marvin Overb, University of Missouri
Erich Saphir, Pima Community College
Linda Trautman, Ohio University-Lancaster

A number of scholars reviewed the previous three editions. They include:

Philip Aka, Chicago State University
Lucas Allen, Michigan State University
Roger Ashby, Peace College
Michael Baranowski, Northern Kentucky University
Jack Citrin, University of California, Berkeley
Zach Courser, Boston College
Stan Crippen, Riverside County Office of Education
Gregory Culver, University of Southern Indiana
Matthew Eshbaugh-Soha, University of North Texas
Glenn David Garrison, Collin County Community College—Spring Creek Campus
Kipling Hagopian
Kathleen C. Hauger, Abington Senior High School
Stephen Kerbow, Southwest Texas Junior College

Halima Asghar Khan, Massasoit Community College
Young-Choul Kim, University of Evansville
Junius H. Koonce, Edgecombe Community College
William Lester, Jacksonville State University
Brad Lockerbie, University of Georgia
Randall McKeever, Forney ISD
Marvin Overby, University of Missouri
Anne F. Presley, McKinney High School
Gayle Randolph, Neosho County Community College
Jonathan Roberts, Portland, OR, schools
P. S. Ruckman, Rock Valley College
Rebecca Small, Herndon High School
Greg Snoad, Mauldin High School
Jennifer Walsh, Azusa Pacific University
David Wigg, St. Louis Community College
Teresa Wright, California State University—Long Beach

About the Authors

John J. DiIulio, Jr.

JOHN J. DIIULIO, JR., is a professor of political science at the University of Pennsylvania. From 1986 to 1999, he was a professor of politics and public affairs at Princeton University's Woodrow Wilson School of Public and International Affairs. He received B.A. and M.A. degrees from the University of Pennsylvania and M.A. and Ph.D. degrees from Harvard University. He is the author, coauthor, or editor of a dozen books, including *Godly Republic* (2007), *Medicaid and Devolution* (1998, with Frank Thompson), *Deregulating the Public Service* (1994), and *Governing Prisons* (1987). He has received many awards for excellence in teaching including Penn's two most prestigious, the Lindback Award and the Abrams Award.

DiIulio advised both Vice President Al Gore and Governor George W. Bush during the 2000 presidential campaign. While on leave in academic year 2000–2001, he served as assistant to the president of the United States. He served as the first Director of the White House Office on Faith-Based Initiatives and assisted the Obama administration in reconstituting it. He has advised officials at the National Performance Review, the Office of Management and Budget, the General Accounting Office, the U.S. Department of Justice, and other federal agencies. He has served on the boards of Big Brothers Big Sisters of America and other nonprofit organizations.

In 1995, the Association of Public Policy Analysis and Management conferred on him the David N. Kershaw Award for outstanding research achievements, and in 1987 he received the American Political Science Association's Leonard D. White Award in public administration. In 1991–1994, he chaired the latter association's standing committee on professional ethics. Since 2005, he has had a leading role in nonprofit initiatives to assist post-Katrina New Orleans.

Meena Bose

MEENA BOSE is Director of the Peter S. Kalikow Center for the Study of the American Presidency at Hofstra University, as well as Peter S. Kalikow Chair in Presidential Studies and Professor of Political Science. Her first book, *Shaping and Signaling Presidential Policy: The National Security Decision Making of Eisenhower and Kennedy* (Texas A&M University Press, 1998), was based on her dissertation, which won the Best Dissertation on the Presidency Award from the Center for Presidential Studies at Texas A&M University in 1997.

Dr. Bose also is editor of the reference volume *The New York Times on the Presidency* (2009) as well as several edited volumes in presidential studies, including *From Votes to Victory: Winning and Governing the White House in the Twenty-First Century* (2011); *President or King? Evaluating the Expansion of Presidential Power from Abraham Lincoln to George W. Bush* (2011); *U.S. Presidential Leadership at the United Nations from 1945 to the Present* (2012); and *Change in the White House: Comparing the Presidencies of George W. Bush and Barack Obama* (2012). She is co-editor (with Rosanna Perotti) of *From Cold War to New World Order: The Foreign Policy of George H. W. Bush* (2002), co-editor (with Mark Landis) of *The Uses and Abuses of Presidential Ratings* (2003), and co-editor (with John J. DiIulio, Jr.) of *Classic Ideas and Current Issues in American Government* (2007).

Dr. Bose has developed non-partisan courses sponsored by The Washington Center in connection with the national party conventions as well as on key issues in American politics. She also has designed and taught courses for Elderhostel on presidential leadership and American politics. Dr. Bose serves on the editorial board of *Political Science Quarterly* and has been a guest editor several times for *White House Studies*.

Dr. Bose taught for six years at the United States Military Academy at West Point, where she also served as Director of American Politics in 2006. Dr. Bose previously was an assistant professor of political science at Hofstra from 1996–2000 and acting director of Hofstra's University Honors Program from 1999–2000. She received her undergraduate degree in international politics from Penn State University (1990), and her master's and doctoral degrees from Princeton University (1992, 1996).

In Memoriam
James Q. Wilson
(May 27, 1931–March 2, 2012)

James Q. Wilson's death made news. There was a front-page story in *The New York Times*. There were stories in *The Wall Street Journal, The Washington Post*, and nearly every other major U.S. newspaper. There were also essays in *The Economist, The New Republic, The Weekly Standard*, and many other magazines; reflections by Ross Douthat, George Will, and many other leading syndicated columnists; postings by think-tank leaders and big-time bloggers; and statements by present and former public officials in both parties.

In 1959, Wilson received his doctoral degree in political science from the University of Chicago. He held endowed chair professorships at Harvard, UCLA, and Pepperdine, and a final post as a Distinguished Scholar at Boston College. Harvard and a half-dozen other universities bestowed honorary degrees on him. He won numerous academic awards, including ones from the American Political Science Association, the Academy of Criminal Justice Sciences, and the Policy Studies Organization. He held board chairmanships, memberships, directorships, or academic advisory group leadership positions with, among other institutions, the Joint Center for Urban Studies of Harvard and MIT, the American Academy of Arts and Sciences, the American Philosophical Society, the American Enterprise Institute, the National Academy of Sciences, the Robert A. Fox Leadership Program at the University of Pennsylvania, and the Pardee Rand Graduate School. He authored or co-authored 17 books, including 13 editions of *American Government* that, all told, sold more than a million copies. He also penned or co-penned several edited volumes and several hundred articles, plus scores of op-eds in leading newspapers.

Predictably, most of the public coverage that followed his passing, even the parts of it that included personal reminiscences or that quoted people who knew him, was mainly about Wilson the eminent and influential public intellectual. That is, it was about the Wilson who Senator Daniel Patrick Moynihan, his friend and former Harvard colleague, famously described to President Richard M. Nixon as "the smartest man in America." It was about the Wilson who served both Democratic and Republican officeholders, including six U.S. presidents, as an advisor. It was about the Wilson who was the chairperson of President Lyndon Johnson's White House Task Force on Crime, the chairperson of President Nixon's National Advisory Commission on Drug Abuse Prevention, and a member of many other public commissions or blue-ribbon bodies, including the President's Foreign Policy Intelligence Board, the President's Council on Bioethics, the Police Foundation's Board of Directors, and the International Council of the Human Rights Foundation. It was about the Wilson who received the Presidential Medal of Freedom in 2003 and was cited by President George W. Bush as "the most influential political scientist in America since the White House was home to Professor Woodrow Wilson."

Wilson, the eminent and influential public intellectual, was a real genius and a laudable giant, but that was not the whole of the man that I was blessed to know over the last 32 years. Even greater, in my view, were Wilson the deeply good family man and neighbor-citizen and Wilson the devoted teacher, dedicated mentor, and pure scholar.

A two-time national high school debate champion, Jim graduated from the University of Redlands and served in the U.S. Navy. He married his high school sweetheart, Roberta. They were happily married for nearly sixty years. Jim is survived by Roberta and their two children, Matthew and Annie, his children's spouses, a sister, and many grandchildren, nieces, and nephews. Somehow, for all his prolific public and professional pursuits, he spent several lifetimes of quality time with his children, time that included reading all of the Sunday comics to them when they were young, never missing an important event in their lives, and leading them on many trips abroad and other adventures. Jim loved to share the things that he loved. Those things included scuba diving and underwater photography. He and Roberta co-authored a book, *Watching Fishes: Life and Behavior on Coral Reefs* (1985). He also loved cars, fast ones, and was into racing. I once described him as "an open-highway patriot," and he smiled at the description. Jim was a model community member. He coached a local youth soccer team and he served on the board of his local library.

Jim was also an amazingly dedicated undergraduate and graduate student classroom teacher. He was an angel-on-the-shoulder thesis supervisor, dissertation advisor, colleague, co-author, editor, and co-editor. He loved to laugh at himself and with others, and his generosity was genuine and unfailing.

For all Jim's influence and diverse intellectual interests, at the core of his professional and civic being he was a proudly card-carrying political scientist who always pursued knowledge more for its intrinsic than for its instrumental value. Indeed, he was supremely skeptical about what policy-oriented public intellectuals (often offering himself as Exhibit A) had to offer real-world public policymakers and administrators.

In *The Politics of Regulation*, an edited volume featuring chapters by many of his former graduate students, Jim wrote:

> (M)uch, if not most, of politics consists of efforts to change wants by arguments, persuasion, threats, bluffs, and education. What people want—or believe they want—is the essence of politics. . . . Both economics and politics deal with problems of scarcity and conflicting preferences. Both deal with persons who ordinarily act rationally. But politics differs from economics in that it manages conflict by forming heterogeneous coalitions out of persons with changeable and incommensurable preferences in order to make binding decisions for everyone. Political science is an effort to make statements about the formation of preferences and nonmarket methods of managing conflict among those preferences; as a discipline, it will be as inelegant, disorderly, and changeable as its subject matter.

Requiescat in Pace: May he rest in peace.

John J. DiIulio, Jr.

A longer version of this essay appeared in PS: Political Science and Politics, *2012. This excerpt is reprinted here by permission.*

© Orhan Cam/Shutterstock.com

The Study of American Government

1

LEARNING OBJECTIVES

LO 1.1   What is meant by "politics"?

LO 1.2   Can you give two definitions of "democracy"?

LO 1.3   How is political power actually distributed in America?

LO 1.4   How can you classify and explain the politics of different issues?

Today, Americans and their elected leaders are hotly debating the federal government's spending, taxing, and future finances.

Some things never change.

THEN

In 1786, a committee of Congress reported that since the Articles of Confederation were adopted in 1781, the state governments had paid only about one-seventh of the monies requisitioned by the federal government. The federal government was broke and sinking deeper into debt, including debt owed to foreign governments. Several states had financial crises, too.

In 1788, the proposed Constitution's chief architect, James Madison, argued that while the federal government needed its own "power of taxation" and "collectors of revenue," its overall powers would remain "few and defined" and its taxing power would be used sparingly.[1] In reply, critics of the proposed Constitution, including the famous patriot Patrick Henry, mocked Madison's view and predicted that if the Constitution were ratified, there would, over time, be "an immense increase of taxes" spent by an ever-growing federal government.[2]

NOW

A bipartisan presidential commission has warned that by 2015, the federal government will be paying well over $300 billion a year in interest on a roughly $20 trillion national debt, much of it borrowed from foreign nations. The federal budget initially proposed for 2014 called for spending about $3.8 trillion, roughly a fifth of it in deficit spending. Projected total state and local government spending for 2014 was about $3.2 trillion (including federal grants), and many states' and cities' finances were in shambles.[3]

So, in the 1780s, as in the 2010s, nearly everyone agreed that the government's finances were a huge mess and that bold action was required, and soon; but in each case, then and now, there was no consensus about what action to take, or when.

Issues and Politics

This might seem odd. After all, it may appear that the government's financial problems—including big budget deficits and revenue shortfalls—could be solved by simple arithmetic: either spend and borrow less, or tax more, or both. But now ask: spend or borrow less for what, and raise taxes on whom, when, how, and by how much? For example, should we cut the defense budget, but continue to fund health care programs, or the reverse? Or should we keep defense and health care funding at current levels, but reduce spending on environmental protection or homeland security? Should we perhaps increase taxes on the wealthy (define *wealthy*) and cut taxes for the middle class (define *middle class*), or ... what?

Then, as now, the fundamental government finance problems were *political*, not mathematical. People disagreed not only over how much the federal government should tax and spend, but also over whether it should involve itself at all in various endeavors. For example, in 2011, the federal government nearly shut down, not mainly over disagreements between the two parties about how much needed to be cut from the federal budget (in the end, the agreed-to cuts totaled $38.5 billion), but primarily over whether any federal funding at all should go to certain relatively small-budget federal health, environmental, and other programs.

Fights over taxes and government finances; battles over abortion, school prayer, and gay rights; disputes about where to store nuclear waste; competing plans on immigration, international trade, welfare reform, environmental protection, or gun control; contention surrounding a new health care proposal. Some of these matters are mainly about money and economic interests; others are more about ideas and personal beliefs. Some people care a lot about at least some of these matters; others seem to care little or not at all.

Regardless, all such matters and countless others have this in common: each is an **issue**, defined as a conflict, real or apparent, between the interests, ideas, or beliefs of different citizens.[4]

An issue may be more apparent than real; for example, people might fight over two tax plans that, despite superficial differences, would actually distribute tax burdens on different groups in exactly the same way. Or an issue may be as real as it seems to the conflicting parties, as, for example, it is in matters that pose clear-cut choices (high tariffs or no tariffs; abortion legal in all cases or illegal in all cases).

And an issue might be more about conflicts over means than over ends. For example, on health care reform or other issues, legislators who are in the same party and have similar ideological leanings (like a group of liberal Democrats, or a group of conservative Republicans) might agree on objectives, but still wrangle bitterly with each other over different means of achieving their goals. Or they might agree on both ends and means, but differ over priorities (which goals to pursue first), timing (when to proceed), or tactics (how to proceed).

Whatever form issues take, they are the raw materials of politics. By **politics** we mean "the activity—negotiation, argument, discussion, application of force, persuasion, etc.—by which an issue is agitated or settled."[5] There are many different ways that any given issue can be agitated (brought to attention, stimulate conflict) or settled (brought to an accommodation, stimulate consensus). And there are many different ways that government can agitate or settle, foster or frustrate political conflict.

Some citizens are quite issue-oriented and politically active: they vote and try to influence others to vote likewise; they join political campaigns or give money to candidates; they keep informed about diverse issues, sign petitions, advocate for new laws, or communicate with elected leaders, and more.

But such politically attentive and engaged citizens are the exception to the rule, most especially among young adult citizens under age 30. According to many experts, ever more young Americans are closer to being "political dropouts" than they are to being "engaged citizens" (a fact that is made no less troubling by similar trends in the United Kingdom, Canada, Scandinavia, and elsewhere).[6] Many high school and college students believe getting "involved in our democracy" means volunteering for community service, but not voting.[7] Most young Americans do not regularly read newspapers (online or otherwise) or closely follow political news; and most know little about how government works, and exhibit no "regular interest in politics."[8] In response to such concerns, various analysts and study commissions have made proposals ranging from compulsory voting to enhanced "civic education" in high schools.[9]

issue A conflict, real or apparent, between the interests, ideas, or beliefs of different citizens.

politics The activity by which an issue is agitated or settled.

power The ability of one person to get another person to act in accordance with the first person's intentions.

Power, Authority, and Legitimacy

Politics, and the processes by which issues are normally agitated or settled, involves the exercise of power. By **power** we mean the ability of one person to get another person to act in accordance with the first person's intentions. Sometimes an exercise of power is obvious, as when the president tells the Air Force that it cannot build a new bomber, or orders soldiers into combat in a foreign land. Other times, an exercise of power is subtle, as when the president's junior speechwriters, reflecting their own evolving views, adopt a new tone when writing for their boss about controversial social issues like abortion. The speechwriters may not think they are using power—after all, they are the president's subordinates and may rarely see

political agenda Issues that people believe require governmental action.

authority The right to use power.

legitimacy Political authority conferred by law or by a state or national constitution.

democracy The rule of the many.

direct or participatory democracy A government in which all or most citizens participate directly.

him face-to-face. But if the president lets their words exit his mouth in public, they have used power.

Power is found in all human relationships, but we shall be concerned here only with power as it is used to affect who will hold government office and how government will behave. We limit our view here to government, and chiefly to the American federal government. However, we shall repeatedly pay special attention to how things once thought to be "private" matters become "public"—that is, how they manage to become objects of governmental action. Indeed, as we will discuss more below, one of the most striking transformations of American politics has been the extent to which, in recent decades, almost every aspect of human life has found its way onto the **political agenda**.

People who exercise political power may or may not have the authority to do so. By **authority**, we mean the right to use power. The exercise of rightful power—that is, of authority— is ordinarily easier than the exercise of power not supported by any persuasive claim of right. We accept decisions, often without question, if they are made by people who we believe have the right to make them; we may bow to naked power because we cannot resist it, but by our recalcitrance or our resentment we put the users of naked power to greater trouble than the wielders of authority. In this book, we will on occasion speak of "formal authority." By this we mean that the right to exercise power is vested in a governmental office. A president, a senator, and a federal judge have formal authority to take certain actions.

What makes power rightful varies from time to time and from country to country. In the United States, we usually say a person has political authority if his or her right to act in a certain way is conferred by a law or by a state or national constitution. But what makes a law or constitution a source of right? That is the question of **legitimacy**. In the United States, the Constitution today is widely, if not unanimously, accepted as a source of legitimate authority, but that was not always the case.

What Is Democracy?

On one matter, virtually all Americans seem to agree: no exercise of political power by government at any level is legitimate if it is not in some sense democratic. That wasn't always the prevailing view. In 1787, as the Constitution was being debated, Alexander Hamilton worried that the new government he helped create might be too democratic, while George Mason, who refused to sign the Constitution, worried that it was not democratic enough. Today, however, almost everyone believes that democratic government is the only proper kind. Most people believe that American government is democratic; some believe that other institutions of public life—schools, universities, corporations, trade unions, churches—also should be run on democratic principles if they are to be legitimate; and some insist that promoting democracy abroad ought to be a primary purpose of U.S. foreign policy.

Democracy is a word with at least two different meanings. First, the term *democracy* is used to describe those regimes that come as close as possible to Aristotle's definition—the "rule of the many."[10] A government is democratic if all—or most—of its citizens participate directly in either holding office or making policy. This often is called **direct or participatory democracy**. In Aristotle's time—Greece in the 4th century B.C.—such a government was possible. The Greek city-state, or *polis*, was quite small, and within it, citizenship was extended to all free adult male property holders. (Slaves, women, minors, and those without property were excluded from participation in government.) In more recent times, the New England town meeting approximates the Aristotelian ideal. In such a meeting, the adult citizens of a community gather once or twice a year to vote directly on all major issues and expenditures of the town. As towns have become larger and issues more complicated, many town governments have abandoned the pure town meeting in favor of either the representative town meeting (in which a large number of elected representatives, perhaps 200–300, meet to vote on town affairs) or representative government (in which a small number of elected city councilors make decisions).

representative democracy
A government in which leaders make decisions by winning a competitive struggle for the popular vote.

The second definition of *democracy* is the principle of governance of most nations that are called democratic. It was most concisely stated by the economist Joseph Schumpeter: "The democratic method is that institutional arrangement for arriving at political decisions in which individuals [that is, leaders] acquire the power to decide by means of a competitive struggle for the people's vote."[11] Sometimes this method is called, approvingly, **representative democracy**; at other times it is referred to, disapprovingly, as the elitist theory of democracy. It is justified by one or both of two arguments: First, it is impractical—owing to limits of time, information, energy, interest, and expertise—for the people to decide on public policy, but it is not impractical to expect them to make reasonable choices among competing leadership groups. Second, some people (including, as we shall see in the next chapter, many of the Framers of the Constitution) believe direct democracy is likely to lead to bad decisions, because people often decide large issues on the basis of fleeting passions and in response to popular demagogues. This concern about direct democracy persists today, as evidenced by the statements of leaders who disagree with voter decisions. For example, voters in many states have rejected referenda that would have increased public funding for private schools. Politicians who opposed the defeated referenda spoke approvingly of the "will of the people," but politicians who favored them spoke disdainfully of "mass misunderstanding."

Whenever we refer to that form of democracy involving the direct participation of all or most citizens, we shall use the term *direct* or *participatory* democracy. Whenever the word *democracy* is used alone in this book, it will have the meaning Schumpeter gave it. Schumpeter's definition usefully implies basic benchmarks that enable us to judge the extent to which any given political system is democratic.[12] A political system is *non*-democratic to the extent that it denies equal voting rights to part of its society and severely limits (or outright prohibits) "the civil and political freedoms to speak, publish, assemble, and organize,"[13] all of which are necessary to a truly "competitive struggle for the people's vote." A partial list of non-democratic political systems would include absolute monarchies, empires, military dictatorships, authoritarian systems, and totalitarian states.[14]

Scholars of comparative politics and government have much to teach about how different types of political systems, democratic and non-democratic, arise, persist, and change. For our present purposes, however, it is most important to understand that America itself was once far less democratic than it is today and that it was so not by accident, but by design. As we discuss in the next chapter, the men who wrote the Constitution did not use the word *democracy* in that document. They wrote instead of a "republican form of government," but by that they meant what we call "representative democracy." And, as we emphasize when discussing civil liberties and civil rights (see Chapter 4 and 5), and again when discussing political participation (see Chapters 7 and 8), America was not born as a full-fledged representative democracy; and, for all the progress of the past half-century or so, the nation's representative democratic character is still very much a work in progress.

For any representative democracy to work, there must, of course, be an opportunity for genuine leadership competition. This requires in turn that individuals and parties be able to run for office; that communications (through speeches or the press, in meetings, and on the internet) be free; and that the voters perceive that a meaningful choice exists. But what, exactly, constitutes a "meaningful choice"? How many offices should be elective and how many appointive? How many candidates or parties can exist before the choices become hopelessly confused? Where will the money come from to finance electoral campaigns? There are many answers to such questions. In some European democracies, for example, very few offices—often just those in the national or local legislature—are elective, and much of the money for campaigning for these offices comes from the government. In the United States, many offices—executive and judicial, as well as legislative—are elective, and most of the money the candidates use for campaigning comes from industry, labor unions, and private individuals.

Some people have argued that the virtues of direct or participatory democracy can and should be reclaimed even in a modern, complex society. This can be done either by allowing individual neighborhoods in big cities to govern themselves (community control), or by requiring those affected by some government program to participate in its formulation (citizen participation). In many states, a measure of direct democracy exists when voters can decide on referendum issues—that is, policy choices that appear on the ballot. The proponents of direct democracy defend it as the only way to ensure that the "will of the people" prevails.

As we discuss in the nearby **Constitutional Connections** feature, and as we explore more in Chapter 2, the Framers of the Constitution did not think that the "will of the people" was synonymous with the "common interest" or the "public good." They strongly favored representative democracy over direct democracy.

Political Power in America: Five Views

Scholars differ in their interpretations of the American political experience. Where some see a steady march of democracy, others see no such thing; where some emphasize how voting and other rights have been steadily expanded, others stress how they were denied to so many for so long, and so forth.

The actual distribution of political power in a representative democracy will depend on the composition of the political elites who are involved in the struggles for power and over policy.

CONSTITUTIONAL CONNECTIONS

Deciding What's Legitimate

Much of American political history has been a struggle over what constitutes legitimate authority. The Constitutional Convention in 1787 was an effort to see whether a new, more powerful federal government could be made legitimate; the succeeding administrations of George Washington, John Adams, and Thomas Jefferson were in large measure preoccupied with disputes over the kinds of decisions that were legitimate for the federal government to make. The Civil War was a bloody struggle over slavery and the legitimacy of the federal union; the New Deal of Franklin Roosevelt was hotly debated by those who disagreed over whether it was legitimate for the federal government to intervene deeply in the economy. Not uncommonly, the federal judiciary functions as the ultimate arbiter of what is legitimate in the context of deciding what is or is not constitutional (see Chapter 12). For instance, in 2012, amidst a contentious debate over the legitimacy of the federal health care law that was enacted in 2010, the U.S. Supreme Court decided that the federal government could require individuals to purchase health insurance, but could not require states to expand health care benefits for citizens participating in the federal-state program known as Medicaid.

By **elite** we mean an identifiable group of persons who possess a disproportionate share of some valued resource—in this case, political power.

There are at least five views about how political power is distributed in America: (1) wealthy capitalists and other economic elites determine most policies; (2) a group of business, military, labor union, and elected officials controls most decisions; (3) appointed bureaucrats ultimately run everything; (4) representatives of a large number of interest groups are in charge; and (5) morally impassioned elites drive political change.

The first view began with the theories of Karl Marx, who, in the 19th century, argued that governments were dominated by business owners (the "bourgeoisie") until a revolution replaced them with rule by laborers (the "proletariat").[15] But strict Marxism has collapsed in most countries. Today, a **class view**, though it may derive inspiration from Marx, is less dogmatic and emphasizes the power of "the rich" or the leaders of multinational corporations.

The second view ties business leaders together with other elites whose perceived power is of concern to the view's adherents. These elites may include: top military officials, labor union leaders, mass media executives, and the heads of a few special-interest groups. Derived from the work of sociologist C. Wright Mills, this **power elite view** argues that American democracy is dominated by a few top leaders, many of them wealthy or privately powerful, who do not hold elective office.[16]

The third view is that appointed officials run everything despite the efforts of elected officials and the public to control them. The **bureaucratic view** was first set forth by the German scholar Max Weber (1864–1920). He argued that the modern state, in order to become successful, puts its affairs in the hands of appointed bureaucrats whose competence is essential to the management of complex affairs.[17] These officials, invisible to most people, have mastered the written records and legislative details of the government and do more than just implement democratic policies; they actually make those policies.

The fourth view holds that political resources—such as money, prestige, expertise, and access to the mass media—have become so widely distributed that no single elite, no social class, no bureaucratic arrangement, can control them. Many 20th-century political scientists—among them David B. Truman—adopted a **pluralist view**.[18] In the United States, they argued, political resources are broadly shared in part because there are so many governmental institutions (cities, states, school boards) and so many rival institutions (legislatures, executives, judges, bureaucrats) that no single group can dominate most, or even much, of the political process.

The fifth view maintains that while each of the other four views is correct with respect to how power is distributed on certain issues or during political "business as usual" periods, each also misses how the most important policy decisions and political changes are influenced by morally impassioned elites who are motivated less by economic self-interest than they are by an almost religious zeal to bring government institutions and policies into line with democratic ideals. Samuel P. Huntington articulated this **creedal passion view**, offering the examples of Patrick Henry and the revolutionaries of the 1770s, the advocates of Jackson-style democracy in the 1820s, the progressive reformers of the early 20th century, and the leaders of the civil rights and anti-war movements in the mid-20th century.[19]

elite Persons who possess a disproportionate share of some valued resource, like money, prestige, or expertise.

class view View that the government is dominated by capitalists.

power elite view View that the government is dominated by a few top leaders, most of whom are outside of government.

bureaucratic view View that the government is dominated by appointed officials.

pluralist view View that competition among all affected interests shapes public policy.

creedal passion view View that morally impassioned elites drive important political changes.

Who Governs—and to What Ends?

So, which view is correct? At one level, all are correct, at least in part: economic class interests, powerful cadres of elites, entrenched bureaucrats, competing pressure groups, and morally impassioned individuals have all at one time or another wielded political power and played a part in shaping our government and its policies.

But, more fundamentally, understanding any political system means being able to give reasonable answers to each of two separate, but related questions about it: who governs, and to what ends?

We want to know the answer to the first question because we believe that those who rule—their personalities and beliefs, their virtues and vices—will affect what they do to and for us. Many people think they already know the answer to the question, and they are prepared to talk and vote on that basis. That is their right, and the opinions they express may be correct. But they also may be wrong. Indeed, many of these opinions must be wrong because they are in conflict. When asked, "Who governs?" some people will say "the unions" and some will say "big business"; others will say "the politicians," "the people," or "the special interests." Still others will say "Wall Street," "the military," "crackpot liberals," "the media," "the bureaucrats," or "white males." Not all these answers can be correct—at least not all of the time.

The answer to the second question is important because it tells us how government affects our lives. We want to know not only who governs, but what difference it makes who governs. In our day-to-day lives, we may not think government makes much difference at all. In one sense that is right, because our most pressing personal concerns—work, play, love, family, health—essentially are private matters on which government touches but slightly. But in a larger and longer perspective, government makes a substantial difference. Consider: in 1935, 96 percent of all American families paid no federal income tax, and for the 4 percent or so who did pay, the average rate was only about 4 percent of their incomes. Today, almost all families pay federal payroll taxes, and the average rate is about 21 percent of their incomes. Or consider: in 1960, in many parts of the country, African Americans could ride only in the backs of buses, had to use washrooms and drinking fountains that were labeled "colored," and could not be served in most public restaurants. Such restrictions have almost all been eliminated, in large part because of decisions by the federal government.

It is important to bear in mind that we wish to answer two different questions, and not two versions of the same question. You cannot always predict what goals government will establish by knowing only who governs, nor can you always tell who governs by knowing what activities government undertakes. Most

Americans felt powerfully connected to their fellow citizens in the immediate aftermath of 9/11.

Matt McDermott

HOW WE COMPARE

Academic Freedom

You are reading a textbook on American government, but how is the freedom to study, teach, or do research protected from undue government interference? And how do European democracies protect academic freedom?

The U.S. Constitution does not mention academic freedom. Rather, in America, the federal and state courts have typically treated academic freedom—at least in tax-supported universities—as "free speech" strongly protected under the First Amendment.

In each of nine European nations, the constitution is silent on academic freedom, but various national laws protect it. In 13 other European nations, academic freedom is protected both by explicit constitutional language and by national legislation. But is academic freedom better protected in these nations than in either the United States or elsewhere in Europe?

Not necessarily. Germany's constitution states that "research and teaching are free," but subject to "loyalty to the constitution." Italy's constitution offers lavish protections for academic freedom, but its national laws severely restrict those same freedoms.

The United Kingdom has no written constitution, but its national laws regarding academic freedom (and university self-governance) are quite restrictive by American standards.

Source: Terence Karran, "Freedom in Europe: A Preliminary Analysis," *Higher Education Policy* 20 (2007):289–313.

people holding national political office are middle-class, middle-aged, white, Protestant males, but we cannot then conclude that the government will adopt only policies that are to the narrow advantage of the middle class, the middle-aged, whites, Protestants, or men. If we thought that, we would be at a loss to explain why the rich are taxed more heavily than the poor, why the War on Poverty was declared, why constitutional amendments giving rights to African Americans and women passed Congress by large majorities, or why Catholics and Jews have been appointed to so many important governmental posts.

This book is chiefly devoted to answering the question: Who governs? It is written in the belief that this question cannot be answered without looking at how government makes—or fails to make—decisions about a large variety of concrete issues. Thus, in this book we shall inspect government policies to see what individuals, groups, and institutions seem to exert the greatest power in the continuous struggle to define the purposes of government.

The Politics of Different Issues

Once an issue is on the political agenda, its nature affects the kind of politicking that ensues. Some issues provoke intense interest group conflict; others allow one group to prevail almost unchallenged. Some issues involve ideological appeals to broad national constituencies; others involve quiet bargaining in congressional offices. We all know that private groups try to influence government policies; we often forget that the nature of the issues with which government is dealing influences the kinds of groups that become politically active.

cost A burden that people believe they must bear if a policy is adopted.

benefit A satisfaction that people believe they will enjoy if a policy is adopted.

One way to understand why government handles a given issue as it does is to examine what appear to be the costs and benefits of the proposed policy. The **cost** is any burden, monetary or nonmonetary, that some people must bear, or believe they must bear, if the policy is adopted. The costs of a government spending program are the taxes it entails; the cost of a foreign policy initiative may be the increased chance of having the nation drawn into war.

The **benefit** is any satisfaction, monetary or nonmonetary, that people believe they will enjoy if the policy is adopted. The benefits of a government spending program are the payments, subsidies, or contracts received by some people; the benefits of a foreign policy initiative may include the enhanced security of the nation, the protection of a valued ally, or the vindication of some important principle such as human rights.

Two aspects of these costs and benefits should be borne in mind. First, it is the *perception* of costs and benefits that affects politics. People may think the cost of an auto emissions control system is paid by the manufacturer, when it is actually passed on to the consumer in the form of higher prices and reduced performance. Political conflict over pollution control will take one form when people think that the polluting industries pay the costs, and another form when they think that the consumers pay.

Second, people take into account not only who benefits, but also whether it is legitimate for that group to benefit. When programs providing financial assistance to women with dependent children were first developed in the early part of the 20th century, they were relatively noncontroversial because people saw the money as going to widows and orphans who deserved such aid. Later on, giving aid to mothers with dependent children became controversial because some people now perceived the recipients not as deserving widows, but as irresponsible women who had never married. Whatever the truth of the matter, the program had lost some of its legitimacy because the beneficiaries were no longer seen as "deserving." By the same token, groups once thought undeserving—such as men out of work—were later thought to be entitled to aid, and thus the unemployment compensation program acquired a legitimacy that it once lacked.

Politics is, in large measure, a process of raising and settling disputes over who *will* benefit or pay for a program and who *ought* to benefit or pay. Because beliefs about the results of a program and the rightness of those results are matters of opinion, it is evident that ideas are at least as important as interests in shaping politics. In recent years, ideas have become especially important with the rise of issues whose consequences are largely intangible, such as abortion, school prayer, and gay rights.

Though perceptions about costs and benefits change, most people most of the time prefer government programs that provide substantial benefits to them at low cost. This rather obvious fact can have important implications for how politics is carried out. In a political system based on some measure of popular rule, public officials have a strong incentive to offer programs that confer—or appear to confer—benefits on people with costs either small in amount, remote in time, or borne by "somebody else." Policies that seem to impose high, immediate costs in return for small or remote benefits will be avoided, enacted with a minimum of publicity, or proposed only in response to a real or apparent crisis.

Ordinarily, no president would propose a policy that would immediately raise the cost of fuel, even if he were convinced that future supplies of oil and gasoline were likely to be exhausted unless higher prices reduced current consumption. But when a crisis occurs, such as the Arab oil cartel's price increases beginning in 1973, it becomes possible for the president to offer such proposals—as did Nixon, Ford, and Carter in varying ways. Even then, however, people are reluctant to bear increased costs, and thus many are led to dispute the president's claim that an emergency actually exists.

These entirely human responses to the perceived costs and benefits of proposed policies can be organized into a simple theory of politics.[20] It is based on the observation that the costs and benefits of a policy may be *widely distributed* (spread over many, most, or even all citizens) or *narrowly concentrated* (limited to a relatively small number of citizens or to some identifiable, organized group).

> **majoritarian politics**
> A policy in which almost everybody benefits and almost everybody pays.

For instance, a widely distributed cost would include an income tax, a Social Security tax, or a high rate of crime; a widely distributed benefit might include retirement benefits for all citizens, clean air, national security, or low crime rates. Examples of narrowly concentrated costs include the expenditures by a factory to reduce its pollution, government regulations imposed on doctors and hospitals participating in the Medicare program, or restrictions on freedom of speech imposed on a dissident political group. Examples of narrowly concentrated benefits include subsidies to farmers or merchant ship companies, the enlarged freedom to speak and protest afforded a dissident group, or protection against competition given to an industry because of favorable government regulation.

Four Types of Politics

The perceived distribution of costs and benefits shapes the *kinds of political coalitions that will form*—but it will not necessarily determine *who wins.* There are four types of politics, and a given popular majority, interest group, client, or entrepreneur may win or lose depending on its influence and the temper of the times.

Majoritarian Politics: Distributed Benefits, Distributed Costs

Some policies promise benefits to large numbers of people at a cost that large numbers of people will have to bear (see Figure 1.1). For example, almost everyone will sooner or later receive Social Security benefits, and almost everyone who works has to pay Social Security taxes.

Such **majoritarian politics** are usually not dominated by pulling and hauling among rival interest groups; instead, they involve making appeals to large segments of voters and their representatives in hopes of finding a majority. The reason why interest groups are not so important in majoritarian politics is that citizens rarely will have much incentive to join an interest group if the policy that such a group supports will benefit everybody, whether or not they are members of the group. This

FIGURE 1.1 **A Way of Classifying and Explaining the Politics of Different Policy Issues**

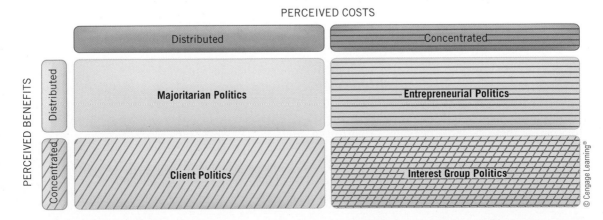

© Cengage Learning®

interest group politics A policy in which one small group benefits and another small group pays.

client politics A policy in which one small group benefits and almost everybody pays.

is the "free-rider" problem. Why join the Committee to Increase (or Decrease) the Defense Budget when what you personally contribute to that committee makes little difference in the outcome and when you will enjoy the benefits of more (or less) national defense even if you have stayed on the sidelines?

Majoritarian politics may be controversial, but the controversy is usually over matters of cost or ideology, not between rival interest groups. For example, there was intense controversy over the health care plan that President Obama signed into law, but the debate was not dominated by interest groups and many different types of politics were at play. The military budget went up during the early 1980s, down in the late 1980s, up after 2001, and down again after 2010. These changes reflected different views on how much we need to spend on our military operations abroad.

Interest Group Politics: Concentrated Benefits, Concentrated Costs

In **interest group politics**, a proposed policy will confer benefits on some relatively small, identifiable group and impose costs on another small, equally identifiable group. For example, when Congress passed a bill requiring companies to give 60 days' notice of a plant closing or a large-scale layoff, labor unions (whose members would benefit) backed the bill, and many business firms (which would pay the costs) opposed it.

Issues of this kind tend to be fought out by organized interest groups. Each side will be so powerfully affected by the outcome that it has a strong incentive to mobilize: union members who worry about layoffs will have a personal stake in favoring the notice bill; business leaders who fear government control of investment decisions will have an economic stake in opposing it.

Interest group politics often produces decisions about which the public is uninformed. For instance, there have been bitter debates between television broadcasters and cable companies over who may send what kind of signals to which homes. But these debates hardly draw any public notice—until after a law is passed and people see their increased cable charges.

Though many issues of this type involve monetary costs and benefits, they can also involve intangible considerations. If the American Nazi Party wants to march through a predominantly Jewish neighborhood carrying flags with swastikas on them, the community may organize itself to resist out of revulsion due to the horrific treatment of Jews by Nazi Germany. Each side may hire lawyers to debate the issue before the city council and in the courts.

Client Politics: Concentrated Benefits, Distributed Costs

With **client politics** some identifiable, often small group will benefit, but everybody—or at least a large part of society—will pay the costs. Because the benefits are concentrated, the group to receive those benefits has an incentive to organize and work to get them. But because the costs are widely distributed, affecting many people only slightly, those who pay the costs may be either unaware of any costs or indifferent to them, because per capita, they are so small.

This situation gives rise to client politics (sometimes called clientele politics); the beneficiary of the policy is the "client" of the government. For example, many farmers benefit substantially from agricultural price supports, but the far more numerous food consumers have no idea what these price supports cost them in taxes and higher food prices. Similarly, for some time airlines benefited from the higher prices they were able to charge on certain routes as a result of government regulations that restricted competition over prices. But the average passenger was either unaware that his or her costs were higher or did not think the higher prices were worth making a fuss about.

Not all clients have economic interests. Localities can also benefit as clients when, for example, a city or county obtains a new dam, a better harbor, or an improved irrigation system. Some of these projects may be worthwhile, others may not; by custom, however, they are referred to as *pork-barrel projects.* Usually, several pieces of "pork" are put into one barrel—that is, several projects are approved in a single piece of **pork-barrel legislation**, such as the "rivers and harbors" bill that Congress passes almost every year. Trading votes in this way attracts the support of members of Congress from each affected area; with enough projects, a majority coalition is formed. This process is called **log-rolling**.

Not every group that wants something from government at little cost to the average citizen will get it. Welfare recipients cost the typical taxpayer a small amount each year, yet there was great resistance to increasing these benefits. The homeless have not organized themselves to get benefits—most do not even vote. Yet benefits are being provided (albeit in modest amounts). These examples show the importance of popular views concerning the legitimacy of client claims as a factor in determining the success of client demands.

By the same token, groups can lose legitimacy that they once had. People who grow tobacco once were supported simply because they were farmers, and were thus seen as both "deserving" and politically important. But when people began worrying about the health risks associated with using tobacco, farmers who produce tobacco lost some legitimacy compared to those who produce corn or cotton. As a result, it became harder to get votes for maintaining tobacco price supports and easier to slap higher taxes on cigarettes.

During the Great Depression, depositors besieged a bank hoping to get their savings out.

Topharr / The Image Works

Entrepreneurial Politics: Distributed Benefits, Concentrated Costs

In **entrepreneurial politics**, society as a whole or some large part of it benefits from a policy that imposes substantial costs on some small, identifiable segment of society. The antipollution and safety requirements for automobiles were proposed as ways of improving the

pork-barrel legislation
Legislation that gives tangible benefits to constituents in several districts or states in the hope of winning their votes in return.

log-rolling A legislator supports a proposal favored by another in return for support of his or hers.

entrepreneurial politics
A policy in which almost everybody benefits and a small group pays.

policy entrepreneurs
Activists in or out of government
who pull together a political
majority on behalf of unorganized
interests.

health and well-being of all people at the expense (at least initially) of automobile manufacturers.

It is remarkable that policies of this sort are ever adopted, and in fact many are not. After all, the American political system creates many opportunities for checking and blocking the actions of others. The Founders deliberately arranged things so that it would be difficult to pass a new law; a determined minority therefore has an excellent chance of blocking a new policy. And any organized group that fears the loss of some privilege or the imposition of some burden will become a very determined minority indeed. The opponent has every incentive to work hard; the large group of prospective beneficiaries may be unconvinced of the benefit, or regard it as too small to be worth fighting for.

Nonetheless, policies with distributed benefits and concentrated costs are in fact adopted, and in recent decades they have been adopted with increasing frequency. A key element in the adoption of such policies has been the work of people who act on behalf of the unorganized or indifferent majority. Such people, called **policy entrepreneurs**, are those both in and out of government who find ways of pulling together a legislative majority on behalf of interests that are not well represented in the government. These policy entrepreneurs may or may not represent the interests and wishes of the public at large, but they do have the ability to dramatize an issue in a convincing manner. Ralph Nader is perhaps the best-known example of a policy entrepreneur, or as he might describe himself, a "consumer advocate." But there are other examples from both ends of the political spectrum, conservative as well as liberal.

Entrepreneurial politics can occur without the leadership of a policy entrepreneur if voters or legislators in large numbers suddenly become disgruntled by the high cost of some benefit that a group is receiving (or become convinced of the urgent need for a new policy to impose such costs). For example, voters may not care about government programs that benefit the oil industry when gasoline costs only one dollar a gallon, but they might care very much when the price rises to three dollars a gallon, even if the government benefits had nothing to do with the price increase. By the same token, legislators may not worry much about the effects of smog in the air until a lot of people develop burning eyes and runny noses during an especially severe smog attack.

Understanding Politics

Whether pondering one's own positions on given issues, attempting to generalize about the politics of different policy issues, or tackling questions about American government, institutions, and policies, an astute student will soon come to know what Aristotle meant when he wrote that it is "the mark of the educated person to look for precision in each class of things just so far as the nature of the subject admits."[21]

Ideally, political scientists ought to be able to give clear answers, amply supported by evidence, to the questions we have posed about American democracy, starting with "who governs?" In reality they can (at best) give partial, contingent, and controversial answers. The reason is to be found in the nature of our subject. Unlike economists—who assume that people have more or less stable preferences and can compare ways of satisfying those preferences by looking at the relative prices of various goods and services—political scientists are interested in how preferences are formed, especially for those kinds of services, such as national defense or pollution control, that cannot be evaluated chiefly in terms of monetary costs.

Understanding preferences is vital to understanding power. Who did what in government is not hard to find out, but who wielded power—that is, who made a difference in the outcome and for what reason—is much harder to discover. *Power* is a word that conjures up images of deals, bribes, power plays, and arm-twisting. In fact, most power exists because of shared understanding, common friendships, communal or organizational loyalties, and different degrees of prestige. These are hard to identify and almost impossible to quantify.

Nor can the distribution of political power be inferred simply by knowing what laws are on the books or what

Federal employees protested the October 2013 federal government shutdown on Capitol Hill.

administrative actions have been taken. The enactment of a consumer protection law does not mean that consumers are powerful, any more than the absence of such a law means that corporations are powerful. The passage of such a law could reflect an aroused public opinion, the lobbying of a small group claiming to speak for consumers, the ambitions of a senator, or the intrigues of one business firm seeking to gain a competitive advantage over another. A close analysis of what the law entails and how it was passed and administered is necessary before much of anything can be concluded.

This book will avoid sweeping claims that we have an "imperial" presidency (or an impotent one), an "obstructionist" Congress (or an innovative one), or "captured" regulatory agencies. Such labels do an injustice to the different roles that presidents, members of Congress, and administrators play in different kinds of issues and in different historical periods.

The view taken in this book is that judgments about institutions and interests can be made only after one has seen how they behave on a variety of important issues or potential issues, such as economic policy, the regulation of business, social welfare, civil rights and liberties, and foreign and military affairs. The policies adopted or blocked, the groups heeded or ignored, the values embraced or rejected—these constitute the raw material out of which one can fashion an answer to the central questions we have asked: Who governs—and to what ends?

The way in which our institutions of government handle social welfare, for example, differs from the way other democratic nations handle it, and it differs as well from the way our own institutions once treated it. The description of our institutions in Chapters 9, 10, 11, and 12 will therefore include not only an account of how they work today, but also a brief historical background on their workings and a comparison with similar institutions in other countries. There is a tendency to assume that how we do things today is the only way they could possibly be done. In fact, there are other ways to operate a government based on some measure of popular rule. History, tradition, and belief weigh heavily on all that we do.

Although political change is not always accompanied by changes in public laws, the policy process is arguably one of the best barometers of changes in who governs. Our way of classifying and explaining the politics of different policy issues has been developed, refined, and tested over more than two decades (longer than most of our readers have been alive!). Our own students and others have valued it mainly because they have found it helps to answer such questions about who governs: How do political issues get on the public agenda in the first place? How, for example, did sexual harassment—which was hardly ever discussed or debated by Congress—burst onto the public agenda? Once on the agenda, how do the politics of issues like income security for older Americans—for example, the politics of Social Security, a program that has been on the federal books since 1935—change over time? And if, today, one cares about expanding civil liberties (see Chapter 4) or protecting civil rights (see Chapter 5), what political obstacles and opportunities will one likely face, and what role will public opinion, organized interest groups, the media, the courts, political parties, and other institutions likely play in frustrating or fostering one's particular policy preferences, whatever they might be?

Peek ahead, if you wish, but understand that the place to begin a search for how power is distributed in national politics and what purposes that power serves is with the founding of the federal government in 1787: the Constitutional Convention and the events leading up to it. Though the decisions of that time were not made by philosophers or professors, the practical men who made them had a philosophic and professorial cast of mind, and thus they left behind a fairly explicit account of what values they sought to protect and what arrangements they thought ought to be made for the allocation of political power.

LEARNING OBJECTIVES

LO 1.1 What is meant by "politics"?

Politics is the activity by which an issue is agitated or settled. Politics occurs because people disagree and the disagreement must be managed. Disagreements over many political issues, including disputes over government budgets and finances, are often at their essence disagreements over what government should or should not do at all.

LO 1.2 Can you give two definitions of "democracy"?

Democracy can mean either that everyone votes on all government issues (direct or participatory democracy) or that the people elect representatives to make most of these decisions (representative democracy).

LO 1.3 How is political power actually distributed in America?

Some believe that political power in America is monopolized by wealthy business leaders, by other powerful elites, or by entrenched government bureaucrats. Others believe that political resources such as money, prestige, expertise, organizational position, and access to the mass media are so widely dispersed in American society, and the governmental institutions and offices in which power may be exercised so numerous and varied, that no single group truly has all or most political power. In this view, political power in America is distributed more or less widely. Still others suggest that morally impassioned leaders have at times been deeply influential in our politics. No one, however, argues that political resources are distributed equally in America.

LO 1.4 How can you classify and explain the politics of different issues?

One way to classify and explain the politics of different issues is in relation to the perceived costs and benefits of given policies and how narrowly concentrated (limited to a relatively small number of identifiable citizens) or widely distributed (spread over many, most, or all citizens) their perceived costs and benefits are. This approach gives us four types of politics: *majoritarian* (widely distributed costs and benefits), *interest group* (narrowly concentrated costs and benefits), *client* (widely distributed costs and narrowly concentrated benefits), and *entrepreneurial* (narrowly concentrated costs and widely distributed benefits). Different types of coalitions are associated with each type of politics. Issues can sometimes "migrate" from one type of politics to another. Some policy dynamics involve more than one type of politics. And the politics of some issues is harder to classify and explain than the politics of others.

TO LEARN MORE

- Huntington, Samuel P. *American Politics: The Promise of Disharmony.* Cambridge, MA: Harvard University Press, 1981. A fascinating analysis of the American political experience as shaped by recurring "creedal passion" periods.

- Marx, Karl, and Friedrich Engels. "The Manifesto of the Communist Party." In *The Marx-Engels Reader,* 2d ed., edited by Robert C. Tucker. New York: Norton, 1978, 469–500. The classic and historic statement suggesting that government is a mere instrument of the economic elite (wealthy capitalists in the modern world).

- Meyerson, Martin, and Edward C. Banfield. *Politics, Planning, and the Public Interest.* New York: Free Press, 1955. An understanding of issues and politics comparable to the approach adopted in this book.

- Schumpeter, Joseph A. *Capitalism, Socialism, and Democracy.* 3d ed. New York: Harper Torchbooks, 1950, chs. 20–23. A lucid statement of the theory of representative democracy and how it differs from participatory democracy.

- Truman, David B. *The Governmental Process: Political Interests and Public Opinion.* New York: Knopf, 1951. A pluralist interpretation of American politics.

- Weber, Max. *From Max Weber: Essays in Sociology.* Translated and edited by H. H. Gerth and C. Wright Mills. London: Routledge & Kegan Paul, 1948, ch. 8. A theory of bureaucracy and its power.

- Wilson, James Q. *Political Organizations.* New York: Basic Books, 1973. It is from a theory originally developed in this treatise that the four-box model of how to classify and explain the politics of different issues that is presented in this chapter was derived.

2

The Constitution

LEARNING OBJECTIVES

LO 2.1   Why was a Bill of Rights adopted so soon after the ratification of the Constitution?

LO 2.2   Why did so many authors of the Constitution fear factions?

LO 2.3   Why did the Framers agree on the idea of a separation of powers?

LO 2.4   What is the difference between a democracy and a republic?

LO 2.5   Whose freedom does the Constitution protect?

THEN

When the Constitutional Convention was held in Philadelphia in 1787, its members were all white men. They were not chosen by popular election, and a few famous men, such as Patrick Henry of Virginia, refused to attend. One state, Rhode Island, sent no delegates at all. They met in secret and there was no press coverage. The delegates met to remedy the defects of the Articles of Confederation, under which the rebellious colonies had been governed, but instead of fixing the Articles, they wrote an entirely new constitution. They then publicized it and said that it would go into effect once it had been ratified, not by state legislatures, but by popular conventions in at least nine states.

NOW

Suppose you think we should have a new constitutional convention to remedy what you and others think are defects in the present document. As you will see later in this chapter, opinions about how our Constitution might be improved are quite diverse. Some critics want the Constitution to create an American version of the parliamentary system of government one finds in the United Kingdom; others would rather that it weaken the federal government by (for example) having a requirement that the budget be balanced or setting a limit on tax revenue each year. Now try to imagine your answers to these questions: How would delegates be picked? How many would there be? Is there any way to limit what the new convention does? Should the meeting be covered by live television, and should the delegates be free to send emails and Twitter messages to outsiders?

The Problem of Liberty

The goal of the American Revolution was liberty. It was not the first revolution with that object (nor was it the last), but it was perhaps the clearest case of a people altering the political order violently, simply in order to protect their liberties. Subsequent revolutions had more complicated or utterly different objectives. The French Revolution in 1789 sought not only liberty, but "equality and fraternity." The Russian Revolution (1917) and the Chinese Revolution (culminating in 1949) chiefly sought equality and were scarcely concerned with liberty as we understand it.

What the American colonists sought to protect when they signed the Declaration of Independence in 1776 were the traditional liberties to which they thought they were entitled as British subjects. These liberties included the right to bring their legal cases before truly independent judges, rather than ones subordinate to the king; to be free of the burden of having British troops quartered in their homes; to engage in trade without burdensome restrictions; and, of course, to pay no taxes levied by a British Parliament in which they had no direct representation. During the ten years or more of agitation and argument leading up to the War of Independence, most colonists believed their liberties could be protected while they remained a part of the British Empire.

Slowly, but surely, opinion shifted. By the time war broke out in 1775, a large number of colonists (though perhaps not a majority) had reached the conclusion that the colonies would have to become independent of Great Britain if their liberties were to be assured. The colonists had many reasons for regarding independence as the only solution, but one is especially important: They no longer had confidence in the English constitution. This constitution was not a single document, but rather a collection of laws, charters, and traditional understandings that proclaimed the liberties of British subjects. In the eyes of the colonists, these liberties were regularly violated, despite their constitutional protection. Clearly, then, the English constitution was an inadequate check on the abuses of political power. The revolutionary leaders sought an explanation of the insufficiency of the constitution and found it in human nature.

The Colonial Mind

"A lust for domination is more or less natural to all parties," one colonist wrote.[1] Men will seek power, many colonists believed, because they are ambitious, greedy, and easily corrupted. John Adams denounced the "luxury, effeminacy, and venality" of English politics; Patrick Henry spoke scathingly of the "corrupt House of Commons"; and Alexander Hamilton described England as "an old, wrinkled, withered, worn-out hag."[2] This was, in part, flamboyant rhetoric designed to whip up enthusiasm for the conflict, but it was also deeply revealing of the colonial mindset. Their belief that English politicians—and by implication, most politicians—tended to be corrupt was the colonists' explanation of why the English constitution was not an adequate guarantee of the liberty of the citizens. This opinion was to persist and, as we shall see, profoundly affect the way the Americans went about designing their own governments.

The liberties the colonists fought to protect were, they thought, widely understood. They were based not on the generosity of the king or the language of statutes, but on a "higher law" embodying "natural rights" that were ordained by God, discoverable in nature and history, and essential to human progress. These rights, John Dickinson wrote, "are born with us; exist with us; and cannot be taken away from us by any human power."[3] There was general agreement that the essential rights included life, liberty, and property long before Thomas Jefferson wrote them into the Declaration of Independence. (Jefferson changed "property" to "the pursuit of happiness," but almost everybody else went on talking about property.)

This emphasis on property did not mean the American Revolution was thought up by the rich and wellborn to protect their interests or that there was a struggle between property owners and the propertyless. In late-18th-century America, most people (except the black slaves) had property of some kind. The overwhelming majority of citizens were self-employed—as farmers or artisans—and rather few people benefited financially by gaining independence from England. Taxes were higher during and after the war than they were before it, trade was disrupted by the conflict, and debts mounted perilously as various expedients were invented to pay for the struggle. There were, of course, war profiteers and those who tried to manipulate the currency to their own advantage, but most Americans at the time of the war saw the conflict in terms of political rather than economic issues. It was a war of ideology.

We all recognize the glowing language with which Jefferson set out the case for independence in the second paragraph of the Declaration:

> We hold these truths to be self-evident, that all men are created equal, that they are endowed by their Creator with certain unalienable Rights, that among these are Life, Liberty, and the pursuit of Happiness.—That to secure these rights, Governments are instituted among Men, deriving their just powers from the consent of the governed—that whenever any Form of Government becomes destructive of these ends, it is the Right of the People to alter or to abolish it, and to institute new Government, having its foundation on such principles, and organizing its powers in such form, as to them shall seem most likely to effect their Safety and Happiness.

What almost no one recalls, but what is an essential part of the Declaration, are the next 27 paragraphs, in which Jefferson listed, item by item, the specific complaints the colonists had against George III and his ministers. None of these items spoke of social or economic conditions in the colonies; all spoke instead of specific violations of political liberties. The Declaration was in essence a lawyer's

Signing the Declaration of Independence, painted by John Trumbull.

brief, prefaced by a stirring philosophical claim that the rights being violated were **unalienable**—that is, based on nature and Providence, and not on the whims or preferences of people. Jefferson, in his original draft, added another complaint—that the king had allowed the slave trade to continue *and* was inciting slaves to revolt against their masters. Congress, faced with so contradictory a charge, instead decided to include a muted reference to slave insurrections and omit all reference to the slave trade.

The Real Revolution

The Revolution was more than the War of Independence. It began before the war, continued after it, and involved more than driving out the British army by force of arms. The *real* Revolution, as John Adams afterward explained in a letter to a friend, was the "radical change in the principles, opinions, sentiments, and affections of the people."[4] This radical change had to do with a new vision of what could make political authority legitimate and personal liberties secure. Government by royal prerogative was rejected; instead, legitimate government would require the consent of the governed. Political power could not be exercised on the basis of tradition, but only as a result of a direct grant of power contained in a written constitution. Human liberty existed before government was organized, and government must respect that liberty. The legislative branch of government, in which the people were directly represented, should be superior to the executive branch.

These were indeed revolutionary ideas. No government at the time had been organized on the basis of these principles. To the colonists, such notions were not empty words, but rules to be put into immediate practice. In 1776, eight states adopted written constitutions. Within a few years, every former colony had adopted one except Connecticut

unalienable A human right based on nature or God.

Articles of Confederation
A weak constitution that governed America during the Revolutionary War.

and Rhode Island, two states that continued to rely on their colonial charters. Most state constitutions had detailed bills of rights defining personal liberties, and most placed the highest political power in the hands of elected representatives.

Written constitutions, representatives, and bills of rights are so familiar to us now that we don't realize how bold and unprecedented those innovations were in 1776. Indeed, many Americans did not think they would succeed: such arrangements would be either so strong that they would threaten liberty, or so weak that they would permit chaos.

The 11 years that elapsed between the Declaration of Independence and the signing of the Constitution in 1787 were years of turmoil, uncertainty, and fear. George Washington headed a bitter, protracted war effort without anything resembling a strong national government to support him. The supply and financing of his army were based on a series of hasty improvisations, most badly administered and few adequately supported by the fiercely independent states. When peace came, many parts of the nation were a shambles. At least a quarter of New York City was in ruins, and many other communities were nearly devastated. Though the British lost the war, they still were powerful on the North American continent, with an army available in Canada (where many Americans loyal to Britain had fled) and a large navy at sea. Spain claimed the Mississippi River Valley and occupied what are now Florida and California. Men who had left their farms to fight came back to discover themselves in debt with no money and heavy taxes. The paper money printed to finance the war was now virtually worthless.

Weaknesses of the Confederation

The 13 states had formed only a faint semblance of a national government with which to bring order to the nation. The **Articles of Confederation**, which went into effect in 1781, created little more than a "league of friendship" that could not levy taxes or regulate commerce. Each state retained its sovereignty and independence, each state (regardless of size) had one vote in Congress, nine (of 13) votes were required to pass any measure, and the delegates who cast these votes were picked and paid for by the state legislatures. Congress did have the power to make peace, and thus it was able to ratify the treaty with England in 1783. It could coin money, but there was precious little to coin; it could appoint the key army officers, but the army was small and dependent for support on independent state militias; it was allowed to run the post office, then, as now, a thankless task that no one else wanted. In 1785, John Hancock was elected to the meaningless office of "president" under the Articles and never showed up to take the job. Several states claimed the unsettled lands in the West, and they occasionally pressed those claims with guns. Pennsylvania and Virginia went to war near Pittsburgh, and Vermont threatened to become part of Canada. There was no national judicial system to settle these or other claims among the states. To amend the Articles of Confederation, all 13 states had to agree.

Many of the leaders of the Revolution, such as George Washington and Alexander Hamilton, believed a stronger national government was essential. They lamented the disruption of commerce and travel caused by the quarrelsome states and deeply feared the possibility of foreign military intervention, with England or France playing one state off against another. A small group of men, conferring at Washington's home at Mount Vernon in 1785, decided to call a meeting to discuss trade regulation. That meeting, held at Annapolis, Maryland, in September 1786, was not well attended (no delegates arrived from New England), and so another meeting, this one in Philadelphia, was called for the following spring—in May 1787—to consider ways of remedying the defects of the Confederation.

The Constitutional Convention

The delegates assembled at Philadelphia at the **Constitutional Convention**, for what was advertised (and authorized by Congress) as a meeting to revise the Articles; they adjourned four months later

having written a wholly new constitution. When they met, they were keenly aware of the problems of the confederacy, but far from agreement as to what should be done about those problems. The protection of life, liberty, and property was their objective in 1787 as it had been in 1776, but they had no accepted political theory that would tell them what kind of national government, if any, would serve that goal.

The Lessons of Experience

They had read ancient and modern political history, only to learn that nothing seemed to work. James Madison spent a good part of 1786 studying books sent to him by Thomas Jefferson, then in Paris, in hopes of finding some model for a workable American republic. He took careful notes on various confederacies in ancient Greece and on the more modern confederacy of the United Netherlands. He reviewed the history of Switzerland and Poland and the ups and downs of the Roman republic. He concluded that there was no model; as he later put it in one of the *Federalist* papers, history consists only of beacon lights "which give warning of the course to be shunned, without pointing out that which ought to be pursued."[5] The problem seemed to be that confederacies were too weak to govern and tended to collapse from internal dissension, while all stronger forms of government were so powerful as to trample the liberties of the citizens.

State Constitutions Madison and the others did not need to consult history, or even the defects of the Articles of Confederation, for illustrations of the problem. These could be found in the government of the American states at the time. Pennsylvania and Massachusetts exemplified two aspects of the problem. The Pennsylvania constitution, adopted in 1776, created the most radically democratic of the new state regimes. All power was given to a one-house (unicameral) legislature, the Assembly, the members of which were elected annually for one-year terms. No legislator could serve more than four years. There was no governor or president, only an Executive Council that had few powers. Thomas Paine, whose pamphlets had helped precipitate the break with England, thought the Pennsylvania constitution was the best in America, and in France philosophers hailed it as the very embodiment of the principle of rule by the people. Though popular in France, it was a good deal less popular in Philadelphia. The Assembly disfranchised the Quakers, persecuted conscientious objectors to the war, ignored the requirement of trial by juries, and manipulated the judiciary.[6] To Madison and his friends, the Pennsylvania constitution demonstrated how a government, though democratic, could be tyrannical as a result of concentrating all powers into one set of hands.

The Massachusetts constitution, adopted in 1780, was a good deal less democratic. There was a clear separation of powers among the various branches of government, the directly elected governor could veto acts of the legislature, and judges served for life. Both voters and elected officials had to be property owners; the governor, in fact, had to own at least £1,000 worth of property. The principal officeholders had to swear they were Christians.

Shays's Rebellion But if the government of Pennsylvania was thought too strong, that of Massachusetts seemed too weak, despite its "conservative" features. In January 1787, a group of ex–Revolutionary War soldiers and officers, plagued by debts and high taxes and fearful of losing their property to creditors and tax collectors, forcibly prevented the courts in western Massachusetts

Shays's Rebellion
A 1787 rebellion in which
ex–Revolutionary War soldiers
attempted to prevent foreclosures
of farms as a result of high
interest rates and taxes.

from sitting. This became known as **Shays's Rebellion**, after one of the officers, Daniel Shays. The governor of Massachusetts asked the Continental Congress to send troops to suppress the rebellion, but it could not raise the money or the manpower. Then he turned to his own state militia, but discovered he did not have one. In desperation, private funds were collected to hire a volunteer army, which marched on Springfield and, with the firing of a few shots, dispersed the rebels, who fled into neighboring states.

Shays's Rebellion, occurring between the aborted Annapolis and the coming Philadelphia conventions, had a powerful effect on opinion. Delegates who might have been reluctant to attend the Philadelphia meeting, especially those from New England, were galvanized by the fear that state governments were about to collapse from internal dissension. George Washington wrote a friend despairingly: "For God's sake, if they [the rebels] have real grievances, redress them; if they have not, employ the force of government against them at once."[7] Thomas Jefferson, living in Paris, took a more detached view: "A little rebellion now and then is a good thing," he wrote. "The tree of liberty must be refreshed from time to time with the blood of patriots and tyrants."[8] Though Jefferson's detachment might be explained by the fact that he was in Paris and not in Springfield, there were others, like Governor George Clinton of New York, who shared the view that no strong central government was required. (Whether Clinton would have agreed about the virtues of spilled blood, especially his, is another matter.)

The Framers

The Philadelphia convention attracted 55 delegates, only about 30 of whom participated regularly in the proceedings. One state, Rhode Island, refused to send anyone. The convention met during a miserably hot Philadelphia summer, with the delegates pledged to keep their deliberations secret. The talkative and party-loving Benjamin Franklin was often accompanied by other delegates to make sure that neither wine nor his delight in telling stories would lead him to divulge delicate secrets.

Those who attended were for the most part young (Hamilton was 30; Madison 36), but experienced. Eight delegates had signed the Declaration of Independence, seven had been governors, 34 were lawyers and reasonably well-to-do, a few were wealthy. They were not "intellectuals," but men of practical affairs. Thirty-nine had served in the ineffectual Congress of the Confederation; a third of all delegates were veterans of the Continental Army.

Some names made famous by the Revolution were conspicuously absent. Thomas Jefferson and John Adams were serving as ministers abroad; Samuel Adams was ill; Patrick Henry was chosen to attend but refused, commenting that he "smelled a rat in Philadelphia, tending toward monarchy."

The key men at the convention were an odd lot. George Washington was a very tall, athletic man who was the best horseman in Virginia and who impressed everyone with his dignity, despite decaying teeth and big eyes. James Madison was the very opposite: quite short with a frail body, and not much of an orator, but possessed of one of the best minds in the country. Benjamin Franklin, though old and ill, was the most famous American in the world as a scientist and writer, and always displayed shrewd judgment, at least when sober. Alexander Hamilton, the illegitimate son of a French woman and a Scottish merchant, had so strong a mind and so powerful a desire that he succeeded in everything he did, from being Washington's aide during the Revolution to serving as a splendid secretary of the treasury during Washington's presidency.

The convention produced not a revision of the Articles of Confederation, as it had been authorized to do, but instead a wholly new written constitution creating a true national government unlike any that had existed before. That document is today the world's oldest written national constitution. Those who wrote it were neither saints nor schemers, and the deliberations were not always lofty or philosophical—much hard bargaining, more than a little confusion, and the accidents of personality and time helped shape the final product. The delegates were split on many issues—what powers should be given to a central government, how the states should be represented, what was to be done about slavery, the role of the people—each of which was resolved by a compromise. The speeches of the delegates (known to us from the detailed notes kept by Madison) did not explicitly draw on political philosophy or quote from the writings of philosophers. Everyone present was quite familiar with the traditional arguments and, on the whole, well read in history. Though the leading political philosophers were only rarely mentioned, the debate was profoundly influenced by philosophical beliefs, some formed by the revolutionary experience and others by the 11-year attempt at self-government.

From the debates leading up to the Revolution, the delegates had drawn a commitment to liberty, which, despite the abuses sometimes committed in its name, they continued to share. Their defense of liberty as a natural right was derived from the writings of the 17th-century English philosopher John Locke. Unlike his English rival, Thomas Hobbes, Locke did not believe that it was necessary to have an all-powerful government or that democracy was impossible. Hobbes had argued that in any society without an absolute, supreme ruler there is bound to be ceaseless violent turmoil—a "war of all against all." Locke disagreed. In a "state of nature," Locke argued, all men cherish and seek to protect their life, liberty, and property. But in a state of nature—that is, a society without a government—the strong can use their liberty to deprive the weak of their own liberty. The instinct for self-preservation leads people to want a government that will prevent this exploitation. But if the government is not itself to deprive its subjects of their liberty, it must be limited. The chief limitation on it, he said, should derive from the fact that it is created, and governs, by the consent of the governed. People will not agree to be ruled by a government that threatens their liberty; therefore, the government to which they freely choose to submit themselves will be a limited government designed to protect liberty.[9]

The Pennsylvania experience, as well as the history of British government led the Framers to doubt whether popular consent alone would be a sufficient guarantor of liberty. A popular government may prove too weak (as in Massachusetts) to prevent

Shays's Rebellion in western Massachusetts in 1786–1787 stirred deep fears of anarchy in America. The ruckus was put down by a hastily assembled militia, and the rebels were eventually pardoned.

one faction from abusing another, or a popular majority can be tyrannical (as in Pennsylvania). In fact, the tyranny of the majority can be an even graver threat than rule by the few. In the former case, there may be no defenses for the individual—one lone person cannot count on the succor of public opinion or the possibility of popular revolt.

The problem, then, was a delicate one: how to devise a government strong enough to preserve order, but not so strong that it would threaten liberty. The answer, the delegates believed, was not "democracy" as it was then understood. To many conservatives in the late 18th century, democracy meant mob rule—it meant, in short, Shays's Rebellion (or, if they had been candid about it, the Boston Tea Party). On the other hand, *aristocracy*—the rule of the few—was no solution, since the few were likely to be self-serving. Madison, writing later in the *Federalist* papers, put the problem this way:

> *If men were angels, no government would be necessary. If angels were to govern men, neither external nor internal controls on government would be necessary. In framing a government which is to be administered by men over men, the great difficulty lies in this: you must first enable the government to control the governed; and in the next place oblige it to control itself.*[10]

Striking this balance could not be done, Madison believed, simply by writing a constitution that set limits on what government could do. The example of British rule over the colonies proved that laws and customs were inadequate checks on political power. As he expressed it, "A mere demarcation on parchment of the constitutional limits [of government] is not a sufficient guard against those encroachments which lead to a tyrannical concentration of all the powers of government in the same hands."[11]

The Challenge

The resolution of political issues, great and small, often depends crucially on how the central question is phrased. The delegates came to Philadelphia in general agreement that there were defects in the Articles of Confederation that ought to be remedied. Had they, after convening, decided to make their business that of listing these defects and debating alternative remedies for them, the document that emerged would in all likelihood have been very different from what in fact was adopted. But immediately after the convention had organized itself and chosen Washington to be its presiding officer, the Virginia delegation, led by Governor Edmund Randolph but relying heavily on the draftsmanship of James Madison, presented to the convention a comprehensive plan for a wholly new national government. The plan quickly became the major item of business at the meeting; it, and little else, was debated for the next two weeks.

The Virginia Plan

When the convention decided to make the **Virginia Plan** its agenda, it had fundamentally altered the nature of its task. The business at hand was not to be the Articles and their defects, but rather how one should go about designing a true national government. The Virginia Plan called for a strong national union organized into three governmental branches—the legislative, executive, and judicial. The legislature was to be composed of two houses, the first elected directly by the people and the second chosen by the first house from among the candidates nominated by state legislatures. The executive was to be chosen by the national legislature, as were members of a national judiciary. The executive and some members of the judiciary were to constitute a "council of revision" that could veto acts of the legislature; that veto, in turn,

Virginia Plan Proposal to create a strong national government.

could be overridden by the legislature. There were other interesting details, but the key features of the Virginia Plan were two: (1) a national legislature would have supreme powers on all matters on which the separate states were not competent to act, as well as the power to veto any and all state laws; and (2) at least one house of the legislature would be elected directly by the people.

New Jersey Plan Proposal to create a weak national government.

Great Compromise Plan to have a popularly elected House based on state population and a state-selected Senate, with two members for each state.

The New Jersey Plan

As the debate continued, the representatives of New Jersey and other small states became increasingly worried that the convention was going to write a constitution in which the states would be represented in both houses of Congress on the basis of population. If this happened, the smaller states feared they would always be outvoted by the larger ones, and so, with William Paterson of New Jersey as their spokesman, they introduced a new plan. The **New Jersey Plan** proposed to amend, not replace, the old Articles of Confederation. It enhanced the power of the national government (though not as much as the Virginia Plan), but it did so in a way that left the states' representation in Congress unchanged from the Articles—each state would have one vote. Thus not only would the interests of the small states be protected, but Congress itself would remain to a substantial degree the creature of state governments.

If the New Jersey resolutions had been presented first and taken up as the major item of business, it is quite possible they would have become the framework for the document that finally emerged. But they were not. Offered after the convention had been discussing the Virginia Plan for two weeks, the resolutions encountered a reception very different from what they may have received if introduced earlier. The debate had the delegates already thinking in terms of a national government that was more independent of the states, and thus it had accustomed them to proposals that, under other circumstances, might have seemed quite radical. On June 19, the first decisive vote of the convention was taken: seven states preferred the Virginia Plan, three states the New Jersey Plan, and one state was split.

With the tide running in favor of a strong national government, the supporters of the small states had to shift their strategy. They now began to focus their efforts on ensuring that the small states could not be outvoted by the larger ones in Congress. One way was to have the members of the lower house elected by the state legislatures rather than the people, with each state getting the same number of seats rather than seats proportional to its population.

The debate was long and feelings ran high, so much so that Benjamin Franklin, the oldest delegate present (at 81 years of age), suggested that each day's meeting begin with a prayer. It turned out that the convention could not even agree on this: Hamilton is supposed to have objected that the convention did not need "foreign aid," and others pointed out that the group had no funds with which to hire a minister. And so the argument continued.

The Compromise

Finally, a committee was appointed to meet during the Fourth of July holidays to work out a compromise, and the convention adjourned to await its report. Little is known of what went on in that committee's session, though some were later to say that Franklin played a key role in hammering out the plan that finally emerged. That compromise, the most important reached at the convention, and later called the **Great Compromise** (or sometimes the Connecticut Compromise), was submitted to the full convention on July 5 and debated for another week and a half. The debate might have gone on even longer, but suddenly the hot weather moderated, and Monday, July 16, dawned cool and fresh after a month of misery. On that day, the plan was adopted: five states were in favor, four were opposed, and two did not vote.* Thus, by the narrowest of margins, the structure of the national legislature was set as follows:

- A House of Representatives consisting initially of 65 members apportioned among the states roughly on the basis of population and elected by the people.

- A Senate consisting of two senators from each state to be chosen by the state legislatures.

The Great Compromise reconciled the interests of small and large states by allowing the former to predominate in the Senate and the latter in the House. This reconciliation was necessary to ensure there would be support for a strong national government from small as well as large states. It represented major concessions on the part of several groups. Madison, for one, was deeply opposed to the idea of having the states equally represented in the Senate. He saw in that a way for the states to hamstring the national government and much preferred some measure of proportional representation in both houses. Delegates from other states worried that representation on the basis of population in the House of Representatives would enable the large states to dominate legislative affairs. Although the margin by which the compromise was accepted was razor-thin, it held firm. In time, most of the delegates from the dissenting states accepted it.

After the Great Compromise, many more issues had to be resolved, but by now a spirit of accommodation had developed. When one delegate proposed having Congress choose the president, another, James Wilson, proposed that he be elected directly by the people. When neither side of that argument prevailed, a committee invented a plan for an "electoral college" that would choose the president. When some delegates wanted the president chosen for a life term, others proposed a seven-year term, and still others wanted the term limited to three years without eligibility for reelection. The convention settled on a four-year term with no bar to reelection. Some states wanted the Supreme Court picked by the Senate; others wanted it chosen by the president. They finally agreed to let the justices be nominated by the president and then confirmed by the Senate.

Finally, on July 26, the proposals that were already accepted, together with a bundle of unresolved issues, were handed over to the Committee of Detail, consisting of five delegates. This committee included Madison and Gouverneur Morris, who was to be the chief draftsman of the document that finally emerged. The committee hardly contented itself with mere "details," however. It inserted some new proposals and made changes in old ones, drawing for inspiration on existing state constitutions and the members' beliefs as to what the other delegates might accept. On August 6, the report—the first complete draft of the Constitution—was submitted to the convention. There it was debated item by item, revised, amended, and finally, on September 17, approved by all 12 states in attendance. (Not all *delegates* approved, however; three, including Edmund Randolph, who first submitted the Virginia Plan, refused to sign.)

The Constitution and Democracy

A debate continues to rage over whether the Constitution created, or was even intended to create, a democratic government. The answer is complex. The Framers did not intend to create a "pure democracy"—one in which the people rule directly. For one thing, the size of the country and the distances between settlements would have made that physically impossible. But more importantly, the Framers worried that a government in which all citizens directly participate, as in the New England town

*The states in favor were Connecticut, Delaware, Maryland, New Jersey, and North Carolina. Those opposed were Georgia, Pennsylvania, South Carolina, and Virginia. Massachusetts was split down the middle; the New York delegates had left the convention. New Hampshire and Rhode Island were absent.

meeting, would be a government excessively subject to temporary popular passions and one in which minority rights would be insecure. They intended instead to create a **republic**, by which they meant a government in which a system of representation operates.

The Framers favored a republic over a direct democracy because they believed that government should mediate, not mirror, popular views, and that elected officials should represent, not register, majority sentiments. They supposed that most citizens did not have the time, information, interest, and expertise to make reasonable choices among competing policy positions. They suspected that even highly educated people could be manipulated by demagogic leaders who played on their fears and prejudices. They knew that representative democracy often proceeds slowly and prevents sweeping changes in policy, but they cautioned that a government capable of doing great good quickly can also do great harm quickly. They agreed that majority opinion should figure in the enactment of many or most government policies, but they insisted that protection of civil rights and civil liberties—the right to a fair trial; the freedom of speech, press, and religion; or the right to vote itself—ought never to hinge on a popular vote. Above all, they embraced representative democracy because they saw it as a way of minimizing the chances that power would be abused either by a tyrannical popular majority or by self-serving officeholders.

The Framers were influenced by philosophers who had discussed democracy. Aristotle, who lived four centuries before Christ, defined democracy as the rule of the many; that is, rule by ordinary people, most of whom would be poor. But democracy, he suggested, can easily decay into an oligarchy (rule of the rich) or a tyranny (the rule of a despot). To prevent this, a good political system will be a mixed regime, combining elements of democracy and oligarchy: most people will vote, but talented people will play a large role in managing affairs.

But, as we noted earlier in this chapter, the Framers were strongly influenced by John Locke, the 17th-century English writer who argued against powerful kings and in favor of popular dissent. In Locke's *Second Treatise of Civil Government* (1690), he argued that people can exist in a state of nature— that is, without any ruler—so long as they can find enough food to eat and a way to protect themselves. But food may not be plentiful and, as a result, life may be poor and difficult.

The human desire for self-preservation will lead people to want a government that will enable them to own property and thereby to increase their supply of food. But unlike his English rival, Thomas Hobbes, Locke did not think it necessary to have an all-powerful government. In *Leviathan* (1651), Hobbes had argued that people live in a "war of all against all" and so an absolute, supreme ruler was essential to prevent civil war. Locke disagreed: people can get along with one another if they can securely own their farms and live off what they produce. But for that to happen, a decent government must exist with the consent of the governed and be managed by majority rule. To prevent a majority from hurting a minority, Locke wrote, the government should separate its powers, with different and competing legislative and executive branches.

Thus, what the Framers tried to do in 1787 was to create a republic that would protect freedom and private property, a moderate regime that would simultaneously safeguard people and leave them alone.

In designing that republic, the Framers chose, not without argument, to have the members of the House of Representatives elected directly by the people. Some delegates did not want to go even that far. Elbridge Gerry of Massachusetts, who refused to sign the Constitution, argued that though "the people do not want [that is, lack] virtue," they often are the "dupes of pretended patriots." Roger Sherman of Connecticut agreed. But George Mason of Virginia and James Wilson of Pennsylvania carried the day when they argued that "no government could long subsist without the confidence of the people," and this required "drawing the most numerous branch of the legislature directly from the people." Popular elections for the House were approved: six states were in favor, two opposed.

judicial review The power
of the courts to declare laws
unconstitutional.

federalism Government
authority shared by national and
local governments.

But though popular rule was to be one element of the new government, it was not to be the only one. State legislatures, not the people, would choose the senators; electors, not the people directly, would choose the president. As we have seen, without these arrangements, there would have been no Constitution at all, for the small states adamantly opposed any proposal that would have given undue power to the large ones. And direct popular election of the president would clearly have made the populous states the dominant ones. In short, the Framers wished to observe the principle of majority rule, but they felt that, on the most important questions, two kinds of majorities were essential—a majority of the voters and a majority of the states.

The power of the Supreme Court to declare an act of Congress unconstitutional—**judicial review**—is also a way of limiting the power of popular majorities. It is not clear whether the Framers intended that there be judicial review, but there is little doubt that in the Framers' minds the fundamental law, the Constitution, had to be safeguarded against popular passions. They made the process for amending the Constitution easier than it had been under the Articles, but still relatively difficult.

An amendment can be proposed either by a two-thirds vote of both houses of Congress *or* by a national convention called by Congress at the request of two-thirds of the states.[†] Once proposed, an amendment must be ratified by three-fourths of the states, either through their legislatures or through special ratifying conventions in each state. Twenty-seven amendments have survived this process, all of them proposed by Congress, and all but one (the Twenty-first Amendment) ratified by state legislatures rather than state conventions.

In short, the answer to the question of whether the Constitution brought into being a democratic government is yes, if by *democracy* one means a system of representative government based on popular consent. The degree of that consent has changed since 1787, and the institutions embodying that consent can take different forms. One form, rejected in 1787, gives all political authority to one set of representatives, directly elected by the people. (That is the case, for example, in most parliamentary regimes, such as the United Kingdom, and in some city governments in the United States.) The other form of democracy is one in which different sets of officials, chosen directly or indirectly by different groups of people, share political power. (That is the case with the United States and a few other nations where the separation of powers is intended to operate.)

Key Principles

The American version of representative democracy was based on two major principles: the separation of powers and federalism. In America, political power was to be shared by three separate branches of government; in parliamentary democracies, that power was concentrated in a single, supreme legislature. In America, political authority was divided between a national government and several state governments—**federalism**—whereas in most European systems authority was centralized in the national government. Neither of these principles was especially controversial at Philadelphia. The delegates began their work in broad agreement that separated powers and some measure of federalism were necessary, and both the Virginia and New Jersey plans contained a version of each. How much federalism should be written into the Constitution was quite controversial, however.

[†]There have been many attempts to assemble a new constitutional convention. In the 1960s, 33 states, one short of the required number, requested a convention to consider the reapportionment of state legislatures. In the 1980s, efforts were made to call a convention to consider amendments to ban abortions and to require a balanced federal budget.

Under these two principles, governmental powers in this country can be divided into three categories. The powers given to the national government exclusively are the delegated or **enumerated powers**. They include the authority to print money, declare war, make treaties, conduct foreign affairs, and regulate commerce among the states and with foreign nations. Those given exclusively to the states are the **reserved powers** and include the power to issue licenses and to regulate commerce wholly within a state. Those shared by both the national and the state governments are called **concurrent powers** and include collecting taxes, building roads, borrowing money, and maintaining courts.

enumerated powers Powers given to the national government alone.

reserved powers Powers given to the state government alone.

concurrent powers Powers shared by the national and state governments.

checks and balances Authority shared by three branches of government.

Government and Human Nature

The desirability of separating powers and leaving the states equipped with a broad array of rights and responsibilities was not controversial at the Philadelphia convention because the Framers' experiences with British rule and state government under the Articles had shaped their view of human nature. These experiences had taught most of the Framers that people would seek their own advantage in and out of politics; this pursuit of self-interest, unchecked, would lead some people to exploit others. Human nature was good enough to make it possible to have a decent government based on popular consent, but it was not good enough to make it inevitable.

One solution to this problem would be to improve human nature. Ancient political philosophers such as Aristotle believed that the first task of any government was to cultivate virtue among the governed.

HOW THINGS WORK

Checks and Balances

The Constitution creates a system of *separate* institutions that *share* powers. Because the three branches of government share powers, each can (partially) check the powers of the others. This is the system of **checks and balances**. The major checks possessed by each branch are listed below.

Congress

1. Can check the president in these ways:

   a. By refusing to pass a bill the president wants

   b. By passing a law over the president's veto

   c. By using the impeachment powers to remove the president from office

   d. By refusing to approve a presidential appointment (Senate only)

   e. By refusing to ratify a treaty the president has signed (Senate only)

(continued)

HOW THINGS WORK (*Continued*)

2. Can check the federal courts in these ways:

   a. By changing the number and jurisdiction of the lower courts

   b. By using the impeachment powers to remove a judge from office

   c. By refusing to approve a person nominated to be a judge (Senate only)

The President

1. Can check Congress by vetoing a bill it has passed

2. Can check the federal courts by nominating judges

The Courts

1. Can check Congress by declaring a law unconstitutional

2. Can check the president by declaring actions by him or his subordinates unconstitutional or not authorized by law

In addition to these checks specifically provided for in the Constitution, each branch has informal ways of checking the others. For example, the president can try to withhold information from Congress (on the grounds of "executive privilege"), and Congress can try to get information by mounting an investigation.

The exact meaning of the various checks is explained in Chapter 9 on Congress, Chapter 10 on the presidency, and Chapter 12 on the judiciary.

Many Americans were of the same mind. To them, Americans would first have to become good people before they could have a good government. Samuel Adams, a leader of the Boston Tea Party, said that the new nation must become a "Christian Sparta." Others spoke of the need to cultivate frugality, industry, temperance, and simplicity.

But to James Madison and the other architects of the Constitution, the deliberate cultivation of virtue would require a government too strong and thus too dangerous to liberty, at least at the national level. Self-interest, freely pursued within reasonable limits, was a more practical and durable solution to the problem of government than any effort to improve the virtue of the citizenry. He wanted, he said, to make republican government possible "even in the absence of political virtue."

Madison argued that the very self-interest that leads people toward factionalism and tyranny might, if properly harnessed by appropriate constitutional arrangements, provide a source of unity and a guarantee of liberty. This harnessing was to be accomplished by dividing the offices of the new government among many people and giving to the holder of each office the "necessary means and personal motives to resist encroachments of the others." In this way, "ambition must be made to counteract ambition" so that "the private interest of every individual may be a sentinel over the public rights."[12]

If men were angels, all this would be unnecessary. But Madison and the other delegates pragmatically insisted on taking human nature pretty much as it was, and therefore they adopted "this policy of supplying, by opposite and rival interests, the defect of better motives."[13] The **separation of powers** would work, not in spite of the imperfections of human nature, but because of them.

So it also is with federalism. By dividing power between the states and the national government, one level of government can serve as a check on the other. This should provide a "double security" to the rights of the people: "The different governments will control each other, at the same time that each will be controlled by itself."[14] This was especially likely to happen in America, Madison thought, because it was a large country filled with diverse interests—rich and poor, Protestant and Catholic, northerner and southerner, farmer and merchant, creditor and debtor. Each of these interests would constitute a **faction** that would seek its own advantage. One faction might come to dominate government, or a part of government, in one place, and a different and rival faction might dominate it in another. The pulling and hauling among these factions would prevent any single government—say, that of New York—from dominating all of government. The division of powers among several governments would provide virtually every faction an opportunity to gain some—but not full—power.

> *separation of powers*
> Constitutional authority is shared by three different branches of government.
>
> *faction* A group with a distinct political interest.
>
> *Federalists* Those who favor a stronger national government.
>
> *Antifederalists* Those who favor a weaker national government.

The Constitution and Liberty

A more difficult question is whether the Constitution created a system of government that would respect personal liberties. In fact, that is the question that was debated in the states when the document was presented for ratification. The proponents of the Constitution called themselves the **Federalists** (though they might more accurately have been called "nationalists"). The opponents came to be known as the **Antifederalists** (though they might more accurately have been called "states' rights advocates").[‡] To be put into effect, the Constitution had to be approved at ratifying conventions in at least nine states. This was perhaps the most democratic feature of the Constitution: It had to be accepted, not by the existing Congress (still limping along under the Articles of Confederation), nor by the state legislatures, but by special conventions elected by the people.

Though democratic, the process established by the Framers for ratifying the Constitution was technically illegal. The Articles of Confederation, which still governed, could be amended only with the approval of all 13 state legislatures. The Framers wanted to bypass these legislatures because they feared that, for reasons of ideology or out of a desire to retain their powers, the legislators would oppose the Constitution. The Framers wanted ratification with less than the consent of all 13 states because they knew that such unanimity could not be attained. And indeed the conventions in North Carolina and Rhode Island did initially reject the Constitution (see Figure 2.1).

The Antifederalist View

The great issue before the state conventions was liberty, not democracy. The opponents of the new Constitution, the Antifederalists, had a variety of objections, but were in general united by the belief that liberty could be secure only in a small republic in which the rulers were physically close to—and

‡To the delegates, a truly "federal" system was one—like the New Jersey Plan—that allowed for very strong states and a weak national government. When the New Jersey Plan lost, the delegates who defeated it began using the word *federal* to describe their plan, even though it called for a stronger national government. Thus, men who began as "Federalists" at the convention ultimately became known as "Antifederalists" during the struggle over ratification.

FIGURE 2.1   Ratification of the Federal Constitution by State Constitutions, 1787–1790

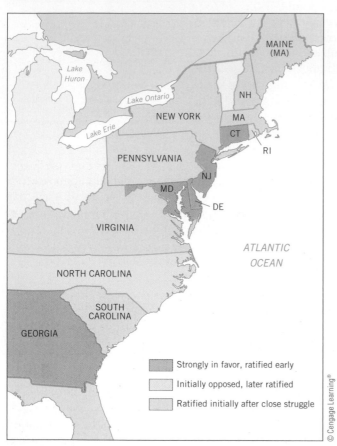

Strongly in favor, ratified early

Initially opposed, later ratified

Ratified initially after close struggle

© Cengage Learning®

closely checked by—the ruled. Their central objection was stated by a group of Antifederalists at the ratifying convention in an essay published just after they had lost: "a very extensive territory cannot be governed on the principles of freedom, otherwise than by a confederation of republics."[15]

These dissenters argued that a strong national government would be distant from the people and would use its powers to annihilate or absorb the functions that properly belonged to the states. Congress would tax heavily, the Supreme Court would overrule state courts, and the president would come to head a large standing army. (Since all these things have occurred, we cannot dismiss the Antifederalists as cranky obstructionists who opposed without justification the plans of the Framers.) These critics argued that the nation needed, at best, a loose confederation of states, with most of the powers of government kept firmly in the hands of state legislatures and state courts.

But if a stronger national government was to be created, the Antifederalists argued, it should be hedged about with many more restrictions than those in the constitution then under consideration. They proposed several such limitations, including narrowing the jurisdiction of the Supreme Court, checking the president's power by creating a council that would review his actions, leaving military affairs in the hands of the state militias, increasing the size of the House of Representatives so that it would reflect a greater variety of popular interests, and reducing or eliminating the power of Congress to levy taxes. And some of them insisted that a *bill of rights* be added to the Constitution.

James Madison gave his answer to these criticisms in *Federalist* No. 10 and No. 51 (reprinted in the Appendix with a reading guide). It was a bold answer, for it flew squarely in the face of widespread popular sentiment and much philosophical writing. Following the great French political philosopher Montesquieu, many Americans believed liberty was safe only in small societies governed either by direct democracy or by large legislatures with small districts and frequent turnover among members.

Madison argued quite the opposite—that liberty is safest in *large* (or as he put it, "extended") republics. In a small community, he said, there will be relatively few differences in opinion or interest; people will tend to see the world in much the same way. If anyone dissents or pursues an individual interest, he or she will be confronted by a massive majority and will have few, if any, allies. But in a large republic there will be many opinions and interests; as a result, it will be hard for a tyrannical majority to form or organize, and anyone with an unpopular view will find it easier to acquire allies. If Madison's argument seems strange or abstract, ask yourself the following question: If I have an unpopular opinion, an exotic lifestyle, or an unconventional interest, will I find greater security living in a small town or a big city?

By favoring a large republic, Madison was not trying to stifle democracy. Rather, he was attempting to show how democratic government really works, and what can make it work better. To rule, different interests must come together and form a **coalition**—that is, an alliance. In *Federalist* No. 51, he argued that the coalitions that formed in a large republic would be more moderate than those that formed in a small one because the bigger the republic, the greater the variety of interests, and thus the more a coalition of the majority would have to accommodate a diversity of interests and opinions if it hoped to succeed. He concluded that in a nation the size of the United States, with its enormous variety of interests, "a coalition of a majority of the whole society could seldom take place on any other principles than those of justice and the general good." Whether he was right in that prediction is a matter to which we shall return repeatedly.

The implication of Madison's arguments was daring, for he was suggesting that the national government should be at some distance from the people and insulated from their momentary passions, because the people did not always want to do the right thing. Liberty was threatened as much (or even more) by public passions and popularly based factions as by strong governments. Now the Antifederalists themselves had no very lofty view of human nature, as is evidenced by the deep suspicion with which they viewed "power-seeking" officeholders. What Madison did was take this view to its logical conclusion, arguing that if people could be corrupted by office, they could also be corrupted by factional self-interest. Thus the government had to be designed to prevent both the politicians and the people from using it for ill-considered or unjust purposes.

To argue in 1787 against the virtues of small democracies was like arguing against motherhood. Moreover, the Federalists' counterargument involved many steps: representative democracy over direct democracy; a large republic over a small republic; diversity of economic, religious, and other interests over homogeneity of such interests; and barriers, not boosts, to majority group formation and influence. Still, the Federalists prevailed, probably because many citizens were convinced that a reasonably strong national government was essential if the nation were to stand united against foreign enemies, facilitate commerce among the states, guard against domestic insurrections, and keep one faction from oppressing another. The political realities of the moment and the recent bitter experiences with the Articles probably counted for more in ratifying the Constitution than Madison's arguments. His cause was helped by the fact that, for all their legitimate concerns and their uncanny instinct for what the future might bring, the Antifederalists could offer no agreed-upon alternative to the new Constitution. In politics, then as now, you cannot beat something with nothing.

But this does not explain why the Framers failed to add a bill of rights to the Constitution. If they were so preoccupied with liberty, why didn't they take this most obvious step toward protecting liberty, especially since the Antifederalists were demanding it? Some historians have suggested that this omission was evidence that liberty was not as important to the Framers as they claimed. In fact, when one delegate suggested that a bill of rights be drawn up, the state delegations at the convention unanimously voted the idea down. There were several reasons for this.

First, the Constitution, as written, *did* contain a number of specific guarantees of individual liberty, including the right of trial by jury in criminal cases and the privilege of the writ of habeas corpus. The liberties guaranteed in the Constitution (before the **Bill of Rights** was added) are listed here:

- Writ of **habeas corpus** may not be suspended (except during invasion or rebellion).

- No **bill of attainder** may be passed by Congress or the states.

coalition An alliance of groups.

Bill of Rights First 10 amendments to the Constitution.

habeas corpus An order to produce an arrested person before a judge.

bill of attainder A law that declares a person, without a trial, to be guilty of a crime.

- No **ex post facto law** may be passed by Congress or the states.

- Right of trial by jury in criminal cases is guaranteed.

ex post facto law A law that makes an act criminal although the act was legal when it was committed.

- The citizens of each state are entitled to the privileges and immunities of the citizens of every other state.

- No religious test or qualification for holding federal office is imposed.

- No law impairing the obligation of contracts may be passed by the states.

Second, most states in 1787 had bills of rights. When Elbridge Gerry proposed to the convention that a federal bill of rights be drafted, Roger Sherman rose to observe that it was unnecessary because the state bills of rights were sufficient.[16]

But third, and perhaps most important, the Framers thought they were creating a government with specific, limited powers. It could do, they thought, only what the Constitution gave it the power to do, and nowhere in that document was there permission to infringe on freedom of speech or of the press or to impose cruel and unusual punishments. Some delegates probably feared that if any serious effort were made to list the rights that were guaranteed, later officials might assume that they had the power to do anything not explicitly forbidden.

Need for a Bill of Rights

Whatever their reasons, the Framers made at least a tactical and perhaps a fundamental mistake. It quickly became clear that without at least the promise of a bill of rights, the Constitution would not be ratified. Though the small states, pleased by their equal representation in the Senate, quickly ratified (in Delaware, New Jersey, and Georgia, the vote in the conventions was unanimous), the battle in the large states was intense and the outcome uncertain. In Pennsylvania, Federalist supporters dragged boycotting Antifederalists to the legislature in order to ensure a quorum was present so a convention could be called. There were rumors of other rough tactics.

In Massachusetts, the Constitution was approved by a narrow majority, but only after key leaders promised to obtain a bill of rights. In Virginia, James Madison fought against the fiery Patrick Henry, whose climactic speech against ratification was dramatically punctuated by a noisy thunderstorm outside. The Federalists won by 10 votes. In New York, Alexander Hamilton argued the case for six weeks against the determined opposition of most of the state's key political leaders; he carried the day, but only by three votes, and then only after New York City threatened to secede from the state if it did not ratify. By June 21, 1788, the ninth state—New Hampshire—had ratified, and the Constitution was law.

Many people think that the first Congress moved quickly to adopt a Bill of Rights—that is, the first 10 amendments to the Constitution—in order to satisfy demands made in state ratifying conventions that this be done. Unfortunately, that is not quite right. Of the many criticisms made of the proposed Constitution, hardly any referred to civil liberties. Take, for example, the Massachusetts convention. Several critics, including John Hancock, said they would vote to ratify the document if the new members of Congress did all they could to get nine amendments adopted. But these amendments had nothing to do with free speech or a free press. Instead, they involved the size of the House of Representatives, congressional influence on local elections, the power of Congress to impose taxes, and the need for grand juries in criminal cases.[17] Other speakers wanted an amendment that would have House members stand for election every year. Critics in other states made the same arguments.

Despite the bitterness of the ratification struggle, the new government that took office in 1789–1790, headed by President Washington, was greeted enthusiastically. By the spring of 1790, all 13 states had ratified. There remained, however, the task of fulfilling the promise of amending the document. To that end, James Madison introduced into the first session of the First Congress a set of proposals, 12 of which were approved by Congress; 10 of these were ratified by the states and went into effect in 1791. But with only a few exceptions, these bore no relationship to the criticisms made in the state conventions. On what, then, did Madison base them? Probably on the Virginia Declaration of Rights, written by George Mason and Madison, and unanimously approved by the Virginia legislature in 1776. These amendments, which no one called a Bill of Rights as late as 1792, did not limit the power of state governments over citizens, only the power of the federal government. Later, the Fourteenth Amendment, as interpreted by the Supreme Court, extended many of the guarantees of the Bill of Rights to cover state governmental action.

HOW THINGS WORK

The Bill of Rights

The First Ten Amendments to the Constitution Grouped by Topic and Purpose

Protections Afforded Citizens to Participate in the Political Process

Amendment 1: Freedom of religion, speech, press, and assembly; the right to petition the government.

Protections Against Arbitrary Police and Court Action

Amendment 4: No unreasonable searches or seizures.

Amendment 5: Grand jury indictment required to prosecute a person for a serious crime.

No "double jeopardy" (being tried twice for the same offense).

Forcing a person to testify against himself or herself prohibited.

No loss of life, liberty, or property without due process.

Amendment 6: Right to speedy, public, impartial trial with defense counsel and right to cross-examine witnesses.

Amendment 7: Jury trials in civil suits where value exceeds $20.

Amendment 8: No excessive bail or fines, no cruel and unusual punishments.

Protections of States' Rights and Unnamed Rights of People

Amendment 9: Unlisted rights are not necessarily denied.

Amendment 10: Powers not delegated to the United States or denied to states are reserved to the states.

Other Amendments

Amendment 2: Right to bear arms.

Amendment 3: Troops may not be quartered in homes in peacetime.

The Constitution and Slavery

Though slaves amounted to one-third of the population of the five southern states, nowhere in the Constitution can one find the word *slave* or *slavery*.

To some, the failure of the Constitution to address the question of slavery was a great betrayal of the promise of the Declaration of Independence that "all men are created equal." For the Constitution to be silent on the subject of slavery, and thereby to allow that odious practice to continue, was to convert, by implication, the wording of the Declaration to "all white men are created equal."

It is easy to accuse the signers of the Declaration and the Constitution of hypocrisy. They knew of slavery, many of them owned slaves, and yet they were silent. Indeed, British opponents of the independence movement took special delight in taunting the colonists about their complaints of being "enslaved" to the British Empire while ignoring the slavery in their very midst.

Increasingly, revolutionary leaders during this period spoke to this issue. Thomas Jefferson had tried to get a clause opposing the slave trade put into the Declaration of Independence. James Otis of Boston had attacked slavery and argued that black as well as white men should be free. As revolutionary fervor mounted, so did northern criticism of slavery. The Massachusetts legislature and then the Continental Congress voted to end the slave trade; Delaware prohibited the importation of slaves; Pennsylvania voted to tax slavery out of existence; and Connecticut and Rhode Island decided that all slaves brought into those states would automatically become free.

Slavery continued unabated in the South, defended by some whites because they thought it right, by others because they found it useful. But even in the South there were opponents, though rarely

American Slave Market, 1852 (oil on canvas), American School, (19th century) / © Chicago History Museum, USA / Bridgeman Images

The Constitution was silent about slavery, so buying and selling slaves continued for many years.

conspicuous ones. George Mason, a large Virginia slaveholder and a delegate to the convention, warned prophetically that "by an inevitable chain of causes and effects, providence punishes national sins [slavery] by national calamities."[18]

The blunt fact, however, was that any effort to use the Constitution to end slavery would have meant the end of the Constitution. The southern states would never have signed a document that seriously interfered with slavery. Without the southern states, there would have been a continuation of the Articles of Confederation, which would have left each state entirely sovereign and thus entirely free of any prospective challenge to slavery.

Thus the Framers compromised with slavery; political scientist Theodore Lowi calls this their Greatest Compromise.[19] Slavery is dealt with in three places in the Constitution, though never by name. In determining the representation each state was to have in the House, "three-fifths of all other persons" (that is, of slaves) are to be added to "the whole number of free persons."[20] The South originally wanted slaves to count fully, even though, of course, none would be elected to the House; they settled for counting 60 percent of them. The Great (or Connecticut) Compromise favored smaller states, which were mostly northern, by giving each state two senators; but the three-fifths compromise even more strongly favored the South's slaveholding states. For example, apportioned according to its free population, the southern states would have had a combined total of 33 House seats rather than the 47 they claimed. The three-fifths compromise is the primary reason why southern-born presidents, House leaders, and Supreme Court justices generally dominated antebellum American national government.[21]

The convention also agreed not to allow the new government by law or even constitutional amendment to prohibit the importation of slaves until 1808.[22] The South thus had 20 years in which it could acquire more slaves from abroad; after that, Congress was free (but not required) to end the importation. Finally, the Constitution guaranteed that if a slave were to escape his or her master and flee to a free state, the slave would be returned by that state to "the party to whom ... service or labour may be due."[23]

The unresolved issue of slavery was to prove the most explosive question of all. Allowing slavery to continue was a fateful decision, one that led to the worst social and political catastrophe in the

HOW WE COMPARE

Does a Constitution Guarantee Freedom?

You may think that the best protection for individual freedom is for a nation to have a written constitution. After all, a constitution is supposed to limit governmental action. But if you look around the world, you will see that a constitution is not enough.

Here are three nations that do not have a written constitution, and yet personal freedom is well established:

Israel   New Zealand   United Kingdom

And here are three nations with a written constitution where personal freedom is rare:

Iran   North Korea   Russia

What else must nations have in order to ensure personal freedom?

nation's history—the Civil War. The Framers chose to sidestep the issue in order to create a union that, they hoped, would eventually be strong enough to deal with the problem when it could no longer be postponed. The legacy of that choice reverberates to this day.

The Motives of the Framers

The Framers were not saints or demigods. They were men with political opinions who also had economic interests and human failings. It would be a mistake to conclude that everything they did in 1787 was motivated by a disinterested commitment to the public good. But it would be an equally great mistake to think that what they did was nothing but an effort to line their pockets by producing a government that would serve their own narrow interests. As in almost all human endeavors, the Framers acted out of a mixture of motives. What is truly astonishing is that economic interests played only a modest role in their deliberations.

Economic Interests

Some of the Framers were wealthy; some were not. Some owned slaves; some had none. Some were creditors (having loaned money to the Continental Congress or to private parties); some were deeply in debt. For nearly a century, scholars have argued over just how important these personal interests were in shaping the provisions of the Constitution.

In 1913, Charles Beard, a historian, published a book—*An Economic Interpretation of the Constitution*—arguing that the better-off urban and commercial classes, especially those members who held the IOUs issued by the government to pay for the Revolutionary War, favored the new Constitution because they stood to benefit from it.[24] But in the 1950s, that view was challenged by historians who, after looking carefully at what the Framers owned or owed, concluded that one could not explain the Constitution exclusively or even largely in terms of the economic interests of those who wrote it.[25] Some of the richest delegates, such as Elbridge Gerry of Massachusetts and George Mason of Virginia, refused to sign the document, while many of its key backers—James Madison and James Wilson, for example—were men of modest means or heavy debts.

In the 1980s, a new group of scholars, primarily economists applying more advanced statistical techniques, found evidence that some economic considerations influenced how the Framers voted on some issues during the Philadelphia convention. Interestingly, however, the economic position of the *states* from which they came had a greater effect on their votes than did their *own* monetary condition.[26]

We have already seen how delegates from small states fought to reduce the power of large states and how those from slave-owning states made certain that the Constitution would contain no provision that would threaten slavery.

But contrary to what Beard asserted, the economic interests of the Framers themselves did not dominate the convention. Some delegates owned a lot of public debt they had purchased for low prices. A strong national government of the sort envisaged by the Constitution was more likely than the weak Continental Congress to pay off this debt at face value, thus making the delegates who owned it much richer. Despite this, the ownership of public debt had no significant effect on how the Framers voted in Philadelphia. Nor did the big land speculators vote their interests. Some, such as George Washington and Robert Morris, favored the Constitution, while others, such as George Mason and William Blount, opposed it.[27]

In sum, the Framers tended to represent their states' interests on important matters. Since they were picked by the states to do so, this is exactly what one would expect. If they had not met in secret, perhaps they would have voted even more often as their constituents wanted.

With the grave and enormous exception of slavery, the Framers usually did not vote their own respective economic interests.

At the popularly elected state ratifying conventions, economic factors played a larger role. Delegates who were merchants, who lived in cities, who owned large amounts of western land, who held government IOUs, and who did not own slaves were more likely to vote to ratify the new Constitution than delegates who were farmers, who did not own public debt, and who did own slaves.[28] There were plenty of exceptions, however. Small farmers dominated the conventions in some states where the vote to ratify was unanimous.

Though interests made a difference, they were not simply elite interests. In most states, the great majority of adult white males could vote for delegates to the ratifying conventions. This means that women and blacks were excluded from the debates, but by the standards of the time—standards that did not change for over a century—the ratification process was remarkably democratic.

The Constitution and Equality

Ideas counted for as much as interests. At stake were two views of the public good. One, espoused by the Federalists, was that a reasonable balance of liberty, order, and progress required a strong national government. The other, defended by the Antifederalists, was that liberty would not be secure in the hands of a powerful, distant government; freedom required decentralization.

Today, that debate has a new focus. The defect of the Constitution, to some contemporary critics, is not that the government it created is too strong, but that it is too weak. In particular, the national government is too weak to resist the pressures of special interests that reflect and perpetuate social inequality.

This criticism reveals how our understanding of the relationship between liberty and equality has changed since the Founding. To Jefferson and Madison, citizens naturally differed in their talents and qualities. What had to be guarded against was the use of governmental power to create unnatural and undesirable inequalities. This might happen, for example, if political power was concentrated in the hands of a few people (who could use that power to give themselves special privileges) or if it was used in ways that allowed some private parties to acquire exclusive charters and monopolies. To prevent the inequality that might result from having too strong a government, its powers must be kept strictly limited.

Today, some people think of inequality quite differently. To them, it is the natural social order—the marketplace and the acquisitive talents of people operating in that marketplace—that leads to undesirable inequalities, especially in economic power. The government should be powerful enough to restrain these natural tendencies and produce, by law, a greater degree of equality than society allows when left alone.

To the Framers, liberty and (political) equality were not in conflict; to some people today, these two principles are deeply in conflict. To the Framers, the task was to keep government so limited as to prevent it from creating the worst inequality—political privilege. To some modern observers, the task is to make government strong enough to reduce what they believe is the worst inequality—differences in wealth.

Constitutional Reform: Modern Views

Almost from the day it was ratified, the Constitution has been the object of debate over ways in which it might be improved. These debates have rarely involved the average citizen, who tends to revere the document even if he or she cannot recall all its details. Because of this deep and broad popular support, scholars and politicians have been wary of attacking the Constitution or suggesting many wholesale changes. But such attacks have occurred. During the 1980s—the decade in which we celebrated the bicentennial of its adoption—we heard a variety of suggestions for improving the Constitution, ranging from particular amendments to wholesale revisions. In general there are today, as in the 18th century, two kinds of critics: those who think the federal government is too weak and those who think it is too strong.

Reducing the Separation of Powers

To the first kind of critic, the chief difficulty with the Constitution is the separation of powers. By making every decision the uncertain outcome of the pulling and hauling between the president and Congress, the Constitution precludes the emergence—except perhaps in times of crisis—of the kind of effective national leadership the country needs. In this view, our nation today faces a number of challenges that require prompt, decisive, and comprehensive action. Our problem is gridlock. Our position of international leadership, the dangerous and unprecedented proliferation of nuclear weapons among the nations of the globe, and the need to find ways of stimulating economic growth while reducing our deficit and conserving our environment—all these situations require the president be able to formulate and carry out policies free of some of the pressures and delays from interest groups and members of Congress tied to local interests.

Not only would this increase in presidential authority make for better policies, these critics argue, it would also help the voters hold the president and his party accountable for their actions. As matters now stand, nobody in government can be held responsible for policies: everyone takes the credit for successes and no one is willing to take the blame for failures. Typically, the president, who tends to be the major source of new programs, cannot get his policies adopted by Congress without long delays and much bargaining, the result of which often is some watered-down compromise that neither the president nor Congress really likes, but that each must settle for if anything is to be done at all.

Finally, critics of the separation of powers complain that the government agencies responsible for implementing a program are exposed to undue interference from legislators and special interests. In this view, the president is supposed to be in charge of the bureaucracy, but in fact must share this authority with countless members of Congress and congressional committees.

Not all critics of the separation of powers agree with all these points, nor do they all agree on what should be done about the problems. But they all have in common a fear that the separation of powers makes the president too weak and insufficiently accountable. Their proposals for reducing the separation of powers include the following:

- Allow the president to appoint members of Congress to serve in the Cabinet (the Constitution forbids members of Congress from holding any federal appointive office while in Congress).

- Allow the president to dissolve Congress and call for a special election (elections now can be held only on the schedule determined by the calendar).

- Allow Congress to require a president who has lost its confidence to face the country in a special election before his term would normally end.

- Require the presidential and congressional candidates to run as a team in each congressional district; thus a presidential candidate who carries a given district could be sure the congressional candidate of his party would also win in that district.

- Have the president serve a single six-year term instead of being eligible for up to two four-year terms; this would presumably free the president to lead without having to worry about reelection.

- Lengthen the terms of members of the House of Representatives from two to four years so that the entire House would stand for reelection at the same time as the president.[29]

Some of these proposals are offered by critics out of a desire to make the American system of government work more like the British parliamentary system, in which the prime minister is the undisputed leader of the majority in the British Parliament. The parliamentary system is the major alternative in the world today to the American separation-of-powers system.

Both the diagnoses and the remedies proposed by these critics of the separation of powers have been challenged. Many defenders of our present constitutional system believe that nations, such as the United Kingdom, with a different, more unified political system have done no better than the United States in dealing with the problems of economic growth, national security, and environmental protection. Moreover, they argue, close congressional scrutiny of presidential proposals has improved these policies more often than it has weakened them. Finally, congressional "interference" in the work of government agencies is a good way of ensuring that the average citizen can fight back against the bureaucracy; without that so-called interference, citizens and interest groups might be helpless before big and powerful agencies.

Each of the specific proposals, defenders of the present constitutional system argue, would either make matters worse or have, at best, uncertain effects. Adding a few members of Congress to the president's Cabinet would not provide much help in getting his program through Congress; there are 535 senators and representatives, and probably only about half a dozen would be in the Cabinet. Giving either the president or Congress the power to call a special election in between the regular elections (every two or four years) would cause needless confusion and great expense; the country would live under the threat of being in a perpetual political campaign with even weaker political parties. Linking the fate of the president and congressional candidates by having them run as a team in each district would reduce the stabilizing and moderating effect of having them elected separately. A Republican presidential candidate who wins in the new system would have a Republican majority in the House; a Democratic candidate winner would have a Democratic majority. We might, as a result, expect dramatic changes in policy as the political pendulum swung back and forth. Giving presidents a single six-year term would indeed free them from the need to worry about reelection, but it is precisely that worry that keeps presidents reasonably concerned about what the American people want.

Making the System Less Democratic

The second kind of critic of the Constitution thinks the government does too much, not too little. Though the separation of powers at one time may have slowed the growth of government and moderated the policies it adopted, in the last few decades government has grown helter-skelter. The problem, these critics argue, is not that democracy is a bad idea, but that democracy can produce bad—or at least unintended—results if the government caters to the special-interest claims of the citizens rather than to their long-term values.

To see how these unintended results might occur, imagine a situation in which every citizen thinks the government grows too big, taxes too heavily, and spends too much. Each citizen wants the government made smaller by reducing the benefits other people get—but not by reducing the benefits he or she gets. In fact, such citizens may even be willing to see their own benefits cut, provided everyone else's benefits are cut as well, and by a like amount.

But the political system attends to individual wants, not general preferences. It gives aid to farmers, contracts to industry, grants to professors, pensions to the elderly, and loans to students. As someone once said, the government is like an adding machine: during elections, candidates campaign by promising to do more for whatever group is dissatisfied with what the incumbents are doing for it. As a result, most elections bring to office men and women committed to doing more for somebody. The grand total of all these additions is more for everybody. Few politicians have an incentive to do less for anybody.

CONSTITUTIONAL CONNECTIONS

Women and the Constitution

Women were mentioned nowhere in the Constitution when it was written in 1787. Moreover, Article I, which set forth the provisions for electing members of the House of Representatives, granted the vote to those people who were allowed to vote for members of the lower house of the legislature in the states in which they resided. In no state at the time could women participate in those elections. In no state could they vote in any elections or hold any offices. Furthermore, wherever the Constitution uses a pronoun, it uses the masculine form—*he* or *him*.

In another sense, no: Wherever the Constitution or the Bill of Rights defines a right that people are to have, it either grants that right to "persons" or "citizens," not to "men," or it makes no mention at all of people or gender. For example:

- "The *citizens* of each State shall be entitled to all privileges and immunities of citizens of the several States."

    [Art. I, sec. 9]

- "No *person* shall be convicted of treason unless on the testimony of two witnesses to the same overt act, or on confession in open court."

    [Art. III, sec. 3]

- "No bill of attainder or ex post facto law shall be passed."

    [Art. I, sec. 9]

- "The right of the *people* to be secure in their persons, houses, papers, and effects, against unreasonable searches and seizures, shall not be violated."

    [Amend. IV]

- "No *person* shall be held to answer for a capital, or otherwise infamous crime, unless on presentment or indictment of a grand jury ... nor shall any *person* be subject for the same offense to be twice put in jeopardy of life or limb; ... nor be deprived of life, liberty, or property, without due process of law."

    [Amend. V]

- "In all criminal prosecutions the *accused* shall enjoy the right to a speedy and public trial, by an impartial jury."

    [Amend. VI]

- Moreover, when the qualifications for elective office are stated, the word *person*, not *man*, is used.

- "No *person* shall be a Representative who shall not have attained to the age of twenty-five years."

    • [Art. I, sec. 2]

- "No *person* shall be a Senator who shall not have attained to the age of thirty years."

    [Art. I, sec. 3]

- "No *person* except a natural born citizen ... shall be eligible to the office of President; neither shall any *person* be eligible to that office who shall not have attained to the age of thirty-five years."

    [Art. II, sec. 1]

In places, the Constitution and the Bill of Rights used the pronoun *he*, but always in the context of referring back to a *person* or *citizen*. At the time, and until quite recently, the male pronoun was often used in legal documents to refer generically to both men and women.

(Continued)

CONSTITUTIONAL CONNECTIONS (*Continued*)

Thus, though the Constitution did not give women the right to vote until the Nineteenth Amendment was ratified in 1920, it did use language that extended fundamental rights, and access to office, to women and men equally.

Of course, what the Constitution permitted did not necessarily occur. State and local laws denied women rights that in principle they ought to have enjoyed. Except for a brief period in New Jersey, no women voted in statewide elections until, in 1869, they were given the right to cast ballots in territorial elections in Wyoming.

When women were first elected to Congress, there was no need to change the Constitution; nothing in it restricted office-holding to men.

When women were given the right to vote by constitutional amendment, it was not necessary to amend any existing language in the Constitution, because nothing in the Constitution itself denied women the right to vote; the amendment simply added a new right:

- "The right of citizens of the United States to vote shall not be denied or abridged by the United States or any state on account of sex."

[Amend. XIX]

Source: Adapted from Robert Goldwin, "*Why Blacks, Women and Jews Are Not Mentioned in the Constitution*," Commentary (May 1987): 28–33.

To remedy this state of affairs, these critics suggest various mechanisms, but principally a constitutional amendment that would either set a limit on the amount of money the government could collect in taxes each year, or require that each year the government have a balanced budget (that is, not spend more than it takes in in taxes), or both. In some versions of these plans, an extraordinary majority (say, 60 percent) of Congress could override these limits, and the limits would not apply in wartime.

The effect of such amendments, the proponents claim, would be to force Congress and the president to look at the big picture—the grand total of what they are spending—rather than just to operate the adding machine by pushing the "add" button over and over again. If they could spend only so much during a given year, they would have to allocate what they spend among all rival claimants. For example, if more money were to be spent on the poor, less could then be spent on the military, or vice versa.

Some critics of an overly powerful federal government think these amendments will not be passed or may prove unworkable; instead, they favor enhancing the president's power to block spending by giving him a **line-item veto**. Most state governors can veto a particular part of a bill and approve the rest using a line-item veto. The theory is that such a veto would better equip the president to stop unwarranted spending without vetoing the other provisions of a bill. In 1996, President Clinton signed the Line Item Veto Act, passed by the 104th Congress. But despite its name, the new law did not give the president full line-item veto power (only a change in the Constitution could confer that power). Instead, the law gave the president authority to selectively eliminate individual items in large appropriations bills, expansions in certain income-transfer programs, and tax breaks (giving the president what budget experts call *enhanced rescission authority*). But it also left Congress free to craft bills in ways that would give the president few opportunities to veto (or *rescind*) favored items. For example, Congress could still force the president to accept or reject an entire appropriations bill simply by tagging on this sentence: "Appropriations provided under this act (or title or section) shall not be subject to the provisions of the Line Item

line-item veto An executive's ability to block a particular provision in a bill passed by the legislature.

amendments A new provision in the Constitution that has been ratified by the states.

Veto Act." In *Clinton et al. v. New York et al.* (1998), the Supreme Court struck down the 1996 law, holding 6 to 3 that the Constitution does not allow the president to cancel specific items in tax and spending legislation. Clinton's successor, President George W. Bush, championed the line-item veto, but to no avail; and, when asked about the line-item veto in February 2009, President Barack Obama's press secretary, Robert Gibbs, quipped that the new president would "love to take that for a test drive."

Finally, some critics of a powerful government feel that the real problem arises not from an excess of "adding-machine" democracy, but from the growth in the power of the federal courts, as described in Chapter 12. These critics would like to devise a set of laws or constitutional amendments that would narrow the authority of federal courts.

The opponents of these suggestions argue that constitutional amendments to restrict the level of taxes or to require a balanced budget are unworkable, even assuming—which they do not—that a smaller government is desirable. There is no precise, agreed-upon way to measure how much the

HOW THINGS WORK

Ways of Amending the Constitution

Under Article V, there are two ways to *propose* amendments to the Constitution and two ways to *ratify* them.

To Propose an Amendment

1. Two-thirds of both houses of Congress vote to propose an amendment, *or*

2. Two-thirds of the state legislatures ask Congress to call a national convention to propose amendments.

To Ratify an Amendment

1. Three-fourths of the state legislatures approve it, *or*

2. Ratifying conventions in three-fourths of the states approve it.

Some Key Facts

- Only the first method of proposing an amendment has been used.

- The second method of ratification has been used only once, to ratify the Twenty-first Amendment (repealing Prohibition).

- Congress may limit the time within which a proposed amendment must be ratified. The usual limitation has been seven years.

- Thousands of proposals have been made, but only 33 have obtained the necessary two-thirds vote in Congress.

- Twenty-seven amendments have been ratified.

- The first 10 amendments, ratified on December 15, 1791, are known as the Bill of Rights.

government spends or to predict in advance how much it will receive in taxes during the year; thus defining and enforcing a "balanced budget" is no easy matter. Since the government can always borrow money, it might easily evade any spending limits. It has also shown great ingenuity in spending money in ways that never appear as part of the regular budget.

The line-item veto may or may not be a good idea. Unless the Constitution is amended to permit it, future presidents will have to do without it. The states—where some governors have long had the veto—are quite different from the federal government in power and responsibilities. Whether a line-item veto would work as well in Washington, D.C., as it does in many state capitals is something that we may simply never know.

Finally, proposals to curtail judicial power are thinly veiled attacks, the opponents argue, on the ability of the courts to protect essential citizens' rights. If Congress and the people do not like the way the Supreme Court has interpreted the Constitution, they can always amend the Constitution to change a specific ruling; there is no need to adopt some across-the-board limitation on court powers.

Who Is Right?

Some of the arguments of these two sets of critics of the Constitution may strike you as plausible or even entirely convincing. Whatever you may ultimately decide, decide nothing for now. One cannot make or remake a constitution based entirely on abstract reasoning or unproven factual arguments. Even when the Constitution was first written in 1787, it was not an exercise in abstract philosophy, but rather an effort to solve pressing, practical problems in the light of a theory of human nature, the lessons of past experience, and a close consideration of how governments in other countries and at other times had worked.

Brendan Hoffman/Getty Images

People write on a large copy of the U.S. Constitution in Washington, D.C., bringing their perspective on the relevance of the 18th-century document today.

Just because the Constitution is more than 200 years old does not mean it is out of date. The crucial questions are these: How well has it worked over the long sweep of American history? How well has it worked compared to the constitutions of other democratic nations?

The only way to answer those questions is to study American government closely—with special attention to its historical evolution and to the practices of other nations. That is what this book is about. Of course, even after close study, people will still disagree about whether our system should be changed. People want different things and evaluate human experience according to different beliefs. But if we first understand how, in fact, the government works and why it has produced the policies it has, we can then argue more intelligently about how best to achieve our wants and give expression to our beliefs.

LEARNING OBJECTIVES

LO 2.1 Why was a Bill of Rights adopted so soon after the ratification of the Constitution?

A Bill of Rights was adopted by the First Congress because so many states had asked for amendments in exchange for their votes to ratify the Constitution. But what they got was quite different from what they requested. James Madison, in writing the amendments, used much of the language of the Virginia Declaration of Rights.

LO 2.2 Why did so many authors of the Constitution fear factions?

Many Framers—but especially Madison—feared factions because human nature divides people, and when they are divided they are likely to oppose one another and so threaten the chances of arriving at the common good.

LO 2.3 Why did the Framers agree on the idea of a separation of powers?

Almost all of the Framers agreed that our government should be based on the separation of powers among its three branches because such a system would provide better checks on power than what they had experienced with England.

LO 2.4 What is the difference between a democracy and a republic?

A democracy means rule by the people; direct democracy means letting every important issue be decided by popular vote. A republic is a government in which authority has been given to elected representatives. The United States is a republic in which members of the House of Representatives are selected in democratic elections, members of the Senate (at least initially) were selected by state legislatures, and the courts are staffed by appointed judges.

LO 2.5 Whose freedom does the Constitution protect?

It was intended to protect everybody's freedom, except that of slaves. To create a national government, it was necessary that the Constitution ignore slavery, but without the Constitution, there would have been no national government to challenge slavery during the Civil War. Though women are not mentioned, in fact there is nothing in the Constitution to prevent them from holding national office or from voting in federal elections. Voting rights were to be decided by each state until the passage of a constitutional amendment (the Nineteenth, ratified in 1920) that prohibited the states from denying the vote to women.

TO LEARN MORE

• To find historical and legal documents: **TeachingAmericanHistory.org**

• National Constitution Center: **www.constitutioncenter.org**

• Congress: **thomas.loc.gov/** (choose Historical Documents)

• To look at court cases about the Constitution: Cornell University, **www.law.cornell.edu/supct**

• Bailyn, Bernard. *The Ideological Origins of the American Revolution*. Cambridge: Harvard University Press, 1967. A brilliant account of how the American colonists formed and justified the idea of independence.

• Becker, Carl L. *The Declaration of Independence*. New York: Vintage, 1942. The classic account of the meaning of the Declaration.

• *Federalist* papers. By Alexander Hamilton, James Madison, and John Jay. The definitive edition, edited by Jacob E. Cooke, was published in Middletown, CT, in 1961, by the Wesleyan University Press.

• Maier, Pauline. *Ratification: The People Debate the Constitution, 1787–1788*. New York: Simon and Schuster, 2010. Not only is this a marvelous study of ratification, but it also is virtually the only one in existence. A splendid, comprehensive account.

• McDonald, Forrest. *Novus Ordo Seclorum*. Lawrence: University of Kansas Press, 1985. A careful study of the intellectual origins of the Constitution. The Latin title means "New World Order," which is what the Framers hoped they were creating.

• Sheldon, Garrett W. *The Political Philosophy of James Madison*. Baltimore: Johns Hopkins University Press, 2001. Masterful account of Madison's political thought and its roots in classical republicanism and Christianity.

• Storing, Herbert J. *What the Anti-Federalists Were For*. Chicago: University of Chicago Press, 1981. Close analysis of the political views of those opposed to the ratification of the Constitution.

• Wood, Gordon S. *The Creation of the American Republic*. Chapel Hill: University of North Carolina Press, 1969. A detailed study of American political thought before the Philadelphia convention.

• ____. *The Radicalism of the American Revolution*. New York: Knopf, 1992. Magisterial study of the nature and effects of the American Revolution and the relationship between the socially radical Revolution and the Constitution.

Visionsof America/Joe Sohm/Getty Images

3

Federalism

LEARNING OBJECTIVES

LO 3.1   Why does the United States have federalism?

LO 3.2   How has American Federalism evolved from the Founding to the present?

LO 3.3   Where is sovereignty located in the American political system?

LO 3.4   How is power divided between the national government and the states under the Constitution?

LO 3.5   What competing values are at stake in federalism?

THEN

When the Framers drafted the Constitution, the Antifederalists opposed it primarily on the grounds that it gave too much power to national government. The Antifederalists recognized the limitations of the Articles of Confederation, but they feared that the Constitution sacrificed liberty and civic responsibility with its expansion of the power of the national government.

NOW

The Federalists prevailed over the Antifederalists with the ratification of the Constitution. Amended only 27 times in more than 225 years, the Constitution is still the law of the land today. But, much as the Antifederalists predicted, the federal government has taken on responsibilities that traditionally were the province of state governments, such as social welfare policy, education, health care, and a minimum wage. States have some flexibility in implementing policies, but the national government sets the direction in many more policy areas today than it did originally; and, as the Antifederalists feared, we now have a large standing army and powerful federal courts.

These changes between then and now do not mean that the Constitution was wrong (if we were forced to take sides, we would have sided with the Federalists—would you?) But there is no denying that the federal government has grown far beyond anything that even the most ardent Federalists had envisioned. Much of that growth has occurred in just the last half-century or so. In 2010, the federal government spent roughly $4 trillion. Adjusted for inflation, that was more than five times what it spent in 1960.

But that is only about half of the story. Over the last half-century, state and local government spending has risen steeply, too. In 2010, state and local governments spent a combined total of nearly $2.5 trillion. Adjusted for inflation, that was nearly six times what they spent in 1960.

No less telling, virtually all of the post-1960 growth in government employees has been concentrated not in Washington, but in state capitals and city halls: the federal government's full-time civilian (nonmilitary) workforce numbers about 2 million (about the same number as in 1960), whereas state and local governments employ a combined total of about 12 million full-time workers (more than double the number they employed in 1960).

Back when the Federalists and the Antifederalists debated the Constitution, neither side anticipated that what today we call "big government" would encompass all three levels of government: federal, state, and local. Then: they fussed and fought over how vast the federal government might someday become. Now: the reality is that, apart from military affairs and international diplomacy, most "national" laws, policies, and programs are shaped, administered, or funded in whole or in part through a complex and often contentious system of federal–state relations.

Why Federalism Matters

Federalism can be defined as a political system in which the national government shares power with local governments (state governments in the case of the United States, but other subnational governments in the case of federal systems including Australia, India, and Switzerland). Constitutionally, in America's federal system, state governments have a specially protected existence and the authority to make final decisions over many governmental activities. Even today, after more than a century during which the government headquartered in Washington, D.C., has grown, state and local governments are not mere junior partners in deciding important

> **Federalism** Government authority shared by national and local governments.

public policy matters. The national government can pass, and the federal courts can uphold, laws to protect the environment, store nuclear waste, expand low-income housing, guarantee the right to an abortion, provide special services for the handicapped, or toughen public-school graduation standards. But whether and how such federal laws are followed or funded often involves decisions by diverse state and local government officials, both elected and appointed.

Federalism or federal–state relations may seem like an arcane or boring subject until you realize that it is behind many things that matter to many people: how much you pay in certain taxes, whether you can drive above 55 miles per hour on certain roadways, whether or where you can buy liquor, how much money gets spent on schools, whether all or most children have health insurance coverage, and much more. For instance, as summarized in the **Constitutional Connections** feature on page 53, the Supreme Court's 2012 ruling on the new federal health care law's "federalism" provisions matters greatly to how Americans shop for health insurance. By the same token, federalism affects almost every aspect of crime and punishment in America: persons convicted of murder are subject to the death penalty in some states, but not in others; penalties for illegal drug sales vary widely from state to state; and there is an unresolved conflict between national law and certain states' laws regarding the use of marijuana. Perhaps most importantly, federalism is critical to how certain civil liberties (Chapter 4) and civil rights (Chapter 5) are defined and protected (for instance, some state constitutions mention God, and some state laws specifically prohibit funding for religious schools).

Federalism matters, but how it matters has changed over time. In 1908, Woodrow Wilson observed that the relationship between the national government and the states "is the cardinal question of our constitutional system," a question that cannot be settled by "one generation, because it is a question of growth, and every successive stage of our political and economic development gives it a new aspect, makes it a new question."[1]

Since the adoption of the Constitution in 1787, the single most persistent source of political conflict has been the relations between the national and state governments. The political conflict

Bill Clark/CQ Roll Call/Getty Images

After the passage of the 2010 health care law, critics declared that it would require thousands of pages of rules and regulations for implementation.

CONSTITUTIONAL CONNECTIONS

States and "Health Exchanges"

In *National Federation of Business v. Sebelius* (2012), the U.S. Supreme Court upheld the constitutionality of the "individual mandate" (effective January 1, 2014, individual citizens must carry health insurance or pay a "tax"), but it struck down provisions of the law that required the states to spend substantially more on Medicaid (the means-tested, federal–state program that pays medical expenses for low-income and elderly people receiving certain other federal welfare benefits). At the same time, however, the Court let stand provisions of the law requiring the District of Columbia and the states to establish (by January 1, 2014) online "health exchanges" for people that are not enrolled in Medicare (the non-means-tested federal program that pays for part of the cost of medical care for retired or disabled people covered by Social Security). The "health exchanges" are supposed to enable consumers to compare different private insurance plans, find out if they are eligible for Medicaid, and choose among four levels of coverage designated as "bronze," "silver," "gold," and "platinum." But the Court's decision left each state free to choose whether to operate the exchange itself ("state-run exchange"), utilize an exchange established by the federal government ("federal exchange"), or set up a federal–state partnership under which the state chooses insurance options, but the federal government runs the exchange ("planned partnership exchange"). According to tracking reports by the Kaiser Family Foundation, by mid-2013, the District of Columbia and 17 states had each opted to create its own exchange, 25 states had opted to utilize the federal exchange, and 8 states had selected the planned partnership exchange.

over slavery, for example, was intensified because some state governments condoned or supported slavery, while others took action to discourage it. The proponents and opponents of slavery were thus given territorial power centers from which to carry on the dispute. Other issues—such as the regulation of business and the provision of social welfare programs—were in large part fought out, for well over a century, in terms of "national interests" versus "states' rights." While other nations, such as Great Britain, were debating the question of whether the national government *ought* to provide old-age pensions or regulate the railroads, the United States debated a different question—whether the national government *had the right* to do these things.

The Founding

The goal of the Founders seems clear: federalism was one device whereby personal liberty was to be protected. (The separation of powers was another.) The Founders feared that placing final political authority in any one set of hands—even in the hands of persons popularly elected—would so concentrate power, as to risk tyranny. But they had seen what happened when independent states tried to form a compact, as under the Articles of Confederation; what the states put together, they could also take apart. The alliance among the states that existed from 1776 to 1787 was a confederation—that is, a system of government in which the people create state governments, which in turn create and operate a national government (see Figure 3.1). Since the national government in a confederation derives its powers from the states, it is dependent on their continued cooperation for its survival. By 1786, that cooperation was barely forthcoming.

FIGURE 3.1 **Lines of Power in Three Systems of Government**

UNITARY SYSTEM

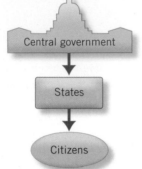

Power centralized.
State or regional governments derive authority from central government. Examples: United Kingdom, France.

FEDERAL SYSTEM

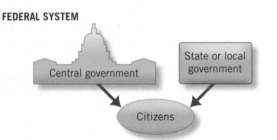

Power divided between central and state or local governments.
Both the government and constituent governments act directly upon the citizens.
Both must agree to constitutional change.
Examples: Canada, United States since adoption of Constitution.

CONFEDERAL SYSTEM (or CONFEDERATION)

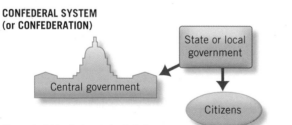

Power held by independent states.
Central government is a creature of the constituent governments.
Example: United States under the Articles of Confederation.

© Cengage Learning®

A Bold, New Plan

A federation—or a "federal republic," as the Founders called it—derives its powers directly from the people, as do the state governments. As the Founders envisioned it, both levels of government—the national and the state—would have certain powers, but neither would have supreme authority over the other. Madison, writing in *Federalist* No. 46, said that both the state and federal governments "are in fact but different agents and trustees of the people, constituted with different powers." In *Federalist* No. 28, Hamilton explained how he thought the system would work: the people could shift their support between state and federal levels of government as needed to keep the two in balance. "If their rights are invaded by either, they can make use of the other as the instrument of redress."

It was an entirely new plan, for which no historical precedent existed. Nobody came to the Philadelphia Convention with a clear idea of what a federal (as opposed to a unitary or a confederal) system would look like, and there was not much discussion at Philadelphia of how the system would work in practice. Few delegates then used the word *federalism* in the sense in which we now employ it (it was originally used as a synonym for *confederation*, and only later came to stand for something different).[2] The Constitution does not spell out the powers that the states are to have, and until the Tenth Amendment was added at the insistence of various states, there was not even a clause in it saying (as did the amendment) that "the powers not delegated to the United States by the Constitution, nor prohibited by it to the states, are reserved to the states respectively, or to the people." The Founders assumed from the outset that the federal government would have only those powers given to it by the Constitution; the Tenth Amendment was an afterthought, added to make that assumption explicit and allay fears that something else was intended.[3]

The Tenth Amendment has rarely had much practical significance, however. From time to time, the Supreme Court has tried to interpret that amendment as putting certain state activities beyond the reach of the federal government, but usually the Court has later changed its mind and allowed Washington to regulate such matters as the hours that employees of a city-owned mass-transit system may work. The Court did not find that running such a transportation system was one of the powers "reserved to the states."[4] But, as we explain later in this chapter, the Court has begun to give new life to the Tenth Amendment and the doctrine of state sovereignty.

Elastic Language

The need to reconcile the competing interests of large and small states and of northern and southern states—especially as they affected the organization of Congress—was sufficiently difficult without trying to spell out exactly what relationship ought to exist between the national and state systems. For example, Congress was given the power to regulate commerce "among the several states." The Philadelphia Convention would have gone on for four years rather than four months if the Founders had decided that it was necessary to describe, in clear language, how one was to tell where commerce *among* the states ended and commerce wholly *within* a single state began. The Supreme Court, as we shall see, devoted more than a century to that task before giving up.

Though some clauses bearing on federal–state relations were reasonably clear (see the box on page 57), other clauses were quite vague. The Founders realized, correctly, that they could not make an exact and exhaustive list of everything the federal government was empowered to do—circumstances would change, and new exigencies would arise. Thus they added the following elastic language to Article I: Congress shall have the power to "make all laws which shall be necessary and proper for carrying into execution the foregoing powers."

The Founders themselves carried away from Philadelphia different views of what federalism meant. One view was championed by Hamilton. Since the people had created the national government, since the laws and treaties made pursuant to the Constitution were "the supreme law of the land" (Article VI), and since the most pressing needs were the development of a national economy and the conduct of foreign affairs, Hamilton thought that the national government was the superior and leading force in political affairs and that its powers ought to be broadly defined and liberally construed.

The other view, championed by Jefferson, was that the federal government, though important, was the product of an agreement among the states, and though "the people" were the ultimate sovereigns, the principal threat to their liberties was likely to come from the national government. (Madison, a strong supporter of national supremacy at the convention, later became a champion of states' rights.) Thus the powers of the federal government should be narrowly construed and strictly limited. As Madison put it in *Federalist* No. 45, in language that probably made Hamilton wince, "The powers delegated by the proposed Constitution to the federal government are few and defined. Those which are to remain in the State governments are numerous and indefinite."

Hamilton argued for national supremacy, Jefferson for states' rights. Though their differences were greater in theory than in practice, the differing interpretations they offered of the Constitution were to shape political debate in this country until well into the 1960s.

The Debate on the Meaning of Federalism

The Civil War was fought, in part, over the issue of national supremacy versus states' rights, but it settled only one part of that argument—namely, that the national government was supreme, its sovereignty derived directly from the people, and thus the states could not lawfully secede from the Union. Virtually every other aspect of the national-supremacy issue continued to animate political and legal debate for another century.

The Supreme Court Speaks

"necessary and proper"
clause Section of the Constitution allowing Congress to pass all laws "necessary and proper" to its duties, and which has permitted Congress to exercise powers not specifically given to it (enumerated) by the Constitution.

As arbiter of what the Constitution means, the Supreme Court became the focal point of that debate. In Chapter 12, we shall see in some detail how the Court made its decisions. For now, it is enough to know that during the formative years of the new Republic, the Supreme Court was led by a staunch and brilliant advocate of Hamilton's position, Chief Justice John Marshall. In a series of decisions, he and the Court powerfully defended the national-supremacy view of the newly formed federal government.

The box on page 61 lists some landmark cases in the history of federal–state relations. Perhaps the most important decision was in a case, seemingly trivial in its origins, which arose when James McCulloch, the cashier of the Baltimore branch of the Bank of the United States—which had been created by Congress—refused to pay a tax levied on that bank by the state of Maryland. He was hauled into state court and convicted of failing to pay the tax. In 1819, McCulloch appealed all the way to the Supreme Court in a case known as *McCulloch v. Maryland.* The Court, in a unanimous opinion, answered two questions in ways that expanded the powers of Congress and confirmed the supremacy of the federal government in the exercise of those powers.

The first question was whether Congress had the right to set up a bank, or any other corporation, since such a right is nowhere explicitly mentioned in the Constitution. Marshall said that, though the federal government possessed only those powers enumerated in the Constitution, the "extent"—that is, the meaning—of those powers required interpretation. Though the word *bank* is not in that document, one finds there the power to manage money: to lay and collect taxes, issue a currency, and borrow funds. To carry out these powers, Congress may reasonably decide that chartering a national bank is "necessary and proper." Marshall's words were carefully chosen to endow the **"necessary and proper" clause** with the widest possible sweep:

> *Let the end be legitimate, let it be within the scope of the Constitution, and all means which are appropriate, which are plainly adapted to that end, which are not prohibited, but consistent with the letter and spirit of the Constitution, are constitutional.*[5]

The second question was whether a federal bank could lawfully be taxed by a state. To answer it, Marshall went back to first principles. The government of the United States was not established by the states, but by the people, and thus the federal government was supreme in the exercise of those powers conferred upon it. Having already concluded that chartering a bank was within the powers of Congress, Marshall then argued that the only way for such powers to be supreme was for their use to be immune from state challenge and for the products of their use to be protected against state destruction. Since "the power to tax involves the power to destroy," and since the power to destroy a federal agency would confer upon the states supremacy over the federal government, the states may not tax any federal instrument. Hence the Maryland law was unconstitutional.

McCulloch won, and so did the federal government. Half a century later, the Court decided that what was sauce for the goose was sauce for the gander. It held that just as state governments could not tax federal bonds, the federal government could not tax the interest people earn on state and municipal bonds. In 1988, the Supreme Court reversed course and decided that Congress was now free, if it wished, to tax the interest on such state and local bonds.[6] Municipal bonds—which for nearly a century were a tax-exempt investment protected (so their holders thought) by the Constitution—were now protected only by politics. So far, Congress hasn't tried to tax them.

Nullification

The Supreme Court can decide a case without settling the issue. The struggle over states' rights versus national supremacy continued to rage in Congress, during presidential elections, and ultimately on the battlefield. The issue came to center on the doctrine of **nullification**. When Congress passed laws (in 1798) to punish newspaper editors who published stories critical of the federal government, James Madison and Thomas Jefferson opposed the laws, suggesting (in statements known as the Virginia and Kentucky Resolutions) that the states had the right to "nullify" (that is, declare null and void) a federal law that, in the states' opinion, violated the Constitution. The laws expired before the claim of nullification could be settled in the courts.

> **nullification** The doctrine that a state can declare null and void a federal law that, in the state's opinion, violates the Constitution.

HOW THINGS WORK

The States and the Constitution

The Framers made some attempt to define the relations between the states and the federal government and how the states were to relate to one another. The following points were made in the original Constitution—before the Bill of Rights was added.

Restrictions on Powers of the States

States may not make treaties with foreign nations, coin money, issue paper currency, grant titles of nobility, pass a bill of attainder or an ex post facto law, or, without the consent of Congress, levy any taxes on imports or exports, keep troops and ships in time of peace, or enter into an agreement with another state or with a foreign power.

[Art. I, sec. 10]

Guarantees by the Federal Government to the States

The national government guarantees to every state a "republican form of government" and protection against foreign invasion and (provided the states request it) protection against domestic insurrection.

[Art. IV, sec. 4]

An existing state will not be broken up into two or more states or merged with all or part of another state without that state's consent.

[Art. IV, sec. 3]

Congress may admit new states into the Union.

[Art. IV, sec. 3]

Taxes levied by Congress must be uniform throughout the United States: they may not be levied on some states but not others.

[Art. I, sec. 8]

(*continued*)

HOW THINGS WORK (*Continued*)

The Constitution may not be amended to give states unequal representation in the Senate.

[Art. V]

Rules Governing How States Deal with Each Other

"Full faith and credit" shall be given by each state to the laws, records, and court decisions of other states. (For example, a civil case settled in the courts of one state cannot be retried in the courts of another.)

[Art. IV, sec. 1]

The citizens of each state shall have the "privileges and immunities" of the citizens of every other state. (No one is quite sure what this is supposed to mean.)

[Art. IV, sec. 2]

If a person charged with a crime by one state flees to another, he or she is subjected to extradition—that is, the governor of the state that finds the fugitive is obliged to return the person to the governor of the state where he or she is wanted.

[Art. IV, sec. 2]

Later, the doctrine of nullification was revived by John C. Calhoun of South Carolina, first in opposition to a tariff enacted by the federal government, and later in opposition to federal efforts to restrict slavery. Calhoun argued that if Washington attempted to ban slavery, the states had the right to declare such acts unconstitutional, and thus null and void. This time, the issue was settled—by war. The Northern victory in the Civil War determined once and for all that the federal union is indissoluble and that states cannot declare acts of Congress unconstitutional, a view later confirmed by the Supreme Court.[7]

Dual Federalism

After the Civil War, the debate about the meaning of federalism focused on the interpretation of the commerce clause of the Constitution. Out of this debate emerged the doctrine of **dual federalism**, which held that though the national government was supreme in its sphere, the states were equally supreme in theirs, and that these two spheres of action should and could be kept separate. Applied to commerce, the concept of dual federalism implied that there were such things as *inter*state commerce, which Congress could regulate, and *intra*state commerce, which only the states could regulate, and that the Court could determine which was which.

dual federalism Doctrine holding that the national government is supreme in its sphere, the states are supreme in theirs, and the two spheres should be kept separate.

For a long period, the Court tried to decide what was interstate commerce based on the kind of business that was conducted. Transporting things between states was obviously interstate commerce, and so subject to federal regulation. Thus federal laws affecting the interstate shipment of lottery tickets,[8] prostitutes,[9] liquor,[10] and harmful foods and drugs[11] were upheld. On the other hand, manufacturing,[12] insurance,[13] and farming[14] were, in the past, considered *intra*state commerce, and so only the state governments were allowed to regulate them.

Such product-based distinctions turned out to be hard to sustain. For example, if you ship a case of whiskey from Kentucky to Kansas, how long is it in interstate commerce (and thus subject to federal law), and when does it enter intrastate commerce and become subject only to state law? For a while, the Court's answer was that the whiskey was in interstate commerce so long as it was in its "original package,"[15] but that only precipitated long quarrels as to what was the original package and how one is to treat things, like gas and grain, which may not be shipped in packages at all. And how could one distinguish between manufacturing and transportation when one company did both, or when a single manufacturing corporation owned factories in different states? And if an insurance company sold policies to customers both inside and outside a given state, were there to be different laws regulating identical policies that happened to be purchased from the same company by persons in different states?

In time, the effort to find some clear principles that distinguished interstate from intrastate commerce was pretty much abandoned. Commerce was like a stream flowing through the country, drawing to itself contributions from thousands of scattered enterprises and depositing its products in millions of individual homes. The Court began to permit the federal government to regulate almost anything that affected this stream, so that by the 1940s, not only had farming and manufacturing been redefined as part of interstate commerce,[16] but even the janitors and window washers in buildings that housed companies engaged in interstate commerce were now said to be part of that stream.[17]

Today, lawyers are engaged in interstate commerce, but professional baseball players are not. If your state has approved marijuana use for medical purposes, you can still be penalized under federal law even when the marijuana you consume was grown in a small container in your backyard.[18]

State Sovereignty

It would be a mistake to think that the doctrine of dual federalism is entirely dead. Until recently, Congress, provided that it had a good reason, could pass a law regulating almost any kind of economic activity anywhere in the country, and the Supreme Court would call it constitutional. But in *United States v. Lopez* (1995), the Court held that Congress had exceeded its commerce clause power by prohibiting guns in a school zone.

The Court reaffirmed the view that the commerce clause does not justify any federal action when, in May 2000, it overturned the Violence Against Women Act of 1994. This law allowed women who were the victims of a crime of violence motivated by gender to sue the guilty party in federal court. In *United States v. Morrison,* the Court, in a five-to-four decision, said that attacks against women are not, and do not substantially affect, interstate commerce, and hence Congress cannot constitutionally pass such a law. Chief Justice William Rehnquist said that "the Constitution requires a distinction between what is truly national and what is truly local." The states, of course, can pass such laws, and many have.

The Court has moved to strengthen states' rights on other grounds as well. In *Printz v. United States* (1997), the Court invalidated a federal law that required local police to conduct background checks on all gun purchasers. The Court ruled that the law violated the Tenth Amendment by commanding state governments to carry out a federal regulatory program. Writing for the five-to-four majority, Justice Antonin Scalia declared, "The Federal government may neither issue directives requiring the states to address particular problems, nor command the states' officers, or those of their political subdivisions, to administer or enforce a Federal regulatory program.... Such commands are fundamentally incompatible with our constitutional system of dual sovereignty."

The Court has also given new life to the Eleventh Amendment, which protects states from lawsuits by citizens of other states or foreign nations. In 1999, the Court shielded states from suits by copyright owners who claimed infringement of copyrights issued by state agencies and immunized states from lawsuits by people who argued that state regulations create unfair economic competition. In *Alden v. Maine* (1999), the Court held that state employees could not sue to force state compliance with federal fair-labor laws. In the Court's five-to-four majority opinion, Justice Anthony M. Kennedy stated, "Although the Constitution grants broad powers to Congress, our federalism requires that Congress treat the states in a manner consistent with their status as residuary sovereigns and joint participants in the governance of the nation." A few years later, in *Federal Maritime Commission v. South Carolina Ports Authority* (2002), the Court further expanded states' sovereign immunity from private lawsuits. Writing for the five-to-four majority, Justice Clarence Thomas declared that dual sovereignty "is a defining feature of our nation's constitutional blueprint," adding that the states "did not consent to become mere appendages of the federal government" when they ratified the Constitution.

Not all Court decisions, however, support greater state sovereignty. In 1999, for example, the Court ruled seven to two that state welfare programs may not restrict new residents to the welfare benefits they would have received in the states from which they moved. In addition, each of the Court's major

HOW THINGS WORK

The Terms of Local Governance

Legally, a **city** is a **municipal corporation** or **municipality** that has been chartered by a state to exercise certain defined powers and provide certain specific services. There are two kinds of charters: special-act charters and general-act charters.

A **special-act charter** applies to a certain city (for example, New York City) and lists what that city can and cannot do. A **general-act charter** applies to a number of cities that fall within a certain classification, usually based on city population. Thus in some states, all cities over 100,000 population will be governed on the basis of one charter, while all cities between 50,000 and 99,999 population will be governed on the basis of a different one.

Under **Dillon's rule,** the terms of these charters are to be interpreted very narrowly. This rule (named after a lawyer who wrote a book on the subject in 1911) authorizes a municipality to exercise only those powers expressly given, implied by, or essential to the accomplishment of its enumerated powers. This means, for example, that a city cannot so much as operate a peanut stand at the city zoo unless the state has specifically given the city that power by law or charter.

A **home-rule charter,** now in effect in many cities, reverses Dillon's rule and allows a city government to do anything not prohibited by the charter or state law. Even under a home-rule charter, however, city laws (called **ordinances**) cannot be in conflict with state laws, and the states can pass laws that preempt or interfere with what home-rule cities want to do.

In this country, there are more than 87,500 local governments, only about a fifth (19,500) of which are cities or municipalities. **Counties** (3,000) are the largest territorial units between a state and a city or town. Every state but Connecticut and Rhode Island has county governments. (In Louisiana, counties are called *parishes,* in Alaska *boroughs.*)

LANDMARK CASES

Federal-State Relations

- *McCulloch v. Maryland* **(1819):** The Constitution's "necessary and proper" clause permits Congress to take actions (in this case, to create a national bank) when it is essential to a power that Congress has (in this case, managing the currency).

- *Gibbons v. Ogden* **(1824):** The Constitution's commerce clause gives the national government exclusive power to regulate interstate commerce.

- *Wabash, St. Louis and Pacific Railroad v. Illinois* **(1886):** The states may not regulate interstate commerce.

- *United States v. Lopez* **(1995):** The national government's power under the commerce clause does not permit it to regulate matters not directly related to interstate commerce (in this case, banning firearms in a school zone).

- *Printz v. United States* **(1997):** The national government's authority to require state officials to administer or enforce a federal regulation is limited.

- *Alden v. Maine* **(1999):** Congress may not act to subject nonconsenting states to lawsuits in state courts.

- *Reno v. Condon* **(2000):** The national government's authority to regulate interstate commerce extends to restrictions on how states gather, circulate, or sell certain information about citizens.

- *U.S. v. Morrison* **(2000):** The national government's power to regulate interstate commerce does not extend to giving female victims of violence the right to sue perpetrators in federal court.

- *Federal Maritime Commission v. South Carolina Ports Authority (2002):* Expanded states' sovereign immunity from private lawsuits and declared that the states "did not consent to become mere appendages of the federal government" when they ratified the Constitution.

- *Kelo v. City of New London (2005):* The Constitution allows a local government to seize property, not only for "public use" such as building highways, but also to "promote economic development" in a "distressed" community.

- *National Federation of Independent Business v. Sebelius (2012):* The national government's authority to "alter" or "amend" programs that it jointly funds and administers with the states is limited.

prostate sovereignty decisions has been decided by a tenuous five-to-four margin. More generally, to empower states is not to disempower Congress, which, as it has done since the late 1930s, can still make federal laws regarding almost anything as long as it does not go too far in "commandeering" state resources or gutting states' rights.

New debates over state sovereignty call forth old truths about the constitutional basis of state and local government. In general, a state can do anything that is not prohibited by the Constitution or preempted by federal policy and that is consistent with its own constitution. One generally recognized

police power State power to enact laws promoting health, safety, and morals.

state power is the **police power**, which refers to those laws and regulations—not otherwise unconstitutional—that promote health, safety, and morals. Thus the states can enact and enforce criminal codes, require children to attend school and citizens to be vaccinated, and restrict (subject to many limitations) the availability of pornographic materials or the activities of prostitutes and drug dealers.

Governmental Structure

Federalism refers to a political system in which there are local (territorial, regional, provincial, state, or municipal) units of government—as well as a national government—that can make final decisions with respect to at least some governmental activities and whose existence is specially protected. Almost every nation in the world has local units of government of some kind, if for no other reason than to decentralize the administrative burdens of governing. But these governments are not federal unless the local units exist independent of the preferences of the national government and can make decisions on at least some matters without regard to those preferences.

The United States, Canada, Australia, India, Germany, and Switzerland are federal systems, as are a few other nations. France, Great Britain, Italy, and Sweden are not: They are unitary systems,

HOW THINGS WORK

Sovereignty, Federalism, and the Constitution

Sovereignty means supreme or ultimate political authority: A sovereign government is one that is legally and politically independent of any other government.

A **unitary system** is one in which sovereignty is wholly in the hands of the national government, so that the states and localities are dependent on its will.

A **confederation or confederal system** is one in which the states are sovereign and the national government is allowed to do only that which the states permit.

A **federal system** is one in which sovereignty is shared, so that in some matters the national government is supreme, and in other matters the states are supreme.

The Founding Fathers often took *confederal* and *federal* to mean much the same thing. Rather than establishing a government in which there was a clear division of sovereign authority between the national and state governments, they saw themselves as creating a government that combined some characteristics of a unitary regime with some of a confederal one. Or, as James Madison expressed the idea in *Federalist* No. 39, the Constitution "is, in strictness, neither a national nor a federal Constitution, but a composition of both." Where sovereignty is located in this system is a matter that the Founders did not clearly answer.

In this text, a **federal regime** is defined in the simplest possible terms—as one in which local units of government have a specially protected existence and can make some final decisions over some governmental activities.

because such local governments as they possess can be altered or even abolished by the national government and cannot plausibly claim to have final authority over any significant governmental activities.

The special protection that subnational governments enjoy in a federal system derives in part from the constitution of the country, but also from the habits, preferences, and dispositions of the citizens and the actual distribution of political power in society. The constitution of the former Soviet Union in theory created a federal system, as claimed by that country's full name—the Union of Soviet Socialist Republics—but for most of their history, none of these "socialist republics" were in the slightest degree independent of the central government. Were the American Constitution the only guarantee of the independence of the American states, they would long since have become mere administrative subunits of the government in Washington. Their independence results in large measure from the commitment of Americans to the idea of local self-government and from the fact that Congress consists of people who are selected by and responsive to local constituencies.

"The basic political fact of federalism," writes David B. Truman, "is that it creates separate, self-sustaining centers of power, prestige, and profit."[19] Political power is locally acquired by people whose careers depend for the most part on satisfying local interests. As a result, though the national government has come to have vast powers, it exercises many of those powers through state governments. What many of us forget when we think about "the government in Washington" is that it spends much of its money and enforces most of its rules not directly on citizens, but on other, local units of government. A large part of the welfare system, all of the interstate highway system, virtually every aspect of programs to improve cities, the largest part of the effort to supply jobs to the unemployed, the entire program to clean up our water, and even much of our military manpower (in the form of the National Guard) are enterprises in which the national government does not govern so much as it seeks—by regulation, grant, plan, argument, and cajolery—to get the states to govern in accordance with nationally (though often vaguely) defined goals.

In France, welfare, highways, education, the police, and the use of land are all matters that are directed nationally. In the United States, highways and some welfare programs are largely state functions (though they make use of federal money), while education, policing, and land-use controls are primarily local (city, county, or special-district) functions.

Sometimes, however, confusion or controversy about which government is responsible for which functions surfaces at the worst possible moment and lingers long after attempts have been made to sort it all out. Sadly, in our day, that is largely what "federalism" has meant in practice to citizens from New Orleans and the Gulf Coast region impacted by Hurricane Katrina in 2005.

Before, during, and after Hurricanes Katrina and Rita struck in 2005, federal, state, and local officials could be found fighting among themselves over everything from who was supposed to maintain and repair the levees to who should lead disaster relief initiatives. In the weeks after the hurricanes hit, it was widely reported that the main first-responders and disaster relief workers came not from government, but from myriad religious and other charitable organizations. Not only that, but government agencies, such as the Federal Emergency Management Agency (FEMA), often acted in ways that made it harder, not easier, for these volunteers and groups to deliver help when and where it was most badly needed.

Federalism needs to be viewed dispassionately through a historical lens wide enough to encompass both its worst legacies (for instance, state and local laws that once legalized racial discrimination against blacks) and its best (for instance, blacks winning mayors' offices and seats in state legislatures when no blacks were in the U.S. Senate and not many blacks had been elected to the U.S. House).

HOW WE COMPARE

American-Style Federalism

The United States has always had a federal form of government. By contrast, most of the nearly 200 nations in existence today have never had a federal form of government.

Depending on the stringency of the criteria used to delineate federal from unitary systems, the United States is one of a dozen to two dozen nations that now have federal forms of government: America, Australia, Belgium, Brazil, Canada, Ethiopia, Germany, India, Malaysia, Mexico, Nigeria, Pakistan, Russia, South Africa, Spain, and Switzerland are on nearly every expert's list of federal nations.

But some of these nations (for instance, Belgium, Spain, and South Africa) once had unitary systems, and many nations that have federal forms of government are multiparty parliamentary democracies. By contrast, American-style federalism has shaped and been shaped by the country's separation-of-powers system (see Chapter 2) and its two-party electoral system.

In some federal nations, public opinion favors the national government over subnational governments: people in these countries tend to trust their national governments as much or more than they trust other levels of government. In contrast, Americans tend to trust their state and local governments more than they trust Washington.

Sources: "Trust in Government Remains Low," Gallup Organization, September 2008; Richard Cole and John Kincaid, "Public Opinion on U.S. Federal and Intergovernmental Issues," *Publius* 36 (Summer 2006): pp. 443–459;John Kincaid and G. Alan Tarr, eds., *Constitutional Origins, Structure, and Change in Federal Countries* (Montreal: McGill-Queens Press, 2005); Pradeep Chhibber and Ken Kollman, *The Formation of National Party Systems: Federalism and Party Competition in Canada, Great Britain, India, and the United States* (Princeton: Princeton University Press, 2004).

Federalism, it is fair to say, has the virtues of its vices and the vices of its virtues. To some, federalism means allowing states to block action, prevent progress, upset national plans, protect powerful local interests, and cater to the self-interests of hack politicians. Harold Laski, a British observer, described American states as "parasitic and poisonous,"[20] and William H. Riker, an American political scientist, argued that "the main effect of federalism since the Civil War has been to perpetuate racism."[21] By contrast, another political scientist, Daniel J. Elazar, argued that the "virtue of the federal system lies in its ability to develop and maintain mechanisms vital to the perpetuation of the unique combination of governmental strength, political flexibility, and individual liberty, which has been the central concern of American politics."[22]

So diametrically opposed are the Riker and Elazar views that one wonders whether they are talking about the same subject. They are, of course, but they are stressing different aspects of the same phenomenon. Whenever the opportunity to exercise political power is widely available (as among the 50 states, 3,000 counties, and many thousands of municipalities in the United States), it is obvious that in different places, different people will make use of that power for different purposes. There is no question that allowing states and cities to make autonomous, binding political decisions will allow some people in some places to make those decisions in ways that maintain racial segregation, protect vested interests, and facilitate corruption. It is equally true, however, that this arrangement also enables other people in other places to pass laws that attack segregation, regulate harmful economic practices, and purify politics, often long before these ideas gain national support or become national policy.

The existence of independent state and local governments means that different political groups pursuing different political purposes will come to power in different places. The smaller the political unit, the more likely it is to be dominated by a single political faction. James Madison understood this fact perfectly and used it to argue (in *Federalist* No. 10) that it would be in a large (or "extended") republic, such as the United States as a whole, that one would find the greatest opportunity for all relevant interests to be heard. When William Riker condemns federalism, he is thinking of the fact that in some places the ruling factions in cities and states have opposed granting equal rights to African Americans. When Daniel Elazar praises federalism, he is recalling that, in other states and cities, the ruling factions have taken the lead (long in advance of the federal government) in developing measures to protect the environment, extend civil rights, and improve social conditions. If you live in California, whether you like federalism depends in part on whether you like the fact that California has, independent of the federal government, cut property taxes, strictly controlled coastal land use, heavily regulated electric utilities, and increased (at one time) and decreased (at another time) its welfare rolls.

Stock Montage/Getty Images

Federalism has permitted experimentation. Women were able to vote in the Wyoming Territory in 1888, long before they could do so in most states.

Increased Political Activity

Federalism has many effects, but its most obvious effect has been to facilitate the mobilization of political activity. Unlike Don Quixote, the average citizen does not tilt at windmills. He or she is more likely to become involved in organized political activity if he or she feels a reasonable chance exists of producing a practical effect. The chances of having such an effect are greater where there are many elected officials and independent governmental bodies, each with a relatively small constituency, than where there are few elected officials, most of whom have the nation as a whole for a constituency. In short, a federal system, by virtue of the decentralization of authority, lowers the cost of organized political activity; a unitary system, because of the centralization of authority, raises the cost. We may disagree about the purposes of organized political activity, but the fact of widespread organized activity can scarcely be doubted—or if you do doubt it, that is only because you have not yet read Chapters 7 and 8.

initiative Process that permits voters to put legislative measures directly on the ballot.

referendum Procedure enabling voters to reject a measure passed by the legislature.

recall Procedure whereby voters can remove an elected official from office.

It is impossible to say whether the Founders, when they wrote the Constitution, planned to produce such widespread opportunities for political participation. Unfortunately, they were not very clear (at least in writing) about how the federal system was supposed to work, and thus most of the interesting questions about the jurisdiction and powers of our national and state governments had to be settled by a century and a half of protracted and often bitter conflict.

What the States Can Do

The states play a key role in social welfare, public education, law enforcement, criminal justice, health and hospitals, roads and highways, and managing water supplies. On these and many other matters, state constitutions are far more detailed and sometimes confer more rights than the federal one. For example, the California constitution includes an explicit right to privacy, says that noncitizens have the same property rights as citizens, and requires the state to use "all suitable means" to support public education.

Many state constitutions are now believed by some to be on the whole more progressive in their holdings on abortion rights (authorizing fewer restrictions on minors), welfare payments (permitting fewer limits on eligibility), employment discrimination (prohibiting discrimination based on sexual preference), and many other matters than federal courts generally are. As we saw in Chapter 2, the federal Constitution is based on a republican, not a democratic, principle: laws are to be made by the representatives of citizens, not by the citizens directly. But many state constitutions open one or more of three doors to direct democracy. About half of the states provide for some form of legislation by initiative. The **initiative** allows voters to place legislative measures (and sometimes constitutional amendments) directly on the ballot by getting enough signatures (usually between 5 and 15 percent of those who voted in the last election) on a petition. About half of the states permit the **referendum**, a procedure that enables voters to reject a measure adopted by the legislature. Sometimes the state constitution specifies that certain kinds of legislation (for example, tax increases) must be subject to a referendum whether the legislature wishes it or not. The **recall** is a procedure, in effect in more than 20 states, whereby voters can remove an elected official from office. If enough signatures are gathered on a petition, the official must go before voters, who can vote to leave the person in office, remove the person from office, or remove the person and replace him or her with someone else.

The existence of the states is guaranteed by the federal Constitution: no state can be divided without its consent, each state must have two representatives in the Senate (the only provision of the Constitution that may not be amended), every state is assured of a republican form of government, and the powers not granted to Congress are reserved for the states. By contrast, cities, towns, and counties enjoy no such protection; they exist at the pleasure of the states. Indeed, states have frequently abolished certain kinds of local governments, such as independent school districts.

This explains why there is no debate about city sovereignty comparable to the debate about state sovereignty. The constitutional division of power between them is settled: the state is supreme. But federal–state relations can be complicated, because the Constitution invites elected leaders to struggle over sovereignty. Which level of government has the ultimate power to decide where nuclear waste gets stored, how much welfare beneficiaries are paid, what rights prisoners enjoy, or whether supersonic jets can land at local airports? American federalism answers such questions, but on a case-by-case basis through intergovernmental politics and court decisions.

Federal–State Relations

Though constitutionally, the federal government may be supreme, politically, it must take into account the fact that the laws it passes have to be approved by members of Congress selected from, and responsive to, state and local constituencies. Thus, what Washington lawfully may do is not the same thing as what it politically may wish to do.

grants-in-aid Money given by the national government to the states.

Grants-In-Aid

The best illustration of how political realities modify legal authority can be found in federal **grants-in-aid**. The first of these programs began even before the Constitution was adopted, in the form of land grants made by the national government to the states in order to finance education. (State universities all over the country were built with the proceeds from the sale of these land grants; hence the name *land-grant colleges*.) Land grants were also made to support the building of wagon roads, canals, railroads,

HOW THINGS WORK

Government Powers: Federal, State, and Both

Federal Government Powers

- Subject to Article V of the Constitution, deciding on the process by which amendments to the Constitution are to be proposed and ratified
- Declaring war
- Maintaining and deploying military forces
- Making foreign policy, international treaties, and trade deals
- Printing money
- Regulating interstate commerce
- Maintaining postal offices and services

State Government Powers

- Ratifying amendments to the Constitution through state legislatures or ratifying conventions
- Conducting elections for public offices, initiatives, and referenda
- Establishing local governments
- Regulating intrastate commerce
- Licensing occupations and land uses
- Enacting laws to promote public safety, health, and morals (the "police power")

(continued)

HOW THINGS WORK (*Continued*)

Powers Exercised by Both the Federal Government and State Governments

- Taxing citizens and businesses
- Chartering banks and corporations
- Building and maintaining roads
- Borrowing money and managing public debts
- Administering criminal justice institutions
- Regulating Native American gaming (casino) businesses

and flood-control projects. These measures were hotly debated in Congress (President Madison thought some were unconstitutional), even though the use to which the grants were put was left almost entirely to the states.

Cash grants-in-aid began almost as early. In 1808, Congress gave $200,000 to the states to pay for their militias, with the states in charge of the size, deployment, and command of these troops. However, grant-in-aid programs remained few in number and small in price until the 20th century, when scores of new ones came into being. Today, federal grants go to hundreds of programs, including such giant federal–state programs as Medicaid (see Table 3.1).

The grants-in-aid system, once under way, grew rapidly because it helped state and local officials resolve a dilemma. On the one hand, they wanted access to the superior taxing power of the federal government. On the other hand, prevailing constitutional interpretation—at least until the late 1930s—held that the federal government could not spend money for purposes not authorized by the Constitution. The solution was obviously to have federal money put into state hands: Washington would pay the bills; the states would run the programs.

To state officials, federal money seemed so attractive for four reasons. First, the money was there. Thanks to the high-tariff policies of the Republicans, Washington in the 1880s had huge budget surpluses. Second, in the 1920s, as those surpluses dwindled, Washington inaugurated the federal income tax. It automatically brought in more money as economic activity (and thus personal

TABLE 3.1 Federal Grants to State and Local Governments (2011)

The federal government spent more than $625 billion on grants to states in 2011.	
Among the biggest items:	
Medicaid	$276.2 billion
Income Security	$116.4 billion
Education and training	$101.4 billion
Transportation	$61 billion
Community development	$18.6 billion

Source: U.S. Census Bureau, *Statistical Abstract of the United States*: 2012, Table 432, p. 269.

income) grew. Third, the federal government, unlike the states, managed the currency and could print more at will. (Technically, it borrowed this money, but it was under no obligation to pay it all back, because, as a practical matter, it had borrowed from itself.) States could not do this: If they borrowed money (and many could not), they had to pay it back, in full.

These three economic reasons for the appeal of federal grants were probably not as important as a fourth reason: politics. Federal money seemed to a state official to be "free" money. Governors did not have to propose, collect, or take responsibility for federal taxes. Instead, a governor could denounce the federal government for being profligate in its use of the people's money. Meanwhile, he or she could claim credit for a new public works or other project funded by Washington and, until recent decades, expect little or no federal supervision in the bargain.[23]

That every state had an incentive to ask for federal money to pay for local programs meant, of course, that it would be very difficult for one state to get money for a given program without every state getting it. The senator from Alabama who votes for the project to improve navigation on the Tombigbee will have to vote in favor of projects improving navigation on every other river in the country if the senator expects his or her Senate colleagues to support such a request. Federalism as practiced in the United States means that when Washington wants to send money to one state or congressional district, it must send money to many states and districts.

Shortly after September 11, 2001, for example, President George W. Bush and congressional leaders in both parties pledged new federal funds to increase public safety payrolls, purchase the latest equipment to detect bioterror attacks, and so on. Since then, New York City and other big cities have received tens of millions of federal dollars for such purposes, but so have scores of smaller cities and towns. The grants allocated by the Department of Homeland Security were based on so-called fair-share formulas mandated by Congress, which are basically the same formulas the federal government uses to allocate certain highway and other funds among the states. These funding formulas not only spread money around, but also generally skew funding toward states and cities with low populations. Thus, Wyoming received seven times as much federal homeland security funding per capita as New York State did, and Grand Forks County, North Dakota (population 70,000), received $1.5 million to purchase biochemical suits, a semi-armored van, decontamination tents, and other equipment to deal with weapons of mass destruction.[24]

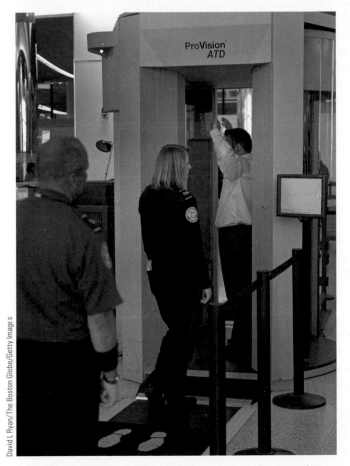

David L Ryan/The Boston Globe/Getty Images

An airline passenger goes through a scanner that searches electronically for any contraband.

Meeting National Needs

Until the 1960s, most federal grants-in-aid were conceived by or in cooperation with the states and were designed to serve essentially state purposes. Large blocs of voters and a variety of organized interests would press for grants to help farmers, build highways, or support vocational education. During the 1960s, however, an important change occurred: the federal government began devising grant programs based less on what states were demanding and more on what federal officials perceived to be important *national* needs (see Figure 3.2). Federal officials, not state and local ones, were the principal proponents of grant programs to aid the urban poor, combat crime, reduce pollution, and deal with drug abuse.

The rise in federal activism in setting goals and the occasional efforts—during some periods—to bypass state officials by providing money directly to cities or even local citizen groups had at least two separate, but related effects: one effect was to increase federal grants to state and local governments, and the other was to change the purposes to which those monies were put. Whereas federal aid amounted to less than 2 percent of state general revenue in 1927, by 2006, federal aid accounted for about 30 percent of state general revenue. In 1960, about 3 percent of federal grants to state and local governments were for health care. Today, however, one federal–state health care program alone, Medicaid, accounts for nearly half of all federal grants. And whereas in 1960, more than 40 percent of all federal grants to state and local governments went to transportation (including highways), today only about 10 percent is used for that purpose (see Figure 3.2). Even in the short term, the purposes to which federal grants are put can shift; for example, after Hurricanes Katrina and Rita, federal grants for "community and regional development" spiked, but returned to pre-2005 levels by 2011.

The Intergovernmental Lobby

State and local officials, both elected and appointed, began to form an important new lobby, the "intergovernmental lobby," made up of mayors, governors, superintendents of schools, state directors of public health, county highway commissioners, local police chiefs, and others who had come to depend on federal funds.[25] Today, federal agencies responsible for health care, criminal justice, environmental protection, and other programs have people on staff who specialize in providing information, technical assistance, and financial support to state and local organizations, including the "Big 7": the U.S. Conference of Mayors; the National Governors Association; the National Association of Counties; the National League of Cities; the Council of State Governments;

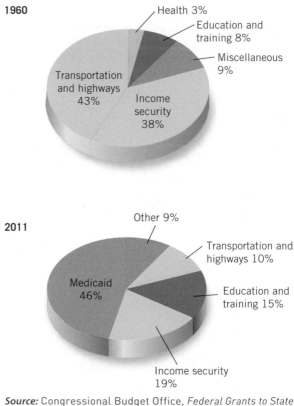

FIGURE 3.2 **The Changing Purpose of Federal Grants to State and Local Governments**

1960

- Health 3%
- Education and training 8%
- Miscellaneous 9%
- Income security 38%
- Transportation and highways 43%

2011

- Other 9%
- Transportation and highways 10%
- Education and training 15%
- Income security 19%
- Medicaid 46%

Source: Congressional Budget Office, *Federal Grants to State and Local Governments*, March 2013, pp. 2–4.

the International City/County Management Association; and the National Conference of State Legislatures. Reports by these groups and publications like *Governing* magazine are read routinely by many federal officials to keep a handle on issues and trends in state and local government.

categorical grants Federal grants for specific purposes, such as building an airport.

National organizations of governors or mayors press for more federal money, but not for increased funding for any particular city or state. Thus most states, dozens of counties, and more than a hundred cities have their own offices in Washington, D.C. Some are small, some share staff with other jurisdictions, but a few are quite large and boast several dozen full-time employees. Back home, state and local governments have created new positions, or redefined old ones, in response to new or changed federal funding opportunities.

The purpose of the intergovernmental lobby has been the same as that of any private lobby—to obtain more federal money with fewer strings attached. For a while, the cities and states did in fact get more money, but since the early 1980s, their success in obtaining federal grants has been more checkered.

Categorical Grants

The effort to loosen the strings took the form of shifting—as much as possible—the federal aid from **categorical grants** to block grants. A categorical grant is one for a specific purpose defined by federal law: to build an airport or a college dormitory, for example, or to make welfare payments to low-income mothers. Such grants usually require that the state or locality put up money to "match" some part of the federal grant, though the amount of matching funds can be quite small (sometimes only 10 percent or less). Governors and mayors complained about these categorical grants because their purposes were often so narrow that it was impossible for a state to adapt federal grants to local needs. A mayor seeking federal money to build parks might have discovered that the city could get money only if it launched an urban-renewal program that entailed bulldozing several blocks of housing or small businesses.

One response to this problem was to consolidate several categorical or project grant programs into a single block grant devoted to some general purpose and with fewer restrictions on its use. Block grants began in the mid-1960s, when such a grant was created in the health field. Though many block grants were proposed between 1966 and 1980, only five were enacted. Of the three largest, one consolidated various categorical grant programs aimed at cities (Community Development Block Grants), another created a program to aid local law enforcement (Law Enforcement Assistance Act), and a third authorized new kinds of locally managed programs for the unemployed (CETA, or the Comprehensive Employment and Training Act).

In theory, block grants and revenue sharing were supposed to give the states and cities considerable freedom in deciding how to spend the money while helping to relieve their tax burdens. To some extent, they did. However, for four reasons, neither the goal of "no strings" nor the one of fiscal relief was really attained. First, the amount of money available from block grants and revenue sharing did not grow as fast as the states had hoped, nor as quickly as did the money available through categorical grants. Second, the federal government steadily increased the number of strings attached to the spending of this supposedly "unrestricted" money.

Third, block grants grew more slowly than categorical grants because of the different kinds of political coalitions supporting each. Congress and the federal bureaucracy liked categorical grants for the same reason the states disliked them—the specificity of these programs enhanced federal control over how the money was to be used. Federal officials, joined by liberal interest groups and organized labor, tended to distrust state governments. Whenever Congress wanted to address some national problem, its natural inclination was to create a categorical grant program so that it, and not the states, would decide how the money would be spent.

Fourth, even though governors and mayors like block grants, these programs cover such a broad range of activities that no single interest group has a vital stake in pressing for their enlargement. Categorical grants, on the other hand, often are a matter of life and death for many agencies—state departments of welfare, of highways, and of health, for example, are utterly dependent on federal aid. Accordingly, the administrators in charge of these programs will press strenuously for their expansion. Moreover, categorical programs are supervised by special committees of Congress, and as we shall see in Chapter 9, many of these committees have an interest in seeing their programs grow.

Rivalry among the States

The more important federal money becomes to the states, the more likely the states are to compete among themselves for the largest share of it. For a century or better, the growth of the United States—in population, business, and income—was concentrated in the industrial Northeast. In recent decades, however, that growth—at least in population and employment, if not in income—has shifted to the South, Southwest, and Far West. This change has precipitated an intense debate over whether the federal government, by the way it distributes its funds and awards its contracts, is unfairly helping some regions and states at the expense of others. Journalists and politicians have dubbed the struggle as one between Snowbelt (or Frostbelt) and Sunbelt states.

Whether in fact there is anything worth arguing about is far from clear: the federal government has had great difficulty in figuring out where it ultimately spends what funds for what purposes. For

New Jersey Governor Chris Christie greets President Barack Obama, who visited the state to see the devastation caused by Superstorm Sandy in October 2012.

example, a $1 billion defense contract may go to a company with headquarters in California, but much of the money may actually be spent in Connecticut or New York, as the prime contractor in California buys from subcontractors in the other states. It is even less clear whether federal funds actually affect the growth rate of the regions. The uncertainty about the facts has not prevented a debate about the issue, however. That debate focuses on the formulas written into federal laws by which block grants are allocated. These formulas take into account such factors as a county's or city's population, personal income in the area, and housing quality. A slight change in a formula can shift millions of dollars in grants in ways that favor either the older, declining cities of the Northeast or the newer, still-growing cities of the Southwest.

conditions of aid Terms set by the national government that states must meet if they are to receive certain federal funds.

mandates Terms set by the national government that states must meet whether or not they accept federal grants.

With the advent of grants based on distributional formulas (as opposed to grants for a particular project), the results of the census, taken every 10 years, assume monumental importance. A city or state shown to be losing population may, as a result, forfeit millions of dollars in federal aid. Senators and representatives now have access to computers that can tell them instantly the effect on their states and districts of even minor changes in a formula by which federal aid is distributed. These formulas rely on objective measures, but the exact measure is selected with an eye to its political consequences. There is nothing wrong with this in principle, since any political system must provide some benefits for everybody if it is to stay together. Given the competition among states in a federal system, however, the struggle over allocation formulas becomes especially acute.

Federal Aid and Federal Control

So important has federal aid become for state and local governments that mayors and governors, along with others, began to fear that Washington was well on its way to controlling other levels of government. "He who pays the piper calls the tune," they muttered. In this view, the constitutional protection of state government to be found in the Tenth Amendment was in jeopardy as a result of the strings attached to the grants-in-aid on which the states were increasingly dependent.

Block grants were an effort to reverse this trend by allowing the states and localities freedom to spend money as they wished. But as we have seen, the new device did not in fact reverse the trend. Categorical grants—those with strings attached—continued to grow even faster.

There are two kinds of federal controls on state governmental activities. The traditional control tells the state government what it must do if it wants to get some grant money. These strings often are called **conditions of aid**. The newer form of control tells the state government what it must do, period. These rules are called **mandates**. Most mandates have little or nothing to do with federal aid—they apply to all state governments whether or not they accept grants.

Mandates

Most mandates concern civil rights and environmental protection. States may not discriminate in the operation of their programs, no matter who pays for them. Initially, the antidiscrimination rules applied chiefly to distinctions based on race, sex, age, and ethnicity, but of late they have broadened to include physical and mental disabilities as well. Various pollution-control laws require the states to comply with federal standards for clean air, pure drinking water, and sewage treatment.[26]

waiver A decision by an administrative agency granting some other part permission to violate a law or rule that would otherwise apply to it.

Stated in general terms, these mandates seem reasonable enough. It is hard to imagine anyone arguing that state governments should be free to discriminate against people because of their race or national origin. In practice, however, some mandates create administrative and financial problems, especially when the mandates are written in vague language, thereby giving federal administrative agencies the power to decide for themselves what state and local governments are supposed to do.

But not all areas of public law and policy are equally affected by mandates. Federal-state disputes about who governs on such controversial matters as minors' access to abortion, same-sex marriage, and medical uses for banned narcotics make headlines. It is mandates that fuel everyday friction in federal–state relations, particularly those that Washington foists upon the states, but funds inadequately or not at all. One study concluded that "the number of unfunded federal mandates is high in environmental policy, low in education policy, and moderate in health policy."[27] But why?

Some think that how much Washington spends in a given policy area is linked to how common federal mandates—funded or not—are in that same area. There is some evidence for that view. For instance, in recent years, annual federal grants to state and local governments for a policy area where unfunded mandates are pervasive—environmental protection—were about $4 billion, while federal grants for health care—an area where unfunded mandates have been less pervasive—amounted to about $200 billion. The implication is that when Washington itself spends less on something it wants done, it squeezes the states to spend more for that purpose. Washington is more likely to grant state and local governments waivers in some areas than in others. A **waiver** is a decision by an administrative agency granting some other party permission to violate a law or administrative rule that would otherwise apply to it. Generally, for instance, education waivers have been easy for state and local governments to get, but environmental protection waivers have proven almost impossible to acquire.[28]

However, caution is in order. Often, the more one knows about federal-state relations in any given area, the harder it becomes to generalize about present-day federalism's fiscal, administrative, and regulatory character, the conditions under which "permissive federalism" prevails, or whether new laws or court decisions will considerably tighten or further loosen Washington's control over the states.

Mandates are not the only way in which the federal government imposes costs on state and local governments. Certain federal tax and regulatory policies make it difficult or expensive for state and local governments to raise revenues, borrow funds, or privatize public functions. Other federal laws expose state and local governments to financial liability, and numerous federal court decisions and administrative regulations require state and local governments to do or not do various things, either by statute or through an implied constitutional obligation.[29]

It is clear that the federal courts have helped fuel the growth of mandates. As interpreted in this century by the U.S. Supreme Court, the Tenth Amendment provides state and local officials no protection against the march of mandates. Indeed, many of the more controversial mandates result not from congressional action, but from court decisions. For example, many state prison systems have been, at one time or another, under the control of federal judges who required major changes in prison construction and management in order to meet standards the judges derived from their reading of the Constitution.

School-desegregation plans are the best-known example of federal mandates. Those involving busing—an unpopular policy—have typically been the result of court orders rather than of federal law or regulation.

Judges—usually, but not always, in federal courts—ordered Massachusetts to change the way it hires firefighters, required Philadelphia to institute new procedures to handle complaints of police brutality, and altered the location in which Chicago was planning to build housing projects. Note that in most of these cases, nobody in Washington was placing a mandate on a local government; rather, a local citizen was using the federal courts to change a local practice.

The Supreme Court has made it much easier of late for citizens to control the behavior of local officials. A federal law, passed in the 1870s to protect newly freed slaves, makes it possible for a citizen to sue any state or local official who deprives that citizen of any "rights, privileges, or immunities secured by the Constitution and laws" of the United States. A century later, the Court decided that this law permitted a citizen to sue a local official if the official deprived the citizen of *anything* to which the citizen was entitled under federal law (and not just those federal laws protecting civil rights). For example, a citizen can now use the federal courts to obtain from a state welfare office a payment to which he or she may be entitled under federal law.

Conditions of Aid

By far, the most important federal restrictions on state action are the conditions attached to the grants the states receive. In theory, accepting these conditions is voluntary—if you don't want the strings, don't take the money. But when the typical state depends for a quarter or more of its budget on federal grants—many of which it has received for years and on which many of its citizens depend for their livelihoods—it is not clear exactly how "voluntary" such acceptance is. During the 1960s, some strings were added, the most important of which had to do with civil rights. But, beginning in the 1970s, the number of conditions began to proliferate and has expanded in each subsequent decade to the present.

Some conditions are specific to particular programs, but most are not. For instance, if a state builds something with federal money, it must first conduct an environmental impact study, it must pay construction workers the "prevailing wage" in the area, it often must provide an opportunity for citizen participation in some aspects of the design or location of the project, and it must ensure that the contractors who build the project have nondiscriminatory hiring policies. The states and the federal government, not surprisingly, disagree about the costs and benefits of such rules. Members of Congress and federal officials feel they have an obligation to develop uniform national policies with respect to important matters and to prevent states and cities from misspending federal tax dollars. State officials, on the other hand, feel these national rules fail to take into account diverse local conditions, require the states to do things that the states must then pay for, and create serious inefficiencies.

What state and local officials discovered, in short, was that "free" federal money was not quite free after all. In the 1960s, federal aid seemed entirely beneficial; what mayor or governor would not want such money? But just as local officials found it attractive to do things that another level of government then paid for, in time federal officials learned the same thing. Passing laws to meet the concerns of national constituencies—leaving the cities and states to pay the bills and manage the problems—began to seem attractive to Congress.

Because they face different demands, federal and local officials find themselves in a bargaining situation in which each side is trying to get some benefit (solving a problem, satisfying a pressure group) while passing on to the other side most of the costs (taxes, administrative problems). The bargains struck in this process used to favor the local officials, because members of Congress were essentially servants of local interests: they were elected by local political parties, they were part of local political organizations, and they supported local autonomy. Beginning in the 1960s, however, changes in American politics that will be described in later chapters—especially the weakening of political parties, the growth of public-interest lobbies in Washington, and the increased activism of the courts—shifted the orientation of many in Congress toward favoring Washington's needs over local needs.

Congress and Federalism

There remains more political and policy diversity in America than one is likely to find in any other large industrialized nation. The reason is not only that state and local governments have retained certain constitutional protections, but also that members of Congress continue to think of themselves as the representatives of localities *to* Washington and not as the representatives *of* Washington to the localities. As we shall see in Chapter 7, American politics, even at the national level, remains local in its orientation.

But if this is true, why do these same members of Congress pass laws that create so many problems for, and stimulate so many complaints from, mayors and governors? One reason is that members of Congress represent different constituencies from the same localities. For example, one member of Congress from Los Angeles may think of the city as a collection of businesspeople, homeowners, and taxpayers, while another may think of it as a group of African Americans, Hispanics, and nature lovers. If Washington wants to simply send money to Los Angeles, these two representatives could be expected to vote together. But if Washington wants to impose mandates or restrictions on the city, these representatives might very well vote on opposite sides, each voting as his or her constituents would most likely prefer.

Another reason is that the organizations that once linked members of Congress to local groups have eroded. As we shall see in Chapter 7, the political parties, which once allowed many localities to speak with a single voice in Washington, have decayed to the point where most members of Congress now operate as free agents, judging local needs and national moods independently. In the 1960s, these needs and moods seemed to require creating new grant programs; in the 1970s, they seemed to require voting for new mandates; in the 1980s and 1990s, they seemed to require letting the cities and states alone experiment with new ways of meeting their needs; and today, some say they require rethinking devolution before it goes "too far."

There are exceptions. In some states, the parties continue to be strong, to dominate decision making in the state legislatures, and to significantly affect the way their congressional delegations behave. Democratic members of Congress from Chicago, for example, typically have a common background in party politics and share at least some allegiance to important party leaders.

But these exceptions are becoming fewer and fewer. As a result, when somebody tries to speak "for" a city or state in Washington, that person has little claim to any real authority. The mayor of Philadelphia may favor one program, the governor of Pennsylvania may favor another, and individual local and state officials—school superintendents, the insurance commissioner, public health administrators—may favor still others. In bidding for federal aid, those parts of the state or city that are best organized often do the best, and increasingly these groups are not the political parties, but rather specialized occupational groups such as doctors or schoolteachers. If one is to ask, therefore, why a member of Congress does not listen to his or her state anymore, the answer is, "What do you mean by *the state?* Which official, which occupational group, which party leader speaks for the state?"

Finally, Americans differ in the extent to which we prefer federal as opposed to local decisions. When people are asked which level of government gives them the most for their money, relatively poor citizens are likely to mention the federal government first, whereas relatively well-to-do citizens are more likely to mention local government. If we add to income other measures of social diversity—race, religion, and region—there emerge even sharper differences of opinion about which level of government works best. It is this social diversity—and the fact that it is represented not only by state and local leaders, but also by members of Congress—that keeps federalism alive and makes it so important. Americans simply do not agree on enough things—or even on which level of government ought to decide on those things—to make possible a unitary system.

LEARNING OBJECTIVES

LO 3.1 Why does the United States have federalism?

The Framers of the Constitution created a federal system of government for the United States because they wanted to balance the power of the central government with states that would exercise independent influence over most areas of people's lives, outside of national concerns such as defense, coining money, and so forth. Liberty would be protected by requiring the federal government to share power and authority with the states.

LO 3.2 How has American federalism evolved from the Founding to the present?

Since the Founding, the balance of power between the national government and the states has shifted over time. Overall, the federal government's power and responsibilities have increased, particularly with the expansion of programs in the 20th century. Still, states exercise broad latitude in implementing policies, and they frequently provide models for the federal government to consider in creating national policies.

LO 3.3 Where is sovereignty located in the American political system?

Strictly speaking, the answer is "nowhere." Sovereignty means supreme or ultimate political authority. A sovereign government is one that is legally and politically independent of any other government. No government in America—including the national government headquartered in Washington, D.C.— meets that definition. In the American political system, federal and state governments share sovereignty in complicated and ever-changing ways. Both constitutional tradition (the doctrine of dual sovereignty) and everyday politicking (fights over federal grants, mandates, and conditions of aid) render the national government supreme in some matters (national defense, for example) and the states supreme in others (education, for instance).

LO 3.4 How is power divided between the national government and the states under the Constitution?

Early in American history, local governments and the states had most of it. In the 20th century, the national government gained power. In the last two decades, the states have won back some of their power because of Supreme Court decisions and legislative efforts to devolve certain federal programs to the states. But the distribution of power between the national government and the states is never as simple or as settled as it may appear.

LO 3.5 What competing values are at stake in federalism?

Basically two: equality versus participation. Federalism means that citizens living in different parts of the country will be treated differently, not only in spending programs, such as welfare, but also in legal systems that assign in different places different penalties to similar offenses or that differentially enforce civil rights laws. But federalism also means that more opportunities exist for participation in making decisions—in influencing what is taught in the schools and in deciding where highways and government projects are to be built. Indeed, differences in public policy—that is, unequal treatment— are in large part the result of participation in decision making. It is difficult, perhaps impossible, to have more of one of these values without having less of the other.

TO LEARN MORE

- State news: **www.stateline.org**

- Council of State Governments: **www.csg.org**

- National Governors Association: **www.nga.org**

- Supreme Court decisions: **www.findlaw.com/casecode/supreme.html**

- Beer, Samuel H. *To Make a Nation: The Rediscovery of American Federalism*. Cambridge: Harvard University Press, 1993. The definitive study of the philosophical bases of American federalism.

- Conlan, Timothy. *From New Federalism to Devolution*. Washington, D.C.: Brookings Institution, 1998. A masterful overview of the politics of federalism from Richard Nixon to Bill Clinton.

- Daniel, Ronald, Donald F. Kettl, and Howard Kureuther, eds. *On Risk and Disaster: Lessons from Hurricane Katrina*. Philadelphia: University of Pennsylvania Press, 2006. Several experts evaluate the government response.

- Derthick, Martha N. *Keeping the Compound Republic*. Washington, D.C.: Brookings Institution, 2001. A masterful analysis of trends in American federalism from the Founding to the present.

- Diamond, Martin. "The Federalist's View of Federalism." In *Essays in Federalism*, edited by George C. S. Benson. Claremont, Calif.: Institute for Studies in Federalism of Claremont Men's College, 1961, pp. 21–64. A profound analysis of what the Founders meant by federalism.

- Grodzins, Morton. *The American System*. Chicago: Rand McNally, 1966. Argues that American federalism has always involved extensive sharing of functions between national and state governments.

- Melnick, R. Shep. *Between the Lines: Interpreting Welfare Rights*. Washington, D.C.: Brookings Institution, 1994. An examination of how trends in statutory interpretation have affected broader policy developments, including the expansion of the agenda of national government, the persistence of divided government, and the resurgence and decentralization of Congress.

- Riker, William H. *Federalism: Origin, Operation, Significance*. Boston: Little, Brown, 1964. A classic explanation and critical analysis of federalism here and abroad.

- Teske, Paul. *Regulation in the States*. Washington, D.C.: Brookings Institution, 2004. States have responded to devolution by adding new regulations of their own.

Chip Somodevilla/Getty Images News/Getty Images

Civil Liberties

4

LEARNING OBJECTIVES

LO 4.1 Why do the courts play so large a role in deciding what our civil liberties should be?

LO 4.2 Must the rights afforded to citizens by the Constitution be respected by not only the federal government but also by the states?

LO 4.3 Are all forms of expression protected by the Constitution?

LO 4.4 Did America ever have state-supported churches, and do some modern democratic nations still have them?

LO 4.5 How does the Constitution protect the liberties of persons accused of crimes or designated "enemy combatants"?

THEN

In 1803, President Thomas Jefferson wrote to the governor of Pennsylvania complaining about the "licentiousness" of newspapers and urging him and other state leaders to bring about "a few prosecutions of the most prominent offenders." This would, Jefferson said, have a "wholesome effect in restoring the integrity of the presses."[1]

NOW

Today, a president writing such a letter to anyone, especially a governor, would be subject to intense criticism. Prosecuting publishers who had attacked the government would strike most people as outrageous.

There are two differences between then and now. First, as you will see later in this chapter, the Supreme Court decided in 1833 that the Bill of Rights only restricted the federal government. The only limits on state governments with regards to free speech, a free press, and religious freedom were those found in state constitutions. This law changed after the ratification of the Fourteenth Amendment in 1868 and was (slowly) interpreted by the Supreme Court to mean that the states must also honor freedom for speech, publications, and churches.

The second change occurred in the minds of the American people. Gradually, but especially in the 20th century, they acquired a libertarian view of personal freedom. According to this perspective, the government at every level ought to leave people alone with respect to what they say, write, read, or worship.

The Framers of the Constitution thought they had written a document that stated what the federal government *could* do, not one that specified what state governments (such as school systems) *could not* do. And they thought they had created a national government of such limited powers that it was not even necessary to add a list—a bill of rights—stating what that government was forbidden from doing. It would be enough, for example, that the Constitution did not authorize the federal government to censor newspapers; an amendment prohibiting censorship would be superfluous.

The people who gathered in the state ratifying conventions weren't so optimistic. They suspected—rightly, as it turned out—that the federal government might well try to do things it was not authorized to do, and so they insisted that the Bill of Rights be added to the Constitution. But even they never imagined that the Bill of Rights would affect what *state* governments could do. Each state would decide that for itself, in its own constitution. And if by chance the Bill of Rights did apply to the states, surely its guarantees of free speech and freedom from unreasonable search and seizure would apply to big issues—the freedom to attack the government in a newspaper editorial, for example, or to keep the police from breaking down the door of your home without a warrant. The courts would not be deciding who could wear what kinds of armbands or under what circumstances a school could expel a student.

Civil liberties are the rights—chiefly, rights to be free of government interference—accorded to an individual by the Constitution: free exercise of religion, free speech, and so on. Civil rights, to

Civil liberties Rights—chiefly, rights to be free of government interference—accorded to an individual by the Constitution: free speech, free press, and so on.

be discussed in the next chapter, usually refers to protecting certain groups—such as women, gays, and African Americans—from discrimination. In practice, however, there is no clear line between civil liberties and civil rights. For example, is the right to an abortion a civil liberty or a civil right? In this chapter, we take a look at free speech, free press, religious freedom, and the rights of the accused. In the next one, we look at discrimination and abortion.

Culture and Civil Liberties

We often think of "civil liberties" as a set of principles that protect the freedoms of all of us all of the time. That is true—up to a point.

Rights in Conflict

In fact, the Constitution and the Bill of Rights contain a list of *competing* rights and duties. That competition becomes obvious when one person asserts one constitutional right or duty and another person asserts a different one. For example:

- At the funeral of a Marine killed in Iraq, Phelps and others from a church picketed it with signs saying "Thank God for Dead Soldiers" and other outrageous remarks. (The opening photo for this chapter shows such picketers outside the Supreme Court.) The Marine's father sued the church, claiming the picketers caused him suffering. Free speech versus extreme emotional distress.

- The U.S. government has an obligation to "provide for the common defense" and, in pursuit of that duty, has claimed the right to keep secret certain military and diplomatic information. The *New York Times* claimed the right to publish such secrets as the "Pentagon Papers" without censorship, citing the Constitution's guarantee of freedom of the press. A duty and a right in conflict.

- Carl Jacob Kunz delivered inflammatory anti-Jewish speeches on the street corners of a Jewish neighborhood in New York City, suggesting, among other things, that Jews be "burnt in incinerators." The Jewish people living in that area were outraged. The New York police commissioner revoked Kunz's license to hold public meetings on the streets. When he continued to air his views on the public streets, Kunz was arrested for speaking without a permit. Freedom of speech versus the preservation of public order.

Even a disruptive high school student's right not to be a victim of arbitrary or unjustifiable expulsion is in partial conflict with the school's obligation to maintain an orderly environment in which learning can take place.

Political struggles over civil liberties follow much the same pattern as interest group politics involving economic issues, even though the claims in question are made by individuals. Indeed, there are formal, organized interest groups concerned with civil liberties. The Fraternal Order of the Police complains about restrictions on police powers, whereas the American Civil Liberties Union defends and seeks to enlarge those restrictions. Catholics have pressed for public support of parochial schools; Protestants and Jews have argued against it. Sometimes the opposing groups are entirely private; sometimes one or both are government agencies. Often, their clashes end up in the courts. (When the Supreme Court decided the cases given earlier, Phelps, the *New York Times,* and Kunz all won.[2])

War has usually been the crisis that has restricted the liberty of some minority. For example:

- The Sedition Act was passed in 1798, making it a crime to write, utter, or publish "any false, scandalous, and malicious writing" with the intention of defaming the president, Congress, or the government or of exciting against the government "the hatred of the people." The occasion was a kind of half-war between the United States and France, stimulated by fear in this country of the violence following the French Revolution of 1789. The policy entrepreneurs were Federalist politicians who believed that Thomas Jefferson and his followers were supporters of the French Revolution and would, if they came to power, encourage here the kind of anarchy that seemed to be occurring in France.

- The Espionage and Sedition Acts were passed in 1917–1918, making it a crime to utter false statements that would interfere with the American military, to send through the mails material "advocating or urging treason, insurrection, or forcible resistance to any law of the United States," or to utter or write any disloyal, profane, scurrilous, or abusive language intended to incite resistance to the United States or to curtail war production. The occasion was World War I; the impetus was the fear that Germans in this country were spies and also that radicals were seeking to overthrow the government. Under these laws, more than 2,000 persons were prosecuted (about half were convicted), and thousands of aliens were rounded up and deported. The policy entrepreneur leading this massive crackdown (the so-called Red Scare) was Attorney General A. Mitchell Palmer.

- The Smith Act was passed in 1940, the Internal Security Act in 1950, and the Communist Control Act in 1954. These laws made it illegal to advocate the overthrow of the U.S. government by force or violence (Smith Act), required members of the Communist Party to register with the government (Internal Security Act), and declared the Communist Party to be part of a conspiracy to overthrow the government (Communist Control Act). The occasion was World War II and the Korean War, which, like earlier wars, inspired fears that foreign agents (Nazi and Soviet) were trying to subvert the government. For the latter two laws, the policy entrepreneur was Senator Joseph McCarthy, who attracted a great deal of attention with his repeated (and sometimes inaccurate) claims that Soviet agents were working inside the U.S. government.

These laws had in common an effort to protect the nation from threats, real and imagined, posed by people who claimed to be exercising their freedom to speak, publish, organize, and assemble. In each case, a real threat (a war) led the government to narrow the limits of permissible speech and activity. Almost every time such restrictions were imposed, the Supreme Court was called upon to decide whether Congress (or sometimes state legislatures) had drawn those limits properly. In most instances, the Court tended to uphold the legislatures. But as time passed and the war or crisis ended, popular passions abated and many of the laws proved unimportant.

Though it is uncommon, some use is still made of the sedition laws. In the 1980s, various white supremacists and Puerto Rican nationalists were charged with sedition. In each case, the government alleged that the accused had not only spoken in favor of overthrowing the government, but had actually engaged in violent actions such as bombings. Later in this chapter, we shall see how the Court has increasingly restricted the power of Congress and state legislatures to outlaw political speech; to be found guilty of sedition now, it usually is necessary to do something more serious than just talk about it.

Cultural Conflicts

In the main, the United States was originally the creation of white European Protestants. Blacks were, in most cases, slaves, and American Indians were not citizens. Catholics and Jews in the colonies composed a small minority, and often a persecuted one. The early schools tended to be religious—that is, Protestant—ones, many of them receiving state aid. It is not surprising that under these circumstances a view of America arose that equated "Americanism" with the values and habits of white Anglo-Saxon Protestants.

But immigration to this country brought a flood of new settlers, many of them coming from very different backgrounds. In the mid-19th century, the potato famine led millions of Irish Catholics to migrate here. At the turn of the century, religious persecution and economic disadvantage brought more millions of people, many Catholic or Jewish, from southern and eastern Europe.

In recent decades, political conflict and economic want have led Hispanics (mostly from Mexico, but increasingly from all parts of Latin America), Caribbeans, Africans, Middle Easterners, Southeast

Asians, and Asians to come to the United States—most legally, but some illegally. Among them have been Buddhists, Catholics, Muslims, and members of many other religious and cultural groups.

Ethnic, religious, and cultural differences have given rise to different views as to the meaning and scope of certain constitutionally protected freedoms. For example:

A Hispanic girl studies both English and Spanish in a bilingual classroom.

- Many Jewish groups find it offensive for a crèche (that is, a scene depicting the birth of Christ in a manger) to be displayed in front of a government building such as city hall at Christmastime, while many Catholics and Protestants regard such displays as an important part of our cultural heritage. Does a religious display on public property violate the First Amendment requirement that the government pass no law "respecting an establishment of religion"?

- Many English-speaking people believe that the public schools ought to teach all students to speak and write English, because the language is part of our nation's cultural heritage. Some Hispanic groups argue that the schools should teach pupils in both English and Spanish, since Spanish is part of the Hispanic cultural heritage. Is bilingual education constitutionally required?

- The Boy Scouts of America refuses to allow homosexual men to become scout leaders even though federal law says that homosexuals may not be the victims of discrimination. Many civil libertarians and homosexuals challenged this policy because it discriminated against gays, while the Boy Scouts defended it because their organization was a private association free to make its own rules. (The Supreme Court in 2000 upheld the Boy Scouts on the grounds of their right to associate freely.)

Even within a given cultural tradition there are important differences of opinion as to the balance between community sensitivities and personal self-expression. To some people, the sight of a store carrying pornographic books or a theater showing a pornographic movie is deeply offensive; to others, pornography is offensive, but such establishments ought to be tolerated to ensure that laws restricting them do not also restrict politically or artistically important forms of speech; to still others, pornography itself is not especially offensive. What forms of expression are entitled to constitutional protection?

Applying the Bill of Rights to the States

For many years after the Constitution was signed and the Bill of Rights was added to it as amendments, the liberties these documents detailed applied only to the federal government. The Supreme Court made this clear in a case decided in 1833.[3] Except for Article I, which, among other things, banned ex post facto laws and guaranteed the right of habeas corpus, the Constitution was silent on what the states could not do to their residents.

due process of law Denies the government the right, without due process, to deprive people of life, liberty, and property.

equal protection of the laws A standard of equal treatment that must be observed by the government.

selective incorporation The process whereby the Court has applied most, but not all, parts of the Bill of Rights to the states.

freedom of expression Right of people to speak, publish, and assemble.

This began to change after the Civil War, when new amendments were ratified in order to ban slavery and protect newly freed slaves. The Fourteenth Amendment, ratified in 1868, was the most important addition. It said that no state shall "deprive any person of life, liberty, or property without **due process of law**" (a phrase now known as the "due process clause") and that no state shall "deny to any person within its jurisdiction the **equal protection of the laws**" (a phrase now known as the "equal protection clause").

Beginning in 1897, the Supreme Court started to use these two phrases as a way of applying certain rights to state governments. It first said that no state could take private property without paying just compensation, and then in 1925 held, in the *Gitlow* case, that the federal guarantees of free speech and free press also applied to the states. In 1937, it went much further and said in *Palko v. Connecticut* that certain rights should be applied to the states because, in the Court's words, they "represented the very essence of a scheme of ordered liberty" and were "principles of justice so rooted in the traditions and conscience of our people as to be ranked fundamental." [4]

The Supreme Court began the process of **selective incorporation** by which most, but not all, federal rights also applied to the states. But which rights are so "fundamental" that they ought to govern the states? There is no entirely clear answer to this question, but in general, the entire Bill of Rights is now applied to the states except for the following:

- The right not to have soldiers forcibly quartered in private homes (Third Amendment)
- The right to be indicted by a grand jury before being tried for a serious crime (Fifth Amendment)
- The right to a jury trial in civil cases (Seventh Amendment)
- The ban on excessive bail and fines (Eighth Amendment)

The Second Amendment that protects "the right of the people to keep and bear arms" may or may not apply to the states. In 2008, the Supreme Court in *District of Columbia v. Heller* held for the first time that this amendment did not allow the federal government to ban the private possession of firearms. But the case arose in the District of Columbia, which is governed by federal law. The decision raised two questions: First, will this ruling be incorporated so that it also applies to state governments? In 2010, the Supreme Court said in *McDonald v. Chicago* that the decision in the *Heller* case also applied to the states. [5] Second, will it still be possible to regulate gun purchases and gun use even if the government cannot ban guns? Based on other court cases, the answer appears to be yes.

Interpreting and Applying the First Amendment

The First Amendment contains the language that has been at issue in most of the cases to which we have thus far referred. It has roughly two parts: one protecting **freedom of expression** ("Congress shall make no law ... abridging the freedom of speech, or of the press, or the right of people peaceably to assemble, and to petition the government for a redress of grievances") and the other protecting

freedom of religion ("Congress shall make no law respecting an establishment of religion; or abridging the free exercise thereof").

Speech and National Security

The traditional view of free speech and a free press was expressed by William Blackstone, the great English jurist, in his *Commentaries,* published in 1765. A free press is essential to a free state, he wrote, but the freedom that the press should enjoy is the freedom from **prior restraint**—that is, freedom from censorship, or rules telling a newspaper in advance what it can publish. Once a newspaper has published an article or a person has delivered a speech, that paper or speaker has to take the consequences if what was written or said proves to be "improper, mischievous, or illegal."[6]

freedom of religion People shall be free to exercise their religion, and government may not establish a religion.

prior restraint Censorship of a publication.

clear-and-present-danger test Law should not punish speech unless there was a clear and present danger of producing harmful actions.

The U.S. Sedition Act of 1798 was in keeping with traditional English law. Like it, the act imposed no prior restraint on publishers; it did, however, make them liable to punishment after the fact. The act was an improvement over the English law, however, because unlike the British model, it entrusted the decision to a jury, not a judge, and allowed the defendant to be acquitted if he or she could prove the truth of what had been published. Although several newspaper publishers were convicted under the act, none of these cases reached the Supreme Court. When Jefferson became president in 1801, he pardoned the people who had been imprisoned under the Sedition Act. Though Jeffersonians objected vehemently to the law, their principal objection was not to the idea of holding newspapers accountable for what they published, but to letting the *federal* government do this. Jefferson was perfectly prepared to have the *states* punish what he called the "overwhelming torrent of slander" by means of "a few prosecutions of the most prominent offenders."[7]

It would be another century before the federal government would attempt to define the limits of free speech and writing. Perhaps recalling the widespread opposition to the sweep of the 1798 act, Congress in 1917–1918 placed restrictions not on publications that were critical of the government, but only on those that advocated "treason, insurrection, or forcible resistance" to federal laws or attempted to foment disloyalty or mutiny in the armed services.

In 1919, this new law was examined by the Supreme Court when it heard the case of Charles T. Schenck, who had been convicted of violating the Espionage Act because he had mailed circulars to men eligible for the draft, urging them to resist. At issue was the constitutionality of the Espionage Act and, more broadly, the scope of Congress's power to control speech. One view held that the First Amendment prevented Congress from passing *any* law restricting speech; the other held that Congress could punish dangerous speech. For a unanimous Supreme Court, Justice Oliver Wendell Holmes announced a rule by which to settle the matter. It soon became known as the **clear-and-present-danger test**:

> The question in every case is whether the words used are used in such circumstances and are of such a nature as to create a clear and present danger that they will bring about the substantive evils that Congress has a right to prevent.[8]

The Court held that Schenck's leaflets did create such a danger, and so his conviction was upheld. In explaining why, Holmes said that not even the Constitution protects a person who has been "falsely shouting fire in a theatre and causing a panic." In this case, things that might safely be said in peacetime may be punished in wartime.

CONSTITUTIONAL CONNECTIONS

Selective Incorporation

The selective incorporation process—the process by which the Supreme Court has applied most, but not all, parts of the Bill of Rights to the states—began in earnest in 1925 and has continued ever since, most recently with the Supreme Court's decision in the Second Amendment case of *McDonald v. Chicago*.

The selective incorporation process has never been straightforward or simple. For instance, in *Palko v. Connecticut* (1937), the Supreme Court held that states must observe all "fundamental" rights, but declared that the Fifth Amendment's protection against "double jeopardy" (being tried, found innocent, and then being tried again for the same crime), which was the issue at hand in the case, was *not* among those rights. It was only about three decades later, in its decision in *Benton v. Maryland* (1969), that the Court partially incorporated the double jeopardy provision of the Fifth Amendment. Still, to this day, no provision of the Fifth Amendment has been fully incorporated, and the provision regarding the right to be indicted by a grand jury has not been incorporated at all.

Similarly, in *Powell v. Alabama* (1932), the Supreme Court incorporated the Sixth Amendment's right to counsel, but only in capital punishment cases. In *Gideon v. Wainwright* (1963), the Court extended that right to all felony defendants that might, if convicted, go to prison for years or for life. In the decade thereafter, the Court issued six more Sixth Amendment selective incorporation decisions. In the last of these, *Argersinger v. Hamlin* (1972), the Court extended the right to legal counsel to any defendant facing a sentence that might result in incarceration.

Year	Amendment	Provision	Case
1925	First	Free speech	*Gitlow v. New York*
1931	First	Free press	*Near v. Minnesota*
1932	Sixth	Legal counsel	*Powell v. Alabama*
1937	First	Free assembly	*De Jonge v. Oregon*
1937	Fifth	Double jeopardy	*Palko v. Connecticut*
1947	First	No religious establishment	*Everson v. Board of Education*
1948	Sixth	Public trial	*In re Oliver*
1949	Fourth	Unreasonable searches and seizures	*Wolf v. Colorado*
1958	First	Free association	*NAACP v. Alabama*
1961	Fourth	Warrantless searches and seizures	*Mapp v. Ohio*
1963	First	Free petition	*NAACP v. Button*
1963	Sixth	Legal counsel	*Gideon v. Wainwright*
1965	Sixth	Confront witnesses	*Pointer v. Texas*
1966	Sixth	Impartial jury	*Parker v. Gladden*
1967	Sixth	Speedy trial	*Klopfer v. North Carolina*
1967	Sixth	Compel witnesses	*Washington v. Texas*
1968	Sixth	Jury trial	*Duncan v. Louisiana*
1972	Sixth	Legal counsel	*Argersinger v. Hamlin*
2010	Second	Keep and bear arms	*McDonald v. Chicago*

(*Continued*)

CONSTITUTIONAL CONNECTIONS (*Continued*)

The Third Amendment, which establishes the right not to have soldiers forcibly "quartered in any home without the consent" of the homeowner, and the Seventh Amendment, which establishes the right to a trial in civil cases, each remains wholly unincorporated. The Eighth Amendment's prohibition against "cruel and unusual punishment" is partially incorporated, while its provision forbidding excessive bail or fines remains wholly unincorporated.

The clear-and-present-danger test may have clarified the law, but it kept no one out of jail. Schenck went, and so did the defendants in five other cases in the period 1919–1927, even though during this time Holmes, the author of the test, shifted his position and began writing dissenting opinions in which he urged that the test had not been met and so the defendant should go free.

In 1925, Benjamin Gitlow was convicted of violating New York's sedition law—a law similar to the federal Sedition Act of 1918—by passing out some leaflets, one of which advocated the violent overthrow of our government. The Supreme Court upheld his conviction, but added, as we have seen, a statement that changed constitutional history: freedom of speech and of the press were now among the "fundamental personal rights" protected by the due process clause of the Fourteenth Amendment from infringements by *state* action.[9] Thereafter, state laws involving speech, the press, and peaceful assembly were struck down by the Supreme Court for being in violation of the freedom-of-expression guarantees of the First Amendment, made applicable to the states by the Fourteenth Amendment.[10]

The clear-and-present-danger test was a way of balancing the competing demands of free expression and national security. As the memory of World War I and the ensuing Red Scare evaporated, the Court began to develop other tests, ones that shifted the balance more toward free expression. Some of these tests arc listed in the box on page 91.

But when a crisis reappears, as it did in World War II and the Korean War, the Court has tended to defer, up to a point, to legislative judgments about the need to protect national security. For example, it upheld the conviction of 11 leaders of the Communist Party for having advocated the violent overthrow of the U.S. government, a violation of the Smith Act of 1940.

This conviction once again raised the hard question of the circumstances under which words can be punished. Hardly anybody would deny that actually *trying* to overthrow the government is a crime; the question is whether *advocating* its overthrow is a crime. In the case of the 11 communist leaders, the Court said that the government did not have to wait to protect itself until "the *putsch* [rebellion] is about to be executed, the plans have been laid and the signal is awaited." Even if the communists were not likely to be successful in their effort, the Court held that specifically advocating violent overthrow could be punished. "In each case," the

LANDMARK CASES

Incorporation

- ***Gitlow v. New York* (1925):** Supreme Court says the First Amendment applies to states.

- ***Palko v. Connecticut* (1937):** Supreme Court says that states must observe all "fundamental" liberties.

- ***McDonald v. Chicago* (2010):** The Second Amendment that allows the people to keep and bear arms applies to state governments as well as the federal one.

MR. PRESIDENT
REMEMBER THE CONSTITUTION
"CONGRESS SHALL MAKE NO LAW---
ABRIDGING THE FREEDOM OF SPEECH,
OR OF THE PRESS---" THE POLITICAL
PRISONERS WHO BELEIVED IN THIS
GUARANTEE, ARE NOW SERVING 20
YEARS IN PRISON

Bettmann/CORBIS

Women picketed in front of the White House, urging President Warren Harding to release political radicals arrested during his administration.

opinion read, the courts "must ask whether the gravity of the 'evil,' discounted by its improbability, justifies such invasion of free speech as is necessary to avoid the danger."[11]

But as the popular worries about communists began to subside and the membership of the Supreme Court changed, the Court began to tip the balance even farther toward free expression. By 1957, the Court made it clear that for advocacy to be punished, the government would have to show not just that a person believed in the overthrow of the government, but also that he or she was using words "calculated to incite" that overthrow.[12]

By 1969, the pendulum had swung to the point where the speech would have to be judged likely to incite "imminent" unlawful action. When Clarence Brandenburg, a Ku Klux Klan leader in Ohio, made a speech before Klan members in which he called for "revengeance" [sic] against blacks and Jews (described with racial slurs) and called for a march on Washington, he was arrested and convicted for "advocating" violence. The U.S. Supreme Court reversed the conviction, holding that the First Amendment protects speech that abstractly advocates violence unless that speech will incite or produce "imminent lawless action."[13]

This means that no matter how offensive or provocative some forms of expression may be, this expression has powerful constitutional protections. In 1977, a group of American Nazis wanted to parade through the streets of Skokie, Illinois, a community with a large Jewish population. The residents, outraged, sought to ban the march. Many feared violence if it occurred. But the lower courts, under prodding from the Supreme Court, held that, noxious and provocative as the anti-Semitic slogans of the Nazis may be, the Nazi party had a constitutional right to speak and parade peacefully.[14]

Similar reasoning led the Supreme Court in 1992 to overturn a Minnesota statute that made it a crime to display symbols or objects, such as a Nazi swastika or a burning cross, that are likely to cause alarm or resentment among an ethnic or racial group, such as Jews or African Americans.[15] On the other hand, if you are convicted of actually hurting someone, you may be given a tougher sentence if it can be shown that you were motivated to assault them by racial or ethnic hatred.[16] To be punished for such a hate crime, your bigotry must result in some direct and physical harm and not just the display of an odious symbol.

What Is Speech?

If most political speaking or writing is permissible—save that which actually incites someone to take illegal actions—what *kinds* of speaking and writing qualify for this broad protection? Though the Constitution says that the legislature may make "no law" abridging freedom of speech or the press, and although some justices have argued that this means literally *no* law, the Court has held that there are at least four forms of speaking and writing that are not automatically granted full constitutional protection: libel, obscenity, symbolic speech, and false advertising.

Libel

A **libel** is a written statement that defames the character of another person. (If the statement is oral, it is called a *slander*.) The libel or slander must harm the person being attacked. In some countries, such as the United Kingdom, it is easy to sue another person for libel and to collect. In this country, it is much harder. For one thing, you must show that the libelous statement was false. If it was true, you cannot collect no matter how badly it harmed you.

A Ku Klux Klan member uses his constitutional right to free speech to utter "white power" chants in Skokie, Illinois.

A beauty contest winner was awarded $14 million (later reduced on appeal) when she proved that *Penthouse* magazine had libeled her. Actress Carol Burnett collected a large sum from a libel suit brought against a gossip newspaper. But when Theodore Roosevelt sued a newspaper for falsely claiming that he was a drunk, the jury awarded him damages of only six cents.[17]

If you are a public figure, it is much harder to win a libel suit. A public figure such as an elected official, a candidate for office, an army general, or a well-known celebrity must prove not only that the publication was false and damaging, but also that the words were published with "actual malice"— that is, with reckless disregard for their truth or falsity or with knowledge that they were false.[18] Israeli General Ariel Sharon was able to prove that the statements made about him by *Time* magazine were false and damaging, but not that they were the result of "actual malice."

For a while, people who felt they had been libeled would bring suit in the United Kingdom against an American author. One Saudi leader sued an American author who had accused him of financing terrorism even though she had not sold her book in the United Kingdom (but word about it had been on the internet). This strategy, called "libel tourism," was ended in 2010 when Congress unanimously passed and the president signed a bill that bars enforcement in U.S. courts of libel actions against Americans if what they published would not be libelous under American law.

Obscenity

Obscenity is not protected by the First Amendment. The Court has always held that obscene materials— because they have no redeeming social value and are calculated chiefly to appeal to one's sexual rather than political or literary interests—can be regulated by the state. The problem, of course, arises with the meaning of *obscene*. In the period from 1957 to 1968, the Court decided 13 major cases involving the definition of obscenity, which resulted in 55 separate opinions.[19] Some justices, such as Hugo Black, believed that the First Amendment protected all publications, even wholly obscene ones. Others believed that obscenity deserved no

libel Writing that falsely injures another person.

protection and struggled heroically to define the term. Still others shared the view of former Justice Potter Stewart, who objected to "hard-core pornography," but admitted that the best definition he could offer was "I know it when I see it."[20]

It is unnecessary to review in detail the many attempts by the Court at defining obscenity. The justices have made it clear that nudity and sex are not, by definition, obscene and that they will provide First Amendment protection to anything that has political, literary, or artistic merit, allowing the government to punish only the distribution of "hard-core pornography." Their most recent definition of this is as follows: to be obscene, the work, taken as a whole, must be judged by "the average person applying contemporary community standards" to appeal to the "prurient interest" or to depict "in a patently offensive way, sexual conduct specifically defined by applicable state law" and to lack "serious literary, artistic, political, or scientific value."[21]

After Albany, Georgia, decided that the movie *Carnal Knowledge* was obscene by contemporary local standards, the Supreme Court overturned the distributor's conviction on the grounds that the authorities in Albany failed to show that the film depicted "patently offensive hard-core sexual conduct."[22]

It is easy to make sport of the problems the Court has faced in trying to decide obscenity cases (one conjures up images of black-robed justices leafing through the pages of *Hustler* magazine, taking notes), but these problems reveal, as do other civil liberties cases, the continuing problem of balancing competing claims. One part of the community wants to read or see whatever it wishes; another part wants to protect private acts from public degradation. The first part cherishes liberty above all; the second values decency above liberty. The former fears that *any* restriction on literature will lead to *pervasive* restrictions; the latter believes that reasonable people can distinguish (or reasonable laws can require them to distinguish) between patently offensive and artistically serious work.

Anyone strolling today through an "adult" bookstore must suppose that no restrictions at all exist on the distribution of pornographic works. This condition does not arise simply from the doctrines of the Court. Other factors operate as well, including the priorities of local law enforcement officials, the political climate of the community, the procedures that must be followed to bring a viable court case, the clarity and workability of state and local laws on the subject, and the difficulty of changing the behavior of many people by prosecuting one person. The current view of the Court is that localities can decide for themselves whether to tolerate hard-core pornography; but if they choose not to, they must meet some fairly strict constitutional tests.

The protections given by the Court to expressions of sexual or erotic interest have not been limited to books, magazines, and films. Almost any form of visual or auditory communication can be considered "speech" and thus protected by the First Amendment. In one case, even nude dancing was given protection as a form of "speech,"[23] although in 1991, the Court held that nude dancing was only "marginally" within the purview of First Amendment protections, and so it upheld an Indiana statute that banned *totally* nude dancing.[24]

Of late, some feminist organizations have attacked pornography on the grounds that it exploits and degrades women. They persuaded Indianapolis, Indiana, to pass an ordinance that defined pornography as portrayals of the "graphic, sexually explicit subordination of women" and allowed people to sue the producers of such material. Sexually explicit portrayals of women in positions of equality were not defined as pornography. The Court disagreed. In 1986, it affirmed a lower-court ruling that such an ordinance was a violation of the First Amendment because it represented a legislative preference for one form of expression (women in positions of equality) over another (women in positions of subordination).[25]

One constitutionally permissible way to limit the spread of pornographic materials has been to establish rules governing where in a city they can be sold. When one city adopted a zoning ordinance prohibiting an "adult" movie theater from locating within 1,000 feet of any church, school, park, or residential area, the Court upheld the ordinance, noting that the purpose of the law was not to regulate speech, but to regulate the use of land. And in any case, the adult theaters still had much of the city's land area in which to find a location.[26]

   With the advent of the internet, it has become more difficult for the government to regulate obscenity. The internet spans the globe. It offers an amazing variety of materials—some educational, some entertaining, some sexually explicit. But it is difficult to apply the Supreme Court's standard for judging whether sexual material is obscene—the "average person" applying "contemporary community standards"—to the internet, because there is no easy way to tell what "the community" is. Is it the place where the recipient lives or the place where the material originates? And since no one is in charge of the internet, who can be held responsible for controlling offensive material? Since anybody can send anything to anybody else without knowing the age or location of the recipient, how can the internet protect children? When Congress tried to ban obscene, indecent, or "patently offensive" materials from the internet, the Supreme Court struck down the law as unconstitutional. The Court went even further with child pornography. Though it has long held that child pornography is illegal even if it is not obscene because of the government's interest in protecting children, it would not let Congress ban pornography involving computer-designed children. Under the 1996 law, it would be illegal to display computer simulations of children engaged in sex even if no real children were involved. The Court said "no." It held that Congress could not ban "virtual" child pornography without violating the First Amendment because, in its view, the law might bar even harmless depictions of children and sex (for example, in a book on child psychology).[27]

HOW THINGS WORK

Testing Restrictions on Expression

The Supreme Court has employed various standards and tests to decide whether a restriction on freedom of expression is constitutionally permissible.

1. **Preferred position** The right of free expression, though not absolute, occupies a higher, or more preferred, position than many other constitutional rights, such as property rights. This is still a controversial rule; nonetheless, the Court always approaches a restriction on expression skeptically.

2. **Prior restraint** With scarcely any exceptions, the Court will not tolerate a prior restraint on expression, such as censorship, even when it will allow subsequent punishment of improper expressions (such as libel).

3. **Imminent danger** Punishment for uttering inflammatory sentiments will be allowed only if there is an imminent danger that the utterances will incite an unlawful act.

4. **Neutrality** Any restriction on speech, such as a requirement that parades or demonstrations not disrupt other people in the exercise of their rights, must be neutral—that is, it must not favor one group more than another.

5. **Clarity** If you must obtain a permit to hold a parade, the law must set forth clear (as well as neutral) standards to guide administrators in issuing that permit. Similarly, a law punishing obscenity must contain a clear definition of obscenity.

(continued)

HOW THINGS WORK (*Continued*)

6. **Least-restrictive means** If it is necessary to restrict the exercise of one right to protect the exercise of another, the restriction should employ the least-restrictive means to achieve its end. For example, if press coverage threatens a person's right to a fair trial, the judge may only do what is minimally necessary to achieve that end, such as transferring the case to another town rather than issuing a "gag order."

Cases cited, by item: (1) *United States v. Carolene Products*, 304 U.S. 144 (1938). (2) *Near v. Minnesota*, 283 U.S. 697 (1931). (3) *Brandenburg v. Ohio*, 395 U.S. 444 (1969). (4) *Kunz v. New York*, 340 U.S. 290 (1951). (5) *Hynes v. Mayor and Council of Oradell*, 425 U.S. 610 (1976). (6) *Nebraska Press Association v. Stuart*, 427 U.S. 539 (1976).

Symbolic Speech

Ordinarily, you cannot claim that an illegal act should be protected because that action is meant to convey a political message. For example, if you burn your draft card in protest against the foreign policy of the United States, you can be punished for the illegal act (burning the card), even if your intent was to communicate your beliefs. The Court reasoned that giving such **symbolic speech** the same protection as real speech would open the door to permitting all manner of illegal actions—murder, arson, rape—if the perpetrator meant thereby to send a message.[28]

On the other hand, a statute that makes it illegal to burn the American flag is an unconstitutional infringement of free speech.[29] Why is there a difference between a draft card and the flag? The Court argues that the government has a right to run a military draft and so can protect draft cards, even if this incidentally restricts speech. But the only motive that the government has in banning flag-burning is to restrict this form of speech, and that would make such a restriction improper.

The American people were outraged by the flag-burning decision, and in response the House and Senate passed by huge majorities (380 to 38 and 91 to 9) a law making it a federal crime to burn the flag. But the Court struck this law down as unconstitutional.[30] Now that it was clear that only a constitutional amendment could make flag-burning illegal, Congress was asked to propose one. But it would not. Earlier members of the House and Senate had supported a law banning flag-burning with more than 90 percent of their votes, but when asked to make that law a constitutional amendment, they could not muster the necessary two-thirds majorities. The reason is that Congress is much more reluctant to amend the Constitution than to pass new laws. Several members decided that flag-burning was wrong, but not so wrong or so common as to justify an amendment.

Commercial and Youthful Speech

If people have a right to speak and publish, do corporations, interest groups, and children have the same right? By and large the answer is yes, though there are some exceptions.

symbolic speech An act that conveys a political message.

When the attorney general of Massachusetts tried to prevent the First National Bank of Boston from spending money to influence votes in a local election, the Court stepped in and blocked him. The Court held that a corporation, like a person, has certain First

Robert Pearce/The Sydney Morning Herald/Fairfax Media/Getty Images

"Symbolic speech:" When young men burned their draft cards during the 1960s to protest the Vietnam War, the Supreme Court ruled that it was an illegal act for which they could be punished.

Amendment rights. Similarly, when the federal government tried to limit the spending of a group called Massachusetts Citizens for Life (an antiabortion organization), the Court held that such organizations have First Amendment rights.[31] The Court has also told states that they cannot forbid liquor stores to advertise their prices and informed federal authorities that they cannot prohibit casinos from plugging gambling.[32]

When the California Public Utility Commission tried to compel one of the utilities it regulates, the Pacific Gas and Electric Company, to enclose in its monthly bills to customers statements written by groups attacking the utility, the Supreme Court blocked the agency, saying that forcing it to disseminate political statements violated the firm's free-speech rights. "The identity of the speaker is not decisive in determining whether speech is protected," the Court said. "Corporations and other associations, like individuals, contribute to the 'discussion, debate, and the dissemination of information and ideas' that the First Amendment seeks to foster." In this case, the right to speak includes the choice of what *not* to say.[33]

Even though corporations have some First Amendment rights, the government can place more limits on commercial than on noncommercial speech. The legislature can place restrictions on advertisements for cigarettes, liquor, and gambling; it can even regulate advertising for some less harmful products provided that the regulations are narrowly tailored and serve a substantial public interest.[34] If the regulations are too broad or do not serve a clear interest, then ads are entitled to some constitutional protection. For example, the states cannot bar lawyers from advertising or accountants from personally soliciting clients.[35]

A big exception to the free-speech rights of corporations and labor unions groups was imposed by the McCain-Feingold campaign finance reform law passed in 2002. Many groups—ranging from the

American Civil Liberties Union and the AFL-CIO to the National Rifle Association and the Chamber of Commerce—felt that the law banned legitimate speech. Under its terms, organizations could not pay for "electioneering communications" on radio or television that "refer" to candidates for federal office within 60 days before the election. But the Supreme Court temporarily struck down these arguments, upholding the law in *McConnell v. Federal Election Commission*. The Court said ads that only mentioned but did not "expressly advocate" a candidate were ways of influencing the election. Some dissenting opinion complained that a Court that had once given free-speech protection to nude dancing ought to give it to political speech.[36] But seven years later, the Court, in *Citizens United v. Federal Election Commission*, decided that the part of the McCain-Feingold law that denied corporations and labor unions the right to run ads (independently of a political party's or candidate's campaign) about the election violated their rights to free speech under the Constitution.

Under certain circumstances, young people may have less freedom of expression than adults. In 1988, the Supreme Court held that the principal of Hazelwood High School could censor articles appearing in the student-edited newspaper. The newspaper was published using school funds and was part of a journalism class. The principal ordered the deletion of stories dealing with student pregnancies and the impact of parental divorce on students. The student editors sued, claiming their First Amendment rights had been violated. The Court agreed that students do not "shed their constitutional rights to freedom of speech or expression at the schoolhouse gate" and that they cannot be punished for

LANDMARK CASES

Free Speech and Free Press

- *Schenck v. United States* (1919): Speech may be punished if it creates a clear-and-present-danger of illegal acts.

- *Chaplinksy v. New Hampshire* (1942): "Fighting words" are not protected by the First Amendment.

- *New York Times v. Sullivan* (1964): To libel a public figure, there must be "actual malice."

- *Tinker v. Des Moines* (1969): Public-school students may wear armbands to class protesting against America's war in Vietnam when such display does not disrupt classes.

- *Miller v. California* (1973): Obscenity defined as appealing to prurient interests of an average person with materials that lack literary, artistic, political, or scientific value.

- *Texas v. Johnson* (1989): There may not be a law to ban flag-burning.

- *Reno v. ACLU* (1997): A law that bans sending "indecent" material to minors over the internet is unconstitutional because "indecent" is too vague and broad a term.

- *FEC v. Wisconsin Right to Life* (2007): Prohibits campaign finance reform law from banning political advocacy.

- *Citizens United v. FEC* (2010): The part of the McCain-Feingold campaign finance reform law that prevents corporations and labor unions from spending money on advertisements (independent of political candidates or parties) in political campaigns is unconstitutional.

expressing on campus their personal views. But students do not have exactly the same rights as adults if the exercise of those rights impedes the educational mission of the school. Students may lawfully say things on campus, as individuals, that they cannot say if they are part of school-sponsored activities (such as plays or school-run newspapers) that are part of the curriculum. School-sponsored activities can be controlled so long as the controls are "reasonably related to legitimate pedagogical concerns."[37]

free-exercise clause First Amendment requirement that law cannot prevent free exercise of religion.

establishment clause First Amendment ban on laws "respecting an establishment of religion."

Church and State

Everybody knows, correctly, the language of the First Amendment that protects freedom of speech and the press, though most people are not aware of how complex the legal interpretations of these provisions have become. But many people also believe, wrongly, that the language of the First Amendment clearly requires the "separation of church and state." It does not.

What that amendment actually says is quite different and maddeningly unclear. It has two parts. The first, often referred to as the **free-exercise clause**, states that Congress shall make no law prohibiting the "free exercise" of religion. The second, which is called the **establishment clause**, states that Congress shall make no law "respecting an establishment of religion."

The Free-Exercise Clause

The free-exercise clause is the clearer of the two, though by no means is it lacking in ambiguity. It obviously means that Congress cannot pass a law prohibiting Catholics from celebrating Mass, requiring Baptists to become Episcopalians, or preventing Jews from holding a bar mitzvah. Since the First Amendment has been applied to the states via the due process clause of the Fourteenth Amendment, it means that state governments cannot pass such laws either. In general, the courts have treated religion like speech: You can pretty much do or say what you want, so long as it does not cause some serious harm to others.

Even some laws that do not appear on their face to apply to churches may be unconstitutional if their enforcement imposes particular burdens on churches or greater burdens on some churches than others. For example, a state cannot apply a license fee on door-to-door solicitors when the solicitor is a Jehovah's Witness selling religious tracts.[38] By the same token, the courts ruled that the city of Hialeah, Florida, cannot ban animal sacrifices by members of an Afro-Caribbean religion called Santeria. Since killing animals generally is not illegal (if it were, there could be no hamburgers or chicken sandwiches served in Hialeah's restaurants, and rat traps would be unlawful), the ban in this case was clearly directed against a specific religion and hence was unconstitutional.[39]

Having the right to exercise your religion freely does not mean, however, that you are exempt from laws binding other citizens, even when the law goes against your religious beliefs. A man cannot have more than one wife, even if (as once was the case with Mormons) polygamy is thought desirable on religious grounds.[40] For religious reasons, you may oppose being vaccinated or having blood transfusions, but if the state passes a compulsory vaccination law or orders that a blood transfusion be given to a sick child, the courts will not block it on grounds of religious liberty.[41] Similarly, if you belong to an Indian tribe that uses a drug—such as peyote, in religious ceremonies—you cannot claim that your freedom was abridged if the state decides to ban the use of that drug, provided the law applies equally to all.[42] Since airports have a legitimate need for tight security measures, begging can be outlawed in them,

Public schools cannot organize prayers, but private ones can.

even if some of the people doing the begging are part of a religious group (in this case, the Hare Krishnas).[43]

Unfortunately, some conflicts between religious belief and public policy are even more difficult to settle. What if you believe on religious grounds that war is immoral? The draft laws have always exempted a conscientious objector from military duty, and the Court has upheld such exemptions. But the Court has gone further: It has said that people cannot be drafted even if they do not believe in a Supreme Being or belong to any religious tradition, so long as their "consciences, spurred by deeply held moral, ethical, or religious beliefs, would give them no rest or peace if they allowed themselves to become part of an instrument of war."[44] Do exemptions on such grounds create an opportunity for some people to evade the draft because of their political preferences? In trying to answer such questions, the courts often have had to try to define religion—no easy task.

And even when there is no question about your membership in a bona fide religion, the circumstances under which you may claim exemption from laws that apply to everybody else are unclear. What if you, a member of the Seventh-Day Adventists, are fired by your employer for refusing on religious grounds to work on Saturday, and then it turns out that you cannot collect unemployment insurance because you refuse to take an available job—one that also requires you to work on Saturday? Or what if you are a member of the Amish sect, which refuses—contrary to state law—to send its children to public schools past the eighth grade? The Court has ruled that the state must pay you unemployment compensation and cannot require you to send your children to public schools beyond the eighth grade.[45]

These last two decisions, and others like them, show that even the "simple" principle of freedom of religion gets complicated in practice and can lead to the courts' giving, in effect, preference to members of one church over members of another.

The Establishment Clause

What in the world did the members of the First Congress mean when they wrote into the First Amendment language prohibiting Congress from making a law "respecting" an "establishment" of religion? The Supreme Court has more or less consistently interpreted this vague phrase to mean that the Constitution erects a "**wall of separation**" between church and state.

That phrase, so often quoted, is not in the Bill of Rights nor in the debates in the First Congress that drafted the Bill of Rights; it comes from the pen of Thomas Jefferson, who was opposed to having the Church of England as the established church of his native Virginia. (At the time of the Revolutionary War, there were established churches—that is, official, state-supported churches—in at least eight of the 13 former colonies.) But it is not clear that Jefferson's view was the majority view.

wall of separation Court ruling that government cannot be involved with religion.

During much of the debate in Congress, the wording of this part of the First Amendment was quite different and much plainer than what finally emerged. Up to the last minute, the clause was intended to read "no religion shall be established by law" or "no national religion shall be established." The meaning of those words seems quite clear: Whatever the states may do, the federal government cannot create an official, national religion or give support to one religion in preference to another.[46]

But Congress instead adopted an ambiguous phrase, and so the Supreme Court had to decide what it meant. It has declared that these words do not simply mean "no national religion," but mean as well no government involvement with religion at all, even on a non-preferential basis. They mean, in short, erecting a "wall of separation" between church and state.[47] Though the interpretation of the establishment clause remains a topic of great controversy among judges and scholars, the Supreme Court has more or less consistently adopted this wall-of-separation principle.

Its first statement of this interpretation was in 1947. The case involved a New Jersey town that reimbursed parents for the costs of transporting their children to school, including parochial (in this case Catholic) schools. The Court decided that this reimbursement was constitutional, but it made it clear that the establishment clause of the First Amendment applied (via the Fourteenth Amendment) to the states, and that it meant, among other things, that the government cannot require a person to profess a belief or disbelief in any religion; it cannot aid one religion, some religions, or all religions; and it cannot spend any tax money, however small the amount might be, in support of any religious activities or institutions.[48] The reader may wonder, in view of the Court's reasoning, why it allowed the town to pay for busing children to Catholic schools. The answer it gave is that busing is a religiously neutral activity, akin to providing fire and police protection to Catholic schools. Busing, available to public- and private-school children alike, does not breach the wall of separation.

Since 1947, the Court has applied the wall-of-separation theory to strike down as unconstitutional most efforts to have any officially conducted or sponsored prayer in public schools, even if it is nonsectarian,[49] voluntary,[50] or limited to reading a passage of the Bible.[51] Since 1992, it has even been unconstitutional for a public school to ask a rabbi or minister to offer a prayer—an invocation or a benediction—at the school's graduation ceremony. Since 2000, it has been unconstitutional for a student to lead a prayer at a public high school football game because it was done "over the school's public address system, by a speaker representing the student body, under the supervision of the school faculty, and pursuant to school policy."[52] The Court made it clear, however, that public-school students could pray voluntarily during school provided that the school or the government did not sponsor that prayer. Moreover, the Court has held that laws prohibiting teaching the theory of evolution or requiring giving equal time to "creationism" (the biblical doctrine that God created mankind) are religiously inspired and thus unconstitutional.[53] A public school may not allow its pupils to take time out from their regular classes for religious instruction if this occurs within the schools, though "released-time" instruction is all right if it is done outside the public-school building.[54] The school prayer decisions in particular have provoked a storm of controversy, but efforts to get Congress to propose to the states a constitutional amendment authorizing such prayers have failed.

Almost as controversial have been Court-imposed restrictions on public aid to parochial schools, though here the wall-of-separation principle has not been used to forbid any and all forms of aid. For example, it is permissible for the federal government to provide aid for constructing buildings on denominational (as well as nondenominational) college campuses[55] and for state governments to loan free textbooks to parochial-school pupils,[56] grant tax-exempt status to parochial schools,[57] allow parents of parochial-school children to deduct their tuition payments on a state's income tax returns,[58] and pay for computers and deaf children's sign language interpreters at private and religious schools.[59] But the government cannot pay a salary supplement to teachers who teach secular subjects in parochial schools,[60] reimburse parents for the cost of parochial-school tuition,[61] supply parochial schools with services such as counseling,[62] give money with which to purchase instructional materials, require that "creationism" be taught in public schools, or create a special school district for Hasidic Jews.[63]

The Court sometimes changes its mind on these matters. In 1985, it said the states could not send teachers into parochial schools to teach remedial courses for needy children, but 12 years later it decided they could. "We no longer presume," the Court wrote, "that public employees will inculcate religion simply because they happen to be in a sectarian environment."[64]

Perhaps the most important establishment-clause decision in recent times was the Court ruling that vouchers can be used to pay for children being educated at religious and other private schools. The case began in Cleveland, Ohio, where the state offered money to any family (especially poor ones) whose children attended a school that had done so badly that it was under a federal court order requiring it to be managed directly by the state superintendent of schools. The money, a voucher, could be used to send a child to any other public or private school, including one run by a religious group. The Court held that this plan did not violate the establishment clause because the aid went, not to the school, but to the families who were to choose a school.[65]

If you find it confusing to follow the twists and turns of Court policy in this area, you are not alone. The wall-of-separation principle has not been easy to apply, and the Court has begun to alter its position on church–state matters. The Court has tried to sort out the confusion by developing a three-prong test to decide under what circumstances government involvement in religious activities is improper.[66] That involvement is constitutional if it meets these tests:

1. It has a strictly secular purpose.

2. Its primary effect neither advances nor inhibits religion.

3. It does not foster an excessive government entanglement with religion.

No sooner had the test been developed than the Court decided that it was all right for the government of Pawtucket, Rhode Island, to erect a Nativity scene as part of a Christmas display in a local park. But five years later, it said Pittsburgh could not put a Nativity scene in front of the courthouse, but could display a menorah (a Jewish symbol of Chanukah) next to a Christmas tree and a sign extolling liberty. The Court ruled that the crèche had to go (because, being too close to the courthouse, a government

HOW WE COMPARE

Church and State

The American government cannot pay for or endorse any church. By contrast, the national governments in the United Kingdom, Greece, Germany, Norway, and Sweden can. Moreover, until recently, there were state-supported churches in France, Italy, and Spain. Despite the absence of any governmental support for churches in this country, attendance in churches and synagogues is very high—by some estimates, as much as 40 percent of our population goes to these institutions every week. By contrast, in countries that have or have had state-supported churches, church attendance is sparse. Only 4 percent of the English and 5 percent of the French go to church at least once a week.

How would you explain high church attendance in a country where churches lack government backing and low attendance where they have that backing?

endorsement was implied), but the menorah could stay (because, being next to a Christmas tree, it would not lead people to think that Pittsburgh was endorsing Judaism).

When the Ten Commandments are displayed in or near a public building, a deeply divided Court has made some complicated distinctions. It held that it was unconstitutional for two Kentucky counties to put up the Ten Commandments in their courthouses because, the Court decided, the purpose was religious. It did no good for one Kentucky courthouse to surround the Ten Commandments with displays of the Declaration of Independence and the Star Spangled Banner, so as to make the Commandments part of America's political heritage. The Court said it was still a religious effort, even though it noted that there was a frieze containing Moses in the Supreme Court's own building. (This, the opinion held, was not religious.) But when the Ten Commandments were put up outside the Texas state capitol, this was upheld. Justice Stephen Breyer, who forbid the Kentucky display, but allowed the Texas one, wrote that in Texas, the Commandments now revealed a secular message and, besides, no one had sued to end this display until 40 years after it was erected.[67]

Though the Court has struck down prayer in public schools, it has upheld prayer in Congress (since 1789, the House and Senate open each session with a prayer).[68] A public school cannot have a chaplain, but the armed services can. The Court has said that the government cannot "advance" religion, but it has not objected to the printing of the phrase "In God We Trust" on the back of every dollar bill.

These distinctions reflect the fact that the Court tends to use the wall-of-separation test when it deals with public schools, but that it tries to strike a reasonable balance when it deals with Congress or state office buildings, perhaps because schools have a young and captive population, whereas public forums have an adult and voluntary membership.

LANDMARK CASES

Religious Freedom

- *Pierce v. Society of Sisters* (1925): Though states may require public education, they may not require that students attend only public schools.

- *Everson v. Board of Education* (1947): The wall-of-separation principle is announced.

- *Zorauch v. Clauson* (1952): States may allow students to be released from public schools to attend religious instruction.

- *Engel v. Vitale* (1962): There may not be a prayer, even a nondenominational one, in public schools.

- *Lemon v. Kurtzman* (1971): Three tests are described for deciding whether the government is improperly involved with religion.

- *Lee v. Weisman* (1992): Public schools may not have clergy lead prayers at graduation ceremonies.

- *Santa Fe Independent School District v. Doe* (2000): Students may not lead prayers before the start of a football game at a public school.

- *Zelman v. Simmons-Harris* (2002): Voucher plan to pay school bills is upheld.

It is obvious that despite its efforts to set forth clear rules governing church-state relations, the Court's actual decisions are hard to summarize. It is deeply divided—some would say deeply confused—on these matters, and so the efforts to define the "wall of separation" will continue to prove to be as difficult as the Court's earlier efforts to decide what is interstate and what is local commerce (see Chapter 3).

Terrorism and Civil Liberties

The attacks of September 11, 2001, raised important questions about how far the government can go in investigating and prosecuting individuals.

A little more than one month after the attacks, Congress passed a new law, the USA Patriot Act, designed to increase federal powers to investigate terrorists.† Its main provisions are these:

- Telephone taps. The government may tap, if it has a court order, any telephone a suspect uses instead of having to get a separate order for each telephone.

- Internet taps. The government may tap, if it has a court order, internet communications.

- Voice mail. The government, with a court order, may seize voice mail.

- Grand jury information. Investigators can now share with other government officials things learned in secret grand jury hearings.

- Immigration. The attorney general may hold any noncitizen who is thought to be a national security risk for up to seven days. If the alien cannot be charged with a crime or deported within that time, he or she may still be detained if he or she is certified to be a security risk.

- Money laundering. The government gets new powers to track the movement of money across U.S. borders and among banks.

- Crime. This provision eliminates the statute of limitation on terrorist crimes and increases the penalties.

About a month later, President Bush, by executive order, proclaimed a national emergency under which any noncitizen who is believed to be a terrorist or to have harbored a terrorist will be tried by a military, rather than a civilian, court. A military trial is carried on before a commission of military officers and not a civilian jury. The tribunal can operate in secret if classified information is used in evidence. Two-thirds of the commission must agree before the suspect can be convicted and sentenced. If convicted, the suspect can appeal to the secretary of defense and the president, but not to a civilian court. These commissions may eventually be used to try some of the men captured by the U.S. military during its campaign in Afghanistan against the Taliban regime and the al Qaeda terrorist network that was created by Osama bin Laden. The detainees held in a prison at our Guantanamo naval base in Cuba are not regarded by the Defense Department as ordinary prisoners of war.

The biggest legal issue created by this country's war on terrorism is whether the people we capture can be held by our government without giving them access to the courts. The traditional view, first announced during World War II, was that spies sent to this country by the Nazis could be tried by a military tribunal instead of by a civilian court. They were neither citizens nor soldiers, but "unlawful combatants."[69] The Bush administration relied on this view when it detained—in our military base in Guantanamo Bay, Cuba—men seized by American forces in Afghanistan. These men were mostly members of the al Qaeda terrorist movement or of the Taliban movement that governed Afghanistan before American armed forces, together with Afghan rebels, defeated them. These men, none of them American citizens, argued that they were neither terrorists nor combatants. They demanded access to American courts. By a vote of six to three, the Supreme Court held that American courts can consider challenges to the legality of the detention of these men. The Court's opinion did not spell out what the courts should do when it hears such petitions.[70]

In another decision given the same day, the Supreme Court ruled on the case of an American citizen who apparently was working with the Taliban regime but was captured by our forces and imprisoned in South Carolina. The Court said that American citizens are entitled to a hearing before a neutral decision maker in order to challenge the basis for detention.[71]

That "neutral decision maker" was created in 2006 by a law authorizing military commissions to try alien enemy combatants. These are foreign fighters not in uniform, such as members of al Qaeda, who are captured by American forces. Each commission is to be composed of at least five military officers and is to allow the defendant certain fundamental rights (such as to see evidence and testify). Appeals from its decisions can be taken to the Court of Military Review, whose members are selected by the secretary of defense. The federal appeals court for the District of Columbia and, if it wishes, the Supreme Court may hear appeals from the Court of Military Review.[72]

Military commissions have conducted hearings about the inmates in the Guantanamo prison. Some were released, some were held, and for some no decision has been made. Right after he became president,

HOW THINGS WORK

The Miranda Rule

The Supreme Court has interpreted the due process clause to require that local police departments issue warnings of the sort shown below to people whom they are arresting.

PHILADELPHIA POLICE DEPARTMENT

STANDARD POLICE INTERROGATION CARD

WARNINGS TO BE GIVEN ACCUSED

We are questioning you concerning the crime of (state specific crime).

We have a duty to explain to you and to warn you that you have the following legal rights:

A. You have a right to remain silent and do not have to say anything at all.

B. Anything you say can and will be used against you in Court.

C. You have a right to talk to a lawyer of your own choice before we ask you any questions, and also to have a lawyer here with you while we ask questions.

D. If you cannot afford to hire a lawyer, and you want one, we will see that you have one provided to you free of charge before we ask you any questions.

E. If you are willing to give us a statement, you have a right to stop any time you wish.

75-Misc.-3   (Over)

(6-24-70)

Philadelphia Police Department

Ernesto A. Miranda was convicted in Arizona of rape and kidnapping. When the Supreme Court overturned the conviction, it issued a set of rules—the "Miranda rule"—governing how police must conduct an arrest and interrogation.

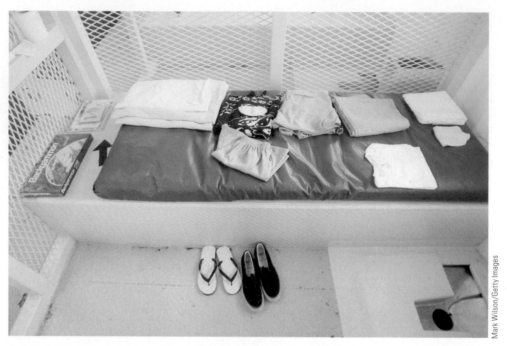

Mark Wilson/Getty Images

Inside a cell at the terrorist prison in Guantanamo, where Muslim inmates receive a copy of the Koran, a chess set, and an arrow pointing toward Mecca.

Barack Obama issued an order to close the Guantanamo prison. But there is a problem: What do you do with the inmates? While George W. Bush was president, 420 of the more than 700 inmates were released, but another 50 or so, though declared eligible for release, could not find a country willing to accept them. Where will they go?

When it was first passed in 2001, the Patriot Act made certain provisions temporary, perhaps to allay the fears of civil libertarians. When the act was renewed in March 2006, only a few changes were made and almost all of its provisions were made permanent.

In addition to the Patriot Act, Congress passed and the president signed in 2005 a law that required all states by 2008 to comply with federal standards when they issue driver licenses. States, not Washington, pass out these licenses, but by mid-2008, the Real ID Act says that no federal agency—including those that manage security at airports—may accept a license or state identification card that does not have the person's photograph, address, signature, and full legal name based on documents that prove he or she is legally in this country. Some people think this amounts to a required national ID card.[73]

Searches Without Warrants

For many decades, presidents of both parties authorized telephone taps without warrants when they believed the person being tapped was a foreign spy. Some did this to capture information about their political enemies. In 1978, Congress decided to bring this practice under legislative control. It passed the Foreign Intelligence Surveillance Act (FISA), which required the president to go before a special court, composed of seven judges selected by the chief justice, to obtain approval for electronic eavesdropping on persons who were thought to be foreign spies. The FISA court would impose a standard lower than that which governs the issuance of warrants against criminals. For criminals, a warrant must be based on showing "probable cause" that the person is engaged in a crime; for FISA warrants, the government need only show that the person is likely to be working for a foreign government.

In late 2005, *The New York Times* and other newspapers revealed that the National Security Agency (NSA), this country's code-breaking and electronic surveillance organization, had a secret program to intercept telephone calls and email messages between certain people abroad and Americans. The Bush administration defended the program, arguing that the intercepts were designed not to identify criminals or foreign spies, but to alert the country to potential terrorist threats. It could not rely on FISA because its procedures took too long and its standards of proof were too high. Critics of the program said that it imperiled the civil liberties of Americans.

The Supreme Court has never spoken on this matter, but every lower federal court—including the court that hears appeals from the FISA court—has agreed that the president, as commander-in-chief, has the "inherent authority" to conduct warrantless searches to obtain foreign intelligence information.[74] The

LANDMARK CASES

- Rights of the Accused or Detained, *Mapp v. Ohio* (1961): Evidence illegally gathered by the police may not be used in a criminal trial.

- *Gideon v. Wainwright* (1963): Persons charged with a crime have a right to an attorney even if they cannot afford one.

- *Miranda v. Arizona* (1966): Court describes warning that police must give to arrested persons.

- *United States v. Leon* (1984): Illegally obtained evidence may be used in a trial if it was gathered in good faith without violating the principles of the *Mapp* decision.

- *Dickerson v. United States* (2000): The *Mapp* decision is based on the Constitution and cannot be altered by Congress passing a law.

- *Rasul v. Bush* and *Hamdi v. Rumsfeld* (2004): Terrorist detainees must have access to a neutral court to decide if they are legally held.

administration also argued that after 9/11, when Congress passed a law authorizing the president to exercise "all necessary and appropriate" uses of military force, it included warrantless intercepts of terrorist communications.

In 2008, Congress passed a bill that allowed the government to intercept foreign communications with people in the United States provided the FISA court had approved the surveillance methods. But the administration could begin the surveillance before the FISA ruling was made if it declared the need to be urgent. However, if Americans living overseas are made the target of this surveillance, then there must first be a FISA warrant. In addition, private telephone and internet companies that aided in the surveillance were exempt from lawsuits so long as they had received "substantial evidence" that the program was authorized by the president. In 2013, a controversy erupted when it was revealed that nine U.S. internet companies had collaborated with the NSA and British intelligence agencies on a secret and extensive surveillance program. Civil liberties questions are in some ways like and in some ways unlike ordinary policy debates. Like most issues, civil liberties problems often involve competing interests—in this case, conflicting rights or conflicting rights and duties—and so we have groups mobilized on both sides of issues involving free speech and crime control. Like some other issues, civil liberties problems also can arise from the successful appeals of a policy entrepreneur, and so we have periodic reductions in liberty resulting from popular fears, usually aroused during or just after a war.

But civil liberties are unlike many other issues in at least one regard: more than struggles over welfare spending or defense or economic policy, debates about civil liberties reach down into our fundamental political beliefs and political culture, challenging us to define what we mean by religion, Americanism, and decency. The most important of these challenges focuses on the meaning of the First Amendment: What is "speech"? How much of it should be free? How far can the state go in aiding religion? How do we strike a balance between national security and personal expression? The zigzag course followed by the courts in judging these matters has, on balance, tended to enlarge freedom of expression.

The resolution of these issues by the courts is political in the sense that differing opinions about what is right or desirable compete, with one side or another prevailing (often by a small majority). In this competition of ideas, federal judges, though not elected, often are sensitive to strong currents of popular opinion. When politics has produced new action against apparently threatening minorities, judges are inclined, at least for a while, to give serious consideration to popular fears and legislative majorities. And when no strong national mood is discernible, the opinions of elites influence judicial thinking (as described in Chapter 12).

At the same time, courts resolve political conflicts in a manner that differs in important respects from the resolution of conflicts by legislatures or executives. First, the very existence of the courts, and the relative ease with which one may enter them to advance a claim, facilitates challenges to accepted values. An unpopular political or religious group may have little or no access to a legislature, but it will have substantial access to the courts. Second, judges often settle controversies about rights not simply by deciding the case at hand, but rather by formulating a general rule to cover like cases elsewhere. This has an advantage (the law tends to become more consistent and better known), but a disadvantage as well: A rule suitable for one case may be unworkable in another. Judges reason by analogy and sometimes assume two cases are similar when in fact important differences exist. For example, a definition of "obscenity" or "fighting words" may suit one situation but be inadequate in another. Third, judges interpret the Constitution, whereas legislatures often consult popular preferences or personal convictions. However, as much as their own beliefs influence what judges read into the Constitution, almost all of them are constrained by its language.

Taken together, the desire to find and announce rules, the language of the Constitution, and the personal beliefs of judges have led to a general expansion of civil liberties.

LEARNING OBJECTIVES

LO 4.1 Why do the courts play so large a role in deciding what our civil liberties should be?

The courts are independent of the executive and legislative branches, both of which will respond to public pressures. In wartime or in other crisis periods, people want "something done." The president and members of Congress know this. The courts usually are a brake on their demands. Of course, the courts can make mistakes or get things confused, as many people believe they have with the establishment clause and the rights of criminal defendants. Still, when it comes to government respecting civil liberties like the freedom to express unpopular beliefs, the courts are often citizens' last best hope.

LO 4.2 Must the rights afforded to citizens by the Constitution be respected by not only the federal government, but also by the states?

Yes, with only a few remaining exceptions. After the Fourteenth Amendment was adopted in 1868, the Supreme Court began the slow, but steady process of "incorporation" by which federal rights deemed "fundamental" also applied to the states. Today, the entire Bill of Rights is now applied to the states except the Third Amendment right not to have soldiers forcibly quartered in private homes, the Fifth Amendment right to be indicted by a grand jury before being tried for a serious crime, the Seventh Amendment right to a jury trial in civil cases, and the Eighth Amendment ban on excessive bail and fines. Although states can still regulate gun purchases and gun use, the latest incorporated right is the Second Amendment right to own and "bear arms," which the Court applied to the states in a 2010 decision.

LO 4.3 Are all forms of expression protected by the Constitution?

No. Four forms of expression that are not protected are the following: libel (injurious written statements about another person); certain types of symbolic speech (actions that convey a political message); "fighting words" that incite others to commit illegal acts or that directly and immediately provoke another person to violent behavior; and obscenity (writing or pictures that the average person, applying the standards of his or her community, believes appeal to the prurient interest and lack literary, artistic, political, or scientific value).

LO 4.4 Did America ever have state-supported churches, and do some modern democratic nations still have them?

Yes and yes. The First Amendment banned the federal government, but not the states, from having an "established," tax-supported church. Some states had tax-funded churches well into the 19th century. Today, the Supreme Court has long since outlawed state-sponsored churches, but the national governments of the United Kingdom, Greece, and several other modern democracies still either have "official" state religions, endorse certain religions, or give certain religions special privileges.

LO 4.5 How does the Constitution protect the liberties of persons accused of crimes or designated "enemy combatants"?

Mainly through a host of rules and procedures that government authorities are required to follow: the exclusionary rule (evidence gathered in violation of the Constitution cannot be used in a trial); the need for a search warrant (an order from a judge authorizing the search of a place); the Miranda rules (warnings that police must give to a person being arrested regarding the rights of the accused); and others. In 2004, the Supreme Court ruled that terrorist detainees and enemy combatants (persons who are neither citizens nor prisoners of war) must have access to a neutral court to decide if they are legally held.

TO LEARN MORE

- Court cases: **www.law.cornell.edu**
- Civil Rights Division of the Department of Justice: **www.usdoj.gov**
- American Civil Liberties Union: **www.aclu.org**

- American Center for Law and Justice: **www.aclj.org**

- Americans United for Separation of Church and State: **www.au.org**

- Institutional Religious Freedom Alliance: **www.irfalliance.org**

- Abraham, Henry J., and Barbara A. Perry, *Freedom and the Court*, 7th ed. New York: Oxford University Press, 1998. Analysis of leading Supreme Court cases on civil liberties and civil rights.

- Amar, Akhil Reed. *The Constitution and Criminal Procedure: First Principles*. New Haven, CT: Yale University Press, 1997. A brilliant critique of how the Supreme Court has interpreted those parts of the Constitution bearing on search warrants, the exclusionary rule, and self-incrimination.

- Berns, Walter. *The First Amendment and the Future of American Democracy*. New York: Basic Books, 1976. A look at what the Founders intended by the First Amendment that takes issue with contemporary Supreme Court interpretations of it.

- Clor, Harry M. *Obscenity and Public Morality*. Chicago: University of Chicago Press, 1969. Argues for the legitimacy of legal restrictions on obscenity.

- Levy, Leonard W. *Legacy of Suppression: Freedom of Speech and Press in Early American History*. Rev. ed. New York: Oxford University Press, 1985. Careful study of what the Founders and the early leaders meant by freedom of speech and press.

Robert W. Kelley/Time Life Pictures/Getty Images

Civil Rights

5

LEARNING OBJECTIVES

LO 5.1 If both African Americans and women benefit from civil rights, why do federal courts allow them to be treated somewhat differently?

LO 5.2 What is the difference between "strict scrutiny" and "intermediate scrutiny"?

LO 5.3 Legally, what is meant by "sexual harassment"?

LO 5.4 Under what circumstances can men and women be treated differently?

LO 5.5 How has Court doctrine and public opinion on gay rights changed over the last decade or so?

THEN

In 1830, Congress passed a law requiring all Indians (they were so called in the law) east of the Mississippi River to move to the Indian Territory west of the river, and the army set about implementing it. In the 1850s, a major political fight broke out in Boston over whether the police department should be obliged to hire an Irish officer. Until 1920, women could not vote in most elections. In the 1930s, the Cornell University Medical School had a strict quota limiting the number of Jewish students who could enroll. In the 1940s, President Franklin D. Roosevelt ordered that all Japanese Americans be removed from their homes in California and placed them in relocation centers far from the coast. Until 1954, public schools in many states were required by law to be segregated by race. Until 1967, 16 states outlawed marriages between whites and nonwhites. Until 2003, 14 states outlawed consensual sexual relations between same-sex partners.

NOW

Now it would be inconceivable that the army would forcibly relocate American Indians. No one can be denied entry into a police department by reason of race, ethnicity, or religion. Women not only have long had the right to vote, but actually now vote at higher rates than men do. Unlike during World War II, today no group of people can be forcibly relocated or held against their will en masse, and even suspected terrorists and "enemy combatants" cannot be detained indefinitely without having their day in court. The quotas that once limited Jews' access to colleges and universities are history. State laws requiring segregated public schools and banning interracial marriage are history, too. And, within just the last decade, state laws forbidding consensual sexual relations between same-sex partners have been eliminated, and the constitutions or statutes that in dozens of states outlaw same-sex marriages or other same-sex unions have been challenged both in courts of law and in the court of public opinion.

Still, then as now, if the government passes a law that treats different groups of people differently, that law is not necessarily unconstitutional.

Civil rights is about cases in which some group, usually defined along racial or ethnic lines, is denied access to facilities, opportunities, or services that are available to other groups. The pertinent question regarding civil rights is not whether the government has the authority to treat different people differently; it is whether such differences in treatment are reasonable. Many laws and policies make distinctions among people—for example, the tax laws require higher-income people to pay taxes at a higher rate than lower-income ones—but not all such distinctions are defensible. The courts have long held that classifying people on the basis of their income and taxing them at different rates is quite permissible because such classifications are not arbitrary or unreasonable and are related to a legitimate public need (that is, raising revenue). Increasingly, however, the courts have said that classifying people on the basis of their race or ethnicity is unreasonable.[1] The tests the courts use are summarized in the box on page 124.

civil rights The rights of people to be treated without unreasonable or unconstitutional differences.

To explain the victimization of certain groups and the methods by which they have begun to overcome it, we shall start with racial classifications and the case of African Americans. The strategies employed by or on behalf of African Americans have typically set the pattern for the strategies employed by other groups. At the end of this chapter, we shall look at the issues of women's rights and gay rights.

Race and Civil Rights

In July 2013, the National Urban League (NUL), led by its president, Marc H. Morial, the former mayor of New Orleans, came to Philadelphia for its annual conference. With the National Association for the Advancement of Colored People (NAACP), the NUL is among the nation's most historic and important civil rights organizations. Its 2013 conference theme was "Redeem the Dream." Fifty years earlier, in 1963, Reverend Dr. Martin Luther King, Jr. delivered his historic "I Have a Dream" speech in Washington, D.C. In its 2013 *State of Black America* report, the NUL credited civil rights laws (see the summary on page 111) for the progress made over the last half-century or so in closing white–black gaps in education and standards of living:

- The white–black high school completion rate gap has closed by 57 points; whereas only 25 percent of blacks graduated from high school in 1963, by 2013 the fraction had risen to 85 percent, and there had been a three-fold increase in the number of blacks enrolled in college.

- The white–black poverty rate gap fell by 23 points; whereas 48 percent of blacks lived in poverty in 1963, by 2013 the fraction had fallen to 28 percent.

- There was a 14 percent increase in the number of black homeowners.

But the same report also documented numerous racial gaps and disparities in housing, education, health care, employment, and overall economic opportunity:

- In 2013, as in 1963, the black–white unemployment ratio was still 2-to-1, regardless of education, gender, region, or income level.

- In 2013, as in 1963, more than a third of all black children (38 percent) still lived in poverty.

- In 2013, as in 1963, blacks employed in the public sector earned less than whites in the same jobs, and a still-wider black–white wage disparity persisted in the private sector.

Citing the history surrounding Reverend Dr. King's "I Have a Dream" speech, Morial and other leaders called on all citizens to come together to eliminate these and other racial gaps and disparities in housing, education, employment, and other areas. As late as the mid-20th century, African Americans in many parts of the country could not vote, attend integrated schools, ride in

National Urban League President Marc Morial speaks to reporters after meeting, along with other political leaders (including Rev. Al Sharpton, who is standing next to him), with President Obama following his re-election.

Roger L. Wollenberg/Getty Images

the front seats of buses, or buy homes in white neighborhoods. Conditions were especially oppressive in those parts of the country, notably the Deep South, where blacks were often in the majority. There, the politically dominant white minority felt keenly the potential competition for jobs, land, public services, and living space posed by large numbers of people of another race. But even in the North, black gains often appeared to be at the expense of lower-income whites who lived or worked near them, not at the expense of upper-status whites who lived in suburbs.

African Americans were not allowed to vote at all in many areas; they could vote only with great difficulty in others; and even in those places where voting was easy, they often lacked the material and institutional support for effective political organization. If your opponent feels deeply threatened by your demands and can deny you access to the political system that will decide the fate of those demands, you are, to put it mildly, at a disadvantage. Yet from the end of Reconstruction to the 1960s—for nearly a century—many blacks in the South found themselves in just such a position.

To the dismay of those who prefer to explain political action in terms of economic motives, people often attach greater importance to the intangible costs and benefits of policies than to the tangible ones. Thus, even though the average black represented no threat to the average white, anti-black attitudes—racism—produced some appalling actions. Between 1882 and 1946, 4,715 people—about three-fourths of them African Americans—were lynched in the United States.[2] Some of these brutalities were perpetrated by small groups of vigilantes acting with much ceremony, but others were the actions of frenzied mobs. In the summer of 1911, a black man charged with murdering a white man in Livermore, Kentucky, was dragged by a mob to the local theater, where he was hanged. The audience, which had been charged admission, was invited to shoot the swaying body (those in the orchestra seats could empty their revolvers; those in the balcony were limited to a single shot).[3]

Though the public in other parts of the country was shocked by such events, little was done: lynching was a local, not a federal, crime. It obviously would not require many killings to tell African Americans in these localities that it would be foolhardy to try to vote or enroll in a white school. And even in those states where blacks did vote, popular attitudes were not conducive to blacks buying homes or taking jobs on an equal basis with whites. Even among those professing to support equal rights, a substantial portion opposed African Americans' efforts to obtain them and federal action to secure them. In 1942, a national poll showed that only 30 percent of whites thought black and white children should attend the same schools; in 1956, the proportion had risen, but only to 49 percent, still less than a majority. (In the South, white support for school integration was even lower—14 percent favored it in 1956, about 31 percent in 1963.) As late as 1956, a majority of Southern whites were opposed to integrated public transportation facilities. Even among whites who generally favored integration, there was in 1963 (*before* the ghetto riots) considerable opposition to the black civil rights movement: nearly half of the whites classified in a survey as moderate integrationists thought demonstrations hurt the black cause; nearly two-thirds disapproved of actions taken by the civil rights movement; and more than a third felt civil rights should be left to the states.[4]

In short, the political position in which African Americans found themselves until the 1960s made it difficult for them to advance their interests through a feasible legislative strategy; their opponents were aroused, organized, and powerful. Thus, if black interests were to be championed in Congress or state legislatures, blacks would have to have white allies. Though some such allies could be found, they were too few to make a difference in a political system that gives a substantial advantage to strongly motivated opponents of any new policy. For that to change, one or both of two things would have to happen: additional allies would have to be recruited (a delicate problem, given that many white integrationists disapproved of aspects of the civil rights movement), or the

HOW THINGS WORK

Key Provisions of Major Civil Rights Laws

1957   **Voting** Made it a federal crime to try to prevent a person from voting in a federal election. Created the Civil Rights Commission.

1960   **Voting** Authorized the attorney general to appoint federal referees to gather evidence and make findings about allegations that African Americans were deprived of their right to vote. Made it a federal crime to use interstate commerce to threaten or carry out a bombing.

1964   **Voting** Made it more difficult to use devices such as literacy tests to bar African Americans from voting.

       Public accommodations Barred discrimination on grounds of race, color, religion, or national origin in restaurants, hotels, lunch counters, gasoline stations, movie theaters, stadiums, arenas, and lodging houses with more than five rooms.

       Schools Authorized the attorney general to bring suit to force the desegregation of public schools on behalf of citizens.

       Employment Outlawed discrimination in hiring, firing, or paying employees on grounds of race, color, religion, national origin, or sex.

       Federal funds Barred discrimination in any activity receiving federal assistance.

1965   **Voter registration** Authorized appointment by the Civil Service Commission of voting examiners who would require registration of all eligible voters in federal, state, and local elections, general or primary, in areas where discrimination was found to be practiced or where less than 50 percent of voting-age residents were registered to vote in the 1964 election.

       Literacy tests Suspended use of literacy tests or other devices to prevent African Americans from voting.

1968   **Housing** Banned, by stages, discrimination in sale or rental of most housing (excluding private owners who sell or rent their homes without the services of a real-estate broker).

       Riots Made it a federal crime to use interstate commerce to organize or incite a riot.

1972   **Education** Prohibited sex discrimination in education programs receiving federal aid.

       Discrimination If any part of an organization receives federal aid, no part of that organization may discriminate on the basis of race, sex, age, or physical disability.

1991   **Discrimination** Made it easier to sue over job discrimination and collect damages; overturned certain Supreme Court decisions. Made it illegal for the government to adjust, or "norm," test scores by race.

struggle would have to be shifted to a policy-making arena in which the opposition enjoyed less of an advantage.

Partly by plan, and partly by accident, black leaders followed both of these strategies simultaneously. By publicizing their grievances and organizing a civil rights movement that (at least in its early stages) concentrated on dramatizing the denial to blacks of essential and widely accepted liberties, African Americans were able to broaden their base of support both among political elites and among the general public, thereby elevating the importance of civil rights issues on the political agenda. By waging a patient, prolonged, but carefully planned legal struggle, black leaders shifted decision-making power on key civil rights issues from Congress—where they had been stymied for generations—to the federal courts.

After this strategy had achieved some substantial successes—once blacks had become enfranchised and legal barriers to equal participation in political and economic affairs had been lowered—the politics of civil rights became more conventional. African Americans were able to assert their demands directly in the legislative and executive branches of government with reasonable (though scarcely certain) prospects of success. Civil rights became less a matter of gaining entry into the political system and more one of waging interest group politics within that system. At the same time, the goals of civil rights politics were broadened. The struggle to gain entry into the system had focused on the denial of fundamental rights (to vote, to organize, to obtain equal access to schools and public facilities); later, the dominant issues were manpower development, economic progress, and the improvement of housing and neighborhoods.

The Campaign in the Courts

The Fourteenth Amendment was both an opportunity and a problem for black activists. Adopted in 1868, it seemed to guarantee equal rights for all: "No state shall make or enforce any law which shall abridge the privileges or immunities of citizens of the United States; nor shall any state deprive any person of life, liberty, or property, without due process of law; nor deny to any person within its jurisdiction the equal protection of the laws."

The key phrase was "equal protection of the laws." Read broadly, it might mean that the Constitution should be regarded as color-blind: no state law could have the effect of treating whites and blacks differently. Thus, a law segregating blacks and whites into separate schools or neighborhoods would be unconstitutional. Read narrowly, "equal protection" might mean only that blacks and whites had certain fundamental legal rights in common (such as the right to sign contracts, to serve on juries, or to buy and sell property), but otherwise they could be treated differently.

In a series of decisions beginning in the 1870s, the Supreme Court took the narrow view, albeit often by narrow majorities. Adopted in 1870, the Fourteenth Amendment had been proposed as a means to reinforce the Civil Rights Act of 1866. That Act was intended by Congress to ensure that former slaves' citizenship rights would be respected not only by the federal government, but also by the state governments, both North and South. But in its 5-to-4 majority decision in the *Slaughter-House Cases* (1873), the Court ruled that the "privileges and immunities" clause of the Fourteenth Amendment did not protect citizens from discriminatory actions by state governments. Though in 1880 it declared unconstitutional a West Virginia law requiring juries to be composed only of white males,[5] the Court decided in 1883 that it was unconstitutional for Congress to prohibit racial discrimination in public accommodations such as hotels.[6] The difference between the two cases seemed, in the eyes of the Court, to be this: serving on a jury was an essential right of citizenship that the state could not deny to any person on racial grounds without violating the Fourteenth

Amendment, but registering at a hotel was a convenience controlled by a private person (the hotel owner) who could treat blacks and whites differently if he or she wished.

    The major decision that determined the legal status of the Fourteenth Amendment for more than half a century was *Plessy v. Ferguson*. Louisiana had passed a law requiring blacks and whites to occupy separate cars on railroad trains operating in that state. When Adolph Plessy, who was seven-eighths white and one-eighth black, refused to obey the law, he was arrested. He appealed his conviction to the Supreme Court, claiming that the law violated the Fourteenth Amendment. In 1896, the Court rejected his claim, holding that the law treated both races equally even though it required them to be separate. The equal protection clause guaranteed political and legal, but not social, equality. "Separate-but-equal" facilities were constitutional because if "one race be inferior to the other socially, the Constitution of the United States cannot put them on the same plane."[7]

Separate But Equal

Thus began the **separate-but-equal doctrine**. Three years later, the Court applied it to schools as well, declaring in *Cumming v. Richmond County Board of Education* that a decision in a Georgia community to close the black high school while keeping open the white high school was not a violation of the Fourteenth Amendment because blacks could always go to private schools. Here the Court seemed to be saying that not only could schools be separate, they could even be unequal.[8]

    What the Court has made, the Court can unmake. But to get it to change its mind requires a long, costly, and uncertain legal battle. The National Association for the Advancement of Colored People (NAACP) was the main organization that waged that battle against the precedent of *Plessy v. Ferguson*. Formed in 1909 by a group of whites and blacks in the aftermath of a race riot, the NAACP did many things, including lobbying in Washington and publicizing black grievances (especially in the pages of *The Crisis*, a magazine edited by W. E. B. Du Bois). But its most influential role was played in the courtroom.

    It was a rational strategy. Fighting legal battles does not require forming broad political alliances or changing public opinion, tasks that would have been very difficult for a small and unpopular organization. A court-based approach also enabled the organization to remain nonpartisan. But it was a slow and difficult strategy. The Court had adopted a narrow interpretation of the Fourteenth Amendment. To get the Court to change its mind would require the NAACP to bring before it cases involving the strongest possible claims that a black had been unfairly treated—and under circumstances sufficiently different from those of earlier cases, so that the Court could find some grounds for changing its mind.

    The steps in that strategy were these: First, persuade the Court to declare unconstitutional laws creating schools that were separate but obviously unequal. Second, persuade it to declare unconstitutional laws supporting schools that were separate but unequal in not-so-obvious ways. Third, persuade it to rule that racially separate schools were inherently unequal and hence unconstitutional.

Can Separate Schools Be Equal?

The first step was accomplished in a series of court cases stretching from 1938 to 1948. In 1938, the Court held that Lloyd Gaines had to be admitted to an all-white law school in Missouri because no black law school of equal quality existed in that state.[9] In 1948, the Court ordered the all-white

University of Oklahoma Law School to admit Ada Lois Sipuel, a black, even though the state planned to build a black law school later. For education to be equal, it had to be equally available.[10] It still could be separate, however: the university admitted Ms. Sipuel, but required her to attend classes in a section of the state capitol, roped off from other students, where she could meet with her law professors.

The second step was taken in two cases decided in 1950. Heman Sweatt, an African American, was treated by the University of Texas Law School much as Ada Sipuel had been treated in Oklahoma: "admitted" to the all-white school, but relegated to a separate building. Another African American, George McLaurin, was allowed to study for his Ph.D in a "colored section" of the all-white University of Oklahoma. The Supreme Court unanimously decided that these arrangements were unconstitutional because, by imposing racially based barriers on the black students' access to professors, libraries, and other students, they created unequal educational opportunities.[11]

The third step, the climax of the entire drama, began in Topeka, Kansas, where Linda Brown wanted to enroll in her neighborhood school, but could not because she was black and the school was by law reserved exclusively for whites. When the NAACP took her case to the federal district court in Kansas, the judge decided the black school Linda could attend was substantially equal in quality to the white school she could not attend and, therefore, denying her access to the white school was constitutional. To change that, the lawyers would have to persuade the Supreme Court to overrule the district judge on the grounds that racially separate schools were unconstitutional even if they were equal. In other words, the separate-but-equal doctrine would have to be overturned by the Court.

It was a risky and controversial step to take. Many states, Kansas among them, were trying to make their all-black schools equal to those of whites by launching expensive building programs. If the NAACP succeeded in getting separate schools declared unconstitutional, the Court might well put a stop to the building of these new schools. Blacks could win a moral and legal victory but suffer a practical defeat—the loss of these new facilities. Despite these risks, the NAACP decided to go ahead with the appeal.

Brown v. Board of Education

On May 17, 1954, a unanimous Supreme Court, speaking through an opinion written and delivered by Chief Justice Earl Warren, found that "in the field of public education the doctrine of 'separate but equal' has no place" because "separate educational facilities are inherently unequal."[12] *Plessy v. Ferguson* was overruled, and "separate but equal" was dead.

The ruling was a landmark decision, but the reasons for it and the means chosen to implement it were as important and as controversial as the decision itself. There were at least three issues. First, how would the decision be implemented? Second, on what grounds were racially separate schools unconstitutional? Third, what test would a school system have to meet in order to be in conformity with the Constitution?

Implementation The *Brown* case involved a class-action suit; that is, it applied not only to Linda Brown, but to all others similarly situated. This meant that black children everywhere now had the right to attend formerly all-white schools. This change would be one of the most far-reaching and conflict-provoking events in modern American history. It could not be effected overnight or by the stroke of a pen. In 1955, the Supreme Court decided it would let local federal district courts oversee the end of segregation by giving them the power to approve or disapprove local desegregation plans. This was to be done "with all deliberate speed."[13]

AP Images/Douglas Martin

Dorothy Counts, the first black student to attend Harding High School in Charlotte, NC, tries to maintain her poise as she is taunted by shouting, gesticulating white students in September 1957.

In the South, "all deliberate speed" turned out to be a snail's pace. Massive resistance to desegregation broke out in many states. Some communities simply defied the Court; some sought to evade its edict by closing their public schools. In 1956, more than 100 Southern members of Congress signed a "Southern Manifesto" that condemned the *Brown* decision as an "abuse of judicial power" and pledged to "use all lawful means to bring about a reversal of the decision."

In the late 1950s and early 1960s, the National Guard and regular Army paratroopers were used to escort black students into formerly all-white schools and universities. It was not until the 1970s that resistance collapsed and most Southern schools were integrated. The use of armed force convinced people that resistance was futile; the disruption of the politics and economy of the South convinced leaders that it was imprudent; and the voting power of blacks convinced politicians that it was suicidal. In addition, federal laws began providing financial aid to integrated schools and withholding it from segregated ones. By 1970, only 14 percent of Southern black schoolchildren still attended all-black schools.[14]

The Rationale As the struggle to implement the *Brown* decision continued, the importance of the rationale for that decision became apparent. The case was decided in a way that surprised many legal scholars.

The Court could have said that the equal protection clause of the Fourteenth Amendment makes the Constitution, and thus state laws, color-blind. Or it could have said that the authors of the Fourteenth Amendment meant to ban segregated schools. It did neither. Instead, it said segregated education is bad because it "has a detrimental effect upon the colored children" by generating "a feeling of inferiority as

MPI/Getty Images

In 1963, Governor George Wallace of Alabama stood in the doorway of the University of Alabama to block the entry of black students. Facing him is U.S. Deputy Attorney General Nicholas Katzenbach.

suspect classification
Classifications of people based on their race or ethnicity; laws so classifying people are subject to "strict scrutiny."

to their status in the community" that may "affect their hearts and minds in a way unlikely ever to be undone."[15] This conclusion was supported by a footnote reference to social science studies of the apparent impact of segregation on black children.

Why did the Court rely on social science as much as or more than the Constitution in supporting its decision? Apparently for two reasons. One was the justices' realization that the authors of the Fourteenth Amendment may *not* have intended to outlaw segregated schools. The schools in Washington, D.C., were segregated when the amendment was proposed, and when this fact was mentioned during the debate, it seems to have been made clear that the amendment was not designed to abolish this segregation. When Congress debated a civil rights act a few years later, it voted down provisions that would have ended segregation in schools.[16] The Court could not easily base its decision on a constitutional provision that had, at best, an uncertain application to schools. The other reason grew out of the first. On so important a matter the chief justice wanted to speak for a unanimous court. Some justices did not agree that the Fourteenth Amendment made the Constitution color-blind.

CONSTITUTIONAL CONNECTIONS

Suspect Classifications

Beginning with the *Brown* case, virtually every form of racial segregation imposed by law has been struck down as unconstitutional. Race has become a **suspect classification** such that any law making racial distinctions is now subject to **strict scrutiny**. To be upheld as constitutional, a suspect classification must be related to a "compelling government interest," be "narrowly tailored" to achieve that interest, and use the "least restrictive means" available. But the Court has also determined that though race is a suspect classification, the Constitution is not "color-blind," and so the government may make racial distinctions for the purpose of remedying past racial discrimination. Later in this chapter we discuss affirmative action, the laws or administrative regulations that require a business firm, government agency, labor union, school, college, or other organization to take positive steps to increase the number of African Americans, other minorities, or women in its membership.

In the interests of harmony, the Court found an ambiguous rationale for its decision.

Desegregation versus Integration That ambiguity led to the third issue. If separate schools were inherently unequal, what would "unseparate" schools look like? Since the Court had not said race was irrelevant, an "unseparate" school could be either one that blacks and whites were free to attend if they chose or one that blacks and whites in fact attended whether they wanted to or not. The first might be called a desegregated school, and the latter an integrated school. Think of the Topeka case. Was it enough that there was now no barrier to Linda Brown's attending the white school in her neighborhood? Or was it necessary that there be black children (if not Linda, then some others) actually going to that school together with white children?

As long as the main impact of the *Brown* decision lay in the South, where laws had prevented blacks from attending white schools, this question did not seem important. Segregation by law (***de jure segregation***) was now clearly unconstitutional. But in the North, laws had not kept blacks and whites apart; instead, all-black and all-white schools were the result of residential segregation, preferred living patterns, informal social forces, and administrative practices (such as drawing school district lines so as to produce single-race schools). This often was called segregation in fact (***de facto segregation***).

In 1968, the Supreme Court settled the matter. In New Kent County, Virginia, the school board had created a "freedom-of-choice" plan under which every pupil would be allowed without legal restriction to attend the school of his or her choice. As it turned out, all the white children chose to remain in the all-white school, and 85 percent of the black children remained in the all-black school. The Court rejected this plan as unconstitutional because it did not produce the "ultimate end," which was a "unitary, nonracial system of education."[17] In the opinion written by Justice William Brennan, the Court seemed to be saying that the Constitution required actual racial mixing in the schools, not just the repeal of laws requiring racial separation.

This impression was confirmed three years later when the Court considered a plan in North Carolina under which pupils in Mecklenburg County (which includes Charlotte) were assigned to the nearest neighborhood school without regard to race. As a result, about half the black children now attended formerly all-white schools, with the other half attending all-black schools. The federal district court held that this was inadequate and ordered some children to be bused into more distant schools in order to achieve a greater degree of integration. The Supreme Court, now led by Chief Justice Warren Burger, upheld the district judge on the grounds that the court plan was necessary to achieve a "unitary school system."[18]

This case—*Swann v. Charlotte-Mecklenburg Board of Education*—pretty much set the guidelines for all subsequent cases involving school segregation. The essential features of those guidelines are as follows:

- To violate the Constitution, a school system, by law, practice, or regulation, must have engaged in discrimination. Put another way, a plaintiff must show intent to discriminate on the part of the public schools.

- The existence of all-white or all-black schools in a district with a history of segregation creates a presumption of intent to discriminate.

strict scrutiny The standard by which "suspect classifications" are judged. To be upheld, such a classification must be related to a "compelling government interest," be "narrowly tailored" to achieve that interest, and use the "least restrictive means" available.

de jure segregation Racial segregation that is required by law.

de facto segregation Racial segregation that occurs in schools, not as a result of the law, but as a result of patterns of residential settlement.

- The remedy for past discrimination will not be limited to freedom of choice, or what the Court called "the walk-in school." Remedies may include racial quotas in the assignment of teachers and pupils, redrawn district lines, and court-ordered busing.

- Not every school must reflect the social composition of the school system as a whole.

Relying on *Swann,* district courts have supervised redistricting and busing plans in localities all over the nation, often in the face of bitter opposition from the community. In Boston, the control of the city schools by a federal judge, W. Arthur Garrity, lasted for more than a decade and involved him in every aspect of school administration. One major issue not settled by *Swann* was whether busing and other remedies should cut across city and county lines. In some places, the central-city schools had become virtually all black. Racial integration could be achieved only by bringing black pupils to white suburban schools or moving white pupils into central-city schools. In a series of split-vote decisions, the Court ruled that court-ordered intercity busing could be authorized only if it could be demonstrated that the suburban areas, as well as the central city, had in fact practiced school segregation. Where that could not be shown, such intercity busing would not be required. The Court was not persuaded that intent had been proved in Atlanta, Detroit, Denver, Indianapolis, and Richmond, but it was persuaded that it had been proved in Louisville and Wilmington.[19]

The importance the Court attaches to intent means that if a school system that was once integrated becomes all black as a result of whites' moving to the suburbs, the Court will not require that district lines constantly be redrawn or new busing plans be adopted to adjust to the changing distribution of the population.[20] This in turn means that as long as blacks and whites live in different neighborhoods for whatever reason, there is a good chance that some schools in both areas will be heavily of one race. If mandatory busing or other integration measures cause whites to move out of a city at a faster rate than they otherwise would (a process often called "white flight"), then efforts to integrate the schools may in time create more single-race schools. Ultimately, integrated schools will exist only in integrated neighborhoods or where the quality of education is so high that both blacks and whites want to enroll in the school even at some cost in terms of travel and inconvenience.

Mandatory busing to achieve racial integration has been a deeply controversial program and has generated considerable public opposition. Surveys show that a majority of people oppose it.[21] As recently as 1992, a poll showed that 48 percent of whites in the Northeast and 53 percent of Southern whites felt it was "not the business" of the federal government to ensure "that black and white children go to the same schools."[22] Presidents Nixon, Ford, and Reagan opposed busing; all three supported legislation to prevent or reduce it, and Reagan petitioned the courts to reconsider busing plans. The courts refused to reconsider, and Congress has passed only minor restrictions on busing.

The reason why Congress has not followed public opinion on this matter is complex. It has been torn between the desire to support civil rights and uphold the courts and the desire to represent the views of its constituents. Because it faces a dilemma, Congress has taken both sides of the issue simultaneously. By the late 1980s, busing was a dying issue in Congress, in part because no meaningful legislation seemed possible and in part because popular passion over busing had somewhat abated.

Then, in 1992, the Supreme Court made it easier for local school systems to reclaim control over their schools from the courts. In DeKalb County, Georgia (a suburb of Atlanta), the schools had been operating under court-ordered desegregation plans for many years. Despite this effort, full integration had not been achieved, largely because the county's neighborhoods had increasingly become either all black or all white. The Court held that local schools could not be held responsible for segregation caused solely by segregated living patterns, and so the courts would have to relinquish their control over the schools. In 2007, the Court said race could not be the decisive factor in assigning students to schools that had either never been segregated (as in Seattle) or where legal segregation had long since ended (as in Jefferson County, Kentucky).[23]

The Campaign in Congress

The campaign in the courts for desegregated schools, though slow and costly, was a carefully managed effort to alter the interpretation of a constitutional provision. But to get new civil rights laws out of Congress required a far more difficult and decentralized strategy, one that was aimed at mobilizing public opinion and overcoming the many congressional barriers to action.

The first problem was to get civil rights on the political agenda by convincing people that something had to be done. This could be achieved by dramatizing the problem in ways that tugged at the conscience of whites who were not racist but were ordinarily indifferent to black problems. Brutal lynching of blacks had shocked these whites, but the practice of lynching was on the wane in the 1950s.

Civil rights leaders could, however, arrange for dramatic confrontations between blacks claiming some obvious right and the whites who denied it to them. Beginning in the late 1950s, these confrontations began to occur in the form of sit-ins at segregated lunch counters and "freedom rides" on segregated bus lines. At about the same time, efforts were made to get blacks registered to vote in counties where whites had used intimidation and harassment to prevent it.

The best-known campaign occurred in 1955–1956 in Montgomery, Alabama, where blacks, led by a young minister named Martin Luther King, Jr., boycotted the local bus system after it had a black woman, Rosa Parks, arrested because she refused to surrender her seat on a bus to a white man.

These early demonstrations were based on the philosophy of **civil disobedience**—that is, peacefully violating a law, such as one requiring blacks to ride in a segregated section of a bus, and allowing oneself to be arrested as a result.

But the momentum of protest, once unleashed, could not be centrally directed or confined to nonviolent action. A rising tide of anger, especially among younger blacks, resulted in the formation of more militant organizations and the spontaneous eruption of violent demonstrations and riots in dozens of cities across the country. From 1964 to 1968, there were in the North, as well as the South, four "long, hot summers" of racial violence.

LANDMARK CASES

Civil Rights

- **Dred Scott case, *Scott v. Sanford* (1857):** Congress had no authority to ban slavery in a territory. A slave was considered a piece of property.

- ***Plessy v. Ferguson* (1896):** Upheld separate-but-equal facilities for white and black people on railroad cars.

- ***Brown v. Board of Education* (1954):** Said separate public schools are inherently unequal, thus starting racial desegregation.

- ***Green v. County School Board of New Kent County* (1968):** Banned a freedom-of-choice plan for integrating schools, suggesting blacks and whites must actually attend racially mixed schools.

- ***Swann v. Charlotte-Mecklenburg Board of Education* (1971):** Approved busing and redrawing district lines as ways of integrating public schools.

civil disobedience
Opposing a law one considers unjust by peacefully disobeying it and accepting the resultant punishment.

The demonstrations and rioting succeeded in getting civil rights on the national political agenda, but at a cost: many whites, opposed to the demonstrations or appalled by the riots, dug in their heels and fought against making any concessions to "lawbreakers," "troublemakers," and "rioters." In 1964, and again in 1968, more than two-thirds of the whites interviewed in opinion polls said the civil rights movement was pushing too fast, had hurt the black cause, and was too violent.[24]

In short, a conflict existed between the agenda-setting and coalition-building aspects of the civil rights movement. This was especially a problem since conservative Southern legislators still controlled many key congressional committees that had for years been the graveyard of civil rights legislation. The Senate Judiciary Committee was dominated by a coalition of Southern Democrats and conservative Republicans, and the House Rules Committee was under the control of a chairman hostile to civil rights bills, Howard Smith of Virginia. Any bill that passed the House faced an almost certain filibuster in the Senate. Finally, President John F. Kennedy was reluctant to submit strong civil rights bills to Congress.

Four developments made it possible to break the deadlock. First, public opinion was changing. From the mid-1950s to the mid-1990s, surveys found that the proportion of whites who were willing to have their children attend a school that was half black increased sharply (though the proportion of whites willing to have their children attend a school that was predominantly black increased by much less). About the same change could be found in white attitudes toward allowing blacks equal access to hotels and buses.[25] Of course, support in principle for these civil rights measures was not necessarily the same as support in practice; nonetheless, clearly a major shift was occurring in popular approval of at least the principles of civil rights. At the leading edge of this change were young, college-educated people.[26]

Second, certain violent reactions by white segregationists to black demonstrators were vividly portrayed by the media (especially television) in ways that gave the civil rights cause a powerful moral force. In May 1963, the head of the Birmingham police, Eugene "Bull" Connor, ordered his men to use attack dogs and high-pressure fire hoses to repulse a peaceful march by African Americans demanding desegregated public facilities and increased job opportunities. The pictures of that confrontation (such as the one on page 121) created a national sensation and contributed greatly to the massive participation—by whites and blacks alike—in the "March on Washington" that summer. About a quarter of a million people gathered in front of the Lincoln Memorial to hear the Reverend Dr. Martin Luther King, Jr., deliver the aforementioned "I Have a Dream" speech, which is now widely regarded as one of the most significant public addresses in American history, and which today is read, studied, or memorized in whole or in part by millions of school children each year (see Appendix). The following summer in Neshoba County, Mississippi, three young civil rights workers (two white and one black) were brutally murdered by Klansmen aided by the local sheriff. When the FBI identified the murderers, the effect on national public opinion was galvanic; no white Southern leader could any longer offer persuasive opposition to federal laws protecting voting rights when white law enforcement officers had killed students working to protect those rights. And the next year, a white woman, Viola Liuzzo, was shot and killed while driving a car used to transport civil rights workers. Her death was the subject of a presidential address.

Third, President John F. Kennedy was assassinated in Dallas, Texas, in November 1963. Many people originally (and wrongly) thought he had been killed by a right-wing conspiracy. Even after the assassin had been caught and shown to have left-wing associations, the shock of the president's murder—in a Southern city—helped build support for efforts by the new president, Lyndon B. Johnson (a Texan), to obtain passage of a strong civil rights bill as a memorial to the slain president.

Fourth, the 1964 elections not only returned Johnson to office with a landslide victory, but also sent a huge Democratic majority to the House and retained the large Democratic margin in the Senate. This made it possible for Northern Democrats to outvote or outmaneuver Southerners in the House.

The cumulative effect of these forces led to the enactment of five civil rights laws between 1957 and 1968. Three (1957, 1960, and 1965) were chiefly directed at protecting the right to vote; one (1968) was aimed at preventing discrimination in housing; and one (1964), the most far-reaching of all, dealt with voting, employment, schooling, and public accommodations.

The passage of the 1964 act was the high point of the legislative struggle. Liberals in the House had drafted a bipartisan bill, but it was now in the House Rules Committee, where such proposals had often disappeared without a trace. In the wake of Kennedy's murder, a discharge petition was filed—with President Johnson's support—to take the bill out of committee and bring it to the floor of the House. But the Rules Committee, without waiting for a vote on the petition (which it probably realized it would lose), sent the bill to the floor, where it passed overwhelmingly. In the Senate, an agreement between Republican minority leader Everett Dirksen and President Johnson smoothed the

This picture of a police dog lunging at a black man during a racial demonstration in Birmingham, Alabama, in May 1963 was one of the most influential photographs ever published. It was widely reprinted throughout the world and was frequently referred to in congressional debates on the civil rights bill of 1964.

way for passage in several important respects. The House bill was sent directly to the Senate floor, thereby bypassing the Southern-dominated Judiciary Committee. Nineteen Southern senators began an eight-week filibuster against the bill. On June 10, 1964, by a vote of 71 to 29, cloture was invoked and the filibuster ended—the first time in history that a filibuster aimed at blocking civil rights legislation had been broken.

Since the 1960s, congressional support for civil rights legislation has grown—so much so, indeed, that labeling a bill a civil rights measure, once the kiss of death, now almost guarantees its passage. For example, in 1984 the Supreme Court decided the federal ban on discrimination in education applied only to the "program or activity" receiving federal aid and not to the entire school or university.[27] In 1988, Congress passed a bill to overturn this decision by making it clear that antidiscrimination rules applied to the entire educational institution and not just to that part (say, the physics lab) receiving federal money. When President Reagan vetoed the bill (because, in his view, it would diminish the freedom of church-affiliated schools), Congress overrode the veto. In the override vote, every Southern Democrat in the Senate and almost 90 percent of those in the House voted for the bill. This was a dramatic change from 1964, when more than 80 percent of the Southern Democrats in Congress voted

AFP/Getty Images

Reverend Dr. Martin Luther King, Jr., delivers his "I Have a Dream" speech on the Washington, D.C., mall in 1963.

against the Civil Rights Act (see Figure 5.1). This change partly reflected the growing political strength of Southern blacks. In 1960, less than one-third of voting-age blacks in the South were registered to vote; by 1971 more than half were, and by 1984 two-thirds were.

In 2008, Barack Obama was elected president and became the first African American to hold the nation's highest elected office. That monumental historic moment, which included Obama winning two Southern states, was preceded by four decades of growth in the number of black elected officials at all levels of government. Between 1970 and 2010, the total number of black elected officials rose from fewer than 1,500 to more than 10,500 (see Table 5.1) In the presidential elections of 2008 and 2012, voter turnout rates among African Americans equaled or exceeded that of whites. Such parity in voter turnout rates and the aforementioned increase in the number of black elected officials could not have happened without civil rights laws like the Voting Rights Act (VRA) of 1965. In 2006, following more than 20 public hearings, and with support from then-President George W. Bush, Congress reauthorized the VRA's key provisions for another quarter-century, including the section (Section 4) designating the "preclearance" formula used to determine which state or local jurisdictions must have any major changes to their voting laws or procedures approved in advance by the U.S. Department of Justice or by a federal court. Along with the need to remain vigilant in checking any recurrence of old methods of discrimination, the bill's

FIGURE 5.1 Increase in Support among Southern Democrats in Congress for Civil Rights Bills, 1957–1991

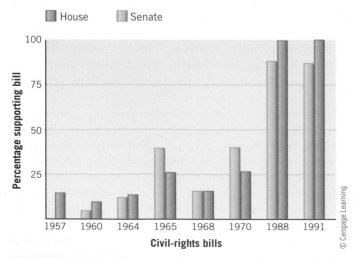

■ House   ■ Senate

Source: Congressional Quarterly, *Congress and the Nation*, vols. 1, 2, 3, 7, 8.

© Cengage Learning

bipartisan backers also cited concerns about "racial gerrymandering," the proliferation of "voter identification" laws, and other measures that could adversely and disproportionately affect minority participation in the electoral process.

But, in 2013, in the case of *Shelby County v. Holder*, the Supreme Court struck down the VRA's preclearance formula as unconstitutional. Writing for the Court's 5-to-4 majority, Chief Justice John Roberts declared that "things have changed dramatically" in the South since 1965; he also issued a statement from the bench indicating that Congress "may draft another formula based on current conditions." Writing for the four dissenting justices, Justice Ruth Bader Ginsburg declared that the majority had "failed to grasp why the VRA has proven effective;" she also issued a statement from the bench stressing that in 2006, Congress "found that 40 years has not been sufficient time to eliminate the vestiges of discrimination following 100 years of disregard for the 15th Amendment." President Obama issued a statement in which he observed that the decision "upsets decades of well-established practices that help to make sure voting is fair, especially in places where voting discrimination has been historically prevalent;" he also called on Congress to pass new voting rights legislation.

TABLE 5.1   Increase in Number of Black Elected Officials

	1970	2010
Federal Office	10	43
State Office	169	642
Local Office	1,290	9,800

Source: Statistical Abstract of the United States, 2003, table 417; Joint Center for Political and Economic Studies, *Roster of Black Elected Officials*, November 2011; "A Time to Reflect: Charting the Quality of Life for Black Americans: Politics," *USA Today*, February 21, 2011.

Women and Equal Rights The political and legal efforts to secure civil rights for African Americans were accompanied by efforts to expand the rights of women. There was an important difference between the two movements, however: whereas African Americans were arguing against a legal tradition that explicitly aimed to keep them in a subservient status, women had to argue against a tradition that claimed to be protecting them. For example, in 1908, the Supreme Court upheld an Oregon law that limited female laundry workers to a 10-hour workday against the claim that it violated the Fourteenth Amendment. The Court justified its decision with this language:

> The two sexes differ in structure of body, in the functions to be performed by each, in the amount of physical strength, in the capacity for long- continued labor, particularly when done standing . . . the self-reliance which enables one to assert full rights, and in the capacity to maintain the struggle for subsistence. This difference justifies a difference in legislation and upholds that which is designed to compensate for some of the burdens which rest upon her.[28]

The origin of the movement to give more rights to women was probably the Seneca Falls Convention held in 1848. Its leaders began to demand the right to vote for women. Though this was slowly granted by several states, especially in the West, it was not until 1920 that the Nineteenth Amendment made it clear that no state may deny the right to vote on the basis of sex. The great change in the status of women, however, took place during World War II when the demand for workers in our defense plants led to the employment of millions of women, such as "Rosie the Riveter," in jobs they had rarely held before. After the war, the feminist movement took flight with the publication in 1963 of *The Feminine Mystique* by Betty Friedan.

Congress responded by passing laws that required equal pay for equal work, prohibited discrimination on the basis of sex in employment and among students in any school or university receiving federal funds, and banned discrimination against pregnant women on the job.[29]

At the same time, the Supreme Court was altering the way it interpreted the Constitution. The key passage was the Fourteenth Amendment, which prohibits any state from denying to "any person" the "equal protection of the laws." For a long time the traditional standard, as we saw in the 1908 case, was a kind of protective paternalism. By the early 1970s, however, the Court had changed its mind. In deciding whether the Constitution bars all, some, or no sexual discrimination, the Court had a choice among three standards.

The first standard is the *reasonableness* standard. This says that when the government treats some classes of people differently from others—for example, applying statutory rape laws to men but not to women—the different treatment must be reasonable and not arbitrary.

The second standard is *intermediate scrutiny*. When women complained that some laws treated them unfairly, the Court adopted a standard somewhere between the reasonableness and strict scrutiny tests. Thus, a law that treats men and women differently must be more than merely reasonable, but the allowable differences need not meet the strict scrutiny test.

And so, in 1971, the Court held that an Idaho statute was unconstitutional because it required that males be preferred over females when choosing people to administer the estates of deceased children. To satisfy the Constitution, a law treating men and women differently "must be reasonable, not arbitrary, and must rest on some ground of difference having a fair and substantial relation to the object of legislation so that all persons similarly circumstanced shall be treated alike."[30] In later decisions, some members of the Court wanted to make classifications based on sex inherently suspect and subject to the strict scrutiny test, but no majority has yet embraced this position.[31]

The third standard is *strict scrutiny*. This says that some instances of drawing distinctions between different groups of people—for example, by treating whites and blacks differently—are inherently suspect; thus, the Court will subject them to strict scrutiny to ensure they are clearly necessary to attain a legitimate state goal.

But sexual classifications can also be judged by a different standard. The Civil Rights Act of 1964 prohibits sex discrimination in the hiring, firing, and compensation of employees. The 1972 Civil

---

HOW THINGS WORK

How the Court Decides If You Discriminate

The Supreme Court has produced three different tests to decide if a government policy produces unconstitutional discrimination. Don't be surprised if you find it a bit hard to tell them apart.

1. **Rational basis** If the policy uses reasonable means to achieve a legitimate government goal, it is constitutional.

   Examples: If the government says you can't buy a drink until you are 21, this meets the rational basis test: the government wants to prevent children from drinking, and age 21 is a reasonable means to define when a person is an adult. And a state can ban advertising on trucks unless the ad is about the truck owner's own business.

2. **Intermediate scrutiny** If the policy "serves an important government interest" and is "substantially related" to serving that interest, it is constitutional.

   Examples: Men can be punished for statutory rape even if women are not punished because men and women are not "similarly situated." And men can be barred from entering hospital delivery rooms even though (obviously) women are admitted.

3. **Strict scrutiny** To be constitutional, the discrimination must serve a "compelling government interest," it must be "narrowly tailored" to attain that interest, and it must use the "least restrictive means" to attain it.

   Examples: Distinctions based on race, ethnicity, religion, or voting must pass the strict scrutiny test. You cannot bar black children from a public school or black adults from voting, and you cannot prevent one religion from knocking on your door to promote its views.

Rights Act bans sex discrimination in local education programs receiving federal aid. These laws apply to *private*, and not just government, actions.

Over the years, the Court has decided many cases involving sexual classification. The following lists provide several examples of illegal sexual discrimination (violating either the Constitution or a civil rights act) and legal sexual distinctions (violating neither).

Illegal Discrimination

- A state cannot set different ages at which men and women legally become adults.[32]

- A state cannot set different ages at which men and women are allowed to buy beer.[33]

- Women cannot be barred from jobs by arbitrary height and weight requirements.[34]

- Employers cannot require women to take mandatory pregnancy leaves.[35]

- Girls cannot be barred from Little League baseball teams.[36]

- Business and service clubs, such as the Junior Chamber of Commerce and Rotary Club, cannot exclude women from membership.[37]

- Though women as a group live longer than men, an employer must pay them monthly retirement benefits equal to those received by men.[38]

- High schools must pay the coaches of girls' sports the same as they pay the coaches of boys' sports.[39]

Decisions Allowing Differences Based on Sex

- A law that punishes males but not females for statutory rape is permissible; men and women are not "similarly situated" with respect to sexual relations.[40]

- All-boy and all-girl public schools are permitted if enrollment is voluntary and quality is equal.[41]

- States can give widows a property-tax exemption not given to widowers.[42]

- The Navy may allow women to remain officers longer than men without being promoted.[43]

The lower federal courts have been especially busy in the area of sexual distinctions. They have said that public taverns may not cater to men only and that girls may not be prevented from competing against boys in noncontact high school sports; on the other hand, hospitals may bar fathers from the delivery room. Women may continue to use their maiden names after marriage.[44]

In 1996, the Supreme Court ruled that women must be admitted to the Virginia Military Institute, until then an all-male, state-supported college that had for many decades supplied what it called an "adversative method" of training to

LANDMARK CASES

Women's Rights

- ***Reed v. Reed*** **(1971):** Gender discrimination violates the equal protection clause of the Constitution.

- ***Craig v. Boren*** **(1976):** Gender discrimination can be justified only if it serves "important governmental objectives" and is "substantially related to those objectives."

- ***Rostker v. Goldberg*** **(1981):** Congress can draft men without drafting women.

- ***United States v. Virginia*** **(1996):** State may not finance an all-male military school.

> **police powers** State power to effect laws promoting health, safety, and morals.

instill physical and mental discipline in cadets. In practical terms, this meant the school was very tough on students. The Court said that for a state to justify spending tax money on a single-sex school, it must supply an "exceedingly persuasive justification" for excluding the other gender. Virginia countered by offering to support an all-female training course at another college, but this was not enough.[45] This decision came close to imposing the strict scrutiny test, and so it has raised important questions about what could happen to all-female or traditionally black colleges that accept state money.

Perhaps the most far-reaching cases defining the rights of women have involved the draft and abortion. In 1981, the Court held in *Rostker v. Goldberg* that Congress may require men but not women to register for the draft without violating the due process clause of the Fifth Amendment.[46] In the area of national defense, the Court will give great deference to congressional policy (Congress had already decided to bar women from combat roles). For many years, women could be pilots and sailors, but not on combat aircraft or combat ships. In 1993, the secretary of defense opened air and sea combat positions to all persons regardless of gender; only ground-troop combat positions were still reserved for men. The issue played a role in preventing the ratification of the Equal Rights Amendment to the Constitution, because of fears that it would reverse *Rostker v. Goldberg.*

Sexual Harassment

When Paula Corbin Jones accused President Clinton of sexual harassment, the judge threw the case out of court because she had not submitted enough evidence such that, if the jury believed her story, she would have made a legally adequate argument that she had been sexually harassed.

What, then, is sexual harassment? Drawing on rulings by the Equal Employment Opportunities Commission, the Supreme Court has held that harassment can take one of two forms. First, it is illegal for someone to request sexual favors as a condition of employment or promotion. This is the "quid pro quo" rule. If a person does this, the employer is "strictly liable." Strict liability means the employer can be found at fault even if he or she did not know a subordinate was requesting sex in exchange for hiring or promotion.

Second, it is illegal for an employee to experience a work environment that has been made hostile or intimidating by a steady pattern of offensive sexual teasing, jokes, or obscenity. But employers are not strictly liable in this case; they can be found at fault only if they were "negligent"—that is, they knew about the hostile environment but did nothing about it.

In 1998, the Supreme Court decided three cases that made these rules either better or worse, depending on your point of view. In one, it determined that a school system was not liable for the conduct of a teacher who seduced a female student because the student never reported the actions. In a second, it held that a city was liable for a sexually hostile work environment confronting a female lifeguard even though she did not report this to her superiors. In the third, it decided that a female employee who was not promoted after having rejected the sexual advances of her boss could recover financial damages from the firm. But, it added, the firm could have avoided paying this bill if it had put in place an "affirmative defense" against sexual exploitation, although the Court never said what such a policy might be.[47]

Sexual harassment is a serious matter, but because there are almost no federal laws governing it, we are left with somewhat vague and often inconsistent court and bureaucratic rules to guide us.

Privacy and Sex

Regulating sexual matters has traditionally been left up to the states, which do so by exercising their **police powers**. These powers include more than the authority to create police departments; they include all laws designed to promote public order and secure the safety and morals of the citizens.

Some have argued that the Tenth Amendment to the Constitution, by reserving to the states all powers not delegated to the federal government, meant that states could do anything not explicitly prohibited by the Constitution. But that changed when the Supreme Court began expanding the power of Congress over business and when it started to view sexual matters under the newly discovered right to privacy.

Until that point, it had been left up to the states to decide whether and under what circumstances a woman could obtain an abortion. For example, New York allowed abortions during the first 24 weeks of pregnancy, while Texas banned it except when the mother's life was threatened. That began to change in 1965 when the Supreme Court held that the states could not prevent the sale of contraceptives because by so doing it would invade a "zone of privacy." Privacy is nowhere mentioned in the Constitution, but the Court argued that it could be inferred from "penumbras" (literally, shadows) cast off by various provisions of the Bill of Rights.[48]

Eight years later the Court, in its famous *Roe v. Wade* decision, held that a "right to privacy" is "broad enough to encompass a woman's decision whether or not to terminate a pregnancy."[49] The case, which began in Texas, produced this view: during the first three months (or first trimester) of pregnancy, a woman has an unfettered right to an abortion. During the second trimester, states may regulate abortions, but only to protect the mother's health. In the third trimester, states might ban abortions.

In reaching this decision, the Court denied that it was trying to decide when human life began—at the moment of conception, at the moment of birth, or somewhere in between. But that is not how critics of the decision saw things. To them, life begins at conception, and so the human fetus is a "person" entitled to the equal protection of the laws guaranteed by the Fourteenth Amendment. People feeling this way began to use the slogans "right to life" and "pro-life." Supporters of the Court's action saw matters differently. In their view, no one can say for certain when human life begins; what one *can* say, however, is that a woman is entitled to choose whether or not to have a baby. These people took the slogans "right to choose" and "pro-choice."

Almost immediately, the congressional allies of pro-life groups introduced constitutional amendments to overturn *Roe v. Wade*, but none passed Congress. Nevertheless, abortion foes did persuade Congress, beginning in 1976, to bar the use of federal funds to pay for abortions except when the life of the mother is at stake. This provision is known as the Hyde Amendment, after its sponsor, Representative Henry Hyde. The chief effect of the amendment has been to deny the use of Medicaid funds to pay for abortions for low-income women.

Despite pro-life opposition, the Supreme Court for 16 years steadfastly reaffirmed and even broadened its decision in *Roe v. Wade*. It struck down laws requiring, before an abortion could be performed, a woman to have the consent of her husband, an "emancipated" but underage girl to have the consent of her parents, or a woman to be advised by her doctor as to the facts about abortion.[50]

LANDMARK CASES

Privacy and Abortion

- *Griswold v. Connecticut* (1965): Found a "right to privacy" in the Constitution that would ban any state law against selling contraceptives.

- *Roe v. Wade* (1973): State laws prohibiting abortion were unconstitutional.

- *Webster v. Reproductive Health Services* (1989): Allowed states to ban abortions from public hospitals and permitted doctors to test to see if fetuses were viable.

- *Planned Parenthood v. Casey* (1992): Reaffirmed *Roe v. Wade* but upheld certain limits on its use.

- *Gonzales v. Carhart* (2007): Federal law may ban certain forms of partial-birth abortion.

equality of results Making certain that people achieve the same result.

affirmative action Laws or administrative regulations that require a business firm, government agency, labor union, school, college, or other organization to take positive steps to increase the number of African Americans, other minorities, or women in its membership.

But in 1989, under the influence of justices appointed by President Reagan, the Court began in the *Webster* case to uphold some state restrictions on abortions. When that happened, many people predicted that in time *Roe v. Wade* would be overturned, especially if President George H.W. Bush was able to appoint more justices. He appointed two (Souter and Thomas), but *Roe* survived. The key votes were cast by Justices O'Connor, Souter, and Kennedy. In 1992, in its *Casey* decision, the Court, by a vote of five to four, explicitly refused to overturn *Roe*, declaring that there was a right to abortion. At the same time, however, it upheld a variety of restrictions imposed by the state of Pennsylvania on women seeking abortions. These included a mandatory 24-hour waiting period between the request for an abortion and the performance of it, the requirement that teenagers obtain the consent of one parent (or, in special circumstances, of a judge), and a requirement that women contemplating an abortion be given pamphlets about alternatives to it. Similar restrictions had been enacted in many other states, all of which looked to the Pennsylvania case for guidance as to whether they could be enforced. In allowing these restrictions, the Court overruled some of its own earlier decisions.[51] On the other hand, the Court did strike down a state law that would have required married women to obtain the consent of their husbands before having an abortion.

After a long political and legal struggle, the Court in 2007 upheld a federal law that bans certain kinds of partial-birth abortions. The law does not allow an abortion in which the fetus, still alive, is withdrawn until its head is outside the mother and then it is killed. But the law does not ban a late-term abortion if it is necessary to protect the physical health of the mother or if it is performed on an already dead fetus, even if the doctor has already killed it.[52]

There is one irony in all of this: "Roe," the pseudonym for the woman who started the suit that became *Roe v. Wade,* never had an abortion and, many years later, using her real name, Norma McCorvey, became an evangelical Christian who published a book and started a ministry to denounce abortions.

Affirmative Action

A common thread running through the politics of civil rights is the argument between **equality of results** and equality of opportunity.

Equality of Results

One view, expressed by most civil rights and feminist organizations, is that the burdens of racism and sexism can be overcome only by taking race or sex into account in designing remedies. It is not enough that people be given rights; they also must be given benefits. If life is a race, everybody must be brought up to the same starting line (or possibly even to the same finish line). This means that the Constitution is not and should not be color-blind or sex-neutral. In education, this implies that the races must actually be mixed in the schools, by busing if necessary. In hiring, it means that affirmative action must be used in the hiring process. **Affirmative action** refers to laws or administrative regulations that require a business firm, government agency, labor union, school, college, or other organization to take positive steps to increase the number of African Americans, other minorities, or women in its membership. It means that it is not enough that women should simply be free to enter the labor force; they should be given the material necessities (for example, free daycare) that will help them enter it. On payday, workers' checks should reflect not just the results of competition in the marketplace, but the results of plans designed to ensure that people earn comparable amounts for comparable jobs. Of late, affirmative action has been defended in the name of diversity or multiculturalism—the view that every institution (firm, school, or agency) and every college curriculum should reflect the cultural (that is, ethnic) diversity of the nation.

reverse discrimination Using race or sex to give preferential treatment to some people.

equality of opportunity Giving people an equal chance to succeed.

Equality of Opportunity

The second view holds that if it is wrong to discriminate *against* African Americans and women, it is equally wrong to give them preferential treatment over other groups. To do so constitutes **reverse discrimination**. The Constitution and laws should be color-blind and sex-neutral.[53] In this view, allowing children to attend the school of their choice is sufficient; busing them to attain a certain racial mixture is wrong. Eliminating barriers to job opportunities is right; using numerical "targets" and "goals" to place minorities and women in specific jobs is wrong. If people wish to compete in the market, they should be satisfied with the market verdict concerning the worth of their work.

Each of these views is intertwined with other deep philosophical differences. Supporters of **equality of opportunity** tend to have orthodox beliefs; they favor letting private groups behave the way that they want (and so may defend the right of a men's club to exclude women). Supporters of the opposite view are likely to be progressive in their beliefs and insist that private clubs meet the same standards as schools or business firms. Adherents to the equality-of-opportunity view often attach great importance to traditional models of the family and so are skeptical of subsidized daycare and federally funded abortions. Adherents to the equality-of-results view prefer greater freedom of choice in lifestyle questions and so take the opposite position on daycare and abortion.

 HOW THINGS WORK

Becoming a Citizen

For persons born in the United States, the rights of U.S. citizenship have been ensured—in constitutional theory, if not in everyday practice—since the passage of the Fourteenth Amendment in 1868 and the civil rights laws of the 1960s. The Fourteenth Amendment conferred citizenship upon "all persons born in the United States . . . and subject to the jurisdiction thereof." Subsequent laws also gave citizenship to children born outside the United States to parents who are American citizens.

But immigrants, by definition, are not born with the rights of U.S. citizenship. Instead, those seeking to become U.S. citizens must, in effect, assume certain responsibilities in order to become citizens. The statutory requirements for naturalization, as they have been broadly construed by the courts, are as follows:

- Five years' residency, or three years if married to a citizen.

- Continuous residency since filing of the naturalization petition.

(continued)

HOW THINGS WORK (*Continued*)

- Good moral character, which is loosely interpreted to mean no evidence of criminal activity.

- Attachment to constitutional principles. This means that potential citizens have to answer basic factual questions about American government (e.g., "Who was the first president of the United States?") and publicly denounce any and all allegiance to their native country and its leaders (e.g., Italy and the king of Italy), but devotion to constitutional principles is now regarded as implicit in the act of applying for naturalization.

- Being favorably disposed to "the good order and happiness of the United States."*

Today, about 97 percent of aliens who seek citizenship are successful in meeting these requirements and becoming naturalized citizens of the United States.

*8 U.S.C. 1423, 1427 (1970); *Girouard v. United States*, 328 U.S. 61 (1946).

Of course, the debate is more complex than this simple contrast suggests. Take, for example, the question of affirmative action. Both the advocates of equality of opportunity and those of equality of results might agree that there is something odd about a factory or university that hires no African Americans or women, and both might press it to prove that its hiring policy is fair. Affirmative action in this case can mean *either* looking hard for qualified women and minorities and giving them a fair shot at jobs *or* setting a numerical goal for the number of women and minorities that should be hired and insisting that that goal be met. Persons who defend the second course of action call these goals "targets"; persons who criticize that course call them "quotas."

The issue has largely been fought in the courts. Between 1978 and 1990, about a dozen major cases involving affirmative action policies were decided by the Supreme Court; in about half the policies were upheld, and in the other half they were overturned. The different outcomes reflect two things—the differences in the facts of the cases and the arrival on the Court of three justices (Kennedy, O'Connor, and Scalia) appointed by a president, Ronald Reagan, who was opposed to (at least) the broader interpretation of affirmative action. As a result of these decisions, the law governing affirmative action is now complex and confusing.

HOW THINGS WORK

The Rights of Aliens

America is a nation of immigrants. Some have arrived legally, others illegally. A person residing in this country who is not a citizen is referred to as an *alien*. An illegal, or undocumented, alien is subject to deportation. With the passage in 1986 of the Immigration Reform and Control Act, illegal aliens who have resided in this country continuously since before January 1, 1982, are entitled to amnesty—that is, they can become legal residents. However, the same legislation

(continued)

HOW THINGS WORK (*Continued*)

stipulated that employers (who once could hire undocumented aliens without fear of penalty) must now verify the legal status of all newly hired employees; if they knowingly hire an illegal alien, they face civil and criminal penalties.

Aliens cannot vote or run for office. Nevertheless, they must pay taxes just as if they were citizens. And they are entitled to many constitutional rights, even if they are in this country illegally. This is because most of the rights mentioned in the Constitution refer to "people" or "persons," not to "citizens." For example, the Fourteenth Amendment bars a state from depriving "*any person* of life, liberty, or property, without due process of law" and from denying "to *any person* within its jurisdiction the equal protection of the laws" [italics added]. As a result, the courts have held that:

- The children of illegal aliens cannot be excluded from the public school system.[1]
- Legally admitted aliens are entitled to welfare benefits.[2]
- Illegal aliens cannot be the object of reprisals if they attempt to form a labor union where they work.[3]
- The First Amendment rights of free speech, religion, press, and assembly and the Fourth Amendment protections against arbitrary arrest and prosecution extend to aliens as well as to citizens.[4]
- Aliens are entitled to own property.
- The government can make rules that apply to aliens only, but they must justify the reasonableness of the rules. For example:
- The Immigration and Naturalization Service has broader powers to arrest and search illegal aliens than police departments have to arrest and search citizens.[5]
- States can limit certain jobs, such as police officer and schoolteacher, to citizens.[6]
- The president or Congress can bar the employment of aliens by the federal government.[7]
- States can bar aliens from serving on a jury.[8]
- Illegal aliens are not entitled to obtain a Social Security card.

[1]*Plyler v. Doe*, 457 U.S. 202 (1982).

[2]*Graham v. Richardson*, 403 U.S. 365 (1971).

[3]*Sure-Tan v. National Labor Relations Board*, 467 U.S. 883 (1984).

[4]*Chew v. Colding*, 344 U.S. 590 (1953).

[5]*United States v. Brignoni-Ponce*, 422 U.S. 873 (1975); *INS v. Delgado*, 466 U.S. 210 (1984); *INS v. Lopez-Mendoza*, 486 U.S. 1032 (1984).

[6]*Cabell v. Chavez-Salido*, 454 U.S. 432 (1982); *Foley v. Connelie*, 435 U.S. 291 (1978); *Amblach v. Norwick*, 441 U.S. 68 (1979).

[7]*Hampton v. Mow Sun Wong*, 436 U.S. 67 (1976).

[8]*Schneider v. New Jersey*, 308 U.S. 147 (1939).

Consider one issue: should the government be allowed to use a quota system to select workers, enroll students, award contracts, or grant licenses? In the *Bakke* decision in 1978, the Court said the medical school of the University of California at Davis could not use an explicit numerical quota in admitting minority students but could "take race into account."[54] So no numerical quotas, right? Wrong. Two years later, the Court upheld a federal rule that set aside 10 percent of all federal construction contracts for minority-owned firms.[55] All right, maybe quotas can't be used in medical schools, but they can be used in the construction industry. Not exactly. In 1989, the Court overturned a Richmond, Virginia, law that set aside 30 percent of its construction contracts for minority-owned firms.[56] Well, maybe the Court just changed its mind between 1980 and 1989. No. One year later it upheld a federal rule that gave preference to minority-owned firms in the awarding of broadcast licenses.[57] Then in 1993, it upheld the right of white contractors to challenge minority set-aside laws in Jacksonville, Florida.[58]

It is too early to try to make sense of these twists and turns, especially since a deeply divided Court is still wrestling with these issues and Congress (as with the Civil Rights Act of 1991) is modifying or superseding some earlier Court decisions. But a few general standards seem to be emerging. In simplified form, they are as follows:

- The courts will subject any quota system created by state or local governments to "strict scrutiny" and will look for a "compelling" justification for it.

HOW THINGS WORK

The Rights of the Disabled

In 1990, the federal government passed the Americans with Disabilities Act (ADA), a sweeping law that extended many of the protections enjoyed by women and racial minorities to disabled persons.

Who Is a Disabled Person?

Anyone who *has* a physical or mental impairment that substantially limits one or more major life activities (for example, holding a job), anyone who has a *record* of such impairment, or anyone who is *regarded* as having such an impairment is considered disabled.

What Rights Do Disabled Persons Have?

Employment

Disabled persons may not be denied employment or promotion if, with "reasonable accommodation," they can perform the duties of that job. (Excluded from this protection are people who currently use illegal drugs, gamble compulsively, or are homosexual or bisexual.) Reasonable accommodation need not be made if this would cause "undue hardship" on the employer.

Government Programs and Transportation

Disabled persons may not be denied access to government programs or benefits. New buses, taxis, and trains must be accessible to disabled persons, including those in wheelchairs.

(continued)

HOW THINGS WORK (*Continued*)

Public Accommodations

Disabled persons must enjoy "full and equal" access to hotels, restaurants, stores, schools, parks, museums, auditoriums, and the like. To achieve equal access, owners of existing facilities must alter them "to the maximum extent feasible"; builders of new facilities must ensure they are readily accessible to disabled persons, unless this is structurally impossible.

Telephones

The ADA directs the Federal Communications Commission to issue regulations to ensure telecommunications devices for hearing- and speech-impaired people are available "to the extent possible and in the most efficient manner."

Congress

The rights under this law apply to employees of Congress.

Rights Compared

The ADA does not enforce the rights of disabled persons in the same way as the Civil Rights Act enforces the rights of African Americans and women. Racial or gender discrimination must end *regardless of cost*; denial of access to disabled persons must end unless "undue hardship" or excessive costs would result.

- Quotas or preference systems cannot be used by state or local governments without first showing that such rules are needed to correct an actual past or present pattern of discrimination.[59]

- In proving there has been discrimination, it is not enough to show that African Americans (or other minorities) are statistically underrepresented among employees, contractors, or union members; the actual practices that have had this discriminatory impact must be identified.[60]

- Quotas or preference systems created by *federal* law will be given greater deference, in part because Section 5 of the Fourteenth Amendment gives to Congress powers not given to the states to correct the effects of racial discrimination.[61]

- It may be easier to justify in court a voluntary preference system (for example, one agreed to in a labor-management contract) than one that is required by law.[62]

- Even when you can justify special preferences in *hiring* workers, the Supreme Court is not likely to allow racial preferences to govern who gets *laid off*. A worker laid off to make room for a minority worker loses more than a worker not hired in preference to a minority applicant.[63]

Complex as they are, these rulings still generate a great deal of passion. Supporters of the decisions barring certain affirmative action plans hail these decisions as steps back from an emerging pattern of reverse discrimination. In contrast, civil rights organizations have denounced those decisions that have overturned affirmative action programs.

In thinking about these matters, most Americans distinguish between compensatory action and preferential treatment. They define *compensatory action* as "helping disadvantaged people catch up, usually by giving them extra education, training, or services." A majority of the public supports this. They define preferential treatment as "giving minorities preference in hiring, promotions, college admissions, and contracts." Large majorities oppose this.[64] These views reflect an enduring element in American political culture—a strong commitment to individualism ("nobody should get something without deserving it") coupled with support for help for the disadvantaged ("somebody who is suffering through no fault of his or her own deserves a helping hand").

Where does affirmative action fit into this culture? Polls suggest that if affirmative action is defined as "helping," people will support it, but if it is defined as "using quotas," they will oppose it. On this matter, blacks and whites see things differently. Blacks think they should receive preferences in employment to create a more diverse workforce and to make up for past discrimination; whites oppose using goals to create diversity or to remedy past ills. In sum, the controversy over affirmative action depends on what you mean by it and on your racial identity.[65]

A small construction company named Adarand tried to get a contract to build guardrails along a highway in Colorado. Though it was the low bidder, it lost the contract because of a government policy that favors small businesses owned by "socially and economically disadvantaged individuals"—that is, by racial and ethnic minorities. In a five-to-four decision, the Court agreed with Adarand and sent the case back to Colorado for a new trial.

The essence of the Court's decision was that *any* discrimination based on race must be subject to strict scrutiny, even if its purpose is to help, not hurt, a racial minority. Strict scrutiny means two things:

- Any racial preference must serve a "compelling government interest."

- The preference must be "narrowly tailored" to serve that interest.[66]

To serve a compelling governmental interest, it is likely that any racial preference will have to remedy a clear pattern of past discrimination. No such pattern had been shown in Colorado.

This decision prompted a good deal of political debate about affirmative action. In California, an initiative was put on the 1996 ballot to prevent state authorities from using "race, sex, color, ethnicity, or national origin as a criterion for either discriminating against, or granting preferential treatment to, any individual or group" in public employment, public education, or public contracting. When the votes were counted, it passed. Michigan, Nebraska, and Washington have adopted similar measures, and other states may do so.

But the *Adarand* case and the passage of the California initiative did not mean affirmative action was dead. Though the federal Court of Appeals for the Fifth Circuit had rejected the affirmative action program of the University of Texas Law School,[67] the Supreme Court did not take up that case. It waited for several more years to rule on a similar matter arising from the University of Michigan. In 2003, the Supreme Court overturned the admissions policy of the University of Michigan that had given to every African American, Hispanic, and Native American applicant a bonus of 20 points out of the 100 needed to guarantee admission to the University's undergraduate program.[68] This policy was not "narrowly tailored." In rejecting the bonus system, the Court reaffirmed its decision in the *Bakke* case made in 1978 in which it had rejected a university using a "fixed quota" or an exact numerical advantage to the exclusion of "individual" considerations.

But that same day, the Court upheld the policy of the University of Michigan Law School that used race as a "plus factor" but not as a numerical quota.[69] It did so even though using race as a plus factor increased by threefold the proportion of minority applicants who were admitted. In short, admitting more minorities serves a "compelling state interest," and doing so by using race as a plus factor is "narrowly

LANDMARK CASES

Affirmative Action

- *Regents of the University of California v. Bakke* **(1978):** In a confused set of rival opinions, the decisive vote was cast by Justice Powell, who said that a quota-like ban on Bakke's admission was unconstitutional, but that "diversity" was a legitimate goal that could be pursued by taking race into account.

- *United Steelworkers v. Weber* **(1979):** Despite the ban on racial classifications in the 1964 Civil Rights Act, this case upheld the use of race in an employment agreement between the steelworkers union and steel plant.

- *Richmond v. Croson* **(1989):** Affirmative action plans must be judged by the strict scrutiny standard that requires any race-conscious plan to be narrowly tailored to serve a compelling interest.

- *Grutter v. Bollinger* **and** *Gratz v. Bollinger* **(2003):** Numerical benefits cannot be used to admit minorities into college, but race can be a "plus factor" in making those decisions.

- *Parents v. Seattle School District* **(2007):** Race cannot be used to decide which students may attend especially popular high schools because this was not "narrowly tailored" to achieve a "compelling" goal.

tailored" to achieve that goal. But, in 2006, Michigan voters approved a ballot measure banning the use of race as a consideration in academic admissions, public employment, and government contracting. In 2012, a U.S. Circuit Court struck down the ban, but only in relation to academic admissions. In 2013, the U.S. Supreme Court agreed to hear a challenge to the Circuit Court's ruling. And in *Fisher v. University of Texas* (2013), the Court, in a 7-to-1 decision, sent another affirmative action case involving college admissions back to the Fifth Circuit Court of Appeals for reconsideration. Invoking the *Bakke* (1978) and *Grutter* (2003) decisions (see Landmark Cases box), the majority declared that the lower court had failed to apply the strict scrutiny test.

Gay Rights

At first, the Supreme Court was willing to let states decide how many rights homosexuals should have. Georgia, for example, passed a law banning sodomy (that is, any sexual contact involving the sex organs of one person and the mouth or anus of another). In *Bowers v. Hardwick* (1986), the Supreme Court decided, by a five-to-four majority, that there was no reason in the Constitution to prevent a state from having such a law. There was a right to privacy, but it was designed simply to protect "family, marriage, or procreation."[70]

But ten years later, the Court seemed to take a different position. The voters in Colorado had adopted a state constitutional amendment that made it illegal to pass any law to protect persons based on their "homosexual, lesbian, or bisexual orientation." The law did not penalize gays and lesbians; instead it said they could not become the object of specific legal protection of the sort that had traditionally been given to racial or ethnic minorities. (Ordinances to give specific protection to homosexuals had been adopted in some Colorado cities.) The Supreme Court struck down the Colorado constitutional amendment because it violated the equal protection clause of the federal Constitution.[71]

Now we faced a puzzle: a state can pass a law banning homosexual sex, as Georgia did, but a state cannot adopt a rule preventing cities from protecting homosexuals, as Colorado did. The matter was finally put to rest in 2003. In *Lawrence v. Texas*, the Court, again by a five-to-four vote, overturned a Texas law that banned sexual contact between persons of the same sex. The Court repeated the language it had used earlier in cases involving contraception and abortion. If "the right to privacy means anything, it is the right of the individual, married or single, to be free from unwanted governmental intrusion" into sexual matters. The right of privacy means the "right to define one's own concept of existence, of meaning, of the universe, and of the mystery of human life." It specifically overruled *Bowers v. Hardwick*.[72]

In 2003, the same year as the *Lawrence* decision, the Massachusetts Supreme Judicial Court decided, by a four-to-three vote, that gays and lesbians must be allowed to be married in the state.[73] In response, the Massachusetts legislature passed a bill that would amend that state's constitution to ban gay marriage. But that amendment required another ratification vote, which took place in 2007, and the amendment was defeated. In the mid-2000s, while Massachusetts legalized same-sex marriage and officials in other states considered doing the same, 13 states amended their state constitutions to prohibit or further restrict it. State-by-state, a complicated set of political and legal actions and counter-actions had begun. For instance, in California, the mayor of San Francisco began issuing marriage licenses to hundreds of gay couples. In 2004, the California Supreme Court overturned the mayor's decisions. The next year, the state legislature voted to make same-sex marriages legal, but Governor Arnold Schwarzenegger vetoed the bill. In 2008, the state's voters approved a ballot measure, Proposition 8, banning gay marriage. But, in 2010, a federal district judge overturned that vote. After a federal appeals court put the lower federal court's decision on hold, a case concerning Proposition 8 made its way before the U.S. Supreme Court.

In March 2013, the Court heard oral arguments in each of two same-sex marriage cases. In *Hollingsworth v. Perry*, the central issue was the constitutionality of California's Proposition 8: Does the Proposition 8 ban on same-sex marriage violate the Constitution's "equal protection" or other provisions? In *United States v. Windsor*, the central issue was the constitutionality of the Defense of Marriage Act (DOMA), a 1996 federal law that bars the federal government from recognizing same-sex marriage couples in relation to health, tax, and other benefits that it affords to heterosexual married couples: Does the DOMA violate the Constitution by depriving all persons that are legally married under the laws of their respective states the same recognition, benefits, and rights, and is same-sex marriage a fundamental right that all states must respect?

In June 2013, the Court issued opinions that in each case were widely understood as victories for same-sex marriage proponents, but that also in each case left the central constitutional questions for another day. In the Proposition 8 case, the Court, by a 5-to-4 majority, held that the private parties that brought the suit did not have standing to defend the law in federal court after California state officials had declined to do so. The practical effect was to let stand the lower federal court's decision striking down

LANDMARK CASES

Gay Rights

- *Boy Scouts of America v. Dale* (2000): A private organization may ban gays from its membership.

- *Lawrence v. Texas* (2003): State law may not ban sexual relations between same-sex partners.

- *United States v. Windsor* (2013): Gay couples married in states where same-sex marriage is legal must receive the same federal health, tax, and other benefits that heterosexual married couples receive.

Justin Sullivar/Getty Images

Proposition 8 opponents celebrate the ruling to overturn the proposition, which denied same-sex couples the right to marry in the state of California.

Proposition 8 as unconstitutional, and to thereby overturn the ban on same-sex marriage in California without, however, affecting laws in other states that prohibit same-sex marriage. In the more significant DOMA case, the Court, by a 5-to-4 majority, held that the 1996 law was unconstitutional because it deprived gay couples married in states where same-sex marriage is legal of the same federal health, tax, and other benefits that heterosexual married couples receive. But the Court stopped far short of declaring that same-sex marriage is a fundamental right that all states must respect. Still, in the months following the Court's decisions on Proposition 8 and the DOMA, new legal challenges to laws banning same-sex marriage were launched in a half-dozen states.

Thus far, the Court has continued to treat sexual orientation cases involving private groups differently from the way that it has treated such cases involving government agencies or benefits. The Court has maintained that private groups are free to exclude homosexuals from their membership. For example, in 2000, by a five-to-four vote, the Court decided that the Boy Scouts of America could exclude gay men and boys because that group had a right to determine its own membership.[74] In May 2013, following more than a decade of controversy over the decision and the policy, the Boy Scouts of America made public a plan that would have the organization admit openly gay boys, but continue to exclude openly gay men from leadership and membership in the organization.

Looking Back—and Ahead

The civil rights movement in the courts and in Congress profoundly changed the nature of African American participation in politics by bringing Southern blacks into the political system so they could become an effective interest group. The decisive move was to enlist Northern opinion in this cause, a job made easier by the Northern perception that civil rights involved simply an unfair contest between two minorities—Southern whites and Southern blacks. That perception changed when it became evident the court rulings and legislative decisions would apply to the North as well as the South, leading to the emergence of Northern opposition to court-ordered busing and affirmative action programs.

By the time this reaction developed, the legal and political system had been changed sufficiently to make it difficult—if not impossible—to limit the application of civil rights laws to the special circumstances of the South or to alter by legislative means the decisions of federal courts. Though the courts can accomplish little when they have no political allies (as revealed by the massive resistance to early school-desegregation decisions), they can accomplish a great deal, even in the face of adverse public opinion, when they have some organized allies. The feminist movement has paralleled in organization and tactics many aspects of the black civil rights movement, but with important differences. Women sought to repeal or reverse laws and court rulings that in many cases were ostensibly designed to protect rather than subjugate them. The conflict between protection and liberation was sufficiently intense to defeat the effort to ratify the Equal Rights Amendment.

Among the most divisive civil rights issues in American politics are abortion and affirmative action. From 1973 to 1989, the Supreme Court seemed committed to giving constitutional protection to all abortions within the first trimester; since 1989, it has approved various state restrictions on the circumstances under which abortions can be obtained.

There has been a similar shift in the Court's view of affirmative action. Though it will still approve some quota plans, it now insists they pass strict scrutiny to ensure they are used only to correct a proven history of discrimination, they place the burden of proof on the party alleging discrimination, and they

HOW WE COMPARE

Same-Sex Marriages at Home and Abroad

During the first quarter of 2013, France, New Zealand, and Uruguay brought to 14 the number of nations that grant legal recognition to same-sex marriages.

Country (Year Legalized Gay Marriage)

The Netherlands (2000)	Argentina (2010)
Belgium (2003)	Iceland (2010)
Canada (2005)	Portugal (2012)
Spain (2005)	Denmark (2012)
South Africa (2006)	France (2013)
Norway (2009)	New Zealand (2013)
Sweden (2009)	Uruguay (2013)

As of mid-2013, in three other nations, same-sex marriage is legal in some, but not all, parts of the country:

United States (2003)	Mexico (2009)
Brazil (2011)	

Source: Pew Forum on Religion and Public Life, *Gay Marriage around the World*, May 3, 2013.

are limited to hiring and not extended to layoffs. Congress has modified some of these rulings with new civil rights legislation.

Finally, while it remains uncertain whether both court doctrines and legislative initiatives on gay rights will follow patterns like those that expanded civil rights protections for African Americans, other minorities, and women, it is clear that the policy dynamics surrounding same-sex marriage are quite different from what they were only a dozen years ago.

LEARNING OBJECTIVES

LO 5.1 If both African Americans and women benefit from civil rights, why do federal courts allow them to be treated somewhat differently?

The Supreme Court allows blacks and women to be treated somewhat differently because race is a skin color (and thus laws affecting it are subjected to strict scrutiny) while gender is a different body type (and so laws affecting it are subjected to intermediate scrutiny).

LO 5.2 What is the difference between "strict scrutiny" and "intermediate scrutiny"?

Strict scrutiny requires that a law be "narrowly tailored" and use "the least restrictive means" to serve a "compelling government interest." Intermediate scrutiny means that a law must be "substantially related" to serving "an important government interest."

LO 5.3 Legally, what is meant by "sexual harassment"?

Sexual harassment exists when an employer requests sexual favors in order to obtain employment or promotions or when an employee experiences a hostile or intimidating work environment that exists because of sexual teasing, jokes, or obscenity.

LO 5.4 Under what circumstances can men and women be treated differently?

A difference in treatment can be justified constitutionally if the difference is fair, reasonable, and not arbitrary. Sex differences need not meet the "strict scrutiny" test. It is permissible to punish men for statutory rape and to bar them from hospital delivery rooms; men are different from women in these respects. Congress may draft men without drafting women.

LO 5.5 How has Court doctrine and public opinion on gay rights changed over the last decade or so?

As late as 1986, the Supreme Court upheld a state law forbidding certain homosexual acts. But, in 2003, the Court struck down state laws banning consensual sexual relations between same-sex partners. In the 2000s, while some states legalized same-sex marriage and other states outlawed it, public opinion shifted in favor of allowing gays and lesbians to marry, rising from 35 percent, a minority, in favor in 2001 to 47 percent, a plurality, in favor in 2012. And, in 2013, the Court struck down as unconstitutional the federal Defense of Marriage Act, declaring that the federal government must provide gay couples married in states where same-sex marriage is legal with the same health, tax, and other benefits that heterosexual married couples receive.

TO LEARN MORE

- Court cases: **www.law.cornell.edu**
- Department of Justice: **www.usdoj.gov**
- Civil rights organizations: National Association for the Advancement of Colored People: **www.naacp.org**
- National Organization for Women: **www.now.org**
- National Gay and Lesbian Task Force: **www.thetaskforce.org**
- National Council of La Raza: **www.nclr.org**
- National Urban League: **http://nul.iamempowered.com**
- American Arab Anti-Discrimination Committee: **www.adc.org**
- Anti-Defamation League: **www.adl.org**

- Branch, Taylor. *Parting the Waters: America in the King Years*. New York: Simon and Schuster, 1988. A vivid account of the civil rights struggle.
- Flexner, Eleanor. *Century of Struggle: The Women's Rights Movement in the United States*, rev. ed. Cambridge: Harvard University Press, 1975. A historical account of the feminist movement and its political strategies.
- Foreman, Christopher A. *The African-American Predicament*. Washington, D.C.: Brookings Institution, 1999. Thoughtful essays on problems faced by African Americans today.
- Franklin, John Hope. *From Slavery to Freedom*, 5th ed. New York: Knopf, 1980. A survey of black history in the United States.
- Friedan, Betty. *The Feminine Mystique*. New York: Norton, 1963. Tenth anniversary edition, 1974. A well-known call for women to become socially and culturally independent.
- Kluger, Richard. *Simple Justice*. New York: Random House/Vintage Books, 1977. Detailed and absorbing account of the school-desegregation issue, from the Fourteenth Amendment to the *Brown* case.
- Kull, Andrew. *The Color-Blind Constitution*. Cambridge: Harvard University Press, 1992. A history of efforts, none yet successful, to make the Constitution color-blind.
- Mansbridge, Jane J. *Why We Lost the ERA*. Chicago: University of Chicago Press, 1986. Explains why the Equal Rights Amendment did not become part of the Constitution.
- Thernstrom, Stephan, and Abigail Thernstrom. *America in Black and White*. New York: Simon and Schuster, 1997. Detailed history and portrait of African Americans.
- Wilhoit, Francis M. *The Politics of Massive Resistance*. New York: George Braziller, 1973. The methods—and ultimate collapse—of all-out Southern resistance to school desegregation.
- Woodward, C. Vann. *The Strange Career of Jim Crow*. New York: Oxford University Press, 1957. Brief, lucid account of the evolution of Jim Crow practices in the South.

© Sergieiev/Shutterstock.com

Public Opinion and the Media

6

LEARNING OBJECTIVES

LO 6.1   What is "public opinion" and how do we measure it?

LO 6.2   What is "political ideology" and how does it matter for what elites and the mass public believe?

LO 6.3   What role do the media play in American politics?

LO 6.4   How has technology changed interactions between public officials and the media?

LO 6.5   Why are there so few restrictions on media coverage of politics and politicians in the United States?

Defined simply, **public opinion** refers to how people think or feel about particular things. In this chapter, we take a close look at what "public opinion" is, how it is formed, and how opinions differ. The **media** are all public sources of news and information—local newspapers, national magazines, talk radio stations, cable television news networks, Internet blogs, and others—that have the potential to influence public opinion. While much research on "media effects" is inconclusive, there is growing evidence that the "media exercise considerable leverage over public opinion."[1] In this chapter, we explore how public opinion is formed and measured, how opinions differ, and what role the media play in American politics. This much is certain: public opinion dynamics and media influences are not the same today as they were only a generation ago. Television and the Internet are key parts of the New Media; newspapers and magazines are part of the Old Media. And when it comes to politics, the New Media are getting stronger and the Old Media weaker.

THEN

In 1972–1974, the Nixon administration's efforts to cover up the burglary of Democratic National Committee headquarters at the Watergate hotel in Washington, D.C., were revealed through a series of articles published in *The Washington Post*, which gained national fame for its riveting news coverage by journalists Bob Woodward and Carl Bernstein.[2] In the summer of 1987, Congress held live, televised hearings about the Iran-Contra scandal, which viewers watched at home, as well as in stores and other public venues that broadcast the hearings on their televisions.[3]

NOW

In 2004, *60 Minutes*, a CBS television news program, ran a story claiming that President Bush had performed poorly during his time in the Air National Guard. Within a few hours, bloggers produced evidence that the documents underlying this charge were forged, something CBS later conceded was true. Not long afterward, the producer and newscaster responsible for the charges left CBS. In 2008, then-presidential candidate Barack Obama stated at a private fundraiser that voters in economic distress "cling to guns or religion," and a freelance writer for *The Huffington Post* who attended the event decided to publish Obama's remarks, creating an uproar in his campaign.[4] In 2011, reports that the United States had captured and killed Osama bin Laden first appeared on the online site Twitter.

Social media are becoming a regular news source for people: a 2012 study found that almost one-fifth of Americans reported seeing news or headlines on a social networking site, almost twice as many as in 2010. Only 13 percent of adults under 30 read a newspaper, either in print or electronically, and the number of people getting news from television or radio continued to decline, while use of online/mobile news sources increased (though more people still watch television news than view online).[5]

public opinion How people think or feel about particular things.

media Sources of news and information that have the potential to influence public opinion.

But not all of the users are convinced that the Internet is entirely trustworthy. One-third of adults think it lets the loudest and most extreme voices prevail and feel that it is full of misinformation. And though newspapers are rapidly losing their audience, they remain vitally important: much of what is on the Internet comes from newspaper reporters, and politicians devote at least as much time to getting good newspaper coverage as they devote to expanding their Internet coverage. Through both Old Media and New Media, politicians seek to cultivate "good press" for themselves and are eager to know "what the voters are thinking." But it is not easy to know what the public thinks. We are so inundated these days with public opinion polls that we may imagine that they tell us what the public believes. That may be true on a few rather simple, clear-cut, and widely discussed issues, but it is not true with respect to most matters on which the government must act. The best pollsters know the limits of their methods, and citizens should know them as well.

What Is Public Opinion?

For businesses, understanding how people think or feel about particular things—for example, knowing whether consumers are likely to want a new product or be willing to pay more for an old one—can spell the difference between profit and loss. In the early 20th century, corporations and marketing firms pioneered attempts to systematically measure public views, and political scientists were not far behind them.

The first major academic studies of public opinion and voting, published in the 1940s, painted a distressing picture of American democracy. The studies found that, while a small group of citizens knew lots about government and had definite ideas on many issues, the vast majority knew next to nothing about government and had only vague notions even on much-publicized public policy matters that affected them directly.[6] In the ensuing decades, however, other studies painted a somewhat more reassuring picture. These studies suggested that, while most citizens are poorly informed about government and care little about most public policy issues, they are nonetheless pretty good at using limited information (or cues) to figure out what policies, parties, or candidates most nearly reflect

CONSTITUTIONAL CONNECTIONS

Majority Opinion and Public Policy

For the most part, the Framers of the Constitution thought that public opinion should play only a limited and indirect role in making public policy (see Chapters 1 and 2). They favored representative democracy over direct democracy. They doubted that most people would have the time, energy, interest, information, or expertise to deliberate and decide well on policy matters. They worried that majority opinion would often be fickle, factious, and overly influenced by short-term thinking. Thus, in *Federalist* No. 63, did James Madison reflect on the need to defend "the people against their own temporary errors and delusions" and the "tyranny of their own passions." On the other hand, however, the Framers believed that while the opinions held by a temporary or "transient" majority should carry little weight with elected policymakers, the opinions expressed by a persistent majority—for example, a majority that persists over the staggered terms of House and Senate and over more than a single presidential term—should be heard and, in many (though not in all) cases heeded. When it came to civil liberties and civil rights, Madison and the other Framers were not willing to empower even persistent majorities or subject fundamental freedoms to a popular vote. Still, they believed that, on most public policy issues, a truly representative democratic government would and should enact the policies persistently favored by most people.

poll A survey of public opinion.

random sample Method of selecting from a population in which each person has an equal probability of being selected.

sampling error The difference between the results of random samples taken at the same time.

exit polls Polls based on interviews conducted on election day with randomly selected voters.

their values or favor their interests, and then acting (or voting) accordingly.[7]

The more closely scholars have studied public opinion on particular issues, the less uniformed, indifferent, or fickle it has appeared to be. For example, a study by political scientist Terry M. Moe analyzed public opinion concerning whether the government should provide parents with publicly funded grants, or vouchers, that they can apply toward tuition at private schools. He found that although most people are unfamiliar with the voucher issue, "they do a much better job of formulating their opinions than skeptics would lead us to expect." When supplied with basic information, average citizens adopt "their positions for good substantive reasons, just as the informed do.[8]

How Polling Works

If properly conducted, a survey of public opinion—popularly called a **poll**—can capture the opinions of 300 million citizens by interviewing as few as 1,500 of them. There are many keys to good polling: posing comprehensible questions (asking people about things they have some basis for forming an opinion about), wording questions fairly (not using "loaded" or "emotional" words or indicating what the "right" answer is), and others.

However, no poll, whatever it asks and however it is worded, can provide us with a reasonably accurate measure of how people think or feel unless the persons polled are a **random sample** of the entire population, meaning that any given voter or adult has an equal chance of being interviewed. Through a process called stratified or multistage area sampling, the pollster makes a list of all the geographical units in the country—say all the counties—and groups (or "stratifies") them by size of their population. The pollster then selects at random units from each group or stratum in proportion to its total population. Within each selected county, smaller and smaller geographical units (down to particular blocks or streets) are chosen, and then, within the smallest unit, individuals are selected at random (by, for example, choosing the occupant of every fifth house).

If this process is repeated using equally randomized methods, the pollster might get slightly different results. The difference between the results of two surveys or samples is called **sampling error**. For example, if one random sample shows that 70 percent of all Americans approve of the way the president is handling the job, and another random sample taken at the same time shows that 65 percent do, the sampling error is 5 percent.

Even if properly conducted, polls are hardly infallible. Since 1952, most major polls have in fact picked the winner of the presidential election. Likewise, **exit polls**—interviews with randomly selected voters conducted at polling places on election day in a representative sample of voting districts—have proven quite accurate. But as a result of sampling error and for other reasons, it is very hard for pollsters to predict the winner in a close election.

For any population over 500,000, pollsters need to make about 15,000 telephone calls to reach a number of respondents (technically, the number computes to 1,065) sufficient to ensure that the opinions of the sample differ only slightly (by a 3 percent plus or minus margin) from what the results would have been had they interviewed the entire population from which the sample was drawn. That can be very expensive to do. Polling firms can economize by using smaller-than-ideal samples or by under-sampling hard-to-contact people, but then they risk getting things wrong.

How Opinions Differ

Nobody fully understands how public opinion influences everything from who wins an election to what gets politicians' attention to whether given bills become law, but a few things are clear: some people care more about certain issues than other people do (*opinion saliency*); on some issues or choices, opinions are pretty steady, while on others they tend to be more volatile (*opinion stability*); and on some issues government seems to be largely in sync with popular views or majority sentiments, while on other issues it seems to be significantly out of sync (*opinion-policy congruence*). For example, most Americans had an opinion on U.S. involvement in Iraq, but some felt more strongly about it than others did, and opinions changed in response to news of positive or negative developments. In the mid-2000s, for example, many news reports on the situation in Iraq were negative, and mass public support for U.S. involvement fell.[9]

Studies also tell us that people with certain characteristics in common sometimes hold certain political beliefs in common. By no means do people with similar or even virtually identical family histories, religious affiliations, formal educations, or job experiences think or vote exactly the same way on all or most issues. But **political socialization**—the process by which personal and other background traits influence one's views about politics and government—matters. It is behind the fact, to be discussed in the next section, that children tend to share their parents' party affiliations; and it helps to explain why, as we shall see, opinions seem to vary in interesting ways associated with age, gender, religion, race, ethnicity, and other characteristics.

Research also has made clear that mass and elite opinions differ. By "elite" we do not mean people who are "better" than others. Rather, as discussed in Chapter 1, **elite** is a term used by social scientists to refer to people who have a disproportionate amount of some valued resource—money, schooling, prestige, political power, or whatever. Not only do political elites *know more* about politics than the rest of us, they *think differently* about it—they have different views and beliefs. As we explain later in this chapter, they are more likely than average citizens to hold a more or less consistent set of opinions about the policies government ought to pursue. The government attends more to the elite views than to popular views, at least on many matters.

> **political socialization** Process by which background traits influence one's political views.
>
> **elite** People who have a disproportionate amount of some valued resource.

Political Socialization

How do people learn about American politics and government, and develop their political beliefs? The process of political socialization begins in childhood and continues throughout our lives, with many influences, from family to religion to profession and more.

The Family

For a long time, scholars believed people acquired their political views from their families. There is a lot of truth in that

People express their opinions on American politics in many ways, including working at polling stations and voting.

Joshua Lott/Getty Images

HOW WE COMPARE

Opinions on Americans

It is not surprising that most Americans have a favorable view of Americans; but what opinions on Americans are held by people in other countries?

By the same token, a majority of Americans typically express confidence in the U.S. president; but do majorities in other nations share that confidence?

For several years now, the Pew Global Attitudes Project has conducted sophisticated, in-depth opinion polls in dozens of nations. Below are two sets of selected results from its 2009 survey.

Percent with "a favorable view of the American people," 2009	
Top Five	**Bottom Five**
1. United States 90%	1. Turkey 14%
2. Kenya 87%	2. Pakistan 20%
	2. Palestinian Territory 20%
3. South Korea 83%	3. Argentina 38%
4. Nigeria 76%	4. Jordan 39%
5. France 75%	5. Egypt 40%

Percent with "confidence in the U.S. president," 2009	
Top Five & U.S.	**Bottom Five**
1. Kenya 94%	1. Pakistan 13%
2. Germany 93%	2. Palestinian Territory 23%
3. Canada 88%	3. Jordan 31%
4. Nigeria 88%	4. Turkey 33%
5. Britain 86%	5. Russia 37%
11. United States 74%	

Source: Data from Pew Charitable Trusts.

argument. The great majority of high school students know the party affiliation of their parents, and only a tiny minority of children supports a party opposite that of their parents.[10]

But of late we have learned that genetic background also explains some of our political ideology, though rather little of our party affiliation. When we compare how identical twins (who are genetically the same) think about politics with how fraternal twins (who share only half of their genes) think about politics, we discover that identical twins are much more likely to have similar political views than fraternal twins. Some research has found that about one-third of the differences among people with regards to political beliefs comes from genetic makeup, but only one-tenth of these differences comes from family influences.[11]

These results should not surprise us. We know that children in the same family have different personalities even though they have the same parents. Genes play a big role in personality, as they also do in basic political beliefs. If you add together the big effect of genes and the smaller effect of parental influences, then half of our political views come from our family backgrounds. The other half comes from our individual life experiences, such as the friends we acquire, the schools we attend, and what happens to us as adults.

But political beliefs are not necessarily the same as party affiliation. One can be a liberal or conservative Democrat, a liberal or conservative Republican. Studies that have shown that genes affect our political beliefs also suggest that they do not have much of an effect on our party affiliation. Whether we are Democrats, Republicans, or something else depends substantially on what we learn from our parents.

Still, the ability of the family to inculcate a strong sense of party identification has declined in recent years. The proportion of citizens who say they consider themselves Democrats or Republicans has become steadily smaller since the early 1950s. Accompanying this decline in partisanship has been a sharp rise in the proportion of citizens describing themselves as independents.[12]

Part of this change has resulted from the fact that young voters have always had a weaker sense of partisanship than older ones. But the youthfulness of the population cannot explain all the changes, for the decline in partisanship has occurred at all age levels. Those who reached voting age in the 1960s were less apt than those who matured in the 1950s to keep the party identification of their parents.[13] Moreover, as personal policy preferences develop into adulthood, the effects of parental socialization on the partisanship of children decrease gradually over time.[14]

There are also sizable age-related differences in opinions on several issues. For example, in 2010, citizens under age 30 supported gay marriage by a margin of 24 percent more than those aged 65 and older.[15] In some ways, the opinions of younger citizens break old ideological molds. Compared to older Americans, for example, citizens aged 18 to 29 have been more likely to favor gay marriage and women's rights (generally labeled the liberal view), but also more likely to favor giving parents tax money in the form of vouchers for private or religious schools and letting people invest some of their Social Security contribution in the stock market (generally labeled the conservative view).[16] More generally, a majority of today's 18- to 24-year-olds think elected officials have priorities different from their own, but only one out of five thinks politics is not relevant to their lives at present (see Table 6.1).

Where do such views about politics come from? In most families, the dinner table is not a seminar in political philosophy, but a place where people discuss school, jobs, dates, and chores. In some families, however, the dinner table is a political classroom. Studies of the participants in various radical student movements in the 1960s suggested that college radicals often were the sons and daughters of people who had themselves been young radicals; some commentators dubbed them the "red-diaper babies." Presumably, deeply conservative people come disproportionately from families that were also deeply conservative. This transfer of political beliefs from one generation to the next reflects both heredity and family teaching.

Children grow up learning, but not always following, their parents' political beliefs.

TABLE 6.1 Young Adults on Politics and Politicians (2010)

Percent of 18- to 29-year-olds who agree that:	
politics has become too partisan	46%
elected officials don't have the same priorities I have	51%
getting involved in politics is an honorable thing to do	31%
people like me don't have any say about what government does	36%
it is difficult to find ways to be involved in politics	22%
politics is not relevant to my life right now	21%

Source: Institute of Politics, *The 17th Biannual Youth Survey on Politics and Public Service*, John F. Kennedy School of Government, Harvard University, Spring 2010.

Bob Daemmrich/The Image Works

But, again, this transfer of political beliefs leaves plenty of room for inter-generational differences in opinion. Whether and on what issues age-related opinion gaps are wider today than they were in the past is a subject on which more research is needed. But this much is clear: today, adults under age 30 differ markedly from senior citizens (persons age 65 or older) in their opinions on many issues pertaining to social change, religiosity, government, immigration, and civic engagement (see Table 6.2).

One way in which the family forms and transmits political beliefs is by its religious tradition. Religious differences make for political differences, but the differences generally are more complicated than first meet the eye.

Although most Americans remain somewhat or deeply religious, most seriously question religion's role in politics and government.[17] Religious influences on public opinion are pronounced with respect to social issues like abortion or gay marriage, but they matter less on most other issues; and when a war is perceived to be going badly or the economy is in trouble, most Americans of all faiths or of no faith agree that these are the issues that matter most.[18]

TABLE 6.2   Opinion Gaps Between Young Adults and Senior Citizens in 2012

	Age 18 to 29 %	Age 65 and Older %	Gap
Social Change			
Favor allowing gay and lesbian couples to marry	65	31	+34
Believe one parent can bring up a child as well as two parents together	65	36	+29
It's all right for blacks and whites to date each other	95	68	+27
Religiosity			
Prayer is an important part of my daily life	61	85	−24
I never doubt the existence of God	67	87	−20
Government			
The Constitution should be interpreted in terms of what it means in modern times*	62	35	+27
A free market economy needs government regulation in order to best serve the public interest	74	57	+17
When something is run by the government it is usually inefficient and wasteful	47	69	−22
Immigrants			
Newcomers from other countries threaten traditional American customs and values	43	58	−15
It bothers me when I come in contact with immigrants who speak little or no English	30	44	−14
Civic Engagement			
I'm Interested in keeping up with national affairs (completely agree)	46	63	−17
I feel it's my duty as a citizen to always vote	84	98	−14

Source: Pew Research Center, "Partisan Polarization Surges in Bush, Obama Years: Trends in American Values, 1987–2012," June 2012, with one point (*) from Pew Research Center, "Ideological Chasm Over Interpreting Constitution," June 2011.

Opinions about politics and government vary not only across, but also within given religious traditions. White Evangelicals and black Protestants hold similar views on environmental regulation, same-sex marriage, and faith-based initiatives, but differ over more

gender gap Difference in political views between men and women.

aid to the poor. People of whatever religion who attend worship services regularly are considerably less likely to vote Democratic than otherwise comparable persons who attend worship services rarely or never.

The Gender Gap

Journalists often point out that women have "deserted" Republican candidates to favor Democratic ones. In some cases, this is true. But it would be equally correct to say that men have "deserted" Democratic candidates for Republican ones. The **gender gap** is the difference in political views between men and women. That gap has existed for a long time, and it is a problem for both political parties.

Women obtained the right to vote in 1920 when the Nineteenth Amendment to the Constitution was ratified. Until 1980, women voted at significantly lower rates than men. Since 1980, however, women have voted at somewhat higher rates than men, a difference amplified by the fact that women are also a larger proportion of the voting-age population. In every presidential election from 1980 through 2012, women were more likely than men to favor the Democratic candidate. In the 2012 presidential election, women favored the Democrat by 12 points and men favored the Republican by 8 points, yielding a 20-point gender gap. Behind the gender gap in partisan self-identification and voting are differences between men and women over prominent political issues and which issues matter most. For example, as results from multiple national surveys have suggested, women are more likely than men to favor activist government, universal health care, environmental protection regulations, anti-poverty programs, and laws supporting same-sex marriage; less likely than men to favor cutting taxes at the expense of social services or to support military interventions; and more likely than men to consider social welfare issues important.

Social Class

Americans speak of "social class" with embarrassment. The norm of equality tugs at our consciences, urging us to judge people as individuals, not as parts of some social group (such as "the lower class"). Social scientists speak of "class" with confusion. They know it exists, but quarrel constantly about how to define it: by income? occupation? wealth? schooling? prestige? personality?

Let's face up to the embarrassment and skip over the confusion. Truck drivers and investment bankers look differently, talk differently, and vote differently. There is nothing wrong with saying that the first group consists of "working-class" (or "blue-collar") people and the latter of "upper-class" (or "management") people. Moreover, though different definitions of class produce slightly different groupings of people, most definitions overlap to such an extent that it does not matter too much which we use.

However defined, public opinion and voting have been less determined by class in the United States than in Europe, and the extent of class cleavage has declined in the last few decades in both the United States and Europe. In the 1950s, V. O. Key, Jr., found that differences in political opinion were closely associated with occupation. He noted that people holding managerial or professional jobs had distinctly more conservative views on social welfare policy and more internationalist views on foreign policy than manual workers.[19] During the next decade, this pattern changed greatly. Opinion surveys done in the late 1960s showed that business and professional people had views quite similar to those of manual workers on matters such as the poverty program, health insurance, American policy in Vietnam, and government efforts to create jobs.[20]

The voting patterns of different social classes also have become somewhat more similar. The differences in whether or not people vote, depending on their social class, have declined sharply since the late 1940s in the United States, France, Great Britain, and Germany, and have declined moderately in Sweden.

Class differences remain, of course. Unskilled workers are more likely than affluent white-collar workers to be Democrats and to have liberal views on economic policy. And when economic issues pinch—for example, when farmers are hurting or steelworkers are being laid off—the importance of economic interests in differentiating the opinions of various groups rises sharply.

Still, many of the issues that now lead us to choose which party to support and that determine whether we think of ourselves as liberals or conservatives are noneconomic issues. In recent years, our political posture has been shaped by the positions we take on race relations, abortion, school prayer, environmentalism, and terrorism, issues that do not clearly affect the rich differently than the poor (or at least do not affect them as differently as do the union movement, the minimum wage, and unemployment). Moral, symbolic, and foreign policy matters do not divide rich and poor in the same way as economic ones. Thus, we have many well-off people who think of themselves as liberals because they take liberal positions on these noneconomic matters, and many not-so-well-off people who think of themselves as conservatives because that is the position they take on these issues.

Race and Ethnicity

African Americans are overwhelmingly Democratic, though younger ones are a bit more likely than older ones to identify with the Republican party.[21] Younger blacks are also much more likely to support the idea of using school vouchers to pay for education than older ones.

There are sharp differences between white and black attitudes on many public policy questions. For example, blacks are much more likely than whites to support affirmative action, to think that the criminal justice system is biased against blacks, to oppose the use of military force, to doubt that we all should be willing to fight for our country, and to think that believing in God is essential for a person to be moral.[22]

But there are also many areas of agreement. Both blacks and whites want our courts to be tougher in handling criminals, oppose the idea of making abortion legal in all cases, agree that people have become too dependent on government aid, and think that everyone has it in his or her own power to succeed.[23]

Latinos are the largest minority group in America, numbering more than 50 million people. Until recently, studies of Latino public opinion were "small, disproportionately oriented toward immigration, and relatively silent on the influence of gender" and other possible intragroup opinion cleavages.[24] An early survey of ethnic groups in California, a state where fully one-third of all recent immigrants to this country live, provided a hint—but only a hint—of how Latinos felt about political parties and issues, and how Latino opinion compared to that of other groups.[25]

Today, however, there is a growing body of survey and other data on Latino opinion, political behavior, and civic engagement. Among the many interesting findings that are emerging from this literature is how the gender gap in presidential voting is narrower among Latino voters than it is in the electorate as a whole; for example, in the 2012 presidential election, 77 percent of Latino women, as well as 73 percent of Latino men, voted for the Democrat. Table 6.3 offers a detailed snapshot of Latino opinion in the months prior to the 2012 presidential election.

Latinos are a diverse mix of Cuban Americans, Mexican Americans, Central Americans, and Puerto Ricans, each with distinct political views. Most studies of Latino voting show that people from Mexico vote heavily Democratic, those from Cuba mostly Republican, and those from Puerto Rico somewhere in between.[26] Local conditions also affect these views. Hispanics in Texas often vote for more conservative candidates than do those in California. Likewise, following the U.S. invasion of Iraq, most Latinos believed U.S. troops should have been withdrawn, but there were important differences between the views of native-born and foreign-born Latinos.[27] Latinos have less money and are younger than non-Hispanic white Americans. In America, about four-fifths of all Latinos, but only half of all non-Hispanic whites, are younger than 45. It is possible that these

Joe Raedle/Getty Images News/Getty Images

Marco Rubio, the Hispanic son of exiles from Cuba, is a Republican elected by Florida to the United States Senate in 2010.

TABLE 6.3   Latino Opinion, 2012

Most Important Issues Facing the Latino Community	
Immigration reform	58%
Create jobs/fix the economy	38
Education reform/schools	19
Health care	15
Immigration Policy	
Strongly/somewhat approve President Obama's handling of immigration policy	70%
Strongly/somewhat approve Democrats in Congress handling of immigration policy	61
Strongly/somewhat approve Republicans in Congress handling of immigration policy	25
Partisan Identification	
Think of myself as a "Strong Democrat"	32%
Think of myself as a "Strong Republican"	7
Think of myself as "Independent"	6
Voting History	
Ever voted for a Democrat for any federal, state, or local elective office	89
Ever voted for a Republican for any federal, state, or local elective office	52
Congress in 2014	
Will vote Democrat for Congress in 2014	56
Will vote Republican for Congress in 2014	14
Undecided/Don't Know how will vote for Congress in 2014	20

Source: Adapted from Latino Decisions, Immigration Poll, March 5, 2012; also see Latino Decisions, "The Untapped Potential of the Latino Electorate," January 15, 2013.

differences affect their views.[28] Despite these differences, there are broad areas of agreement between Latinos and non-Hispanic whites. For instance, almost exactly the same percentage of both groups favor allowing people to invest some of their Social Security taxes into stock-market funds.[29]

Political Ideology

Up to now the words *liberal* and *conservative* have been used as though everyone agrees on what they mean and as if they accurately describe general sets of political beliefs held by large segments of the population. Neither of these assumptions is correct. Like many useful words—*love, justice, happiness*—they are as vague as they are indispensable.

When we refer to people as liberals, conservatives, socialists, or radicals, we are implying that they have a patterned set of beliefs about how government and other important institutions in fact operate and how they ought to operate, and in particular about what kinds of policies government ought to pursue. These groups are said to display to some degree a **political ideology**—that is, a more or less consistent set of beliefs about what policies government ought to pursue.

Political scientists measure the extent to which people have a political ideology in two ways. The first is by seeing how frequently people use broad political categories (such as "liberal," "conservative," "radical") to describe their own views or to justify their preferences for various candidates and policies, or, by seeing to what extent the policy preferences of a citizen are consistent over time or are based at any one time on consistent principles. This second method involves a simple mathematical procedure: measuring how accurately one can predict a person's view on a subject at one time based on his or her view on that subject at an earlier time, or measuring how accurately one can predict a person's view on one issue based on his or her view on a different issue. The higher the accuracy of such predictions (or correlations), the more we say a person's political opinions display "constraint" or ideology.

Despite annual fluctuations, ideological self-identification surveys show that over the last two decades, "conservative" and "moderate" have each been chosen by about 37 to 40 percent, while "liberal" has been chosen by about 20 percent.[30] For instance, from 2008 to 2011, 20 to 21 percent chose "liberal," 35 to 36 percent chose "moderate," and 38 to 39 percent chose "conservative." For three reasons, however, these self-identification survey averages do not really tell us much at all about how or whether most people think about politics in an ideological manner. First, except when asked by pollsters, most Americans do not actually employ the words *liberal, conservative,* or *moderate* in explaining or justifying their preferences for parties, candidates, or policies, and not many more than half can give plausible definitions of these terms. The vast majority of Americans simply do not think about politics in an ideological or very coherent manner.

Second, over the last decade, survey research scholars have rediscovered old truths about the limitations of polling as a window into "the public mind."[31] Public opinion polls must of necessity ask rather simple questions. The apparent "inconsistency" in the answers people give at different times may mean only that the nature of the problem and the wording of the question have changed. Or it could simply mean that many people consistently want from politics or government things that, as a practical matter, they cannot have, or at least cannot have all at once or at a price they are willing to pay—for instance, a bigger military, more expansive public health insurance coverage for all, and greater funding for public schools, but no military draft, no new or increased taxes, and no government budget deficits. Ideological liberals might consistently covet everything on that list except the bigger military,

political ideology A more or less consistent set of beliefs about what policies government ought to pursue.

and they might be willing to pay higher taxes to get it. Ideological conservatives might want only the bigger military, but only if getting it requires no tax increases. But most citizens are more inclined to pick and choose their positions without regard to conventional liberal or conservative views, and without feeling any need to be "consistent."

Third, when surveyed in person (including by telephone), some people will hide what they think are socially or morally unacceptable self-identifications or positions behind a "don't know" or "middle-ground" response.[32] This can happen not only when the questions concern specific labels like "liberal" or "conservative," or particular issues like racial integration or immigration restrictions, but also when the questions seem to ask about fundamental values, patriotism, or "Americanism."

> ***political elites*** Persons with a disproportionate share of political power.

Liberal and Conservative Elites

Although the terms *liberal* and *conservative* do not adequately describe the political views held by most average Americans, they do capture the views held by many, perhaps most, people who are in the country's political elite. As we discussed in Chapter 1, every society has an elite, because in every society government officials have more power than ordinary folk, some persons make more money than others, and some people are more popular than others. The former Soviet Union even had an official name for the political elite—the *nomenklatura.*

In America, we often refer to **political elites** more casually as "activists"—people who hold office, run for office, work in campaigns or on newspapers, lead interest groups and social movements, and speak out on public issues. Being an activist is not an all-or-nothing proposition: people display differing degrees of activism, from full-time politicians to persons who occasionally get involved in a campaign (see Chapter 8). But the more a person is an activist, the more likely it is that he or she will display ideological consistency on the conventional liberal-conservative spectrum.

The reasons for this greater consistency seem to be information and peers. First, we consider information. In general, the better informed people are about politics and the more interest they take in politics, the more likely they are to have consistently liberal or conservative views.[33] This higher level of information and interest may lead them to find relationships among issues that others don't see and to learn from the media and elsewhere what are the "right" things to believe. This does not mean there are no differences among liberal elites (or among conservative ones), only that the differences occur within a liberal (or conservative) consensus that is more well-defined, more consistent, and more important to those who share it than would be the case among ordinary citizens.

Second is the matter of peers. Politics does not make strange bedfellows. On the contrary, politics is a process of likes attracting likes. The more active you are in politics, the more you will associate with people who agree with you on some issues; the more time you spend with those people, the more your other views will shift to match theirs.

The greater ideological consistency of political elites can be seen in Congress. As we shall note in Chapter 9, Democratic members of Congress tend to be consistently liberal, and Republican members of Congress tend to be consistently conservative—*far more* consistently than Democratic voters and Republican voters. By the same token, we shall see in Chapter 7 that the delegates to presidential nominating conventions are far more ideological (liberal in the Democratic convention, conservative in the Republican one) than is true of voters who identify with the Democratic or Republican parties.

Still, on a large number of issues, the policy preferences of average Republican and Democratic voters do differ significantly from one another. Some political scientists argue that Republican and Democratic leaders in Congress are more polarized because voters are more polarized. Other political scientists, however, analyze the available polling and election data differently. They find that ideological changes among voters have been small, while public opinion among Democrats voting in districts represented by Democrats and among Republicans voting in districts represented by Republicans has been remarkably stable. Which side is right? We have no data that allow us to compare in each district what voters think and how their representatives behave. To amass such data would require polls of perhaps 500 voters in each congressional district taken several years apart. Nobody thinks it is worth spending millions of dollars to interview more than 10,000 voters at different times just to answer this one academic puzzle.

The Media and Politics

One way that politicians and other elites attempt to influence public opinion is through the media. The Internet is an important new venue for politics, but it presents similar challenges for politicians as earlier technological advances in communication. From the beginning of the Republic, public officials have tried to get the media on their side while knowing that, because the media love controversy, they are as likely to attack as to praise. The Internet may strike some politicians as the solution to this problem: they think that if they put their own web pages out there, they can reach the voters directly. They can, but so can rival politicians with their own web pages and with their allies attacking their competitors.

All of this takes place in a country so committed to a free press that there is little the government can do to control the process. As we shall see, there have been efforts to control radio and television as a result of the government's right to license broadcasters, but most of these attempts have evaporated.

Even strongly democratic nations restrict the press more than the United States. For example, the laws governing libel are much stricter in the United Kingdom than in the United States. As a result, it is easier in the United Kingdom for politicians to sue newspapers for publishing articles that defame or ridicule them. In this country, the libel laws make it almost impossible to prevent press criticisms of public figures. Moreover, England has an Official Secrets Act that can be used to punish any past or present public officials who leak information to the press.[34] In this country, leaking information occurs all the time, and our Freedom of Information Act makes it relatively easy for the press to extract documents from the government.

European governments can be much tougher on people who make controversial statements than the American political system. In 2006, an Austrian court sentenced a man to three years in prison for having denied that the Nazi death camp at Auschwitz killed its inmates. A French court convicted a distinguished American historian for telling a French newspaper that the slaughter of Armenians may not have been the result of planned effort. An Italian journalist stood trial for having written things "offensive to Islam." In this country, such statements would be protected by the Constitution, even if— as with the man who denied the existence of the Holocaust—they were profoundly wrong.[35]

America has a long tradition of privately owned media. By contrast, private ownership of television has come only recently to France. And the Internet is not owned by anybody: here, and in many nations, people can say or read whatever they want on their computers. Newspapers in this country require no government permission to operate, but radio and television stations need licenses granted by the Federal Communications Commission (FCC). These licenses must be renewed periodically. On occasion, the White House has made efforts to use license renewals as a way of influencing station owners who were out of political favor, but of late the level of FCC control over what is broadcast has lessened.

One potential limit to the freedom of privately owned newspapers and broadcast stations is their need make a profit. Some critics believe the need for profit will lead media outlets to distort the news in order to satisfy advertisers or to build an audience. Though there is some truth to this argument, it is too simple. Every media outlet must satisfy a variety of people—advertisers, subscribers, listeners, reporters, and editors—and balancing those demands is complicated and will be done differently by different owners.

Blogs, both conservative and liberal, have become an important form of political communication.

Journalism in American Political History

Important changes in the nature of American politics have gone hand in hand with major changes in the organization and technology of the press. It is the nature of politics, essentially a form of communication, to respond to changes in how communications are carried on. This can be seen by considering five important periods in journalistic history.

The Party Press

In the early years of the Republic, politicians of various factions and parties created, sponsored, and controlled newspapers to further their interests. This was possible because circulation was of necessity small (newspapers could not easily be distributed to large audiences, owing to poor transportation) and newspapers were expensive (the type was set by hand and the presses printed copies slowly). Furthermore, there were few large advertisers to pay the bills. These newspapers circulated chiefly among the political and commercial elites who could afford the high subscription prices. Even with high prices, the newspapers often required subsidies that frequently came from the government or a political party.

During the Washington administration, the Federalists, led by Alexander Hamilton, created the *Gazette of the United States.* The Republicans, led by Thomas Jefferson, retaliated by creating the *National Gazette* and made its editor, Philip Freneau, "clerk for foreign languages" in the State Department at $250 a year to help support him. After Jefferson became president, he induced another publisher, Samuel Harrison Smith, to start the *National Intelligencer,* subsidizing him by giving him a contract to print government documents. Andrew Jackson, when he became president, aided in the creation of *The Washington Globe.* By some estimates, there were more than 50 journalists on the government payroll during this era. Naturally, these newspapers were relentlessly partisan in their views. Citizens could choose among different party papers, but only rarely could they find a paper that presented both sides of an issue.

The Popular Press

Changes in society and technology made possible the rise of a self-supporting, mass-readership daily newspaper. The development of the high-speed rotary press enabled publishers to print thousands of copies of a newspaper cheaply and quickly. The invention of the telegraph in the 1840s meant that news from Washington could be flashed almost immediately to New York, Boston, Philadelphia, and Charleston, thus providing local papers with access to information that once only the Washington papers enjoyed. The creation in 1848 of the Associated Press allowed telegraphic dissemination of information to newspaper editors on a systematic basis. Since the AP provided stories that had to be brief and that went to newspapers of every political hue, it could not afford to be partisan or biased; to attract as many subscribers as possible, it had to present the facts objectively.

Meanwhile, the nation was becoming more urbanized, with large numbers of people brought together in densely settled areas. These people could support a daily newspaper by paying only a penny per copy and by patronizing merchants who advertised in its pages. Newspapers no longer needed political patronage to prosper, and soon such subsidies began to dry up. In 1860, the Government Printing Office was established, thereby putting an end to most of the printing contracts that Washington newspapers had once enjoyed.

The mass-readership newspaper was scarcely nonpartisan, but the partisanship it displayed arose from the convictions of its publishers and editors rather than from the influence of its party sponsors. And these convictions blended political beliefs with economic interest. The way to attract a large readership was with sensationalism: violence, romance, and patriotism, coupled with exposés of government, politics, business, and society. As practiced by Joseph Pulitzer and William Randolph Hearst, founders of large newspaper empires, this editorial policy had great appeal for the average citizen and especially for the immigrants flooding into the large cities.

Strong-willed publishers could often become powerful political forces. Hearst used his papers to agitate for war with Spain when the Cubans rebelled against Spanish rule. Conservative Republican political leaders were opposed to the war, but a steady diet of newspaper stories about real and imagined

Spanish brutalities whipped up public opinion in favor of intervention. At one point, Hearst sent the noted artist Frederic Remington to Cuba to supply paintings of the conflict. Remington cabled back: "Everything is quiet.... There will be no war." Hearst supposedly replied: "Please remain. You furnish the pictures and I'll furnish the war."[36] When the battleship USS *Maine* blew up in Havana harbor, President William McKinley felt helpless to resist popular pressure, and war was declared in 1898.

For all their excesses, the mass-readership newspapers began to create a common national culture, to establish the feasibility of a press free of government control or subsidy, and to demonstrate how exciting (and profitable) the criticism of public policy and the revelation of public scandal could be.

Magazines of Opinion

The growing middle class often was repelled by what it called "yellow journalism," and was developing, around the turn of the century, a taste for political reform and a belief in the doctrines of the progressive movement. To satisfy this market, a variety of national magazines appeared that—unlike those devoted to manners and literature—discussed issues of public policy. Among the first of these were the *Nation*, the *Atlantic Monthly*, and *Harper's*, founded in the 1850s and 1860s; later came the more broadly based mass-circulation magazines such as *McClure's*, *Scribner's*, and *Cosmopolitan*. They provided the means for developing a national constituency for certain issues such as regulating business (or in the language of the times, "trust-busting"), purifying municipal politics, and reforming the civil service system. Lincoln Steffens and other so-called muckrakers were frequent contributors to the magazines, setting a pattern for what we now call "investigative reporting."

The national magazines of opinion provided an opportunity for individual writers to gain a nationwide following. The popular press, though initially under the heavy influence of founder-publishers, made the names of certain reporters and columnists household words. In time, the great circulation wars between the big-city daily newspapers started to wane, as the more successful papers bought up or otherwise eliminated their competition. This reduced the need for the more extreme forms of sensationalism, a change reinforced by the growing sophistication and education of America's readers. And the founding publishers gradually were replaced by less flamboyant managers. All of these changes—in circulation needs, audience interests, managerial style, and the emergence of nationally known writers—helped increase the power of editors and reporters and make them a force to be reckoned with.

Although politics dominated the pages of most national magazines in the late 19th century, today national magazines that focus mainly on politics and government affairs account for only a small and declining portion of the national magazine market. Among all magazines in circulation today, only a fraction focus on politics—the majority of today's magazines focus on popular entertainment and leisure activities

Electronic Journalism

Radio came on the national scene in the 1920s, television in the late 1940s. They represented a major change in the way news was gathered and disseminated, though few politicians at first understood the importance of this change. A broadcast permits public officials to speak directly to audiences without their remarks being filtered through editors and reporters. This was obviously an advantage to politicians, provided they were skilled enough to use it: they could in theory reach the voters directly on a national scale without the services of political parties, interest groups, or friendly editors.

But there was an offsetting disadvantage—people could easily ignore a speech broadcast on a radio or television station, either by not listening at all or by tuning to a different station. By contrast, the views of at least some public figures would receive prominent and often unavoidable display in newspapers, and

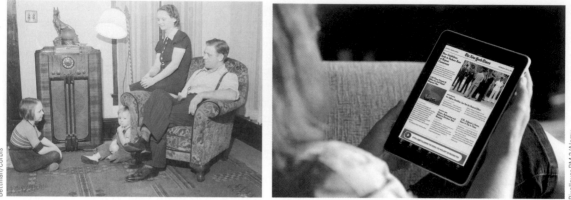

News used to come by radio, but today many people read news on iPads and other electronic devices.

in a growing number of cities there was only one daily paper. Moreover, space in a newspaper is cheap compared to time on a television broadcast.

Adding one more story, or one more name to an existing story, costs the newspaper little. By contrast, less news can be carried on radio or television, and each news segment must be quite brief to avoid boring the audience. As a result, the number of political personalities that can be covered by radio and television news is much smaller than is the case with newspapers, and the cost (to the station) of making a news item or broadcast longer often is prohibitively large.

Thus, to obtain the advantages of electronic media coverage, public officials must do something sufficiently bold or colorful to gain free access to radio and television news—or they must find the money to purchase radio and television time. The president of the United States, of course, is routinely covered by radio and television and can ordinarily get free time to speak to the nation on matters of importance. All other officials must struggle for media attention by making controversial statements, acquiring a national reputation, or purchasing expensive time.

The rise of the talk show as a political forum has increased politicians' access to the electronic media, as has the televised "town meeting." But such developments need to be understood as part of a larger story.

Until the 1990s, the "big three" television networks (ABC, CBS, and NBC) together claimed 80 percent or more of all viewers. Their evening newscasts dominated electronic media coverage of politics and government affairs. When it came to presidential campaigns, for example, the three networks were the only television games in town—they reported on the primaries, broadcast the party conventions, and covered the general election campaigns, including any presidential debates. But over the last few decades, the networks' evening newscasts have changed in ways that have made it harder for candidates to use them to get their messages across. For instance, the average **sound bite**—a video clip of a presidential contender speaking—dropped from about 42 seconds in 1968 to 7.3 seconds in 2000.[37] Furthermore, as Figure 6.1 shows, the audience for the evening news has been in decline since the 1980s.

Today, politicians have sources other than the network news for sustained and personalized television exposure. Cable television, early-morning news and entertainment programs, and prime-time "newsmagazine" shows have greatly increased and diversified politicians' access to the electronic media.

sound bite A radio or video clip of someone speaking.

Naturally, many politicians favor the call-in format, town-meeting setups, lengthy human interest interviews, and casual appearances on

FIGURE 6.1   Evening News Audience Continues a 30-Year Decline

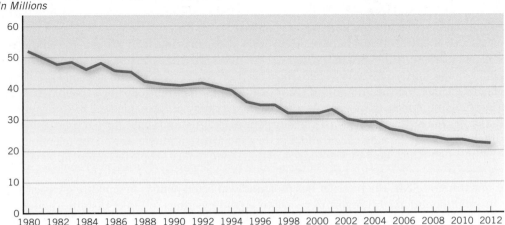

November-to-November Average Viewers per Night In Millions

Source: Nielsen Media Research, used under license. Pew Research Center's Project for Excellence in Journalism, 2013 State of the News Media.

entertainment shows to televised confrontations on policy issues with seasoned network journalists who push, probe, and criticize. And naturally, they favor being a part of visually interesting programs rather than traditional "talking heads" news shows. But what is preferable to candidates is not necessarily helpful to the selection process that voters must go through in choosing a candidate.

One thing is clear: most politicians crave the media spotlight, both on the campaign trail and in office. The efforts made by political candidates to get "visuals"—filmed stories—on television continue after they are elected. Since the president is always news, a politician wishing to make news is well advised to attack the president.

The Internet

More than half of all Americans used the Internet to get political news about the 2010 midterm elections.[38] The political news found there ranges from summaries of stories from newspapers and magazines to political rumors and hot gossip. For example, viewers may scan political ideas posted on a **blog**; many blogs specialize in offering liberal, conservative, or libertarian perspectives. The Internet is the ultimate free market in political news: no one can ban, control, or regulate it, and no one can keep facts, opinions, or nonsense off of it.

The Internet is beginning to play a big role in politics. When Howard Dean ran for the Democratic presidential nomination in 2004, he raised most of his money from Internet appeals. When John Kerry, who won the nomination, was campaigning, the Internet and the blogs on it were a major source of discussion of the criticisms made of him by former Vietnam War veterans. Now every candidate for important offices has a website.

The rise of the Internet has completed a remarkable transformation in American journalism. In the days of the party press, only a few people read newspapers. When mass-circulation newspapers arose, mass politics also arose. When magazines of opinion developed, interest groups also developed. When radio and television became

blog A series, or log, of discussion items on a page of the World Wide Web.

dominant, politicians could build their own bridges to voters without party or interest group influence. And now, with the Internet, voters and political activists can talk to each other. This is true in many dictatorships. When popular revolutions broke out against the autocratic leaders of Egypt and Libya, the activists used the Internet (namely, Twitter) to inform their colleagues. It is becoming much harder for a powerful leader to control what other people can learn.

Most users think the Internet is a wonderful innovation, but some worry that using email, YouTube, Facebook, text messaging, blogs, and Twitter to communicate will isolate people from one another and make public opinion more extreme. There have been several studies of this possibility, but they have not produced a clear answer. A Stanford study argued that the Internet isolates people from ordinary human contact and makes them become anonymous. A study at Carnegie Mellon University came to much the same conclusion. By contrast, a study done at UCLA found that Internet users are more likely to consult newspapers and magazines, and that they spend just as much time on the telephone as people not on the Internet. And a Pew survey suggested that email makes people feel more, not less, connected to others.[39]

But one thing is clear: the Internet has profoundly affected politics by making it easier to (1) raise money in small donations, (2) organize people to attend meetings, (3) take instant (though probably unreliable) opinion polls, (4) disseminate instant criticism of your opponent, (5) mobilize local followers, and (6) provide campaigners with the names of people they should contact.

The Structure of the Media

The relationship between journalism and politics is a two-way street: though politicians take advantage as best they can of the communications media available to them, these media in turn attempt to use politics and politicians as a way of both entertaining and informing their audiences. The mass media, whatever their disclaimers, are not simply a mirror held up to reality or a messenger that carries the news. There is inevitably a process of selection, of editing, and of emphasis, and this process reflects, to some degree, the way in which the media are organized, the kinds of audiences they seek to serve, and the preferences and opinions of the members of the media.

Degree of Competition

There has been a large decline in the number of daily newspapers that serve large communities. There were competing papers in 60 percent of American cities in 1900, but in only 4 percent in 1972. Several large cities—Boston, Chicago, Detroit, Los Angeles, New York, Philadelphia, and Washington, D.C.—have more than one paper, but in some of these cities the same business owns both papers. And newspaper circulation has fallen in recent years, with more and more people getting their news from radio and television. Young people especially have turned away from political news. In the 1940s and 1950s, age did not make much difference; people under the age of 30 read about the same amount of news as people over the age of 50. But by the 1970s, that had changed dramatically: young people read less political news than older people, a trend that continues today. In Figure 6.2, we can see that today only half as many people between the ages of 18 and 34 read newspapers as did in 2000.

To a degree that would astonish most foreigners, the American press—radio, television, and newspapers—is made up of locally owned and managed enterprises. In the United Kingdom, France, Germany, Japan, Sweden, and elsewhere, the media are owned and operated with a national audience in mind. *The Times* of London may be published in that city, but it is read throughout the United Kingdom, as are *The Guardian, The Daily Telegraph,* and the *Daily Mirror.* Radio and television broadcasts are centrally planned and nationally aired.

FIGURE 6.2   Newspaper Readership Falls for Most Age Groups

Percentage Nationally Who Read Any Daily Newspaper Yesterday

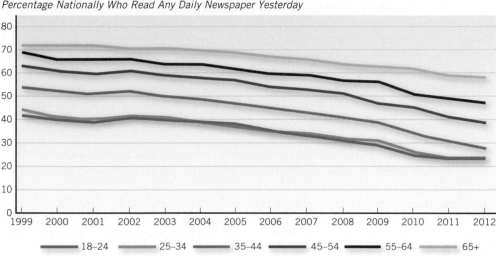

Source: Data adapted from Pew Research Center's Project for Excellence in Journalism, 2013 State of the News Media.

The American newspaper, however, is primarily oriented to its local market and local audience, and there is typically more local than national news in it. Radio and television stations accept network programming, but the early- and late-evening news programs provide a heavy diet of local political, social, and sports news. Government regulations developed by the Federal Communications Commission (FCC) are in part responsible for this. Until the mid-1990s, no one could own and operate more than one newspaper, one AM radio station, one FM radio station, or one television station in a given market. The networks still today may not compel a local affiliate to accept any particular broadcast. (In fact, almost all network news programs are carried by the affiliates.) The result has been the development of a decentralized broadcast industry.

The National Media

The local orientation of much of the American communications media is partially offset, however, by the emergence of certain publications and broadcast services that constitute a kind of national press. The wire services—the Associated Press and United Press International—supply most of the national news that local papers publish. Certain newsmagazines, such as *Time* and *Newsweek*, have a national readership. The network evening news broadcasts produced by ABC, CBS, and NBC are carried by most television stations with a network affiliation. Both CNN (Cable News Network) and Fox News broadcast news around the clock and have large audiences, as does MSNBC. Though most newspapers have only local audiences, several have acquired national influence. *The New York Times* and *The Wall Street Journal* are printed in several locations and can be delivered to many homes early in the morning. *USA Today* was created as a national newspaper and is distributed everywhere, aimed especially at people who travel a lot.

These newspapers have national standing for several reasons. First, they distribute a lot of copies: more than 1 million each day for the *Times* and the *Journal*, and more than 2 million a day for *USA Today.* Second, these papers, as well as *The Washington Post*, are carefully followed by political elites. Unlike most people, the elites even read the editorials. By contrast, local newspapers and radio stations may be invisible to Washington politicians. Third, radio and television stations often decide what to broadcast by looking at the front pages of the *Times* and the *Post*. The front page of the *Times* is a model for each network's evening news broadcast.[40] Finally, the editors and reporters for the national press tend to be better educated and more generously paid than their counterparts in local outlets. And as we shall see, the writers for the national press tend to have distinctly liberal political views. Above all they seek—and frequently obtain—the opportunity to write stories that are not accounts of a particular news event but "background," investigative, or interpretive stories about issues and policies.

Rules Governing the Media

Ironically, the least competitive media outlets—the big-city newspapers—are almost entirely free from government regulation, while the most competitive ones—radio and television stations—must have a government license to operate and must adhere to a variety of government regulations.

Newspapers and magazines need no license to publish, their freedom to publish may not be restrained in advance, and they are liable for punishment for what they do publish only under certain highly restricted circumstances. The First Amendment has been interpreted as meaning that no government, federal or state, can place "prior restraints" (that is, censorship) on the press except under very narrowly defined circumstances.[41] When the federal government sought to prevent *The New York Times* from publishing the Pentagon Papers—a set of secret government documents stolen by an antiwar activist—the Supreme Court held that the paper was free to publish them.[42]

Once something is published, a newspaper or magazine may be sued or prosecuted if the material is libelous or obscene or if it incites someone to commit an illegal act. But these usually are not very serious restrictions, because the courts have defined *libelous, obscene,* and *incitement* so narrowly as to make it more difficult here than in any other nation to find the press guilty of such conduct. For example, for a paper to be found guilty of libeling a public official or other prominent person, the person must not only show that what was printed was wrong and damaging, but must also show, with "clear and convincing evidence," that it was printed maliciously—that is, with "reckless disregard" for its truth or falsity.[43] When in 1984 Israeli General Ariel Sharon sued *Time* magazine for libel, the jury decided the story *Time* printed was false and defamatory, but that *Time* had not published it as the result of malice, and so Sharon did not collect any damages.

There are also laws intended to protect the privacy of citizens, but they do not really inhibit newspapers. In general, your name and picture can be printed without your consent if they are part of a news story of some conceivable public interest. And if a paper attacks you in print, the paper has no legal obligation to give you space for a reply.[44]

It is illegal to use printed words to advocate the violent overthrow of the government if by your advocacy you incite others to action, but this rule has only rarely been applied to newspapers.[45]

Regulating Broadcasting

Although newspapers and magazines by and large are not regulated, broadcasting is regulated by the government. No one may operate a radio or television station without a license from the Federal Communications Commission, renewable every seven years for radio and every five for television stations. An application for renewal is rarely refused, but until recently the FCC required the broadcaster to submit detailed information about its programming and how it planned to serve "community needs" in order to get a renewal. Based on this information or on the complaints of some group, the FCC could use its powers of renewal to influence what the station put on the air. For example, it could induce stations to reduce the amount of violence shown, increase the proportion of "public service" programs on the air, or alter the way it portrayed various ethnic groups.

Of late a movement has arisen to deregulate broadcasting, on the grounds that so many stations are now on the air that competition should be allowed to determine how each station defines and serves community needs. In this view, citizens can choose what they want to hear or see without the government's shaping the content of each station's programming. For example, since the early 1980s, a station can simply submit a postcard requesting that its license be renewed, a request automatically granted unless some group formally opposes the renewal. In that case, the FCC holds a hearing. As a result, some of the old rules—for instance, that each hour on TV could contain only 16 minutes of commercials—are no longer rigidly enforced.

Radio broadcasting has been deregulated the most. Before 1992, one company could own

LANDMARK CASES

The Rights of the Media

- *Near v. Minnesota* (1931): Freedom of the press applies to state governments, so that they cannot impose prior restraint on newspapers.

- *New York Times v. Sullivan* (1964): Public officials may not win a libel suit unless they can prove that the statement was made knowing it to be false or with reckless disregard of its truth.

- *Miami Herald v. Tornillo* (1974): A newspaper cannot be required to give someone a right to reply to one of its stories.

one AM and one FM station in each market. In 1992, this number was doubled. And in 1996, the Telecommunications Act allowed one company to own as many as eight stations in large markets (five in smaller ones) and as many as it wished nationally. This trend has had two results. First, a few large companies now own most of the big-market radio stations. Second, the looser editorial restrictions that accompanied deregulation mean that a greater variety of opinions and shows can be found on radio. There are many more radio talk shows than would have been heard when content was more tightly controlled.

Deregulation has also lessened the extent to which the federal government shapes the content of broadcasting. At one time, for example, a "fairness doctrine" required broadcasters that air one side of a story to give time to opposing points of view. But there are now so many radio and television stations that the FCC relies on competition to manage differences of opinion. The abandonment of the fairness doctrine permitted the rise of controversial talk radio shows. If the doctrine had stayed in place, there would be no Rush Limbaugh or Al Franken. The FCC decided that competition among news outlets protected people by giving them many different sources of news.

There still exists an **equal time rule** that obliges stations that sell advertising time to one political candidate to sell equal time to that person's opponents. When candidates wish to campaign on radio or television, the equal time rule applies.

Campaigning

During campaigns, a broadcaster must provide equal access to candidates for office and charge them rates no higher than the cheapest rate applicable to commercial advertisers for comparable time. At one time, this rule meant that a station or network could not broadcast a debate between the Democratic and Republican candidates for an office without inviting all other candidates as well—Libertarian, Prohibitionist, or whatever. Thus, a presidential debate in 1980 could be limited to the major candidates, Reagan and Carter (or Reagan and Anderson), only by having the League of Women Voters sponsor it and then allowing

equal time rule An FCC rule that if a broadcaster sells time to one candidate, it must sell equal time to other candidates.

horse-race journalism
News coverage that focuses on
who is ahead rather than on the
issues.

selective attention Paying
attention only to those news
stories with which one already
agrees.

radio and TV to cover it as a "news event." Now stations and networks can themselves sponsor debates limited to major candidates.

Though laws guarantee that candidates can buy time at favorable rates on television, not all candidates take advantage of this. The reason is that television is not always an efficient way to reach voters. A television message is literally "broad cast"—spread out to a mass audience without regard to the boundaries of the district in which a candidate is running. Presidential candidates, of course, always use television because their constituency is the whole nation. Candidates for senator or representative, however, may or may not use television, depending on whether the boundaries of their state or district conform well to the boundaries of a television market.

A *market* is an area easily reached by a television signal; there are about 200 such markets in the country. If you are a member of Congress from South Bend, Indiana, you come from a television market based there. You can buy ads on the TV stations in South Bend at a reasonable fee. But if you are a member of Congress from northern New Jersey, the only television stations are in nearby New York City. In that market, the costs of a TV ad are very high because they reach a lot of people, most of whom are not in your district and so cannot vote for you. Buying a TV ad is a waste of money. As a result, a much higher percentage of Senate than House candidates use television ads.

One aspect of campaigning that worries scholars is the media's reliance on **horse-race journalism**, that is, covering a campaign based on guesses about who is ahead rather than on candidates' positions on the issues. For example, in 2008, the journalists talked about how Barack Obama would win the New Hampshire primary because that is what the polls and political insiders told them. But then Hillary Clinton won. Nowhere in the press coverage was any attention given to the positions Clinton and Obama had on the issues. The public says they want more such coverage, though one suspects that they actually like horse-race journalism.

Another concern is that public distrust of the media has grown. As shown in Figure 6.3, the percentage of people saying they believe news organizations has declined significantly in just the first decade of the 21st century.

Media's Influence

Some people will be influenced by what they read or hear, but others will not be. There is a well-known psychological process called **selective attention**. It means that people remember or believe only what they want to. If they see or hear statements inconsistent with their existing beliefs, they will tune out these messages.[46]

But after the 1964 presidential election, one study suggested that in the northern part of the United States a newspaper endorsement favoring Democratic candidate Lyndon Johnson added about five percentage points to the vote he received.[47]

Another study examined the vote in more than 60 contests for the U.S. Senate held over a five-year period. Newspaper stories about the rival candidates were scored as positive, negative, or neutral. Voters' feelings about the candidates were learned from public opinion polls. Obviously, many things other than newspaper stories will affect how voters feel, and so the authors of this study tried to control for these factors. They held constant the seniority of incumbent candidates, the level of political experience of challengers, the amount of campaign spending, how close each race was, and the political ideology and party identification of voters. After doing all of this, they discovered two things. First, newspapers that endorsed incumbents on their editorial pages gave more positive news coverage to them than newspapers that did not endorse them. Second, the voters had more positive

FIGURE 6.3 **Credibility Ratings for Many News Organizations Have Declined in the 21st Century**

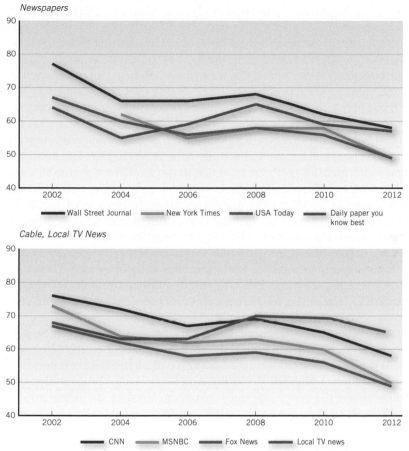

Newspapers

Wall Street Journal — New York Times — USA Today — Daily paper you know best

Cable, Local TV News

CNN — MSNBC — Fox News — Local TV news

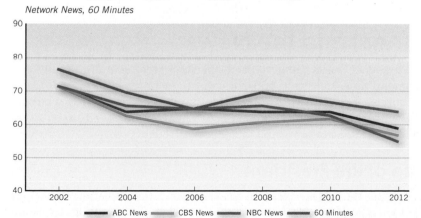

Network News, 60 Minutes

ABC News — CBS News — NBC News — 60 Minutes

Source: Pew Research Center for the People & the Press, "Further Decline in Credibility Ratings for Most News Organizations," August 16, 2012.

feelings about endorsed incumbents than they did about non-endorsed ones. In short, editorial views affect news coverage, and news coverage affects public attitudes.[48]

A fascinating natural experiment occurred when Fox News, a network that generally favors Republicans, began to air in an increasing number of cities. When two scholars compared the effects on voting patterns in cities where Fox News was on the air with similar cities in which it was not, they found that there was a 3 to 8 percent increase in the vote for Republican candidates and about a half a percent increase in the Republican vote for president in the Fox towns.[49] Another study even manufactured an experiment: the authors gave, at no charge, *The Washington Post* (a liberal newspaper) or *The Washington Times* (a conservative newspaper) to people who subscribed to neither in a northern Virginia county. In the next election, those people receiving the *Post* were more likely to vote for the Democratic candidate for governor.[50]

What the press covers affects the policy issues that people think are important. Experiments conducted in New Haven, Connecticut, and a study done in North Carolina show that what citizens believe about some policy questions reflects what newspapers and television stations say about them.[51] But there are limits to media influence. If people are unemployed, the victims of crime, or worried about high gasoline prices, they do not have to be told these things by the media.[52] But most people have no personal knowledge of highway fatalities, the condition of the environment, or American foreign policy in Europe. On these matters, the media are likely to have much more influence.

The best evidence of how important the media are comes from the behavior of people trying to get elected. In 1950, Estes Kefauver was a little-known senator from Tennessee. Then he chaired a Senate committee investigating organized crime. When these dramatic hearings were televised, Kefauver became a household name. In 1952, he ran for the Democratic nomination for president and won a lot of primary votes before losing to Adlai Stevenson.

From that time on, developing a strong media presence became a top priority for political candidates. Sometimes it backfires. In 2004, Howard Dean, then a candidate for the Democratic presidential nomination, saw his campaign start to sputter after television carried a speech he gave to his supporters that seemed to end in a kind of anguished scream. And every White House staffer spends a lot of time worrying about how to get the press, especially television, to cover the president. Studies show that television commentary about presidents affects their popularity.[53] President Lyndon Johnson reportedly concluded that the war he was supporting in Vietnam was a hopeless cause after Walter Cronkite, then the star of the popular CBS News program, turned against the war.

Government and the News

Every government agency, every public official, spends a great deal of time trying to shape public opinion. From time to time, somebody publishes an exposé of the efforts of the Pentagon, the White House, or some bureau to "sell" itself to the people, but in a government of separated powers, weak parties, and a decentralized legislature, any government agency that fails to cultivate public opinion will sooner or later find itself weak, without allies, and in trouble.

Prominence of the President

Theodore Roosevelt was the first president to raise the systematic cultivation of the press to an art form. From the day he took office, he made it clear that he would give inside stories to friendly reporters and withhold them from hostile ones. He made sure that scarcely a day passed without his doing something newsworthy. In 1902, he built the West Wing of the White House and included in it, for the first time, a special room for reporters near his office, and he invited the press to become fascinated by the antics of his children. In return, the reporters adored him. Teddy's nephew Franklin Roosevelt institutionalized this system by making his press secretary (a job created by Herbert Hoover) a major instrument for cultivating and managing, as well as informing, the press.

Today, the press secretary heads a large staff that meets with reporters, briefs the president on questions he is likely to be asked, attempts to control the flow of news from Cabinet departments to the press, and arranges briefings for out-of-town editors (to bypass what many presidents think are the biases of the White House press corps).

All this effort is directed primarily at the White House press corps, a group of men and women who have a lounge in the White House where they wait for a story to break, attend the daily press briefing, or take advantage of a "photo op"—an opportunity to photograph the president with some newsworthy person.

No other nation in the world has brought the press into such close physical proximity to the head of its government. The result is that the actions of our government are personalized to a degree not found in most other democracies. Whether the president rides a horse, comes down with a cold, greets a Boy Scout, or takes a trip, the press is there. The prime minister of the United Kingdom does not share his home with the press or expect to have his every sneeze recorded for posterity.

Coverage of Congress

Congress has watched all this with irritation and envy. It resents the attention given the president, but it is not certain how it can compete. The 435 members of the House are so numerous and play such specialized roles that they do not get much individualized press attention. In the past, the House was quite restrictive about television or radio coverage of its proceedings. Until 1978, it prohibited television cameras on the floor except on purely ceremonial occasions (such as the annual State of the Union message delivered by the president). From 1952 to 1970, the House would not even allow electronic coverage of its committee hearings (except for a few occasions during those periods when the Republicans were in the majority). Significant live coverage of committee hearings began in 1974 when the House Judiciary Committee was discussing the possible impeachment of President Nixon. Since 1979, cable TV (C-SPAN) has provided gavel-to-gavel coverage of speeches on the House floor.

The Senate has used television much more fully, heightening the already substantial advantage that senators have over representatives in getting the public eye. Although radio and television coverage of the Senate floor was not allowed until 1978 (when the debates on the Panama Canal treaties were broadcast live), Senate committee hearings have frequently been televised for either news films or live broadcasts ever since Estes Kefauver demonstrated the power of this medium in 1950. Since 1986, the Senate has allowed live C-SPAN coverage of its sessions.

Senatorial use of televised committee hearings has helped turn the Senate into the incubator for presidential candidates. At least in most states, if you are a governor, you are located far from network television news cameras; news cameras are most likely to focus on your leadership in times of crisis or major disaster, during a flood or a blizzard, for example. But senators all work in Washington, a city filled with cameras. No disaster is necessary to get on the air; only an investigation, a scandal, a major political conflict, or an articulate and telegenic personality is needed.

Even if the press and the politicians loved each other, the competition between the various branches of government would guarantee plenty of news leaks. But since the Vietnam War, the Watergate scandal, and the Iran-Contra affair, the press and the politicians have come to distrust one another. As a result, journalists today are far less willing to accept at face value the statements of elected officials and are far more likely to try to find somebody who will leak "the real story." We have come, in short, to have an

adversarial press The tendency of the national media to be suspicious of officials and eager to reveal unflattering stories about them.

adversarial press—that is, one that (at least at the national level) is suspicious of officialdom and eager to break an embarrassing story that will win for its author honor, prestige, and (in some cases) a lot of money.

Given their experiences with Watergate and Irangate, given the highly competitive nature of national newsgathering, and given their political ideology (which tends to put them to the left of any administration in power), American editors and reporters—at least at the national level—are likely to have an adversarial relationship with government for a long time to come. Given our constitutional

HOW WE COMPARE

Freedom of the Press

The Antifederalists insisted on adding a Bill of Rights to the Constitution because they feared government intrusion into citizens' lives. Their first concern, as reflected in the First Amendment, was to protect speech and expression, which includes freedom of the press. Although the protection is not absolute—the Supreme Court has ruled that there are times when that freedom may be restricted by the government for national security, for example—the burden of proof is on the government to demonstrate when imposing a restriction is constitutionally necessary.

Not all advanced industrialized democracies provide such broad protection for the media. In the United Kingdom, for example, libel laws are stricter than in the United States, which is why celebrities and business sometimes seek restitution in the former over the latter. Some European democracies have prohibitions on hate speech, which the United States does not (though the United States does impose restrictions on other types of speech that can appear in media outlets, such as obscenity or threats of violence). According to a recent report by Freedom House, an organization that tracks various measurements of freedom cross-nationally, access to free and independent media has declined worldwide to its lowest level in more than 10 years. Of 197 countries and territories for which Freedom House evaluated media coverage in 2012, 63 (32 percent) were rated Free, 70 (36 percent) were rated Partly Free, and 64 (32 percent) were rated Not Free.

Countries at Top of Global Press Freedom Rankings, Freedom House, 2012

1. Norway and Sweden (tied for first place)

2. Belgium, Finland, Netherlands (tied for next ranking)

(The United States is tied for 23rd place.)

Countries at Bottom of Global Press Freedom Rankings, Freedom House, 2012

1. Turkmenistan and North Korea (tied for first place)

2. Uzbekistan

3. Eritrea

4. Belarus

Source: Freedom House, "Freedom of the Press 2013."

system, there will always be plenty of people in government eager to help them with leaks hostile to one faction or another.

background A public official's statement to a reporter given on condition that the official not be named.

Government Constraints on Journalists

An important factor works against the influence of ideology and anti-official attitudes on reporters—the need every reporter has for access to key officials. A reporter is only as good as his or her sources, and it is difficult to cultivate good sources if you regularly antagonize them. Thus, Washington reporters must constantly strike a balance between expressing their own views (and risk losing a valuable source) and keeping a source (and risk becoming its mouthpiece).

The great increase in the number of congressional staff members has made striking this balance easier than it once was. Since it is almost impossible to keep anything secret from Congress, the existence of 15,000 to 20,000 congressional staffers means there is a potential source for every conceivable issue and cause. Congress has become a gold mine for reporters. If a story annoys one congressional source, another source can easily be found.

The government is not without means to fight back. The number of press officers on the payroll of the White House, Congress, and the executive agencies has grown sharply in recent decades. Obviously, these people have a stake in putting out news stories that reflect favorably on their elected superiors. They can try to do this with press releases, but adversarial journalists are suspicious of "canned news" (although they use it nonetheless). Or the press officers can try to win journalistic friends by offering leaks and supplying background stories to favored reporters.

There are four ways in which reporters and public officials, or their press officers, can communicate:

- On the record: The reporter can quote the official by name.

- Off the record: What the official says cannot be used.

- On **background**: What the official says can be used but may not be attributed to him or her by name. Reporters often call such an anonymous source "a high-ranking official" or "a knowledgeable member of Congress."

- On deep background: What the official says can be used but not attributed to anybody, even an anonymous source.

To get around the national press, public officials and their press officers can try to reach the local media directly by giving interviews or appearing on radio talk shows. The local media are a bit less likely than the national media to have an adversarial attitude toward the national government, and one can select talk-show hosts on the basis of their known ideology.

The ultimate weapon in the government's effort to shape the press to its liking is the president's rewarding of reporters and editors who treat him well and his punishing of those who treat him badly. President Kennedy regularly called in offending reporters for brutal tongue-lashings and favored friendly reporters with tips and inside stories. Johnson did the same, with special attention to television reporters. Nixon made the mistake of attacking the press publicly, thereby allowing it to defend itself with appeals to the First Amendment. (Kennedy's and Johnson's manipulative skills were used privately.) Probably every president tries to use the press with whatever means are at his disposal, but in the long run it is the press, not the president, who wins. Johnson decided not to run again in 1968 in part because of press hostility to him; Nixon was exposed by the press; Carter and Bush came to be disliked by national reporters. The press and the president need, but do not trust, one another; it is inevitably a stormy relationship.

LEARNING OBJECTIVES

LO 6.1 What is "public opinion" and how do we measure it?

Public opinion refers to how people think or feel about particular things, including but not limited to politics and government. Today, it is commonly measured by means of scientific survey research or polls based on random samples of given populations.

LO 6.2 What is "political ideology" and how does it matter for what elites and the mass public believe?

Political ideology is defined as a more or less consistent set of beliefs about what policies government ought to pursue. Elites are more prone to think ideologically than average citizens are, but there are mass ideologies, and the relationship between what diverse elites believe and what the public at large believes allows for no easy generalizations. Political scientists measure the extent to which people have a political ideology by seeing how frequently people use broad political categories (such as "liberal" and "conservative") to describe their own views or to justify their preferences for candidates and policies. They also measure it by seeing to what extent the policy preferences of a citizen are consistent over time or are based at any one time on consistent principles. Many scholars believe that Americans are becoming more ideological. On many issues, for example, the policy preferences of average Republican and Democratic voters now differ significantly from one another. There is clear evidence that political elites are more ideological today than they were just a generation or two ago. The government attends more to the elite views than to popular views, at least on many matters.

LO 6.3 What role do the media play in American politics?

The media serve three major roles in American politics: gatekeeper, scorekeeper, and watchdog. They identify priorities for policymaking, keep track of which candidates are doing well and which are doing poorly in political campaigns, and oversee the workings of government to ensure that public officials are meeting their responsibilities.

LO 6.4 How has technology changed interactions between public officials and the media?

Changes in technology, particularly the advent of the Internet, have fundamentally changed how politicians and the media interact. Elected officials now can reach constituents directly via email, websites, instant messages, and so forth, whereas previously they were primarily dependent on the media for conveying their messages. Electronic media, in turn, are able to cover elected officials 24 hours a day, further narrowing the zone of privacy that politicians may realistically expect.

LO 6.5 Why are there so few restrictions on media coverage of politics and politicians in the United States?

The First Amendment to the Constitution explicitly guarantees that Congress may not pass a law abridging freedom of speech or of the press. While this protection is not absolute—journalists may be required by courts, for example, to divulge information about confidential sources in the interest of national security—the burden of proof is on the government to explain why violating this constitutional guarantee is necessary. Government officials have fewer protections from media coverage of their actions than private citizens because of their public responsibilities.

TO LEARN MORE

Public Opinion:

- CBS News/*New York Times* poll:
- **Topics.nytimes.com/top/reference/timestopics/subjects/n/newyorktimes-poll-watch/**
- Gallup opinion poll: **www.gallup.com**
- The Pew Research Center for the People & the Press: **www.people-press.org**
- Rasmussen Reports: **www.rasmussenreports.com**
- Roper Center for Public Opinion Research: **www.ropercenter.uconn.edu**
- *Wall Street Journal*/NBC News poll: **topics.wsj.com/subject/W/wall-street-journal/nbc- news-polls/ 6052**
- Berinsky, Adam J. *Silent Voices: Public Opinion and Political Participation in America*. Princeton, NJ: Princeton University Press, 2004. Shows how opinion polls can bias the results and induce people with unpopular views to say "don't know."
- Key, V. O., Jr. *The Responsible Electorate*. Cambridge: Harvard University Press, 1966. An argument, with evidence, that American voters are not fools.
- Lewis-Beck, Michael S., et al. *The American Voter Revisited*. Ann Arbor, MI: University of Michigan Press, 2008. A careful comparison of how voters in the early 2000s compare to those in the mid-1950s.
- Lipset, Seymour Martin. *Political Man: The Social Bases of Politics*. Garden City, NY: Doubleday, 1959. An exploration of the relationship between society, opinion, and democracy in America and abroad.
- Weissberg, Robert. *Polling, Policy, and Public Opinion*. New York: Palgrave Macmillan, 2002. A critique of what we think we know from opinion polling, showing the many ways in which polls can give us misleading answers.
- Zaller, John. *The Nature and Origins of Mass Opinion*. Cambridge, England: Cambridge University Press, 1992. A path-breaking study of how the public forms an opinion, illustrating the ways in which elite views help shape mass views.

The Media:

- To search many news sources: **www.ipl.org**
- To get analyses of the press nonpartisan view: **www.cmpa.com**
- Liberal view: **www.fair.org**
- Conservative view: **www.mrc.org**
- Public opinion about the press Pew Research Center: **www.people-press.org**
- National media: *The New York Times:* **www.nytimes.com**
- *The Wall Street Journal:* **www.wsj.com**

political party A group that seeks to elect candidates to public office.

interest group An organization of people sharing a common interest or goal that seeks to influence public policy.

Later in this book, you will study each of four major governmental institutions: Congress (Chapter 9), the presidency (Chapter 10), the bureaucracy (Chapter 11), and the judiciary (Chapter 12). Together with the media (covered in Chapter 6), political parties and interest groups are major *non*-governmental institutions. A **political party** is a group that seeks to elect candidates to public office by supplying them with a label—a "party identification"—by which they are known to the electorate.[1] An **interest group** is an organization of people sharing a common goal that seeks to influence public policy.

It is tempting to distinguish between political parties and interest groups by saying that the former seek to influence government "from the inside" while the latter seek to influence it "from the outside." But that distinction is a bit too simple now because, as we shall see, many interest groups are deeply involved in raising money for political campaigns and employing people to influence legislation.

While the Framers of the Constitution believed that the media—"a free press"—was both necessary and desirable, they disliked political parties and thought that America's representative democracy would best develop without them. They were only slightly more sanguine about interest groups. On the one hand, they believed that, as James Madison explained in *Federalist Papers* Nos. 10 and 51 (see the Appendix), a "landed interest, a manufacturing interest, a moneyed interest, and many lesser interests, grow up of necessity in civilized nations," and that in "a free government the security for civil rights" actually depended on their being a "multiplicity of interests." On the other hand, they feared that both political parties and what today we term "interest groups" would form and function as "factions" motivated by narrow self-interest and driven by passions that were "adverse to the rights of other citizens" and to "the public good."

In this chapter, we explore how political parties arose and changed, explain how interest groups formed and proliferated, and assess how each of these two non-governmental institutions matters to the present and future of American politics and government.

THEN

The Founders disliked parties, thinking of them as "factions" motivated by ambition and self-interest. George Washington, dismayed by the quarreling between Alexander Hamilton and Thomas Jefferson in his Cabinet, devoted much of his Farewell Address to condemning parties. This hostility toward parties was understandable: the legitimacy and success of the newly created federal government were still very much in doubt. When Jefferson organized his followers to oppose Hamilton's policies, it seemed to Hamilton and *his* followers that Jefferson was opposing not just a policy or a leader but also the very concept of a national government. Jefferson, for his part, thought Hamilton was not simply pursuing bad policies but was subverting the Constitution itself. Before political parties could become legitimate, it was necessary for people to separate in their minds quarrels over policies and elections from disputes over the legitimacy of the new government itself. The ability to make that distinction was slow in coming; thus, parties were objects of profound suspicion, at first defended only as temporary expedients.

NOW

American political parties are the oldest in the world, dating back to the first decade of the republic. They may be in decline, but they are not dead or dying. New parties (like the Green Party launched in 2000 by consumer advocate Ralph Nader, or the Tea Party movement that developed after the 2008 presidential election) may come and go, but two parties, the Democratic and Republican, still dominate the country's campaigns and elections. Nor have party leaders been wholly replaced by media consultants, pollsters, or others whose profession is raising money or devising strategies for whichever candidates bid highest for their services. What distinguishes political parties from other groups, and why are they a fundamental feature of American politics?

Parties—Here and Abroad

Our definition of **political party**—a group that seeks to elect candidates to public office by supplying them with a label—a "party identification"—by which they are known to the electorate—is purposefully broad. It includes both familiar parties (Democratic, Republican) and unfamiliar ones (Whig, Libertarian, Socialist Workers) and covers periods in which a party is very strong (having an elaborate and well-disciplined organization that provides money and workers to its candidates) as well as periods in which it is quite weak (supplying nothing but the label to candidates). The label by which a candidate is known may or may not actually be printed on the ballot opposite the candidate's name: in the United States, it does appear on the ballot in all national elections, but in only a minority of municipal ones; in Australia and Israel (and in the United Kingdom before 1969), it never appears on the ballot at all.

America's political parties do not matter as much, or in the same ways, as they once did. For instance, one reason voter turnout is higher abroad than in this country is that political parties in other democratic nations are more effective at mobilizing voters. The sense of belonging to a party and the inclination to vote the party ticket are greater in France, Italy, and Sweden than in the United States.

It was not always thus. At one time, being a Democrat or a Republican was a serious commitment that people did not make lightly or abandon easily. In those days, it would have been hard to find anything in Europe that could match the vote-getting power of such party organizations as those in Chicago, New York, and Philadelphia.

Parties in the United States are relatively weak today mainly because the laws and rules under which they operate have taken away much of their power at the same time that many voters have lost their sense of commitment to party identification. This weakening has proceeded unevenly, however, because our constitutional system has produced a decentralized party system just as it has produced a decentralized governmental system, with the result that parties are strong in some places and almost nonexistent in other places.

There are three political arenas in which parties may be found and in which changes in their strength may be assessed. A party exists as a *label* in the minds of the voters, as an *organization* that recruits and campaigns for candidates, and as a *set of leaders* who try to organize and control the legislative and executive branches of government. A powerful party is one whose label has a strong appeal for voters, whose organization can decide

When Andrew Jackson ran for president in 1828, more than a million votes were cast for the first time in American history. This poster, from the 1832 election, was part of the emergence of truly mass political participation.

CONSTITUTIONAL CONNECTIONS

"The Spirit of Party"

The noted historian Richard Hofstadter wrote about the Constitution as "A Constitution against Parties." That was the title Hofstadter gave to the second chapter of his 1969 book, *The Idea of a Party System: The Rise of Legitimate Opposition in the United States, 1780–1840*. For the republic's first half-century, most national leaders did not accept the idea that parties were a necessary and desirable feature of American government. For example, near the end of his second term as president, George Washington wrote a letter that later became known as his "Farewell Address." It reads in part:

...Let me now take a more comprehensive view, and warn you in the most solemn manner against the baneful effects of the spirit of party generally. This Spirit, unfortunately, is inseparable from our nature, having its root in the strongest passions of the human mind...The alternate domination of one faction over another, sharpened by the spirit of revenge natural to party dissension ... is itself a frightful despotism...(The) common and continual mischiefs of the spirit of party are sufficient to make it the interest and the duty of a wise people to discourage and restrain it.

who will be candidates and how their campaigns will be managed, and whose leaders can dominate one or all branches of government.

American parties have become weaker in all three arenas. As a *label* with which voters identify, the parties probably are much weaker than they were in the 19th century, but only somewhat weaker than they were several decades ago (see Figure 7.1). In 1952, a total of 36 percent of the electorate identified strongly as Democrats (22 percent) or Republicans (14 percent), while a total of 23 percent of the electorate identified as independents. By 2012, total strong party identifiers had dropped to 34 percent of the electorate, while all independents had risen to 38 percent of the electorate. But the best evidence of weakening party identification is what voters *do*. As we shall see in the next chapter, in some elections many people vote split tickets— supporting a president from one party and members of Congress from the other.

FIGURE 7.1   Decline in Party Identification, 1952–2012

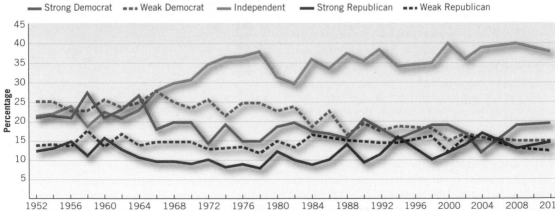

Source: American National Election Studies, Table 2A.1, "Party Identification, 1952–2012."

As a *set of leaders* who organize government, especially Congress, political parties remain somewhat strong in ways that will be described in Chapter 9. As *organizations* that nominate and elect candidates, parties have become dramatically weaker since the 1960s. In most states, parties have very little control over who gets nominated to office. The causes and consequences of that change are the subject of this chapter.

In Europe, things are very different. Almost the only way a person can become a candidate for elective office is to be nominated by party leaders. Campaigns are run by the party, using party funds and workers, not by the candidate. Once in office, the elected officials are expected to vote and act together with other members of their party.

The principal criterion by which voters choose among candidates is their party identification or label. This has been changing somewhat of late: European parties, like American ones, have not been able to count as heavily as in the past on party loyalty among the voters.

Several factors explain the striking differences between American and European political parties. First, the federal system of government in the United States decentralizes political authority and thus decentralizes political party organizations. For nearly two centuries, most of the important governmental decisions were made at the state and local levels—decisions regarding education, land use, business regulation, and public welfare—and thus it was at the state and local levels that the important struggles over power and policy occurred. Moreover, most people with political jobs—either elective or appointive—worked for state and local government, and thus a party's interest in obtaining these jobs for its followers meant it had to focus attention on who controlled city hall, the county courthouse, and the state capitol. Federalism, in short, meant political parties would acquire jobs and money from local sources and fight local contests. This, in turn, meant the national political parties would be coalitions of local parties, and though these coalitions would have a keen interest in capturing the presidency (with it, after all, went control of large numbers of federal jobs), the national party leaders rarely had as much power as the local ones. The Republican leader of Cuyahoga County, Ohio, for example, could often ignore the decisions of the Republican national chair and even the Ohio state chair.

Political authority in the United States has recently become far more centralized: the federal government now makes decisions affecting almost all aspects of our lives, including those—such as schooling and welfare—once left entirely in local hands. Yet the political parties have not become more centralized as a result. If anything, they have become even weaker and more decentralized. One reason for this apparent paradox is that in the United States, unlike in most other democratic nations, political parties are closely regulated by state and federal laws, and these regulations have weakened the power of parties substantially. Perhaps the most important of these regulations are those that prescribe how a party's candidates are selected.

In the great majority of American states, the party leaders do not select people to run for office; by law, those people are chosen by the voters in primary elections. Though sometimes the party can influence who will win a primary contest, in general people running for state or national office in this country owe little to party leaders. In Europe, by contrast, there is no such thing as a primary election—the only way to become a candidate for office is to persuade party leaders to put your name on the ballot.

John Van Hasselt/Corbis

Ten political parties competed in the French presidential elections in 2012.

HOW WE COMPARE

How Many Political Parties?

The United States has two political parties in Congress. Other countries have fewer or more parties in their national legislatures:

China 1

Canada 5

United Kingdom 8

Germany 6

Mexico 7

Russia 4

Israel 17

France 14

Brazil 22 (more or less)

India 43 (more or less)

Source: *Congressional Quarterly.* "Political Parties and Groups." *Political Handbook of the World.* Last Modified 2012. Accessed May 31, 2013.

In a later section of this chapter, the impact of the direct primary will be discussed in more detail; for now, it is enough to note that its use removes from the hands of the party leadership its most important source of power over officeholders.

Furthermore, if an American political party wins control of Congress, it does not—as in most European nations with a parliamentary system of government—also win the right to select the chief executive of the government. The American president, as we have seen, is independently elected, and this means that the president will choose his or her principal subordinates not from among members of Congress but from among persons out of Congress. Should the president pick a representative or senator for his or her Cabinet, the Constitution requires that person to resign from Congress in order to accept the job. Thus, an opportunity to be a Cabinet secretary is not an important reward for members of Congress, and so the president cannot use the prospect of that reward as a way of controlling congressional action. All this weakens the significance and power of parties in terms of organizing the government and conducting its business.

The Rise and Decline of the Political Party

Our nation began without parties, and today's parties, though far from extinct, are about as weak as at any time in our history. There are four broad periods of party history: when political parties were created (roughly from the Founding to the 1820s); when the more or less stable two-party system emerged (roughly from the time of President Jackson to the Civil War); when parties developed a comprehensive organizational form and appeal (roughly from the Civil War to the 1930s); and finally when party "reform" began to alter the party system (beginning in the early 1900s, but taking effect chiefly since the New Deal).

The Founding

The first organized political party in American history was made up of the followers of Jefferson, who, beginning in the 1790s, called themselves *Republicans* (hoping to suggest thereby that their opponents were secret monarchists). The followers of Hamilton kept the label *Federalist*, which once referred to all supporters of the new Constitution (hoping to imply that their opponents were "Antifederalists," or enemies of the Constitution).

These early parties were loose caucuses of political notables in various localities, with New England strongly Federalist and much of the South passionately Republican. Jefferson and ally James Madison thought their Republican Party was a temporary arrangement designed to defeat John Adams, a Federalist, in his bid to succeed Washington in 1796. (Adams narrowly defeated Jefferson, who, under the system then in effect, became vice president because he had the second most electoral votes.) In 1800, Adams's bid to succeed himself intensified party activity even more, but this time Jefferson won and the Republicans assumed office. The Federalists feared that Jefferson would dismantle the Constitution, but Jefferson adopted a conciliatory posture, saying in his inaugural address that "we are all Republicans, we are all Federalists."[2] It was not true, of course: the Federalists detested Jefferson, and some were planning to have New England secede from the Union. But it was good politics, expressive of the need that every president has to persuade the public that, despite partisan politics, the presidency exists to serve all the people.

So successful were the Republicans that the Federalists virtually ceased to exist as a party. Thomas Jefferson was reelected in 1804 with almost no opposition; James Madison easily won two terms; James Monroe carried 16 out of 19 states in 1816 and was reelected without opposition in 1820. Political parties had seemingly disappeared, just as Jefferson had hoped. The parties that existed in these early years were essentially small groups of local notables. Political participation was limited, and nominations for most local offices were arranged rather casually.

The Jacksonians

What often is called the second party system emerged around 1824 with Andrew Jackson's first run for the presidency, and lasted until the dawn of the Civil War. Its distinctive feature was that political participation became a mass phenomenon. For one thing, the number of voters to be reached had become quite large. Only about 365,000 popular votes were cast in 1824. But as a result of laws that enlarged the number of people eligible to vote and an increase in the population, by 1828, well over a million votes were tallied. By 1840, the figure was well over 2 million. In addition, by 1832 presidential electors were selected by popular vote in virtually every state. (As late as 1816, electors were chosen by the state legislatures, rather than by the people, in about half the states.) Presidential politics had become a truly national, genuinely popular activity; in many communities, election campaigns had become the principal public spectacle.

The party system of the Jacksonian era was built from the bottom up rather than—as during the period of the Founding—from the top down. No change better illustrates this transformation than the abandonment of the system of having caucuses composed of members of Congress nominate presidential candidates. The caucus system was an effort to unite the legislative and executive branches by giving the former some degree of control over who would have a chance to capture the latter. The caucus system became unpopular when the caucus candidate for president in 1824 ran third in a field of four in the general election. It was completely discredited that same year when Congress denied the presidency to Jackson, the candidate with the greatest share of the popular vote.

To replace the caucus, the party convention was invented. The first convention in American history was held by the Anti-Masonic Party in 1831; the first convention of a major political party was held by the anti-Jackson Republicans later that year (it nominated Henry Clay for president). The Democrats held a convention in 1832 that ratified Jackson's nomination for reelection and picked Martin Van Buren as his running mate. The first convention to select a man who would be elected president and who was not already the incumbent president was held by the Democrats in 1836; they chose Van Buren.

The Civil War and Sectionalism

The party system created in the Jacksonian period was the first truly national system, with Democrats (followers of Jackson) and Whigs (opponents of Jackson), but it could not withstand the deep split in

mugwumps or ***progressives***
Republican party faction of the
1890s to the 1910s, composed of
reformers who opposed patronage.

opinion created by the agitation over slavery. Both parties tried, naturally, to straddle the issue, but slavery and sectionalism were issues that could not be straddled. The old parties divided and new ones emerged. The modern Republican Party (not the old Democratic-Republican Party of Thomas Jefferson) began as a third party. As a result of the Civil War, it became a major party (the only third party ever to gain major-party status) and dominated national politics, with only occasional interruptions, for three-quarters of a century.

Republican control of the White House, and to a lesser extent Congress, was in large measure the result of two events that gave to Republicans a marked advantage in the competition for the loyalties of voters. The first of these was the Civil War. This bitter, searing crisis deeply polarized popular attitudes. Those who supported the Union side became Republicans for generations; those who supported the Confederacy, or who had opposed the war, became Democrats.

As it turned out, this partisan division was nearly even for a while: though the Republicans usually won the presidency and the Senate, they often lost control of the House. There were many northern Democrats. In 1896, however, another event—the presidential candidacy of William Jennings Bryan—further strengthened the Republican Party. Bryan, a Democrat, alienated many voters in the populous northeastern states while attracting voters in the South and Midwest. The result was to confirm and deepen the split in the country, especially North versus South, begun by the Civil War. From 1896 to the 1930s, with rare exceptions, northern states were solidly Republican, southern ones solidly Democratic.

This split had a profound effect on the organization of political parties, for it meant that most states were now one-party states. As a result, competition for office at the state level had to go on *within* a single dominant party (the Republican Party in Massachusetts, New York, Pennsylvania, Wisconsin, and elsewhere; the Democratic Party in Georgia, Mississippi, South Carolina, and elsewhere). Consequently, there emerged two major factions within each party, but especially within the Republican Party. One was composed of the party regulars—the professional politicians, the "stalwarts," the Old Guard. They were preoccupied with building up the party machinery, developing party loyalty, and acquiring and dispensing patronage—jobs and other favors—for themselves and their faithful followers. Their great skills were in organization, negotiation, bargaining, and compromise; their great interest was in winning.

The other faction, variously called **mugwumps** or **progressives** (or "reformers"), was opposed to the heavy emphasis on patronage; disliked the party machinery because it permitted only bland candidates to rise to the top; was fearful of the heavy influx of immigrants into American cities and of the ability of the party regulars to organize them into "machines;" and wanted to see the party take unpopular positions on certain issues (such as free trade). Their great skills lay in the areas of advocacy and articulation; their great interest was in principle.

At first the mugwumps tried to play a balance-of-power role, sometimes siding with the Republican Party of which they were members, at other times defecting to the Democrats (as when they bolted the Republican Party to support Grover Cleveland, the Democratic nominee, in 1884). But later, as the Republican strength in the nation grew, progressives within that party became increasingly less able to play a balance-of-power role, especially at the state level. If the progressives were to have any power, they came to believe, it would require an attack on the very concept of partisanship itself.

The Era of Reform

Progressives began to espouse measures to curtail or even abolish political parties. They favored primary elections to replace nominating conventions because the latter were viewed as manipulated by party bosses; they favored nonpartisan elections at the city level and in some cases at the state level as well; they argued against corrupt alliances between parties and businesses. They wanted strict voter registration requirements that would reduce voting fraud (but would also, as it turned out, keep ordinary citizens who found the requirements cumbersome from voting); they pressed for civil service reform to eliminate patronage; and they made heavy use of the mass media as a way of attacking the abuses of partisanship and of promoting their own ideas and candidacies.

The progressives were more successful in some places than in others. In California, for example, progressives led by Governor Hiram Johnson in 1910–1911 were able to institute the direct primary and to adopt procedures—called the *initiative* and the *referendum*—so citizens could vote directly on proposed legislation, thereby bypassing the state legislature. Governor Robert La Follette brought about similar changes in Wisconsin.

The effect of these changes was to reduce substantially the worst forms of political corruption and ultimately to make boss rule in politics difficult if not impossible. But they also had the effect of making political parties—whether led by bosses or by statesmen—weaker, less able to hold officeholders accountable, and less able to assemble the power necessary for governing the fragmented political institutions created by the Constitution. In Congress, party lines began to grow fainter, as did the power of congressional leadership. Above all, the progressives did not have an answer to the problem first faced by Jefferson: If there is not a strong political party, by what other means will candidates for office be found, recruited, and supported?

Party Realignments

There have clearly been important turning points in the strength of the major parties, especially in the 20th century, when for long periods we have not so much had close competition between two parties as we have had an alternation of dominance by one party and then the other. To help explain these major shifts in the tides of politics, scholars have developed the theory of **critical** or **realignment periods**. During such periods a sharp, lasting shift occurs in the popular coalition supporting one or both parties. The issues that separate the two parties change, and so the kinds of voters supporting each party change. This shift may occur at the time of the election or just after, as the new administration draws in new supporters.[3] There seem to have been five realignments so far, during or just after these elections: 1800, when the Jeffersonian Republicans defeated the Federalists; 1828, when the Jacksonian Democrats came to power; 1860, when the Whig party collapsed and the Republicans under Lincoln came to power; 1896, when the Republicans defeated William Jennings Bryan; and 1932, when the Democrats under Roosevelt came into office.

There are at least two kinds of realignments—one in which a major party is so badly defeated that it disappears and a new party emerges to take its place (this happened to the Federalists in 1800 and to the Whigs in 1856–1860), and another in which the two existing parties continue, but voters shift their support from one to the other (this happened in 1896 and 1932).

The three clearest cases seem to be 1860, 1896, and 1932. By 1860, the existing parties could no longer straddle the fence on the slavery issue. The Republican Party was formed in 1856 on the basis of clear-cut opposition to slavery; the Democratic Party split in half in 1860, with one part (led by Stephen A. Douglas and based in the North) trying to waffle on the issue and the other (led by John C. Breckinridge and drawing its support from the South) categorically denying that any government had any right to outlaw slavery. The remnants of the Whig party, renamed the Constitutional Union party, tried to unite the nation by writing no platform at all, thus remaining silent on slavery. Lincoln and the antislavery Republicans won in 1860; Breckinridge and the

critical or realignment periods A period when a major, lasting shift occurs in the popular coalition supporting one or both parties.

pro-slavery Southern Democrats came in second. From that moment on, the two major political parties acquired different sources of support and stood (at least for a decade) for different principles. The parties that had tried to straddle the fence were eliminated. The Civil War fixed these new party loyalties deep in the popular mind, and the structure of party competition was set for nearly 40 years.

In 1896, a different kind of realignment occurred. Economics, rather than slavery, was at issue. A series of depressions during the 1880s and 1890s fell especially hard on farmers in the Midwest and parts of the South. The prices paid to farmers for their commodities had been falling more or less steadily since the Civil War, making it increasingly difficult for them to pay their bills. A bitter reaction against the two major parties, which were straddling this issue as they had straddled slavery, spread like a prairie fire, leading to the formation of parties of economic protest—the Greenbackers and the Populists. Reinforcing the economic cleavages were cultural ones: Populists tended to be fundamentalist Protestants; urban voters were increasingly Catholic.

Matters came to a head in 1896 when William Jennings Bryan captured the Democratic nomination for president and saw to it that the party adopted a Populist platform. The existing Populist Party endorsed the Bryan candidacy. In the election, anti-Bryan Democrats deserted the party in droves to support the Republican candidate, William McKinley. Once again, a real issue divided the two parties: the Republicans stood for industry, business, hard money, protective tariffs, and urban interests; the Democrats for farmers, small towns, low tariffs, and rural interests. The Republicans won, carrying the cities, workers, and businesspeople; the Democrats lost, carrying most of the southern and midwestern farm states.

The old split between North and South that resulted from the Civil War was now replaced in part by an East versus West, city versus farm split.[4] It was not, however, only an economic cleavage—the Republicans had been able to appeal to Catholics and Lutherans who disliked fundamentalism and its hostility toward liquor and immigrants.

This alignment persisted until 1932. Again, change was triggered by an economic depression; again, more than economic issues were involved. The New Deal coalition that emerged was based on bringing together into the Democratic Party urban workers, northern blacks, southern whites, and Jewish voters. Unlike in 1860 and 1896, it was not preceded by any third-party movement; it occurred suddenly (though some groups had begun to shift their allegiance in 1928) and gathered momentum throughout the 1930s. The Democrats, isolated since 1896 as a southern and midwestern sectional party, had now become the majority party by finding a candidate and a cause that could lure urban workers, blacks, and Jews away from the Republican Party, where they had been for decades. It was obviously a delicate coalition—blacks and southern whites disagreed on practically everything except their liking for Roosevelt; Jews and the Irish bosses of the big-city machines also had little in common. But the federal government under Roosevelt was able to supply enough benefits to each of these disparate groups to keep them loyal members of the coalition and to provide a new basis for party identification.

In short, an electoral realignment occurs when a new issue of utmost importance to the voters (slavery, the economy) cuts across existing party divisions and replaces old issues that formerly were the basis of party identification.

Some people wondered whether the election of 1980—since it brought into power the most conservative administration in half a century—signaled a new realignment. Many of President Reagan's supporters began talking of a "mandate" to adopt major new policies in keeping with the views of the "new majority." But Reagan won in 1980 less because of what he stood for than because he was not Jimmy Carter, and he was reelected in 1984 primarily because people were satisfied with how the country was doing, especially economically.[5]

Just because we have had periods of one-party dominance in the past does not mean we will have them in the future. Reagan's election could not have been a traditional realignment, because it left Congress in the hands of the Democratic Party. Moreover, some scholars are beginning to question the theory of critical elections, or at least the theory that they occur with some regularity.

Nevertheless, one major change has occurred of late—the shift in the presidential voting patterns of the South. From 1972 through 2008, the South was more Republican than the nation as a whole. The proportion of white southerners describing themselves to pollsters as "strongly Democratic" fell from more than one-third in 1952 to about one-seventh in 1984. There has been a corresponding increase in "independents." As it turns out, southern white independents have voted overwhelmingly Republican in recent presidential elections.[6] If you lump independents together with the parties for which they actually vote, the party alignment among white southerners has gone from 6 to 1 Democratic in 1952 to about 50/50 Democrats and Republicans. If this continues, it will constitute a major realignment in a region of the country that is growing rapidly in population and political clout.

In general, however, the kind of dramatic realignment that occurred in the 1860s or after 1932 may not occur again, because party labels have lost their meaning for a growing number of voters. For these people politics may *de*align rather than *re*align.

split ticket Voting for candidates of different parties for various offices in the same election.

straight ticket Voting for candidates of the same party.

office-bloc ballot A ballot listing all candidates of a given office under the name of that office; also called a "Massachusetts" ballot.

party-column ballot A ballot listing all candidates of a given party together under the name of that party; also called an "Indiana" ballot.

Party Decline

The evidence that the parties are decaying, not realigning, is of several sorts. We have already noted that the proportion of people identifying with one or the other party declined between 1960 and 1980. Simultaneously, the proportion of those voting a **split ticket** (as opposed to a **straight ticket**) increased.

Split-ticket voting rose between 1952 and 1972 and hovered around 25 percent until it declined somewhat after 1992 (see Figure 7.2). For example, in 1988, more than *half* of all House Democrats

FIGURE 7.2 Split-Ticket Voting for President/House, 1952–2008

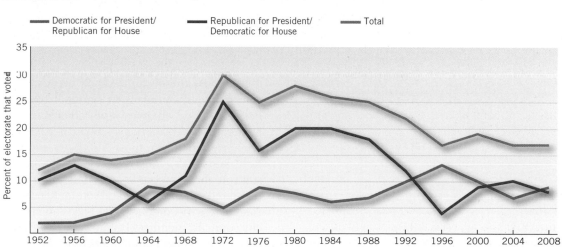

Source: American National Election Studies, Table 9B.2, "Split-Ticket Voting for President/Congress, 1952–2008."

FIGURE 7.3 Cleavages and Continuity in the Two-Party System

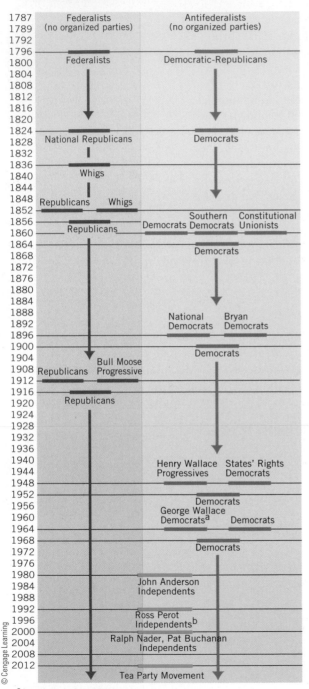

[a]American Independent party.

[b]United We Stand America or Reform Party.

© Cengage Learning

were elected in districts that voted for Republican George Bush as president. This ticket splitting was greatest in the South, but it was common everywhere. If every district that voted for Bush had also elected a Republican to Congress, the Republican Party would have held a 2-to-1 majority in the House of Representatives. Ticket splitting creates divided government—the White House and Congress are controlled by different parties. Ticket splitting helped the Democrats keep control of the House of Representatives from 1954 to 1994.

Ticket splitting was almost unheard of in the 19th century, and for a very good reason. In those days, the voter was either given a ballot by the party of his choice and he dropped it, intact, into the ballot box (thereby voting for everybody listed on the ballot), or he was given a government-printed ballot that listed in columns all the candidates of each party. All the voter had to do was mark the top of one column in order to vote for every candidate in that column. (When voting machines came along, they provided a single lever that, when pulled, cast votes for all the candidates of a particular party.) Around the turn of the century, progressives began to persuade states to adopt the **office-bloc** (or "Massachusetts") **ballot** in place of the **party-column** (or "Indiana") **ballot**. The office-bloc ballot lists all candidates by office; there is no way to vote a straight party ticket by making one mark. Not surprisingly, states using the office-bloc ballot show much more ticket splitting than those without it.[7]

It would be a mistake, however, to conclude that parties have declined simply because many voters now split tickets in national elections. Despite many changes and challenges (see Figure 7.3), America's two-party system remains strong. In most elections—national, state, and local—voters registered as Democrats still vote for Democratic candidates, and voters registered as Republicans still vote for Republican candidates. In Congress, state legislatures, and city councils, members still normally vote along party lines. Local political machines have died, but, as we shall now explain, national party structures remain alive and well.

The National Party Structure Today

Since political parties exist at the national, state, and local levels, you might suppose they are arranged like a big corporation, with a national board of directors giving orders to state managers who in turn direct the activities of rank-and-file workers at the county and city level. Nothing could be further from the truth. At each level, a separate and almost entirely independent organization exists that does pretty much what it wants, and in many counties and cities there is virtually no organization at all.

State party organizations, all determined to pick their delegates to the presidential nominating convention first, have moved their primary elections to earlier and earlier dates. For example, the Iowa caucus and the New Hampshire primary in the 1980s were held in March; in 2008, they were held in January. California moved its primary from June to February. This front-loaded set of primaries has made the campaign much longer and more expensive, but the national party organizations have been almost powerless to prevent it.

On paper, the national Democratic and Republican parties look quite similar. In both parties, ultimate authority is in the hands of the **national convention** that meets every four years to nominate a presidential candidate. Between these conventions, party affairs are managed by a **national committee** made up of delegates from each state and territory. In Congress, each party has a **congressional campaign committee** that helps members of Congress running for reelection or would-be members running for an open seat or challenging a candidate from the opposition party. The day-to-day work of the party is managed by a full-time, paid **national chair** elected by the committee.

For a long time, the two national parties were alike in behavior as well as description. The national chair, if his or her party held the White House, would help decide who among the party faithful would get federal jobs. Otherwise, the parties did very little.

But beginning in the late 1960s and early 1970s, the Republicans began to convert their national party into a well-financed, highly staffed organization devoted to finding and electing Republican candidates, especially to Congress. At about the same time, the Democrats began changing the rules governing how presidential candidates are nominated in ways that profoundly altered the distribution of power within the party. As a consequence, the Republicans became a bureaucratized party and the Democrats became a factionalized one. After the Republicans won four out of five presidential elections from 1968 to 1984 and briefly took control of the Senate, the Democrats began to suspect that maybe an efficient bureaucracy was better than a collection of warring factions, and so they made an effort to emulate the Republicans.

The Republicans had taken advantage of a new bit of technology—computerized mailings. They built up a huge file of names of people who had given or might give money to the party, usually in small amounts, and used that list to raise a big budget for the national party. The Republican National Committee (RNC) used this money to run, in effect, a national political consulting firm. Money went to recruit and train Republican candidates, give them legal and financial advice, study issues and analyze voting trends, and conduct national advertising campaigns on behalf of the party as a whole.

When the Democratic National Committee (DNC) decided to play catch-up, it followed the RNC strategy. Using the same computerized direct-mail techniques, the Democratic Party committees—the National Committee, Senatorial Committee, and Congressional Committee—raised more money than ever before, though not as

national convention A meeting of party delegates held every four years.

national committee Delegates who run party affairs between national conventions.

congressional campaign committee A party committee in Congress that provides funds to members and would-be members.

national chair Day-to-day party manager elected by the national committee.

much as the Republicans. In 2004, the Democrats and their allies outspent the Republicans. The Democrats, like the Republicans, ship a lot of their national party money to state organizations to finance television ads supporting their parties.

Despite the recent enactment of campaign finance laws intended to check the influence of money on national elections, in 2004 both Democrats and Republicans redoubled efforts to raise *soft money*—that is, funds to aid parties (and their ads and polls). In the Democratic presidential primary, Howard Dean alone raised $30 million over the Internet with average contributions under $100. In 2010, new records were also set for spending on congressional races: the average cost for successful House candidates was more than $1.4 million, while the average cost for successful Senate candidates was close to $9 million. In contrast, the average numbers in 2002 were just under $1 million for successful House candidates and about $4.5 million for successful Senate candidates; and, by 2012, successful House candidates spent, on average, more than $1.5 million, while successful Senate candidates spent, on average, more than $10 million (see Figure 7.4).

National Conventions

The national committee selects the time and place of the next national convention and issues a "call" for the convention that sets forth the number of delegates each state and territory is to have and the rules under which delegates must be chosen. The number of delegates and their manner of selection

FIGURE 7.4   **Cost of Winning a Congressional Election, 2002–2012**

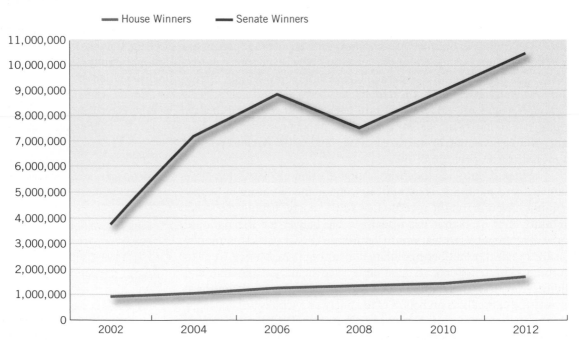

Source: Campaign Finance Institute, updated data from Vital Statistics on Congress, ed. Michael J. Malbin, Norman J. Ornstein, and Thomas E. Mann (Washington, D.C.: Brookings Institution Press, 2008); Jesse Crosson, reporting figures from the Federal Election through February 2013 as compiled by Jay Costa, "What's the Cost of a Seat in Congress?" MapLight.org (http://maplight.org/content/73190).

can significantly influence the chances of various presidential candidates, and considerable attention is thus devoted to these matters. In the Democratic Party, for example, a long struggle took place between those who wished to see southern states receive a large share of delegates to the convention, in recognition of their firm support of Democratic candidates in presidential elections, and those who preferred to see a larger share of delegates allotted to northern and western states, which, though less solidly Democratic, were larger or more liberal. A similar conflict within the Republican Party has pitted conservative Republican leaders in the Midwest against liberal ones in the East.

A compromise formula usually is chosen; nevertheless, over the years these formulas have gradually changed, shifting voting strength in the Democratic convention away from the South and toward the North and West and in the Republican convention away from the East and toward the South and Southwest. These delegate allocation formulas are but one sign (others will be mentioned later in this chapter) of the tendency of the two parties' conventions to move in opposite ideological directions—Democrats more to the left, Republicans more to the right.

The exact formula for apportioning delegates is extremely complex. For the Democrats, it takes into account the vote each state cast for Democratic candidates in past elections and the number of electoral votes of each state; for the Republicans, it takes into account the number of representatives in Congress and whether the state in past elections cast its electoral votes for the Republican presidential candidate and elected Republicans to the Senate, the House, and the governorship. Thus, the Democrats give extra delegates to large states, while the Republicans give extra ones to loyal states.

The way in which delegates are chosen can be even more important than their allocation. The Democrats, beginning in 1972, developed an elaborate set of rules designed to weaken the control over delegates by local party leaders and to increase the proportion of women, young people, African Americans, and Native Americans attending the convention. These rules were first drafted by a party commission chaired by Senator George McGovern (who later made skillful use of these new procedures in his successful bid for the Democratic presidential nomination). They were revised in 1974 by another commission, chaired by Barbara Mikulski, whose decisions were ratified by the 1974 midterm convention. After the 1976 election, a third commission, chaired by Morley Winograd, produced still another revision of the rules, which took effect in 1980. Then a fourth commission, chaired by North Carolina governor James B. Hunt, recommended in 1981 another set of rules, which became effective with the 1984 convention.

The general thrust of the work of the first three rules commissions was to broaden the antiparty changes started by the progressives at the beginning of the 20th century. Whereas the earlier reformers had tried to minimize the role of parties in the election process, those of the 1970s sought to weaken the influence of

President Obama participated in the first White House Twitter Town Hall meeting in 2011, answering questions that were tweeted to him.

KEVIN DIETSCH/UPI/Newscom

leaders within the party. In short, the newer reforms were aimed at creating *intra*party democracy as well as *inter*party democracy. Rules for the 1980 Democratic convention required:

superdelegates Party leaders and elected officials who become delegates to the national convention without having to run in primaries or caucuses.

- Equal division of delegates between men and women
- Establishment of "goals" for the representation of African Americans, Hispanics, and other groups in proportion to their presence in a state's Democratic electorate
- Open delegate selection procedures, with advance publicity and written rules
- Selection of 75 percent of the delegates at the level of the congressional district or lower
- No "unit rule" that would require all delegates to vote with the majority of their state delegation
- Restrictions on the number of party leaders and elected officials who could vote at the convention
- A requirement that all delegates pledged to a candidate vote for that candidate

In 1981, the Hunt Commission changed some of these rules—in particular, the last two—in order to increase the influence of elected officials and to make the convention a somewhat more deliberative body. The commission reserved about 14 percent of the delegate seats for party leaders and elected officials (the "**superdelegates**"), who would not have to commit themselves in advance to a presidential candidate, and it repealed the rule requiring that delegates pledged to a candidate vote for that candidate.

But the "reform" of the parties, especially the Democratic Party, has had far more profound consequences than merely helping one candidate or another. Before 1968, the Republican Party represented, essentially, white-collar voters and the Democratic Party represented blue-collar ones. After a decade of "reform," the Republican and the Democratic parties each represented two ideologically different sets of upper-middle-class voters. The Republicans came to represent the more conservative wing of the traditional middle class and the Democrats the more leftist wing of the liberal middle class.

The DNC changed the rules for the 1992 campaign. Former DNC chair Ronald H. Brown (later President Clinton's secretary of commerce) won approval for three important requirements:

- The winner-reward systems of delegate distribution—which gave the winner of a primary or caucus extra delegates—were banned. (In 1988, fifteen states used winner-reward systems, including such vote-rich states as Florida, Illinois, New Jersey, and Pennsylvania.)
- The proportional representation system was put into use. This system divides a state's publicly elected delegates among candidates who receive at least 15 percent of the vote.
- States that violate the rules are now penalized with the loss of 25 percent of their national convention delegates.

Even though the Democrats have retreated a bit from the reforms of the 1960s and 1970s, the conventions of both parties have changed fundamentally, and probably permanently. Delegates once selected by party leaders are now chosen by primary elections and grassroots caucuses. As a result, the national party conventions are no longer places where party leaders meet to bargain over the selection of their presidential candidates; they are instead places where delegates come together to ratify choices already made by party activists and primary voters.

Most Americans dislike bosses, deals, and manipulation and prefer democracy, reform, and openness. These are commendable instincts. But such instincts, unless carefully tested against practice, may mislead us into supposing that anything carried out in the name of reform is a good idea. Rules must be judged by their practical results, as well as by their conformity to some principle of fairness.

Rules affect the distribution of power: they help some people win and others lose. Later in this chapter, we shall try to assess delegate selection rules by looking more closely at how they affect who attends conventions and which presidential candidates are selected there.

State and Local Parties

While the national party structures have changed, the grassroots organizations have withered. In between, state party systems have struggled to redefine their roles.

In every state, a Democratic and a Republican state party is organized under state law. Each typically consists of a state central committee, below which are county committees and sometimes city, town, or even precinct committees. The members of these committees are chosen in a variety of ways—sometimes in primary elections, sometimes by conventions, sometimes by a building-block process whereby people elected to serve on precinct or town committees choose the members of county committees, who in turn choose state committee members.

Knowing these formal arrangements is much less helpful than knowing the actual distribution of power in each state party. In a few places strong party bosses handpick the members of these committees; in other places, powerful elected officials—key state legislators, county sheriffs, or judges—control the committees. And in many places no one is in charge, so that either the party structure is largely meaningless or it is made up of the representatives of various local factions.

To understand how power is distributed in a party, we must first know what *incentives* motivate people in a particular state or locality to become active in a party organization. Different incentives lead to different ways of organizing parties.

The Machine

A **political machine** is a party organization that recruits its members by the use of tangible incentives—money, political jobs, an opportunity to get favors from government—and is characterized by a high degree of leadership control over member activity. At one time, many local party organizations were machines, and the struggle over political jobs—patronage—was the chief concern of their members. Though Tammany Hall in New York City began as a caucus of well-to-do notables in the local Democratic Party, by the late 19th century, it had become a machine organized on the basis of political clubs in each assembly district. These clubs were composed of party workers whose job it was to get out the straight party vote in their election districts and who hoped for a tangible reward if they were successful.

And there were abundant rewards to hope for. During the 1870s, it was estimated that one out of every eight voters in New York City had a federal, state, or city job.[8] The federal bureaucracy was one important source of those jobs. The New York Customhouse alone employed thousands of people, virtually all of whom were replaced if their party lost the presidential election. The postal system was another source, and it was frankly recognized as such. When James N. Tyner became postmaster general in 1876, he was "appointed not to see that the mails were carried, but to see that Indiana was carried."[9] Elections and conventions were so frequent and the intensity of party competition so great that being a party worker was for many a full-time, paid occupation.

Well before the arrival of vast numbers of poor immigrants from Ireland, Italy, and elsewhere, old-stock Americans had perfected the machine, run up the cost of government, and systematized voting

political machine A party organization that recruits members by dispensing patronage.

ideological party A party that values principled stands on issues above all else.

fraud. Kickbacks on contracts, payments extracted from officeholders, and funds raised from businesspeople made some politicians rich, but also paid the huge bills of the elaborate party organization. When the immigrants began flooding the eastern cities, the party machines were there to provide them with all manner of services in exchange for their support at the polls: the machines were a vast welfare organization operating before the creation of the welfare state.

The abuses of the machine were well known and gradually curtailed. Stricter voter registration laws reduced fraud, civil service reforms cut down the number of patronage jobs, and competitive bidding laws made it harder to award overpriced contracts to favored businesses. The Hatch Act (passed by Congress in 1939) made it illegal for federal civil service employees to take an active part in political management or political campaigns by serving as party officers, soliciting campaign funds, running for partisan office, working in a partisan campaign, endorsing partisan candidates, taking voters to the polls, counting ballots, circulating nominating petitions, or being delegates to a party convention. (They may still vote and make campaign contributions.)

These restrictions gradually took federal employees out of machine politics, but they did not end the machines. In many cities—Chicago, Philadelphia, and Albany—ways were found to maintain the machines even though city employees were technically under the civil service. Far more important than the various progressive reforms that weakened the machines were changes among voters. As voters grew in education, income, and sophistication, they depended less and less on the advice and leadership of local party officials. And as the federal government created a bureaucratic welfare system, the parties' welfare systems declined in value.

It is easy either to scorn the political party machine as a venal and self-serving organization or to romanticize it as an informal welfare system. In truth, it was a little of both. Above all, it was a frank recognition of the fact that politics requires organization; the machine was the supreme expression of the value of organization. Even allowing for voting fraud, in elections where party machines were active, voter turnout was huge: more people participated in politics when mobilized by a party machine than when appealed to via television or good-government associations.[10] Moreover, because the party machines were interested in winning, they would subordinate any other consideration to that end. This has meant that the machines usually were willing to support the presidential candidate with the best chance of winning, regardless of his policy views (provided, of course, that he was not determined to wreck the machines once in office). Republican machines helped elect Abraham Lincoln, as well as Warren G. Harding; Democratic machines were of crucial importance in electing Franklin D. Roosevelt and John F. Kennedy.

The old-style machine is almost extinct, though important examples still can be found in the Democratic organization in Cook County (Chicago) and the Republican organization in Nassau County (New York). But a new-style machine has emerged in a few places. It is a machine in the sense that it uses money to knit together many politicians, but it is new in that the money comes not from patronage and contracts but from campaign contributions supplied by wealthy individuals and the proceeds of direct-mail campaigns.

Ideological Parties

At the opposite extreme from the machine is the **ideological party**. Where the machine values winning above all else, the ideological party values principle above all else. Where the former depends on money incentives, the latter spurns them. Where the former is hierarchical and disciplined, the latter usually is contentious and factionalized.

The most firmly ideological parties have been independent "third parties," such as the Socialist, Socialist Workers, Libertarian, and Right-to-Life parties. But there have been ideological factions within the Democratic and Republican parties as well, and in some places these ideological groups have taken over the regular parties.

solidary incentives The social rewards (sense of pleasure, status, or companionship) that lead people to join political organizations.

In the 1950s and 1960s, these ideological groups were "reform clubs" within local Democratic and Republican parties. In Los Angeles, New York, and many parts of Wisconsin and Minnesota, issue-oriented activists fought to take over the party from election-oriented regulars. Democratic reform clubs managed to defeat the head of Tammany Hall in Manhattan; similar activist groups became the dominant force in California state politics.[11] Democratic club leaders were more liberal than rank-and-file Democrats, and Republican club leaders were often more conservative than rank-and-file Republicans.

The 1960s and 1970s saw these "reform" movements replaced by more focused social movements. The reform movement was based on a generalized sense of liberalism (among Democrats) or conservatism (among Republicans). With the advent of social movements concerned with civil rights, peace, feminism, environmentalism, libertarianism, and abortion, the generalized ideology of the clubs was replaced by the specific ideological demands of single-issue activists.

The result is that in many places, the party has become a collection of people drawn from various social movements. For a candidate to win the party's support, he or she often has to satisfy the "litmus test" demands of the ideological activists in the party. Democratic senator Barbara Mikulski put it this way: "The social movements are now our farm clubs."

With social movements as their farm clubs, the big-league teams—the Democrats and Republicans at the state level—behave very differently than they did when political machines were the farm clubs. Internal factionalism is more intense, and the freedom of action of the party leader (say, the chair of the state committee) has been greatly reduced. A leader who demands too little or gives up too much, or who says the wrong thing on a key issue, is quickly accused of having "sold out." Under these circumstances, many are "leaders" in name only.

Solidary Groups

Many people who participate in state and local politics do so not in order to earn money or vindicate some cause, but simply because they find it fun. They enjoy the game, they meet interesting people, and they like the sense of being "in the know" and rubbing shoulders with the powerful. When people get together out of gregarious or game-loving instincts, they are responding to **solidary incentives**; if they form an organization, it is a solidary association.

Some of these associations were once machines. When a machine loses its patronage, some of its members—especially the older ones—may continue to serve in the organization out of a desire for camaraderie. In other cases precinct, ward, and district committees are built up on the basis of friendship networks. One study of political activists in Detroit found that most of them mentioned friendships and a liking for politics—rather than an interest in issues—as their reasons for joining the party organization.[12] Members of ward and town organizations in St. Louis County gave the same answers when asked why they joined.[13] Since patronage has declined in value and since the appeals of ideology are limited to a minority of citizens, the motivations for participating in politics have become very much like those for joining a bowling league or a bridge club.

The advantage of such groups is that they are neither corrupt nor inflexible; the disadvantage is that they often do not work very hard. Knocking on doors on a rainy November evening to try to talk people into voting for your candidate is a chore under the best of circumstances; it is especially

sponsored party A local or state political party largely supported by another organization in the community.

personal following The political support provided to a candidate on the basis of personal popularity and networks.

unappealing if you joined the party primarily because you like to attend meetings or drink coffee with your friends.[14]

Sponsored Parties

Sometimes a relatively strong party organization can be created among volunteers without heavy reliance on money or ideology and without depending entirely on people's finding the work fun. This type of **sponsored party** occurs when another organization exists in the community that can create, or at least sponsor, a local party structure. The clearest example of this is the Democratic Party in and around Detroit, which has been developed, led, and to a degree financed by the political-action arm of the United Auto Workers (UAW) union. The UAW has had a long tradition of rank-and-file activism, stemming from its formative struggles in the 1930s, and since the city virtually is a one-industry town, it was not hard to transfer some of this activism from union organizing to voter organizing.

By the mid-1950s, union members and leaders made up over three-fourths of all the Democratic Party district leaders within the city.[15] On election day, union funds were available for paying workers to canvass voters; between elections, political work on an unpaid basis was expected of union leaders. Though the UAW–Democratic Party alliance in Detroit has not always been successful in city elections (the city is nonpartisan), it has been quite successful in carrying the city for the Democratic Party in state and national elections. Not many areas have organizations as effective or as dominant as the UAW that can bolster, sponsor, or even take over the weak formal party structure. Thus sponsored local parties are not common in the United States.

Personal Following

Because most candidates can no longer count on the backing of a machine, because sponsored parties are limited to a few unionized areas, and because solidary groups are not always productive, a person wanting to get elected often will try to form a **personal following** that will work for him or her during a campaign and then disband until the next election rolls around. Sometimes a candidate tries to meld a personal following with an ideological group, especially during the primary election campaign, when candidates need the kind of financial backing and hard work that only highly motivated activists are likely to supply.

To form a personal following, the candidate must have an appealing personality, a lot of friends, or a big bank account. The Kennedy family has all three, and the electoral success of the personal followings of John F. Kennedy, Edward M. Kennedy, Robert Kennedy, and Joseph P. Kennedy II are legendary. President George H. W. Bush also established such a following. After he left office, one son (Jeb) became governor of Florida and another one (George W.) became governor of Texas and the 43rd president of the United States.

Southern politicians who operate in one-party states with few, if any, machines have become grand masters at building personal followings, such as those of the Talmadge family in Georgia, the Long family in Louisiana, and the Byrd family in Virginia. But this strategy is increasingly followed wherever party organization is weak. The key asset is to have a known political name. This has helped the electoral victories of the son of Hubert Humphrey in Minnesota, the son and daughter of Pat Brown in California, the son of Birch Bayh in Indiana, the son of George Wallace in Alabama, and the son and grandson of Robert La Follette in Wisconsin.

By the mid-1980s, the traditional party organization—one that is hierarchical, lasting, based on material incentives, and capable of influencing who gets nominated for office—existed, according to political scientist David Mayhew, in only about eight states, mostly the older states of the Northeast. Another five states, he found, had faction-ridden versions of the traditional party organization.[16] The states in the rest of the country displayed the weak party system of solidary clubs, personal followings, ideological groups, and sponsored parties. What that meant could be seen in the composition of Democratic national conventions. In 1984, over half of the delegates were drawn from the ranks of the AFL-CIO, the National Education Association, and the National Organization for Women.[17] By 2004, both national party organizations and their respective conventions had been dominated for at least two decades by ideological groups and the like.

The personal following of former President George H. W. Bush was passed on to his sons, George W. (left) and Jeb (right), both of whom became governors of large states, and the former of whom became president.

The Two-Party System

With so many different varieties of local party organizations (or nonorganizations), and with such a great range of opinion found within each party, it is remarkable that we have had only two major political parties for most of our history. In the world at large a **two-party system** is a rarity; by one estimate only 18 nations have one.[18] Most European democracies are multiparty systems. We have only two parties with any chance of winning nationally, and these parties have been, over time, rather evenly balanced—between 1888 and 2012, the Republicans won 17 presidential elections and the Democrats 15. Furthermore, whenever one party has achieved a temporary ascendancy and its rival has been pronounced dead (as were the Democrats in the first third of the 20th century and the Republicans during the 1930s and the 1960s), the "dead" party has displayed remarkable powers of recuperation, coming back to win important victories.

At the state and congressional district levels, however, the parties are not evenly balanced. For a long time, the South was so heavily Democratic at all levels of government as to be a one-party area, while upper New England and the Dakotas were strongly Republican. All regions are more competitive today than once was the case. Parties are not as competitive in state elections as they are in presidential ones. States have rarely had—at least for any extended period— political parties other than Democratic and Republican.

Scholars do not entirely agree on why the two-party system should be so permanent a feature of American political life, but two explanations are of major importance. The first has to do with the system of elections, the second with the distribution of public opinion.

two-party system An electoral system with two dominant parties that compete in national elections.

plurality system An electoral system in which the winner is the person who gets the most votes, even if he or she does not receive a majority; used in almost all American elections.

Elections at every level of government are based on the plurality, winner-take-all method. The **plurality system** means that in all elections for representative, senator, governor, or president, and in almost all elections for state legislator, mayor, or city councilor, the winner gets the *most* votes, even if he or she does not get a *majority* of all votes cast. We are so familiar with this system that we sometimes forget there are other ways of running an election. For example, one could require that the winner get a majority of the votes, thus producing runoff elections if nobody got a majority on the first try. France does this in choosing its national legislature. In the first election, candidates for parliament who win an absolute majority of the votes cast are declared elected. A week later, remaining candidates who received at least one-eighth, but less than one-half of the vote, go into a runoff election; those who then win an absolute majority are also declared elected.

The French method encourages many political parties to form, each hoping to win at least one-eighth of the vote in the first election and then to enter into an alliance with its ideologically nearest rival in order to win the runoff. In the United States, the plurality system means that a party must make all the alliances it can before the first election—there is no second chance. Hence, every party must be as broadly based as possible; a narrow, minor party has no hope of winning.

The winner-take-all feature of American elections has the same effect. Only one member of Congress is elected from each district. In many European countries, the elections are based on proportional representation. Each party submits a list of candidates for parliament, ranked in order of preference by the party leaders. The nation votes. A party winning 37 percent of the vote gets 37 percent of the seats in parliament; a party winning 2 percent of the vote gets 2 percent of the seats. Since even the smallest parties have a chance of winning something, minor parties have an incentive to organize.

The most dramatic example of the winner-take-all principle is the Electoral College (see Chapter 8). In every state but Maine and Nebraska, the candidate who wins the most popular votes in a state wins *all* of that state's electoral votes. In 1992, for example, Bill Clinton won only 45 percent of the popular vote in Missouri, but he got all of Missouri's 11 electoral votes because his two rivals (George H. W. Bush and Ross Perot) each got fewer popular votes. Minor parties cannot compete under this system. Voters often are reluctant to "waste" their votes on a minor-party candidate who cannot win.

The United States has experimented with other electoral systems. Proportional representation was used for municipal elections in New York City at one time and still is in use in Cambridge, Massachusetts. Many states have elected more than one state legislator from each district. In Illinois, for example, three legislators have been elected from each district, with each voter allowed to cast two votes, thus virtually guaranteeing that the minority party will be able to win one of the three seats. But none of these experiments has altered the national two-party system, probably because of the existence of a directly elected president chosen by a winner-take-all electoral college.

The presidency is the great prize of American politics; to win it, you must form a party with as broad appeal as possible. As a practical matter, this means there will be, in most cases, only two serious parties—one made up of those who support the party already in power, and the other made up of everybody else. Only one third party ever won the presidency—the Republican Party in 1860—and it had by then pretty much supplanted the Whig party. No third party is likely to win, or even come close to winning, the presidency anytime soon. Despite the decline in mass party attachment, among Americans who actually vote in presidential elections, party voting is almost as strong today as it was in the early 1950s. As Table 7.1 shows, in the presidential elections of 1992 through 2012, the vast majority of Democrats voted for the Democrat, and the vast majority of Republicans voted for the Republican. Meanwhile, most independents voted for the winning Republican in 1988 and 2000, and pluralities of independents voted for the winning Democrat

TABLE 7.1   Party Voting in Presidential Elections

Party Affiliation of Voter	1992			1996			2000			2004			2008			2012		
	Dem.	Rep.	Ind.	Dem.	Rep.	Ind.	Dem.	Rep.	Ind.	Dem.	Rep.	Ind.	Dem.	Rep.	Ind.	Dem.	Rep.	Ind.
Democrat	82%	8%	10%	84%	10%	5%	85%	10%	3%	89%	11%	0%	89%	10%	0%	92%	6%	1%
Republican	7	77	16	13	80	6	7	91	1	6	93	0	9	89	0	7	93	1
Independent	39	30	31	43	35	17	37	42	9	49	48	1	52	44	0	45	50	5

Source: Data from CNN exit polls for each year.

in 1992 and 1996 and again in 2008; but, in 2012, the Democrat got 45 percent of the Independent vote, while the Republican got half of it.

The second explanation for the persistence of the two-party system is found in the opinions of the voters. National surveys have found that most Americans see "a difference in what Democratic and Republican parties stand for."[19] For the most part, the majority has deemed Democrats better at handling such issues as poverty, the environment, and health care and the Republicans better at handling such issues as national defense, foreign trade, and crime; but voters generally have split on which party is best at handling the economy and taxes.[20] And when it comes to which party is best able to handle whatever individuals see as the "most important problem" facing the nation, normally about 15 percent to a quarter each choose either Democrats or Republicans, while about 45 to 55 percent answer "not much difference."[21]

As we learned in Chapter 6, however, public opinion often is dynamic, not static. Mass perceptions concerning the parties are no exception. For instance, by 2004, a few years after President George W. Bush passed his No Child Left Behind education plan, Republicans cut into the Democrats' traditional slight edge in public school support concerning which party does better on public schools. After 2004, as the war in Iraq became unpopular, Republicans lost ground to Democrats on national defense. And on certain complicated or controversial issues, such as immigration policy, opinions can shift overnight in response to real or perceived changes in policy by those the public views as each party's respective leaders or spokespersons.

Though there have been periods of bitter dissent, most of the time most citizens have agreed enough to permit them to come together into two broad coalitions. There has not been a massive and persistent body of opinion that has rejected the prevailing economic system (and thus we have not had a Marxist party with mass appeal); there has not been in our history an aristocracy or monarchy (and thus there has been no party that has sought to restore aristocrats or monarchs to power). Churches and religion have almost always been regarded as matters of private choice that lie outside politics (and thus there has not been a party seeking to create or abolish special government privileges for one church or another). In some European nations, the organization of the economy, the prerogatives of the monarchy, and the role of the church have been major issues with long and bloody histories. So divisive have these issues been that they have helped prevent the formation of broad coalition parties.

But Americans have had other deep divisions—between white and black, for example, and between North and South—and yet the two-party system has endured. This suggests that our electoral procedures are of great importance—the winner-take-all, plurality election rules have made it useless for anyone to attempt to create an all-white or an all-black national party except as an act of momentary defiance or in the hope of taking enough votes away from the two major parties to force the presidential election into the House of Representatives. (That may have been George Wallace's strategy in 1968.)

For many years, there was an additional reason for the two-party system: the laws of many states made it difficult, if not impossible, for third parties to get on the ballot. In 1968, for example, the

FIGURE 7.5 **Americans are Divided on the Need for a Third Party**

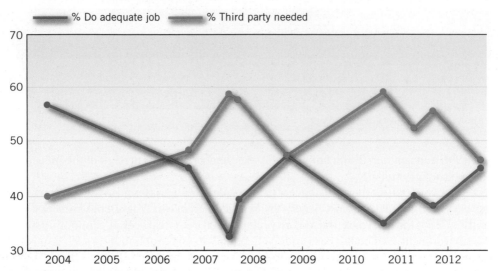

Source: Gallup Poll, *Americans Split on Need for Third Party*, September 12, 2012: http://www.gallup.com/poll/157427/americans-split-need-third-party.aspx

American Independent party of George Wallace found that it would have to collect 433,000 signatures (15 percent of the votes cast in the last statewide election) in order to get on the presidential ballot in Ohio. Wallace took the issue to the Supreme Court, which ruled, six to three, that such a restriction was an unconstitutional violation of the equal protection clause of the Fourteenth Amendment.[22] Wallace got on the ballot. In 1980, John Anderson, running as an independent, was able to get on the ballot in all 50 states; in 1992, Ross Perot did the same. But for the reasons already indicated, the two-party system will probably persist even without the aid of legal restrictions. Furthermore, the public appears ambivalent over whether a third party is needed in American politics, as a Gallup poll taken during the 2012 presidential campaign shows (see Figure 7.5).

Minor Parties

The electoral system may prevent minor parties from winning, but it does not prevent them from forming. Minor parties—usually called, erroneously, "third parties"—have been a permanent feature of American political life. Four major kinds of minor parties, with examples of each, are described in the box on pages 197–198.

The minor parties that have endured are the ideological ones. Their members feel outside the mainstream of American political life and sometimes, as in the case of various Marxist parties, look forward to a time when a revolution or some other dramatic change in the political system will vindicate them. They usually are not interested in immediate electoral success and thus persist despite their poor showing at the polls. One such party, however, the Socialist party of Eugene Debs, won nearly 6 percent of the popular vote in the 1912 presidential election. During its heyday, 1,200 candidates were elected to local offices, including 79 mayors. Part of the Socialist appeal arose from its opposition to municipal corruption, its opposition to American entry into World War I, and its critique of American society. No ideological party has ever carried a state in a presidential election.

Apart from the Republicans, who quickly became a major party, the only minor parties to carry states and thus win electoral votes were one party of economic protest (the Populists, who carried five states in 1892) and several factional parties (most recently, the States' Rights Democrats in 1948 and the American Independent party of George Wallace in 1968). Though factional parties may hope to cause the defeat of the party from which they split, they have not always been able to achieve this. Harry Truman was elected in 1948 despite the defections of both the leftist progressives, led by Henry Wallace, and the right-wing Dixiecrats, led by J. Strom Thurmond. In 1968, it seems likely that Hubert Humphrey would have lost even if George Wallace had not been in the race (Wallace voters would probably have switched to Nixon rather than to Humphrey, though of course one cannot be certain). It is quite possible, on the other hand, that a Republican might have beaten Woodrow Wilson in 1912 if the Republican Party had not split in two (the regulars supporting William Howard Taft, the progressives supporting Theodore Roosevelt).

What is striking is not that we have had so many minor parties, but that we have not had more. There have been several major political movements that did not produce a significant third party: the civil rights movement of the 1960s, the antiwar movement of the same decade, and, most important, the labor movement of the 20th century. African Americans were part of the Republican Party after the Civil War and part of the Democratic Party after the New Deal (even though the southern wing of that party for a long time kept them from voting). The antiwar movement found candidates with whom it could identify within the Democratic Party (Eugene McCarthy, Robert F. Kennedy, George McGovern), even though it was a Democratic president, Lyndon B. Johnson, who was chiefly responsible for the U.S. commitment in Vietnam. After Johnson only narrowly won the 1968 New Hampshire primary, he withdrew from the race. Unions have not tried to create a labor party—indeed, they were for a long time opposed to almost any kind of national political activity. Since labor became a major political force in the 1930s, the largest industrial unions have been content to operate as a part (a very large part) of the Democratic Party.

HOW THINGS WORK

Types of Minor Parties

1. **Ideological parties:** Parties professing a comprehensive view of American society and government radically different from the established parties. Most have been Marxist in outlook, but some are quite the opposite, such as the Libertarian party.

Examples:

Socialist party (1901 to 1960s)

Socialist Labor party (1888 to present)

Socialist Workers party (1938 to present)

Communist party (1920s to present)

Libertarian party (1972 to present)

Green party (1984 to present)

(continued)

HOW THINGS WORK (*Continued*)

2. **One-issue parties:** Parties seeking a single policy, usually revealed by their names, and avoiding other issues.

Examples:

Free-Soil party—to prevent the spread of slavery (1848–1852)

American or "Know-Nothing" party—to oppose immigration and Catholics (1856)

Prohibition party—to ban the sale of liquor (1869 to present)

Woman's party—to obtain the right to vote for women (1913–1920)

3. **Economic-protest parties:** Parties, usually based in a particular region, especially involving farmers, that protest against depressed economic conditions. These tend to disappear as conditions improve.

Examples:

Greenback party (1876–1884)

Populist party (1892–1908)

4. **Factional parties:** Parties created by a split in a major party, usually over the identity and philosophy of the major party's presidential candidate.

Examples:

Split off from the Republican party:

"Bull Moose" Progressive party (1912)

La Follette Progressive party (1924)

Split off from the Democratic Party:

States' Rights ("Dixiecrat") party (1948)

Henry Wallace Progressive party (1948)

American Independent (George Wallace) party (1968)

Split off from both Democrats and Republicans:

Reform party (Ross Perot)

Tea Party movement

One reason some potential sources of minor parties never formed such parties, in addition to the dim chance of success, is that the direct primary and the national convention made it possible for dissident elements of a major party—unless they become completely disaffected—to remain in the party and influence the choice of candidates and policies. The antiwar movement had a profound effect on the Democratic conventions of 1968 and 1972; African Americans have played a growing role in the Democratic Party, especially with the candidacy of Jesse Jackson in 1984 and 1988; only in 1972 did the unions feel that the Democrats nominated a presidential candidate (McGovern) unacceptable to them.

The impact of minor parties on American politics is hard to judge. One bit of conventional wisdom holds that minor parties develop ideas that the major parties later come to adopt. The Socialist party, for example, supposedly called for major social and economic policies that the Democrats under Roosevelt later embraced and termed the New Deal. It is possible the Democrats did steal the thunder of the Socialists, but it hardly seems likely that they did it because the Socialists had proposed these things or proved them popular. (In 1932, the Socialists received only 2 percent of the vote, and in 1936, less than one-half of 1 percent.) Roosevelt probably adopted the policies in part because he thought them correct, and in part because dissident elements within his *own* party—leaders such as Huey Long of Louisiana— were threatening to bolt the Democratic Party if it did not move to the left. Even Prohibition was adopted more as a result of the efforts of interest groups such as the Anti-Saloon League than as the consequence of its endorsement by the Prohibition Party.

The minor parties that have probably had the greatest influence on public policy have been the factional parties. Mugwumps and liberal Republicans, by bolting the regular party, may have made that party more sensitive to the issue of civil service reform; the Bull Moose and La Follette Progressive parties probably helped encourage the major parties to pay more attention to issues of business regulation and party reform; the Dixiecrat and Wallace movements probably strengthened the hands of those who wished to go slow on desegregation. The threat of a factional split is a risk that both major parties must face, and it is in the efforts that each makes to avoid such splits that one finds the greatest impact of minor parties, or at least that was the case in the 20th century.

In 1992 and again in 1996, Ross Perot led the most successful recent third-party movement. It began as United We Stand America and was later renamed the Reform Party. Perot's appeal seemed to reflect a growing American dissatisfaction with the existing political parties and a heightened demand for bringing in a leader who would "run the government without politics." In 2000 and again in 2004, Ralph Nader led the Green party and rallied supporters by promising to remain above partisan politics and avoid making compromises if elected. Of course, it is no more possible to take politics out of governing than it is to take churches out of religion. Though unrealistic, some people seem to want policies without bargaining.

The Tea Party movement that has evolved in recent years is not a single national party, but it shares characteristics with minor parties: Tea Party supporters were active in the 2010 congressional midterm elections, and they seek to influence the national policy agenda. Although there are many groups within the movement with differing views, Tea Party activists seem to agree on the need to reduce taxes, government spending, budget deficits, and the national debt. They appear to have some influence within the Republican Party, where they have overturned a few establishment candidates for office whom they viewed as insufficiently dedicated to fiscal discipline. Whether the movement will turn into a cohesive minor party that shapes the major-party agenda remains to be seen.

The Rise of Interest Groups

The weakness of our political parties, the size and diversity of our country, and the decentralizing effects of our Constitution make it certain that interest groups will be an important way for people to have their voices heard. But while interest groups are as old as the republic itself, the number of interest groups has grown rapidly since 1960, and the number of interest groups that have lobbyists working full-time in Washington has reached new highs in just the last decade.

During the 1770s, many groups arose to agitate for American independence; during the 1830s and 1840s, the number of religious associations increased sharply, and the antislavery movement began. In the 1860s, craft-based trade unions emerged in significant numbers, farmers formed the Grange, and various fraternal organizations were born. In the 1880s and 1890s, business associations proliferated.

The great era of organization building, however, was in the first two decades of the 20th century. Within this 20-year period, many of the best-known and largest associations with an interest in national politics were formed: the Chamber of Commerce, the National Association of Manufacturers, the American Medical Association, the National Association for the Advancement of Colored People (NAACP), the Urban League, the American Farm Bureau Federation, the Farmers' Union, the National Catholic Welfare Conference, the American Jewish Committee, and the Anti-Defamation League.

The wave of interest group formation that occurred in the 1960s led to the emergence of environmental, consumer, and political reform organizations such as those sponsored by consumer activist Ralph Nader. In 1973, a new federal campaign finance law made it legal for interest groups to create political action committees. A political action committee (PAC) is an organization created by a business firm, labor union, trade association, or ideological group that recruits members from whom it obtains campaign contributions. By the mid-1990s, there were about six times as many PACs (more than 4,000) as there had been in the mid-1970s, about a quarter of them ideological in character.

The growth in ideological groups has been equaled and, of late, exceeded only by the growth in business groups. For instance, between 1981 and 2005, the number of full-time and part-time lobbyists— (a lobbyist tries to influence legislation on behalf of an interest group) in Washington representing just the S&P 500 corporations increased from 1,475 to 2,765.[23] Today, about 14,000 lobbyists for business, union, and other groups are listed in the (over 2,000-page) Washington Directory, up from about 7,000 lobbyists (and 531 pages) three decades ago. Adjusted for inflation, the roughly $3.5 billion spent on lobbying in 2009 was nearly seven times the amount spent on lobbying a quarter-century earlier.[24]

Why are associations in general and political interest groups in particular created more rapidly in some periods than in others? After all, there have always been farmers in this country, but there were no national farm organizations until the latter part of the 19th century. Blacks were victimized by various white-supremacy policies from the end of the Civil War on, but the NAACP did not emerge until 1910. Men and women worked in factories for decades before industrial unions were formed. Every political era featured activists who believed strongly in liberal or conservative ideology, but only in recent decades have ideological groups become so pervasive. Organized business interests have battled organized labor interests over public policy for more than a hundred years, but only in recent decades has the big business lobbying presence in Washington expanded so dramatically both in absolute terms and relative to big labor.

At least four factors help explain the rise of interest groups. The first consists of broad economic developments that create new interests and redefine old ones. Farmers had little reason to become organized for political activity so long as most of them consumed what they produced. The importance of regular political activity became evident only after most farmers began to produce cash crops for sale in markets that were unstable or affected by forces (the weather, the railroads, foreign competition) that farmers could not control. Similarly, for many decades most workers were craftspeople working alone or in small groups. Such unions as existed were little more than craft guilds interested in protecting members' jobs and in training apprentices. The impetus for large, mass-membership unions did not exist until there arose mass-production industry operated by large corporations.

Second, government policy itself helps to create interest groups. Wars create veterans, who in turn demand pensions and other benefits. The first large veterans' organization, the Grand Army of the Republic, was made up of Union veterans of the Civil War. By the 1920s, these men were receiving about a quarter of a billion dollars a year from the government, and naturally they created organizations to watch over the distribution of this money. The federal government encouraged the formation of the American Farm Bureau Federation (AFBF) by paying for county agents who would serve the needs of farmers under the supervision of local farm organizations; these county bureaus eventually came together as the AFBF. The Chamber of Commerce was launched at a conference attended by President William Howard Taft. Professional societies, such as those made up of lawyers and doctors, became important in part because state governments gave to such groups the authority to decide who was qualified to become a lawyer or a doctor.

Tea Party activists protest in Washington, D.C., against the Internal Revenue Service's extra scrutiny of their organizations.

Workers had a difficult time organizing as long as the government—by the use of injunctions enforced by the police and the army—prevented strikes. Unions, especially those in mass-production industries, began to flourish after Congress passed laws in the 1930s that prohibited the use of injunctions in private labor disputes, that required employers to bargain with unions, and that allowed a union representing a majority of the workers in a plant to require all workers to join it.[25]

Third, political organizations do not emerge automatically, even when government policy permits them and social circumstances seem to require them. Somebody must exercise leadership, often at substantial personal cost. These organizational entrepreneurs are found in greater numbers at certain times than at others. Often they are young, caught up in a social movement, drawn to the need for change, and inspired by some political or religious doctrine.

Antislavery organizations were created in the 1830s and 1840s by enthusiastic young people influenced by a religious revival sweeping the country. The period from 1890 to 1920, when so many national organizations were created, was a time when the college-educated middle class was growing rapidly. (The number of men and women who received college degrees each year tripled between 1890 and 1920.[26]) During this era, natural science and fundamentalist Christianity were locked in a bitter contest, with the Gospels and Darwinism offering competing ideas about personal salvation and social progress. The 1960s, when many new organizations were born, was a decade in which young people were powerfully influenced by the civil rights and antiwar movements and when college enrollments more than doubled.

Finally, the more government does, the more interest groups will arise or expand and try to influence public policy. Most Washington offices representing corporations, labor unions, and trade and professional associations were established before 1960—in some cases many decades before—because it was during the 1930s or even earlier that the government began making policies important to business and labor. The great majority of "public-interest" lobbies (those concerned with the environment or consumer protection), social welfare associations, and organizations concerned with civil rights, the elderly, and the disabled established offices in Washington after major new federal laws in these respective areas were enacted.

The most recent and dramatic example is what happened in the post-9/11 years after the USA Patriot Act was enacted in 2001 and the Department of Homeland Security (DHS) was created in 2002. By 2010,

LANDMARK CASES

Lobbying Congress

• *United States v. Harriss* (1954): The Constitution protects the lobbying of Congress, but the government may require information from groups that try to influence legislation.

with billions of dollars a year in federal funding for the purpose flowing, more than 500 new private companies specializing in work related to security and counterterrorism had come into being, and most of another 1,400 or so private companies that existed and did related work prior to 2001 had expanded.[27] New lobbies quickly formed to represent those firms and keep their homeland security grants and contracts coming; for example, the "full body scanner" lobby represents firms that sell body-scanning equipment used in airports to a DHS subunit, the Transportation Security Administration (TSA).[28] Moreover, many local governments, from big cities to small towns, have hired lobbyists to work on getting or sustaining their fair share of federal homeland security money.

HOW THINGS WORK

Incentives to Join

Every interest group faces a free rider problem.[29] That is, many people who do not give it money or join as members are likely to benefit if the organization achieves its goal. They ride free on the organization's efforts. To overcome this, interest groups must offer people some incentive to join them. There are three kinds.

Solidary incentives are the sense of pleasure, status, or companionship that arises out of meeting together in small groups. Such rewards are extremely important, but because they tend to be available only from face-to-face contact, national interest groups offering them often have to organize themselves as coalitions of small local units. Forming organizations made up of small local chapters is probably easier in the United States than in Europe because of the great importance of local government in our federal system. There is plenty for a PTA, an NAACP, or a League of Women Voters to do in its own community, and so its members can be kept busy with local affairs while the national staff pursues larger goals.

A second kind of incentive consists of material incentives—that is, money, or things and services readily valued in monetary terms. Farm organizations have recruited many members by offering a wide range of services. Similarly, the American Association of Retired Persons (AARP) has recruited tens of millions of members by supplying them with everything from low-cost life insurance and mail-order discount drugs to tax advice and group travel plans. Almost half of the nation's population aged 50 and older—one out of every four registered voters— belongs to the AARP.

The third—and most difficult—kind of incentive is the purpose of the organization. Many associations rely chiefly on this purposive incentive—the appeal of their stated goals—to recruit members. If the attainment of those goals will also benefit people who do not join, individuals who do join will have to be those who feel passionately about the goal, who have a strong sense of duty

(continued)

HOW THINGS WORK (*Continued*)

(or who cannot say no to a friend who asks them to join), or for whom the cost of joining is so small that they are indifferent to joining or not. Organizations that attract members by appealing to their interest in a coherent set of (usually) controversial principles are sometimes called ideological interest groups.

When the purpose of the organization, if attained, will principally benefit nonmembers, it is customary to call the group a public-interest lobby. (Whether the public at large will really benefit, of course, is a matter of opinion, but at least the group members think they are working selflessly for the common good.)

Though some public-interest lobbies may pursue relatively noncontroversial goals (for example, persuading people to vote or raising money to house orphans), the most visible of these organizations are highly controversial. It is precisely the controversy that attracts the members, or at least those members who support one side of the issue. Many of these groups can be described as markedly liberal or decidedly conservative in outlook.

Interest Groups and Social Movements

Because it is difficult to attract people with purposive incentives, interest groups employing them tend to arise out of social movements. A social movement is a widely shared demand for change in some aspect of the social or political order. The civil rights movement of the 1960s was such an event, as was the environmentalist movement of the 1970s.

A social movement need not have liberal goals. In the 19th century, for example, there were various nativist movements that sought to reduce immigration to this country or to keep Catholics or Masons out of public office. Broad-based religious revivals are social movements. In recent years, the conservative Tea Party movement, which has taken hold around issues like restraining government growth, has played a role in both local and national elections.[30]

No one is quite certain why social movements arise. At one moment, people are largely indifferent to some issue; at another moment, many of these same people care passionately about religion, civil rights, immigration, or conservation. A social movement may be triggered by a disaster (an oil spill on the Santa Barbara beaches helped launch the environmental movement), the dramatic and widely publicized activities of a few leaders (lunch counter sit-ins helped stimulate the civil rights movement), or the coming of age of a new generation that takes up a cause advocated by eloquent writers, teachers, or evangelists.

Whatever its origin, the effect of a social movement is to increase the value some people attach to purposive incentives. As a consequence, new interest groups are formed that rely on these incentives.

The environmental movement provides a good example of how a social movement gives rise to interest groups formed from reliance on purposive incentives. In the 1890s, as a result of the emergence of conservation as a major issue, the Sierra Club was organized. In the 1930s, conservation once again became popular, and the Wilderness Society and the National Wildlife Federation took form. In the 1960s and 1970s, environmental issues again came to the fore, and we saw the emergence of the Environmental Defense Fund and Environmental Action.

The smallest of these organizations (Environmental Action and the Environmental Defense Fund) tend to have the most liberal members. This often is the case with organizations that arise from social movements. A movement will spawn many organizations. The most passionately aroused people will be the fewest in number, and they will gravitate toward the organizations that take the most extreme positions; as a result, these organizations are small, but vociferous. The more numerous and less passionate people will gravitate toward more moderate, less vociferous organizations, which will tend to be larger.

As happens over the years to most politically successful movements, the environmental movement has become more fragmented than it was in the 1970s. Different leading voices and organizations within it have begun to advocate somewhat different policy approaches to achieving the same basic (in this case, environmental protection and sustainability) goals.[31]

Similarly, there have been several feminist social movements in this country's history—in the 1830s, in the 1890s, in the 1920s, and in the 1960s. Each period brought about new organizations, some of which have endured to the present. For example, the League of Women Voters was founded in 1920 to educate and organize women for the purpose of effectively using their newly won right to vote.

Though a strong sense of purpose may lead to the creation of organizations, each will strive to find some incentive that will sustain it over the long haul. These permanent incentives will affect how the organization participates in politics.

At least three kinds of feminist organizations exist. First, there are those that rely chiefly on solidary incentives, enroll middle-class women with relatively high levels of schooling, and tend to support those causes that command the widest support among women generally. The League of Women Voters and the Federation of Business and Professional Women are examples. Both supported the campaign to ratify the Equal Rights Amendment (ERA), but as Jane Mansbridge has observed in her history of the ERA, they were uneasy with the kind of intense, partisan fighting displayed by some other women's organizations and with the tendency of more militant groups to link the ERA to other issues, such as abortion. The reason for their uneasiness is clear: to the extent they relied on solidary incentives, they had a stake in avoiding issues and tactics that would divide their membership or reduce the extent to which membership provided camaraderie and professional contacts.[32]

Second, there are women's organizations that attract members with purposive incentives. The National Organization for Women (NOW) and the National Abortion Rights Action League (NARAL) are two of the largest such groups, though there are many smaller ones. Because they rely on purposes, these organizations must take strong positions, tackle divisive issues, and employ militant tactics. Anything

Zuma Press/Alamy

After the horrific school shooting in Newtown, Connecticut, in December 2012, thousands of people participated in the March on Washington for Gun Control.

less would turn off the committed feminists who make up the rank and file and contribute the funds. But because these groups take controversial stands, they are constantly embroiled in internal quarrels between those who think they have gone too far and those who think they have not gone far enough, between women who want NOW or NARAL to join with lesbian and socialist organizations and those who want them to steer clear. Moreover, as Jane Mansbridge showed, purposive organizations often cannot make their decisions stick on the local level (local chapters will do pretty much as they please).[33]

The third kind of women's organization is the caucus that takes on specific issues that have some material benefit to women.

The Women's Equity Action League (WEAL) is one such group. Rather than relying on membership dues for financial support, it obtains grants from foundations and government agencies. Freed of the necessity of satisfying a large rank-and-file membership, WEAL has concentrated its efforts on bringing lawsuits aimed at enforcing or enlarging the legal rights of women in higher education and other institutions. In electoral politics, the National Women's Political Caucus (officially nonpartisan, but generally liberal and Democratic) and the National Federation of Republican Women (openly supportive of the Republican Party) work to get more women active in politics and more women elected or appointed to office.

The feminist movement has, of course, spawned an antifeminist movement, and thus feminist organizations have their antifeminist counterparts. The campaign by NOW for the ERA was attacked by a women's group called STOP ERA; the pro-choice position of NARAL has been challenged by the various organizations associated with the right-to-life movement. These opposition groups have their own tactical problems, which arise in large part from their reliance on different kinds of incentives. In the chapter on civil rights, we shall see how the conflict between these opposing groups shaped the debate over the ERA.

Business Interests

Despite the rise of social movements and the proliferation of public-interest lobbies, for-profit businesses dominate the interest group landscape. There are two reasons for this: first, well-off people are more likely than poor people to join and be active in interest groups; and second, interest groups representing business and the professions are much more numerous and better financed than organizations representing minorities, consumers, or the disadvantaged.

Farmers once had great influence in Congress and could get their way with a few telephone calls. Today, they often must use mass-protest methods.

One study found that between 1981 and 2006, the ratio of business lobbyists to union plus public-interest lobbyists prone to oppose business interests rose from about 12 to 1 to nearly 16 to 1; and 72 percent of all money spent on lobbying is spent by for-profit companies and their associations.[34] Some now argue that the nation's 2007–2010 economic crises were due in part to the disproportionate political influence wielded during the preceding decade by rich Wall Street executives and related business interests. There is some truth to this view. In 1999, corporate lawyers and lobbyists won a long legislative battle to repeal the Banking Act of 1933, better known as the Glass-Steagall Act, which strictly separated investment from commercial banking and imposed many other restrictions on financial companies. The repeal permitted the home mortgage business to change in ways that made it easier to offer risky loans to people with poor credit histories, and it gave birth to new financial products and services that were weakly regulated by government and incomprehensible to most consumers.

But note that the 1933 law, albeit with certain changes made in subsequent decades, remained on the books for more than 60 years before it was repealed. And—strongly opposed though it was by myriad powerful business interests—today the Wall Street Reform and Consumer Protection Act of 2010 is law. Better known as Dodd-Frank, this law did not restore the Glass-Steagall Act's strict separation between depository banking and financial trading, but it did tighten regulations on virtually all financial companies and broaden consumer protections for all, including first-time mortgage-seekers and small investors.

As this example suggests, even though big business executives and other wealthy people typically have more (and more high-priced) lobbyists looking out for their interests than other citizens do, business interests are often divided and corporate lobbyists can often be found on opposite side of major economic policy, international trade, or tax reform issues.

HOW THINGS WORK

The Activities of Interest Groups

Moreover, size and wealth are no longer entirely accurate measures of an interest group's influence—if indeed they ever were. Depending on the issue, the key to political influence may be the ability to generate a dramatic newspaper headline, mobilize a big letter-writing campaign, stage a protest demonstration, file a suit in federal court to block (or compel) some government action, or quietly supply information to key legislators. All of these things require organization, but only some of them require big or expensive organizations.

Information

Of all these tactics, the single most important one—in the eyes of virtually every lobbyist and every academic student of lobbying—is supplying credible information. The reason why information is so valuable is that, to busy legislators and bureaucrats, information is in short supply. Legislators in particular must take positions on a staggering number of issues about which they cannot possibly become experts.

Nobody needs a lobbyist to access publicly available information via the Internet, but politicians often covet information that is highly detailed, specific, up-to-date, and not publicly available in any easy-to-find form. This kind of information ordinarily will be gathered only by a group that

(continued)

HOW THINGS WORK (*Continued*)

has a strong interest in some issue. Lobbyists, for the most part, are not flamboyant, party-giving arm-twisters; they are specialists who gather information (favorable to their clients, naturally) and present it in as organized, persuasive, and factual a manner as possible. All lobbyists no doubt exaggerate, but few can afford to misrepresent the facts or mislead a legislator, and for a very simple reason: almost every lobbyist must develop and maintain the confidence of a legislator over the long term, with an eye on tomorrow's issues as well as today's.

Misrepresentation or bad advice can embarrass a legislator who accepts it or repel one who detects it, leading to distrust of the lobbyist. Maintaining contacts and channels of communication is vital; to that end, maintaining trust is essential.

The value of the information provided by a lobbyist often is greatest when the issue is fairly narrow, involving only a few interest groups or a complex economic or technical problem. The value of information, and thus the power of the lobbyist, is likely to be least when the issue is one of broad and highly visible national policy.

Public officials not only want technical information, but they also want political cues. A political cue is a signal telling the official what values are at stake in an issue—who is for, who is against a proposal—and how that issue fits into his or her own set of political beliefs. Some legislators feel comfortable when they are on the liberal side of an issue, and others feel comfortable when they are on the conservative side, especially when they are not familiar with the details of the issue. A liberal legislator will look to see whether the AFL-CIO, the NAACP, and various consumer organizations favor a proposal; if so, that is often all he or she has to know. If these liberal groups are split, then the legislator will worry about the matter and try to look into it more closely. Similarly, a conservative legislator will feel comfortable taking a stand on an issue if the Chamber of Commerce, the National Rifle Association, and various business associations are in agreement about it; he or she will feel less comfortable if such conservative groups are divided. As a result of this process, lobbyists often work together in informal coalitions based on general political ideology.

One important way in which these cues are made known is by ratings that interest groups make of legislators. These are regularly compiled by the AFL-CIO (on who is pro-labor), by the Americans for Democratic Action (on who is liberal), by the Americans for Constitutional Action (on who is conservative), by the Consumer Federation of America (on who is pro-consumer), and by the League of Conservation Voters (on who is pro-environment). These ratings are designed to generate public support for (or opposition to) various legislators. They can be helpful sources of information, but they are sometimes biased by the arbitrary determination of what constitutes a liberal, pro-consumer, or conservative vote.

Information can be linked to influence. Lobbyists not only tell members of Congress facts, but they also learn from these members what Washington is doing and then look for ways to sell that information to their clients. What often results is an earmark, that is, a provision in a law that provides a direct benefit to a client without the benefit having been reviewed on the merits by all of Congress.

Earmarks have always existed, but they became much more common in the 1970s and later. There are two reasons for this. First, the federal government was doing much more and thus affecting more parts of society. Second, lobbying organizations figured out that clients would pay for information about how to convert some bit of federal activity to their benefit.

Money and PACs

Contrary to popular suspicions, money is probably one of the less effective ways by which interest groups advance their causes. That was not always the case. Only a few decades ago, powerful interests used their bulging wallets to buy influence in Congress. The passage of campaign finance legislation in the early 1970s changed that. The laws had two effects. First, they sharply restricted the amount any interest could give to a candidate for federal office (see Chapter 8). Second, they made legal the creation by organizations of political action committees (PACs) that could make political contributions.

Once PACs became legal, they grew rapidly in numbers. Today there are more than 4,500 PACs. Over the last few years, so-called leadership PACs and super PACs have proliferated and received media attention. The former type of PAC is headed by a member of Congress who raises money for other candidates, while the latter type of PAC is an "independent, expenditure-only committee" that is not allowed to coordinate with candidates or political party leaders. Among the best-known leadership PACs is the one formed by former House Speaker Nancy Pelosi to help fund Democratic candidates (Team Majority). Among the best-known super PACs is the one launched by former White House aide to President George W. Bush, Karl Rove, to assist Republican candidates (American Crossroads). The leadership PACs are a type of so-called nonconnected PACs that do not act on behalf of a particular corporation, labor union, or trade association, but are instead commonly organized around ideological views, particular issues, or leading political personalities. Still, the vast majority of PACs, including most of the 50 largest PAC contributors, are traditional so-called connected PACs, set up by and connected to business corporations, labor unions, or other interest groups that raise and spend campaign money from voluntary donations. The top ten PAC contributors alone combine to give millions of dollars a year to candidates of their choice (see Table 7.2). But there are strict limits on how much a member can contribute and how much the PAC can give to candidates and parties. How they work is shown in Table 7.3.

TABLE 7.2 Ten Largest PAC Contributors, 2011–2012

PAC Affiliation	Amount
American Federation of Teachers, AFL-CIO Committee on Political Education	$7,274,645
Senate Conservatives Fund	$6,488,757
Committee on Letter Carriers Political Education (Letter Carriers Political Action Fund)	$5,833,823
International Brotherhood of Electrical Workers Political Action Committee	$4,836,450
Honeywell International Political Action Committee	$4,809,325
National Association of Realtors Political Action Committee	$4,774,993
SEIU Cope (Service Employees International Union Committee on Political Education)	$4,618,455
D.R.I.V.E. (Democrat, Republican, Independent Voter Education—The PAC of the International Brotherhood)	$4,526,410
National Air Traffic Controllers Association PAC	$4,407,550
Engineers Political Education Committee (EPEC)/International Union of Operating Engineers	$4,241,689

Source: Federal Election Commission, "Top 50 PACs by Contributions to Candidates and Other Committees, January 1, 2011–December 31, 2012," 2013.

TABLE 7.3 Political Action Committees (PACs)

Can be formed by:
• Business firms
• Labor unions
• Trade associations
• Ideological organizations
Must have at least 50 individual members
• Each member can give up to $5,000 per election
• The sponsoring firm, union, association, or ideological group cannot contribute money
A PAC that contributes to at least five candidates may contribute the following:
• $5,000 to any federal candidate in any election
• $15,000 to any national political party
• $5,000 to any state or local party
(Non-multicandidate PACs have different contribution limits.)
Where the money goes:
• Business PACs give slightly more to Republicans than to Democrats
• Labor unions give more than 90 percent to Democrats
• Ideological PACs give to Democrats and Republicans in about equal amounts

Almost any kind of organization—corporation, labor union, trade association, public-interest lobby, citizens group—can form a PAC. Over half of all PACs are sponsored by corporations or trade associations, about 6 percent by labor unions, and the rest by various groups, including independent and ideological ones. The rise of ideological PACs has been the most remarkable development in interest group activity in recent years. At various points over the last several decades, they have increased in number at a faster rate than business or labor PACs, and in several elections they raised more money than either business or labor.

In the 2011–2012 election cycle, PACs gave more than $437 million to candidates running for the House and Senate. The PACs that gave the most money to candidates included business organizations, labor unions, and groups that represented banks, realtors, and public employees. Incumbents received more PAC money than challengers. Labor PACs gave almost exclusively to Democrats. Business PACs favored Republicans.[35]

Both parties have become dependent on PAC money. Still, the popular image of rich PACs stuffing huge sums into political campaigns and thereby buying the attention and possibly the favors of the grateful candidates is a bit overdrawn. For one thing, the typical PAC contribution is rather small. The average PAC donation to a House candidate is only a few hundred dollars. Most PACs spread small sums of money over many candidates, and despite their great growth in numbers and expenditures, PACs still provide only about one-third of all the money spent by candidates for the House ($356 million of about $1.1 billion in 2011–2012). Moreover, scholars have yet to find systematic evidence that PAC contributions generally affect how members of Congress vote. On most issues, how legislators vote can be explained primarily by their general ideological outlooks and the characteristics of their constituents; how much PAC money they have received turns out to be a small factor. On the other hand, when an issue arises in which most of their constituents have no interest and ideology provides little guidance, there is a slight statistical correlation between PAC contributions and votes. But even here the correlation may be misleading. The same groups that give money also wage intensive lobbying campaigns, flooding representatives with information, press releases, and letters from interested constituents.

In 2010, in *Citizens United v. Federal Election Commission*, the U.S. Supreme Court struck down as unconstitutional provisions of a 2002 federal campaign finance law that prohibited independent expenditures by business corporations, nonprofit organizations, and unions to fund "electioneering communications" within 30 days of a primary election or 60 days of a general election. This decision was the seedbed for the aforementioned super PACs, but it is too soon to know whether, as many observers seem to fear, the decision will increase even more the vast amounts of money that interests groups of all sorts spend to influence lawmakers. But even if that fear is realized, it is not entirely certain that increased expenditures will result in increased influence over how lawmakers vote.

The "Revolving Door"

Every year, hundreds of people leave important jobs in the federal government to take more lucrative positions in private industry. Some go to work as lobbyists, others as consultants to business, still others as key executives in corporations, foundations, and universities. Many people worry that this "revolving door" may give private interests a way of improperly influencing government decisions. If a federal official uses his or her government position to do something for a corporation in exchange for a cushy job after leaving government, or if a person who has left government uses his or her personal contacts in Washington to get favors for private parties, then the public interest may suffer.

Over the years, more than a few scandals have emerged concerning corrupt dealings between federal department officials and industry executives. Many have involved contractors or their consultants bribing procurement officials. Far more common, however, have been major breakdowns in the procurement process itself. For example, in 2006, the Department of Homeland Security revealed the results from an internal audit.[36] In the previous year, the department had spent $17.5 billion on contracts for airport security, radiation-monitor detectors, and other goods and services. But records for nearly three dozen contracts were completely missing, and records for many other contracts lacked evidence that the department had followed federal rules in negotiating best prices. (The internal audit itself was performed by private consultants, presumably in compliance with all relevant rules.)

HOW THINGS WORK

Public-Interest Law Firms

A special kind of public-interest lobby is an organization that advances its cause by bringing lawsuits to challenge existing practices or proposed regulations. A public-interest law firm will act in one of two ways: First, it will find someone who has been harmed by some public or private policy and bring suit on his or her behalf. Second, it will file a brief with a court supporting somebody else's lawsuit (this is called an amicus curiae brief; it is explained in Chapter 12).

(continued)

HOW THINGS WORK (*Continued*)

Here are some examples of liberal and conservative public-interest law firms:

Liberal	*Conservative*
American Civil Liberties Union	Atlantic Legal Foundation
Asian American Legal Defense Fund	The Center for Individual Rights
Lawyers' Committee for Civil Rights	Center for Law and Justice
Mexican American Legal Defense Fund	Institute for Justice
NAACP Legal Defense and Education Fund	National Legal Center for the Public Interest
Natural Resources Defense Council	Pacific Legal Foundation
Women's Legal Defense Fund	Washington Legal Foundation

Civil Disobedience

Public displays and disruptive tactics—protest marches, sit-ins, picketing, and violence—have always been a part of American politics. Indeed, they were among the favorite tactics of the American colonists seeking independence in 1776.

Both ends of the political spectrum have used display, disruption, and violence. On the left feminists, antislavery agitators, coal miners, autoworkers, welfare mothers, African Americans, antinuclear power groups, public housing tenants, the American Indian Movement, the Students for a Democratic Society, and the Weather Underground have created "trouble" ranging from peaceful sit-ins at segregated lunch counters to bombings and shootings. On the right, the Ku Klux Klan has used terror, intimidation, and murder; parents opposed to forced busing of schoolchildren have demonstrated; business firms have used strong-arm squads against workers; right-to-life groups have blockaded abortion clinics; and an endless array of "anti-" groups (anti-Catholics, anti-Masons, anti-Jews, anti-immigrants, anti-saloons, anti-blacks, anti-protesters, and probably even anti-antis) have taken their disruptive turns on stage. These various activities are not morally the same—a sit-in demonstration is quite different from a lynching—but politically they constitute a similar problem for a government official.

There is of course a long history of the use of disruptive methods by "proper" people. For example, in a movement that began in England at the turn of the 20th century and then spread to America, feminists would chain themselves to lampposts or engage in what we now call "sit-ins" as part of a campaign to win the vote for women. The object then was much the same as the object of similar tactics today: to disrupt the working of some institution so that it is forced to negotiate with you, or, failing that, to enlist the sympathies of third parties (the media, other interest groups) who will come to your aid and press your target to negotiate with you, or, failing that, to goad the police into making attacks and arrests so that martyrs are created.

The civil rights and antiwar movements of the 1960s gave experience in these methods to thousands of young people and persuaded others of the effectiveness of such methods under certain conditions. Though these movements have abated or disappeared, their veterans and emulators have

HOW THINGS WORK

Conflict of Interest

In 1978, a new federal law, the Ethics in Government Act, codified and broadened the rules governing possible conflicts of interest among senior members of the executive branch. The key provisions were as follows.

The president, vice president, and top-ranking (GS-16 and above) executive branch employees must each year file a public financial disclosure report that lists:

- The source and amount of all earned income as well as income from stocks, bonds, and property; the worth of any investments or large debts; and the source of a spouse's income, if any

- Any position held in business, labor, or certain nonprofit organizations

Employment after government service is restricted. Former executive branch employees may *not:*

- Represent anyone before their former agencies in connection with any matter that the former employees had been involved in before leaving the government

- Appear before an agency, for two years after leaving government service, on matters that came within the former employees' official sphere of responsibility, even if they were not personally involved in the matter

- Represent anyone on any matter before their former agencies, for one year after leaving them, even if the former employees had no connection with the matter while in the government

In addition, another law prohibits bribery. It is illegal to ask for, solicit, or receive anything of value in return for being influenced in the performance of one's duties.

Finally, an executive order forbids outside employment. An official may not hold a job or take a fee, even for lecturing or writing, if such employment or income might create a conflict of interest or an apparent conflict of interest.

Sources: National Journal (November 19, 1977): 1796–1803; *Congressional Quarterly Weekly Report* (October 28, 1978): 3121–3127.

put such tactics to new uses—trying to block the construction of a nuclear power plant, for example, or occupying the office of a Cabinet secretary to obtain concessions for a particular group.

Government officials dread this kind of trouble. They usually find themselves in a no-win situation. If they ignore the disruption, they are accused of being "insensitive," "unresponsive," or "arrogant." If they give in to the demonstrators, they encourage more demonstrations by proving that this is a useful tactic. If they call the police, they run the risk of violence and injuries, followed not only by bad publicity, but also by lawsuits.

Regulating Interest Groups

Interest group activity is a form of political speech protected by the First Amendment to the Constitution: it cannot lawfully be abolished or even much curtailed. In 1946, Congress passed the Federal Regulation of Lobbying Act, which requires groups and individuals seeking to influence legislation to register with the secretary of the Senate and the clerk of the House and to file quarterly financial reports. The Supreme Court upheld the law, but restricted its application to lobbying efforts involving direct contacts with members of Congress.[37] More general "grassroots" interest group activity may not be restricted by the government. The 1946 law had little practical effect. Not all lobbyists took the trouble to register, and there was no guarantee that the financial statements were accurate. There was no staff in charge of enforcing the law.

After years of growing popular dissatisfaction with Congress, prompted in large measure by the (exaggerated) view that legislators were the pawns of powerful special interests, Congress in late 1995 unanimously passed a bill that tightened up the registration and disclosure requirements. Signed by the president, the law restated the obligation of lobbyists to register with the House and Senate, but it broadened the definition of a lobbyist to include the following:

People celebrate after the Supreme Court overturns the Defense of Marriage Act, ruling that supporters of California's Proposition 8 prohibiting same-sex marriage did not have standing in the case.

- People who spend at least 20 percent of their time lobbying
- People who are paid at least $5,000 in any six-month period to lobby
- Corporations and other groups that spend more than $20,000 in any six-month period on their own lobbying staffs

The law covered people and groups who lobbied the executive branch and congressional staffers as well as elected members of Congress, and it included law firms that represent clients before the government. Twice a year, all registered lobbyists were required to report the following:

- The names of their clients
- Their income and expenditures
- The issues on which they worked

The registration and reporting requirements did not, however, extend to so-called grassroots organizations—that is, campaigns (sometimes led by volunteers, sometimes by hired professionals) to mobilize citizens to write or call the government about some issue. Nor was any new enforcement organization created, although congressional officials could refer violations to the Justice Department for investigation. Fines for breaking the law could amount to $50,000. In addition, the law barred tax-exempt, nonprofit advocacy groups that lobby from getting federal grants.

Just as the Republicans moved expeditiously to pass new regulations on interest groups and lobbying when they regained majorities in Congress in the November 1994 elections, the Democrats' first order of business after retaking Congress in the November 2006 elections was to adopt sweeping reforms. Beginning March 1, 2007, many new regulations took effect, including the following:

- No gifts of any value from registered lobbyists or firms that employ lobbyists
- No reimbursement for travel costs from registered lobbyists or firms that employ lobbyists
- No reimbursement for travel costs, no matter the source, if the trip is in any part organized or requested by a registered lobbyist or firm that employs lobbyists

Strictly speaking, these and related new rules mean that a House member cannot go on a "fact-finding" trip to a local site or a foreign country and have anyone associated with lobbying arrange to pay for it. Even people who are not themselves registered lobbyists, but who work for a lobbying firm, are not permitted to take members of Congress to lunch or give them any other "thing of value," no matter how small.

But if past experience is any guide, "strictly speaking" is not how the rules will be followed or enforced. For instance, buried in the fine print of the new rules are provisions that permit members of Congress to accept reimbursement for travel from lobbyists if the travel is for "one-day trips," so long as the lobbyists themselves do not initiate the trip, make the reservations, or pick up incidental expenses unrelated to the visit. Moreover, these rules have not yet been adopted in precisely the same form by the Senate; and neither chamber has yet clarified language or closed loopholes related to lobbying registration and reporting.

Do not suppose, however, that such remaining gaps in lobbying laws render the system wide open to abuses or evasions. For one thing, loopholes and all, the lobbying laws are now tighter than ever. For another, as we intimated earlier in this chapter, the most significant legal constraints on interest groups come not from the current federal lobbying law (though that may change) but from the tax code and the campaign finance laws. A nonprofit organization—which includes not only charitable groups, but also almost all voluntary associations that have an interest in politics—need not pay income taxes, and financial contributions to it can be deducted on the donor's income tax return, provided that the organization does not devote a "substantial part" of its activities to "attempting to influence legislation."[38] Many tax-exempt organizations do take public positions on political questions and testify before congressional committees. If the organization does any serious lobbying, however, it will lose its tax-exempt status (and thus find it harder to solicit donations and more expensive to operate). Exactly this happened to the Sierra Club in 1968 when the Internal Revenue Service revoked its tax-exempt status because of its extensive lobbying activities. Some voluntary associations try to deal with this problem by setting up separate organizations to collect tax-exempt money—for example, the NAACP, which lobbies, must pay taxes, but the NAACP Legal Defense and Education Fund, which does not lobby, is tax-exempt.

Finally, the campaign finance laws, described in detail in Chapter 8, limit to $5,000 the amount any political action committee can spend on a given candidate in a given election. These laws have sharply curtailed the extent to which any single group can give money, though they have increased the total amount that different groups are providing.

Beyond making bribery or other manifestly corrupt forms of behavior illegal and restricting the sums that campaign contributors can donate, there is probably no system for controlling interest groups that would both make a useful difference and leave important constitutional and political rights unimpaired. Ultimately, the only remedy for imbalances or inadequacies in interest group representation is to devise and sustain a political system that gives all affected parties a reasonable chance to be heard on matters of public policy. That, of course, is exactly what the Founders thought they were doing. Whether they succeeded or not is a question to which we shall return at the end of this book.

Lobbying

In a representative democracy, elected officials make the laws, but we, the public, vote those officials into office and share our views on public policy, from taxes to education to U.S. responsibilities abroad. As we have seen in this chapter, we can share our views in many ways: communicating with elected officials in writing or in person; donating money to campaigns; organizing rallies or protests. We do not all have the same resources to exercise our lobbying rights, of course, but we have the opportunity to develop or find those resources, if we choose.

Sound about right? Not so fast. We all have the right to "lobby" elected officials, but lobbying has become a full-time occupation for political professionals, especially those representing large corporations. As Table 7.2 shows, the top contributions from Political Action Committees (PACs) in the 2011–2012 election cycle represented the defense and telecommunications industries, among others. This is not necessarily a problem—businesses have legitimate public interests, and those interests may well coincide with what many of us support as well—but it does mean that interest-group influence in American politics skews generally (though not always) toward larger, and typically well-funded, lobbying organizations.

Does the current American political system provide sufficient opportunity for anyone to lobby for change, if they have the time, inclination, and willingness to do the hard work necessary to be heard? Even if major lobbying firms have the ability to make large financial donations to campaigns, can we as individuals counter that potential influence through other resources, such as mobilizing grassroots organizations to convey their views to Washington? Or, has political influence tilted so far toward elite special interests that the general public has little, if any, say in what the government does? And if you lean toward the latter view, then how can the system be changed to promote greater diversity in lobbying while still protecting everyone's First Amendment right of free speech?

LEARNING OBJECTIVES

LO 7.1 What is a political party, and why were the Framers of the Constitution concerned about the influence of political parties?

A political party is an organization that works to elect candidates to public office and identifies candidates by a clear name or label. The Framers of the Constitution viewed political parties as "factions" that would promote the interests of a few over the public good. By the early 19th century, though, public parties were viewed as an inevitable feature of democratic politics.

LO 7.2 Why does the United States have a two-party system?

The United States has a two-party political system because of two structural features in American politics: single-member districts and winner-take-all elections. Both features encourage the existence of two major parties, as smaller parties face great difficulty in winning elective office.

LO 7.3 How has America's two-party system changed, and how does it differ from the party systems of other representative democracies?

American parties during the 19th century and the first half of the 20th century were strong organizations that picked their candidates for office. Parties in European democracies still do that, but America has changed. Now, candidates usually are picked by direct primary elections, as the American voters' loyalty to parties has weakened.

LO 7.4 What are interest groups and how did they arise in America?

An interest group is an organization of people sharing a common interest or goal that seeks to influence public policy. Interest groups were present from the first days of the republic, but they proliferated thereafter in several different periods. The latest period of interest group expansion began in the 1960s and has accelerated over the last decade.

LO 7.5 How do interest groups attempt to influence public policy, and how does government regulate interest group activities?

Among other things, interest groups use specialized information, political cues, ratings of legislators, and earmarks to sway politicians and influence policy. Government influences interest groups as much as interest groups influence government: detailed rules and regulations now govern most aspects of what lobbyists do.

TO LEARN MORE

Political Parties:

- Democratic National Committee: **www.democrats.org**
- Republican National Committee: **www.rnc.org**
- Green party: **www.greens.org**
- Libertarian party: **www.lp.org**
- Reform party: **www.reformparty.org**

Interest Groups:

Conservative interest groups

- American Conservative Union: **www.conservative.org**
- Christian Coalition: **www.cc.org**

Liberal interest groups

- American Civil Liberties Union: **www.aclu.org**
- Americans for Democratic Action: **www.adaction.org**

Environmental groups

- Environmental Defense: **www.environmentaldefense.org**
- National Resources Defense Council: **www.nrdc.org**

Civil rights groups

- NAACP: **www.naacp.org**
- Center for Equal Opportunity: **www.ceousa.org**

Feminist group

- National Organization for Women: **www.now.org**

- Aldrich, John H. *Why Parties?: The Origin and Transformation of Political Parties in America* (Chicago: University of Chicago Press, 1995). Explains why we have parties.
- Baumgartner, Frank R., Jeffrey M. Berry, Marie Hojnacki, David C. Kimball, and Beth L. Leech. *Lobbying and Policy Change: Who Wins, Who Loses, and Why.* Chicago: University of Chicago Press, 2009. Thorough empirical assessment of which interest groups exercise influence in Washington.
- Cigler, Allan J., and Burdett A. Loomis, eds. *Interest Group Politics*, 8th ed. Washington, D.C.: Congressional Quarterly Press, 2011. Essays on interest groups active in American politics today.
- Grossman, Matt. *The Not-So-Special Interests: Interest Groups, Public Representation, and American Governance.* Stanford: Stanford University Press, 2012. A comprehensive study of which interest groups become more influential in American politics and why.
- Hofstadter, Richard. *The Idea of a Party System: The Rise of Legitimate Opposition in the United States, 1780–1840.* Berkeley: University of California Press, 1969. Brilliant history of how political parties came to be viewed by most leaders as necessary and desirable political institutions.
- Key, V. O., Jr. *Southern Politics.* New York: Knopf, 1949. A classic account of the one-party South.
- Lowi, Theodore J. *The End of Liberalism.* New York: Norton, 1969. A critique of the role of interest groups in American government
- Mansbridge, Jane J. *Why We Lost the ERA.* Chicago: University of Chicago Press, 1986. Insightful analysis of the relationship between organizational incentives and tactics in the ERA campaign.
- Nader, Ralph. *Crashing the Party: Taking on the Corporate Government in an Age of Surrender.* New York: St. Martin's Press, 2002. An impassioned attack on the two-party system by a well-known activist who ran for president as a minor-party candidate in 2000 and 2004.
- Olson, Mancur. *The Logic of Collective Action.* Cambridge: Harvard University Press, 1965. An economic analysis of interest groups, especially the "free-rider" problem.
- Polsby, Nelson W. *Consequences of Party Reform.* New York: Oxford University Press, 1983. Fine analysis of how changed party rules affected the parties and the government.

- Riordan, William L. *Plunkitt of Tammany Hall*. New York: Knopf, 1948. (First published in 1905.) Insightful account of how an old-style party boss operated.

- Sabato, Larry. *PAC Power*. New York: Norton, 1985. A full discussion of the nature and activities of political action committees.

- Schattschneider, E. E. *Party Government*. New York: Holt, Rinehart and Winston, 1942. An argument for a more disciplined and centralized two-party system.

- Schlozman, Kay Lehman, and John T. Tierney. *Organized Interests and American Democracy*. New York: Harper and Row, 1985. Comprehensive treatise on interest groups based on original research.

- Shafer, Byron E. *Quiet Revolution: The Struggle for the Democratic Party and the Shaping of Post-Reform Politics*. New York: Russell Sage Foundation, 1983. Detailed, insightful history of how the Democratic Party came to be reformed.

- Sundquist, James L. *Dynamics of the Party System*, Rev. ed. Washington, D.C.: Brookings Institution, 1983. History of the party system, emphasizing the impact of issues on voting.

- Truman, David B. *The Governmental Process*, 2d ed. New York: Knopf, 1971. First published in 1951, this was the classic analysis—and defense—of interest group pluralism.

- Wilson, James Q. *Political Organizations*, rev. ed. Princeton, NJ: Princeton University Press, 1995. A theory of interest groups emphasizing the incentives they use to attract members.

- Wilson, James Q. *The Amateur Democrat*. Chicago: University of Chicago Press, 1962. Analysis of the issue-oriented political clubs that rose in the 1950s and 1960s.

Elections and Campaigns

8

LEARNING OBJECTIVES

LO 8.1   What is "political participation"?

LO 8.2   How are voter turnout rates measured?

LO 8.3   Who votes, who doesn't?

LO 8.4   What is the difference between a primary and a general election?

LO 8.5   What matters most in deciding who wins presidential and congressional elections?

political participation
The many different ways that people take part in politics and government.

Defined simply, **political participation** refers to the many different ways that people take part in politics and government: voting or trying to influence others to vote, joining a political party or giving money to a candidate for office, keeping informed about government or debating political issues with others, signing a petition, protesting a policy, advocating for a new law, or just writing a letter to an elected leader. Some scholars of the subject profess that, in addition to these activities, almost any form of civic engagement—like helping out at a local homeless shelter or attending a school board meeting—should count as political participation. And some believe that the rise of the Internet, political blogs, and social media make traditional ideas about what constitutes political participation obsolete.

But no matter how they define it, most academics who study political participation pay close attention to voting and begin with a puzzle: despite successive legal and other changes that might be expected to increase electoral participation, voter turnout rates in America today are lower than they were for previous generations, and scores of millions of Americans now sit out each presidential and midterm national election.

THEN

In most states, well into the 19th century, only property-owning white males could vote. After the Civil War and into the mid-20th century, many states used all manner of stratagems to keep blacks from voting. Women did not receive the right to vote until 1920 when the Nineteenth Amendment to the Constitution was ratified. Before 1961, residents of the District of Columbia could not vote in presidential elections; the Twenty-third Amendment to the Constitution gave them the right. Into the 1960s, most whites had only limited formal education; women and many minority groups faced legal, social, and other barriers or disincentives to voting; and there was nothing resembling today's steady stream of political news via multiple media outlets.

NOW

National laws extend voter eligibility to all persons age 18 or older (courtesy of the Twenty-sixth Amendment to the Constitution ratified in 1971). No state may restrict voting based on discriminatory tests, taxes, or residency requirements. In areas where many non-English speakers live, election authorities must supply ballots written in their own language. People in all 50 states can register to vote when applying for a driver's license, and most states now allow voters to vote by absentee ballot prior to election day even if they are not residing outside their home state. Many states also now permit people to register on the same day that they vote. Over the last half-century, formal education levels have risen among all groups, and news, information, and opinion about politics and government are just about everywhere one turns (or clicks).

And yet, between 1860 and 1900, the percentage of eligible voters participating in presidential elections ranged between 65 percent and 80 percent. By comparison, over the last several decades, the percentage of eligible voters participating in presidential elections has dipped as low as half. Over the same period, voter turnout in midterm national elections has averaged below 50 percent. In 2006, the Democrats took majority control of the U.S. House of Representatives, and then in 2010, the Republicans won the House majority back from the Democrats; but in each of these two recent, power-shifting midterm national elections, about 80 million U.S. residents age 18 or older did not vote. Young voters, despite averaging more years of formal education, facing fewer legal barriers, and enjoying more access to information than any previous generation could have imagined, are nonetheless mostly nonvoters; for example, in the four midterm national elections since 1998, approximately one in five 18- to 24 year-olds cast a ballot.

What explains nonvoting? Are voter turnout rates in America today really as bad as they seem, either in historical terms or relative to rates in other modern democracies; and what about other forms of political participation in America today?

A Close Look at Nonvoting

Start with the fact that there are at least two different ways to measure voter turnout, and they give different answers about the prevalence of nonvoting.[1] All U.S. residents age 18 or older constitute the **voting-age population (VAP)**. But many residents of the United States who are of voting age (18 or older) are not, in fact, eligible to vote. Two such groups are noncitizens who reside in America and convicted felons who, in most states, are disenfranchised by state laws. Unlike the VAP, the **voting-eligible population (VEP)** measure excludes from the calculation U.S. residents age 18 or older who are not legally permitted to cast a ballot. For example, in 2008 the VAP numbered nearly 231 million, but that included about 18 million noncitizens and disenfranchised convicted felons. So, for example, measured by the VAP, the national voter turnout rate was 53.6 percent in 2012, but measured by the VEP it was 58.2 percent; and since 1948, as the percentage of the population age 18 and older that consists of noncitizens and disenfranchised convicted felons has grown, the gap between the VAP and the VEP measures of voter turnout has grown (see Table 8.1).

Another important nuance about nonvoting concerns registered versus unregistered voters. Take a look at Table 8.2. Column A compares democratic nations in terms of the average percentage of their VAP that went to the polls in dozens of post-1945 national legislative (congressional or parliamentary) elections. The United States ranks dead last with 47.7 percent voter turnout.

Now, however, look at Column B. It compares the same nations in terms of percentage of **registered voters** (those

voting-age population (VAP) Citizens who are eligible to vote after reaching the minimum age requirement.

voting-eligible population (VEP) Citizens who have reached the minimum age to be eligible to vote, excluding those who are not legally permitted to cast a ballot.

registered voters People who are registered to vote.

TABLE 8.1 Two Methods of Calculating Turnout in Presidential Elections, 1948–2012

Year	Voting-Age Population (VAP)	Voting-Eligible Population (VEP)
1948	51.1%	52.2%
1952	61.6	62.3
1956	59.3	60.2
1960	62.8	63.8
1964	61.9	62.8
1968	60.9	61.5
1972	55.2	56.2
1976	53.5	54.8
1980	52.8	54.7
1984	53.3	57.2
1988	50.3	54.2
1992	55.0	60.6
1996	48.9	52.6
2000	51.2	55.6
2004	55.0	60.0
2008	56.8	61.7
2012	53.6	58.2

Source: Updated from Michael P. McDonald and Samuel L. Popkin, "The Myth of the Vanishing Voter," *American Political Science Review* 95 (December 2001): table 1, 966. Michael P. McDonald, "2008 General Election Turnout Rates," updated April 26, 2009, at http://elections.gmu.edu, accessed May 8, 2009; *Michael P. McDonald, George Mason University, United States Elections Project, 2012 General Elections Turnout Rate, March 25, 2013.*

TABLE 8.2 Two Ways of Calculating Voting Turnout, Here and Abroad

A		B	
	Turnout as Percentage of Voting-Age Population		Turnout as Percentage of Registered Voters
Italy	92.0%	Australia	94.5%
New Zealand	86.0	Belgium	92.5
Belgium	84.8	Austria	83.1
Austria	84.4	New Zealand	90.8
Australia	84.2	Italy	89.8
Sweden	84.1	Netherlands	87.5
Netherlands	83.8	Sweden	87.1
Denmark	83.6	Denmark	85.9
Canada	82.6	Germany	85.4
Germany	80.2	Norway	80.4
Norway	79.2	United Kingdom	75.2
United Kingdom	73.8	Canada	73.9
France	67.3	France	73.8
Switzerland	51.9	**United States**	66.5
United States	47.7	Switzerland	56.5

Source: Rafael Lopez Pintor, Maria Gratschew, and Kate Sullivan, "Voter Turnout Rates from a Comparative Perspective," in Voter Turnout Since 1945: A Global Report *(Stockholm, Sweden: International Institute for Democracy and Electoral Assistance, 2002).*

eligible voters who have completed a registration form by a set date) who went to the polls in the same legislative elections. The United States still ranks low but looks somewhat better, with 66.5 percent registered voter turnout; and the registered voter turnout in post-1968 U.S. presidential elections is about 70 percent.

Nonvoting rates vary by age largely because voter registration rates vary by age. For example, in midterm and presidential elections alike, Americans ages 18 to 20 register at much lower rates and also fail to vote at much higher rates than do Americans age 65 and older (see Table 8.3). Yet the same data tell us that, without regard to age, citizens who register are highly likely to vote: for example, in the 2010 midterm congressional election, about half of all younger voters, and about four-fifths of all voters age 65 and older, who were registered to vote did cast a ballot.

Still, simply getting more people registered to vote is not a cure-all for nonvoting, for in each national election since 2006, about half of all nonvoters were registered. When registered nonvoters were asked why they did not vote, three answers were most common: about a quarter of registered nonvoters said they were too busy or had scheduling conflicts (work or school mostly); about 12 percent cited family chores or obligations; and another 12 percent believed their vote would make no difference.[2]

In response to the number one reason why registered voters fail to vote (school, work, or other scheduling conflicts), some have proposed making election day a national holiday or holding national elections on weekends. Such proposals, though popular, remain only proposals; but all states now give

TABLE 8.3 Voter Registration and Turnout by Age

Age	Percent Registered/Voted, Midterm Elections				
	1994	1998	2002	2006	2010
18–20	37/17	32/14	33/15	37/17	34/16
21–24	46/22	35/19	43/19	45/22	47/22
25–34	52/32	52/28	50/27	50/28	50/27
65+	76/61	75/60	76/61	75/61	73/59

Age	Percent Registered/Voted, Presidential Elections				
	1996	2000	2004	2008	
18–20	46/31	41/28	51/41	53/44	
21–24	51/33	49/35	52/43	62/52	
25–34	57/43	55/44	56/47	66/57	
65+	77/67	76/68	77/69	77/70	

Source: Adapted from U.S. Bureau of the Census, *Current Population Reports*, June 2008, Table 400, and *Statistical Abstract of the United States: 2012*, Table 399, p. 246.

voters the option to vote prior to election day via mail-in ballots, and by 2012, 27 states afforded voters the option of "no-fault" absentee voting, meaning that voters can vote absentee without having to demonstrate they are residing outside their home state or giving any other explanation. So far as most researchers have been able to determine, and with a few dramatic exceptions (for example, Oregon's 1996 all-mail-in election for the U.S. Senate), there is no definitive evidence that either the greater flexibility and convenience of these voting procedures, or the proliferation of less restrictive registration procedures, has increased voter turnout.[3]

If voter turnout rates are to rise substantially in the United States, then nonregistered voters must become registered to vote in ever greater numbers. In addition to the roughly 40 million registered nonvoters, another 40 million or so voting-age citizens were not registered to vote in each of several recent national elections.

In most European nations, registration is done for you—automatically—by the government. By contrast, in America, the entire burden of registering to vote falls on the individual voters: they must learn how and when and where to register; they must take the time and trouble to go somewhere and fill out a registration form; and they must register if they happen to move. It takes more effort to register to vote in this country than it does to register in other democracies; it should not be surprising that fewer people are registered here than abroad.

But would making it less burdensome to register necessarily result in higher percentages of Americans becoming registered voters *and* voting? In 1993, Congress passed a law designed to make it easier to register to vote. Known as the motor-voter law, the law allows people in all 50 states to register to vote when applying for driver's licenses and to provide registration through the mail and at some state offices that serve the disabled or provide public assistance (such as checks for eligible low-income families).

As with early, mail-in and absentee balloting (see the Constitutional Connections feature on page 225–226), the evidence regarding the motor-voter law's impact on voter participation remains

FIGURE 8.1   Method of Registration to Vote, 2010
Percent Distribution of Registered Voters

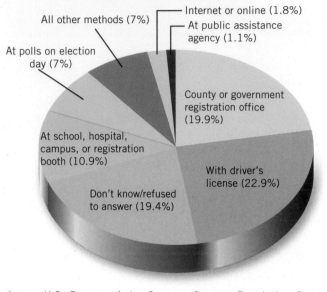

All other methods (7%)

Internet or online (1.8%)

At public assistance agency (1.1%)

At polls on election day (7%)

County or government registration office (19.9%)

At school, hospital, campus, or registration booth (10.9%)

With driver's license (22.9%)

Don't know/refused to answer (19.4%)

Source: U.S. Bureau of the Census, Current Population Survey, "Voting and Registration," November 2010.

hard to interpret definitively. In 2001, eight years after the law was enacted, millions of citizens had registered to vote via state motor vehicles bureaus or other state offices, but a study found "that those who register when the process is costless are less likely to vote."[4] By 2010, motor-voter law-related means of registration were the single most widely used (see Figure 8.1). But between 1993 and 2010, while voter registration rates had increased somewhat over pre-1993 levels, there still was no solid evidence that the law had substantially increased voter turnout.

Mounting a get-out-the-vote (GOTV) drive can make only a small difference depending on what tactic is used. In a 2008 study, political scientists Donald P. Green and Alan Gerber examined the findings from more than a hundred scientific studies of diverse GOTV tactics: door-to-door canvassing, leaflets, direct mail, email, phone calls, radio ads, television ads, and election-day festivals.[5] Door-to-door canvassing and phone calls were the only two tactics that demonstrated statistically significant results; but even most prospective voters touched by these tactics did not turn out. In a separate 2008 study, they found that "social pressure" exerted through mailings increased turnout, yet 62 percent of those pressured still did not vote.[6]

Of course, voting is only one way of participating in politics. It is important (we could hardly be considered a democracy if nobody voted), but it is not all-important. Joining civic associations, supporting social movements, writing to legislators, fighting city hall—all these and other activities are ways of participating in politics. It is possible that, by these measures, Americans participate in politics *more* than most Europeans—or anybody else, for that matter. Moreover, it is possible that low rates of registration indicate that people are reasonably well satisfied with how the country is governed. If 100 percent of all adult Americans registered and voted (especially under a system that makes registering relatively difficult), it could mean that people were deeply upset about how things were run. In short, it is not at all clear whether low voter turnout is a symptom of political disease or a sign of political good health.

The important question about participation is not how much participation there is but how different kinds of participation affect the kind of government we get. This question cannot be answered just by looking at voter turnout, the subject of this chapter; it also requires us to look at the composition and activities of political parties, interest groups, and the media (the subjects of later chapters).

Nonetheless, voting is important. To understand why participation in American elections takes the form that it does, we must first understand how laws have determined who shall vote and under what circumstances.

HOW WE COMPARE

Laws on Voting

Ratified in 1971, the Twenty-sixth Amendment to the U.S. Constitution forbids states to deny "on account of age" the right to vote to citizens who are age 18 or older. But most states deny voting rights to voting-age citizens who have been convicted of felony crimes. Relevant state laws vary; for instance, Kentucky and Virginia have largely maintained laws that disenfranchise felons for life, while Maine and Vermont have permitted certain presently incarcerated felons to vote.

The legal voting age in almost all other nations is also 18. In about a dozen other countries, however, the legal voting age has been 16 (as in Brazil) or 17 (as in Indonesia); and in about twenty other nations the legal voting age is 19 (as in South Korea), 20 (as in Japan), or 21 (as in Lebanon).

Some democracies (for example, the United Kingdom) deny prisoners the right to vote, but it is far more common for democracies to permit all prisoners (save, in some nations, persons convicted of electoral fraud or related crimes) to vote. America is almost alone among democracies in the extent to which laws deny ex-prisoners the right to vote.

America is also in the international minority with respect to laws on voter registration. In most other nations it is legally compulsory for voters to register; a central, regional, or local government, or, most commonly, a specialized "Electoral Management Body," is expressly responsible for registering voters in national elections.

In America, voter registration is not legally required, and under a diverse array of state laws, individual voting-age citizens remain responsible for registering to vote.

Source: ACE Electoral Knowledge Network and United Nations Development Program, data on Voter Registration and Voting Age, http://www.aceproject.org, accessed May 2010; "Felony Disenfranchisement in the United States," The Sentencing Project, September 2008.

CONSTITUTIONAL CONNECTIONS

State Voting Laws and Procedures

"The Times, Places and Manner of holding Elections for Senators and Representatives, shall be prescribed in each State by the Legislature thereof..."

Thus begins Article I, Section 4, of the Constitution. As indicated in the nearby **How We Compare** feature, the United States is unique among modern democracies in the extent to which the laws and procedures under which its citizens vote vary according to where in the nation they reside. As discussed elsewhere in this chapter, the states are no longer free as they once were to decide who could vote for what office, but the shift to federal control has not eliminated differences in state voting laws and procedures. With few exceptions, the federal courts, including the

(*continued*)

CONSTITUTIONAL CONNECTIONS (*Continued*)

U.S. Supreme Court, have let present-day differences in states' voting laws and procedures stand.

On the eve of the 2012 national election, in addition to the traditional Election Day trek to a polling place or "voting booth" in one's home voting district, there were three other ways for voting-age Americans to cast ballots.

- *Early Voting*: Thirty-two states and the District of Columbia permitted people to cast in-person ballots prior to Election Day, and without requiring that they furnish any excuse for doing so. The early voting periods ranged from the Friday before Election Day to 45 days before Election Day. The average early voting period was about 20 days.

- *Absentee Voting*: All states permitted absentee voting by mail for military personnel, their voting-age dependents, and U.S. citizens living overseas. All states also would mail absentee ballots to certain other voters; but in 27 states and the District of Columbia, no excuse for absentee voting was required, while in 21 other states, an excuse was required. In 7 states, certain citizens receive "permanent

absentee ballot" privileges; in most, the citizens granted this status must give evidence of a chronic illness or disability; in Alaska, the status was also afforded to citizens that lived in remote parts of the state.

- *Mail Voting*: A ballot is automatically mailed to every eligible citizen, no request required. There are no traditional Election Day voting sites. Two states, Washington and Oregon, used this system.

It happens that the 15 states with the most restrictive voting laws and procedures—no early voting, and an excuse required for absentee voting—are all located in the eastern half of the country, with the highest concentration of them in the Northeast. Constitutionally, states have also been permitted to decide whether to deny voting rights to voting-age citizens who have been convicted of felony crimes. There continue to be wide state-by-state disparities in felon disenfranchisement laws and procedures. For instance, in 2012, a couple of states permitted convicted felons to vote; a dozen states permitted convicted felons on probation or parole, but not those in prison, to vote; and several states disenfranchised all convicted felons for life.

The Rise of the American Electorate

It is ironic that relatively few citizens vote in American elections, since it was in this country that the mass of people first became eligible to vote. At the time the Constitution was ratified, the vote was limited to property owners or taxpayers, but by the administration of Andrew Jackson (1829–1837) it had been broadened to include virtually all white male adults. Only in a few states did property restrictions persist: they were not abolished in New Jersey until 1844 or in North Carolina until 1856. And, of course, African American males could not vote in many states, in the North as well as the South, even if they were not slaves. Women could not vote in most states until the 20th century; Chinese Americans were widely denied the vote; and being in prison is grounds for losing the franchise even today. Aliens, on the other hand, often were allowed to vote if they had at least begun the process of becoming citizens. By 1880, only an estimated 14 percent of all adult males in the United States could not vote; in England in the same period, about 40 percent of adult males were disfranchised.[7]

From State to Federal Control

Initially, it was left entirely to the states to decide who could vote and for what offices. The Constitution gave Congress the right to pick the day on which presidential electors would gather and to alter state regulations regarding congressional elections. The only provision of the Constitution requiring a popular election was the clause in Article I stating that members of the House of Representatives be chosen by the "people of the several states."

Because of this permissiveness, early federal elections varied greatly. Several states picked their members of the House at large (that is, statewide) rather than by district; others used districts but elected more than one representative from each. Some had their elections in odd-numbered years, and some even required that a congressional candidate win a majority, rather than simply a plurality, of votes to be elected (when that requirement was in effect, runoff elections—in one case, as many as 12—were necessary). Furthermore, presidential electors were at first picked by state legislatures rather than by the voters directly.

Congress, by law and constitutional amendment, has steadily reduced state prerogatives in these matters. In 1842, a federal law required that all members of the House be elected by districts; other laws over the years required that all federal elections be held in even-numbered years on the Tuesday following the first Monday in November.

The most important changes in elections have been those that extended the suffrage to women, African Americans, and 18-year-olds and made mandatory the direct popular election of U.S. senators. The Fifteenth Amendment, adopted in 1870, said that the "right of citizens of the United States to vote shall not be denied or abridged by the United States or by any state on account of race, color, or previous condition of servitude." Reading those words today, one would assume they gave African Americans the right to vote. That is not what the Supreme Court of the 1870s thought they meant. By a series of decisions, it held that the Fifteenth Amendment did not necessarily confer the right to vote on anybody; it merely asserted that if someone was denied that right, the denial could not be explicitly on the grounds of race. And the burden of proving that it was race that led to the denial fell on the black citizen who was turned away at the polls.[8]

This interpretation opened the door to three especially notorious but then-legal devices to keep blacks from voting. One was a **literacy test** (a large proportion of former slaves were illiterate); another was a requirement that a **poll tax** be paid (most former slaves were poor); and the third was the practice of keeping blacks from voting in primary elections (in the one-party South, the only meaningful election was the Democratic primary). To allow whites who were illiterate or poor to vote, a **grandfather clause** was added to the law, saying that a person could vote, even if he did not meet the legal requirements, if he or his ancestors voted before 1867 (blacks, of course, could not vote before 1867). When all else failed, blacks were intimidated, threatened, or harassed if they showed up at the polls.

There began a long, slow legal process of challenging in court each of these restrictions in turn. One by one, the Supreme Court set most of them aside. The grandfather clause was

literacy test A requirement that citizens show that they can read before registering to vote.

poll tax A requirement that citizens pay a tax in order to register to vote.

grandfather clause A clause in registration laws allowing people who do not meet registration requirements to vote if they or their ancestors had voted before 1867.

LANDMARK CASES

Right to Vote

- ***Smith v. Allwright (1944):*** Because political parties select candidates for public office, they may not exclude blacks from voting in their primary elections.

white primary The practice of keeping blacks from voting in the Southern states' primaries through arbitrary use of registration requirements and intimidation.

declared unconstitutional in 1915,[9] and the **white primary** finally fell in 1944.[10] Some of the more blatantly discriminatory literacy tests also were overturned.[11] The practical result of these rulings was slight: only a small proportion of voting-age blacks were able to register and vote in the South, and they were found mostly in the larger cities. A dramatic change did not begin until 1965, with the passage of the Voting Rights Act. This act suspended the use of literacy tests and authorized the appointment of federal examiners who could order the registration of blacks in states and counties (mostly in the South) where fewer than 50 percent of the voting-age population were registered or had voted in the last presidential election. It also provided criminal penalties for interfering with the right to vote.

Though implementation in some places was slow, the number of African Americans voting rose sharply throughout the South. For example, in Mississippi the proportion of voting-age blacks who registered rose from 5 percent to over 70 percent from 1960 to 1970. These changes had a profound effect on the behavior of many white southern politicians: Governor George Wallace stopped making pro-segregation speeches and began courting the black vote.

Women were kept from the polls by law more than by intimidation, and when the laws changed, women almost immediately began to vote in large numbers. By 1915, several states, mostly in the West, had begun to permit women to vote. But it was not until the Nineteenth Amendment to the Constitution was ratified in 1920, after a struggle lasting many decades, that women generally were allowed to vote. At one stroke, the size of the eligible voting population almost doubled. Contrary to the hopes of some and the fears of others, no dramatic changes occurred in the conduct of elections, the identity of the winners, or the substance of public policy. Initially, at least, women voted more or less in the same manner as men, though not quite as frequently.

The political impact of the youth vote was also less than expected. The Voting Rights Act of 1970 gave 18-year-olds the right to vote in federal elections beginning January 1, 1971. It also contained a provision lowering the voting age to 18 in state elections, but the Supreme Court declared this unconstitutional. As a result a constitutional amendment, the Twenty-sixth, was proposed by Congress and ratified by the states in 1971. The 1972 elections became the first in which all people between the ages of 18 and 21 could cast ballots (before then, four states had allowed those under 21 to vote). About 25 million people suddenly became eligible to participate in elections, but their turnout (42 percent) was lower than for the population as a whole, and they did not flock to any particular party or candidate.

Every presidential election year since 1972 has been accompanied by predictions that the "youth vote" is likely to surge. Such predictions were especially prevalent in 2008. In 2008, 23 million citizens under age 30, representing 52 percent of the 18- to 29-year-old voting population, voted. That was a higher fraction than in 1996 (37 percent), 2000 (41 percent), and 2004 (48 percent), but lower than 1972 (55 percent) and the same as 1992 (52 percent). Moreover, in every presidential election from 1996 through 2004, the under-30 youth vote accounted for 17 percent of the total election-day electorate; in 2008 the fraction rose, but only to 18 percent.

Voter Turnout

The proportion of the voting-age population that has gone to the polls in presidential elections has remained about the same—between 50 and 63 percent of those eligible—at least since 1928, and appears today to be much smaller than it was in the latter part of the 19th century (see Figure 8.2). In every presidential election between 1860 and 1900, at least 70 percent of the eligible population apparently went to the polls, and in some years (1860 and 1876) almost 80 percent seem to have voted. Since 1900,

FIGURE 8.2   **Voter Participation in Presidential Elections, 1860–2012**

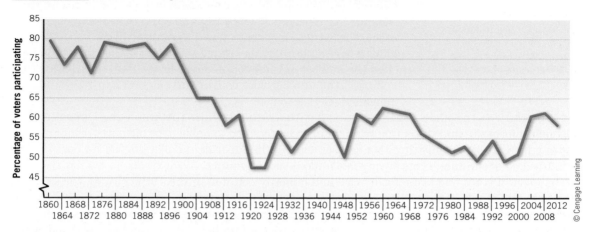

Note: Several Southern states did not participate in the 1864 and 1868 elections.

Source: For 1860–1928: Bureau of the Census, Historical Statistics of the United States, Colonial Times to 1970, part 2, p. 1071; 1932–1944: Statistical Abstract of the United States, 1992, p. 517; 1948–2000: Michael P. McDonald and Samuel L. Popkin, "The Myth of the Vanishing Voter," *American Political Science Review 95* (December 2001): table 1, p. 966; 2004–2012 elections, American National Election Studies (ANES).

in not a single presidential election has turnout reached 70 percent, and on two occasions (1920 and 1924), it did not even reach 50 percent.[12] Even outside the South, where efforts to disenfranchise African Americans make data on voter turnout especially hard to interpret, turnout seems to have declined: over 84 percent of the voting-age population participated in presidential elections in nonsouthern states between 1884 and 1900, but only 68 percent participated between 1936 and 1960, and even fewer have done so since 1960.[13]

Scholars have vigorously debated the meaning of these figures. One view is that this decline in turnout, even allowing for the shaky data on which the estimates are based, has been real and is the result of a decline of popular interest in elections and a weakening of the competitiveness of the two major parties. During the 19th century, according to this theory, the parties fought hard, worked strenuously to get as many voters as possible to the polls, afforded the mass of voters a chance to participate in party politics through caucuses and conventions, kept the legal barriers to participation (such as complex registration procedures) low, and looked forward to close, exciting elections. After 1896, by which time the South had become a one-party Democratic region and the North heavily Republican, both parties became more conservative, national elections usually resulted in lopsided victories for the Republicans, and citizens began to lose interest in politics because it no longer seemed relevant to their needs. The parties ceased functioning as organizations to mobilize the mass of voters and fell under the control of leaders, mostly conservative, who resisted mass participation.[14]

There is another view, however. It argues that the decline in voter turnout has been more apparent than real. Though elections were certainly more of a popular sport in the 19th century than they are today, the parties were no more democratic then than now, and voters then may have been more easily manipulated. Until around the beginning of the 20th century, voting fraud was commonplace, because it was easy to pull off. The political parties, not the government, printed the ballots; they often were cast in public, not private, voting booths; there were few serious efforts to decide who was eligible to vote, and the rules that did operate were easily evaded.

Australian ballot A government-printed ballot of uniform dimensions to be cast in secret that many states adopted around 1890 to reduce voting fraud associated with party-printed ballots cast in public.

Under these circumstances, it was easy for a person to vote more than once, and the party machines made heavy use of these "floaters," or repeaters. "Vote early and often" was not a joke; it was a fact. The parties often controlled the counting of votes, padding the totals whenever they feared losing. As a result of these machinations, often the number of votes counted was larger than the number cast, and often the number cast was in turn larger than the number of individuals eligible to vote.

Around 1890, the states began adopting the **Australian ballot**. This was a government-printed ballot of uniform size and shape that was cast in secret, created to replace the old party-printed ballots cast in public. By 1910, only three states were without the Australian ballot. Its use cut back on (but certainly did not eliminate) vote buying and fraudulent vote counts.

In short, if votes had been legally cast and honestly counted in the 19th century, the statistics on election turnout might well be much lower than the inflated figures we now have.[15] To the extent that this is true, we may not have had a decline in voter participation as great as some have suggested. Nevertheless, most scholars believe that turnout probably did actually decline somewhat after the 1890s. One reason was that voter registration regulations became more burdensome: there were longer residency requirements; aliens who had begun but not completed the process of becoming citizens could no longer vote in most states; it became harder for African Americans to vote; educational qualifications for voting were adopted by several states; and voters had to register long in advance of the elections. These changes, designed to purify the electoral process, were aspects of the progressive reform impulse (described in Chapter 7) and served to cut back on the number of people who could participate in elections.

Strict voter registration procedures tended—like most reforms in American politics—to have unintended as well as intended consequences. These changes not only reduced fraudulent voting, but also reduced voting generally, because they made it more difficult for certain groups of perfectly honest voters—those with little education, for example, or those who had recently moved—to register and vote. This was not the first time, and it will not be the last, that a reform designed to cure one problem created another.

Following the controversy over Florida's vote count in the 2000 presidential election, many proposals were made to overhaul the nation's voting system. In 2002, Congress passed a measure that for the first time requires each state to have in place a system for counting the disputed ballots of voters whose names were left off official registration lists. In addition, the law provides federal funds for upgrading voting equipment and procedures and for training election officials. But it stops short of creating a uniform national voting system. Paper ballots, lever machines, and punch-card voting systems will still be used in some places, while optical scan and direct recording electronic equipment will be used in others. Following the 2004 national elections, however, calls to overhaul the nation's voting system were more muted, partly because the popular vote for president was not terribly close (President Bush received 51 percent, John Kerry received 48 percent), and partly because in most states there were few reported problems.

Even after all the legal changes are taken into account, there seems to have been a decline in citizen participation in elections. Between 1960 and 1980, the proportion of voting-age people casting a ballot in presidential elections fell by about 10 percentage points, a drop that cannot be explained by how ballots were printed or how registration rules were rewritten. Nor can these factors explain why 1996 witnessed not only the lowest level of turnout (49 percent) in a presidential election since 1924, but also the single steepest four-year decline (from 55 percent in 1992) since 1920.

Actual trends in turnout aside, what if they gave an election and everyone came? Would universal turnout change national election outcomes and the content of public policy? It has long been argued that because the poor, less educated, and minorities are overrepresented among nonvoters, universal turnout would strongly benefit Democratic candidates and liberal causes. But careful studies of this question have found that the "party of nonvoters" largely mirrors the demographically diverse and ideologically divided population that goes to the polls, and that "while nonvoters are more liberal and more Democratic than voters, the difference is so small that it would hardly change election outcomes if every American citizen voted.".[16]

Campaigns Today

Within the lifetimes of many a still-living national political leader, campaigns and elections have changed dramatically: parties have become less important; media or "media buys" have become more important and polling has become ubiquitous (see Chapter 7); and money—and the nonstop fundraising that keeps it coming—now matters more than ever.

With the parties' ability to control nominations weakened, candidates are now pretty much on their own. Most, however, do not go it alone. Rather, they hire people to perform several separate but related campaign tasks.[17]

• *Media consultants* who create advertisements and buy airtime from stations and networks.

• *Direct-mail firms* that design and produce mailings to promote the candidate or solicit money.

• *Polling firms* to survey voters on their attitudes toward issues and candidates and to run focus groups.

• *Political technology firms* to supply services such as website design, online advertising, online fundraising, and voter-targeting.

To pay for all this help, today's candidates must raise and spend enormous sums of money. As Table 8.4 shows, in the 2010 midterm elections, all candidates for national office raised and spent more than $1.8 billion: more than $1 billion in House races, and about $765 million in Senate races. These campaign finance sums were unprecedented for a midterm congressional election. According to an April 2013 report by the Federal Election Commission, during the national election cycle that ended in 2012, presidential and congressional candidates combined total receipts (about $3.2 billion), plus those of party committees (about $1.6 billion) and PACs (about $2.2 billion), totaled about $7.1 billion.

Thus, we have entered the era of the $7 billion federal election cycle. The climb there has been steep but steady. For instance, in 1980, all presidential candidates raised about $162 million. In 2012, all presidential candidates raised about $1.3 billion. Adjusted for inflation, the 2012 total is about five times the 1980 total.

TABLE 8.4   **The 2010 Midterm Elections: Money Raised and Spent**

	Total Raised	Total Spent
House Candidates	$1,102,340,257	$1,094,911,271
Senate Candidates	$766,716,134	$764,967,246
Total, All Candidates	$1,869,056,391	$1,859,878,517

Source: Federal Election Commission, 2010 House and Senate Campaign Finance Summary.

TABLE 8.5 **2000–2012 Campaign Receipts**

Presidential Candidates	Number of candidates/ Total receipts
2012	14/$1.37 billion
2008	20/$1.67 billion
2004	12/$904 billion
2000	17/$578 million
Congressional Candidates	
2012	$1.87 billion
2010	$1.86 billion
2008	$1.41 billion
2006	$1.44 billion
2004	$1.29 billion
2002	$979 million

Source: Federal Election Commission, FEC Summary of the 2011–2012 Election Cycle, April 19, 2013.

FIGURE 8.3 **2012 Campaign Spending, Selected Items**

Includes spending by presidential candidates, parties, and political action committees

(rounded to nearest $1 million)

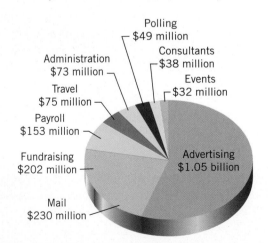

Polling — $49 million
Consultants — $38 million
Administration $73 million
Events — $32 million
Travel $75 million
Payroll $153 million
Advertising $1.05 billion
Fundraising $202 million
Mail $230 million

Source: Federal Election Commission Reports, December 2012, as compiled by *The Washington Post*, 2012 Campaign Finance Explorer, December 7, 2012.

As Table 8.5 shows, between 2000 and 2012, the amount of money received by all presidential candidates (including the two party nominees and all their respective primary challengers) more than doubled: in 2000, 17 presidential candidates had total receipts of about $578 million, while in 2012, 14 presidential candidates had receipts of roughly $1.3 billion. Adjusted for inflation, the 2012 total is about 1.7 times the 2000 total. Congressional fundraising tells much the same tale. Between 2002 and 2012, the total receipts of congressional candidates about doubled; adjusted for inflation, the 2012 total is about 1.5 times the 2002 total. Whether we will witness $8 billion (or $9 billion, or more) national election cycles before the decade is out remains to be seen, but there would appear to be no end in sight to increases in the amount of money that candidates, parties, and PACs collect.

Today's presidential candidates spend more on media consultants, television and radio ads, and diverse other forms of "media messages" than on any other category of campaign expenses. For example, 2008 presidential candidates spent about $569 million on media, representing about 31 percent of all their campaign expenditures. In 2012, campaigns spent more than $1 billion on advertising alone (see Figure 8.3). With so much money spent by candidates for media outlets and media consultants, you might think there is clear and convincing evidence that media exposure makes a critical difference in who wins elections, or that some types of televised appeals work better than others, or both.

But you would be wrong. About the only safe generalization one can presently make on the subject is not that "media buys" matter, but how common it is for today's candidates to purchase political ads embodying emotional appeals.

A comprehensive study carefully analyzed thousands of political ads[18]. A plurality, it found, were purposely designed (everything from the images used to the music playing in the background) to appeal mainly to voters' fears (impending war, losing a job, and so on). A smaller but significant fraction was more focused on stirring positive emotions (patriotism and community pride). You might suppose that candidates favor ads that appeal to such emotions because they are particularly effective in reaching voters who know little and care less about politics.

Once again, you would be wrong. The political ads, televised and other, that appealed to emotion (fear or enthusiasm, mainly) wielded the greatest influence over voters with the greatest interest in politics and the most information about government.[19] Still, experts do not know how or whether televised political ads influence election outcomes.

Here and Abroad

Even the best American political consultants probably would have trouble exporting their wares. A campaign plan that will work here would be useless in almost any other democratic nation; one that would work abroad would be useless here.

Unlike in many other democratic nations, in America, elections have not one, but two crucial phases—getting nominated and getting elected. Getting nominated means getting your name on the ballot. In the great majority of states, winning your party's nomination for either the presidency or Congress requires an *individual* effort—*you* decide to run, *you* raise money, *you* and your friends collect signatures to get your name on the ballot, and *you* appeal to voters in primary elections on the basis of your personality and your definition of the issues. In most European nations, winning your party's nomination for parliament involves an *organizational* decision—*the party* looks you over, *the party* decides whether to allow you to run, and *the party* puts your name on its list of candidates.

American political parties do play a role in determining the outcome of the final election, but even that role involves parties more as labels in the voters' minds than as organizations that get out the vote. By contrast, many other democratic nations conduct campaigns almost entirely as a contest between parties as organizations. In Israel and the Netherlands, the names of the candidates for the legislature do not even appear on the ballot; only the party names are listed there. And even where candidate names are listed, as in Great Britain, the voters tend to vote "Conservative" or "Labour" more than they vote for Smith or Jones. European nations (except France) do not have a directly elected president; instead, the head of the government—the prime minister—is selected by the party that has won the most seats in parliament.

Paul Marotta/WireImage/Getty Images

After working in the Obama administration to create the Consumer Financial Protection Bureau, Elizabeth Warren won election to the U.S. Senate from Massachusetts in 2012.

Presidential versus Congressional Campaigns

Presidential and congressional races differ in important ways. The most obvious, of course, is size: more voters participate in the former than the latter contests, and so presidential candidates must work harder and spend more. But there are some less obvious differences that are equally important.

First, presidential races are more competitive than those for the House of Representatives. In the 41 elections

incumbent The person already holding an elective office.

coattails The alleged tendency of candidates to win more votes in an election because of the presence at the top of the ticket of a better-known candidate, such as the president.

from 1932 to 2012 the Republicans won control of the House 10 times (about 25 percent of the time); in the 21 presidential elections during the same period the Republicans won the White House on nine occasions (about 43 percent of the time). In the typical presidential race, the winner gets less than 55 percent of the two-party vote; in the typical House race, the **incumbent** wins with over 60 percent of the vote.

Second, a much smaller proportion of people vote in congressional races during off years (that is, when there is no presidential contest) than vote for president. This lower turnout (typically about one-third fewer voters than in presidential-election years) means that candidates in congressional races must be appealing to the more motivated and partisan voter.

Third, members of Congress can do things for their constituents that a president cannot. They take credit—sometimes deserved, sometimes not—for every grant, contract, bridge, canal, and highway that the federal government provides the district or state. They send letters (at the government's expense) to large factions of their constituents and visit their districts every weekend. Presidents get little credit for district improvements and must rely on the mass media to communicate with voters.

Fourth, a candidate for Congress can deny that he or she is responsible for "the mess in Washington," even when the candidate is an incumbent. Incumbents tend to run as individuals, even to the point of denouncing the very Congress of which they are a part. An incumbent president cannot get away with this; rightly or wrongly, he often is held responsible for whatever has gone wrong, not only in the government but in the nation as a whole.

These last three factors—low voter turnout, services to constituents, and the ability to duck responsibility—probably help explain why so high a percentage of congressional incumbents get reelected. But they do not enjoy a completely free ride. Members of Congress who belong to the same party as the president often feel voters' anger about national affairs, particularly economic conditions. When the economy turns sour and a Republican is in the White House, Republican congressional candidates lose votes; if a Democrat is in the White House, Democratic congressional candidates lose votes.

At one time the **coattails** of a popular presidential candidate could help congressional candidates in his or her own party. But there has been a sharp decline in the value of presidential coattails; indeed, some scholars doubt they still exist.

The net effect of all these factors is that, to a substantial degree, congressional elections have become independent of presidential ones. Though economic factors may still link the fate of a president and some members of his or her party, by and large the incumbent members of Congress enjoy enough of a cushion to protect them against whatever political storms engulf an unpopular president. This fact further reduces the meaning of party—members of Congress can get reelected even though their party's "leader" in the White House has lost popular support, and non-incumbent candidates for Congress may lose despite the fact that a very popular president from their party is in the White House.

Running for President

The first task facing anyone who wishes to be president is to get "mentioned" as someone who is of "presidential caliber." No one is quite sure why some people are mentioned and others are not. Journalist David Broder once suggested that somewhere there is "The Great Mentioner" who announces from time to time who is of presidential caliber (and only The Great Mentioner knows how big that caliber is).

But if The Great Mentioner turns out to be as unreal as the Easter Bunny, you have to figure out for yourself how to get mentioned. One way is to let it be known to reporters, "off the record," that you are thinking about running for president. Another is to travel around the country making speeches (Ronald Reagan, while working for General Electric, made a dozen or more speeches *a day* to audiences all over the country). Another way is to already have a famous name (John Glenn, the former astronaut, was in the public eye long before he declared for the presidency in 1984). Another way to get mentioned is to be identified with a major piece of legislation. Former Senator Bill Bradley of New Jersey was known as an architect of the Tax Reform Act of 1986; Representative Richard Gephardt of Missouri was known as an author of a bill designed to reduce foreign imports. Still

Journalists have many questions for David Plouffe, campaign manager for Barack Obama in 2008 and 2012.

another way is to be the governor of a big state. Former New York governors, such as Mario Cuomo, often are viewed as presidential prospects, partly because New York City is the headquarters of the television and publishing industries.

Once you are mentioned, it is wise to set aside a lot of time to run, especially if you are only "mentioned" as opposed to being really well known. Ronald Reagan devoted the better part of six years to running; Walter Mondale spent four years campaigning; Howard Baker resigned from the Senate in 1984 to prepare to run in 1988 (he finally dropped out of the race). However, many post-1988 candidates—senators Bob Dole, John Kerry, John McCain, and Barack Obama; governors Michael Dukakis, Bill Clinton, and George W. Bush; vice presidents George Bush and Al Gore; and House members Ron Paul and Dennis Kucinich—made the run while holding elective office.

Though presidential candidates come from various backgrounds, in general the voters tend to prefer those with experience as governors or military leaders rather than those who come immediately from Congress. Some candidates, such as John F. Kennedy and Barack Obama, have been elected president directly after being a senator, but most are either war heroes (Dwight Eisenhower), former governors (George W. Bush, Bill Clinton, Ronald Reagan, Jimmy Carter, and Franklin D. Roosevelt), or former members of Congress who have already had experience as vice presidents (Gerald Ford, Richard Nixon, Lyndon Johnson, and Harry Truman).

Money One reason why running takes so much time is that it takes so long to raise the necessary money and build up an organization of personal followers. As we shall see later in this chapter, federal law restricts the amount that any single individual can give a candidate to $2,000 in each election. (A **political action committee,** or **PAC**, which is a committee set up by and representing a corporation, labor union, or other special-interest group, can give up to $5,000.) Moreover, to be eligible for federal matching grants to pay for your primary campaign, you must first raise at least $5,000, in individual contributions of $250 or less, in each of 20 states.

Organization Raising and accounting for money to campaign requires a staff of fundraisers, lawyers, and accountants. You also need a press secretary, a travel scheduler, an advertising specialist, a

political action committee (PAC) A committee set up by a corporation, labor union, or interest group that raises and spends campaign money from voluntary donations.

direct-mail company, and a pollster, all of whom must be paid, plus a large number of volunteers in at least those states that hold early primary elections or party caucuses. These volunteers will brief you on the facts of each state, try to line up endorsements from local politicians and celebrities, and put together a group of people who will knock on doors, make telephone calls, organize receptions and meetings, and try to keep you from mispronouncing the name of the town in which you are speaking. Finally, you have to assemble advisers on the issues. These advisers will write "position papers" for you on all sorts of things you are supposed to know about (but probably don't). Because a campaign usually is waged around a few broad themes, these position papers rarely get used or even read. The papers exist so you can show important interest groups that you have taken "sound" positions, so you can be prepared to answer tough questions, and so journalists can look up your views on matters that may become topical.

Strategy and Themes Every candidate picks a strategy for the campaign. In choosing one, much depends on whether you are the incumbent. Incumbents must defend their records, like it or not. (An incumbent ran for president in 1964, 1972, 1976, 1980, 1984, 1992, 1996, 2004, and 2012.) The challenger attacks the incumbent. When there is no incumbent (as in 1960, 1968, 1988, 2000, and 2008), both candidates can announce their own programs; however, the candidate from the party that holds the White House must take, whether or not the candidate thinks he deserves it, some of the blame for whatever has gone wrong in the preceding four years. Within these limits, a strategy consists of the answers to questions about tone, theme, timing, and targets:

- What *tone* should the campaign have? Should it be a positive (build-me-up) or negative (attack-the-opponent) campaign? In 1988, George H. W. Bush began with a negative campaign; Michael Dukakis followed suit.

- What *theme* can I develop? A theme is a simple, appealing idea that can be repeated over and over again. For Jimmy Carter in 1976, it was "trust"; for Ronald Reagan in 1980, it was "competence," and in 1984, it was "it's morning again in America"; for Bush in 1988, it was "stay the course"; for Clinton in 1992, it was "we need to change"; for George W. Bush in 2000, it was "compassionate conservatism"; for Barack Obama in 2008, it was "yes we can" and "change you can believe in."

- What should be the *timing* of the campaign? If you are relatively unknown, you will have to put everything into the early primaries and caucuses, try to emerge a frontrunner, and then hope for the best. If you are already the frontrunner, you may either go for broke early (and try to drive out all your opponents) or hold back some reserves for a long fight.

- Whom should you *target*? Only a small percentage of voters change their vote from one election to the next. Who is likely to change this time—unemployed steelworkers? Unhappy farmers? People upset by inflation?

Getting Elected to Congress

A president cannot serve more than two terms, so at least once every eight years you have a chance of running against a non-incumbent; members of Congress can serve for an unlimited number of terms, and so chances are you will run against an incumbent. If you decide to run for the House, the odds are very much against you. Since 1962, over 90 percent of the House incumbents who sought reelection won it.

But the incredible incumbency advantage enjoyed by modern-day House members is hardly the whole story of getting elected to Congress. Who serves in Congress, and what interests are represented there, is affected by how its members are elected. Each state is entitled to two senators who serve six-year terms and at least one representative who serves a two-year term. How many more representatives a state has depends on its population; what local groups these representatives speak for depends in part on how the district lines are drawn.

The Constitution says very little about how representatives will be selected except to require that they be inhabitants of the states from which they are chosen. It says nothing about districts and originally left it up to the states to decide who would be eligible to vote for representatives. The size of the first House was set by the Constitution at 65 members, and the apportionment of the seats among the states was spelled out in Article I, section 2. From that point on, it has been up to Congress to decide how many representatives each state would have (provided that each had at least one).

malapportionment
Drawing the boundaries of legislative districts so that they are unequal in population.

gerrymandering Drawing the boundaries of legislative districts in bizarre or unusual shapes to favor one party.

Initially, some states did not create congressional districts; all their representatives were elected at large. In other states, representatives were elected from multimember as well as single-member districts. In time, all states with more than one representative elected each from a single-member district. How those district boundaries were drawn, however, could profoundly affect the outcomes of elections. There were two problems. One was **malapportionment**, which results from having districts of very unequal size. If one district is twice as populous as another, twice as many votes are needed in the larger district to elect a representative. Thus, a citizen's vote in the smaller district is worth twice as much as a vote in the larger.

The other problem was **gerrymandering**, which means drawing a district boundary in some bizarre or unusual shape to make it easy for the candidate of one party to win election in that district. In a state entitled to 10 representatives, where half the voters are Democrats and half are Republicans, district lines could be drawn so that eight districts would have a slight majority of citizens from one party and two districts would have lopsided majorities from the other. Thus, it can be made easy for one party to win eight of the 10 seats.

Malapportionment and gerrymandering have been conspicuous features of American congressional politics. In 1962, for example, one district in Texas had nearly a million residents, while another had less than a quarter million. In California, Democrats in control of the state legislature drew district lines in the early 1960s so that two pockets of Republican strength in Los Angeles separated by many miles were connected by a thin strip of coastline. In this way, most Republican voters were thrown into one district, while Democratic voters were spread more evenly over several.

Hence, there are four problems to solve in deciding who gets represented in the House:

1. Establishing the total size of the House

2. Allocating seats in the House among the states

3. Determining the size of congressional districts within states

4. Determining the shape of those districts

By and large, Congress has decided the first two questions, and the states have decided the last two—but under some rather strict Supreme Court rules.

In 1911, Congress decided the House had become large enough and voted to fix its size at 435 members. There it has remained ever since (except for a brief period when it had 437 members owing to the admission of Alaska and Hawaii to the Union in 1959). Once the size was decided, it was necessary to find a formula for performing the painful task of apportioning seats among the states as they gained and lost population. The Constitution requires such reapportionment every 10 years. A more or less automatic method was selected in 1929 based on a complex statistical system that has withstood decades of political and scientific testing. Since 1990, under this system 18 states have lost representation in the House and 11 have gained it. Florida and California posted the biggest gains, while New York and Pennsylvania suffered the largest losses (see Table 8.6).

The states did little about malapportionment and gerrymandering until ordered to do so by the Supreme Court. In 1964, the Court ruled that the Constitution requires districts be drawn so that, as nearly as possible, one person's vote would be worth as much as another's.[20] The Court rule, "one person, one vote," seems clear, but in fact leaves a host of questions unanswered. How much deviation from equal size is allowable? Should other factors be considered besides population? (For example, a state legislature might want to draw district lines to make it easier for African Americans, Italian Americans, farmers, or some other group with a distinct interest to elect a representative; the requirement of exactly equal districts might make this impossible.) And the gerrymandering problem remains: districts of the same size can be drawn to favor one party or another. The courts have struggled to find answers to these questions, but they remain far from settled.

Winning the Primary However the district lines are drawn, getting elected to Congress first requires getting one's name on the ballot. At one time, the political parties nominated candidates and even printed ballots with the party slates listed on them. All the voter had to do was take the ballot of the preferred party and put it in the ballot box. Today, with rare exceptions, a candidate wins a party's nomination by gathering enough voter signatures to get on the ballot in a primary election, the outcome of which often is beyond the ability of political parties to influence. Candidates tend to form organizations of personal followings and win "their party's" nomination simply by getting more primary votes than the next candidate. It is quite unusual for an incumbent to lose a primary: from 1990 through 2008, only about 10 percent of incumbent senators and 5 percent of incumbent representatives seeking reelection failed to win renomination in

TABLE 8.6 Changes in State Representation in the House of Representatives

States	Number of Seats			
	After 1990 Census	After 2000 Census	After 2010 Census	Change
Gained/Maintained Seats				
Arizona	6	8	9	+3
California	52	53	53	+1
Florida	23	25	27	+4
Georgia	11	13	14	+3
North Carolina	12	13	13	+1
Texas	30	32	36	+6
Lost Seats				
Illinois	20	19	18	−2
Michigan	16	15	14	−2
New York	31	29	27	−4
Ohio	19	18	16	−3
Pennsylvania	21	19	18	−3

Source: U.S. Bureau of the Census

primaries. These statistics suggest how little opportunity parties have to control or punish their congressional members.

Most newly elected members become strong in their districts very quickly; this is called the **sophomore surge**. It is the difference between the votes candidates get the first time they are elected (and thus become freshman members) and the votes they get when they run for reelection (in hopes of becoming sophomore members). Before the 1960s, House candidates did not do much better the second time they ran. Beginning then, however, the sophomore surge kicked in, so that today freshman candidates running for reelection will get 8 to 10 percent more votes than when they were first elected. Senate candidates also benefit now from a sophomore surge, though to a lesser degree.

sophomore surge An increase in the votes congressional candidates usually get when they first run for reelection.

The reason for this surge is that members of Congress have figured out how to use their offices to run *personal* rather than party campaigns. They make use of free ("franked") mail, frequent trips home, radio and television broadcasts, and the distribution of services to their districts to develop among their constituents a good opinion of themselves, not their party. They also cater to their constituents' distrust of the federal government by promising to "clean things up" if reelected. They run *for* Congress by running *against* it.[21]

To the extent that they succeed, they enjoy great freedom in voting on particular issues and have less need to explain away votes that their constituents might not like. If, however, any single-issue groups are actively working in their districts for or against abortion, gun control, nuclear energy, or tax cuts, muting the candidates' voting record may not be possible.

Staying in Office The way people get elected to Congress has two important effects. First, it produces legislators closely tied to local concerns (their districts, their states), and second, it ensures that party leaders will have relatively weak influence over them (because those leaders cannot determine who gets nominated for office).

The local orientation of legislators has some important effects on how policy is made. For example:

- Every member of Congress organizes his or her office to do as much as possible for people back home.

- If your representative serves on the House Transportation and Infrastructure Committee, your state has a much better chance of getting a new bridge or canal than if you do not have a representative on this committee.[22]

- If your representative serves on the House Appropriations Committee, your district is more likely to get approval for a federal grant to improve your water and sewage-treatment programs than if your representative does not serve on that committee.[23]

Former House Speaker Thomas P. "Tip" O'Neill had this in mind when he said, "All politics is local." Some people think this localism is wrong; in their view members of Congress should do what is best for "the nation as a whole." This argument is about the role of legislators: Are they supposed to be *delegates* who do what their district wants or *trustees* who use their best judgment on issues without regard to the preferences of their district?

Naturally, most members are some combination of delegate and trustee, with the exact mix depending on the nature of the issue. But some, as we shall see, definitely lean one way or the other. All members want to be reelected, but "delegates" tend to value this over every other consideration and so seek out committee assignments and projects that will produce benefits for their districts. On the other hand, "trustees" will seek out committee assignments that give them a chance to address large questions, such as foreign affairs, that may have no implications at all for their districts.

Primary versus General Campaigns

When you run for federal office, you must run in two elections, not just one. The first consists of primary elections designed to choose each party's nominee, and the second is the general election that picks the winner who will hold office. If you are running for president, some states, such as Iowa, hold caucuses instead of primary elections. A caucus is a meeting of people, often in an auditorium or church basement, where they vote on who they would like for their party's nominee.

Each election or caucus attracts a different mix of voters. What may help you win a primary or a caucus may be very different from what will help you win the general election. To win a primary or a caucus, you must mobilize political activists who will give money, do volunteer work, and attend local caucuses. To motivate these activists, you must be more liberal (if you are a Democrat) in your tone and theme than rank-and-file Democrats, or more conservative (if you are a Republican) than rank-and-file Republicans. The activists matter lots when it comes to a caucus—a meeting of party members to select delegates backing one or another primary candidate. Consider the caucuses held in Iowa in the winter preceding a presidential election year. This is the first real test of the candidates vying for the nomination. Anyone who does poorly here is at a disadvantage, in terms of media attention and contributor interest, for the rest of the campaign. The several thousand Iowans who participate in their parties' caucuses are not representative of the followers of their party in the state, much less nationally. In 1988, Senator Robert Dole came in first and evangelist Pat Robertson came in second in the Iowa Republican caucus, with Vice President George Bush finishing third. As it turned out, there was little support for Dole or Robertson in the rest of the country.

Democrats who participate in the Iowa caucus tend to be more liberal than Democrats generally. Moreover, the way the caucuses are run is a far cry from how most elections are held. To vote in the Republican caucus, you need not prove you are a Republican or even a voter. The Democratic caucus is not an election at all; instead, a person supporting a certain candidate stands in one corner of the room with people who also support that candidate, while those supporting other candidates stand in other corners with other groups. There is a lot of calling back and forth, intended to persuade people to leave one group and join another. No group with fewer than 15 percent of the people in attendance gets to choose any delegates, so people in these small groups then go to other, larger ones. It is a cross between musical chairs and fraternity pledge week.

Suppose you are a Democrat running for president and you do well in the Iowa caucus. Suppose you go on to win your party's nomination. Now you have to go back to Iowa to campaign for votes in the general election. Between 1940 and 2008, Iowa has voted Republican in every presidential election but eight (1948, 1964, 1988, 1992, 1996, 2000, 2008, and 2012). Your Republican opponent is not going to let you forget all of the liberal slogans you uttered nine months before. The Republican candidate faces the mirror image of this problem—sounding very conservative to get support from Republican activists in states such as Massachusetts and New York and then having to defend those speeches when running against his or her Democratic opponent in those states.

clothespin vote The vote cast by a person who does not like either candidate and so votes for the less objectionable of the two, putting a clothespin over his or her nose to keep out the unpleasant stench.

The problem is not limited to Iowa, but exists in every state where activists are more ideologically polarized than the average voter. To get activist support for the nomination, candidates move to the ideological extremes; to win the general election, they try to move back to the ideological center. The typical voter looks at the results and often decides that neither candidate appeals to him or her very much, and so casts a **"clothespin vote."**

Early in the 2004 presidential caucuses and primaries, John Kerry claimed he was an opponent of the American invasion of Iraq in order to defeat Howard Dean, the Vermont governor who seemed to be capturing the antiwar vote among Democrats. But after he won his party's nomination, Kerry backed away from an antiwar stance in order to be more attractive to centrist voters. He had learned a lesson that George McGovern did not understand in 1972. McGovern maintained his liberal views on the war in Vietnam, decriminalizing marijuana, and providing amnesty for draft dodgers.[24] His opponent, Richard Nixon, defeated him easily by taking more centrist positions.

One last thing: if you decide to run for president as a Democrat, do not trust too much in the early polls indicating the frontrunner for the nomination. Edmund Muskie (1972), George Wallace (1976), Ted Kennedy (1980), Gary Hart (1988), Mario Cuomo (1992), and Joseph Lieberman (2004) were all early frontrunners among Democrats, but none got the party's nomination. Only frontrunners Walter Mondale (1984) and Al Gore (2000) prevailed (though neither went on to win the office). By contrast, since 1972, every early Republican frontrunner except one has won the nomination. In 2007, the Republican frontrunner was former New York City Mayor Rudolph Giuliani, and the Democratic frontrunner was then New York State Senator Hillary Rodham Clinton. By early 2008, Giuliani faded, and Arizona Senator John McCain went on to win the Republican nomination. McCain lost the general election to Illinois Senator Barack Obama following Obama's protracted nomination battle with Clinton.

HOW THINGS WORK

Qualifications for Entering Congress and Privileges of Serving in Congress

Representative

- Must be 25 years of age (when seated, not when elected)

- Must have been a citizen of the United States for seven years

- Must be an inhabitant of the state from which elected (*Note:* Custom, but *not* the Constitution, requires that a representative live in the district that he or she represents.)

Senator

- Must be 30 years of age (when seated, not when elected)

- Must have been a citizen of the United States for nine years

- Must be an inhabitant of the state from which elected

Judging Qualifications

Each house is the judge of the "elections, returns, and qualifications" of its members. Thus, Congress alone can decide disputed congressional elections. On occasion, it has excluded a person from taking a seat on the grounds that the election was improper. Either house can punish a member—by reprimand, for example—or, by a two-thirds vote, expel a member.

(continued)

HOW THINGS WORK (*Continued*)

Privileges

Members of Congress have certain privileges, the most important of which, conferred by the Constitution, is that "for any speech or debate in either house they shall not be questioned in any other place." This doctrine of "privileged speech" has been interpreted by the Supreme Court to mean that members of Congress cannot be sued or prosecuted for anything that they say or write in connection with their legislative duties.

When Senator Mike Gravel read the Pentagon Papers—some then-secret government documents about the Vietnam War—into the *Congressional Record* in defiance of a court order restraining their publication, the Court held that this was "privileged speech" and beyond challenge (*Gravel v. United States*, 408 U.S. 606, 1972). But when Senator William Proxmire issued a press release critical of a scientist doing research on monkeys, the Court decided the scientist could sue him for libel because a press release was not part of the legislative process (*Hutchinson v. Proxmire*, 443 U.S. 111, 1979).

HOW THINGS WORK

Kinds of Elections

There are two kinds of elections in the United States: general and primary. A **general election** is used to fill an elective office. A **primary election** is used to select a party's candidates for an elective office, though in fact those who vote in a primary election may not consider themselves party members. Some primaries are closed. In a **closed primary**, you must declare in advance (sometimes several weeks in advance) that you are a registered member of the political party in whose primary you wish to vote. About 40 states have closed primaries.

Other primaries are open. In an **open primary**, you can decide when you enter the voting booth which party's primary you wish to participate in. You are given every party's ballot; you may vote on one. Idaho, Michigan, Minnesota, Montana, North Dakota, Utah, Vermont, and Wisconsin have open primaries. A variant on the open primary is the **blanket** (or "free love") **primary**—in the voting booth, you mark a ballot that lists the candidates of all the parties, and thus you can help select the Democratic candidate for one office and the Republican candidate for another. Alaska and Washington have blanket primaries.

The differences among these kinds of primaries should not be exaggerated, for even the closed primary does not create any great barrier for a voter who wishes to vote in the Democratic primary in one election and the Republican in another. Some states also have a **runoff primary**: if no candidate gets a majority of the votes, there is a runoff between the two with the most votes. Runoff primaries are common in the South.

A special kind of primary, a presidential primary, is used to pick delegates to the presidential nominating conventions of the major parties. Presidential primaries come in a bewildering variety. A simplified list looks like this:

(*continued*)

HOW THINGS WORK (*Continued*)

- **Delegate selection only** Only the names of prospective delegates to the convention appear on the ballot. They may or may not indicate their presidential preferences.

- **Delegate selection with advisory presidential preference** Voters pick delegates and indicate their preferences among presidential candidates. The delegates are not legally bound to observe these preferences.

- **Binding presidential preference** Voters indicate their preferred presidential candidates. Delegates must observe these preferences, at least for a certain number of convention ballots. The delegates may be chosen in the primary or by a party convention.

In 1981, the Supreme Court ruled that political parties, not state legislatures, have the right to decide how delegates to national conventions are selected. Thus, Wisconsin could not retain an open primary if the national Democratic Party objected (*Democratic Party v. La Follette*, 101 S. Ct. 1010, 1981). Now the parties can insist that only voters who declare themselves Democrats or Republicans can vote in presidential primaries. The Supreme Court's ruling may have relatively little practical effect, however, since the "declaration" might occur only an hour or a day before the election.

The Sources of Campaign Money

Presidential candidates get part of their money from private donors and part from the federal government; congressional candidates get all of their money from private sources. In the presidential primaries, candidates raise money from private citizens and interest groups. The federal government will provide matching funds, dollar for dollar, for all monies raised from individual donors who contribute no more than $250. (To prove they are serious candidates, they must first raise $5,000 in each of 20 states from such small contributors.) The government also gives a lump-sum grant to each political party to help pay the costs of its nominating convention. In the general election, the government pays all the costs (up to a legal limit) of major-party candidates and part of the costs of minor-party candidates (those winning between 5 and 25 percent of the vote).

Congressional candidates get no government funds; all their money must come out of their own pockets or be raised from individuals, interest groups (PACs), or the political parties. Contrary to what many people think, most of that money comes from—and has always come from—individual donors. Because the rules sharply limit how much any individual can give, these donors tend not to be fat cats, but people of modest means who contribute $100 or $200 per person.

general election An election held to choose which candidate will hold office.

primary election An election held to choose candidates for office.

closed primary A primary election in which voting is limited to already registered party members.

open primary A primary election in which voters may choose in which party to vote as they enter the polling place.

blanket primary A primary election in which each voter may vote for candidates from both parties.

runoff primary A second primary election held when no candidate wins a majority of the votes in the first primary.

John F. Kennedy and Richard Nixon debate during the 1960 presidential campaign.

Paul Schutzer/Time Life Pictures/Getty Images

Campaign Finance Rules

During the 1972 presidential election, men hired by President Nixon's campaign staff broke into the headquarters of the Democratic National Committee in the Watergate office building. They were caught by an alert security guard. The subsequent investigation disclosed that the Nixon people had engaged in dubious or illegal money-raising schemes, including taking large sums from wealthy contributors in exchange for appointing them to ambassadorships. Many individuals and corporations were indicted for making illegal donations (since 1925, it had been against the law for corporations or labor unions to contribute money to candidates, but the law had been unenforceable). Some of the accused had given money to Democratic candidates as well as to Nixon.

When the break-in was discovered, the Watergate scandal unfolded. It had two political results: President Nixon was forced to resign, and a new campaign finance law was passed.

Under the new law, individuals could not contribute more than $1,000 to a candidate during any single election. Corporations and labor unions had for many decades been prohibited from spending money on campaigns, but the new law created a substitute: political action committees. A PAC must have at least 50 members (all of whom enroll voluntarily), give to at least five federal candidates, and must not give more than $5,000 to any candidate in any election or more than $15,000 per year to any political party. In addition, the law made federal tax money available to help pay for presidential primary campaigns and for paying all of the campaign costs of a major-party candidate and a fraction of the costs of a minor-party candidate in a presidential general election.

The new law helped increase the amount of money spent on elections and, in time, changed the way money was spent. As Figure 8.4 shows, over the last several decades, different types of PACs have proliferated or dropped off. In each election since 2002, PACs have given over $250 million to congressional candidates. In its April 2013 report on the 2011–2012 federal election cycle, the Federal Election Commission reported that 7,311 PACs had total receipts of nearly $2.3 billion. The PACs that figured most prominently in that funding were the 1,851 corporate PACs (which had $361 million in receipts) and the 1,251 "non-connected" independent-expenditure only PACs (which had $824 million in receipts). These latter PACs, many organized around a particular political ideology or set of issues, included the so-called "super PACS" (see the nearby How Things Work feature).

By contrast, when George McGovern ran against Richard Nixon in 1972, he was chiefly supported by the large contributions of one wealthy donor, and when Eugene McCarthy ran against Lyndon Johnson in 1968, he benefited from a few big donations and did not have to rely on massive fundraising appeals.

A candidate gets federal money to match, dollar for dollar, what he or she has raised in contributions of $250 or less. But a presidential candidate can decide to forgo federal primary funding and raise his

FIGURE 8.4 Growth of PACs 1979–2010

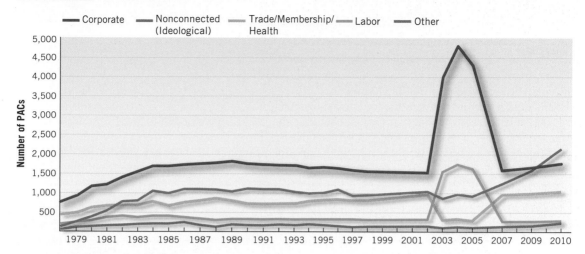

Source: Federal Election Commission.

or her own money. In 2000, George W. Bush relied entirely on his own fundraising, while his chief rival, John McCain, used federal matching funds. In 2004, Bush, Kerry, and Dean all declined federal matching funds in the primary elections. In 2008, John McCain declined public financing for the primaries but accepted it for the general election; Barack Obama relied entirely on his own fundraising for both the primaries and the general election. He did the same in 2012, as did his general election challenger, Mitt Romney.

If you are a minor-party candidate, you can get some support from the federal government provided you have won at least 5 percent of the vote in the last election. In 2000, both Pat Buchanan (Reform party) and Ralph Nader (Green party) got partial support from Washington because their parties had won more than 5 percent of the vote in 1996. But no minor party won more than 5 percent in either 2004, 2008, or 2012, so none received partial support.

The 1973 campaign finance law produced two problems. The first was **independent expenditures**. A PAC, a corporation, or a labor union could spend whatever it wanted supporting or opposing a candidate, so long as this spending was "independent," that is, not coordinated with or made at the direction of the candidate's wishes. Simply put, independent expenditures are ordinary advertising directed at or against candidates.

The second was **soft money**. Under the law, individuals, corporations, labor unions, and other groups could give unlimited amounts of money to political parties provided the money was not used to back candidates by name. But the money could be used in ways that helped candidates by financing voter registration and get-out-the-vote drives. Over half a billion dollars in soft money was spent during each of the last four presidential campaigns (2000, 2004, 2008, 2012). If money is, indeed, the mother's milk of politics, efforts to make the money go away are not likely to work. As soon as the Bipartisan Campaign Reform Act of 2002 began to

independent expenditures
Spending by political action committees, corporations, or labor unions to help a party or candidate but done independently of them.

soft money Funds obtained by political parties that are spent on party activities, such as get-out-the-vote drives, but not on behalf of a specific candidate.

HOW THINGS WORK

Super PACs

Their technical name is "independent expenditure-only committees," but they are more widely known as "super PACs," political action committees that raise and spend unlimited amounts of money from corporations, labor unions, individuals, and other groups. The traditional PAC can accept only so much money from individuals. But super PACs have no limits on who contributes or how much they give, with just this catch: the super PACs are not allowed to act "in concert or cooperation with" the candidate, his or her campaign organization, or a political party. So, for example, a super PAC television ad for a given candidate must be funded and fashioned without that candidate, his or her campaign managers, or the candidate's party leaders being involved in any way.

In 2010, the Supreme Court—in the case of *Citizens United v. Federal Elections Commission*—struck down the ban on corporate and labor union spending on campaign advertisements for and against candidates. This ruling, together with a few other court decisions and rule changes, was behind the proliferation of super PACs in the 2012 national elections. According to an April 2013 report by the Federal Election Commission, in 2011–2012, the "independent-expenditure only" committees spent nearly $800 million, more than was spent by traditional corporate, union, and trade PACs combined. With super PACs, all PACs spent more than $2.1 billion, and PACS outspent the party committees, which spent "only" about $1.6 billion.

HOW THINGS WORK

Major Federal Campaign Finance Rules

General

- All federal election contributions and expenditures are reported to a Federal Election Commission.

- All contributions over $100 must be disclosed, with name, address, and occupation of contributor.

- No *cash* contributions over $100 or foreign contributions.

- No ceiling on how much candidates may spend out of their own money (unless they accept federal funding for a presidential race).

Individual Contributions

- Individuals have limits on how much money they may contribute to a candidate per election or to a Political Action Committee (PAC) or national party committee every year.

- However, the Supreme Court ruled in 2014 that an overall limit on how much money an individual may donate over a two-year period to candidates, political parties, and PACs in total is unconstitutional.

(continued)

HOW THINGS WORK (*Continued*)

Political Action Committees (PACs)

- Each corporation, union, or association may establish one.

- A PAC must register six months in advance, have at least 50 contributors, and give to at least five candidates.

- PAC contributions may not exceed $5,000 per candidate per election or $15,000 to a national political party.

Ban on Soft Money

- No corporation or union may give money from its own treasury to any national political party.

Independent Expenditures

- Corporations, unions, and associations may use their own money to fund "electioneering communications." PACs may fund electioneering communications up to their expenditure limits.

Presidential Primaries

- Federal matching funds can be given to match individual contributions of $250 or less.

- To be eligible, a candidate must raise $5,000 in each of 20 states in contributions of $250 or less.

Presidential Election

- The federal government will pay all campaign costs (up to a legal limit) of major-party candidates and part of the costs of minor-party candidates (those winning between 5 and 25 percent of the vote).

be enforced, people started to find other ways to spend political money. The most common were **527 organizations**. These groups, named after a provision of the Internal Revenue Code, are designed to permit the kind of soft money expenditures once made by political parties. In 2004, the Democrats created the Media Fund, America Coming Together, America Votes, and many other groups. George Soros, the wealthy businessman, gave more than $23 million to organizations pledged to defeat George Bush. The Republicans responded by creating Progress for America, The Leadership Forum, America for Job Security, and other groups. Under the law, as it is now interpreted, 527 organizations can spend their money on politics so long as they do not coordinate with a candidate or lobby directly for that person. As early as the 2004 elections, 527 organizations raised and spent over one-third of a billion dollars. So far, the lesson seems to be this: campaign finance laws are not likely to take money out of politics.

527 organizations
Organizations under section 527 of the Internal Revenue Code that raise and spend money to advance political causes.

HOW THINGS WORK

2014 Election

Forecasts for the 2014 congressional midterm elections uniformly predicted victories for the Republican Party. The 113th Congress, which governed in 2013–14, had a solid Republican majority in the House with more than 230 Republican members, and a solid Democratic majority in the Senate, with 53 Democrats plus two Independents who participated in the Democratic caucus. With nine competitive Senate seats, a party change seemed likely, and Republicans were poised to pick up as many as a dozen or more seats in the House as well.

On election night, the results were clear: President Barack Obama would face fully divided government in Congress. In the Senate, Republicans picked up several seats previously held by Democrats, including seats in Colorado and Iowa, both states that had played significant roles in Obama's presidential victories in 2008 and 2012. Republicans prevailed in all four Senate races with open seats, in Iowa, Montana, South Dakota, and West Virginia. With more than 51 Senate seats, Republicans had confirmed governing power. In the House, Republicans picked up additional seats as well, getting their largest majority in the chamber since at least World War II.

In some respects, the losses were unsurprising. After all, the president's party typically loses seats in midterm elections – since the Great Depression, the only exceptions have been 1934, 1998, and 2002. But the 2014 election results did illustrate a continuing volatility in recent American politics. From 1954–1994, Democrats won control of the House continuously and of the Senate for all but six years of that period (1980–1986). In 1994, Republicans won control of both chambers of Congress, which continued until 2006 (except for a brief period of Democratic control of the Senate from mid-2001 through the 2002 elections, due to a Republican deciding to become Independent and caucus with the Democrats). In 2006, Democrats regained control of both chambers of Congress until 2010, when they lost the House, and then in 2014, when they lost the Senate. What message were voters sending to Washington?

For 2014, the immediate message appeared to a rebuke of the Obama administration's leadership and policies, particularly the controversial health-care law as well as the response to terrorist groups in the Middle East. But exit polls also indicated broad voter dissatisfaction with governance, or the lack thereof, in Washington. More generally, the ever-shortening period between shifts in party control of Congress may indicate pessimism from voters about the likelihood of either political party achieving major policy change in Washington.

Of the 36 Senate races, a few stood out for historic significance. Iowa elected its first woman senator, Joni Ernst, an Iraq war veteran and state senator. Both Iowa and Colorado elected Republican senators in 2014 after casting their electoral-college votes for Obama in 2012. For a Democratic president who was the first since Franklin Delano Roosevelt to win a majority of the popular vote twice (and with strong support from a wide range of voters, as Table 8.7 shows), this marked a significant loss for his political party.

The 2014 elections quickly sparked questions about consequences for 2016. Did the Republican takeover of the Senate and gains in the House indicate a path to the White House in two years? What role, if any, would Tea Party-affiliated candidates play in the campaign? And would Republican control of Congress endure, or might the next elections continue to demonstrate volatility in American politics?

What Decides the Election?

To the voter, it all seems quite simple—he or she votes for "the best person" or maybe "the least-bad person." To scholars, it is all a bit mysterious. How do voters decide who the best person is? What does "best" mean, anyway?

Party

One answer to these questions is party identification. People may say they are voting for the "best person," but for many people the best person is always a Democrat or a Republican. Moreover, we have seen in Chapter 6 that many people consume little political news and know rather little about the details of political issues. They may not even know what position their favored candidate has taken on issues they care about. Given these facts, many scholars have argued that party identification is the principal determinant of how people vote.[25]

If it were only a matter of party identification, though, the Democrats would always win the presidency, since usually more people identify with the Democratic than the Republican party. But we know that the Democrats lost seven of the 12 presidential elections between 1968 and 2012. There are three reasons for this.

First, those people who consider themselves Democrats were less firmly wedded to their party than Republicans. Table 8.8 shows how people identifying themselves as Democrats, Republicans, or independents voted in presidential elections from 1960 to 2012. In every election except those of 1964, 1992, 1996, and 2012, Republicans were more likely to vote for the Republican candidate than Democrats were to vote for the Democratic candidate (with a tie in 2008). In every election except 1992, at least 80 percent of Republican voters supported the Republican candidate. By contrast, there have been a few dramatic defections among Democratic voters—in 1972,

LANDMARK CASES

Financing Elections

- ***Buckley v. Valeo* (1976):** Held that a law limiting contributions to political campaigns was constitutional, but that one restricting a candidate's expenditures of his or her own money was not.

- ***McConnell v. Federal Election Commission* (2002):** Upheld 2002 Bipartisan Campaign Reform Act (popularly known as "McCain-Feingold" law) prohibiting corporations and labor unions from running ads that mention candidates and their positions for 60 days before a federal general election.

- ***Federal Election Commission v. Wisconsin Right to Life, Inc.* (2007):** Held that issue ads may not be prohibited before a primary or general election.

- ***Citizens United v. Federal Election Commission* (2010):** Overturned part of 2002 law that had prohibited corporate and union funding of campaign ads.

- ***McCutcheon, et al v. Federal Election Commission* (2014):** Overturned total spending limits for individual donations in a two-year election cycle to candidates, political parties, and PACs.

TABLE 8.7   2012 Presidential Exit Poll Results

Candidate Receiving Largest Share of the Vote, % Received	
SEX	
Male	Romney, 52%
Female	Obama, 55%
MARITAL STATUS	
Married	Romney, 56%
Unmarried	Obama, 62%
PARTY	
Democrat	Obama, 92%
Republican	Romney, 93%
Independent/Other	Romney, 50%

(Continued)

TABLE 8.7   2012 Presidential Exit Poll Results (*Continued*)

Candidate Receiving Largest Share of the Vote, % Received	
RACE AND ETHNICITY	
White	Romney, 59%
Black	Obama, 93%
Hispanic	Obama, 71%
Asian	Obama, 73%
AGE	
Age 18-29	Obama, 60%
Age 30-44	Obama, 52%
Age 45-64	Romney, 51%
Age 65 and older	Romney, 56%
EDUCATION	
No college	Obama, 51%
Some college	Obama, 49%
College graduate	Romney, 51%
Postgraduate study	Obama, 55%
INCOME	
Under $30,000/year	Obama, 63%
$30,000-$49,999/year	Obama, 57%
$50,000 or more/year	Romney, 53%
$100,000 or more/year	Romney, 54%
LOCATION	
Big cities	Obama, 69%
Mid-sized cities	Obama, 58%
Small cities	Romney, 56%
Suburbs	Romney, 50%
IDEOLOGY	
Liberal	Obama, 86%
Conservative	Romney, 82%
Moderate	Obama, 56%
VIEW OF ECONOMY	
Excellent/good	Obama, 90%
Not so good/poor	Romney, 60%

Source: *The New York Times* 2012 Presidential Election Poll.

a third of Democrats supported Nixon, and in 1984, 26 percent supported Reagan.

The second reason, also clear from Table 8.8, is that the Republicans, from the election of 1960 through the election of 1988, did better than the Democrats among the self-described "independent" voters. In the 14 presidential elections from 1960 to 2012, the Democratic candidate won a larger share of the independent vote six times (1964, 1992, 1996, 2000, 2004, and 2008) while the Republican candidate won it eight times (1960, 1968, 1972, 1976, 1980, 1984, 1988, and 2012). But in five of the last six elections (2012 being the one exception), the Democratic candidate won a larger share of the independent vote than the Republican candidate did.

Finally, a higher percentage of Republicans than Democrats voted in most post-1960 elections, and those describing themselves as "strongly Republican" were more likely to vote than those describing themselves as "strongly Democratic." But those Republican edges in partisan voter participation have ebbed in recent years just as minority voters that traditionally favor the Democratic presidential candidate have increased their participation. For instance, in 2012, Obama won 93 percent of the African American vote; and, at 66.2 percent, voter turnout among African Americans exceeded voter turnout for the electorate as a whole. In 2012, Latino voter turnout was higher than it was in 2008, and Obama won more than 70 percent of all Latino votes.

Issues, Especially the Economy

Even though voters may not know a lot about the issues, that does not mean issues play no role in elections or that voters respond irrationally to them. For example, V. O. Key Jr. looked at those voters who switched from one party to another between elections and found that most of them switched in a direction consistent with their own interests. As Key put it, the voters are not fools.[26]

TABLE 8.8 Percentage of Popular Vote by Groups in Presidential Elections, 1960–2012

		National	Republicans	Democrats	Independents
1960	Kennedy	50%	5%	84%	43%
	Nixon	50	95	16	57
1964	Johnson	61	20	87	56
	Goldwater	39	80	13	44
1968	Humphrey	43	9	74	31
	Nixon	43	86	12	44
	Wallace	14	5	14	25
1972	McGovern	38	5	67	31
	Nixon	62	95	33	69
1976	Carter	51	11	80	48
	Ford	49	89	20	52
1980[a]	Carter	41	11	66	30
	Reagan	51	84	26	54
	Anderson	7	4	6	12
1984	Mondale	41	7	73	35
	Reagan	59	92	26	63
1988	Dukakis	46	8	82	43
	Bush	54	91	17	55
1992	Clinton	43	10	77	38
	Bush	38	73	10	32
	Perot	19	17	13	30
1996	Clinton	49	13	84	43
	Dole	41	80	10	35
	Perot	8	6	5	17
2000	Gore	49	8	86	45
	Bush	48	91	11	47
2004	Kerry	49	6	89	49
	Bush	51	93	11	48
2008	Obama	52	9	89	52
	McCain	46	89	10	44
2012	Obama	51	6	92	45
	Romney	48	90	10	49

[a]The figures for 1980, 1984, 1988, 1996, and 2012 fail to add up to 100 percent because of missing data.

© Cengage Learning

prospective voting Voting for a candidate because you favor his or her ideas for handling issues.

retrospective voting
Voting for a candidate because you like his or her past actions in office.

Moreover, voters may know a lot more than we suppose about issues that really matter to them. They may have hazy, even erroneous views about monetary policy, business regulation, and the trade deficit, but they likely have a very good idea about whether unemployment is up or down, prices at the supermarket are stable or rising, or crime is a problem in their neighborhoods. And on some issues—such as abortion, school prayer, and race relations—they likely have some strong principles they want to see politicians obey.

Contrary to what we learn in our civics classes, representative government does not require voters to be well informed on the issues. If it were our duty as citizens to have accurate facts and sensible ideas about how best to negotiate with foreign adversaries, stabilize the value of the dollar, revitalize failing industries, and keep farmers prosperous, we might as well forget about citizenship and head for the beach. It would be a full-time job, and then some, to be a citizen. Politics would take on far more importance in our lives than most of us would want, given our need to earn a living and our belief in the virtues of limited government.

To see why our system can function without well-informed citizens, we must understand the differences between two ways in which issues can affect elections.

Prospective Voting *Prospective* means "forward-looking"—we vote prospectively when we examine the views the rival candidates have on the issues of the day and then cast our ballots for the person we think has the best ideas for handling these matters. **Prospective voting** requires a lot of information about issues and candidates. Some of us vote prospectively. Those who do tend to be political junkies. They are either willing to spend a lot of time learning about issues or are so concerned about some big issue (abortion, school busing, nuclear energy) that all they care about is how a candidate stands on that question.

Prospective voting is more common among people who are political activists, have a political ideology that governs their voting decision, or are involved in interest groups with a big stake in the election. They are a minority of all voters, but (as we saw in Chapter 7 and as we see here in Chapter 8) they are more influential than their numbers would suggest. Some prospective voters (by no means all) are organized into single-issue groups, to be discussed in the next section.

Retrospective Voting *Retrospective* means "backward-looking"—**retrospective voting** involves looking at how things have gone in the recent past and then voting for the party that controls the White House if we like what has happened and voting against that party if we do not like what has happened. Retrospective voting does not require us to have a lot of information—all we need to know is whether things have, in our view, gotten better or worse.

Elections are decided by retrospective voters.[27] In 1980, they decided to vote against Jimmy Carter because inflation was rampant, interest rates were high, and we seemed to be getting the worst of things overseas. The evidence suggests rather clearly that they did not vote *for* Ronald Reagan; they voted for *an alternative to* Jimmy Carter. (Some people did vote for Reagan and his philosophy; they were voting prospectively, but they were in the minority.) In 1984, people voted for Ronald Reagan because unemployment, inflation, and interest rates were down and because we no longer seemed to be getting pushed around overseas. In 1980, retrospective voters wanted change; in 1984, they wanted continuity. In 1988, there was no incumbent running, but George H. W. Bush portrayed himself as the candidate who would continue the policies that had led to prosperity and depicted Michael Dukakis as a "closet liberal" who would change those policies. In 1992, the economy had once again turned sour, and so voters turned away from Bush and toward his rivals, Bill Clinton and Ross Perot.

Though most incumbent members of Congress get re-elected, those who lose do so, it appears, largely because they are the victims of retrospective voting. After Reagan was first elected, the economy went into a recession in 1981–1982. As a result, Republican members of Congress were penalized by the voters, and Democratic challengers were helped. But it is not just the economy that can hurt congressional candidates. In most midterm elections, the party holding the White House has lost seats in Congress. Just why this should be is not entirely clear, but it probably has something to do with the tendency of some voters to change their opinions of the presidential party once that party has had a chance to govern—which is to say, a chance to make some mistakes, disappoint some supporters, and irritate some interests.

Some scholars believe that retrospective voting is based largely on economic conditions. Figure 8.5 certainly provides support for this view. Each dot represents a presidential election (17 of them, from 1948 to 2012). The horizontal axis is the percentage increase or decrease in per capita disposable income (adjusted for inflation) during the election year. The vertical axis is the percentage of the two-party vote won by the party already occupying the White House. You can see that, as per capita income goes up (as you move to the right on the horizontal axis), the incumbent political party tends to win a bigger share of the vote.

Other scholars feel that matters are more complicated than this. As a result, a small industry has grown up consisting of people who use different techniques to forecast the outcome of elections. If you know how the president stands in the opinion polls several months before the election and how well the economy is performing, you can make a pretty good guess as to who is going to win the presidency. For congressional races, predicting the result is a lot tougher because so many local factors affect these contests. Election forecasting remains an inexact science. As one study of the performance of presidential election forecasting models concluded: "Models may be no improvement over pundits.[28]

The Campaign

If party loyalty and national economic conditions play so large a role in elections, is the campaign just sound and fury, signifying nothing?

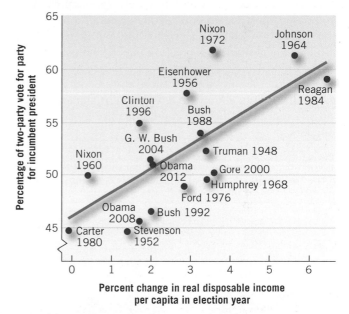

FIGURE 8.5 **The Economy and Vote for President 1948–2012**

Notes: (1) Each dot represents a presidential election, showing the popular vote received by the incumbent president's party. (2) 1992 data do not include votes for independent candidate H. Ross Perot. (3) 2004 value on RDI is projection from data available in December 2004.

Source: From *American Public Opinion*, 5th ed., by Robert S. Erikson and Kent L. Tedin. Copyright © 1995 by Addison-Wesley Educational Publishers, Inc. Reprinted by permission of Pearson Education, Inc. 2008 update from Bureau of Economic Analysis, U.S. Department of Commerce. Federal Reserve of St. Louis. "FRED Economic Data: Real Disposable Personal Income Per Capita." Economic Research. Accessed June 2, 2013. http://research.stlouisfed.org/fred2/graph/? s[1][id]=A229RX0.

No. Campaigns can make a difference in three ways. First, they reawaken the partisan loyalties of voters. Right after a party's nominating convention selects a presidential candidate, that person's standing with voters of both parties goes way up in the polls. The reason is that the just-nominated candidate has received a lot of media attention during the summer months, when not much else is happening. When the campaign gets underway, however, both candidates get publicity, and voters return to their normal Democratic or Republican affiliations.

Second, campaigns give voters a chance to watch how the candidates handle pressure, and they give candidates a chance to apply that pressure. The two rivals, after promising to conduct a campaign "on the issues" without mudslinging, immediately start searching each other's personal histories and records to find acts, statements, or congressional votes that can be shown in the worst possible light in newspaper or television ads. Many voters don't like these "negative ads"—but they work. Careful statistical studies based on actual campaigns (as opposed to voter surveys or laboratory-like focus group studies) suggest that negative ads work by stimulating voter turnout.[29] As a result, every politician constantly worries about how an opponent might portray his or her record, a fact that helps explain why so many politicians never do or say anything that cannot be explained in a 30-second television spot.

Third, campaigns allow voters an opportunity to judge the character and core values of the candidates. Most voters don't study in detail a candidate's positions on issues; even if they had the time, they know you can't predict how politicians will behave just from knowing what a campaign manager has written in a position paper. The voters want some guidance as to how a candidate will behave once elected. They get that guidance by listening not to the details of what a candidate says but to the themes and tone of those statements. Is the candidate tough on crime and drugs? Are his or her statements about the environment sincere or perfunctory? Does the candidate favor having a strong military? Does the candidate care more about not raising taxes or more about helping the homeless?

The desire of voters to discern character, combined with the mechanics of modern campaigning—short radio and television ads and both online and printed direct mail—lend themselves to an emphasis on themes at the expense of details. This tendency is reinforced by the expectations of ideological party activists and single-issue groups.

Thematic campaigning, negative ads, and the demands of single-issue groups are not new; they are as old as the republic. In the 19th century, the theme was slavery and the single-issue groups were abolitionists and their opponents; their negative ads make the ones we have today sound like Sunday school sermons. At the turn of the century, the themes were temperance and the vote for women; both issues led to no-holds-barred, rough-and-tumble campaigning. In the 1970s and 1980s, new themes were advanced by fundamentalist Christians and by pro- and anti-abortion groups.

What has changed is not the tone of campaigning but the advent of primary

AP Images/Mark Duncan

Union members were once heavily Democratic, but since Ronald Reagan began winning white union votes in 1980, these votes have been up for grabs.

elections. Once, political parties picked candidates out of a desire to win elections. Today, activists and single-issue groups influence the selection of candidates, sometimes out of a belief that it is better to lose with the "right" candidate than to win with the wrong one. In a five-candidate primary, a minority of the voters can pick the winner. Single-issue groups can make a big difference under these conditions, even though they may not have much influence in the general election.

Finding a Winning Coalition

Putting together a winning electoral coalition means holding on to your base among committed partisans and attracting the swing voters who cast their ballots in response to issues (retrospectively or prospectively) and personalities.

There are two ways to examine the nature of the parties' voting coalitions. One is to ask what percentage of various identifiable groups in the population supported the Democratic or Republican candidate for president. The other is to ask what proportion of a party's total vote came from each of these groups. The answer to the first question tells us how *loyal* African Americans, farmers, union members, and others are to the Democratic or Republican party or candidate; the answer to the second question tells us how *important* each group is to a candidate or party.

For the Democratic coalition, African Americans are the most loyal voters. In every election but one since 1952, two-thirds or more of all African Americans voted Democratic; since 1964, more than four-fifths have gone Democratic. Usually, Jewish voters are almost as solidly Democratic. Most Latinos have been Democrats, though there are differences among Cuban Americans (who often vote Republican) and Mexican Americans and Puerto Ricans (who are strongly Democratic). In recent elections, turnout rates among Latino voters have begun to rise. After losing the growing Latino vote by a lopsided margin again in 2012, many Republican leaders vowed to make new and concerted efforts to win more Latino votes in time for the 2016 presidential campaign season; we shall see what happens.

The Democrats have lost their once strong hold on Catholics, southerners, and union members. In 1960, Catholics supported John F. Kennedy (a Democrat and fellow Catholic), but they also voted for Eisenhower, Nixon, and Reagan—all Republicans. Union members deserted the Democrats in 1968 and 1972, came back in 1980 and 1988, and divided about evenly between the two parties in 1952, 1956, and 1980. As Table 8.9 shows, in the 13 presidential elections from 1964 through 2012, a majority of Catholics voted for the Democrat in five elections, for the Republican in six elections, and were split 50-50 in two elections (2000 and 2012). Thus, for any president and for either party, a winning coalition must be assembled anew in every election.

The Republican Party often is described as the party of business and professional people. The loyalty of these groups to Republicans is strong: only in 1964 did they desert the Republican candidate to support Lyndon Johnson. Farmers usually have been Republican,

Former Speaker of the U.S. House of Representatives Newt Gingrich campaigned for the Republican presidential nomination in 2012.

TABLE 8.9   Percentage of Various Groups Saying They Voted for the Democratic Presidential Candidate, 1964–2012

		1964	1968[a]	1972	1976	1980[b]	1984	1988	1992[c]	1996	2000	2004	2008	2012
Sex	Men	60	41	37	53	37	37	41	41	43	42	45	49	45
	Women	62	45	38	48	45	42	49	46	54	54	52	56	55
Race	White	59	38	32	46	36	34	40	39	44	45	42	43	40
	Black	94	85	87	85	82	90	86	82	84	90	89	95	93
Education	College	52	37	37	42	35	40	43	44	44	45	47	49	47
	Grade school	66	52	49	58	43	49	56	55	59	52	51	63	63
Age	Under 30	64	47	48	53	43	41	47	44	53	48	54	66	60
	50 and over	59	41	36	52	41[d]	39	49	50	48	48	46	48	47
Religion	Protestant	55	35	30	46	na	na	33[e]	38	41	42	41	45	42
	Catholic	76	59	48	57	40	44	47	42	53	50	48	54	50
	Jewish[f]	89	85	66	68	45	66	64	68	78	79	76	78	69
Southerners		52	31	29	54	47	36	41	42	na	na	41	na	na

[a]1968 election had three major candidates (Humphrey, Nixon, and Wallace).

[b]1980 election had three major candidates (Carter, Reagan, and Anderson).

[c]1992 election had three major candidates (Clinton, George H. W. Bush, and Perot).

[d]For 1980–1992 and 2004, refers to age 60 and over.

[e]For 1988, white Protestants only.

[f]Jewish vote estimated from various sources; because the number of Jewish persons interviewed is often less than 100, the error in this figure, as well as that for nonwhites, may be large.

na, not available.

Source: Gallup poll data as tabulated in Jeane J. Kirkpatrick, "Changing Patterns of Electoral Competition," in Anthony King, ed., *The New American Political System* (Washington, D.C.: American Enterprise Institute, 1978), pp. 264–265. 1980, 1984, 1988, 1992, 1996, 2000, 2004, and 2008 data from CBS News/New York Times survey and CNN poll. 2012 data on Protestant, Catholic, and Jewish, Prof. John Lapinski, University of Pennsylvania, other 2012 data from NEP exit poll data 2012 as reported in Wall Street Journal, November 8, 2012.

but they are a volatile group, highly sensitive to the level of farm prices—and thus quick to change parties. In sum, the loyalty of most identifiable groups of voters to either party is not overwhelming. Only African Americans, businesspeople, and Jews usually give two-thirds or more of their votes to one party or the other; other groups display tendencies, but none that cannot be overcome.

The contribution that each of these groups makes to the party coalitions is a different matter. Though African Americans are overwhelmingly and persistently Democratic, they make up so small a portion of the total electorate that they have never accounted for more than a quarter of the total Democratic vote. The groups that make up the largest part of the Democratic vote—Catholics, union members, southerners—are also the least dependable parts of that coalition.[30]

When representatives of various segments of society make demands on party leaders and presidential candidates, they usually stress their numbers or their loyalty, but rarely both. African American leaders, for example, sometimes describe the black vote as of decisive importance to Democrats and thus deserving of special consideration from a Democratic president. But African Americans are so loyal that a Democratic candidate can almost take their votes for granted, and in any event they are not as numerous as other groups. Union leaders emphasize how many union voters there are, but a president will know that union leaders cannot "deliver" the union vote and that this vote may go to the president's opponent, whatever the leaders say. For any presidential candidate, a winning coalition must be put together anew for each election. Only a few voters can be taken for granted or written off as a lost cause.

Elections in ordinary times are not "critical"—they do not produce any major party realignment, they are not fought out over a dominant issue, and they provide the winners with no clear mandate. In most cases, an election is little more than a retrospective judgment on the record of the incumbent president and the existing congressional majority. If times are good, incumbents win easily; if times are bad, incumbents may lose—even though their opponents may have no clear plans for change. But even a "normal" election can produce dramatic results if the winner is a person such as Ronald Reagan, who helped give his party a distinctive political philosophy, or Barack Obama, the nation's first African American president.

LEARNING OBJECTIVES

LO 8.1 What is "political participation"?

Political participation refers to the many different ways that people take part in politics and government. Voting is one of the most common and widely studied forms of political participation.

LO 8.2 How are voter turnout rates measured?

There are at least two ways to measure voter turnout, by voting-age population (all residents age 18 and older) and voting-eligible population (all residents age 18 and older excluding noncitizens, disenfranchised convicted felons, and others who are not eligible to vote); voter turnout rates are higher when measured according to the voter-eligible population.

LO 8.3 Who votes, who doesn't?

The most powerful determinants of voting are age (older people vote more than younger people) and education (college graduates vote more than high school graduates or adults who have not completed high school).

LO 8.4 What is the difference between a primary election and a general election?

A primary election selects a political party's nominee for office, while a general election determines who will hold that office.

LO 8.5 What matters most in deciding who wins presidential and congressional elections?

The party identification of the voters matters the most. Only 10 to 20 percent of the voters are available to have their votes changed. For them, the state of the economy, and in wartime the success or failures we have while fighting abroad, makes the most difference. Closely allied with those issues, at least for presidential candidates, is the voters' assessment of their character.

TO LEARN MORE

- Federal Election Commission: **www.fec.gov**

- Project Vote Smart: **www.vote-smart.org**

- Election history: **clerk.house.gov**

- Electoral college: **www.archives.gov/federal-register/electoral-college/**

- Campaign finance: **www.opensecrets.org**

Information for voters

- Congress.org: **www.congress.org/**

- League of Women Voters: **www.lwv.org/**

- Voter Information Services: **www.vis.org/**

- Voting Guide: **www.vote411.org/**

- National Mail Voter Registration Form: **www.fec.gov/votregis/vr.shtml**

- Voter turnout statistics: **www.census.gov/compendia/statab/cats/elections/voting-age_ population_and_voter_participation.html**

- Bader, Ted. *Campaigning for Hearts and Minds: How Emotional Appeals in Political Ads Work*. Chicago: University of Chicago Press, 2006. Masterful analysis of how ads move voters and influence people who are most well-informed about politics.

- Black, Earl, and Merle Black. *Divided America: The Ferocious Power Struggle in American Politics*. New York: Simon and Schuster, 2007. Detailed account of how evenly balanced the two parties are in all parts of the country.

- Burnham, Walter Dean. *Critical Elections and the Mainsprings of American Politics*. New York: Norton, 1970. An argument about the decline in voting participation and the significance of the realigning election of 1896.

- Green, Donald P., and Alan S. Gerber. *Get Out the Vote!: How to Increase Voter Turnout*. Washington, D.C.: Brookings Institution Press, 2nd edition, 2008. Excellent review of the evidence on what works—and what doesn't—to get more people to the polls.

- Klein, Joe. *Politics Lost*: *How American Democracy Was Trivialized by People Who Think You're Stupid*. New York: Doubleday, 2006. A veteran political reporter claims that political consultants are to blame for negative political developments.

- Niemi, Richard, Herbert F. Weisberg, and David C. Kimball, eds. *Controversies in Voting Behavior*, 5th edition. Washington, D.C. : Congressional Quarterly Press, 2010. Essays on voting and related topics that summarize the most advanced empirical research and offer competing perspectives on what the data show.

- Sniderman, Paul M., and Benjamin Highton, eds. *Facing the Challenge of Democracy: Explorations in the Analysis of Public Opinion and Political Participation*. Princeton, NJ: Princeton University Press, 2011. Essays on political participation and related topics that highlight new and unresolved research questions and, in many cases, update classic studies.

- Sundquist, James L. *Dynamics of the Party System: Alignment and Realignment of Political Parties in the United States*, rev. ed. Washington, D.C.: Brookings Institution, 1983. Historical analysis of realigning elections from 1860 to the non-realignment of 1980.

- Wattenberg, Martin P. *Is Voting for Young People?* New York: Pearson, 3rd edition, 2012. An account of why youth voter turnout in America has been so low and a case for compulsory voting.

- Wilson, Catherine E. *The Politics of Latino Faith: Religion, Identity, and Urban Community*. New York: New York University Press, 2008. Richly detailed study of how Latino religious life intersects with politics in three cities.

Jeff Malet Photography/Newscom

9 Congress

If you are like most Americans, you trust the Supreme Court, respect the presidency (whether or not you like the president), and dislike Congress (even if you like your own representative and senators). Congress is the most unpopular branch of government. But it is also the most important one. You cannot understand the national government without first understanding Congress. Glance at the Constitution and you will see why Congress is so important: the first four-and-a-half pages are about Congress, while the presidency gets only a page and a half and the Supreme Court about three-quarters of one page.

To the Framers of the Constitution, the bicameral (two-chamber) Congress was "the first branch." They expected Congress to wield most of the national government's powers, including its most important ones like the "power of the purse" (encompassing taxation and spending decisions) and the ultimate authority to declare war. They understood Congress as essential to sustaining federalism (guaranteeing two senators to each state without regard to state population) and maintaining the separation of powers (ensuring that no lawmaker would be allowed to serve in either of the other two branches while in Congress). They also viewed Congress as the linchpin of the system of checks and balances, constitutionally empowered as it was both to override presidential vetoes and to determine the structure and the appellate jurisdiction of the federal judiciary, including the Supreme Court.

Most contemporary Americans and many experts, however, think of Congress not as the first branch, but as "the broken branch," unable to address the nation's most pressing domestic, economic, and international problems in an effective way; unduly responsive to powerful organized special interests; awash in nonstop campaign fundraising and other activities that many believe border on political corruption; and unlikely to fix itself through real reforms.[1]

Consistent with this broken branch view, in recent decades, public approval of Congress has rarely ranged much above a third. In the 2000s, ratings in the 20s or 30s were the norm. In recent years, several ratings in the teens have been recorded. In July 2008, the Gallup Organization, which has tracked public approval of Congress for decades, recorded an all-time low of 14 percent public approval. In March 2010, public approval of Congress stood at 16 percent. In November 2010, Republicans regained control of the House after four years of Democratic control; and in March 2011, public approval of Congress was at 18 percent. The 2012 elections also resulted in little change: Republicans retained control of the House, and during the first half of 2014, Congress's approval dipped as low as 12 percent.

Many academic analysts and veteran Washington journalists echo the popular discontent with Congress as the broken branch, but the experts focus more on two things, the first a paradox and the second a puzzle. The paradox is that most Americans consistently disapprove of Congress yet routinely reelect their own members to serve in it. In political scientist Richard F. Fenno's famous phrase, if "Congress is the broken branch, then how come we love our congressmen so much more than our Congress?"[2] Despite public approval ratings that almost never reach as high as half, since 1980 over 90 percent of all congressional incumbents who have sought reelection have won it, most by comfortable margins. Even in elections in which "anti-incumbent" public sentiment seems rife and voters effect a change in party control of one or both chambers of Congress, incumbents prevail and dominate the institution. For example, in the 2010 midterm elections, Democrats suffered historic losses in the House and then lost control of the Senate in the 2014 midterm elections, but most Democratic and Republican incumbents alike who sought reelection won it. The puzzle is why the post-1970 Congress has become ever more polarized by partisanship and divided by ideology, and whether this development reflects ever-widening political cleavages among average Americans or instead constitutes a disconnect between the people and their representatives on Capitol Hill.

partisan polarization A vote in which a majority of Democratic legislators oppose a majority of Republican legislators.

THEN

During 1890–1910, about two-thirds of all votes in Congress evoked a party split, and in several sessions more than half the roll calls found about 90 percent of each party's members opposing the other party.[3] But, during the 1970s, such **partisan polarization** in Congress was very much the exception to the rule. Well into the 1960s, Congress commonly passed major legislation on most issues on a bipartisan basis, and there were liberal members and conservative members in leadership positions in both parties and in both chambers. Such liberal and conservative voting blocs as existed typically crossed party lines, like the mid-20th-century conservative bloc featuring Republicans and Southern Democrats. Leaders in Congress in each party were usually veteran politicians interested mainly in winning elections, dispensing patronage, obtaining tangible benefits for their own districts or states and constituents, and keeping institutional power and perks. Even members with substantial seniority did not get the most coveted committee chairmanships unless they were disposed to practice legislative politics as the art of the possible and the art of the deal. This meant forging interparty coalitions and approaching interbranch (legislative–executive) relations in ways calculated to result ultimately in bipartisan bargains and compromises, and doing so even on controversial issues and even when congressional leaders and the president were not all in the same party.

HOW THINGS WORK

The Powers of Congress

The powers of Congress are found in Article I, section 8, of the Constitution.

- To lay and collect taxes, duties, imposts, and excises

- To borrow money

- To regulate commerce with foreign nations and among the states

- To establish rules for naturalization (that is, becoming a citizen) and bankruptcy

- To coin money, set its value, and punish counterfeiting

- To fix the standard of weights and measures

- To establish a post office and post roads

- To issue patents and copyrights to inventors and authors

- To create courts inferior to (below) the Supreme Court

- To define and punish piracies, felonies on the high seas, and crimes against the law of nations

- To declare war

- To raise and support an army and navy and make rules for their governance

(continued)

HOW THINGS WORK (*Continued*)

- To provide for a militia (reserving to the states the right to appoint militia officers and to train the militia under congressional rules)

- To exercise exclusive legislative powers over the seat of government (the District of Columbia) and other places purchased to be federal facilities (forts, arsenals, dockyards, and "other needful buildings")

- To "make all laws which shall be necessary and proper for carrying into execution the foregoing powers, and all other powers vested by this Constitution in the government of the United States." (*Note*: This "necessary and proper," or "elastic," clause has been generously interpreted by the Supreme Court, as explained in Chapter 12.)

NOW

When the 91st Congress ended in 1970, the more liberal half of the House had 29 Republicans and the more conservative half of the House had 59 Democrats.[4] By the time the 105th Congress ended in 1998, the more liberal half of the House had only 10 Republicans while the more conservative half of the House had zero Democrats.[5] (Zero!) In the 2000s, liberal Republicans and conservative Democrats became virtually extinct in both the House and the Senate. For example, in 2010, the major health care reform bill (the Patient Protection and Affordable Care Act) proposed by Democrats passed in the House without a single Republican member of the House voting for it. In 2011, the far-reaching fiscal year 2012 budget plan (cutting trillions of dollars in spending over the next decade) drafted by Republicans passed in the House without a single Democratic member of the House voting for it. The 112th Congress began in January 2011, and during its first quarter-year, a post-1945 record high of about 80 percent of all roll-call votes in the House pitted a majority of Democrats against a majority of Republicans.[6] Or consider: In the 93rd Congress that began in 1973, the GOP's House "conservative caucus" (the Republican Study Committee) claimed just 4 of the chamber's 192 Republican House members (or about 2 percent); but, four decades later, in the 113th Congress that began in 2013, it claimed 171 of the 233 Republican members of the House (or about 74 percent).[7]

Congress is now home to ideologically distinct political parties that seem more unified than ever with respect to how their respective members vote, but the body still does not come close to matching the near-total party unity that has been typical in the national legislatures of the United Kingdom and other parliamentary democracies.

Madison and the other Framers expressly rejected a parliamentary system like Great Britain's in favor of a system featuring both a separation of powers and checks and balances. They understood the fundamental differences between a "congress" and a "parliament," and so must every present-day student who hopes to really understand the U.S. Congress.

Congress versus Parliament

The United States (along with many Latin American nations) has a congress; the United Kingdom (along with most Western European nations) has a parliament. A hint as to the difference between the two kinds of legislatures can be found in the original meanings of the words. *Congress* derives from a Latin term that means "a coming together," a meeting, as of representatives from various places. *Parliament* comes from a French word, *parler,* that means "to talk."

There is of course plenty of talking—some critics say there is nothing *but* talking—in the U.S. Congress, and certainly members of a parliament represent, to a degree, their local districts. But the differences implied by the names of the lawmaking groups are real ones, with profound significance for how laws are made and how the government is run. These differences affect two important aspects of lawmaking bodies: how one becomes a member and what one does as a member.

Ordinarily, a person becomes a member of a parliament (such as the British House of Commons) by persuading a political party to put his or her name on the ballot. Though usually a local party committee selects a person to be its candidate, that committee often takes suggestions from national party headquarters. The local group selects as its candidate someone willing to support the national party program and leadership. In the election, voters in the district choose not between two or three personalities running for office, but between two or three national parties.

By contrast, a person becomes a candidate for representative or senator in the U.S. Congress by running in a primary election. Except in a very few places, political parties exercise little control over the choice of who is nominated to run for congressional office. (This is the case even though the person who wins the primary will describe himself or herself in the general election as a Democrat or a Republican.) Voters select candidates in the primaries because of their personalities, positions on issues, or overall reputation. Even in the general election, where the party label affects who votes for whom, many citizens vote "for the man" (or for the woman), not for the party.

As a result of these different systems, a parliament tends to be made up of people loyal to the national party leadership who meet to debate and vote on party issues. A congress, on the other hand, tends to be made up of people who think of themselves as independent representatives of their districts or states and who, while willing to support their party on many matters, expect to vote as their (or their constituents') beliefs and interests require.

Once they are in the legislature, members of a parliament discover they can make only one important decision—whether or not to support the government. The government in a parliamentary system such as that of the United Kingdom consists of a prime minister and various Cabinet officers selected from the party that has the most seats in parliament. As long as the members of that party vote together, that government will remain in power (until the next election). Should members of a party in power in parliament decide to vote against their leaders, the leaders lose office, and a new government must be formed. With so much at stake, the leaders of a party in parliament have a powerful incentive to keep their followers in line. They insist that all members of the party vote together on almost all issues. If someone refuses, the penalty is often drastic: the party does not renominate the offending member in the next election.

Members of the U.S. Congress do not select the head of the executive branch of government— that is done by the voters when they choose a president. Far from making members of Congress less powerful, this makes them more powerful. Representatives and senators can vote on proposed laws without worrying that their votes will cause the government to collapse and without fearing that a failure to support their party will lead to their removal from the ballot in the next election. Congress has independent powers, defined by the Constitution, that it can exercise without regard to presidential preferences. Political parties do not control nominations for office, and thus they cannot discipline members of Congress who fail to support the party leadership. Because Congress is constitutionally independent of the president, and because its members are not tightly disciplined by a party leadership, individual members of Congress are free to express their views and vote as they wish. They are also free to become involved in the most minute details of lawmaking, budget making, and supervision of the administration of laws. They do this through an elaborate set of committees and subcommittees.

A real parliament, such as that in Britain, is an assembly of party representatives who choose a government and discuss major national issues. The principal daily work of a parliament is debate. A congress, such as that in the United States, is a meeting place of the representatives of local constituencies—districts and states. Members of the U.S. Congress can initiate, modify, approve, or reject laws, and they share with the president supervision of the administrative agencies of the government. The principal work of a congress is representation and action, most of which takes place in committees.

What this means in practical terms to the typical legislator is easy to see. Since members of the British House of Commons have little independent power, they get rather little in return. They are poorly paid, may have no offices of their own and virtually no staff, are allowed only small sums to buy stationery, and can make a few free local telephone calls. Each is given a desk, a filing cabinet, and a telephone, but not always in the same place.

By contrast, a member of the U.S. House of Representatives, even a junior one, has power and is rewarded accordingly. For example, in 2013, each member earned a substantial base salary ($174,000) plus generous health care and retirement benefits, and was entitled to a large office (or "clerk-hire") allowance, to pay for about two dozen staffers. (Each chamber's majority and minority leaders earned $193,400 a year, and the Speaker of the House earned $223,500.) Each member also received individual allowances for travel, computer services, and the like. In addition, each member could mail newsletters and certain other documents to constituents for free using the "franking privilege." Senators, and representatives with seniority, received even larger benefits. Each senator is entitled to a generous office budget and legislative assistance allowance and is free to hire as many staff members as he or she wishes with the money. These examples are not given to suggest that members of Congress

Three powerful Speakers of the House: Thomas B. Reed (1889–1891, 1895–1899) (left), Joseph G. Cannon (1903–1911) (center), and Sam Rayburn (1941–1947, 1949–1953, 1955–1961) (right). Reed put an end to a filibuster in the House by refusing to allow dilatory motions and by counting as "present"—for purposes of a quorum—members in the House even though they were not voting. Cannon further enlarged the Speaker's power by refusing to recognize members who wished to speak without Cannon's approval and by increasing the power of the Rules Committee, over which he presided. Cannon was stripped of much of his power in 1910. Rayburn's influence rested more on his ability to persuade than on his formal powers.

are overrewarded, but only that their importance as individuals in our political system can be inferred from the resources they command.

Because the United States has a congress made up of people chosen to represent their states and districts, rather than a parliament made up to represent competing political parties, no one should be surprised to learn that members of the U.S. Congress are more concerned with their own constituencies and careers than with the interests of any organized party or program of action. And since Congress does not choose the president, members of Congress know that worrying about the voters they represent is much more important than worrying about whether the president succeeds with his programs. These two factors taken together mean that Congress tends to be a decentralized institution, with each member more interested in his or her own views and those of his or her voters than with the programs proposed by the president.

Indeed, Congress was designed by the Founders in ways that almost inevitably make it unpopular with voters. Americans want government to take action, follow a clear course of action, and respond to strong leaders. Americans dislike political arguments, the activities of special-interest groups, and the endless pulling and hauling that often precede any congressional decision. But the people who feel this way are deeply divided about what government should do: Be liberal? Be conservative? Spend money? Cut taxes? Support abortions? Stop abortions? Since they are divided, and since members of Congress must worry about how voters feel, it is inevitable that on controversial issues Congress will engage in endless arguments, worry about what interest groups (who represent different groups of voters) think, and work out compromise decisions. When it does those things, however, many people feel let down and say they have a low opinion of Congress.

Of course, a member of Congress might explain all these constitutional facts to the people, but not many members are eager to tell their voters that they do not really understand how Congress was created and organized. Instead they run for re-election by promising voters they will go back to Washington and "clean up that mess."

The Evolution of Congress

The Framers chose to place legislative powers in the hands of a congress rather than a parliament for philosophical and practical reasons. They did not want to have all powers concentrated in a single governmental institution, even one that was popularly elected, because they feared such a concentration could lead to rule by an oppressive or impassioned majority. At the same time, they knew the states were jealous of their independence and would never consent to a national constitution if it did not protect their interests and strike a reasonable balance between large and small states. Hence, they created a **bicameral** (two-chamber) **legislature**—with a House of Representatives, elected directly by the people, and a Senate, consisting of two members from each state, chosen by the legislatures of each state. Though "all legislative powers" were vested in Congress, those powers would be shared with the president (who could veto acts of Congress), limited to powers explicitly conferred on the federal government, and, as it turned out, subject to the power of the Supreme Court to declare acts of Congress unconstitutional.

bicameral legislature A lawmaking body made up of two chambers or parts.

For decades, critics of Congress complained that the body cannot plan or act quickly. They are right, but two competing values are at stake: centralization versus decentralization. If Congress acted quickly and decisively as a body, then there would have to be strong central leadership, restrictions on debate, few opportunities for stalling tactics, and minimal committee interference. If, on the other hand, the interests of individual members—and the constituencies they represent—were protected or enhanced, then there would have to be weak leadership, rules allowing for delay and discussion, and many opportunities for committee activity.

Though there have been periods of strong central leadership in Congress, the general trend, especially since the mid-20th century, has been toward decentralizing decision making and enhancing the power of the individual member at the expense of the congressional leadership. This decentralization may not have been inevitable. Most American states have constitutional systems quite similar to the federal one, yet in many state legislatures, such as those in New York, Massachusetts, and Indiana, the leadership is quite powerful. In part, the position of these strong state legislative leaders may be the result of the greater strength of political parties in some states than in the nation as a whole. In large measure, however, it is a consequence of permitting state legislative leaders to decide who shall chair what committee and who shall receive what favors.

The House of Representatives, though always powerful, often has changed the way in which it is organized and led. In some periods, it has given its leader, the Speaker, a lot of power; in other periods, it has given much of that power to the chairs of the House committees; and in still other periods, it has allowed individual members to acquire great influence. To simplify a complicated story, the box starting on page 269 outlines six different periods in the history of the House.

The House faces fundamental problems: it wants to be big (it has 435 members) and powerful, and its members want to be powerful as individuals and as a group. But being big makes it hard for the House to be powerful unless some small group is given the authority to run it. If a group runs the place, however, the individual members lack much power. Individuals can gain power, but only at the price of making the House harder to run and thus reducing its collective power in government. There is no lasting solution to these dilemmas, and so the House will always be undergoing changes.

The Senate does not face any of these problems. It is small enough (100 members) that it can be run without giving much authority to any small group of leaders. In addition, it has escaped some of the problems the House once faced. During the period leading up to the Civil War, it was carefully balanced so that the number of senators from slave-owning states exactly equaled the number from free states. Hence, fights over slavery rarely arose in the Senate.

From the first, the Senate was small enough that no time limits had to be placed on how long a senator could speak. This meant there never was anything like a Rules Committee that controlled the amount of debate.

Finally, senators were not elected by the voters until the 20th century. Prior to that, they were picked instead by state legislatures. Thus senators often were the leaders of local party organizations, with an interest in funneling jobs back to their states.

The big changes in the Senate came not from any fight about how to run it (nobody ever really ran it), but from a dispute over how its members should be chosen. For more than a century after the Founding, members of the Senate were chosen by state legislatures. Though often these legislatures picked popular local figures to be senators, just as often there was intense political maneuvering among the leaders of various factions, each struggling to win (and sometimes buy) the votes necessary to become senator. By the end of the 19th century, the Senate was known as the Millionaires' Club because of the number of wealthy party leaders and businessmen in it.

There arose a demand for the direct, popular election of senators. Naturally, the Senate resisted, and without its approval the necessary constitutional amendment could not pass Congress. When some states threatened to demand a new constitutional convention, the Senate feared that such a convention would change more than just the way in which senators were chosen. A protracted struggle ensued,

CONSTITUTIONAL CONNECTIONS

From Convention to Congress

Article I of the Constitution (on Congress) is several times longer than Articles II (on the presidency and executive branch) and Article III (on the federal judiciary) combined. The Framers treated Congress as "the first branch" of American national government. As evidenced by the records of the debates among the 55 men that convened the Constitutional Convention, they had good philosophical reasons for treating the new republic's new legislature with special care. Besides, most of the delegates were themselves former legislators: 41 of the 55 had served, or at the time of the Convention, were still serving, as members of the Continental Congress. Moreover, 28 of the 55 delegates would go on to serve in the new Congress created by Article I: 4 served in both the House and the Senate; 9 served in the House only; and 15 served in the Senate only. Among those that went on to serve in the House was the Constitution's chief intellectual architect, James Madison. Madison would also go on to serve as Secretary of State (under President Thomas Jefferson) and, of course, as the nation's fourth president (succeeding Jefferson).

Source: Adapted from The U.S. National Archives & Records Administration, "The Founding Fathers: A Brief Overview," 2013.

during which many state legislatures devised ways to ensure that the senators they picked would already have won a popular election. The Senate finally agreed to a constitutional amendment that required the popular election of its members, and in 1913 the Seventeenth Amendment was approved by the necessary three-fourths of the states. Ironically, given the intensity of the struggle over this question, no great change in the composition of the Senate resulted; most of those members who had first been chosen by state legislatures managed to win re-election by popular vote.

The other major issue in the development of the Senate was the filibuster. A **filibuster** is a prolonged speech, or series of speeches, made to delay action in a legislative assembly. It had become a common—and unpopular—feature of Senate life by the end of the 19th century. It was used by liberals and conservatives alike and for lofty as well as self-serving purposes. The first serious effort to restrict the filibuster came in 1917, after an important foreign policy measure submitted by President Wilson had been talked to death by, as Wilson put it, "eleven willful men." Rule 22 was adopted by a Senate fearful of tying a president's hands during a wartime crisis. The rule provided that debate could be cut off if two-thirds of the senators present and voting agreed to a "cloture" motion. Two years later, it was first invoked successfully when the Senate voted cloture to end, after 55 days, the debate over the Treaty of Versailles. The cloture rule was later changed so that just 60 votes could end a filibuster.

filibuster An attempt to defeat a bill in the Senate by talking indefinitely, thus preventing the Senate from taking action on the bill.

Despite the existence of Rule 22, the tradition of unlimited debate remains strong in the Senate. In late 2013, however, Senate Democrats changed chamber rules so that only a simple majority of 51 votes, rather than 60 votes, would be needed to advance presidential nominees for executive branch positions or federal judgeships. The change did not, however, extend to Supreme Court nominees: they would still be subject to the filibuster.

HOW THINGS WORK

House History: Six Phases

Phase One: The Powerful House

During the first three administrations—of George Washington, John Adams, and Thomas Jefferson—leadership in Congress often was supplied by the president or his Cabinet officers. Rather quickly, however, Congress began to assert its independence. The House of Representatives was the preeminent institution, overshadowing the Senate.

Phase Two: The Divided House

In the late 1820s, the preeminence of the House began to wane. Andrew Jackson asserted the power of the presidency by vetoing legislation he did not like. The party unity necessary for a Speaker, or any leader, to control the House was shattered by the issue of slavery. Of course, representatives from the South did not attend during the Civil War, and their seats remained vacant for several years after it ended. A group called the Radical Republicans, led by men such as Thaddeus Stevens of Pennsylvania, produced strong majorities for measures aimed at punishing the defeated South. But as time passed, the hot passions the war had generated began to cool, and it became clear that the leadership of the House remained weak.

Phase Three: The Speaker Rules

Toward the end of the 19th century, the Speaker of the House gained power. When Thomas B. Reed of Maine became Speaker in 1889, he obtained by vote of the Republican majority more authority than any of his predecessors, including the right to select the chairs and members of all committees. He chaired the Rules Committee and decided what business would come up for a vote, any limitations on debate, and who would be allowed to speak and who would not. In 1903, Joseph G. Cannon of Illinois became Speaker. He tried to maintain Reed's tradition, but he had many enemies within his Republican ranks.

Phase Four: The House Revolts

In 1910–1911, the House revolted against "Czar" Cannon, voting to strip the Speaker of his right to appoint committee chairs and to remove him from the Rules Committee. The powers lost by the Speaker flowed to the party caucus, the Rules Committee, and the chairs of the standing committees. It was not, however, until the 1960s and 1970s that House members struck out against all forms of leadership.

Phase Five: The Members Rule

Newly elected Democrats could not get the House to vote on a meaningful civil rights bill until 1964 because powerful committee chairs, most of them from the South, kept such legislation bottled up. In response, Democrats changed the rules so that chairpersons lost much of their authority. Beginning in the 1970s, committee chairs would no longer be selected simply on the basis of seniority: they had to be elected by the members of the majority party. Chairpersons

(continued)

HOW THINGS WORK (*Continued*)

could no longer refuse to call committee meetings, and most meetings had to be public. Committees without subcommittees had to create them and allow their members to choose subcommittee chairs. Individual members' staffs were greatly enlarged, and half of all majority-party members were chairs of at least one committee or subcommittee.

Phase Six: The Leadership Returns

Since every member had power, it was harder for the House to get anything done. By slow steps, culminating in some sweeping changes made in 1995, there were efforts to restore some of the power the Speaker had once had. The number of committees and subcommittees was reduced. Republican Speaker Newt Gingrich dominated the choice of committee chairs, often passing over more senior members for more agreeable junior ones. But Gingrich's demise was as quick as his rise. His decision not to pass some

One of the most powerful Speakers of the House, Henry Clay, is shown here addressing the U.S. Senate around 1850.

Library of Congress Prints and Photographs Division (LC-DIG-ppmsca-09398)

appropriations bills forced many government offices to close for a short period, he had to pay a fine for using tax-exempt funds for political purposes, and then the Republicans lost a number of seats in the 1998 election. Gingrich resigned as Speaker and as a member of the House and was replaced by a more moderate Speaker, Republican Dennis Hastert of Illinois, with a penchant for accommodating his colleagues. When the 110th Congress began in 2007, Democrat Nancy Pelosi of California held the Speaker's gavel. Pelosi was the sixtieth Speaker in House history but the first woman to lead the House. She presided over many battles with the House's GOP leaders, but her most memorable role as Speaker occurred in 2010 when she struck assorted (and some critics claimed sordid) deals with members of her own party to garner their votes for the president's sweeping health care overhaul plan. Following heavy Democratic losses in the 2010 midterm elections, in January 2011, Pelosi was succeeded as Speaker by Republican John Boehner of Ohio. Even some liberal Democratic members of his state's congressional delegation (for example, Ohio Representative Dennis Kucinich) characterized Boehner as a committed, but pragmatic conservative and professional legislator. With additional Republican victories in the 2014 midterm elections, Boehner faces high expectations for enacting a policy agenda that will continue his party's electoral success in 2016.

Who Is in Congress?

With power so decentralized in Congress, the kind of person elected to it is especially important. Since each member exercises some influence, the beliefs and interests of each individual affect policy. Viewed simplistically, most members of Congress seem the same: the typical representative or senator is a middle-aged white Protestant male lawyer. If all such persons usually thought and voted alike, that would be an interesting fact, but they do not, and so it is necessary to explore the great diversity of views among seemingly similar people.

Gender and Race

Congress has gradually become less male and less white. Between 1950 and 2013, the number of women in the House increased from nine to 78, and the number of African Americans from two to 42. There are also 29 Latino members.

Until recently, the Senate changed much more slowly (see Table 9.1). Before the 1992 election, there were no African Americans, and only two women in the Senate. But in 1992, four more women,

TABLE 9.1   Blacks, Latinos, and Women in Congress, 1971–2014

Congress	Senate			House		
	Blacks	Latinos	Women	Blacks	Latinos	Women
113th (2013–2014)	2	3	20	42	29	82
112th	0	2	17	42	30	79
111th	1	3	17	42	25	77
110th	1	3	16	38	23	74
109th	1	0	14	37	23	59
108th	0	0	13	39	23	62
107th	0	0	13	36	19	59
106th	0	0	9	39	19	58
105th	1	1	9	37	18	51
104th	1	0	8	38	18	48
103rd	1	0	6	38	17	47
102nd	0	0	2	26	10	29
101st	0	0	2	24	11	25
100th	0	0	2	23	11	23
99th	0	0	2	20	11	22
98th	0	0	2	21	10	22
97th	0	0	2	17	6	19
96th	0	0	1	16	6	16
95th	1	0	2	16	5	18
94th	1	1	0	15	5	19
93rd	1	1	0	15	5	14
92nd (1971–1972)	1	1	2	12	5	13

Source: Congressional Quarterly, various years.

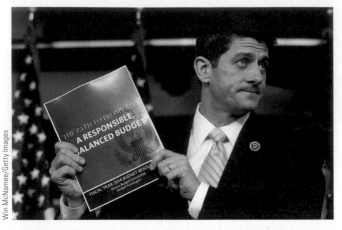

Win McNamee/Getty Images

U.S. House Budget Chairman Paul Ryan, who was the Republican vice-presidential candidate in 2012, presents his party's budget plan.

including one black woman, Carol Mosely Braun of Illinois, were elected. Two more were elected in 1994, when a Native American, Ben Nighthorse Campbell of Colorado, also became a senator. Today there are 20 women in the Senate.

The relatively small number of African Americans and Latinos in the House understates their influence, at least when the Democrats are in the majority. In 1994, four House committees were chaired by blacks and three by Latinos. In the same year, however, no woman chaired a committee. The reason for this difference in power is that the former tend to come from districts in which incumbents have normally won re-election by comfortable margins and thus have more seniority than the latter. When the Democrats retook control of Congress in 2007, African Americans and Latinos became chairpersons of several important committees.

Similarly, the first woman to become Speaker (Nancy Pelosi in 2007) was a Democrat, and the post-1970 increase of women in Congress has been led by Democrats: in the 113th Congress that began in 2013, 16 of the 20 women in the Senate, and 62 of the 82 women in the House, were Democrats. Among the notable women in the 112th Congress was Gabrielle Dee "Gabby" Giffords, a 41-year-old Democrat of Arizona elected to her third House term in 2010, and only the third woman from Arizona to serve in Congress. Representative Giffords served on the House Armed Services Committee and was a member of the "Blue Dog" Caucus of moderately conservative House Democrats. In January 2011, she was shot in the head by a would-be assassin, but made such remarkable and rapid progress toward recovery that in spring 2011 she was able to attend the scheduled but aborted launch of a NASA shuttle co-commanded by her husband. In 2012, she retired from Congress to concentrate more fully on her recovery, received a public tribute from all members of the House, and vowed that she would return to public service in the future.

Middle-aged white males with law degrees are still prevalent in Congress, but as Table 9.2 shows, compared to the makeup of the 102nd Congress that began in 1991, the 113th Congress that began in 2013 had not only more women, blacks, and Latinos, but also fewer lawyers, fewer persons who had served in the armed forces, more businesspeople, more people over the age of 55, and more members (about 1 in 6 overall) serving their first term.

Chip Somodevilla/Getty Images

U.S. House Minority Leader Nancy Pelosi, who previously was the first female Speaker of the House, speaks at a weekly press conference.

Incumbency

The recent spike in first-termers in Congress is interesting, but the most important change that has occurred in the composition of Congress has been so gradual that most people have not noticed it. In the 19th century, a large fraction—often a majority—of congressmen served only one term. In 1869, for example, more than half the members of the House were serving their first term in Congress. Being a congressman in those days was not regarded as a career. This was in part because the federal government was not very important (most of the interesting political decisions were made by the states); in part because travel to Washington, D.C., was difficult and the city was not a pleasant place in which to live; and in part because being a congressman did not pay well. Furthermore, many congressional districts were highly competitive, with the two political parties fairly evenly balanced in each.

TABLE 9.2 Who's in Congress, 1991–1992 versus 2013–2014

	102nd Congress (1991–1992)	113th Congress (2013–2014)
Average Age		
House	53	57
Senate	57	62
Occupation		
Law	244	211
Business	189	214
Military		
Had served	277	108
Incumbency		
In first term	44	89

Source: Adapted from chart based on Congressional Research Service and Military Officers Association data in John Harwood, "For New Congress, Data Shows Why Polarization Abounds," *The New York Times*, March 6, 2011. Updated from *Congressional Directory 2013.*

By the 1950s, however, serving in Congress had become a career. Between 1863 and 1969, the proportion of first-termers in the House fell from 58 percent to 8 percent.[8] As the public took note of this shift, people began to complain about "professional politicians" being "out of touch with the people." A movement to impose term limits was started. In 1995, the House approved a constitutional amendment to do just that, but it died in the Senate. Then the Supreme Court struck down an effort by a state to impose term limits on its own members of Congress.

As it turned out, natural political forces were already doing what the term limits amendment was supposed to do. The 1992 and 1994 elections brought scores of new members to the House, with the result that by 1995 the proportion of members who were serving their first or second terms had risen sharply. Three things were responsible for this change. First, when congressional district lines were redrawn after the 1990 census, a lot of incumbents found themselves running in new districts they couldn't carry. Second, voter disgust at a variety of Washington political scandals made them receptive to appeals from candidates who could describe themselves as "outsiders." And third, the Republican victory in 1994—made possible in part by the conversion of the South from a Democratic bastion to a Republican stronghold—brought a lot of new faces to the Capitol. In the 2006 midterm elections, the Democrats regained control of the House from Republicans; they retained control in 2008 but then lost it again in the 2010 midterm elections and lost additional seats in the 2014 midterm elections.

But these periodic power shifts accompanied by the arrival of scores of new faces in Congress should not obscure an important fact that was documented decades ago by political scientists[9] and is still true today: even in elections that result in the out party regaining power, most incumbent House members who seek re-election not only win but win big in their districts. And while Senators have been somewhat less secure than House members, most Senate incumbents who have sought re-election have won it by a comfortable margin.

marginal districts
Political districts in which candidates elected to the House of Representatives win in close elections, typically by less than 55 percent of the vote.

safe districts Districts in which incumbents win by margins of 55 percent or more.

Figure 9.1 shows the 1964–2012 re-election rates for incumbent House and Senate members who sought re-election. Over that span of two dozen elections, the average re-election rate for House incumbents was 93 percent and the average re-election rate for Senate incumbents was 82 percent. For the 16 elections from 1980 through 2012, the House and Senate incumbent re-election averages are 94 percent and 87 percent, respectively. In the 2010 midterm election, despite polls showing mass disaffection with Congress and a strongly "anti-incumbent" mood, 87 percent of House incumbents who sought re-election won it (53 House incumbents who sought re-election lost), and 84 percent of Senate incumbents who sought re-election won it (4 Senate incumbents who sought re-election lost, two in primary elections and two in the general election). In 2012, among re-election-seeking incumbents, 90 percent of House incumbents and 91 percent of Senate incumbents won re-election.

House incumbents who seek re-election normally beat their opponents by 10 points or more. Political scientists call districts that have close elections (when the winner gets less than 55 percent of the vote) **marginal districts** and districts where incumbents win by wide margins (55 percent or more) **safe districts**. Even by a more exacting standard—winning with 60 percent or more of the vote—in all but one of the two elections from 1964 to 2010 (the election of 1994), between 60 and 80 percent of House incumbents who were re-elected won with 60 percent or more of the vote.[10] By contrast, over the same period, well under half of all Senate incumbents who won re-election did so by such a wide margin. In 1998 and again in 2008, about two-thirds of Senate incumbents won with 60 percent or more of the vote, but "safe states" remain far less common than safe districts.

Why congressional seats have become less marginal—that is, safer—is a matter on which scholars do not agree. Some feel it is the result of television and other media. But challengers can

FIGURE 9.1 **Re-election Rates for House and Senate Incumbents, 1964–2012**

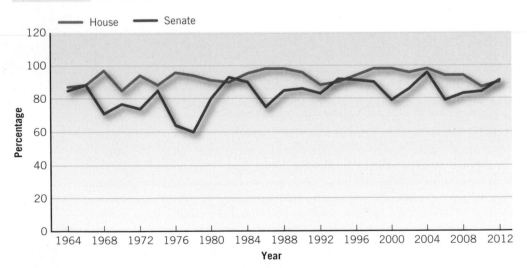

Sources: For 1964–2008 data, The Center for Responsive Politics; 2010 data compiled by author; and 2012 data drawn from The Center for Responsive Politics, OpenSecrets.org, accessed by Jesse Crosson, May 28, 2013.

go on television, too, so why should this benefit incumbents? Another possibility is that voters are becoming less and less likely to automatically support whatever candidate wins the nomination of their own party. They are more likely, in short, to vote for the person rather than the party. And they are more likely to have heard of a person who is an incumbent: incumbents can deluge the voter with free mailings, they can travel frequently (and at public expense) to meet constituents, and they can get their names in the headlines by sponsoring bills or conducting investigations. Simply having a familiar name is important in getting elected, and incumbents find it easier than challengers to make their names known.

Finally, some scholars argue that incumbents can use their power to get programs passed or funds spent to benefit their districts—and thereby to benefit themselves.[11] They can help keep an army base open, support the building of a new highway (or block the building of an unpopular one), take credit for federal grants to local schools and hospitals, make certain a particular industry or labor union is protected by tariffs against foreign competition, and so on.

Probably all of these factors make some difference. Whatever the explanation, the tendency of voters to return incumbents to office means that in ordinary times no one should expect any dramatic changes in the composition of Congress. Even when elections effect a change in party control in one or both chambers, even when new leaders are in charge and new members abound, many old hands will still be on hand in Congress.

Party

Forty-one Congresses convened between 1933 and 2013 (a new Congress convenes every two years). The Democrats controlled both houses in 27 of these Congresses and at least one house in 31 of them. Scholars differ in their explanations of why the Democrats have so often had the upper hand in Congress. Most of the research on the subject has focused on the reasons for Democratic control of the House.

In every election from 1968 to 1992, the percentage of the popular vote for Republican candidates to the House was higher than the percentage of House seats that actually went to Republicans. For example, in 1976, the Republicans won 42.1 percent of the vote, but received only 32.9 percent of the seats. Some argued that this gap between votes and seats occurred because Democratic-controlled state legislatures redrew congressional district maps in ways that make it hard for Republicans to win House seats. Some striking anecdotal evidence supports this conclusion. For example, following the 1990 census, the Democratic-controlled Texas legislature crafted a new congressional district map clearly designed to benefit Democrats. In 1992, Republicans won 48 percent of the House vote in Texas but received only 30 percent of the seats. But after Republicans won control of more state legislatures, matters began to change. In Texas, a new districting plan was adopted that ensured more House seats would be won by Republicans. And when a court, rather than the Democratic legislature, redrew California's district lines, both parties won the same proportion of seats as their share of the popular vote.[12] In 2006, things had evened out nationally: both parties won about the same share of House seats as their percentage of the vote.

Partisan tinkering with district maps and other structural features of House elections is not a sufficient explanation of why Democrats dominated the House in the four decades prior to 1994. As one study concluded, "Virtually all the political science evidence to date indicates that the electoral system has little or no partisan bias, and that the net gains nationally from redistricting for one party over another are very small."[13] To control the redistricting process, one party must control both houses of the legislature, the governor's office, and, where necessary, the state courts. These conditions simply do not exist in most states. For these and related reasons, the gains made by Republicans in the 2010 elections

conservative coalition
An alliance between Republican and conservative Democrats.

are unlikely to be expanded to any significant degree in the decade ahead purely by virtue of the redistricting required by the results of the 2010 Census.[14]

Congressional incumbents have come to enjoy certain built-in electoral advantages over challengers. Democrats were in the majority as the advantages of incumbency grew, but Republicans enjoyed the same or greater advantages from 1994 to 2006. Studies suggest the incumbency advantage was worth about 2 percentage points prior to the 1960s, but has grown to 6 to 8 points today.

It is important to remember that from time to time major electoral convulsions do alter the membership of Congress. For example, in the election of 1938 the Democrats lost 70 seats in the House; in 1942, they lost 50; in 1950, they lost 29; and, in 1966, they lost 48. Despite these big losses, the Democrats retained a majority in the House in each of these years. Not so, however, in 1994, when the Democrats lost 52 House seats (the largest loss by either party since the Republicans had lost 75 seats in 1948), and Republicans gained majorities in both the House and the Senate. And not so in 2010, when Republicans gained more than 60 House seats and narrowly failed to take the Senate as well.

In the past, the Democratic Party was more deeply divided than the Republicans because of the presence in Congress of conservative Democrats from the South. These Southern Democrats often would vote with the Republicans in the House or Senate, thereby forming what came to be called the **conservative coalition**. During the 1960s and 1970s, that coalition came together in about one-fifth of all roll-call votes. When it did, it usually won, defeating Northern Democrats. But since the 1980s, and especially since the watershed election of 1994, the conservative coalition has become much less important. The reason is simple: many Southern Democrats in Congress have been replaced by Southern Republicans, and the Southern Democrats who remain (many of them African Americans) are as liberal as Northern Democrats. The effect of this change is to make Congress, and especially the House, more ideologically partisan—Democrats are liberals, Republicans are conservatives—and this in turn helps explain why there is more party unity in voting—no matter which party is in charge.

The Organization of Congress: Parties and Interests

Congress is not a single organization; it is a vast and complex collection of organizations by which the business of Congress is carried on and through which members of Congress form alliances. Unlike the British Parliament, in which the political parties are the only important kind of organization, parties are only one of many important units in Congress. In fact, other organizations have grown in number as party influence has declined.

Party Organizations

The Democrats and Republicans in the House and the Senate are organized by party leaders, who in turn are elected by the full party membership within the House and Senate.

The Senate The majority party chooses one of its members—usually the person with the greatest seniority—to be president pro tempore of the Senate. This is usually an honorific position, required by the Constitution so that the Senate will have a presiding officer when the vice president of the United States (according to the Constitution, the president of the Senate) is absent. In fact, both the president pro tem and the vice president usually assign the tedious chore of presiding to a junior senator.

The real leadership is in the hands of the majority and minority leaders. The principal task of the **majority leader** is to schedule the business of the Senate, usually in consultation with the **minority leader**. A majority leader who has a strong personality and is skilled at political bargaining (such as Lyndon Johnson, the Democrats' leader in the 1950s) may also acquire much influence over the substance of Senate business.

A **whip**, chosen by each party, helps party leaders stay informed about what the party members are thinking, rounds up members when important votes are taken, and attempts to keep a nose count of how voting on a controversial issue is likely to go. Several senators assist each party whip.

Each party also chooses a Policy Committee composed of a dozen or so senators who help the party leader schedule Senate business, choosing what bills will be given major attention and in what order.

For individual senators, however, the key party organization is the group that assigns senators to the Senate's standing committees: for the Democrats, a 22-member Steering Committee; for the Republicans, an 18-member Committee on Committees. For newly elected senators, their political careers, opportunities for favorable publicity, and chances for helping their states and constituents depend in great part on the committees to which they are assigned.

Achieving ideological and regional balance is a crucial—and delicate—aspect of selecting party leaders, making up important committees, and assigning freshmen senators to committees. Liberals and conservatives in each party fight over the choice of majority and minority leaders.

The House of Representatives The party structure is essentially the same in the House as in the Senate, though the titles of various posts are different. But leadership carries more power in the House than in the Senate because of the House rules. Being so large (435 members), the House must restrict debate and schedule its business with great care; thus leaders who manage scheduling and determine how the rules shall be applied usually have substantial influence.

The **Speaker**, who presides over the House, is the most important person in that body and is elected by whichever party has a majority. Unlike the president pro tem of the Senate, this position is anything but honorific, for the Speaker is also the principal leader of the majority party. Though Speakers as presiders

majority leader The legislative leader elected by party members holding the majority of seats in the House or the Senate.

minority leader The legislative leader elected by party members holding a minority of seats in the House or the Senate.

whip A senator or representative who helps the party leader stay informed about what party members are thinking.

Speaker The presiding officer of the House of Representatives and the leader of his or her party in the House.

SAUL LOEB/AFP/Getty Images

John Boehner became Speaker of the U.S. House of Representatives in 2011.

party vote There are two measures of such voting. By the stricter measure, a party vote occurs when 90 percent or more of the Democrats in either house of Congress vote together against 90 percent or more of the Republicans. A looser measure counts as a party vote any case where at least 50 percent of the Democrats vote together against at least 50 percent of the Republicans.

are expected to be fair, Speakers as party leaders are expected to use their powers to help pass legislation favored by their party.

In helping his or her party, the Speaker has some important formal powers. He or she decides who shall be recognized to speak on the floor of the House, rules whether a motion is relevant and germane to the business at hand, and decides (subject to certain rules) the committees to which new bills shall be assigned. He or she influences what bills are brought up for a vote and appoints the members of special and select committees. Since 1975, the Speaker has been able to select the majority-party members of the Rules Committee, which plays an important role in the consideration of bills.

The Speaker also has some informal powers. He or she controls some patronage jobs in the Capitol building and the assignment of extra office space. Though now far less powerful than some of his or her predecessors, the Speaker is still an important person to have on one's side.

In the House, as in the Senate, the majority party elects a floor leader, called the majority leader. The other party chooses the minority leader. Traditionally, the majority leader becomes Speaker when the person in that position dies or retires—provided, of course, that his or her party is still in the majority. Each party also has a whip, with several assistant whips in charge of rounding up votes. For the Democrats, committee assignments are made and the scheduling of legislation is discussed in a Steering and Policy Committee chaired by the Speaker. The Republicans have divided responsibility for committee assignments and policy discussion between two committees. Each party also has a congressional campaign committee to provide funds and other assistance to party members running for election or re-election to the House.

Party Voting

The effect of this elaborate party machinery can be crudely measured by the extent to which party members vote together in the House and the Senate. A **party vote** can be defined in various ways; naturally, the more stringent the definition, the less party voting we will observe.

Figure 9.2 shows two measures of party voting in the House of Representatives during the last century. By the strictest measure, a party vote occurs when 90 percent or more of the Democrats vote together against 90 percent or more of the Republicans. A looser measure counts as a party vote one in which at least 50 percent of the Democrats vote together against 50 percent of the Republicans. By the 90 percent measure, the extent of party voting is low and has declined since the turn of the century. By the 50 percent measure, it is as high today as it was in 1920 and has risen sharply since 1970.

Given that political parties as organizations do not tightly control a legislator's ability to get elected, what is surprising is not that strict party votes are relatively rare, but that they occur at all. There are several reasons that congressional members of one party sometimes do vote together against a majority of the other party. First, members of Congress do not randomly decide to be Democrats or Republicans; at least for most members, these choices reflect some broad policy agreements. By tabulating the ratings that several interest groups give members of Congress for voting on important issues, it is possible to rank each member of Congress from most to least liberal in three policy areas: economic affairs, social questions, and foreign and military affairs. Democrats in the House and Senate are much more liberal than Republicans, and this has been true for many years. The ideological differences between the parties are so pronounced that even the average Southern Democrat in the House is more liberal than the average Northern Republican.

FIGURE 9.2   Party Votes in the House, 1877–2010

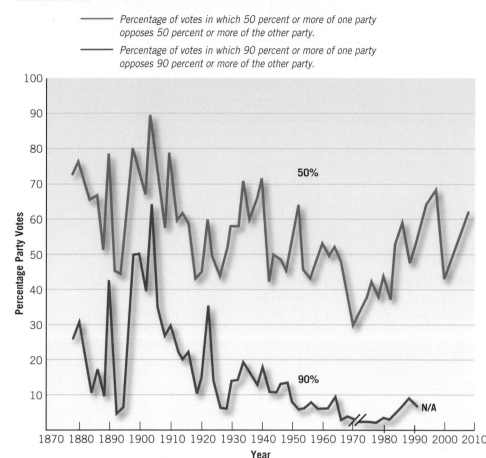

——— Percentage of votes in which 50 percent or more of one party opposes 50 percent or more of the other party.

——— Percentage of votes in which 90 percent or more of one party opposes 90 percent or more of the other party.

Note: A party vote occurs when the specified percentage (or more) of one party votes against the specified percentage (or more) of the other party.

Sources: Updated through 2008 by Zach Courser; NES data as reported in 2001–2002; Harold W. Stanley and Richard G. Niemi, *Vital Statistics on American Politics* (CQ Press, 2001), 211.

In addition to their personal views, members of Congress have other reasons for supporting their party's position at least some of the time. On many matters that come up for vote, members of Congress often have little information and no opinions. It is only natural that they look to fellow party members for advice. Furthermore, supporting the party position can work to the long-term advantage of a member interested in gaining status and influence in Congress. Though party leaders are weaker today than in the past, they are hardly powerless. Sam Rayburn reputedly told freshman members of Congress that "if you want to get along, go along." That is less true today, but still good advice.

In short, party *does* make a difference—though not as much as it did 90 years ago and not nearly as much as it does in a parliamentary system—party affiliation is still the single most important thing to know about a member of Congress. Because party affiliation in the House today embodies strong ideological preferences, the mood of the House is often testy and strident. Members no longer get along

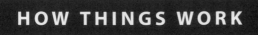

HOW THINGS WORK

Key Facts About Congress

Qualifications

Representative

- Must be 25 years of age (when seated, not when elected).

- Must have been a citizen of the United States for seven years.

- Must be an inhabitant of the state from which elected. (*Note:* Custom, but *not* the Constitution, requires that a representative live in the district he or she represents.)

Senator

- Must be 30 years of age (when seated, not when elected).

- Must have been a citizen of the United States for nine years.

- Must be an inhabitant of the state from which elected.

Judging Qualifications

Each house is the judge of the "elections, returns, and qualifications" of its members. Thus, Congress alone decides disputed congressional elections. On occasion it has excluded a person from taking a seat on the grounds that the election was improper.

Privileges

Members of Congress have certain privileges, the most important of which, conferred by the Constitution, is that "for any speech or debate in either house they shall not be questioned in any other place." This doctrine of "privileged speech" has been interpreted by the Supreme Court to mean that members of Congress cannot be sued or prosecuted for anything they say or write in connection with their legislative duties.

When Senator Mike Gravel read the Pentagon Papers—some then-secret government documents about the Vietnam War—into the *Congressional Record* in defiance of a court order restraining their publication, the Court held this was "privileged speech" and beyond challenge (*Gravel* v. *United States,* 408 U.S. 606, 1972). But when Senator William Proxmire issued a press release critical of a scientist doing research on monkeys, the Court decided the scientist could sue him for libel because a press release was not part of the legislative process (*Hutchinson* v. *Proxmire,* 443 U.S. 111, 1979).

The Size of Congress

Congress decides the size of the House of Representatives. The House began with 65 members in 1790 and has had 435 members since 1912. Each state must have at least one representative. Regardless of its population, each state has two senators. Equal suffrage for states in the Senate is enshrined in Article I of the Constitution, the only provision that cannot be amended (see Article V).

with each other as well as they did 40 years ago. Many liberals and conservatives dislike each other intensely, despite their routine use of complimentary phrases.

Although political parties may be less powerful in Congress than once was the case, ideology is more influential. In the last several Congresses, the 20 most liberal representatives were all Democrats and the 20 most conservative were all Republicans.

Caucuses

Congressional caucuses are a growing rival to the parties as a source of policy leadership. A **caucus** is an association of members of Congress created to advocate a political ideology or to advance a regional, ethnic, or economic interest. In 1959, only four such caucuses existed; by the early 1980s, there were more than 70. The more important among them have included the Democratic Study Group (uniting more than 200 liberal Democrats, though their names are not publicized to avoid embarrassing them with constituents), the Coalition (more popularly known as the Blue Dog Democrats), a group of moderate-to-conservative Democrats, and the Tuesday Lunch Bunch. Other caucuses include the delegations from certain large states who meet on matters of common interest, as well as the countless groups dedicated to racial, ethnic, regional, and policy interests. The Congressional Black Caucus in the House is one of the best known of these and is probably typical of many in its operations. It meets regularly and employs a staff. As with most other caucuses, some members are very active, others only marginally so. On some issues it simply registers an opinion; on others it attempts to negotiate with leaders of other blocs so that votes can be traded in a mutually advantageous way. It keeps its members informed and on occasion presses to put a member on a regular congressional committee that has no blacks. In 1995, the House Republican majority decided to eliminate government funding of caucuses, forcing some to shrivel and others to seek outside support.

The Organization of Congress: Committees

The most important organizational feature of Congress is the set of legislative committees of the House and Senate. In the chairmanship of these committees, and their subcommittees, most of the power of Congress is found. The number and jurisdiction of these committees are of the greatest interest to members of Congress because decisions on these subjects determine what groups of legislators with what political views will pass on legislative proposals, oversee the workings of agencies in the executive branch, and conduct investigations. A typical Congress has, in each house, about two dozen committees and well over 100 subcommittees.

Periodically, efforts have been made to cut the number of committees to give each a broader jurisdiction and to reduce conflict between committees over a single bill. But as the number of committees declined, the number of subcommittees rose, leaving matters much as they had been.

There are three kinds of committees: **standing committees** (more or less permanent bodies with specific legislative responsibilities), **select committees** (groups appointed for a limited purpose, which do not introduce legislation and which exist for only a few years), and **joint committees** (on which both representatives and senators serve). An especially important kind of joint committee is the

caucus An association of congressional members created to advance a political ideology or a regional, ethnic, or economic interest.

standing committees Permanently established legislative committees that consider and are responsible for legislation within a certain subject area.

select committees Congressional committees appointed for a limited time and purpose.

joint committees Committees on which both senators and representatives serve.

conference committee Joint committees appointed to resolve differences in the Senate and House versions of the same bill.

conference committee, made up of representatives and senators appointed to resolve differences in the Senate and House versions of a bill before final passage. Though members of the majority party could in theory occupy all the seats on all the committees, in practice they take the majority of the seats, name the chairperson, and allow the minority party to have the remainder of the seats. The number of seats varies from about 6 to more than 50.

Usually the ratio of Democrats to Republicans on a committee roughly corresponds to their ratio in the House or Senate. Standing committees are more important because, with a few exceptions, they are the only committees that can propose legislation by reporting a bill out to the full House or Senate. Each member of the House usually serves on two standing committees (but members of the Appropriations, Rules, or Ways and Means committees are limited to one committee). Each senator may serve on two major committees and one minor committee (see the box on pages 282–283), but this rule is not strictly enforced.

In the past, when party leaders were stronger, committee chairs were picked on the basis of loyalty to the leader. When this leadership weakened, seniority on the committee came to govern the selection of chairpersons. Of late, however, seniority has been under attack. In 1971, House Democrats decided in their caucus to elect committee chairs by secret ballot; four years later, they used that procedure to remove three committee chairs who held their positions by seniority. Between 1971 and 1992, the Democrats replaced a total of seven senior Democrats with more junior ones as committee chairs. When Republicans took control of the House in 1995, Speaker Newt Gingrich ignored seniority in selecting several committee chairs, picking instead members who he felt would do a better job. In this and other ways, Gingrich enhanced the Speaker's power to a degree not seen since 1910.

Throughout most of the 20th century, committee chairs dominated the work of Congress. In the early 1970s, their power came under attack, mostly from liberal Democrats upset at the opposition by

HOW THINGS WORK

Standing Committees of the Senate

Major Committees

*No senator is supposed to serve on more than two.**

Agriculture, Nutrition, and Forestry

Appropriations

Armed Services

Banking, Housing, and Urban Affairs

Budget Commerce, Science, and Transportation Energy and Natural Resources

Environment and Public Works

Finance

(continued)

HOW THINGS WORK (*Continued*)

Foreign Relations

Health, Education, Labor, and Pensions

Homeland Security and Governmental Affairs

Judiciary

Minor Committees

No senator is supposed to serve on more than one.

Rules and Administration

Small Business and Entrepreneurship

Veterans' Affairs

Select Committees

Aging

Ethics

Indian Affairs

Intelligence

*Despite the rules, some senators serve on more than two major committees.

conservative Southern Democratic chairs to civil rights legislation. The liberals succeeded in getting the House to adopt rules that weakened the chairs and empowered individual members. Among the changes were these:

- Committee chairs must be elected by the majority party, voting by secret ballot.

- The ability of committee chairs to block legislation by refusing to refer it to a subcommittee for a hearing is banned.

- All committees and subcommittees must hold public meetings unless the committee has voted to close them.

- Subcommittee chairs must be elected by committee members.

- Subcommittee chairs can hire their own staffs, independent of the committee chair.

The effect of these and other changes was to give individual members more power and committee chairs less. When the Republicans took control of the House in 1995, they made more changes, including the following:

- They reduced the number of committees and subcommittees.

- They authorized committee chairs to hire subcommittee staffs.

- They imposed term limits on committee and subcommittee chairs of three consecutive terms (or six years) and on the Speaker of four consecutive terms (or eight years).

- They prohibited chairs from casting an absent committee member's vote by proxy.

The House Republican rules gave back some power to chairpersons (for example, by letting them pick all staff members) but further reduced it in other ways (for example, by imposing term limits and banning proxy voting). The commitment to public meetings remained.

In the Senate there have been fewer changes, in part because individual members of the Senate have always had more power than their counterparts in the House. There were, however, three important changes made by the Republicans in 1995:

- A six-year term limit was set on all committee chairs (but not on the term of majority leader).

- Committee members were required to select their chairs by secret ballot

- Beginning in 1997, the chairs of Senate committees were limited to one six-year term.

Despite these new rules, the committees remain the place where the real work of Congress is done. These committees tend to attract different kinds of members. Some, such as the committees that draft tax legislation (the Senate Finance Committee and the House Ways and Means Committee) or that oversee foreign affairs (the Senate and House Foreign Relations Committees), have been attractive to members who want to shape public policy, become experts on important issues, and have influence with their colleagues. Others, such as the House and Senate committees dealing with public lands, small business, and veterans' affairs, are attractive to members who want to serve particular constituency groups.[15]

The Organization of Congress: Staffs and Specialized Offices

In 1900, representatives had no personal staff, and senators averaged fewer than one staff member each. By 1979, the average representative had 16 assistants and the average senator had 36. Since then the numbers have remained about the same. To the more than 10,000 people on the personal staffs of members of Congress must be added another 3,000 who work for congressional committees and yet another 3,000 employed by various congressional research agencies. Congress has produced the most rapidly growing bureaucracy in Washington: the personal staffs of legislators have increased more than fivefold since 1947.[16] Though many staffers perform routine chores, many others help draft legislation, handle constituents, and otherwise shape policy and politics.

Tasks of Staff Members

A major function of a legislator's staff is to help constituents solve problems and thereby help that member of Congress get re-elected. Indeed, over the last two decades, a growing portion of congressional staffs have worked in the local (district or state) offices of the legislator rather than in Washington. Almost all members of Congress have at least one such home office, and most have two or more. Some scholars believe that this growth in constituency-serving staff helps explain why it is so difficult to defeat an incumbent.[17]

The legislative function of congressional staff members is also important. With each senator serving on an average of more than two committees and seven subcommittees, it is virtually impossible for

HOW THINGS WORK

Standing Committees of the House

Exclusive Committees

Member may not serve on any other committee, except Budget.

Appropriations

Rules

Ways and Means

Major Committees

Member may serve on only one major committee.

Agriculture

Armed Services

Education and Labor

Energy and Commerce

Financial Services

Foreign Affairs

Homeland Security

Judiciary

Transportation and Infrastructure

Nonmajor Committees

Member may serve on one major and one nonmajor or two nonmajor committees.

Budget

House Administration

Natural Resources

Oversight and Government Reform

Science and Technology

Small Business

Standards of Official Conduct

Veterans' Affairs

Select Committees

Intelligence

Note: In 1995, the House Republican majority abolished three committees—District of Columbia, Post Office and Civil Service, and Merchant Marine and Fisheries—and gave their duties to other standing committees.

members of Congress to become familiar with the details of all the proposals that come before them or to write all the bills that they feel ought to be introduced.[18] The role of staff members has expanded in proportion to the tremendous growth in Congress's workload.

The orientation of committee staff members differs. Some think of themselves as—and to a substantial degree they are—politically neutral professionals whose job it is to assist members of a committee, whether Democrats or Republicans, in holding hearings or revising bills. Others see themselves as partisan advocates, interested in promoting Democratic or Republican causes, depending on who hired them.

Those who work for individual members of Congress, as opposed to committees, see themselves entirely as advocates for their bosses. They often assume an entrepreneurial function, taking the initiative in finding and selling a policy to their boss—a representative or senator—who can take credit for it. Lobbyists and reporters understand this completely and therefore spend a lot of time cultivating congressional staffers.

The increased reliance on staff has changed Congress, mainly because the staff has altered the environment within which Congress does its work. In addition to their role as entrepreneurs promoting new policies, staffers act as negotiators: members of Congress today are more likely to deal with one another through staff intermediaries than through personal contact. Congress has thereby become less collegial, more individualistic, and less of a deliberative body.[19]

Staff Agencies

In addition to increasing the number of staff members, Congress also has created a set of staff agencies that work for Congress as a whole. These have come into being in large part to give Congress specialized knowledge equivalent to what the president has by virtue of his or her position as chief of the executive branch. One of these, the *Congressional Research Service* (*CRS*), is part of the Library of Congress and employs almost 900 people; it is politically neutral, responding to requests by members of Congress for information and giving both sides of arguments. The *Government Accountability Office* (*GAO*), once merely an auditing agency, now has about 5,000 employees and investigates policies and makes recommendations on almost every aspect of government; its head, though appointed by the president for a 15-year term, is very much the servant of Congress rather than the president. The *Congressional Budget Office* (*CBO*), created in 1974, advises Congress on the likely impact of different spending programs and attempts to estimate future economic trends.

How a Bill Becomes Law

Some bills zip through Congress; others make their way painfully and slowly, sometimes emerging in a form very different from their original one. Congress is like a crowd, moving either sluggishly or, when excited, with great speed. While reading the following account of how a bill becomes law (see Figure 9.3), keep in mind that the complexity of congressional procedures ordinarily gives powerful advantages to the opponents of any new policy. There are many points at which action can be blocked. This does not mean that nothing gets done, but that to get something done, a member of Congress must *either* slowly and painstakingly assemble a majority coalition or take advantage of enthusiasm for some new cause that sweeps away the normal obstacles to change.

Introducing a Bill

Any member of Congress may introduce a bill—in the House by handing it to a clerk or dropping it in a box; in the Senate by being recognized by the presiding officer and announcing the bill's introduction.

FIGURE 9.3 **How a Bill Becomes Law**

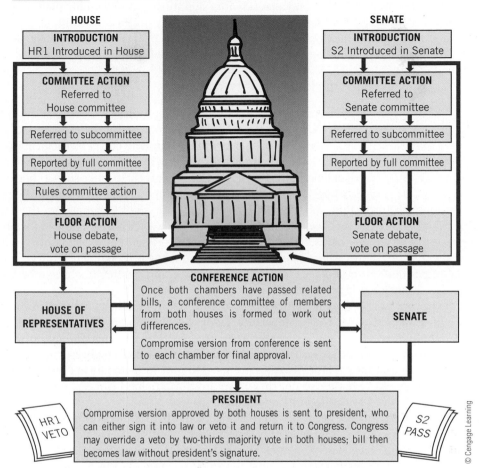

Bills are then numbered and printed. If a bill is not passed within one session of Congress, it is dead and must be reintroduced during the next Congress.

We often hear that legislation is initiated by the president and enacted by Congress. The reality is more complicated. Congress often initiates legislation (for example, most consumer and environmental laws passed since 1966 originated in Congress), and even laws formally proposed by the president have often been incubated in Congress. Even when he is the principal author of a bill, a president usually submits it (if he is prudent) only after careful consultation with key congressional leaders. In any case, he cannot himself introduce legislation; he must get a member of Congress to do it for him.

In addition to bills, Congress can also pass resolutions. Either house can use a **simple resolution** for such matters as establishing operating rules. A **concurrent resolution** is used to settle housekeeping and procedural matters that affect both houses. Simple and concurrent resolutions are not signed by the president and do not

simple resolution An expression of opinion either in the House or Senate to settle procedural matters in either body.

concurrent resolution An expression of opinion without the force of law that requires the approval of both the House and the Senate, but not the president.

joint resolution A formal expression of congressional opinion that must be approved by both houses of Congress and by the president; constitutional amendments need not be signed by the president.

discharge petition A device by which any member of the House, after a committee has had the bill for 30 days, may petition to have it brought to the floor.

have the force of law. A **joint resolution** requires approval by both houses and a presidential signature; it is essentially the same as a law. A joint resolution is also used to propose a constitutional amendment, in which case it must be approved by a two-thirds vote in each house, but does not require the signature of the president.

Study by Committees

A bill is referred to a committee for consideration by either the Speaker of the House or the Senate's presiding officer. If a chairperson or committee is known to be hostile to a bill, assignment can be a crucial matter. Rules govern which committee will get which bill, but sometimes a choice is possible. In the House, the Speaker's right to make such a choice (subject to appeal to the full House) is an important source of his or her power.

The Constitution requires that "all bills for raising revenue shall originate in the House of Representatives." The Senate can and does amend such bills, but only after the House has acted first. Bills that are not for raising revenue—that is, that do not alter tax laws—can originate in either chamber. In practice, the House also originates *appropriations bills* (bills that direct the spending of money). Because of the House's special position on revenue legislation, the committee that handles tax bills—the Ways and Means Committee—is particularly powerful.

Most bills die in committee. They are often introduced only to get publicity for various members of Congress or to enable them to say to a constituent or pressure group that they "did something" on some matter. Bills of general interest—many of them drafted in the executive branch, though introduced by members of Congress—are assigned to a subcommittee for a hearing where witnesses appear, evidence is taken, and questions are asked. These hearings are used to inform members of Congress, to permit interest groups to speak out (whether or not they have anything helpful to say), and to build public support for a measure favored by the majority on the committee.

Though committee hearings are necessary and valuable, they also fragment the process of considering bills dealing with complex matters. Both power and information are dispersed in Congress, and thus it is difficult to take a comprehensive view of matters cutting across committee boundaries. This has made it harder to pass complex legislation. For example, President George W. Bush's proposals to expand government support for religious groups that supply social services were dissected into small sections for the consideration of the various committees that had jurisdiction; after three years, no laws emerged. But strong White House leadership and supportive public opinion can push through controversial measures without great delay, as in the cases of Bush's tax cuts in 2001 and homeland security plans in 2002.

After the hearings, the committee or subcommittee makes revisions and additions (sometimes extensive) to the bill, but these changes do not become part of the bill unless they are approved by the entire house. If a majority of the committee votes to report a bill favorably to the House or Senate, it goes forward, accompanied by an explanation of why the committee favors it and why it wishes to see its amendments, if any, added; committee members who oppose the bill may include their dissenting opinions.

If the committee does not report the bill out to the house favorably, that ordinarily kills it, though there are complex procedures whereby the full House can get a bill that is stalled in committee out and onto the floor. The process involves getting a majority of all House members to sign a **discharge petition**. If 218 members sign, then the petition can be voted on; if it passes, then the stalled bill goes directly to the floor for a vote. These procedures are rarely attempted and even more rarely succeed.

For a bill to come before either house, it must first be placed on a calendar. There are five of these in the House and two in the Senate. Though the bill goes onto a calendar, it is not necessarily considered in chronological order or even considered at all. In the House, the powerful Rules Committee—an arm of the party leadership, especially of the Speaker—reviews most bills and sets the *rule*—that is, the procedures—under which they will be considered by the House. A **restrictive** or **closed rule** sets strict limits on debate and confines amendments to those proposed by the committee; an **open rule** permits amendments from the floor. The Rules Committee is no longer as mighty as it once was, but it can still block any House consideration of a measure and can bargain with the legislative committee by offering a helpful rule in exchange for alterations in the substance of a bill. In the 1980s, closed rules became more common.

The House needs the Rules Committee to serve as a traffic cop; without some limitations on debate and amendment, nothing would ever get done. The House can bypass the Rules Committee in a number of ways, but it rarely does so unless the committee departs too far from the sentiments of the House.

No such barriers to floor consideration exist in the Senate, where bills may be considered in any order at any time whenever a majority of the Senate chooses. In practice, bills are scheduled by the majority leader in consultation with the minority leader.

Floor Debate

Once on the floor, the bills are debated. In the House all revenue and most other bills are discussed by the *Committee of the Whole*—that is, whoever happens to be on the floor at the time, so long as at least 100 members are present. The Committee of the Whole can debate, amend, and generally decide the final shape of a bill, but technically cannot pass it—that must be done by the House itself, for which the **quorum** is half the membership (218 representatives). The sponsoring committee guides the discussion, and normally its version of the bill is the version that the full House passes.

Procedures are a good deal more casual in the Senate. Measures that have already passed the House can be placed on the Senate calendar without a committee hearing. There is no Committee of the Whole and no rule (as in the House) limiting debate, so that filibusters (lengthy speeches given to prevent votes from being taken) and irrelevant amendments, called **riders**, are possible. Filibusters can be broken if three-fifths of all senators resolve to invoke the **cloture rule**. This is a difficult and rarely used procedure. (Both conservatives and liberals have found the filibuster useful, and therefore its abolition is unlikely.)

The sharp increase in Senate filibusters has been made easier by a new process called **double tracking**. When a senator filibusters against a bill, it is temporarily put aside so the Senate can move on to other business. Because of double tracking, senators no longer have to speak around the clock to block a bill. Once they talk long enough, the bill is shelved. So common has this become that, for all practical purposes, any controversial bill can pass the Senate only if it gets enough votes (60) to end a filibuster.

The Senate has made an effort to end filibusters aimed at blocking the nomination of federal judges. In 2005, seven Democrats and seven Republicans agreed not to filibuster a nomination except in "exceptional circumstances." A few nominees whose appointment had been blocked managed to

restrictive An order from the House Rules Committee that permits certain kinds of amendments, but not others, to be made into a bill on the floor.

closed rule An order from the House Rules Committee that sets a time limit on debate; forbids a bill from being amended on the floor.

open rule An order from the House Rules Committee that permits a bill to be amended on the floor.

quorum The minimum number of members who must be present for business to be conducted in Congress.

riders Amendments on matters unrelated to a bill that are added to an important bill so that they will "ride" to passage through the Congress. When a bill has many riders, it is called a Christmas-tree bill.

cloture rule A rule used by the Senate to end or limit debate.

double tracking A procedure to keep the Senate going during a filibuster in which the disputed bill is shelved temporarily so that the Senate can get on with other business.

HOW THINGS WORK

House and Senate Differences: A Summary

House

435 members serving two-year terms

House members have only one major committee assignment, and thus tend to be policy specialists

Speaker referral of bills to committee is hard to challenge

Committees almost always consider legislation first

Scheduling and rules controlled by majority party

Rules Committee powerful; controls time of debate, admissibility of amendments

Debate usually limited to one hour

Non-germane amendments may not be introduced from floor

Senate

100 members serving six-year terms

Senators have two or more major committee assignments, and thus tend to be policy generalists

Referral decisions easy to challenge

Committee consideration easily bypassed

Scheduling and rules generally agreed to by majority and minority leaders

Rules Committee weak; few limits on debate or amendments

Unlimited debate unless shortened by unanimous consent or by invoking cloture

Non-germane amendments may be introduced

get confirmed by this arrangement. Whether it holds for the future depends on how senators define "exceptional circumstances."

One rule was once common to both houses: courtesy, often of the most exquisite nature, was required. Members always referred to each other as "distinguished" even if they were mortal political enemies. Personal or ad hominem criticism was frowned upon, but of late it has become more common. In recent years, members of Congress—especially of the House—have become more personal in their criticisms of one another, and human relationships have deteriorated.

Methods of Voting

There are several methods of voting in Congress, which can be applied to amendments to a bill, as well as to the question of final passage. Some observers of Congress make the mistake of deciding who was for and who against a bill by the final vote. This can be misleading. Often, a member of Congress will vote for final passage of a bill after having supported amendments that, if they had passed, would have made the bill totally different. To keep track of someone's voting record, therefore, it is often more important to know how that person voted on key amendments than how he or she voted on the bill itself.

Finding that out is not always easy, though it has become simpler in recent years. The House has three procedures for voting. A **voice vote** consists of the members shouting "aye" or "no"; a **division** (or standing) **vote** involves the members standing and being counted. In neither case are the names recorded of who voted which way. This is done only with a **roll-call vote**. Since 1973, an electronic voting system has been in use that greatly speeds up roll-call votes, and the number of recorded votes has thus increased sharply. To ensure a roll-call vote, one-fifth of house members present must request it. Voting in the Senate is simpler: it votes by voice or by roll call; they do not use a **teller vote** or electronic counters.

If a bill passes the House and Senate in different forms, the differences must be reconciled if the bill is to become law. If they are minor, the last house to act may simply refer the bill back to the other house, which then accepts the alterations. Major differences must be ironed out in a conference committee, though only a minority of bills requires a conference. Each house must vote to form such a committee. The members are picked by the chairs of the standing committees that have been handling the legislation; the minority as well as the majority party is represented. No decision can be made unless approved by a majority of *each* delegation. Bargaining is long and hard; in the past it was also secret, but some sessions are now public. Often—as with Carter's energy bill—the legislation is substantially rewritten in conference. Theoretically nothing already agreed to by both the House and Senate is to be changed, but in the inevitable give-and-take, even those matters already approved may be modified.

Conference reports on spending bills usually split the difference between the House and Senate versions. Overall, the Senate tends to do slightly better than the House.[20] But whoever wins, conferees report their agreement back to their respective houses, which usually consider the report immediately. The report can be accepted or rejected; it cannot be amended. In the great majority of cases, it is accepted—the alternative is to have no bill at all, at least for that Congress.

The bill, now in final form, goes to the president for signature or **veto**. A vetoed bill returns to the house of origin, where an effort can be made to override the veto. Two-thirds of those present (provided there is a quorum) must vote, by roll call, to override. If both houses override, the bill becomes law without the president's approval.

voice vote A congressional voting procedure in which members shout "yea" in approval or "nay" in disapproval, permitting members to vote quickly or anonymously on bills.

division vote A congressional voting procedure in which members stand and are counted.

roll-call vote A congressional voting procedure that consists of members answering "yea" or "nay" to their names.

teller vote A congressional voting procedure in which members pass between two tellers, the "yeas" first and the "nays" second.

veto Literally, "I forbid": it refers to the power of a president to disapprove a bill; it may be overridden by a two-thirds vote of each house of Congress.

AP Images/Charles Dharapak

Bipartisanship in the 114th Congress will depend upon the cooperation of President Barack Obama and Republican congressional leaders John Boehner and Mitch McConnell.

Legislative Productivity

divided government One party controls the White House and another party controls one or both houses of Congress.

unified government The same party controls the White House and both houses of Congress.

In recent years, political scientists have studied how productive Congress has been and whether the post-9/11 Congress has performed especially well or especially poorly. The first issue concerns how best to measure the body's major and minor "legislative productivity." It is clear that Congress passed and funded an enormous number of bills in response to the Great Depression in the 1930s and in the mid-1960s, mainly in conjunction with that era's "war on poverty." And most scholars agree that in recent decades the body's legislative output has often slowed or declined.[21]

The second issue is how best to evaluate changes in the legislation Congress produces from one time period to the next. For instance, some scholars argue that the relatively low levels of legislative output of the late 1990s, together with decreases in the body's oversight hearings and related activities, betokened an institutional decline of Congress; others, however, reject the view that Congress, by passing fewer laws and holding fewer hearings, had thereby become a "broken branch."[22]

The third issue is whether **divided government** (one party in control of the presidency and the other in charge of one or both chambers of Congress) decreases legislative productivity. Although there are some exceptions, most studies of the subject suggest that divided party government only reduces the passage of the most far-reaching and costly legislation.[23] As we shall discuss in Chapter 10, divided party government does not lead inevitably to "policy gridlock" any more than having **unified government** (a single party in power in the White House and in both chambers of Congress) makes enacting ever more sweeping laws easy or inevitable.

HOW WE COMPARE

Number of Legislators

Writing in *Federalist* paper No. 55, James Madison insists that in any legislative body the number of legislators "ought at most to be kept within a certain limit, in order to avoid the confusion and intemperance of a multitude."

America has heeded Madison's advice. With 435 members of the House and 100 members of the Senate, the Congress has a total of 535 members representing more than 310 million citizens, or roughly one national legislator for every 590,000 citizens.

In most democracies, the ratio of national legislators to citizens is far higher than it is in the United States. For example, with a population of just over 60 million, the British Parliament's two houses total more than 1,300 members, or roughly one national legislator for every 48,000 citizens; and, with a population of about 10 million, Sweden's legislature has nearly 350 members, or roughly one national legislator for every 27,100 citizens.

At the same time, however, America has more numerous and more powerful subnational legislators (more than 7,300 in all) than most other nations do, including, in Madison's home state of

(continued)

HOW WE COMPARE (*Continued*)

Virginia, 140 state lawmakers representing about 8 million citizens, or roughly one state lawmaker for every 57,000 citizens.

Also, the U.S. Constitution would permit the U.S. House to expand enough to approximate the representation ratios of nations like the United Kingdom and Sweden and states like Virginia: Article 1, section 2 states that "the Number of Representatives shall not exceed one for every thirty Thousand."

Thus, given 300 million citizens, the Constitution would allow there to be as many as 10,000 members of the U.S. House (300 million divided by 30,000). But the mere thought heralds Madison's warning, harkening back to ancient Greece's large legislatures, that even if "every Athenian citizen had been a Socrates, every Athenian assembly would have been a mob."

The fourth issue involves so-called **earmarks**—congressional provisions that direct the federal government to fund specific projects or exempt specific persons or groups from needing to pay specific federal taxes or fees. Earmarks have tripled since 1994; in 2006 alone, nearly 13,000 earmarks cost about $64 billion.[24] Earmarks are legally binding, but few appear in a bill's text; rather, most are "hidden" in conference reports not subject to amendment.

Reforming Congress

While most citizens are only vaguely familiar with the rules and procedures under which Congress operates, they do care whether Congress as an institution serves the public interest and fulfills its mission as a democratic body. Over the last several decades, many proposals have been made to reform and improve Congress—term limitations, new ethics and campaign finance laws, and organizational changes intended to reduce the power and perks of members while making it easier for Congress to pass needed legislation in a timely fashion. Some of these proposals—for example, campaign finance reforms (see Chapter 8)—have recently become law.

Many would-be reformers share the view that Congress is overstaffed and self-indulgent. It is, they complain, quick to impose new laws on states, cities, businesses, and average citizens, but slow to apply those same laws to itself and its members. It is quick to pass **pork-barrel legislation**—bills that give tangible benefits (highways, dams, post offices) to constituents in the hope of winning their votes in return—but slow to tackle complex and controversial questions of national policy. The reformers' image of Congress is unflattering, but is it wholly unwarranted?

No perk is more treasured by members of Congress than the frank. Members of Congress are allowed by law to send material through the mail free of charge by substituting their facsimile signature (*frank*) for postage. But rather than using this **franking privilege**

earmarks "Hidden" congressional provisions that direct the federal government to fund specific projects or that exempt specific persons or groups from paying specific federal taxes or fees.

pork-barrel legislation Legislation that gives tangible benefits to constituents in several districts or states in the hope of winning their votes in return.

franking privilege The ability of members to mail letters to their constituents free of charge by substituting their facsimile signature for postage.

to keep their constituents informed about the government, most members use franked newsletters and questionnaires as campaign literature. That is why use of the frank soars in the months before an election. Thus, the frank amounts to a taxpayer subsidy of members' campaigns, a perk that bolsters the electoral fortunes of incumbents. Some reformers do not believe it is possible to fence in congressional use of the frank for public education or other legitimate purposes, and so they propose abolishing it outright. Other reformers argue that the frank can be fenced in by prohibiting mailings just before primaries and general elections.

For years, Congress routinely exempted itself from many of the laws it passed. In defense of this practice, members said that if members of Congress were subject to, for example, the minimum wage laws, the executive branch, charged with enforcing these laws, would acquire excessive power over Congress. This would violate the separation of powers. But as public criticism of Congress grew and confidence in government declined, more and more people demanded that Congress subject itself to the laws that applied to everybody else. In 1995, the 104th Congress did this by passing a bill that obliges Congress to obey 11 important laws governing things such as civil rights, occupational safety, fair labor standards, and family leave.

The bipartisan Congressional Accountability Act of 1995 had to solve a key problem: under the constitutional doctrine of separated powers, it would have been unwise and perhaps unconstitutional for the executive branch to enforce congressional compliance with executive-branch regulations. So Congress created the independent Office of Compliance and an employee grievance procedure to deal with implementation. Now Congress, too, must obey laws such as the Civil Rights Act, the Equal Pay Act, the Age Discrimination Act, and the Family and Medical Care Leave Act.

As already mentioned, bills containing money for local dams, bridges, roads, and monuments are referred to disparagingly as pork-barrel legislation. Reformers complain that when members act to "bring home the bacon," Congress misallocates tax dollars by supporting projects with trivial social benefits in order to bolster their re-election prospects.

No one can doubt the value of trimming unnecessary spending, but pork is not necessarily the villain it is made out to be. For example, the main cause of the budget deficit was the increase in spending on entitlement programs (like health care and interest on the national debt) without a corresponding increase in taxes. Spending on pork is a small fraction of total annual federal spending (about 2.5 percent, on average, from 1993 to 2005).[25] By 2013, what most observers would count as pork spending was below 1 percent of total federal spending. But many categories of pork spending have increased in the last 10 or 15 years. Of course, one person's pork is another person's necessity. No doubt some congressional districts get an unnecessary bridge or highway, but others get bridges and highways that are long overdue. The notion that every bridge or road a member of Congress gets for his or her district is wasteful pork is tantamount to saying that no member attaches any importance to merit.

Even if all pork were bad, it would still be necessary. Congress is an independent branch of government, and each member is, by constitutional design, the advocate of his or her district or state. No member's vote can be won by coercion, and few can be had by mere appeals to party loyalty or presidential needs. Pork is a way of obtaining consent. The only alternative is bribery, but bribery, besides being wrong, would benefit only the member, whereas pork usually benefits voters in the member's district. If you want to eliminate pork, you must eliminate Congress, by converting it into a parliament under the control of a powerful party leader or prime minister. In a tightly controlled parliament, no votes need be bought; they can be commanded. But members of such a parliament can do little to help their constituents cope with government or to defend them against bureaucratic abuses, nor can they investigate the conduct of the executive branch. The price of a citizen-oriented Congress is a pork-oriented Congress.

HOW THINGS WORK

Rules on Congressional Ethics

Senate

Gifts: No gifts (in money, meals, or things) totalling $100 or more from anyone except a spouse or personal friend.

Lobbyists may not pay for gifts, official travel, legal defense funds, or charitable contributions to groups controlled by senators.

Fees: No fees for lectures or writing ("honoraria"), except that fees of up to $2,000 may go to a senator-designated charity.

Outside earned income may not exceed 15 percent of a senator's salary.

Ex-senators may not try to influence members of Congress for one year after leaving the Senate.

Mass mailings: No senator may receive more than $50,000 from the Senate to send out a mailing to constituents.

House

Gifts: No gifts (in money, meals, or things) totalling $100 or more from anyone except a spouse or personal friend.

Lobbyists may not offer gifts or pay for travel, even if a lobbyist is a spouse or personal friend.

Travel: House members may travel at the expense of others if travel is for officially connected meetings.

Fees: No honoraria for House members.

Ex–House members may not lobby Congress for one year after leaving office.

HOW THINGS WORK

How Congress Raises Its Pay

For more than 200 years, Congress has tried to find a politically painless way to raise its own pay. It has managed to vote itself a pay increase 23 times in those two centuries, but usually at the price of a hostile public reaction. Twice during the 19th century, a pay raise led to a massacre of incumbents in the next election.

(continued)

HOW THINGS WORK (*Continued*)

Knowing this, Congress has invented various ways to get a raise without actually appearing to vote for it. These have included the following:

• Voting for a tax deduction for expenses incurred as a result of living in Washington

• Creating a citizens' commission that could recommend a pay increase that would take effect automatically, provided Congress did not vote against it

• Linking increases in pay to decreases in honoraria (that is, speaking fees)

In 1989, a commission recommended a congressional pay raise of over 50 percent (from $89,500 to $135,000) and a ban on honoraria. The House planned to let it take effect automatically. But the public wouldn't have it, demanding that Congress vote on the raise—and vote it down. It did.

Embarrassed by its maneuvering, Congress retreated. At the end of 1989, it voted itself (as well as most top executive and judicial branch members) a small pay increase (7.9 percent for representatives, 9.9 percent for senators) that also provided for automatic cost-of-living adjustments (up to 5 percent a year) in the future. But the automatic adjustments in congressional pay have been rejected every year in recorded roll-call votes. Apparently, nobody in Congress wants to be accused of "getting rich" at the taxpayers' expense.

LEARNING OBJECTIVES

LO 9.1 In what respects is Congress "the first branch" of American national government?

Congress is one of three co-equal branches, but it is "the first branch" by virtue of the especially extensive and important powers bestowed on it by Article I of the Constitution, and with respect to the Framers' belief that Congress was pivotal to making federalism, the separation of powers, and checks and balances work.

LO 9.2 Why do most Americans and many experts now view Congress as "the broken branch"?

Most Americans and many experts express disapproval of Congress and believe that it is ineffective at solving important problems, beholden to contributors and special interests, and unable to reform itself. Yet upward of 90 percent of the "broken branch's" incumbents who seek re-election win it, usually by wide margins. And the experts offer conflicting views regarding why Congress remains "broken" and how, if at all, it can be fixed.

LO 9.3 What are the main differences between a congress and a parliament?

A congress differs from a parliament in two basic ways: how one becomes a member and what one does as a member. To run for a seat in a parliament like the United Kingdom's, you first need a political party to put your name on a ballot, but to become a candidate for representative or senator in Congress, you first need to enter a primary election (political parties exercise relatively little control over who runs). In a parliament, the head of the executive branch (the prime minister) is selected by the majority party from among its members, and once in office a member of parliament has only one important decision to make—whether or not to support the government. By contrast, the voters, not the congress, pick the president, and once elected a member of congress has powers that he or she can exercise without regard to presidential preferences.

LO 9.4 How has the legislative productivity of the U.S. Congress varied over time?

In some periods, like the 1930s (the New Deal) and the 1960s (the Great Society), Congress has produced lots of major legislation. In other periods, however, its legislative output has been less robust. But scholars disagree about what explains these changes and also over how to measure "legislative productivity" in the first place.

LO 9.5 Are the American people as deeply divided in partisan and ideological terms as their representatives in Congress now appear to be?

Nobody disputes that Congress in recent decades has become more polarized in partisan and ideological terms, but some leading scholars argue that the trend reflects the growing political polarization in the American electorate, while others argue instead that voters remain far less polarized than those elected political elites who now represent them.

TO LEARN MORE

- House of Representatives: **www.house.gov**

- Senate: **www.senate.gov**

- Library of Congress: **www.loc.gov**

- For news about Congress *Roll Call* magazine: **www.rollcall.com** C-SPAN: **www.c-span.org**

- Abramowitz, Alan I. *The Disappearing Center: Engaged Citizens, Polarization, and American Democracy.* New Haven and London: Yale University Press, 2010. Claims that polarization in Congress reflects how politically attentive and active voters are polarized, while less informed but more moderate voters are disengaged.

- Arnold, R. Douglas. *The Logic of Congressional Action.* New Haven and London: Yale University Press, 1990. Masterful analysis of how Congress sometimes passes bills that serve the general public, not just special interests.

- Black, Amy E. *From Inspiration to Legislation: How an Idea Becomes a Bill.* Upper Saddle River, NJ: Pearson, 2007. An insider's account of the creation of the Safe Haven Act of 2001.

- Fenno, Richard F., Jr. *Congressmen in Committees.* Boston: Little, Brown, 1973. Classic study of the styles of 12 standing committees.

• Fiorina, Morris P. *Disconnect: The Breakdown of Representation in American Politics*. Oklahoma: University of Oklahoma Press, 2009. Offers evidence suggesting that the increasingly ideological and partisan Congress represents the still-centrist and moderate American people far less well than it did in the past.

• Fiorina, Morris P. *Congress: Keystone of the Washington Establishment*, 2nd ed. New Haven, CT: Yale University Press, 1989. Argues that congressional behavior is aimed at guaranteeing the members' chances for re-election.

• Jacobson, Gary. *The Politics of Congressional Elections*, 6th ed. New York: Longman, 2004. Authoritative study of how members of Congress are elected.

• Maass, Arthur. *Congress and the Common Good*. New York: Basic Books, 1983. Insightful account of congressional operations, especially those involving legislative–executive relations. Disputes Fiorina's argument that re-election needs explain congressional behavior.

• Mann, Thomas E., and Norman J. Ornstein, *Broken Branch: How Congress Is Failing America and How to Get It Back on Track*, 2nd ed. New York: Oxford University Press, 2008. Critically compares the post-1994 Congress to its predecessors and suggests several major reforms.

• Poole, Keith T., and Howard Rosenthal. *Congress: A Political-Economic History of Roll Call Voting*. New York: Oxford University Press, 1997. Sophisticated study of why members of Congress vote as they do and how relatively stable congressional voting patterns have been throughout American history.

• Sundquist, James L. *The Decline and Resurgence of Congress*. Washington, D.C.: Brookings Institution, 1981. A history of the fall and, after 1973, the rise of congressional power vis-à-vis the president.

• Taylor, Andrew J. *Congress: A Performance Appraisal*. Boulder, CO: Westview Press, 2013. Offers evidence and arguments to suggest that the present-day Congress is not the dysfunctional body that the public and many scholars believe it to be.

White House Photo/Alamy

The Presidency

LEARNING OBJECTIVES

LO 10.1 How do presidents differ from prime ministers?

LO 10.2 Did the Founders expect the presidency to be the most important political institution?

LO 10.3 How have the constitutional and political powers of the presidency evolved from the founding of the United States to the present?

LO 10.4 How do presidents make policy?

LO 10.5 Is it harder to govern when the presidency and the Congress are controlled by different political parties?

THEN

When the Framers wrote the Constitution in the summer of 1787, they did not have a ready consensus on how to select the chief executive or define the powers of the office. James Wilson of Pennsylvania wanted the president to be elected by the people, Roger Sherman of Connecticut wanted him elected by Congress. Wilson's view got almost no support because the size of the United States (in 1787 it was as large as England, Ireland, France, Germany, and Italy combined) made it unlikely that anybody save George Washington could obtain a popular majority. Sherman's view got a lot of support, but many delegates worried that the president would become nothing more than a tool of Congress. Ultimately, a small subset of the group, the Committee on Postponed Matters, came up with the idea of creating an electoral college to choose the president. The Framers approved the plan, but they expected that most elections would ultimately be decided by the House of Representatives, as they thought candidates would have difficulty winning a majority in the Electoral College.

NOW

More than two hundred years later, the Electoral College endures, and the House has not chosen a president since 1824. The stability of this institution is surprising, given that the Framers settled on it as a last-minute compromise, and yet it is the only part of the presidential campaign process that the Framers would recognize in the 21st century. The lengthy road to the nomination, extensive fundraising required (in the 2012 presidential race, the two major-party candidates and their parties raised approximately $2 billion for campaign spending),[1] and 24-hour media coverage are all standard features of modern presidential selection, and the weighty demands of winning the White House affect how the victorious candidate governs as president. As you read this chapter, think about which features of the American presidency make sense today and which might merit change, keeping in mind that the Framers were not necessarily wedded to all aspects of the institution they created, nor could they have anticipated how technology and other factors would change it.

Presidents and Prime Ministers

The popularly elected president is an American invention. Of the roughly five dozen countries in which there is some degree of party competition and thus, presumably, some measure of free choice for the voters, only 16 have a directly elected president, and 13 of these are nations of North and South America. The democratic alternative is for the chief executive to be a prime minister, chosen by and responsible to the parliament. This system prevails in most Western European countries, as well as in Israel and Japan. There is no nation with a purely presidential political system in Europe; France combines a directly elected president with a prime minister and parliament.[2]

In a parliamentary system, the prime minister is the chief executive. The prime minister is chosen not by the voters but by the legislature, and he or she in turn selects the other ministers from the members of parliament. If the parliament has only two major parties, the ministers usually will be chosen from the majority party; if there are many parties (as in Israel), several parties may participate in a coalition Cabinet. The prime minister remains in power as long as his or her party has a majority of the seats in the legislature or as long as the coalition he or she has assembled holds together. The voters choose who is to be a member of parliament—usually by voting for one or another party—but cannot choose who is to be the chief executive officer. Whether a nation has a presidential or a parliamentary system makes a big difference in the identity and powers of the chief executive.

A prime minister's party (or coalition) always has a majority in parliament; if it did not, somebody else would be prime minister. A president's party often does not have a congressional majority; instead, Congress often is controlled by the opposite party, creating a divided government. Divided government means that cooperation between the two branches—hard to achieve under the best of circumstances—is often further reduced by partisan bickering. Even when one party controls both the White House and Congress, the two branches often work at cross-purposes. The U.S. Constitution created a system of separate branches sharing powers. The authors of the document expected there would be conflict between the branches, and they have not been disappointed.

divided government One party controls the White House and another party controls one or both houses of Congress.

unified government The same party controls the White House and both houses of Congress.

When Kennedy was president, his party, the Democrats, held a big majority in the House and the Senate. Yet Kennedy was frustrated by his inability to get Congress to approve proposals to enlarge civil rights, supply federal aid for school construction, create a Department of Urban Affairs and Housing, or establish a program of subsidized medical care for the elderly. During his last year in office, Congress passed only about one-fourth of his proposals. Carter did not fare much better; even though the Democrats controlled Congress, many of his most important proposals were defeated or greatly modified. Only Franklin Roosevelt (1933–1945) and Lyndon Johnson (1963–1969) had even brief success in leading Congress, and for Roosevelt most of that success was confined to his first term or to wartime.

Divided Government

In the 60 years from 1952 through 2012, there were 31 congressional elections and 16 presidential elections. Nineteen of the 31 produced **divided government**—a government in which one party controls the White House and a different party controls one or both houses of Congress. When Barack Obama became president in 2009, it was only the fourth time since 1969 that the same party controlled the White House and Congress, creating a **unified government**. Eight years earlier, the inauguration of President George W. Bush marked the first time since 1953 that the Republicans were fully in charge of both branches of government (they controlled the White House and the Senate from 1981 to 1987). But not long after the Senate convened, one Republican, James Jeffords of Vermont, announced that he was an independent and voted with the Democrats. Divided government returned until an additional Republican was elected to the Senate in 2002. But the Democrats retook control in 2007 and increased their majorities in both chambers two years later, even gaining the 60 votes necessary to halt filibusters in the Senate following a contested Minnesota race that ended with Democrat Al Franken being declared the winner and seated. They lost their filibuster-proof majority in 2010, when Republican Scott Brown won a surprise victory to fill the seat of recently deceased Senator Ted Kennedy of Massachusetts. And President Obama faced partially divided government after two years in office, with a Republican-led House and a narrowly Democratic Senate, a division of power that continued even after Obama won re-election in 2012.

Americans say they don't like divided government. They—or at least the pundits who claim to speak for them—think divided government produces partisan bickering, political paralysis, and policy gridlock. During the 1990 battle between President Bush and a Democratic Congress, one magazine compared it to a movie featuring the Keystone Kops, characters from the silent movies who wildly chased each other around while accomplishing nothing.[3] In the 1992 campaign, Bush, Clinton, and Ross Perot bemoaned the "stalemate" that had developed in Washington. When Clinton was sworn in as president, many commentators spoke approvingly of the "end of gridlock."

> **gridlock** The inability of the government to act because rival parties control different parts of the government.

There are two things wrong with these complaints. First, it is not clear that divided government produces a gridlock that is any worse than that which exists with unified government. Second, it is not clear that, even if **gridlock** does exist, it is always, or even usually, a bad thing for the country.

Does Gridlock Matter?

Despite the well-publicized stories about presidential budget proposals being ignored by Congress (Democrats used to describe Reagan's and Bush's budgets as being "dead on arrival"), it is not easy to tell whether divided governments produce fewer or worse policies than unified ones. The scholars who have looked closely at the matter have, in general, concluded that divided governments do about as well as unified ones in passing important laws, conducting important investigations, and ratifying significant treaties.[4] Political scientist David Mayhew studied 267 important laws that were enacted between 1946 and 1990. These laws were as likely to be passed when different parties controlled the White House and Congress as when the same party controlled both branches.[5] For example, divided governments produced the 1948 Marshall Plan to rebuild war-torn Europe and the 1986 Tax Reform Act. The box below lists six examples of divided government in action.

Why do divided governments produce about as much important legislation as unified ones? The main reason is that "unified government" is something of a myth. Just because the Republicans control both the presidency and Congress does not mean that the Republican president and the Republican senators and representatives will see things the same way. For one thing, Republicans are themselves divided between conservatives (mainly from the South) and liberals (mainly from the Northeast and Midwest). They disagree about policy almost as much as Republicans and Democrats disagree. For another thing, the Constitution ensures that the president and Congress will be rivals for power and thus rivals in policymaking. That's what the separation of powers and checks and balances are all about.

As a result, periods of unified government often turn out not to be so unified. Democratic president Lyndon Johnson could not get many Democratic members of Congress to support his war policy in Vietnam. Democratic President Jimmy Carter could not get the Democratic-controlled Senate to ratify his strategic arms-limitation treaty. Democratic president Bill Clinton could not get the Democratic Congress to go along with his policy on gays in the military or his health proposals; and when the heavily revised Clinton budget did pass in 1993, it was by just one vote.

The only time there really is a unified government is when not just the same party but the same *ideological wing* of that party is in effective control of both branches of government. This was true in 1933 when Franklin Roosevelt was president and change-oriented Democrats controlled Congress, and it was true again in 1965 when Lyndon Johnson and liberal Democrats dominated Congress. Both were periods when many major policy initiatives became law: Social Security, business regulations, Medicare, and civil rights legislation. But these periods of ideologically unified government are very rare.

Gridlock, to the extent that it exists, is a necessary consequence of a system of representative democracy. Such a system causes delays, intensifies deliberations, forces compromises, and requires the creation of broad-based coalitions to support most new policies. This system is the opposite of direct democracy. If you believe in direct democracy, you believe that what the people want on some issue should become law with as little fuss and bother as possible. Political gridlocks are like traffic gridlocks—people get overheated, things boil over, nothing moves, and nobody wins except journalists who write about the

HOW THINGS WORK

Divided Government at Work: Six Examples

President George W. Bush and the partly Democratic-controlled Congress (Senate) passed legislation to institute assessment requirements in primary and secondary education.

President Bill Clinton and the Republican-controlled Congress overhauled the nation's welfare system and balanced the federal budget.

President George H. W. Bush and the Democratic-controlled Congress enacted historic legislation to aid disabled persons.

President Ronald Reagan and the partly Democratic-controlled Congress (House) reformed the federal tax system.

President Richard Nixon and the Democratic-controlled Congress created many new federal environmental policies and programs.

President Dwight D. Eisenhower and the Democratic-controlled Congress established the interstate highway system.

Source: Eisenhower to Clinton examples adapted from Associated Press, "Major Laws Passed in Divided Government," November 9, 2006.

HOW WE COMPARE

Presidential Systems

Most modern democracies feature one of three systems:

- Parliamentary systems (like the United Kingdom) in which prime ministers are selected by a legislative majority and can be removed by a legislative majority at virtually any time;

- Presidential systems (like the United States) in which the president and the legislators are separately elected and serve fixed terms, with the president subject to removal by the legislature only under extreme circumstances (for example, in the United States, impeachment by the House and removal from office by the Senate); or

- Semi-presidential systems (like France) in which there is a prime minister selected and subject to removal by a parliamentary majority, as well as a president who is separately elected.

Using a multidimensional definition of "democratic," in 1950, about 60 percent of democratic nations had parliamentary systems, 30 percent had semi-presidential systems, and 10 percent had presidential systems. Today, however, about two-thirds of all democratic nations have either semi-presidential (about 36 percent) or presidential (about 30 percent) systems.

(*continued*)

HOW WE COMPARE (*Continued*)

Are elected officials and party leaders in presidential systems like that in the United States more or less likely to deliver on campaign promises than are their counterparts in the other two systems? The most in-depth studies to date say "less likely": The rate at which a party in power pursues the policies it offered to voters in its platform is generally lower in presidential systems; and the incidence of "policy-switching" (pursuing policies directly contrary to those promised during the campaign) is more than four times as common in presidential systems as it is in parliamentary systems, with semi-presidential systems being in the middle.

Source: David Samuels and Matthew Shugart, *Presidents, Parties, and Prime Ministers: How the Separation of Powers Affects Party Organization and Behavior* (Cambridge University Press, 2010); "Presidents, Prime Ministers, and Mandate Representation: A Global Test," paper prepared for presentation at the 2006 Annual Meeting of the American Political Science Association, Philadelphia, Pennsylvania.

mess and lobbyists who charge big fees to steer their clients around the tie-up. In a direct democracy, the president would be a traffic cop with broad powers to decide in what direction the traffic should move and to make sure that it moves that way.

But if unified governments are not really unified—if in fact they are split by ideological differences within each party and by the institutional rivalries between the president and Congress—then this change is less important than it may seem. What *is* important is the relative power of the president and Congress. That has changed greatly.

The Powers of the President

Though the president, unlike a prime minister, cannot command an automatic majority in the legislature, he does have some formidable, albeit vaguely defined, powers. These are mostly set forth in Article II of the Constitution and are of two sorts: those he can exercise in his own right without formal legislative approval, and those that require the consent of the Senate or of Congress as a whole.

Powers of the President Alone

- Serve as commander in chief of the armed forces

- Commission officers of the armed forces

- Grant reprieves and pardons for federal offenses (except impeachment)

- Convene Congress in special sessions

- Receive ambassadors

- Take care that the laws be faithfully executed

- Wield the "executive power"

- Appoint officials to lesser offices

Powers the President Shares with the Senate

- Make treaties

- Appoint ambassadors, judges, and high officials

Powers the President Shares with Congress as a Whole

- Approve legislation

Taken alone and interpreted narrowly, this list of powers is not very impressive. Obviously, the president's authority as commander in chief is important, but literally construed, most of the other constitutional grants seem to provide for little more than a president who is chief clerk of the country. A hundred years after the Founding, that is about how matters appeared to even the most astute observers. In 1884, Woodrow Wilson wrote a book about American politics titled *Congressional Government,* in which he described the business of the president as "usually not much above routine," mostly "*mere* administration." The president might as well be an officer of the civil service. To succeed, he need only obey Congress and stay alive.[6]

But even as Wilson wrote, he was overlooking some examples of enormously powerful presidents, such as Lincoln, and was not sufficiently attentive to the potential for presidential power to be found in the more ambiguous clauses of the Constitution as well as in the political realities of American life. The president's authority as commander in chief has grown—especially, but not only, in wartime—to encompass not simply the direction of the military forces, but also the management of the economy and the direction of foreign affairs as well. A quietly dramatic reminder of the awesome implications of the president's military powers occurs at the precise instant that a new president assumes office. A military

A military aide to the president carries a leather briefcase containing the classified nuclear war plan, popularly known as the "football," up the steps of Air Force One.

officer carrying a locked briefcase moves from the side of the outgoing president to the side of the new one. In the briefcase are the secret codes and orders that permit the president to authorize the launching of American nuclear weapons.

The president's duty to "take care that the laws be faithfully executed" has become one of the most elastic phrases in the Constitution. By interpreting this broadly, Grover Cleveland was able to use federal troops to break a labor strike in the 1890s, and Dwight Eisenhower was able to send troops to help integrate a public school in Little Rock, Arkansas, in 1957.

The greatest source of presidential power, however, is not found in the Constitution at all but in politics and public opinion. Increasingly since the 1930s, Congress has passed laws that confer on the executive branch broad grants of authority to achieve some general goals, leaving it up to the president and his deputies to define the regulations and programs that will actually be put into effect. In Chapter 11 we shall see how this delegation of legislative power to the president has contributed to the growth of the bureaucracy. Moreover, the American people—always in times of crisis, but increasingly as an everyday matter—look to the president for leadership and hold him responsible for a large and growing portion of our national affairs. The public thinks, wrongly, that the presidency is the "first branch" of government.

The Evolution of the Presidency

Not surprisingly, given the preeminence of the presidency in American politics today, few issues inspired as much debate or concern among the Framers in 1787 as the problem of defining the chief executive. The delegates feared anarchy and monarchy in about equal measure. When the Constitutional Convention met, the existing state constitutions gave most, if not all, power to the legislatures. In eight states, the governor actually was chosen by the legislature, and in 10 states, the governor could not serve more than one year. Only in New York, Massachusetts, and Connecticut did governors have much power or serve for any length of time.

Concerns of the Founders

The delegates in Philadelphia—and later the critics of the new Constitution during the debate over its ratification—worried about aspects of the presidency that were quite different from those that concern us today. In 1787–1789, some Americans suspected that the president, by being able to command the state militia, would use the militia to overpower state governments. Others were worried that if the president were allowed to share treaty-making power with the Senate, he would be "directed by minions and favorites" and become a "tool of the Senate."

But the most frequent concern was over the possibility of presidential re-election: Americans in the late 18th century were sufficiently suspicious of human nature and sufficiently experienced in the arts of mischievous government to believe that a president, once elected, would arrange to stay in office in perpetuity by resorting to bribery, intrigue, and force. This might happen, for example, every time the presidential election was thrown into the House of Representatives because no candidate had received a majority of the votes in the Electoral College, a situation that most people expected to happen frequently.

In retrospect, these concerns seem misplaced, even foolish. The power over the militia has had little significance; the election has gone to the House only twice (1800 and 1824); and though the Senate dominated the presidency off and on during the second half of the 19th century, it has not done so recently. The real sources of the expansion of presidential power—the president's role in foreign affairs, his ability to shape public opinion, his position as head of the executive branch, and his claims to have certain "inherent" powers by virtue of his office—were hardly predictable in 1787.

There was nowhere in the world at that time, nor had there been at any time in history, an example of an American-style presidency. It was a unique and unprecedented institution, and the Framers and their critics can easily be forgiven for not predicting accurately how it would evolve. At a more general level, however, they understood the issue quite clearly. Gouverneur Morris of Pennsylvania put the problem of the presidency this way: "Make him too weak: the Legislature will usurp his powers. Make him too strong: he will usurp on the Legislature."

> ***Electoral College*** The people chosen to cast each state's votes in a presidential election. Each state can cast one electoral vote for each senator and representative it has. The District of Columbia has three electoral votes, even though it cannot elect a representative or senator.

The Framers knew very well that the relations between the president and Congress and the manner in which the president is elected were of profound importance, and they debated both at great length. The first plan was for Congress to elect the president—in short, for the system to be quasi-parliamentary. But if that were done, some delegates pointed out, Congress could dominate an honest or lazy president, while a corrupt or scheming president might dominate Congress.

After much discussion, it was decided that the president should be chosen directly by voters. But by which voters? The emerging nation was large and diverse. It seemed unlikely that every citizen would be familiar enough with the candidates to cast an informed vote for a president directly. Worse, a direct popular election would give inordinate weight to the large, populous states, and no plan with that outcome had any chance of adoption by the smaller states.

The Electoral College

Thus the **Electoral College** was invented, whereby each of the states would select electors in whatever manner it wished. The electors would then meet in each state capital and vote for president and vice president. Many Framers expected that this procedure would lead to each state's electors' voting for a favorite son, and thus no candidate would win a majority of the popular vote. In this event, it was decided, the House of Representatives should make the choice, with each state delegation casting one vote.

The plan seemed to meet every test: large states would have their say, but small states would be protected by having a minimum of three electoral votes no matter how tiny their population. The small states together could wield considerable influence in the House, where—it was widely expected—most presidential elections would ultimately be decided. Of course, it did not work out quite this way: the Framers did not foresee the role that political parties would play in producing nationwide support for a slate of national candidates.

The First Presidents

Those who first served as president were among the most prominent men in the new nation, all active either in the movement for independence or in the Founding or in both. Of the first five presidents, four (all but John Adams) served two full terms. Washington and Monroe were not even opposed. The first administration had at the highest levels the leading spokesmen for all of the major viewpoints: Alexander Hamilton was Washington's secretary of the treasury (and was sympathetic to the urban commercial interests), and Thomas Jefferson was secretary of state (and more inclined toward rural, small-town, and farming views). Washington spoke out strongly against political parties, and though parties soon emerged, there was a stigma attached to them: many people believed that it was wrong to take advantage of divisions in the country, to organize deliberately to acquire political office, or to make legislation depend upon party advantage. As it turned out, this hostility to party (or "faction," as it was more commonly called) was unrealistic: parties are as natural to democracy as churches are to religion.

The Jacksonians

At a time roughly corresponding to the presidency of Andrew Jackson (1829–1837), broad changes began to occur in American politics. These changes, together with the personality of Jackson himself, altered the relations between the president and Congress and the nature of presidential leadership. As so often happens, few people at the time Jackson took office had much sense of what his presidency would be like. Though he had been a member of the House of Representatives and of the Senate, he was elected as a military hero—and an apparently doddering one at that. Sixty-one years old and seemingly frail, he nonetheless used the powers of his office as no one before him had.

Jackson vetoed 12 acts of Congress, more than all his predecessors combined and more than any subsequent president until Andrew Johnson 30 years later. His vetoes were not simply on constitutional grounds but on policy ones: as the only official elected by the entire voting citizenry, he saw himself as the "Tribune of the People." None of his vetoes were overridden. He did not initiate many new policies, but he struck out against the ones he did not like. He did so at a time when the size of the electorate was increasing rapidly, and new states, especially in the West, had entered the Union. (There were then 24 states in the Union, nearly twice the original number.)

Jackson demonstrated what could be done by a popular president. He did not shrink from conflict with Congress, and the tension between the two branches of government that was intended by the Framers became intensified by the personalities of those in government: Jackson in the White House, and Henry Clay, Daniel Webster, and John Calhoun in Congress. These powerful figures walked the political stage at a time when bitter sectional conflicts—over slavery and commercial policies—were beginning to split the country. Jackson, though he was opposed to a large and powerful federal government and wished to return somehow to the agrarian simplicities of Jefferson's time, was nonetheless a believer in a strong and independent presidency. This view, though obscured by nearly a century of subsequent congressional dominance of national politics, was ultimately to triumph—for better or for worse.

With the end of Jackson's second term, Congress quickly reestablished its power, and except for the wartime presidency of Lincoln and brief flashes of presidential power under James Polk (1845–1849) and Grover Cleveland (1885–1889, 1893–1897), the presidency for a hundred years was the subordinate branch of the national government. Of the eight presidents who succeeded Jackson, two (William H. Harrison and Zachary Taylor) died in office, and none of the others served more than one term. Schoolchildren, trying to memorize the list of American presidents, always stumble in this era of the "no-name" presidents. This is hardly a coincidence: Congress was the leading institution, struggling, unsuccessfully, with slavery and sectionalism.

During this long period of congressional—and usually senatorial—dominance of national government, only Lincoln broke new ground for presidential power. Lincoln's expansive use of that power, like Jackson's, was totally unexpected. He was first elected in 1860 as a minority president, receiving less than 40 percent of the popular vote in a field of four candidates. Though a member of the new Republican Party, he had been a member of the Whig party, a group that had stood for limiting presidential power. He had opposed America's entry into the Mexican War and had been critical of Jackson's use of executive authority. But as president during the Civil War, he made unprecedented use of the vague powers in Article II of the Constitution, especially those that he felt were "implied" or "inherent" in the phrase "take care that the laws be faithfully executed" and in the express authorization for him to act as commander-in-chief. Lincoln raised an army, spent money, blockaded Southern ports,

HOW THINGS WORK

The President: Qualifications and Benefits

Qualifications

- A natural-born citizen (can be born abroad of parents who are American citizens)

- 35 years of age

- A resident of the United States for at least 14 years (but not necessarily the 14 years just preceding the election)

Benefits

- A nice house

- A salary of $400,000 per year (taxable)

- An expense account of $50,000 per year (tax-free)

- Travel expenses of $100,000 per year (tax-free)

- A pension, on retirement, equal to the pay of a Cabinet member (taxable)

- Staff support and Secret Service protection for 10 years on leaving the presidency

- A White House staff of 400 to 500

- A place in the country—Camp David

- A personal airplane—Air Force One

- A fine chef

temporarily suspended the writ of habeas corpus, and issued the Emancipation Proclamation to free the slaves—all without prior congressional approval. He justified this, as most Americans probably would have, by the emergency conditions created by civil war. In this he acted little differently from Thomas Jefferson, who while president waged undeclared war against various North African pirates.

After Lincoln, Congress reasserted its power and became, during Reconstruction and for many decades thereafter, the principal federal institution. But it had become abundantly clear that a national emergency could equip the president with great powers and that a popular and strong-willed president could expand his powers even without an emergency.

Except for the administrations of Theodore Roosevelt (1901–1909) and Woodrow Wilson (1913–1921), the president was, until the New Deal, at best a negative force—a source of opposition to Congress, not a source of initiative and leadership for it. Grover Cleveland was a strong personality, but for all his efforts he was able to do little more than veto bills that he did not like. He cast 414 vetoes—more than any other president until Franklin Roosevelt. Frequent targets of his vetoes were bills to confer special pensions on Civil War veterans.

Today we are accustomed to thinking that the president formulates a legislative program to which Congress then responds, but until the 1930s, the opposite was more the case. Congress ignored the initiatives of such presidents as Grover Cleveland, Rutherford Hayes, Chester Arthur, and Calvin Coolidge. Woodrow Wilson in 1913 was the first president since John Adams to deliver personally the State of the Union address, and he was one of the first to develop and argue for a presidential legislative program.

Our popular conception of the president as the central figure of national government, devising a legislative program and commanding a large staff of advisers, is very much a product of the modern era and of the enlarged role of government. In the past, the presidency became powerful only during a national crisis (the Civil War, World War I) or because of an extraordinary personality (Andrew Jackson, Theodore Roosevelt, Woodrow Wilson). Since the 1930s, however, the presidency has been powerful no matter who occupied the office and whether or not there was a crisis. Because government now plays such an active role in our national life, the president is the natural focus of attention and the titular head of a huge federal administrative system (whether he is the real boss is another matter).

The Power to Persuade

The sketchy constitutional powers given to the president, combined with the lack of an assured legislative majority, mean that he must rely heavily on persuasion if he is to accomplish much. Here, the Constitution gives him some advantages: he and the vice president are the only officials elected by the whole nation, and he is the ceremonial head of state as well as the chief executive of the government. The president can use his national constituency and ceremonial duties to enlarge his power, but he must do so quickly: the second half of his first term in office will be devoted to running for re-election, especially if he faces opposition for his own party's nomination (as was the case with Carter and Ford).

The Three Audiences

The president's persuasive powers are aimed at three audiences. The first, and often the most important, is his Washington, D.C., audience of fellow politicians and leaders. As Richard Neustadt points out in his book *Presidential Power*, a president's reputation among his Washington colleagues is of great importance in affecting how much deference his views receive and thus how much power he can wield.[7] If a president is thought to be "smart," "sure of himself," "cool," "on top of things," or "shrewd," and thus "effective," he *will* be effective. Franklin Roosevelt had that reputation, and so did Lyndon Johnson, at least for his first few years in office. Truman, Ford, and Carter often did not have that reputation, and they lost ground accordingly. Power, like beauty, exists largely in the eye of the beholder.

A second audience is composed of party activists and officeholders outside Washington—the partisan grassroots. These persons want the president to exemplify their principles, trumpet their slogans, appeal to their fears and hopes, and help them get re-elected. Since, as we explained in Chapter 7, partisan activists increasingly have an ideological orientation toward national politics, these people will expect "their" president to make fire-and-brimstone speeches that confirm in them a shared sense of purpose and, incidentally, help them raise money from contributors to state and local campaigns.

The third audience is "the public." But of course that audience is really many publics, each with a different view or set of interests. A president on the campaign trail speaks boldly of what he will accomplish; a president in office speaks quietly of the problems that must be overcome. Citizens often are irritated at the apparent tendency of officeholders—including the president—to sound mealy-mouthed and equivocal. But it is easy to criticize the cooking when you haven't been the cook. A president learns quickly that every utterance will be scrutinized closely by the media and by organized groups here and abroad, and errors of fact, judgment, timing, or even inflection will be immediately and forcefully pointed out. Given the risks of saying too much, it is a wonder that presidents say anything at all.

Presidents have made fewer and fewer impromptu remarks in the years since Franklin Roosevelt held office and have instead relied more and more on prepared speeches from which political errors can be removed in advance. Hoover and Roosevelt held six or seven press conferences each month, but every president from Nixon through Clinton has held barely one a month. Instead, modern presidents make formal speeches. A president's use of these speeches often is called the **bully pulpit**, a phrase that means taking advantage of the prestige and visibility of the presidency to try to guide or mobilize the American people.

bully pulpit The president's use of his prestige and visibility to guide or enthuse the American public.

Popularity and Influence

The object of all this talk is to convert personal popularity into congressional support for the president's legislative programs (and improve chances for re-election). It is not obvious, of course, why Congress should care about a president's popularity. After all, as we saw in Chapter 9, most members of Congress are secure in their seats, and few need fear any "party bosses" who might deny them re-nomination. Moreover, the president cannot ordinarily provide credible electoral rewards or penalties to members of Congress. By working for their defeat in the 1938 congressional election, President Franklin Roosevelt attempted to "purge" members of Congress who opposed his program, but he failed. Nor does presidential support help a particular member of Congress: most representatives win re-election anyway, and the few who are in trouble are rarely saved by presidential intervention. When President Reagan campaigned hard for Republican senatorial candidates in 1986, he, too, failed to have much impact.

For a while, scholars thought congressional candidates might benefit from the president's coattails: they might ride into office on the strength of the popularity of a president of their own party. It is true, as can be seen from Table 10.1, that a winning president will often find that his party's strength in Congress increases.

TABLE 10.1 Partisan Gains or Losses in Congress in Presidential Election Years

Year	President	Party	Gains or Losses of President's Party In: House	Gains or Losses of President's Party In: Senate
1932	Roosevelt	Dem.	+90	+9
1936	Roosevelt	Dem.	+12	+7
1940	Roosevelt	Dem.	+7	−3
1944	Roosevelt	Dem.	+24	−2
1948	Truman	Dem.	+75	+9
1952	Eisenhower	Rep.	+22	+1
1956	Eisenhower	Rep.	−3	−1
1960	Kennedy	Dem.	−20	+1
1964	Johnson	Dem.	+37	+1
1968	Nixon	Rep.	+5	+7
1972	Nixon	Rep.	+12	−2
1976	Carter	Dem.	+1	+1
1980	Reagan	Rep.	+33	+12
1984	Reagan	Rep.	+16	−2
1988	Bush	Rep.	−3	−1
1992	Clinton	Dem.	−9	+1
1996	Clinton	Dem.	+9	−2
2000	Bush	Rep.	−3	−4
2004	Bush	Rep.	+4	+4
2008	Obama	Dem.	+21	+9
2012	Obama	Dem.	+8	+2

Sources: *Updated from* Congress and the Nation, *vol. 4 (1973–1976),* 28; *Congressional Quarterly,* Guide to U.S. Elections, *928; U.S. House of Representatives website.*

FIGURE 10.1 **Presidential Popularity** *(continued on opposite page)*

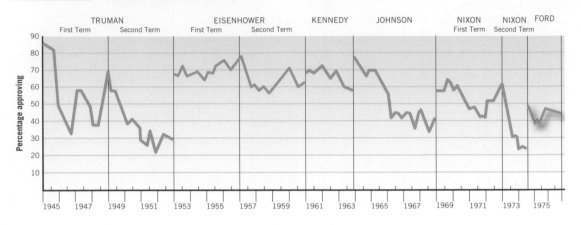

But there are good reasons to doubt whether the pattern observed in Table 10.1 is the result of presidential coattails. For one thing, there are some exceptions. Eisenhower won 57.4 percent of the vote in 1956, but the Republicans lost seats in the House and Senate. Kennedy won in 1960, but the Democrats lost seats in the House and gained but one in the Senate. When Nixon was re-elected in 1972 with one of the largest majorities in history, the Republicans lost seats in the Senate.

Careful studies of voter attitudes and of how presidential and congressional candidates fare in the same districts suggest that, whatever may once have been the influence of coattails, their effect has declined in recent years and is quite small today. The weakening of party loyalty and of party organizations, combined with the enhanced ability of members of Congress to build secure relations with their constituents, has tended to insulate congressional elections from presidential ones. When voters choose as members of Congress people of the same party as an incoming president, they probably do so out of desire for a general change and as an adverse judgment about the outgoing party's performance as a whole, not because they want to supply the new president with members of Congress favorable to him.[8] The big increase in Republican senators and representatives that accompanied the election of Ronald Reagan in 1980 was probably as much a result of the unpopularity of the outgoing president and the circumstances of various local races as it was of Reagan's coattails.

Nonetheless, a president's personal popularity may have a significant effect on how much of his program Congress passes, even if it does not affect the re-election chances of those members of Congress. Though they do not fear a president who threatens to campaign against them (or cherish one who promises to support them), members of Congress do have a sense that it is risky to oppose too adamantly the policies of a popular president. Politicians share a sense of a common fate: they tend to rise or fall together. Statistically, a president's popularity, as measured by the Gallup poll (see Figure 10.1), is associated with the proportion of his legislative proposals approved by Congress (see Figure 10.2). Other things equal, the more popular the president, the higher the proportion of his bills Congress will pass.

But use these figures with caution. How successful a president is with Congress depends not just on the numbers reported here, but on a lot of other factors as well. First, he can be "successful" on a big bill or on a trivial one. If he is successful on a lot of small matters and never on a big one, the measure of presidential victories does not tell us much. Second, a president can keep his victory score high

(continued from opposite page)

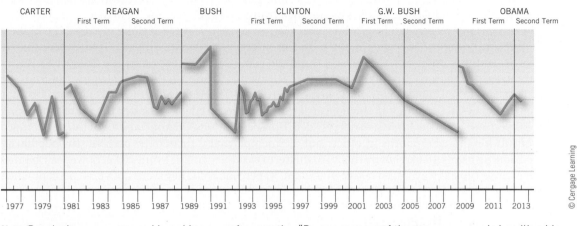

Note: Popularity was measured by asking every few months, "Do you approve of the way _____ is handling his job as president?"

Source: Thomas E. Cronin, *The State of the Presidency* (Boston: Little, Brown, 1975), 110–111. Updated with Gallup poll data, 1976 to present.

FIGURE 10.2   Presidential Victories on Votes in Congress, 1953–2012

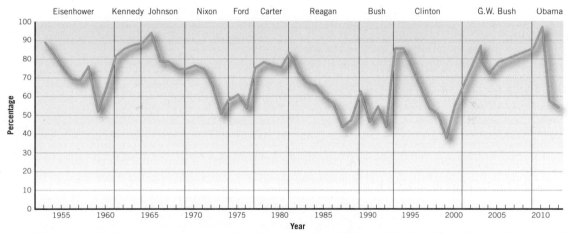

Note: Percentages indicate number of congressional votes supporting the president divided by the total number of votes on which the president has taken a position.

Source: *Congressional Quarterly Weekly*, various years

by not taking a position on any controversial measure. (President Carter made his views known on only 22 percent of the House votes, while President Eisenhower made his views known on 56 percent of those votes.) Third, a president can appear successful if a few bills he likes are passed, but most of his legislative program is bottled up in Congress and never comes to a vote. Given these problems, "presidential victories" are hard to measure accurately.

A fourth general caution: presidential popularity is hard to predict and can be greatly influenced by factors over which nobody, including the president, has much control. For example, when he took office in 2001, President George W. Bush's approval rating was 57 percent, nearly identical to what President Bill Clinton received in his initial rating (58 percent) in 1993. But Bush also had the highest initial *dis*approval rating (25 percent) of any president since polling began. This was undoubtedly partly due to his becoming president on the heels of the Florida vote-count controversy (see Chapter 8). Bush's approval ratings through his first six months were fairly typical for post-1960 presidents. But from the terrorist attack on the United States on September 11, 2001, through mid-2002, his approval ratings never dipped below 70 percent, and the approval ratings he received shortly after the attack (hovering around 90 percent) were the highest ever recorded. President Barack Obama's approval rating averaged 63 percent in his first six months in office, but as unemployment neared 10 percent, his popularity decreased, falling below 45 percent by the 2010 midterm elections. In 2011 and 2012, however, Obama's approval ratings typically averaged between 45 and 50 percent, and they were above 50 percent when he won re-election.

The Decline in Popularity

Though presidential popularity is an asset, its value tends inexorably to decline. As can be seen from Figure 10.1, every president except Eisenhower, Reagan, and Clinton lost popular support between his inauguration and the time that he left office, except when his re-election gave him a brief burst of renewed popularity. Truman was hurt by improprieties among his subordinates and by the protracted Korean War; Johnson was crippled by the increasing unpopularity of the Vietnam War; Nixon was severely damaged by the Watergate scandal; Ford was hurt by having pardoned Nixon for his part in Watergate; Carter was weakened by continuing inflation, staff irregularities, and the Iranian kidnapping of American hostages; George H. W. Bush was harmed by an economic recession. George W. Bush suffered from public criticism of the war in Iraq.

Because a president's popularity tends to be highest right after an election, political commentators like to speak of a "honeymoon," during which, presumably, the president's love affair with the people and with Congress can be consummated. Certainly, Roosevelt enjoyed such a honeymoon. In the legendary "first hundred days" of his presidency, from March to June 1933, FDR obtained from a willing Congress a vast array of new laws creating new agencies and authorizing new powers. But those were extraordinary times: the most serious economic depression of that century had put millions out of work, closed banks, impoverished farmers, and ruined the stock market. It would have been political suicide for Congress to have blocked, or even delayed, action on measures that appeared designed to help the nation out of the crisis.

Other presidents, serving in more normal times, have not enjoyed such a honeymoon. Truman had little success with what he proposed; Eisenhower proposed little. Kennedy, Nixon, Ford, and Carter had some victories in their first year in office, but nothing that could be called a honeymoon. Only Lyndon Johnson enjoyed a highly productive relationship with Congress; until the Vietnam War sapped his strength, he rarely lost. Reagan began his administration with important victories in his effort to cut expenditures and taxes, but in his second year in office he ran into trouble.

veto message A message from the president to Congress stating that he will not sign a bill it has passed. Must be produced within 10 days of the bill's passage.

The decay in the reputation of the president and his party in midterm is evident in Table 10.2. Since 1934, in every off-year election but two, the president's party has lost seats in one or both houses of Congress. In 1998, the Democrats won five seats in the House and lost none in the Senate; in 2002, the Republicans gained eight House seats and two in the Senate. The ability of the president to persuade is important but limited. However, he also has a powerful bargaining chip to play: the ability to say no.

The Power to Say No

The Constitution gives the president the power to veto legislation. In addition, most presidents have asserted the right of "executive privilege," or the right to withhold information that Congress may want to obtain from the president or his subordinates, and some presidents have tried to impound funds appropriated by Congress. These efforts by the president to say no are not only a way of blocking action but also a way of forcing Congress to bargain with him over the substance of policies.

Veto

If a president disapproves of a bill passed by both houses of Congress, he may veto it in one of two ways. One is by a **veto message**. This is a statement that the president sends to Congress accompanying the bill, within 10 days (not counting Sundays) after the bill has been passed. In it he sets forth his reasons for not signing the bill. The other is the **pocket veto**. If the president does not sign the bill within 10 days *and* Congress has adjourned within that time, then the bill will not become law. Obviously, a pocket veto can be used only during a certain time of the year—just before Congress adjourns at the end of its second session. At times, however, presidents have pocket-vetoed a bill just before Congress recessed for a summer vacation or to permit its members to campaign during an off-year election. In 1972, Senator Edward M. Kennedy of Massachusetts protested that this was unconstitutional, since a recess is not the same thing as an adjournment. In a case brought to federal court, Kennedy was upheld, and it is now understood that the pocket veto can be used only just before the life of a given Congress expires.

TABLE 10.2 Partisan Gains or Losses in Congress in Off-Year Elections

Year	President	Party	Gains or Losses of President's Party in:	
			House	Senate
1934	Roosevelt	Dem.	+9	+9
1938	Roosevelt	Dem.	−70	−7
1942	Roosevelt	Dem.	−50	−8
1946	Truman	Dem.	−54	−11
1950	Truman	Dem.	−29	−5
1954	Eisenhower	Rep.	−18	−1
1958	Eisenhower	Rep.	−47	−13
1962	Kennedy	Dem.	−5	+2
1966	Johnson	Dem.	−48	−4
1970	Nixon	Rep.	−12	+1
1974	Ford	Rep.	−48	−5
1978	Carter	Dem.	−12	−3
1982	Reagan	Rep.	−26	0
1986	Reagan	Rep.	−5	−8
1990	Bush	Rep.	−9	−1
1994	Clinton	Dem.	−52	−9
1998	Clinton	Dem.	+5	0
2002	G. W. Bush	Rep.	+8	+2
2006	G. W. Bush	Rep.	−30	−6
2010	Obama	Dem.	−64	−6
2014*	Obama	Dem.	−12	−7

*Preliminary data

Sources: Norman J. Ornstein, Thomas E. Mann, and Michael J. Malbin, *Vital Statistics on Congress, 2001–2002* (Washington, D.C.: Congressional Quarterly Press, 2001), 207; websites of U.S. House of Representatives and U.S. Senate.

pocket veto A bill fails to become law because the president did not sign it within 10 days before Congress adjourns.

line-item veto An executive's ability to block a particular provision in a bill passed by the legislature.

A bill not signed or vetoed within 10 days while Congress is still in session becomes law automatically, without the president's approval. A bill returned to Congress with a veto message can be passed over the president's objections if at least two-thirds of each house votes to override the veto. A bill that has received a pocket veto cannot be brought back to life by Congress (since Congress has adjourned), nor does such a bill carry over to the next session of Congress. If Congress wants to press the matter, it will have to start all over again by passing the bill anew in its next session, and then hope the president will sign it or, if he does not, that they can override his veto.

The president must either accept or reject the entire bill. Presidents do not have the power, possessed by most governors, to exercise a **line-item veto**, with which the chief executive can approve some provisions of a bill and disapprove others. Congress could take advantage of this by putting items the president did not like into a bill he otherwise favored, forcing him to approve those provisions along with the rest of the bill or reject the whole thing. In 1996, Congress passed a bill, which the president signed into law, that gives the president the power of "enhanced rescission." This means the president could cancel parts of a spending bill passed by Congress without vetoing the entire bill. The president had five days after signing a bill to send a message to Congress rescinding some parts of what he had signed. These rescissions would take effect unless Congress, by a two-thirds vote, overturned them. Congress could choose which parts of the president's cancellations it wanted to overturn. But the Supreme Court has decided that this law is unconstitutional. The Constitution gives the president no such power to carve up a bill: he must either sign the whole bill, veto the whole bill, or allow it to become law without his signature.[9]

Nevertheless, the veto power is a substantial one, because Congress rarely has the votes to override it. From George Washington to Barack Obama, more than 2,500 presidential vetoes were cast; about 4 percent were overridden (see Table 10.3). Cleveland, Franklin Roosevelt, Truman, and Eisenhower made the most extensive use of vetoes, accounting for 65 percent of all vetoes ever cast. George W. Bush did not veto a single bill in his first term, though he issued 12 vetoes in his second term, of which four were overridden. In his first term in office, Barack Obama vetoed just two bills. Often the vetoed legislation is revised by Congress and passed in a form suitable to the president. There is no tally of how often this happens, but it is frequent enough so that both branches of government recognize that the veto, or even the threat of it, is part of an elaborate process of political negotiation in which the president has substantial powers.

Executive Privilege

The Constitution says nothing about whether the president is obliged to divulge private communications between himself and his principal advisers, but presidents have acted as if they do have that privilege of confidentiality. The presidential claim is based on two grounds. First, the doctrine of the separation of powers means that one branch of government does not have the right to inquire into the internal workings of another branch headed by constitutionally named officers. Second, the principles of statecraft and of prudent administration require that the president have the right to obtain confidential and candid advice from subordinates; such advice could not be obtained if it would quickly be exposed to public scrutiny.

For almost 200 years, there was no serious challenge to the claim of presidential confidentiality. The Supreme Court did not require the disclosure of confidential communications to or from the president.[10] Congress was never happy with this claim, but until 1973, did not seriously dispute it. Indeed, in 1962, a Senate committee explicitly accepted a claim by President Kennedy that his secretary of defense, Robert S. McNamara, was not obliged to divulge the identity of Defense Department officials who had censored certain speeches by generals and admirals.

In 1974, the Supreme Court for the first time met the issue directly. A federal special prosecutor sought tape recordings of White House conversations between President Nixon and his advisers as part of his investigation of the Watergate scandal. In the case of *United States v. Nixon*, the Supreme Court, by a vote of 8 to 0, held that while there may be a sound basis for the claim of executive privilege, especially where sensitive military or diplomatic matters are involved, there is no "absolute unqualified Presidential privilege of immunity from judicial process under all circumstances."[11] To admit otherwise would be to block the constitutionally defined function of the federal courts to decide criminal cases.

Thus, Nixon was ordered to hand over the disputed tapes and papers to a federal judge so that the judge could decide which were relevant to the case at hand and allow those to be introduced into evidence. In the future, another president may well persuade the Court that a different set of records or papers is so sensitive as to require protection, especially if there is no allegation of criminal misconduct requiring the production of evidence in court. As a practical matter, it seems likely that presidential advisers will be able, except in unusual cases such as Watergate, to continue to give private advice to the president.

In 1997 and 1998, President Clinton was sued while in office by a private person, Paula Jones, who claimed he had solicited sex from her in ways that hurt her reputation. In defending himself against that and other matters, his lawyers attempted to

TABLE 10.3 Presidential Vetoes, 1789–2014

	Regular Vetoes	Pocket Vetoes	Total Vetoes	Vetoes Overridden
Washington	2	—	2	—
Madison	5	2	7	—
Monroe	1	—	1	—
Jackson	5	7	12	—
Tyler	6	3	9	1
Polk	2	1	3	—
Pierce	9	—	9	5
Buchanan	4	3	7	—
Lincoln	2	4	6	—
A. Johnson	21	8	29	15
Grant	45	49	94	4
Hayes	12	1	13	1
Arthur	4	8	12	1
Cleveland	304	109	413	2
Harrison	19	25	44	1
Cleveland	43	127	170	5
McKinley	6	36	42	—
T. Roosevelt	42	40	82	1
Taft	30	9	39	1
Wilson	33	11	44	6
Harding	5	1	6	—
Coolidge	20	30	50	4
Hoover	21	16	37	3
F. Roosevelt	372	263	635	9
Truman	180	70	250	12
Eisenhower	73	108	181	2
Kennedy	12	9	21	—
L. Johnson	16	14	30	—
Nixon	26	17	43	7
Ford	48	18	66	12
Carter	13	18	31	2
Reagan	39	39	78	9
Bush	29	15	44	1
Clinton	36	1	37	2
G. W. Bush	12	0	12	4
Obama	2		2	0

Source: Norman J. Ornstein, Thomas E. Mann, and Michael J. Malbin, Vital Statistics on Congress, 2002–2003 (Washington, D.C.: Congressional Quarterly Press, 2003), 207; The American Presidency Project of the University of California at Santa Barbara; Office of the Clerk of the U.S. House of Representatives website United States Senate website

claim executive privilege for Secret Service officers and government-paid lawyers who worked with him, but federal courts held that not only could a president be sued, but these other officials could not claim executive privilege.[12] One unhappy consequence of this episode is that the courts have greatly weakened the number of officials with whom the president can speak in confidence. It is not easy to run an organization when the courts can later compel your associates to testify about everything you said.

Impoundment of Funds

From time to time, presidents have refused to spend money appropriated by Congress. Truman did not spend all that Congress wanted spent on the armed forces, and Johnson did not spend all that Congress made available for highway construction. Kennedy refused to spend money appropriated for new weapons systems that he did not like. Indeed, the precedent for impounding funds goes back at least to the administration of Thomas Jefferson.

But what has precedent is not thereby constitutional. The Constitution is silent on whether the president *must* spend the money that Congress appropriates; all it says is that the president cannot spend money that Congress has *not* appropriated. The major test of presidential power in this respect occurred during the Nixon administration. Nixon wished to reduce federal spending. He proposed in 1972 that Congress give him the power to reduce federal spending so that it would not exceed $250 billion for the coming year. Congress, under Democratic control, refused. Nixon responded by pocket-vetoing 12 spending bills and then impounding funds appropriated under other laws that he had not vetoed.

Congress in turn responded by passing the Budget Reform Act of 1974, which, among other things, requires the president to spend all appropriated funds unless he first tells Congress what funds he wishes not to spend and Congress, within 45 days, agrees to delete the items. If he wishes simply to delay spending the money, he need only inform Congress, but Congress then can refuse the delay by passing a resolution requiring the immediate release of the money. Federal courts have upheld the rule that the president must spend, without delay for policy reasons, money that Congress has appropriated.

LANDMARK CASES

Powers of the President

- *United States v. Nixon* (1974): Though the president is entitled to receive confidential advice, he can be required to reveal material related to a criminal prosecution.

- *Nixon v. Fitzgerald* (1982): The president may not be sued while in office.

- *Clinton v. Jones* (1997): The president may be sued for actions taken before he became president.

Signing Statements

Since at least the presidency of James Monroe, the White House has issued statements at the time the president signs a bill that has been passed by Congress. These statements have had several purposes: to express presidential attitudes about the law, to tell the executive branch how to implement it, or to declare that the president thinks some part of the law is unconstitutional. President Andrew Jackson, for example, issued a statement in 1830 saying that a law designed to build a road from Chicago to Detroit should not cross the Michigan boundary (and so not get to Chicago). Congress complained, but Jackson's view prevailed and the road did not get to Chicago.

In the 20th century, these statements became common. President Reagan issued 71, President George H. W. Bush signed 141, and President Clinton inked 105. By the late 1980s, they were published in legal documents as part of the legislative history of a bill.[13] During his two terms, President George W. Bush signed more than 150, and in so doing, he challenged more than 1,200 sections of legislation, about double the number challenged by all of his predecessors. As of mid-2013, President Obama (who campaigned against the use of signing statements) had signed 23.[14]

> **signing statement** A presidential document that reveals what the president thinks of a new law and how it ought to be enforced.

Naturally, members of Congress are upset by this practice. To them, a **signing statement** often blocks the enforcement of a law Congress has passed, and so it is equivalent to an unconstitutional line-item veto. But presidential advisers have defended these documents, arguing (as did an assistant attorney general in the Clinton administration) that they not only clarify how the law should be implemented but also allow the president to declare what part of the law is in his view unconstitutional and thus ought not to be enforced at all.[15]

While the Supreme Court has allowed signing statements to clarify the unclear legislative intent of a law, it has never given a clear verdict about the constitutional significance of such documents.[16] By 2007, the Democratic Congress was considering a challenge to the practice, and President Barack Obama issued a memo less than three months after taking office stating that he would use signing statements only to protest unconstitutional provisions on legislation, not for policy disagreements. But even with unified government, President Obama issued a few signing statements during his first year in office, and members of Congress criticized him for doing so. The struggle over signing statements is another illustration of what one scholar has called the "invitation to struggle" that the Constitution has created between the president and Congress.[17]

The Office of the President

It was not until 1857 that the president was allowed to have a private secretary paid for with public funds, and it was not until after the assassination of President McKinley in 1901 that the president was given a Secret Service bodyguard. The president was not able to submit a single presidential budget until after 1921, when the Budget and Accounting Act was passed and the Bureau of the Budget (now called the Office of Management and Budget) was created. Grover Cleveland personally answered the White House telephone, and Abraham Lincoln often answered his own mail.

Today, of course, the president has hundreds of people assisting him, and the trappings of power—helicopters, guards, limousines—are plainly visible. The White House staff has grown enormously. (Just how big the staff is, no one knows. Presidents like to pretend that the White House is not the large bureaucracy that it in fact has become.) Add to this the opportunities for presidential appointments to the Cabinet, the courts, and various agencies, and the resources at the disposal of the president would appear to be awesome. That conclusion is partly true and partly false, or at least misleading, and for a simple reason. If the president was once helpless for lack of assistance, he now confronts an army of assistants so large that it constitutes a bureaucracy he has difficulty controlling.

The White House Office

The president's closest assistants have offices in the White House, usually in the West Wing of that building. Their titles often do not reveal the functions that they actually perform: "counsel," "counselor," "assistant to the president," "special assistant," "special consultant," and so forth. The actual titles

pyramid structure A president's subordinates report to him through a clear chain of command headed by a chief of staff.

circular structure Several of the president's assistants report directly to him.

ad hoc structure Several subordinates, Cabinet officers, and committees report directly to the president on different matters.

vary from one administration to another, but in general the men and women who hold them oversee the political and policy interests of the president. As part of the president's personal staff, these aides do not have to be confirmed by the Senate; the president can hire and fire them at will. In 2012, the Obama White House had more than 460 staff members and a budget of almost $38 million.

There are essentially three ways in which a president can organize his personal staff—through the "pyramid," "circular," and "ad hoc" methods. In a **pyramid structure**, used by Eisenhower, Nixon, Reagan, both Presidents Bush, and (after a while) Clinton, most assistants report through a hierarchy to a chief of staff, who then deals directly with the president. In a **circular structure**, used by Carter, Cabinet secretaries and assistants report directly to the president. In an **ad hoc structure**, used for a while by President Clinton, task forces, committees, and informal groups of friends and advisers deal directly with the president. For example, the Clinton administration's health care policy planning was spearheaded not by Health and Human Services Secretary Donna E. Shalala, but by First Lady Hillary Rodham Clinton and a White House adviser, Ira Magaziner. Likewise, its initiative to reform the federal bureaucracy (the National Performance Review) was led not by Office of Management and Budget director Leon E. Panetta, but by an adviser to Vice President Gore, Elaine Kamarck.[18]

It is common for presidents to mix methods. For example, Franklin Roosevelt alternated between the circular and ad hoc methods in the conduct of his domestic policy and sometimes employed a pyramid structure when dealing with foreign affairs and military policy.

Taken individually, each method of organization has advantages and disadvantages. A pyramid structure provides for an orderly flow of information and decisions, but does so at the risk of isolating or misinforming the president. The circular method has the virtue of giving the president a great deal of information, but at the price of confusion and conflict among cabinet secretaries and assistants. An ad hoc structure allows great flexibility, minimizes bureaucratic inertia, and generates ideas and information from disparate channels, but it risks cutting the president off from the government officials who are ultimately responsible for translating presidential decisions into policy proposals and administrative action.

All presidents claim they are open to many sources of advice, and some presidents try to guarantee that openness by using the circular method of staff organization. President Carter liked to describe his office as a wheel, with himself as the hub and his several assistants as spokes. But most presidents discover, as did Carter, that the difficulty of managing the large White House bureaucracy and of conserving their own limited supply of time and energy makes it necessary for them to rely heavily on one or two key subordinates. Carter, in July 1979, dramatically altered the White House staff organization by elevating Hamilton Jordan to the post of chief of staff, with the job of coordinating the work of the other staff assistants.

At first, President Reagan adopted a compromise between the circle and the pyramid, putting the White House under the direction of three key aides. At the beginning of his second term in 1985, however, the president shifted to a pyramid, placing all his assistants under a single chief of staff. Clinton began with an ad hoc system and then changed to one more like a pyramid. Each assistant has, of course, others working for him or her, sometimes a large number. There are, at a slightly lower level of status, "special assistants to the president" for various purposes. (Being "special" means, paradoxically, being less important.)

Typically, senior White House staff members are drawn from the ranks of the president's campaign staff—longtime associates in whom he has confidence. A few members, however, will be experts

HOW THINGS WORK

The Electoral College

Until November 2000, it was almost impossible to get a student interested in the Electoral College. But in the 2000 presidential election, Florida's electoral vote hung in the balance for weeks, with Bush finally winning it and (though he had fewer popular votes than Al Gore) the presidency.

Here are the essential facts: each state gets electoral votes equal to the number of its senators and representatives (the District of Columbia also gets 3, even though it has no representatives in Congress). There are 538 electoral votes. To win, a candidate must receive at least half, or 270.

In all but two states, the candidate who wins the most popular votes wins all of the state's electoral votes. Maine and Nebraska have a different system. They allow electoral votes to be split by awarding some votes on the basis of a candidate's statewide total and some on the basis of how the candidate did in each congressional district.

Electoral Votes per State

The distribution of electoral college votes per state is for the 2012 presidential election, based on the 2010 Census. The colors indicate which states voted Democratic and Republican in 2012.

The winning slates of electors assemble in their state capitals about six weeks after the election to cast their ballots. Ordinarily this is a pure formality. Occasionally, however, an elector will vote for a presidential candidate other than the one who carried the state. Such "faithless electors" have appeared in several elections since 1796. The state electoral ballots are opened and counted before a joint session of Congress during the first week of January. The candidate with a majority is declared elected.

If no candidate wins a majority, the House of Representatives chooses the president from among the three leading candidates, with each state casting one vote. By House rules, each state's vote is allotted to the candidate preferred by a majority of the state's House delegation. If there is a tie within a delegation, that state's vote is not counted.

The House has had to decide two presidential contests. In 1800, Thomas Jefferson and Aaron Burr tied in the electoral college because of a defect in the language of the Constitution—each state cast two electoral votes, without indicating which was for president and which for vice president. (Burr was supposed to be vice president, and after much maneuvering he was.) This problem was corrected by the Twelfth Amendment, ratified in 1804. The only House decision under the modern system was in 1824, when it chose John Quincy Adams over Andrew Jackson and William H. Crawford, even though Jackson had more electoral votes (and probably more popular votes) than his rivals.

Today the winner-takes-all system in effect in 48 states makes it possible for a candidate to win at least 270 electoral votes without winning a majority of the popular votes. This happened in

(continued)

HOW THINGS WORK (*Continued*)

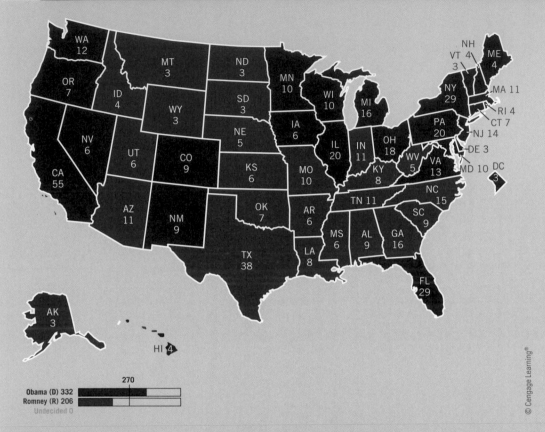

Obama (D) 332
Romney (R) 206
Undecided 0

270

2000, 1888, and 1876, and almost happened in 1960 and 1884. Today a candidate who carries the 10 largest states wins 256 electoral votes, only 14 short of a presidential victory.

This means that the candidates have a strong incentive to campaign hard in big states they have a chance of winning. In 2000, Gore worked hard in California, New York, and Pennsylvania but pretty much ignored Texas, where Bush was a shoo-in. Bush campaigned hard in Florida, Illinois, and Ohio, but not so much in New York, where Gore was an easy winner. But the Electoral College can also help small states. South Dakota, for example, has 3 electoral votes (about 0.5 percent of the total), even though it casts only about 0.3 percent of the popular vote. South Dakota and other small states are thus overrepresented in the Electoral College.

Most Americans would like to abolish the Electoral College. But doing away with it entirely would have some unforeseen effects. If we relied just on the popular vote, there might have to be a runoff election among the two leading candidates if neither got a majority because third-party candidates won a lot of votes. This would encourage the formation of third parties (we might have a Jesse Jackson party, a Pat Buchanan party, a Pat Robertson party, and a Ralph

(*continued*)

HOW THINGS WORK (*Continued*)

Nader party). Each third party would then be in a position to negotiate with one of the two major parties between the first election and the runoff about favors it wanted in return for its support. American presidential politics might come to look like the multiparty systems in France and Italy.

There are other changes that could be made. One is for each state to allocate its electoral votes proportional to the popular vote the candidates receive in that state. Voters in Colorado acted on that measure in November 2004, but that proposal failed. If every state did that, several past elections would have been decided in the House of Representatives because no candidate got a majority of the popular vote.

And the Electoral College serves a larger purpose: it makes candidates worry about carrying states as well as popular votes, and so heightens the influence of states in national politics.

brought in after the campaign: such was the case, for example, with Henry Kissinger, a former Harvard professor who became President Nixon's assistant for national security affairs. The offices these men and women occupy often are small and crowded (Kissinger's was not much bigger than the one he had while a professor at Harvard), but their occupants willingly put up with any discomfort in exchange for the privilege (and the power) of being *in* the White House. The arrangement of offices—their size, and especially their proximity to the president's Oval Office—is a good measure of the relative influence of the people in them.

The Executive Office of the President

Agencies in the Executive Office report directly to the president and perform staff services for him but are not located in the White House itself. Their members may or may not enjoy intimate contact with him; some agencies are rather large bureaucracies. The top positions in these organizations are filled by presidential appointment, but unlike the White House staff positions, these appointments must be confirmed by the Senate.

The principal agencies in the Executive Office are:

- Office of Management and Budget (OMB)

- Director of National Intelligence (DNI)

- Council of Economic Advisers (CEA)

- Office of Personnel Management (OPM)

- Office of the U.S. Trade Representative

Of all the agencies in the Executive Office of the President, perhaps the most important in terms of the president's need for assistance in administering the federal government is the Office of Management and Budget. First called the Bureau of the Budget when it was created in 1921, it became OMB in 1970 to reflect its broader responsibilities. Today it does considerably more than assemble and analyze the figures that go each year into the national budget the president submits to Congress. It also studies the

Cabinet The heads of the 15 executive branch departments of the federal government.

organization and operations of the executive branch, devises plans for reorganizing various departments and agencies, develops ways of getting better information about government programs, and reviews proposals that cabinet departments want included in the president's legislative program.

TABLE 10.4   The Cabinet Departments

Department	Created	Approximate Employment (2012)
State	1789	39,200*
Treasury	1789	104,100
Defense[a]	1947	761,533
Justice	1789	116,303
Interior	1849	69.702
Agriculture[b]	1889	91,278
Commerce	1913	44,996
Labor	1913	16,816
Health and Human Services[c]	1953	86,532
Housing and Urban Development	1965	9,114
Transportation	1966	57,042
Energy	1977	15,715
Education	1979	4,294
Veterans Affairs	1989	328,088
Homeland Security	2002	197,627

[a]Formerly the War Department, created in 1789. Figures are for civilians only.

[b]Agriculture Department created in 1862; made part of Cabinet in 1889.

[c]Originally Health, Education and Welfare; reorganized in 1979.

Subcabinet refers to undersecretary, deputy secretary, and assistant secretaries in each Cabinet department.

Note: Department of State figure taken from: US Census Bureau. "The 2012 Statistical Abstract: The National Data Book." Census.gov. Last modified September 30, 2011. This figure is used due to the fact that there are major discrepancies in how to count foreign service and foreign service national employees. The figure in the FedScope source is inordinately low, compared to most State Department estimates.

Source: US Office of Personnel Management. "Employment - December 2012: Cabinet-Level Agencies." *FedScope*.

The Cabinet

The **Cabinet** is a product of tradition and hope. At one time, the heads of the federal departments met regularly with the president to discuss matters, and some people, especially those critical of strong presidents, would like to see this kind of collegial decision making reestablished. But in fact this role of the Cabinet is largely a fiction. Indeed, the Constitution does not even mention the Cabinet (though the Twenty-fifth Amendment implicitly defines it as consisting of "the principal offices of the executive departments"). When Washington tried to get his Cabinet to work together, its two strongest members—Alexander Hamilton and Thomas Jefferson—spent most of their time feuding. The Cabinet, as a presidential committee, did not work any better for John Adams or Abraham Lincoln, for Franklin Roosevelt or John Kennedy. Dwight Eisenhower is almost the only modern president who came close to making the Cabinet a truly deliberative body: he gave it a large staff, held regular meetings, and listened to opinions expressed there. But even under Eisenhower, the Cabinet did not have much influence over presidential decisions, nor did it help him gain more power over the government.

By custom, Cabinet officers are the heads of the 15 major executive departments. These departments, together with the dates of their creation and the approximate number of their employees, are given in Table 10.4. The order of their creation is unimportant except in terms of protocol: where one sits at cabinet meetings is determined by the age of the department that one heads. Thus, the secretary of state sits next to the president on one side and the secretary of the treasury next to him on the other. Down at the foot of the table are the heads of the newer departments.

Independent Agencies, Commissions, and Judgeships

The president also appoints people to four dozen or so agencies and commissions that are not considered part of the Cabinet and that by law often have a quasi-independent status. The difference between an "executive" and an "independent" agency is not precise. In general, it means the heads of executive agencies serve at the pleasure of the president and can be removed at his discretion. On the other hand, the heads of many independent agencies serve for fixed terms of office and can be removed only "for cause."

The president can also appoint federal judges, subject to the consent of the Senate. Judges serve for life unless they are removed by impeachment and conviction. The reason for the special barriers to the removal of judges is that they represent an independent branch of government as defined by the Constitution, and limits on presidential removal powers are necessary to preserve that independence.

Who Gets Appointed

As we have seen, a president can make a lot of appointments, but he rarely knows more than a few of the people whom he does appoint.

Unlike Cabinet members in a parliamentary system, the president's Cabinet officers and their principal deputies usually have not served with the chief executive in the legislature. Instead they come from private business, universities, think tanks, foundations, law firms, labor unions, and the ranks of former and present members of Congress as well as past state and local government officials. A president is fortunate if most Cabinet members turn out to agree with him on major policy questions. President Reagan made a special effort to ensure that his Cabinet members were ideologically in tune with him, but even so Secretary of State Alexander Haig soon got into a series of quarrels with senior members of the White House staff and had to resign.

The men and women appointed to the Cabinet and to the subcabinet usually will have had some prior federal experience. One study of more than a thousand such appointments made by five presidents (Franklin Roosevelt through Lyndon Johnson) found that about 85 percent of the Cabinet, subcabinet, and independent-agency appointees had some prior federal experience. In fact, most were in government service (at the federal, state, or local levels) just before they received their cabinet or subcabinet appointment.[19] Clearly, the executive branch is not, in general, run by novices.

Many of these appointees are what Richard Neustadt has called "in-and-outers": people who alternate between jobs in the federal government and ones in the private sector, especially in law firms and in universities. Donald Rumsfeld, before becoming secretary of defense to President George W. Bush, had been secretary of defense and chief of staff under President Ford and before that a member of Congress. Between his Ford and Bush services, he was an executive in a large pharmaceutical company. This pattern is quite different from that of parliamentary systems, where all the cabinet officers come from the legislature and typically are full-time career politicians.

The President's Program

Imagine you have just spent three or four years running for president, during which time you have given essentially the same speech over and over again. You have had no time to study the issues in any depth. To reach a large television audience, you have couched your ideas largely in rather simple—if not simple-minded—slogans. Your principal advisers are political aides, not legislative specialists.

Secretary of Labor Frances Perkins (left), appointed by President Franklin Roosevelt, was the first woman cabinet member. When Condoleezza Rice was selected by President George W. Bush to be national security advisor, she became the first woman to hold that position (and later the first African American woman to be secretary of state).

You win. You are inaugurated. Now you must *be* a president instead of just talking about it. You must fill hundreds of appointive posts, but you know personally only a handful of the candidates. You must deliver a State of the Union message to Congress only two or three weeks after you are sworn in. It is quite possible you have never read, much less written, such a message before. You must submit a new budget; the old one is hundreds of pages long, much of it comprehensible only to experts. Foreign governments, as well as the stock market, hang on your every word, interpreting many of your remarks in ways that totally surprise you. What will you do?

The Constitution is not much help. It directs you to report on the state of the union and to recommend "such measures" as you shall judge "necessary and expedient." Beyond that, you are charged to "take care that the laws be faithfully executed."

At one time, of course, the demands placed on a newly elected president were not very great, because the president was not expected to do very much. The president, on assuming office, might speak of the tariff, or relations with England, or the value of veterans' pensions, or the need for civil service reform, but he was not expected to have something to say (and offer) to everybody. Today he is.

There are essentially two ways for a president to develop a program. One, exemplified by Presidents Carter and Clinton, is to have a policy on almost everything. To do this, they worked endless hours and studied countless documents, trying to learn something about and then state their positions on, a large number of issues. The other method, illustrated by President Reagan, is to concentrate on three or four major initiatives or themes and leave everything else to subordinates.

But even when a president has a governing philosophy, as did Reagan, he cannot risk plunging ahead on his own. He must judge public and congressional reaction to this program before he commits himself fully to it. Therefore, he often will allow parts of his program to be "leaked" to the press, or "floated" as a trial balloon. Reagan's commitment to a 30 percent tax cut and larger military expenditures was so well known that it required no leaking, but he did have to float his ideas on Social Security and certain budget cuts to test popular reaction. His opponents in the bureaucracy did exactly the same thing, hoping for the opposite effect. They leaked controversial parts of the program in an effort to discredit the whole policy. This process of testing the winds by a president and his critics helps explain why so many news stories coming from Washington mention no person by name but only an anonymous "highly placed source."

In addition to the risks of adverse reaction, the president faces three other constraints on his ability to plan a program. One is the sheer limit of his time and attention span. Every president works harder than he has ever worked before. A 90-hour week is typical. Even so, he has great difficulty keeping up with all the things he is supposed to know and make decisions about. For example, Congress during an average year passes between 400 and 600 bills, each of which the president must sign, veto, or allow to take effect without his signature. Scores of people wish to see him. Hundreds of phone calls must be made to members of Congress and others in order to ask for help, to smooth ruffled feathers, or to get information. He must receive all newly appointed ambassadors and visiting heads of state and in addition have his picture taken with countless people, from a Nobel Prize winner to a child whose likeness will appear on the Easter Seal.

The second constraint is the unexpected crisis. Franklin Roosevelt obviously had to respond to a depression and to the mounting risks of world war. But most presidents get their crises when they least expect them.

The third constraint is that the federal government and most federal programs, as well as the federal budget, can only be changed marginally, except in special circumstances. The vast bulk of federal expenditures are beyond control in any given year: the money must be spent whether the president likes it or not. Many federal programs have such strong congressional or public support that they must be left intact or modified only slightly. And this means that most federal employees can count on being secure in their jobs, whatever a president's views on reducing the bureaucracy.

The result of these constraints is that the president, at least in ordinary times, has to be selective about what he wants. He can be thought of as having a stock of influence and prestige the way that he might have a supply of money. If he wants to get the most "return" on his resources, he must "invest" that influence and prestige carefully in enterprises that promise substantial gains—in public benefits and political support—at reasonable costs. Each president tends to speak in terms of changing everything at once, calling his approach a "New Deal," a "New Frontier," a "Great Society," or the "New Federalism." But beneath the rhetoric, he must identify a few specific proposals on which he wishes to bet his resources while remaining mindful of the need to leave a substantial stock of resources in reserve to handle the inevitable crises and emergencies. In recent decades, events have required every president to devote much of his time and resources to two key issues: the state of the economy and foreign affairs. What he manages to do beyond this will depend on his personal views and his sense of what the nation, as well as his re-election, requires.

Presidential Transition

No president but Franklin Roosevelt has ever served more than two terms, and since the ratification of the Twenty-second Amendment in 1951, no president will ever again have the chance. But more than tradition or the Constitution escorts presidents from office. Only about one-third of the presidents since George Washington have been elected to a second term. Of the 27 not re-elected, four died in office

President Reagan, moments before he was shot on March 30, 1981, by a would-be assassin. The Twenty-fifth Amendment solves the problem of presidential disability by providing for an orderly transfer of power to the vice president.

during their first term. But the remainder either did not seek or (more usually) could not obtain re-election.

Of the eight presidents who died in office, four were assassinated: Lincoln, Garfield, McKinley, and Kennedy. At least six other presidents were the objects of unsuccessful assassination attempts: Jackson, Theodore Roosevelt, Franklin Roosevelt, Truman, Ford, and Reagan. (There may have been attempts on other presidents that never came to public notice; the attempts mentioned here involved public efforts to fire weapons at presidents.)

The presidents who served two or more terms fall into certain periods, such as the Founding (Washington, Jefferson, Madison, Monroe) or wartime (Lincoln, Wilson, Roosevelt), or they happened to be in office during especially tranquil times (Monroe, McKinley, Eisenhower, Clinton), or some combination of the above. When the country was deeply divided, as during the years just before the Civil War and during the period of Reconstruction after it, it was the rare president who was re-elected.

The Vice President

Eight times a vice president has become president because of the death of his predecessor. It first happened to John Tyler, who became president in 1841 when William Henry Harrison died peacefully after only one month in office. The question for Tyler and for the country was substantial: Was Tyler simply to be the acting president and a kind of caretaker until a new president was elected, or was he to be *president* in every sense of the word? Despite criticism and despite what might have been the contrary intention of the Framers of the Constitution, Tyler decided on the latter course and was confirmed in that opinion by a decision of Congress. Ever since, the vice president has automatically become president, in title and in powers, when the occupant of the White House has died or resigned.

But if vice presidents frequently acquire office because of death, they rarely acquire it by election. Since the earliest period of the Founding, when John Adams and Thomas Jefferson were each elected president after having first served as vice president under their predecessors, there have only been three occasions when a vice president was later able to win the presidency without his president's having died in office. One was in 1836, when Martin Van Buren was elected president after having served as Andrew Jackson's vice president; the second was in 1968, when Richard Nixon became president after having served as Dwight Eisenhower's vice president eight years earlier; the third was in 1988, when George Bush succeeded Ronald Reagan. Many vice presidents who entered the Oval Office because their predecessors died were subsequently elected to terms in their own right—Theodore Roosevelt, Calvin Coolidge, Harry Truman, and Lyndon Johnson. But no one who wishes to become president should assume that to become vice president first is the best way to get there.

The vice presidency is just what so many vice presidents have complained about its being: a rather empty job. The only official task of the vice president is to preside over the Senate and to vote in case of a tie. Even this is scarcely time-consuming, as the Senate chooses from among its members a president pro tempore, as required by the Constitution, who (along with others) presides in the absence of the vice president. The vice president's leadership powers in the Senate are weak, especially when the vice president is of a different party from the majority of the senators. But on occasion the vice president can become very important. Right after the terrorists attacked the United States in 2001, President Bush was in his airplane while his advisers worried that he might be attacked next. Vice President Cheney was quickly hidden away in a secret, secure location so he could run the government if anything happened to President Bush. And for many months thereafter, Cheney stayed in this location in case he suddenly became president. But absent a crisis, the vice president is, at best, only an adviser to the president.

Problems of Succession

If the president should die in office, the right of the vice president to assume that office has been clear since the time of John Tyler. But two questions remain: What if the president falls seriously ill, but does not die? And if the vice president steps up, who then becomes the new vice president?

The first problem has arisen on a number of occasions. After President James A. Garfield was shot in 1881, he lingered through the summer before he died. President Woodrow Wilson collapsed from a stroke in 1919, became a virtual recluse for several months, and then sharply curtailed activity for the rest of his term. Eisenhower had three serious illnesses while in office; Reagan was shot during his first term and hospitalized during his second.

The second problem has arisen on eight occasions when the vice president became president owing to the death of the incumbent. In these cases, no elected person was available to succeed the new president, should he die in office. For many decades, the problem was handled by law. The Succession Act of 1886, for example, designated the secretary of state as next in line for the presidency should the vice president die, followed by the other Cabinet officers in order of seniority. But this meant that a vice president who became president could pick his own successor by choosing his own secretary of state. In 1947, the law was changed to make the Speaker of the House and then the president pro tempore of the Senate next in line for the presidency. But that created still other problems: a Speaker or a president pro tempore is likely to be chosen because of seniority, not executive skill, and in any event might well be of the party opposite to that occupying the White House.

Both problems were addressed in 1967 by the Twenty-fifth Amendment to the Constitution. It deals with the disability problem by allowing the vice president to serve as "acting president" whenever the president declares he is unable to discharge the powers and duties of his office or whenever the vice president and a majority of the Cabinet declare that the president is incapacitated. If the president disagrees with the opinion of his vice president and a majority of the Cabinet, then Congress decides the issue. A two-thirds majority is necessary to confirm that the president is unable to serve.

The amendment deals with the succession problem by requiring a vice president who assumes the presidency (after a vacancy is created by death or resignation) to nominate a new vice president. This person takes office if the nomination is confirmed by a majority vote of both houses of Congress. When there is no vice president, then the 1947 law governs: next in line are the Speaker, the Senate president, and the 15 Cabinet officers, beginning with the secretary of state.

The disability problem has not arisen since the adoption of the amendment, but the succession problem has. In 1973, Vice President Spiro Agnew resigned, having pleaded no contest to criminal charges. President Nixon nominated Gerald Ford as vice president, and after extensive hearings he was confirmed by both houses of Congress and sworn in. Then on August 9, 1974, Nixon resigned the presidency—the first man to do so—and Ford became president. He nominated as his vice president Nelson Rockefeller, who was confirmed by both houses of Congress—again, after extensive hearings—and was sworn in on

impeachment Charges against a president approved by a majority of the House of Representatives.

December 19, 1974. For the first time in history, the nation had as its two principal executive officers men who had not been elected to either the presidency or the vice-presidency. It is a measure of the legitimacy of the Constitution that this arrangement caused no crisis in public opinion.

Impeachment

There is one other way—besides death, disability, or resignation—by which a president can leave office before his term expires, and that is by impeachment. Not only the president and vice president, but also all "civil officers of the United States" can be removed by being impeached and convicted. As a practical matter civil officers—Cabinet secretaries, bureau chiefs, and the like—are not subject to impeachment, because the president can remove them at any time and usually will if their behavior makes them a serious political liability. Federal judges, who serve during "good behavior"‡ and who are constitutionally independent of the president and Congress, have been the most frequent objects of impeachment.

An **impeachment** is like an indictment in a criminal trial: a set of charges against somebody, voted by (in this case) the House of Representatives. To be removed from office, the impeached officer must be convicted by a two-thirds vote of the Senate, which sits as a court, is presided over by the Chief Justice, hears the evidence, and makes its decision under whatever rules it wishes to adopt. Sixteen persons have been impeached by the House, and seven have been convicted by the Senate. The last conviction was in 1989, when two federal judges were removed from office.

Only two presidents have ever been impeached—Andrew Johnson in 1868 and Bill Clinton in 1998. Richard Nixon would surely have been impeached in 1974, had he not resigned after the House Judiciary Committee voted to recommend impeachment.

The Senate did not convict either Johnson or Clinton by the necessary two-thirds vote. The case against Johnson was entirely political—Radical Republicans, who wished to punish the South after the Civil War, were angry at Johnson, a Southerner, who had a soft policy toward the South. The argument against him was flimsy.

The case against Clinton was more serious. The House Judiciary Committee, relying on the report of independent counsel Kenneth Starr, charged Clinton with perjury (lying under oath about his sexual affair with Monica Lewinsky), obstruction of justice (trying to block the Starr investigation), and abuse of power (making false written statements to the Judiciary Committee). The vote to impeach was passed by the House along party lines. The Senate vote fell far short of the two-thirds required for conviction.

Why did Clinton survive? There were many factors. The public disliked his private behavior, but did not think it amounted to an impeachable offense. (In fact, right after Lewinsky revealed her sexual affair with him, his standing in opinion polls went up.) The economy was strong, and the nation was at peace. Clinton was a centrist Democrat who did not offend most voters.

The one casualty of the entire episode was the death of the law creating the office of the Independent Counsel. Passed in 1978 by a Congress that was upset by the Watergate crisis, the law directed the attorney general to ask a three-judge panel to appoint an independent counsel whenever a high official is charged with serious misconduct. (In 1993, when the 1978 law expired, President Clinton asked that it be passed again. It was.) Eighteen people were investigated by various independent counsels from 1978 to 1999. In about half the cases, no charges were brought to court.

For a long time, Republicans disliked the law because the counsels were investigating them. After Clinton came to office, the counsels started investigating him and his associates, and so the Democrats began to oppose it. In 1999, when the law expired, it was not renewed.

---

‡"Good behavior" means a judge can stay in office until he retires or dies, unless he or she is impeached and convicted.

A problem remains, however. How will any high official, including the president, be investigated when the attorney general, who does most investigations, is part of the president's team? One answer is to let Congress do it, but Congress may be controlled by the president's party. No one has yet solved this puzzle.

Some Founders may have thought that impeachment would be used frequently against presidents, but as a practical matter it is so complex and serious an undertaking that we can probably expect it to be reserved in the future only for the gravest forms of presidential misconduct. No one quite knows what a high crime or misdemeanor is, but most scholars agree that the charge must involve something illegal or unconstitutional, not just unpopular. Unless a president or vice president is first impeached and convicted, many experts believe he is not liable to prosecution as would be an ordinary citizen. (No one is certain, because the question has never arisen.) President Ford's pardon of Richard Nixon meant that he could not be prosecuted under federal law for things he may have done while in office.

How Powerful Is the President?

In the face of modern problems, all branches of government, including the presidency, seem both big and ineffectual. Add to this the much closer and more critical scrutiny of the media and the proliferation of interest groups, and it is small wonder that both presidents and members of Congress feel that they have lost power.

Presidents have come to acquire certain rules of thumb for dealing with their political problems. Among them are these:

- *Move it or lose it.* A president who wants to get something done should do it early in his term, before his political influence erodes.

- *Avoid details.* President Carter's lieutenants regret having tried to do too much. Better to have three or four top priorities and forget the rest.

- *Cabinets don't get much accomplished; people do.* Find capable White House subordinates and give them well-defined responsibility; then watch them closely.[20]

LEARNING OBJECTIVES

LO 10.1 How do presidents differ from prime ministers?

Unlike prime ministers, American presidents are elected independently of Congress, which gives them both more independence in governing and more challenges in building political coalitions.

LO 10.2 Did the Founders expect the presidency to be the most important political institution?

Most did not. They worried about whether the presidency would be too strong or too weak, but designed a Constitution hoping that Congress would be the most important institution. And it was, with a few exceptions, until the 20th century. Today, the strength of the presidency depends chiefly on two things: the importance of military and foreign affairs and the president's personal popularity.

LO 10.3 How have the constitutional and political powers of the presidency evolved from the founding of the United States to the present?

Presidential power has grown significantly from its constitutional origins. Since the 1930s, the president has become the central figure in American politics, even though the president's ability to achieve political success remains highly dependent on other individuals and institutions.

LO 10.4 How do presidents make policy?

To make policy, a president must work closely with Congress and the federal bureaucracy, while being attentive to public and political party expectations, as well as media scrutiny.

LO 10.5 Is it harder to govern when the presidency and Congress are controlled by different political parties?

Not really. Both the Democratic and Republican parties have legislators who often vote with their party rivals. Unless the president has a big ideological majority in Congress, something that does not happen too often, he can easily lose legislative struggles. Gridlock does not in fact prevent major new pieces of legislation from being passed.

TO LEARN MORE

- Official White House blog: **www.whitehouse.gov**
- Studies of presidents:
Miller Center of Public Affairs, University of Virginia:
www.millercenter.virginia.edu/academic/americanpresident
- The American Presidency Project, University of California at Santa Barbara:
www.presidency.ucsb.edu
- Cohen, Jeffrey E. *Going Local: Presidential Leadership in the Post-Broadcast Age*. New York: Cambridge University Press, 2010. Examines how party polarization and an increasingly decentralized media have led presidents to target their public communications to local audiences over the national arena.
- Corwin, Edward S. *The President: Office and Powers*, 5th ed. New York: New York University Press, 1985. Historical, constitutional, and legal development of the office.
- Greenstein, Fred I. *The Presidential Difference: Leadership Style from FDR to Barack Obama*, 3rd ed. Princeton, NJ: Princeton University Press, 2009. Explores how, independent of other influences, modern presidents' respective leadership styles account for consequential changes in domestic and foreign policy decisions.
- Kernell, Samuel. *Going Public: New Strategies of Presidential Leadership*, 4th ed. New Haven, CT: Yale University Press, 2007. Examines how modern presidents develop policies with an eye fixed on how best to communicate with multiple public audiences.

- Neustadt, Richard E. *Presidential Power and the Modern Presidents: The Politics of Leadership from Roosevelt to Reagan.* New York: The Free Press, 1990 (original edition published in 1960). How presidents try to acquire and hold political power in the competitive world of official Washington, by a man who was both a scholar and an insider.

- Peterson, Mark A. *Legislating Together: The White House and Congress from Eisenhower to Reagan.* Cambridge: Harvard University Press, 1990. Challenges the conventional view that "the president proposes, Congress disposes." Contains many excellent examples of bargaining and cooperation between Congress and the executive branch.

- Polsby, Nelson W., and Aaron Wildavsky. *Presidential Elections*, 10th ed. New York: Chatham House, 2000. Excellent analysis of how campaigns and the electoral college shape the presidency.

- Tulis, Jeffrey K. *The Rhetorical Presidency.* Princeton, NJ: Princeton University Press, 1987. Fascinating study of how once-powerful constitutional customs that proscribed presidents rallying the public for political support on a routine basis changed in the early 20th century.

On Franklin D. Roosevelt

- Leuchtenburg, William E. *Franklin D. Roosevelt and the New Deal, 1932–1940.* New York: Harper & Row, 1963.

- Maney, Richard J. *The Roosevelt Presence.* New York: Twayne, 1992.

On Harry S. Truman

- Hamby, A. L. *Beyond the New Deal: Harry S. Truman and American Liberalism.* New York: Columbia University Press, 1973.

- McCullough, David. *Truman.* New York: Simon and Schuster, 1984.

On Dwight D. Eisenhower

- Ambrose, Stephen E. *Eisenhower.* New York: Simon and Schuster, 1984.

- Greenstein, Fred I. *The Hidden-Hand Presidency: Eisenhower as Leader.* New York: Basic Books, 1982.

On John F. Kennedy

- Paper, Lewis J. *The Promise and the Performance: The Leadership of John F. Kennedy.* New York: Crown, 1975.

- Parmet, Herbert C. *Jack.* New York: Dial Press, 1980.

On Lyndon B. Johnson

- Caro, Robert A. *The Years of Lyndon Johnson.* 3 vols. New York: Alfred Knopf, 1982–2002.

- Dallek, Robert. *Lone Star Rising and Flawed Giant.* New York: Oxford University Press, 1991 and 1996.

- Kearns, Doris. *Lyndon Johnson and the American Dream.* New York: Harper and Row, 1976.

On Richard M. Nixon

- Ambrose, Stephen E. *Nixon.* 3 vols. New York: Simon and Schuster, 1987, 1989, 1991.

On Jimmy Carter

- Bourne, Peter G. *Jimmy Carter.* New York: Scribner, 1997.

On Ronald Reagan

- Cannon, Lou. *President Reagan*. New York: Simon and Schuster, 1991.

On George H. W. Bush

- Han, Lori Cox. *A Presidency Upstaged: The Public Leadership of George H.W. Bush*. College Station, TX: Texas A&M University Press, 2011.

- Parmet, Herbert C. *George Bush*. New York: Scribner, 1997.

On Bill Clinton

- Klein, Joe. *The Natural: The Misunderstood Presidency of Bill Clinton*. New York: Doubleday, 2002.

On George W. Bush

- Draper, Robert. *Dead Certain: The Presidency of George W. Bush*. New York; Free Press, 2007.

- Jacobson, Gary C. *A Divider, Not a Uniter: George W. Bush and the American People*. 2d ed. (New York: Longman, 2010).

- Pfiffner, James P. *Power Play: The Bush Presidency and the Constitution*. Washington, D.C.: Brookings Institution Press, 2008.

On Barack Obama

- Remnick, David. *The Bridge: The Life and Rise of Barack Obama*. New York: Knopf, 2010.

- Renshon, Stanley A. *Barack Obama and the Politics of Redemption*. New York: Routledge, 2011.

SAUL LOEB/Stringer/Getty Images

The Bureaucracy

LEARNING OBJECTIVES

LO 11.1 What is "bureaucracy," and in what ways is the American bureaucracy distinctive?

LO 11.2 What is "discretionary authority" and why do some bureaucrats have lots of it?

LO 11.3 How does Congress exert control over the bureaucracy?

LO 11.4 What happened to make the bureaucracy a "fourth branch" of American national government?

LO 11.5 What are the actual size and scope of the federal bureaucracy?

bureaucracy A large, complex organization composed of appointed officials.

For most people and politicians, *bureaucracy* is a pejorative word implying waste, confusion, red tape, and rigidity. But for scholars—and for bureaucrats themselves—*bureaucracy* is a word with a neutral, technical meaning. A **bureaucracy** is a large, complex organization composed of appointed officials. By *complex*, we mean that authority is divided among several managers; no one person is able to make all the decisions. A large corporation is a bureaucracy; so also are a big university and a government agency. With its sizable staff, even Congress has become, to some degree, a bureaucracy.

What is it about complex organizations in general, and government agencies in particular, that leads so many people to complain about them? In part, the answer is to be found in their very size and complexity. But in large measure the answer is to be found in the political context within which such agencies must operate. If we examine that context carefully, we will discover that many of the problems that we blame on "the bureaucracy" are in fact the result of what Congress, the courts, and the president do. And, if we dig just a bit deeper, we will also discover that behind just about every government bureaucracy is some set of new or old public demands. Consider, for example, Washington bureaucracies' roles with respect to keeping us safe from street criminals, cleaning up toxic waste sites, and making sure that poor children have nutritious school lunches.

THEN

The U.S. Department of Justice (USDOJ—this is bureaucracy, so enjoy all the alphabet soup) was established in 1789, but until a series of federal "crime bills" was enacted beginning in the 1960s, it had only an incidental role in crime control. For the most part, it neither funded nor worked at all closely with state and local criminal justice agencies. A USDOJ subunit, the Federal Bureau of Prisons (FBOP), was a tiny agency that held fewer inmates than many small state prison systems did.

NOW

With public support for successive federal "wars on crime" and "wars on drugs," the USDOJ and other federal agencies now spend billions of dollars each year to fund federal, state, and local agencies engaged in combating street crime, and the FBOP now runs one of the largest prison systems in the world.

THEN

Before the Environmental Protection Agency (EPA) was launched in 1970, the federal government's environmental protection activities were virtually nonexistent.

NOW

The media stories and public outcries that accompanied the discovery of lethal toxic waste sites in and around New York's Love Canal area led in 1978 to the creation of the so-called Superfund program. To administer Superfund, in 1980, the EPA expanded, and there has been an expansion in federal environmental protection efforts, and in federally directed state and local efforts as well, in most years ever since.

The first federal law providing for subsidized school lunches was passed in 1946, but it was not until the 1960s that Washington began expanding its programs in this area to include ever greater numbers of children eligible for both free (or reduced price) breakfasts and lunches.

It was only in 2010 that the U.S. Department of Agriculture (USDA)—created in 1862, made into a Cabinet department in 1889, and long concerned mainly with the nation's farms and agri-businesses— was mandated by law to work with local school districts and other organizations so as to make nutritious meals (breakfasts, lunches, and snacks) available to low-income children year-round, including in the summer months when school is out.

Whatever else it may be, bureaucracy is an outgrowth of representative democracy. If people demanded that government do less or do nothing, in due course public laws would change and the agencies that exist to translate those laws into administrative action would dissolve. But that has rarely happened. Instead, six of the federal government's 15 Cabinet agencies, including (next to the U.S. Department of Defense) its two largest and newest (the U.S. Department of Veterans Affairs, created in 1989, and the U.S. Department of Homeland Security, created in 2002), were created after 1964.

Distinctiveness of the American Bureaucracy

As you might expect, much the same can be said for the growth of bureaucracy in other democratic nations. Indeed, bureaucratic government has become an obvious feature of all modern societies, democratic and nondemocratic alike.

In the United States, however, three aspects of our constitutional system and political traditions give to the bureaucracy a distinctive character. First, political authority over the bureaucracy is not in one set of hands but is shared among several institutions. In a parliamentary regime, such as in the United Kingdom, the appointed officials of the national government work for the Cabinet ministers, who are in turn dominated by the prime minister. In theory, and to a considerable extent in practice, British bureaucrats report to and take orders from the ministers in charge of their departments, do not deal directly with Parliament, and rarely give interviews to the press. In the United States, the Constitution permits both the president and Congress to exercise authority over the bureaucracy. Every senior appointed official has at least two masters: one in the executive branch and the other in the legislative. Often there are many more than two: Congress, after all, is not a single organization but a collection of committees, subcommittees, and individuals. This divided authority encourages bureaucrats to play one branch of government against the other and to make heavy use of the media.

Second, most of the agencies of the federal government share their functions with related agencies in state and local government. Though some federal agencies deal directly with American citizens—the Internal Revenue Service collects taxes from them, the Federal Bureau of Investigation looks into crimes for them, the Postal Service delivers mail to them—many agencies work with other organizations at other levels of government. For example, the Department of Education gives money to local school systems; the Centers for Medicare and Medicaid Services in the Department of Health and Human Services reimburses states for money spent on health care for the poor; the Department of Housing and Urban Development gives grants to cities for community development; and the Employment and Training Administration in the Department of Labor supplies funds to local governments so that they can run job-training programs. In France, by

government by proxy
Washington pays state and local governments and private groups to staff and administer federal programs.

contrast, government programs dealing with education, health, housing, and employment are centrally run, with little or no control exercised by local governments.

Third, the institutions and traditions of American life have contributed to the growth of what some writers have described as an "adversary culture," in which the definition and expansion of personal rights, and the defense of rights and claims through lawsuits as well as political action, are given central importance. A government agency in this country operates under closer public scrutiny and with a greater prospect of court challenges to its authority than in almost any other nation. Virtually every important decision of the Occupational Safety and Health Administration or of the Environmental Protection Agency is likely to be challenged in the courts or attacked by an affected party; in Sweden the decisions of similar agencies go largely uncontested.

The scope as well as the style of bureaucratic government differs. In most Western European nations, the government owns and operates large parts of the economy: the French government operates the railroads and owns companies that make automobiles and cigarettes, and the Italian government owns many similar enterprises and also the nation's oil refineries. In just about every large nation except the United States, the telephone system is owned by the government. Publicly operated enterprises account for about 12 percent of all employment in France but less than 3 percent in the United States.[1] The U.S. government regulates privately owned enterprises to a degree not found in many other countries, however. Why we should have preferred regulation to ownership as the proper government role is an interesting question to which we shall return.

Proxy Government

Much of our federal bureaucracy operates on the principle of **government by proxy**.[2] In every representative government, the voters elect legislators who make the laws, but in this country the bureaucrats often pay other people to do the work. These "other people" include state and local governments, business firms, and nonprofit organizations.

Among the programs run this way are Social Security, Medicare, much environmental protection, and the collection of income taxes by withholding money from your paycheck. Even many military duties are contracted out.[3] In the first Gulf War in 1991, American soldiers outnumbered private contractors in the region by 60 to 1. But by 2006, there were nearly as many private workers as soldiers in Iraq. One company was paid $7.2 billion to get food and supplies to our troops there.[4]

When Hurricanes Katrina and Rita hit our Gulf Coast, the nation's response was managed by a small and weak group, the Federal Emergency Management Agency (FEMA). When the levees broke, it had only 2,600 employees; most of the help it was to provide came through "partners," such as state and local agencies, and some of these were not very competent.

Critics of our government-by-proxy system argue that it does not keep track of

After Hurricane Katrina in 2005, many people in New Orleans were rescued from their damaged homes by boat.

Mario Tama/Getty Images

how the money we send to public and private agencies is used. Congress, of course, could change matters around, but it has an interest in setting policies and defining goals, not in managing the bureaucracy or levying taxes. Moreover, the president and Congress like to keep the size of the federal bureaucracy small by giving jobs to people not on the federal payroll.[5]

Defenders of government by proxy claim that the system produces more flexibility, takes advantage of private and nonprofit skills, and defends the principle of federalism embodied in our Constitution. The defenders make fair points, but the system does produce certain everyday oddities, such as the fact that many average citizens receive costly federal government services over long periods of time without ever directly interacting with civil servants. Donald F. Kettl, a University of Maryland political scientist, dubbed this the "Mildred Paradox": in her last several years of life, his aged and ill mother-in-law, Mildred, applied successfully for multiple federal health insurance programs and received several years' worth of different types of expensive institutional care and top-quality medical treatment—all at government expense—but without ever actually encountering a single government worker.[6]

Or look a bit closer at what we noted above regarding the U.S. Department of Agriculture (USDA). As a result of a new federal law (the Healthy, Hunger-Free Kids Act of 2010), the USDA is now required to expand and improve its "food security" programs by, among other measures, seeing to it that all eligible low-income children have daily access to free meals (breakfast or lunch plus a snack) during the summer months when school is out. The new law, however, does not even begin to specify just how the USDA and its scores and scores of state and local government proxy agencies (not to mention their tens of thousands of administrative partners) are to accomplish that objective. Among big cities, Philadelphia has had the largest USDA-funded summer food program in the country (almost 4 million meals served each summer through more than 1,000 local "sites" including churches, recreation centers, and private homes on streets closed off for the purpose by local police). But the city's summer participation rate among eligible children has still been only about 50 percent.

The Growth of the Bureaucracy

The Constitution made scarcely any provision for an administrative system other than to allow the president to appoint, with the advice and consent of the Senate, "ambassadors, other public ministers and consuls, judges of the Supreme Court, and all other officers of the United States whose appointments are not herein otherwise provided for, and which shall be established by law."[7] Departments and bureaus were not mentioned.

In the first Congress, in 1789, James Madison introduced a bill to create a Department of State to assist the new secretary of state, Thomas Jefferson, in carrying out his duties. People appointed to this department were to be nominated by the president and approved by the Senate, but they were "to be removable by the president" alone. These six words, which would confer the right to fire government officials, occasioned six days of debate in the House. At stake was the locus of power over what was to become the bureaucracy. Madison's opponents argued that the Senate should consent to the removal of officials as well as their appointment. Madison responded that, without the unfettered right of removal, the president would not be able to control his subordinates, and without this control he would not be able to discharge his constitutional obligation to "take care that the laws be faithfully executed."[8] Madison won, 29 votes to 22. When the issue went to the Senate, another debate resulted in a tie vote, broken in favor of the president by Vice President John Adams. The Department of State, and all cabinet departments subsequently created, would be run by people removable only by the president.

That decision did not resolve the question of who would really control the bureaucracy, however. Congress retained the right to appropriate money, to investigate the administration, and to shape the laws that would be executed by that administration—more than ample power to challenge any president who claimed to have sole authority over his subordinates. And many members of Congress expected the Cabinet departments, even though headed by people removable by the president, to report to Congress.

The government in Washington was at first minuscule. The State Department started with only nine employees; the War Department did not have 80 civilian employees until 1801. Only the Treasury Department, concerned with collecting taxes and finding ways to pay the public debt, had much power, and only the Post Office Department provided any significant service.

The Appointment of Officials

Small as the bureaucracy was, people struggled, often bitterly, over who would be appointed to it. From George Washington's day to modern times, presidents have found appointment to be one of their most important and difficult tasks. The officials they select affect how the laws are interpreted (thus the political ideology of the job holders is important), what tone the administration will display (thus personal character is important), how effectively the public business is discharged (thus competence is important), and how strong the political party or faction in power will be (thus party affiliation is important). Presidents trying to balance the competing needs of ideology, character, fitness, and partisanship have rarely pleased most people. As John Adams remarked, every appointment creates one ingrate and 10 enemies.

Because Congress, during most of the 19th and 20th centuries, was the dominant branch of government, congressional preferences often controlled the appointment of officials. And since Congress was, in turn, a collection of people who represented local interests, appointments were made with an eye to rewarding the local supporters of members of Congress or building up local party organizations. These appointments made on the basis of political considerations—patronage—were later to become a major issue. They galvanized various reform efforts that sought to purify politics and to raise the level of competence of the public service. Many of the abuses the reformers complained about were real enough, but patronage served some useful purposes as well. It gave the president a way to ensure that his subordinates were reasonably supportive of his policies; it provided a reward the president could use to induce recalcitrant members of Congress to vote for his programs; and it enabled party organizations to be built up to perform the necessary functions of nominating candidates and getting out the vote.

Though at first there were not many jobs to fight over, by the middle of the 19th century, there were a lot. From 1816 to 1861, the number of federal employees increased eightfold. This expansion was not, however, the result of the government's taking on new functions, but simply a result of the increased demands on its traditional functions. The Post Office alone accounted for 86 percent of this growth.[9]

The Civil War was a great watershed in bureaucratic development. Fighting the war led, naturally, to hiring many new officials and creating many new offices. Just as important, the Civil War revealed the administrative weakness of the federal government and led to demands by the civil service reform movement for an improvement in the quality and organization of federal employees. And finally, the war was followed by a period of rapid industrialization and the emergence of a national economy. The effects of these developments could no longer be managed by state governments acting alone. With the creation of a nationwide network of railroads, commerce among the states became increasingly important. The constitutional powers of the federal government to regulate interstate commerce, long dormant for want of much commerce to regulate, now became an important source of controversy.

A Service Role

From 1861 to 1901, new agencies were created, many to deal with particular sectors of society and the economy. More than 200,000 new federal employees were added, with only about half of this increase in the Post Office. The rapidly growing Pension Office began paying benefits to Civil War veterans; the

Department of Agriculture was created in 1862 to help farmers; the Department of Labor was founded in 1882 to serve workers; and the Department of Commerce was organized in 1903 to assist businesspeople. Many more specialized agencies, such as the National Bureau of Standards, also came into being.

> ***laissez-faire*** An economic theory that government should not regulate or interfere with commerce.

These agencies had one thing in common: their role was primarily to serve, not to regulate. Most did research, gathered statistics, dispensed federal lands, or passed out benefits. Not until the Interstate Commerce Commission (ICC) was created in 1887 did the federal government begin to regulate the economy (other than by managing the currency) in any large way. Even the ICC had, at first, relatively few powers.

There were several reasons why federal officials primarily performed a service role. The values that had shaped the Constitution were still strong: these included a belief in limited government, the importance of states' rights, and the fear of concentrated discretionary power. The proper role of government in the economy was to promote, not to regulate, and a commitment to **laissez-faire**—a freely competitive economy—was strongly held. But just as important, the Constitution said nothing about giving any regulatory powers to bureaucrats. It gave to *Congress* the power to regulate commerce among the states. Now, obviously, Congress could not make the necessary day-to-day decisions to regulate, for example, the rates that interstate railroads charged to farmers and other shippers. Some agency or commission composed of appointed officials and experts would have to be created to do that. For a long time, however, the prevailing interpretation of the Constitution was that no such agency could exercise such regulatory powers unless Congress first set down clear standards that would govern the agency's decisions. As late as 1935, the Supreme Court held that a regulatory agency could not make rules on its own; it could only apply the standards enacted by Congress.[10] The Court's view was that the legislature may not delegate its powers to the president or to an administrative agency.[11]

These restrictions on what administrators could do were set aside in wartime. During World War I, for example, President Woodrow Wilson was authorized by Congress to fix prices, operate the railroads, manage the communications system, and even control the distribution of food.[12] This kind of extraordinary grant of power usually ended with the war.

Some changes in the bureaucracy did not end with the war. During the Civil War, World War I, World War II, the Korean War, and the war in Vietnam, the number of civilian (as well as military) employees of the government rose sharply. These increases were not simply in the number of civilians needed to help serve the war effort; many of the additional people were hired by agencies, such as the Treasury Department, not obviously connected with the war. Furthermore, the number of federal officials did not return to prewar levels after each war. Though there was some reduction, each war left the number of federal employees larger than before.[13]

It is not hard to understand how this happens. During wartime, almost every government agency argues that its activities have *some* relation to the war effort, and few legislators want to be caught voting against something that may help that effort. Hence in 1944, the Reindeer Service in Alaska, an agency of the Interior Department, asked for more employees because reindeer are "a valued asset in military planning."

A Change in Role

Today's bureaucracy is largely a product of two events: the depression of the 1930s (and the concomitant New Deal program of President Roosevelt) and World War II. Though many agencies have been added since then, the basic features of the bureaucracy were set mainly as a result of changes in public attitudes and in constitutional interpretation that occurred during these periods. The government was now expected to play an active role in dealing with economic and social problems. In the late 1930s, the Supreme Court reversed its earlier decisions (see Chapter 12) on the question of delegating legislative powers to administrative agencies and upheld laws by which Congress merely instructs agencies to make decisions that serve "the public interest" in some area.[14] As a result, it was possible for President Nixon to set up in 1971 a system of price and wage controls based on a statute that simply authorized the president "to issue such orders and regulations as he may deem appropriate to stabilize prices, rents, wages, and salaries."[15] The Cost of Living Council and other agencies that Nixon established to carry out this order were run by appointed officials who had the legal authority to make sweeping decisions based on general statutory language.

World War II was the first occasion during which the government made heavy use of federal income taxes—on individuals and corporations—to finance its activities. Between 1940 and 1945, total federal tax collections increased from about $5 billion to nearly $44 billion. The end of the war brought no substantial tax reduction: the country believed that a high level of military preparedness continued to be necessary and that various social programs begun before the war should enjoy the heavy funding made possible by wartime taxes. Tax receipts continued, by and large, to grow. Before 1913, when the Sixteenth Amendment to the Constitution was passed, the federal government could not collect income taxes at all (it financed itself largely from customs duties and excise taxes). From 1913 to 1940, income taxes were small (in 1940, the average American paid only $7 in federal income taxes). World War II created the first great financial boom for the government, permitting the sustained expansion of a wide variety of programs and thus entrenching a large number of administrators in Washington.[16]

Although it is still too soon to tell, a third event—the September 11, 2001, terrorist attacks on the United States—could affect bureaucracy as profoundly as the depression of the 1930s and World War II. A law creating a massive new Cabinet agency, the Department of Homeland Security (DHS), was passed in late 2002. Within two years of its creation, the DHS had consolidated under its authority 22 smaller federal agencies with nearly 180,000 federal employees (third behind Defense and Veterans Affairs) and over $40 billion in budgets (fourth behind Defense, Health and Human Services, and Education). In addition, dozens of intergovernmental grant-making programs came under the authority of the DHS. In late 2004, Congress passed another law that promised, over time, to centralize under a single director of national intelligence the work of the more than 70 federal agencies authorized to spend money on counterterrorist activities. But even after related reforms in 2006, dozens of different agencies were still authorized to spend money on counterterrorism activities; and in 2013, the DHS faced sharp questioning from the House Subcommittee on Oversight

CONSTITUTIONAL CONNECTIONS

Beyond Checks and Balances?

The Framers of the Constitution did not envision anything akin to today's federal bureaucracy with its several million full-time employees and its millions more part-time employees. But far more surprising to the Framers than the sheer size of today's federal bureaucracy (after all, the country and its population have grown, too) would be its scope: Cabinet departments, bureaus, independent agencies, government corporations,

(continued)

CONSTITUTIONAL CONNECTIONS (*Continued*)

and regulatory commissions touching virtually every facet of the nation's economic, social, and civic life—trade, banking, labor, environmental protection, broadcasting, transportation, human services, health, housing, education, energy, environmental protection, space exploration, national parks, homeland security, and more. Beyond the contemporary federal bureaucracy's size and scope, the Framers might be mystified by the "proxy government" system described on pages 338–339, and by how so many "federal" programs are actually jointly funded and administered by federal, state, and local governments in conjunction with for-profit firms and nonprofit organizations.

But would the Framers, in turn, view today's federal bureaucracy not only as a "fourth branch" of American national government but one that operates outside their system of separated powers and checks and balances, and that has transformed federalism (see Chapter 3) into Washington-controlled "intergovernmental administration"?

Some think so. They argue that federal agencies, including the Internal Revenue Service, the Environmental Protection Agency, and many others, routinely exercise not only executive powers but also lawmaking and judicial powers as well, and that state governments are required to fund or co-fund and administer many federal programs including large ones like Medicaid. Moreover, they claim, Congress now commonly passes long and complicated laws and leaves it almost entirely to the discretion of federal bureaucrats to decide what the laws mean, how to apply them, and even in some cases how much to spend on them.

Others, however, think not. They argue that through federal laws that set boundaries on administrators' authority (like the Administrative Procedures Act of 1946), routine oversight of federal agencies by congressional committees and subcommittees, and federal court decisions limiting how far Washington can go in requiring state governments to fund or administer its programs, the federal bureaucracy's powers and the discretion exercised by Washington's appointed officials normally remain duly limited. We share this view: the "fourth branch" is far bigger and broader than the Framers could ever have envisioned, but most federal government agencies most of the time are checked and balanced by Congress and by other means.

and Management Efficiency, and the Government Accountability Office (GAO) once again ranked the DHS, which by then employed more than 220,000 employees, among those agencies with serious management problems.[17]

The Federal Bureaucracy Today

No president wants to admit that he has increased the size of the bureaucracy. He can avoid saying this by pointing out that the number of civilians working for the federal government, excluding postal workers, has not increased significantly in recent years and is about the same today (2 million persons) as it was in 1960, and less than it was during World War II. This explanation is true but misleading, for it neglects the roughly 13 million people who work *indirectly* for Washington as employees of private firms and state or local agencies that are largely, if not entirely, supported by federal funds. There are nearly three persons earning their living indirectly from the federal government for every one earning it directly. While federal employment has remained quite stable, employment among federal contractors and consultants and in state and local governments has mushroomed. Indeed, most federal bureaucrats, like most other people who work for the federal government, live outside Washington, D.C.

As Table 11.1 shows, from 1990 to 2012, 11 of the 15 federal executive departments reduced their workforce. The U.S. Department of State grew by more than half, but that represented fewer than 15,000 new staff. The Department of Veterans Affairs expanded after 2007 as veterans from the wars in Iraq and Afghanistan began to return home. Since its creation in 2003, the Department of Homeland Security grew by about a quarter. The largest growth was in the U.S. Department of Justice (DOJ). This growth is explained mainly by the growth in just one DOJ unit—and one of the few federal agencies anywhere in the bureaucracy that was slow to join the trend toward what we described earlier in this chapter as government

TABLE 11.1   Federal Civilian Employment, 1990–2012

	1990	2012	Percent Change
All executive departments (in millions) (In thousands)	2.065	1.937	−6.2
State	25.2	39.2	+55.5
Treasury	158.6	110.1	−30.6
Defense	1,034	772.6	−25.3
Justice	83.9	117.9	+40.5
Interior	77.6	70.2	−9.5
Agriculture	122.5	106.9	−12.7
Commerce	69.9	56.9	−18.6
Labor	17.7	17.6	−0.6
Health and Human Services	123.9	69.8	−43.7
Housing and Urban Development	13.5	9.6	−28.9
Transportation	67.3	58.0	−1.3
Energy	17.7	16.1	−9.0
Education	4.70	4.5	−4.3
Veterans Affairs	248.1	304.7	+22.8
Homeland Security	N/A	183.5	+22.0*

*Since its creation in 2003

Source: *Statistical Abstract of the United States*, 2009 and 2012

Federal Bureau of Prisons	1990	2013	Percent Change
Staff	19.0	38.6	+103
Inmates	58.0	218.1	+276

Source: Federal Bureau of Prisons Weekly Population Report and Quick Facts, available at http://www.bop.gov/locations/weekly_report.jsp; and http://www.bop.gov/news/quick.jsp#5.

by proxy—the Federal Bureau of Prisons (BOP). The BOP administers nearly 200 facilities, from maximum-security prisons to community corrections centers, all across the country. Between 1990 and 2013, its staff doubled to nearly 39,000, while the prisoner populations these federal workers supervised more than doubled to about 276,000.

> ***discretionary authority***
> The extent to which appointed bureaucrats can choose courses of action and make policies not spelled out in advance by laws.

The power of the federal bureaucracy cannot be measured by the number of employees, however. A bureaucracy of 5 million persons would have little power if each employee did nothing but type letters or file documents, whereas a bureaucracy of only 100 persons would have awesome power if each member were able to make arbitrary life-and-death decisions affecting the rest of us. The power of the bureaucracy depends on the extent to which appointed officials have **discretionary**

> ***competitive service*** The government offices to which people are appointed on the basis of merit, as ascertained by a written exam or by applying certain selection criteria.

authority—that is, the ability to choose courses of action and to make policies not spelled out in advance by laws. As Figure 11.1 on the next page shows, the volume of regulations issued has risen much faster than the rate of government spending (relative to gross domestic product) and the number of federal employees who write the regulations and spend the money (federal employees who, as we have explained, often work mainly through state and local government employees and other administrative proxies).

By this test, the power of the federal bureaucracy has grown enormously. Congress has delegated substantial authority to administrative agencies in three areas: (1) paying subsidies to particular groups and organizations in society (farmers, veterans, scientists, schools, universities, hospitals); (2) transferring money from the federal government to state and local governments (the grant-in-aid programs described in Chapter 3); and (3) devising and enforcing regulations for various sectors of society and the economy. Some of these administrative functions, such as grants-in-aid to states, are closely monitored by Congress; others, such as the regulatory programs, usually operate with a greater degree of independence. These delegations of power, especially in the areas of paying subsidies and regulating the economy, did not become commonplace until the 1930s, and then only after the Supreme Court decided that such delegations were constitutional. Today, by contrast, appointed officials can decide, within rather broad limits, who shall own a television station, what safety features automobiles shall have, what kinds of scientific research shall be specially encouraged, what drugs shall appear on the market, which dissident groups shall be investigated, what fumes an industrial smokestack may emit, which corporate mergers shall be allowed, what use shall be made of national forests, and what prices crop and dairy farmers shall receive for their products.

If appointed officials have this kind of power, then how they use it is of paramount importance in understanding modern government. There are, broadly, four factors that may explain the behavior of these officials:

1. The manner in which they are recruited and rewarded

2. Their personal attributes, such as their socioeconomic backgrounds and their political attitudes

3. The nature of their jobs

4. The constraints that outside forces—political superiors, legislators, interest groups, journalists—impose on their agencies

Recruitment and Retention

The federal civil service system was designed to recruit qualified people on the basis of merit, not political patronage, and to retain and promote employees on the basis of performance, not political favoritism. Many appointed federal officials belong to the **competitive service**. This means they are appointed

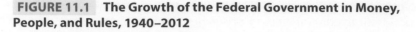

FIGURE 11.1 **The Growth of the Federal Government in Money, People, and Rules, 1940–2012**

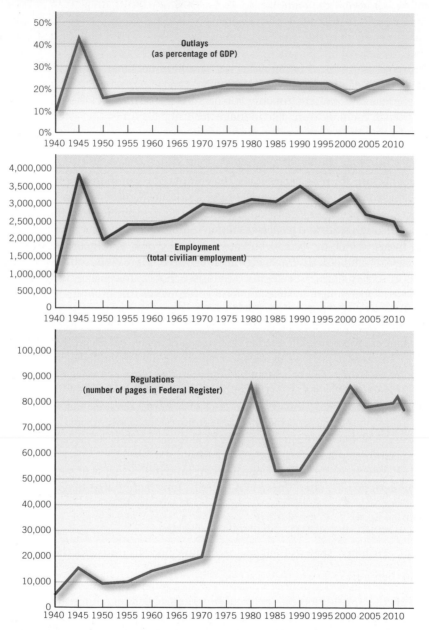

Source: Data for 2011 and 2012 compiled by Jesse Crosson from reports of the Office of Management and Budget, the U.S. Department of Labor, and the *Federal Register*.

only after they have passed a written examination administered by the Office of Personnel Management (OPM) or met certain selection criteria (such as training, educational attainments, or prior experience) devised by the hiring agency and approved by the OPM. Where competition for a job exists and candidates can be ranked by their scores or records, the agency must usually appoint one of the three top-ranking candidates.

Employees hired outside the competitive service are part of the excepted service. They now make up almost half of all workers. Though not hired by the OPM, they still are typically hired in a nonpartisan fashion. Some are hired by agencies—such as the CIA, the FBI, and the Postal Service—that have their own selection procedures.

About 3 percent of the excepted employees are appointed on grounds other than or in addition to merit. These legal exceptions exist to permit the president to select, for policymaking and politically sensitive posts, people who are in agreement with his policy views. Such appointments are generally of three kinds:

1. Presidential appointments authorized by statute (Cabinet and subcabinet officers, judges, U.S. marshals and U.S. attorneys, ambassadors, and members of various boards and commissions).

2. "Schedule C" appointments to jobs described as having a "confidential or policy-determining character" below the level of cabinet or subcabinet posts (including executive assistants, special aides, and confidential secretaries).

3. Non-career executive assignments (NEAs) given to high-ranking members of the regular competitive civil service or to persons brought into the civil service at these high levels. These people are deeply involved in the advocacy of presidential programs or participate in policymaking.

These three groups of excepted appointments constitute the patronage available to a president and his administration. When President Kennedy took office in 1961, he had 451 political jobs to fill. When President Barack Obama took office in 2009, he had more than four times that number, including nearly four times the number of top Cabinet posts. Scholars disagree over whether this proliferation of political appointees has improved or worsened Washington's performance, but one thing is clear: widespread presidential patronage is hardly unprecedented. In the 19th century, practically every federal job was a patronage job. For example, when Grover Cleveland, a Democrat, became president in 1885, he replaced some 40,000 Republican postal employees with Democrats.

Ironically, two years earlier, in 1883, the passage of the Pendleton Act had begun a slow but steady transfer of federal jobs from the patronage to the merit system. It may seem strange that a political party in power (the Republicans) would be willing to relinquish its patronage in favor of a merit-based appointment system. Two factors made it possible for the Republicans to pass the Pendleton Act: (1) public outrage over the abuses of the spoils system, highlighted by the assassination of President James Garfield by a man always described in the history books as a "disappointed office seeker" (*lunatic* would be a more accurate term); and (2) the fear that if the Democrats came to power on a wave of anti-spoils sentiment, existing Republican office-holders would be fired. (The Democrats won anyway.)

Fire erupting from the offshore oil rig operated by BP in the Gulf of Mexico near American land.

HOW THINGS WORK

Firing a Bureaucrat

To fire or demote a member of the competitive civil service, these procedures must be followed:

1. The employee must be given written notice at least 30 days in advance that he or she is to be fired or demoted for incompetence or misconduct.

2. The written notice must contain a statement of reasons, including specific examples of unacceptable performance.

3. The employee has the right to an attorney and to reply, orally or in writing, to the charges.

4. The employee has the right to appeal any adverse action to the Merit Systems Protection Board (MSPB), a three-person, bipartisan body appointed by the president with the consent of the Senate.

5. The MSPB must grant the employee a hearing, at which the employee has the right to have an attorney present.

6. The employee has the right to appeal the MSPB decision to a U.S. court of appeals, which can hold new hearings.

The merit system spread to encompass most of the federal bureaucracy, generally with presidential support. Though presidents may have liked in theory the idea of hiring and firing subordinates at will, most felt that the demands for patronage were impossible either to satisfy or to ignore. Furthermore, by increasing the coverage of the merit system a president could "blanket in" patronage appointees already holding office, thus making it difficult or impossible for the next administration to fire them.

Why So Many Constraints?

The biggest difference between a government agency and a private organization is the vastly greater number of constraints on the agency. Unlike a business firm, the typical government bureau cannot hire, fire, build, or sell without going through procedures set down in laws. How much money it pays its members is determined by statute, not by the market. Not only the goals of an agency, but often its exact procedures, are spelled out by Congress.

At one time, the Soil Conservation Service was required by law to employ at least 14,177 full-time workers. The State Department has been forbidden by law from opening a diplomatic post in Antigua or Barbuda but forbidden from closing a post anywhere else. The Agency for International Development (which administers our foreign-aid program) has been given by Congress 33 objectives and 75 priorities and must send to Congress 288 reports each year. When it buys military supplies, the Defense Department must give a "fair proportion" of its contracts to small businesses, especially those operated by "socially and economically disadvantaged individuals," and must buy from American firms even if, in some cases, buying abroad would be cheaper. Some of the more general constraints include the following:

- Administrative Procedure Act (1946). Before adopting a new rule or policy, an agency must give notice, solicit comments, and (often) hold hearings.

- Freedom of Information Act (1966). Citizens have the right to inspect all government records except those containing military, intelligence, or trade secrets or revealing private personnel actions.

- National Environmental Policy Act (1969). Before undertaking any major action affecting the environment, an agency must issue an environmental impact statement.

- Privacy Act (1974). Government files about individuals, such as Social Security and tax records, must be kept confidential.

- Open Meeting Law (1976). Every part of every agency meeting must be open to the public unless certain matters (for example, military or trade secrets) are being discussed.

One of the biggest constraints on bureaucratic action is that Congress rarely gives any job to a single agency. Stopping drug trafficking is the task of the Customs Service, the FBI, the Drug Enforcement Administration, the Border Patrol, and the Defense Department (among others). Disposing of the assets of failed savings-and-loan associations is the job of the Resolution Funding Corporation, Resolution Trust Corporation, Federal Housing Finance Board, Office of Thrift Supervision in the Treasury Department, Federal Deposit Insurance Corporation, Federal Reserve Board, and Justice Department (among others).

The effects of these constraints on agency behavior are not surprising.

- The government will often act slowly. (The more constraints that must be satisfied, the longer it will take to get anything done.)

- The government will sometimes act inconsistently. (What is done to meet one constraint—for example, freedom of information—may endanger another constraint—for example, privacy.)

- It will be easier to block action than to take action. (The constraints ensure that lots of voices will be heard; the more voices heard, the more they may cancel each other out.)

- Lower-ranking employees will be reluctant to make decisions on their own. (Having many constraints means having many ways to get into trouble; to avoid trouble, let your boss make the decision.)

- Citizens will complain of red tape. (The more constraints to serve, the more forms to fill out.)

These constraints do not mean government bureaucracy is powerless, only that, however great its power, it tends to be clumsy. That clumsiness arises not from the fact that the people who work for agencies are dull or incompetent, but from the complicated political environment in which that work must be done.

The moral of the story: the next time you get mad at a bureaucrat, ask yourself, why would a rational, intelligent person behave that way? Chances are you will discover there are good reasons for that action. You would probably behave the same way if you were working for the same organization.

Government agencies behave as they do in large part because of the many different goals they must pursue and the complex rules they must follow. Where does all this red tape come from?

From us. From us, the people.

Every goal, every constraint, every bit of red tape, was put in place by Congress, the courts, the White House, or the agency itself responding to the demands of some influential faction. Civil rights groups want every agency to hire and buy from women and minorities. Environmental groups want every agency

A U.S. Air Force F-35 stealth fighter aircraft undergoes preflight checks before launching.

to file environmental impact statements. Industries being regulated want every new agency policy to be formulated only after a lengthy public hearing with lots of lawyers present. Labor unions also want those hearings so that they can argue against industry lawyers. Everybody who sells something to the government wants a "fair chance" to make the sale, and so everybody insists that government contracts be awarded only after complex procedures are followed. A lot of people don't trust the government, and so they insist that everything it does be done in the sunshine—no secrets, no closed meetings, no hidden files.

If we wanted agencies to pursue their main goal with more vigor and less encumbering red tape, we would have to ask Congress, the courts, or the White House to repeal some of these constraints. In other words, we would have to be willing to give up something we want in order to get something else we want even more. But politics does not encourage people to make these trade-offs; instead it encourages us to expect to get everything—efficiency, fairness, help for minorities—all at once.

Agency Allies

Despite these constraints, government bureaucracies are not powerless. In fact, some of them actively seek certain constraints. They do so because it is a way of cementing a useful relationship with a congressional committee or an interest group.

At one time scholars described the relationship between an agency, a committee, and an interest group as an **iron triangle**. For example, the Department of Veterans Affairs, the House and Senate committees on veterans' affairs, and veterans' organizations (such as the American Legion) would form a tight, mutually advantageous alliance. The department would do what the committees wanted and in return get political support and budget appropriations; the committee members would do what the veterans' groups wanted and in return get votes and campaign contributions. Iron triangles are examples of what are called *client politics*.

Many agencies still have important allies in Congress and the private sector, especially those bureaus that serve the needs of specific sectors of the economy or regions of the country. The Department of Agriculture works closely with farm organizations, the Department of the Interior with groups interested in obtaining low-cost irrigation or grazing rights, and the Department of Housing and Urban Development with mayors and real-estate developers.

Sometimes these allies are so strong that they can defeat a popular president. For years, President Reagan tried to abolish the Small Business Administration (SBA), arguing that its program of loans to small firms was wasteful and ridden with favoritism. But Congress, reacting to pressures from small-business groups, rallied to the SBA's defense. As a result, Reagan had to oversee an agency that he didn't want.

iron triangle A close relationship between an agency, a congressional committee, and an interest group.

But iron triangles are much less common today than once was the case. Politics of late has become far more complicated. For one thing, the number and variety of interest groups have increased so much in recent years that scarcely any agency is not subject to pressures from several competing interests instead of only from one powerful interest. For another, the growth of subcommittees in Congress has meant most agencies are subject to control by many different legislative groups, often with very different concerns. Finally, the courts have made it much easier for all kinds of individuals and interests to intervene in agency affairs.

issue network A network of people in Washington, D.C.-based interest groups, on congressional staffs, in universities and think tanks, and in the mass media, who regularly discuss and advocate public policies.

authorization legislation Legislative permission to begin or continue a government program or agency.

As a result, nowadays government agencies face a bewildering variety of competing groups and legislative subcommittees that constitute not a loyal group of allies, but a fiercely contentious collection of critics. The Environmental Protection Agency is caught between the demands of environmentalists and those of industry organizations, the Occupational Safety and Health Administration between the pressures of labor and those of business, and the Federal Communications Commission between the desires of broadcasters and those of cable television companies. Even the Department of Agriculture faces not a unified group of farmers, but many different farmers split into rival groups, depending on the crops they raise, the regions in which they live, and the attitudes they have toward the relative merits of farm subsidies or free markets.

Political scientist Hugh Heclo has described the typical government agency today as being embedded not in an iron triangle, but in an **issue network**.[18] These issue networks consist of people in Washington-based interest groups, on congressional staffs, in universities and think tanks, and in the mass media, who regularly debate government policy on a certain subject—say, health care or auto safety. The networks are contentious, split along political, ideological, and economic lines. When a president takes office, he often recruits key agency officials from those members of the issue network who are most sympathetic to his views.

When Jimmy Carter, a Democrat, became president, he appointed to key posts in consumer agencies people who were from that part of the consumer issue network associated with Ralph Nader. Ronald Reagan, a conservative Republican, filled these same jobs with people who were from that part of the issue network holding free-market or anti-regulation views. When George Bush the elder, a more centrist Republican, took office, he filled these posts with more centrist members of the issue network. Bill Clinton brought back the consumer activists. George W. Bush reversed Clinton, and Barack Obama reversed Bush.

Congressional Oversight

The main reason why some interest groups are important to agencies is that they are important to Congress. Not every interest group in the country has substantial access to Congress, but those that do and that are taken seriously by the relevant committees or subcommittees must also be taken seriously by the agency. Furthermore, even apart from interest groups, members of Congress have constitutional powers over agencies and policy interests in how agencies function.

Congressional supervision of the bureaucracy takes several forms. First, no agency may exist (except for a few presidential offices and commissions) without congressional approval. Congress influences—and sometimes determines precisely—agency behavior by the statutes it enacts.

Second, no money may be spent unless it has first been authorized by Congress. **Authorization legislation** originates in a legislative committee (such as Agriculture, Education and Labor, or Public

appropriation A legislative grant of money to finance a government program or agency.

Works) and states the maximum amount of money that an agency may spend on a given program. This authorization may be permanent, it may be for a fixed number of years, or it may be annual (that is, it must be renewed each year, or the program or agency goes out of business).

Third, even funds that have been authorized by Congress cannot be spent unless (in most cases) they are also appropriated. Appropriations usually are made annually, and they originate not with the legislative committees but with the House Appropriations Committee and its various (and influential) subcommittees. An **appropriation** (money formally set aside for a specific use) may be, and often is, for less than the amount authorized. The Appropriations Committee's action thus tends to have a budget-cutting effect. There are some funds that can be spent without an appropriation, but in virtually every part of the bureaucracy, each agency is keenly sensitive to congressional concerns at the time that the annual appropriations process is going on.

But is fidelity to the constitutional principle of separation of powers (see Chapter 2) called into question when Congress engages in oversight of agencies that are in the executive branch? Members of Congress themselves once debated that issue, but the aforementioned Administrative Procedure Act of 1946 and a dozen subsequent laws that built on it (the latest being the Data Quality Act of 2000, and all upheld when challenged in the courts) are predicated on the idea that agencies are "adjuncts for legislative functions.... Congress lacks the capacity to legislate on all matters it touches and perforce must delegate a great deal of legislative authority to the agencies."[19]

This idea was challenged during the George W. Bush presidency by administration officials and others who, especially but not exclusively with respect to military, national, and homeland security issues, argued that agencies were bound to act in accordance with the president's directives whenever they conflicted with directives from Congress. While Bush's executive-centered approach sparked many controversies, most scholars seem to think that it effected no major or lasting changes, and some suggest that it stirred Congress to pursue even more comprehensive (and aggressive) oversight policies and practices.[20]

The Appropriations Committee and Legislative Committees

The fact that an agency budget must be both authorized and appropriated means that each agency serves not one congressional master but several, and that these masters may be in conflict. The real power over an agency's budget is exercised by the Appropriations Committee; the legislative committees are especially important when a substantive law is first passed or an agency is first created, or when an agency is subject to annual authorization.

In the past, the power of the Appropriations Committee was rarely challenged: from 1947 through 1962, fully 90 percent of the House Appropriations Committee's recommendations on expenditures were approved by the full House without change.[21] Furthermore, the Appropriations Committee tends to recommend less money than an agency requests (though some specially favored agencies, such as the FBI, the Soil Conservation Service, and the Forest Service, have tended to get almost everything that they have asked for). Finally, the process of "marking up" (revising, amending, and approving) an agency's budget request gives to the Appropriations Committee, or one of its subcommittees, substantial influence over the policies that the agency follows.

Of late, the appropriations committees have lost some of their great power over government agencies. This has happened in three ways.

First, Congress has created trust funds to pay for the benefits many people receive. The Social Security trust fund is the largest of these. In 2012, it took in $729 billion in Social Security taxes and paid out $635 billion in old-age benefits. There are several other trust funds as well. **Trust funds** operate outside the regular government budget, and the appropriations committees have no control over these expenditures. They are automatic.

Second, Congress has changed the authorization of many programs from permanent or multiyear to annual authorizations. This means that every year the legislative committees, as part of the reauthorization process, get to set limits on what these agencies can spend. This limits the ability of the appropriations committees to determine the spending limits. Before 1959, most authorizations were permanent or multiyear. Now a long list of agencies must be reauthorized every year—the State Department, NASA, military procurement programs of the Defense Department, the Justice Department, the Energy Department, and parts or all of many other agencies.

Third, the existence of huge budget deficits during the 1980s and in the 2000s has meant that much of Congress's time has been taken up with trying (usually not very successfully) to keep spending down. As a result, there has rarely been much time to discuss the merits of various programs or how much ought to be spent on them; instead, attention has been focused on meeting a target spending limit. In 1981, the budget resolution passed by Congress mandated cuts in several programs before the appropriations committees had even completed their work.[22]

In addition to the power of the purse, there are informal ways by which Congress can control the bureaucracy. An individual member of Congress can call an agency head on behalf of a constituent. Most such calls merely seek information, but some result in, or attempt to obtain, special privileges for particular people. Congressional committees may also obtain the right to pass on certain agency decisions. This is called **committee clearance**, and though it usually is not legally binding on the agency, few agency heads will ignore the expressed wish of a committee chair that he or she be consulted before certain actions (such as transferring funds) are taken.

trust funds Funds for government programs collected and spent outside the regular government budget.

committee clearance The ability of a congressional committee to review and approve certain agency decisions in advance and without passing a law.

legislative veto The authority of Congress to block a presidential action after it has taken place. The Supreme Court has held that Congress does not have this power.

The Legislative Veto

For many decades, Congress made frequent use of the legislative veto to control bureaucratic or presidential actions. A **legislative veto** is a requirement that an executive decision must lie before Congress for a specified period (usually 30 or 90 days) before it takes effect. Congress could then veto the decision if a resolution of disapproval was passed by either house (a "one-house veto") or both houses (a "two-house veto"). Unlike laws, such resolutions were not signed by the president. Between 1932 and 1980, about 200 laws were passed providing for a legislative veto, many of them involving presidential proposals to sell arms abroad.

But in June 1983, the Supreme Court declared the legislative veto to be unconstitutional. In the *Chadha* case, the Court held that the Constitution clearly requires in Article I that "every order, resolution, or vote to which the concurrence of the Senate and House of Representatives may be necessary" (with certain minor exceptions) "shall be presented to the President of the United States," who must either approve it or return it with his veto attached. In short, Congress cannot take any action that has the force of law unless the president concurs in that action.[23] With a stroke of the pen, parts of 200 laws suddenly became invalid. At least that happened in theory. In fact, since the *Chadha* decision, Congress has passed a number of laws that contain legislative vetoes, despite the Supreme

Court having ruled against them! (Someone will have to go to court to test the constitutionality of these new provisions.)

Opponents of the legislative veto hope future Congresses will have to pass laws that state much more clearly than before what an agency may or may not do. But it is just as likely that Congress will continue to pass laws stated in general terms and require that agencies implementing those laws report their plans to Congress, so that it will have a chance to enact and send to the president a regular bill disapproving the proposed action. Or Congress may rely on informal (but scarcely weak) means of persuasion, including threats to reduce the appropriations of an agency that does not abide by congressional preferences.

Congressional Investigations

Perhaps the most visible and dramatic form of congressional supervision of an agency is the investigation. Since 1792, when Congress investigated an army defeat by a Native American tribe, congressional investigations of the bureaucracy have been a regular feature—sometimes constructive, sometimes destructive—of legislative–executive relations. The investigative power is not mentioned in the Constitution but has been inferred from the power to legislate. The Supreme Court has consistently upheld this interpretation, though it has also said that such investigations should not be solely for the purpose of exposing the purely personal affairs of private individuals and must not operate to deprive citizens of their basic rights.[24] Congress may compel a person to attend an investigation by issuing a subpoena; anyone who ignores the subpoena may be punished for contempt. Congress can vote to send the person to jail or can refer the matter to a court for further action. As explained in Chapter 10, the president and his principal subordinates have refused to answer certain congressional inquiries on grounds of "executive privilege."

Although many areas of congressional oversight—budgetary review, personnel controls, investigations—are designed to control the exercise of bureaucratic discretion, other areas are intended to ensure the freedom of certain agencies from effective control, especially by the president. In dozens of cases, Congress has authorized department heads and bureau chiefs to operate independent of presidential preferences. Congress has resisted, for example, presidential efforts to ensure that policies to regulate pollution do not impose excessive costs on the economy, and interest groups have brought suit to prevent presidential coordination of various regulatory agencies. If the bureaucracy sometimes works at cross-purposes, it usually is because Congress—or competing committees in Congress—wants it that way.

Bureaucratic "Pathologies"

Everyone complains about bureaucracy in general (though rarely about bureaucratic agencies that everyone believes are desirable). This chapter should persuade you that it is difficult to say anything about bureaucracy "in general"; there are too many different kinds of agencies, kinds of bureaucrats, and kinds of programs to label the entire enterprise with some single adjective. Nevertheless, many people who recognize the enormous variety among government agencies still believe they all have some general features in common and suffer from certain shared problems or pathologies.

This is true enough, but the reasons for it—and the solutions, if any—are often not understood. There are five major (or at least frequently mentioned) problems with bureaucracies: red tape, conflict, duplication, imperialism, and waste. **Red tape** refers to the complex

red tape Complex bureaucratic rules and procedures that must be followed to get something done.

rules and procedures that must be followed to get something done. (As early as the seventh century, legal and government documents in England were bound together with a tape of pinkish-red color. Since then *red tape* has come to mean "bureaucratic delay or confusion," especially that accompanied by unnecessary paperwork.[25]) *Conflict* exists because some agencies seem to be working at cross-purposes with other agencies. (For example, the Agricultural Research Service tells farmers how to grow crops more efficiently, while the Agricultural Stabilization and Conservation Service pays farmers to grow fewer crops or to produce less.) *Duplication* (usually called "wasteful duplication") occurs when two government agencies seem to be doing the same thing, as when the Customs Service and the Drug Enforcement Administration both attempt to intercept illegal drugs being smuggled into the country. *Imperialism* refers to the tendency of agencies to grow without regard to the benefits that their programs confer or the costs that they entail. *Waste* means spending more than is necessary to buy some product or service.

These problems all exist, but they do not necessarily exist because bureaucrats are incompetent or power hungry. Most exist because of the very nature of government itself. Take red tape: partly we encounter cumbersome rules and procedures because any large organization, governmental or not, must have some way of ensuring that one part of the organization does not operate out of step with another. Business corporations have red tape also; it is to a certain extent a consequence of bigness. But a great amount of governmental red tape is also the result of the need to satisfy legal and political requirements. Government agencies must hire on the basis of "merit," must observe strict accounting rules, must supply Congress with detailed information on their programs, and must allow for citizen access in countless ways. Meeting each need requires rules; enforcing the rules requires forms.

Or take conflict and duplication: they do not occur because bureaucrats enjoy conflict or duplication. (Quite the contrary!) They exist because Congress, in setting up agencies and programs, often wants to achieve a number of different, partially inconsistent goals or finds that it cannot decide which goal it values the most. Congress has 535 members and little strong leadership; it should not be surprising that 535 people will want different things and will sometimes succeed in getting them.

Imperialism results in large measure from government agencies' seeking goals so vague and so difficult to measure that it is hard to tell when they have been attained. When Congress is unclear as to exactly what an agency is supposed to do, the agency will often convert that legislative vagueness into bureaucratic imperialism by taking the largest possible view of its powers. It may do this on its own; more often it does so because interest groups and judges rush in to fill the vacuum left by Congress. In 1973, the Rehabilitation Act was passed with a provision barring discrimination against people with disabilities in any program receiving federal aid. Under pressure from people with disabilities, that lofty but vague goal was converted by the Department of Transportation into a requirement that virtually every big-city bus have a device installed to lift people in wheelchairs onboard.

Waste is probably the biggest criticism that people have of the bureaucracy. Everybody has heard stories of the Pentagon's paying $91 for screws that

At the world's busiest border crossing, cars line up to enter the United States in Tijuana, Mexico.

David McNew/Getty Images

cost 3 cents in the hardware store. President Reagan's "Private Sector Survey on Cost Control," generally known as the Grace Commission (after its chairman, J. Peter Grace), publicized these and other tales in a 1984 report. No doubt there is waste in government. After all, unlike a business firm worried about maximizing profits, in a government agency there are only weak incentives to keep costs down. If a business employee cuts costs, he or she often receives a bonus or raise, and the firm gets to add the savings to its profits. If a government official cuts costs, he or she receives no reward, and the agency cannot keep the savings—they go back to the Treasury.

But many of the horror stories are either exaggerations or unusual occurrences.[26] Most of the screws, hammers, and light bulbs purchased by the government are obtained at low cost by means of competitive bidding among several suppliers. When the government does pay outlandish amounts, the reason typically is that it is purchasing a new or one-of-a-kind item not available at your neighborhood hardware store—for example, a new bomber or missile.

Even when the government is not overcharged, it still may spend more money than a private firm in buying what it needs. The reason is red tape—the rules and procedures designed to ensure that when the government buys something, it will do so in a way that serves the interests of many groups. For example, it often must buy from American rather than foreign suppliers, even if the latter charge a lower price; it must make use of contractors that employ minorities; it must hire only union laborers and pay them the "prevailing" (that is, the highest) wage; it must allow public inspection of its records; it frequently is required to choose contractors favored by influential members of Congress; and so on. Private firms do not have to comply with all these rules and thus can buy for less.

From this discussion, it should be easy to see why these five basic bureaucratic problems are so hard to correct. To end conflicts and duplication, Congress would have to make some policy choices and set some clear priorities, but with all the competing demands that it faces, Congress finds it difficult to do that. You make more friends by helping people than by hurting them, and so Congress is more inclined to add new programs than to cut old ones, whether or not the new programs are in conflict with existing ones. To check imperialism, some way would have to be found to measure the benefits of government, but that is often impossible; government exists in part to achieve precisely those goals—such as national defense—that are least measurable. Furthermore, what might be done to remedy some problems would make other problems worse: if you simplify rules and procedures to cut red tape, you are also likely to reduce the coordination among agencies and thus to increase the extent to which there is duplication or conflict. If you want to reduce waste, you will have to have more rules and inspectors—in short, more red tape. The problem of bureaucracy is inseparable from the problem of government generally.

Just as people are likely to say they dislike Congress but like their own member of Congress, they are inclined to express hostility toward "the bureaucracy," but goodwill for that part of the bureaucracy with which they have dealt personally. While most Americans have unfavorable impressions of government agencies and officials in general, they have quite favorable impressions about government agencies and officials with whom they have had direct contact or about which they claim to know something specific.

For example, Table 11.2 shows that wide majorities have very or somewhat favorable impressions of diverse federal government agencies. Surveys dating back decades suggest that, despite persistent public complaints about "the bureaucracy," most Americans have judged, and continue to judge, each federal agency to be fair and useful.[27] Even the tax-collecting IRS has more public fans than foes, as did the new Transportation Safety Administration (TSA), whose workers people routinely encounter at airport security checkpoints.

This finding helps explain why government agencies are rarely reduced in size or budget: whatever the popular feelings about the bureaucracy, any given agency tends to have many friends. Even the much-criticized FEMA, viewed unfavorably by half the public, was able to fend off budget cuts in the several years following its failed response to Hurricane Katrina.

TABLE 11.2 How the Public Views Particular Federal Agencies

AGENCY	% FAVORABLE Very/Somewhat/Total	% UNFAVORABLE Very/Somewhat/Total	Favorable Minus Unfavorable
Postal Service	58/31/89	5/5/10	+79
FBI	31/46/77	10/7/17	+60
Defense Department	31/34/65	15/2/17	+48
Social Security Admin.	24/40/64	19/13/32	+32
EPA	23/40/63	15/15/31	+32
CIA	22/36/58	16/14/30	+28
Homeland Security	24/36/60	17/17/34	+26
Transportation Safety	15/41/56	16/9/25	+26
Education Department	22/37/59	19/19/38	+21
IRS	14/42/56	21/18/39	+17
FEMA	16/33/49	24/26/50	−1

Percent reporting a "favorable or unfavorable impression"*

*Other response categories were "never heard of" and "can't rate," and only the newest agency, the Transportation Safety Administration, drew significant numbers in each category (9 percent for each).

Source: Adapted from results of a nationally representative Associated Press/IPSOS Public Agenda poll conducted December 17–19, 2007.

Reforming the Bureaucracy

The history of American bureaucracy has been punctuated with countless efforts to make it work better and cost less. There were 11 major attempts in the 20th century alone. The latest was the National Performance Review (NPR)—popularly called the plan to "reinvent government"—led by Vice President Al Gore.

The NPR differed from many of the preceding reform efforts in one important way. Most of the earlier ones suggested ways of increasing central (that is, presidential) control of government agencies: the Brownlow Commission (1936–1937) recommended giving the president more assistants, the First Hoover Commission (1947–1949) suggested ways of improving top-level management, and the Ash Council (1969–1971) called for consolidating existing agencies into a few big "super departments." The intent was to make it easier for the president and his cabinet secretaries to run the bureaucracy. The key ideas were efficiency, accountability, and consistent policies.

The NPR, by contrast, emphasized customer satisfaction (the "customers" in this case being the citizens who come into contact with federal agencies). To the authors of the NPR report, the main problem with the bureaucracy was that it had become too centralized, too rule bound, too little concerned with making programs work, and too much concerned with avoiding scandal. The NPR report contained many horror stories about useless red tape, excessive regulations, and cumbersome procurement systems that make it next to impossible for agencies to do what they were created to do. (For example, before it could buy an ashtray, the General Services Administration issued a nine-page document that described an ashtray and specified how many pieces it must break into, should it be hit with a hammer.)[28]

To solve these problems, the NPR called for less centralized management and more employee initiative, fewer detailed rules and more emphasis on customer satisfaction. It sought to create a new kind of organizational culture in government agencies, one more like that found in the more innovative, quality-conscious American corporations. The NPR was reinforced legislatively by the Government Performance and Results Act (GPRA) of 1993, which required agencies "to set goals, measure performance, and report on the results."

President George W. Bush built on the Clinton-Gore NPR efforts and the GPRA using the Performance Assessment Rating Tool (PART). The main goal of the PART was to link management reform to the budget process. During the 2008 presidential campaign, Barack Obama harkened back to the Clinton-Gore NPR, but also pledged to keep but improve Bush's PART. By 2011, however, administrative reform was not widely mentioned among Obama's main priorities or accomplishments in office.

Reforming the bureaucracy is easier said than done. Most of the rules and red tape that make it hard for agency heads to do a good job are the result either of the struggle between the White House and Congress for control over the agencies or of the agencies' desire to avoid irritating influential voters. Silly as the rules

HOW WE COMPARE

Outsourcing Government

In the United States, government by proxy is the norm. Bureaucrats in Washington pay state and local governments and private groups to staff and administer most federal programs.

For instance, Medicaid, the main federal health program for low-income citizens, is administered mainly by state agencies. The federal government has co-funded nonprofit groups to lead recovery efforts in the hurricane-ravaged Gulf Coast. At points during the second Gulf War, there were nearly as many for-profit workers as U.S. soldiers in Iraq.

The Canadian and Indian central governments each administer many policies via provincial or territorial governments; and every European government uses private contractors for at least some functions.

But most other democracies restrict and regulate outsourcing more than the United States does; for example, German law directs that all persons involved in administering national policies must be directly supervised by a government official.

And no other nation follows the American practice whereby government bureaucracies give tax-exempt organizations, including local faith-based groups, grants to administer myriad health and human services programs.

Many experts argue that outsourcing and proxy government have gone too far in this country; but none is sure whether or how it can be reined in, and most admit that public administration in other democracies is also far from perfect.

Source: Donald F. Kettl, The Next Government of the United States: Why Our Institutions Fail Us and How to Fix Them (New York: W. W. Norton, 2008); *Paul R. Verkuil*, Outsourcing Sovereignty: Why Privatization of Government Functions Threatens Democracy and What We Can Do About It *(Cambridge: Cambridge University Press, 2007)*; John J. Dilulio, Jr., "Government by Proxy: A Faithful Overview," Harvard Law Review, March 2003, pp. 1271–1284.

for ashtrays may sound, they were written so that the government could say it had an "objective" standard for buying ashtrays. If it simply went out and bought ashtrays at a department store the way ordinary people do, it would risk being accused by the Acme Ashtray Company of buying trays from its competitor, the A-1 Ashtray Company, because of political favoritism.

The rivalry between the president and Congress for control of the bureaucracy makes bureaucrats nervous about irritating either branch, and so they issue rules designed to avoid getting into trouble, even if these rules make it hard to do their job. Matters become even worse during periods of divided government when different

Former Los Angeles Mayor Antonio Villaraigosa goes through a full-body scanner at Los Angeles International Airport.

parties control the White House and Congress. As we saw in Chapter 10, divided government may not have much effect on *making* policy, but it can have a big effect on *implementing* it. Presidents of one party have tried to increase political control over the bureaucracy ("executive micromanagement"), and Congresses of another party have responded by increasing the number of investigations and detailed rule-making ("legislative micromanagement"). Divided government intensifies the cross fire between the executive and legislative branches, making bureaucrats dig into even deeper layers of red tape to avoid getting hurt.

This does not mean that reform is impossible, only that it is very difficult. For example, despite a lack of clear-cut successes in other areas, the NPR's procurement reforms stuck: government agencies can now buy things costing as much as $100,000 without following any complex regulations. Still, the main effect of the NPR, the GPRA, and the PART was to get federal agencies collecting far more information than in the past concerning what they do, without, however, using the information to improve the way they do it.[29]

It might be easier to make desirable changes if the bureaucracy were accountable to only one master—say, the president—instead of to several. But that situation, which exists in many parliamentary democracies, creates its own problems. When the bureaucracy has but one master, it often ends up having none: it becomes so powerful that it controls the prime minister and no longer listens to citizen complaints. A weak, divided bureaucracy, such as exists in the United States, may strike us as inefficient, but that very inefficiency may help protect our liberties.

LEARNING OBJECTIVES

LO 11.1 What is "bureaucracy" and in what ways is the American bureaucracy distinctive?

A bureaucracy is a large, complex organization composed of appointed officials. American bureaucracy is distinctive in three ways: political authority over the bureaucracy is shared by several institutions; most national government agencies share their functions with state and local government agencies;

and government agencies are closely scrutinized and frequently challenged by both individuals and nongovernmental groups.

LO 11.2 What is "discretionary authority" and why do some bureaucrats have lots of it?

Discretionary authority refers to the extent to which appointed bureaucrats can choose courses of action and make policies not spelled out in advance by laws. It is impossible for Congress to specify every last detail regarding how a law it passes is to be implemented. Many laws are administered by persons with special information and expertise, and many private citizens administer public laws by working as government contractors or grantees.

LO 11.3 How does Congress exert control over the bureaucracy?

Congress exerts control over the bureaucracy in many different ways. It decides whether an agency may exist and how much money an agency spends. It can hold oversight hearings and launch investigations into just about any aspect of agency decision making or operations it chooses. And it traditionally has enjoyed wide latitude from the president in exercising its oversight functions.

LO 11.4 What happened to make the bureaucracy a "fourth branch" of American national government?

The Constitution made no provision for an administrative system other than to allow the president to appoint, with the advice and consent of the Senate, ambassadors, Supreme Court judges, and "all other officers . . . which shall be provided by law." By the early 20th century, however, Washington's role in making, administering, and funding public policies had already grown far beyond what the Framers had contemplated. Two world wars, the New Deal, and the Great Society each left the government with expanded powers and requiring new batteries of administrative agencies to exercise them. Today, the federal bureaucracy is as vast as most people's expectations about Washington's responsibility for every public concern one can name. It is the appointed officials—the bureaucrats—not the elected officials or policymakers, who command the troops, deliver the mail, audit the tax returns, run the federal prisons, decide who qualifies for public assistance, and do countless other tasks. Unavoidably, many bureaucrats exercise discretion in deciding what public laws and regulations mean and how to apply them. Still, the president, Cabinet secretaries, and thousands of political appointees are ultimately their bosses. Congress and the courts have ample, if imperfect, means of checking and balancing even the biggest bureaucracy, old or new.

LO 11.5 What are the actual size and scope of the federal bureaucracy?

A few million civil servants work directly for the federal government, but more than five times as many people work indirectly for Washington as employees of business firms or of nonprofit organizations that receive federal grants or contracts, or as state and local government employees working under federal mandates. For example, the U.S. Department of Health and Human Services (HHS) has about 70,000 employees, runs more than 300 different programs, and makes more than 60,000 grants a year. But millions more people work indirectly for the HHS—as state and local government employees whose entire jobs involve the administration of one or more HHS programs (for example, Medicaid), and as people who work for community-serving nonprofit organizations that receive HHS grants to administer social services.

TO LEARN MORE

For addresses and reports of various cabinet departments:

- Web addresses: **www.whitehouse.gov**

- Documents and bulletin boards: **http://fedworld.ntis.gov**

- National Partnership for Reinventing Government: **http://govinfo.library.unt.edu/npr/index.htm**

A few specific websites of federal agencies:

- Department of Defense: **www.defenselink.mil**

- Department of Education: **www.ed.gov**

- Department of Health and Human Services: **www.dhhs.gov**

- Department of State: **www.state.gov**

- Federal Bureau of Investigation: **www.fbi.gov**

- Department of Labor: **www.dol.gov**

- Burke, John P. *Bureaucratic Responsibility*. Baltimore: Johns Hopkins University Press, 1986. Examines the problem of individual responsibility—for example, when to be a whistle blower—in government agencies.

- Downs, Anthony. *Inside Bureaucracy*. Boston: Little, Brown, 1967. An economist's explanation of why bureaucrats and bureaus behave as they do.

- Durant, Robert F., ed. *The Oxford Handbook of American Bureaucracy*. New York: Oxford University Press, 2010. Thirty-three largely up-to-date academic essays covering just about every facet of the subject.

- Halperin, Morton H. *Bureaucratic Politics and Foreign Policy*. Washington, D.C.: Brookings Institution, 1974. Insightful account of the strategies by which diplomatic and military bureaucracies defend their interests.

- Heclo, Hugh. *A Government of Strangers*. Washington, D.C.: Brookings Institution, 1977. Analyzes how political appointees attempt to gain control of the Washington bureaucracy and how bureaucrats resist those efforts.

- Kettl, Donald F. *Government by Proxy*. Washington, D.C.: Congressional Quarterly Press, 1988. An account of how the federal government pays others to staff and run its programs.

- Kettl, Donald F. *The Next Government of the United States: Why Our Institutions Fail Us and How to Fix Them*. New York: W. W. Norton, 2008. A masterful study of how proxy government functions and often fails today, and what might be done to remedy its worst failures.

- Moore, Mark H. *Creating Public Value: Strategic Management in Government*. Cambridge: Harvard University Press, 1995. A thoughtful account of how wise bureaucrats can make government work better.

- Parkinson, C. Northcote. *Parkinson's Law*. Boston: Houghton Mifflin, 1957. Half-serious, half-joking explanation of why government agencies tend to grow.

- Wilson, James Q. *Bureaucracy: What Government Agencies Do and Why They Do It*. New York: Basic Books, 1989. A comprehensive review of what we know about bureaucratic behavior in the United States.

12

The Judiciary

LEARNING OBJECTIVES

LO 12.1   Where in the Constitution does it say that the Supreme Court has the power of judicial review?

LO 12.2   What is meant by an "Article III" federal judge?

LO 12.3   What is the difference between original and appellate jurisdiction?

LO 12.4   Why should federal judges serve for life?

LO 12.5   Why should federal courts be able to declare laws unconstitutional?

THEN

When the states were debating the ratification of the Constitution, Alexander Hamilton wrote in *Federalist* paper No. 78 that the new system of federal courts would be "the least dangerous" branch of government because, unlike the president, it would not command the sword and, unlike Congress, it would not control the purse strings. The courts, he argued, could take "no active resolution whatever." Nowhere in the Constitution was the Supreme Court given the right to declare laws of Congress or decisions of the president to be unconstitutional, though Hamilton argued that such a power was necessary. That document was our fundamental law and expressed the will of the people, and so it ought to be preferred to a law passed by Congress if there were an "irreconcilable variance between the two."

NOW

Within a few years after the Constitution was ratified, the Supreme Court took Hamilton's position by asserting that the Court could decide if a law was unconstitutional. A dozen years later, the same Court said that Congress could not only pass laws on the basis of powers explicitly given it by the Constitution, but also do things that were "necessary and proper" in order to implement those powers. By the middle of the 19th century, the Supreme Court had begun to declare many federal and scores of state laws to be unconstitutional.

As a result of its newfound powers, justices began serving on the Supreme Court for much longer periods. The 11 justices nominated by President George Washington served, on average, seven years, while the five nominated 40 years later by President Andrew Jackson served on average 20 years. The Court had become not the least dangerous branch, but a powerful one.

In time, the identity of the justices became an important political issue. Until recently, most justices were confirmed by the Senate, and from 1947 to 1985, almost all persons nominated to be a federal appeals court judge were approved. But of late, these nominations have had a less certain reception in the Senate. When President Ronald Reagan nominated Antonin Scalia for the Supreme Court, he was confirmed by the Senate in 1986 by a vote of 98 to 0. But one year later, when President Reagan nominated Robert Bork, he was rejected by the Senate. Four years after that, Clarence Thomas barely survived a confirmation vote (52 to 48). In 2006, President George W. Bush's nominee Samuel Alito won confirmation by a vote of 58 to 42 after Senate Democrats tried to block the vote by means of a filibuster. During President Barack Obama's first term, each of his two nominees won conformation: Sonia Sotomayor won confirmation in 2009 by a vote of 68 to 31, and Elena Kagan won confirmation in 2010 by a vote of 63 to 37. But in each case many Republicans voted against the nominee.

Beyond the Supreme Court, there has been a sharp drop in the percentage of nominees to federal appeals courts who are confirmed. From 1945 until 1970, almost every appeals court nominee was confirmed, but by 1995 only about half got through the Senate and by 2000 it was less than 40 percent. Table 12.1 shows a decline in the confirmation rate for the federal appeals courts that occurred from the Carter administration (92 percent) to the George W. Bush administration (71 percent). During President Obama's first term, the confirmation rate for his nominees to the federal appeals courts was 71 percent, slightly higher than the confirmation rate (67 percent) for the preceding administration.[1] Nominees to the federal district court are much less controversial than nominees to the federal appeals courts because the president rarely nominates for a federal district court someone who is not known to and supported by the nominee's two home state senators. Still, the confirmation rate for President Obama's nominees to the federal district courts (78 percent) was well below the confirmation rate (95 percent) for

TABLE 12.1   Judicial Nominations and Confirmations U.S. Court of Appeals

Presidency	Nominations	Confirmations	Confirmation Rate
Jimmy Carter	61	56	92%
Ronald Reagan	94	83	88
George H.W. Bush	53	42	79
Bill Clinton	90	66	73
George W. Bush	84	60	71

Source: Adapted from Russell Wheeler, *Judicial Nominations and Confirmations in the 11th Senate and What to Look for in the 112th*, Governance Studies, Brookings Institution, January 4, 2011, p. 2.

TABLE 12.2   Federal Court Nominees, Time From Hearings to Confirmation

Presidency	U.S. District Court Nominees	U.S. Appeals Court Nominees
	Average Number of Days	
Bill Clinton	30	43
George W. Bush	54	63
Barack Obama (first term)	139	177

Source: Adapted from Russell Wheeler, *Judicial Nominations and Confirmations in Obama's First Term*, Governance Studies, Brookings Institution, December 13, 2012, p. 9.

the preceding administration.[2] Also, as Table 12.2 shows, over the last three presidencies, the average number of days between a nominee's Senate hearings and his or her confirmation has increased steeply for both federal appeals court nominees and for federal district court nominees.

Why the changes? One reason is that the federal judiciary has played an increasingly important role in making public policy. It, and not Congress, decided that abortions should be legal, settled the closely contested 2000 presidential election, and allowed private homes to be seized in order to build a residential hotel and other private structures aimed at affluent clientele. In these and many other cases, the federal courts have become major political actors; as a result, Congress has become concerned about who will be federal judges. Especially during certain periods of divided government (see Chapter 10), the increased partisan polarization in Congress (see Chapter 9) has made its mark on the Senate's confirmation process. For example, during President Clinton's first two years in office, a period of unified government, 86 percent of his nominees for the U.S. Court of Appeals were confirmed; but, during his second two years in office, a period of divided government, the confirmation rate dropped to 55 percent.[3]

As federal judges make more policy decisions, and as partisan rancor over those decisions rises, the process by which the Senate considers nominees for the federal bench has become longer, more ideologically charged, and less certain to result in confirmations. By long-standing tradition, senators from the home state of an appeals court nominee are allowed to file a private objection—what is called registering a negative "blue slip" complaint. If filed by a Judiciary Committee member, this will prevent a hearing on the nominee from being held. Sometimes these blue slips indicate that a senator doesn't like the nominee's political views, but other times it can mean that the senator is blocking a judicial appointment as a way of inducing the president to do something he or she wants on a totally unrelated matter. But, over the last three presidencies, that tradition has been used ever more as just another tool of partisan politics.

Judicial Review

One aspect of the power of the federal courts is **judicial review**—the right of the federal courts to declare laws of Congress and acts of the executive branch void and unenforceable if they are judged to be in conflict with the Constitution. Since 1789, the Supreme Court has declared more than 160 federal laws to be unconstitutional. In Britain, by contrast, Parliament is supreme. The UK Supreme Court, established quite recently by the Constitutional Reform Act of 2005, started work in 2009 and is much more limited in its powers of judicial review. It cannot overturn primary legislation made by Parliament. As the second earl of Pembroke supposedly said, "A parliament can do anything but make a man a woman and a woman a man." All that prevents Parliament from acting contrary to the (unwritten) constitution of Britain are the consciences of its members and the opinions of the citizens.

About 60 nations do have something resembling judicial review, but in only a few cases does this power mean much in practice. Where it means something—in Australia, Canada, Germany, India, and some other nations—one finds a stable, federal system of government with a strong tradition of an independent judiciary.[4] Some other nations—France, for example—have special councils, rather than courts, that can under certain circumstances decide that a law is not authorized by the constitution.

Judicial review is the federal courts' chief weapon in the system of checks and balances on which the American government is based. Today, few people would deny to the courts the right to decide that a legislative or executive act is unconstitutional, though once that right was controversial. What remains controversial is the method by which such review is conducted.

There are two competing views, each ardently pressed during the fight to confirm Clarence Thomas. The first holds that judges should only judge—that is, they should confine themselves to applying those rules stated in or clearly implied by the language of the Constitution. This often is called the **judicial restraint approach**. The other argues that judges should discover the general principles underlying the Constitution and its often vague language, amplify those principles on the basis of some moral or economic philosophy, and apply them to cases. This is sometimes called the **activist approach**.

Note that the difference between activist and strict-constructionist judges is not necessarily the same as the difference between liberals and conservatives. Judges can be political liberals and still believe they are bound by the

judicial review The power of courts to declare laws unconstitutional.

judicial restraint approach The view that judges should decide cases strictly on the basis of the language of the laws and the Constitution.

activist approach The view that judges should discern the general principles underlying laws or the Constitution and apply them to modern circumstances.

TABLE 12.3   Chief Justices of the United States

Chief Justice	Appointed by	Years of Service
John Jay	Washington	1789–1795
Oliver Ellsworth	Washington	1796–1800
John Marshall	Adams	1801–1835
Roger B. Taney	Jackson	1836–1864
Salmon P. Chase	Lincoln	1864–1873
Morrison R. Waite	Grant	1874–1888
Melville W. Fuller	Cleveland	1888–1910
Edward D. White	Taft	1910–1921
William Howard Taft	Harding	1921–1930
Charles Evans Hughes	Hoover	1930–1941
Harlan Fiske Stone	F. Roosevelt	1941–1946
Fred M. Vinson	Truman	1946–1953
Earl Warren	Eisenhower	1953–1969
Warren E. Burger	Nixon	1969–1986
William H. Rehnquist	Reagan	1986–2005
John G. Roberts, Jr.	Bush	2005–present

Note: Omitted is John Rutledge, who served for only a few months in 1795 and who was not confirmed by the Senate.

© Cengage Learning

language of the Constitution. A liberal justice, Hugo Black, once voted to uphold a state law banning birth control because nothing in the Constitution prohibited such a law. Or judges can be conservative and still think they have a duty to use their best judgment in deciding what is good public policy. Rufus Peckham, one such conservative, voted to overturn a state law setting maximum hours of work because he believed the Fourteenth Amendment guaranteed something called "freedom of contract," even though those words are not in the amendment. Seventy years ago, judicial activists tended to be conservatives and strict-constructionist judges tended to be liberals; today the opposite usually is the case.

The Development of the Federal Courts

Most of the Founders probably expected the Supreme Court to have the power of judicial review (though they did not say that in so many words in the Constitution), but they did not expect federal courts to play so large a role in making public policy. The traditional view of civil courts was that they judged disputes between people who had direct dealings with each other—they had entered into a contract, for example, or one had dropped a load of bricks on the other's toe—and decided which of the two parties was right. The court then supplied relief to the wronged party, usually by requiring the other person to pay him or her money ("damages").

This traditional understanding was based on the belief that judges would find and apply existing law. The purpose of a court case was not to learn what the judge believes but what the law requires. The later rise of judicial activism occurred when judges questioned this traditional view and argued instead that judges do not merely find the law, they make the law.

The view that judges interpret the law, not make policy, made it easy for the Founders to justify the power of judicial review. It also led them to predict that the courts would play a relatively neutral, even passive, role in public affairs. Alexander Hamilton, writing in *Federalist* No. 78, described the judiciary as the branch "least dangerous" to political rights. The president is commander in chief and thus holds the "sword of the community"; Congress appropriates money and thus "commands the purse," as well as decides what laws shall govern. But the judiciary "has no influence over either the sword or the purse" and "can take no active resolution whatever." It has "neither force nor will but merely judgment," and thus is "beyond comparison the weakest of the three departments of power." As a result, "liberty can have nothing to fear from the judiciary alone." Hamilton went on to state clearly that the Constitution intended to give to the courts the right to decide whether a law is contrary to the Constitution. But this authority, he explained, was designed not to enlarge the power of the courts but to confine that of the legislature.

Obviously, things have changed since Hamilton's time. The evolution of the federal courts, especially the Supreme Court, toward the present level of activism and influence has been shaped by the political, economic, and ideological forces of three historical eras. From 1787 to 1865, nation building, the legitimacy of the federal government, and slavery were the great issues; from 1865 to 1937, the great issue was the relationship between the government and the economy; from 1938 to the present, the major issues confronting the Court have involved personal liberty and social equality and the potential conflict between the two. In the first period, the Court asserted the supremacy of the federal government; in the second, it placed important restrictions on the powers of that government; and in the third, it enlarged the scope of personal freedom and narrowed that of economic freedom.

National Supremacy and Slavery

"From 1789 until the Civil War, the dominant interest of the Supreme Court was in that greatest of all the questions left unresolved by the Founders—the nation-state relationship."[5] The answer the Court gave, under the leadership of Chief Justice John Marshall, was that national law was in all instances the dominant law, with state law having to give way, and that the Supreme Court had the power to decide what the Constitution meant. In two cases of enormous importance—*Marbury v. Madison* in 1803 and *McCulloch v. Maryland* in 1819—the Court, in decisions written by Marshall, held that the Supreme Court could declare an act of Congress unconstitutional; that the power granted by the Constitution to the federal government flows from the people and thus should be generously construed (and thus any federal laws that are "necessary and proper" to the attainment of constitutional ends are permissible); and that federal law is supreme over state law, even to the point that a state may not tax an enterprise (such as a bank) created by the federal government.[6]

The supremacy of the federal government was reaffirmed by other decisions as well. In 1816, the Supreme Court rejected the claim of the Virginia courts that the Supreme Court could not review the decisions of state courts. The Virginia courts were ready to acknowledge the supremacy of the U.S. Constitution but believed they had as much right as the U.S. Supreme Court to decide what the Constitution meant. The Supreme Court felt otherwise, and in this case and another like it, the Court asserted its own broad powers to review any state court decision if that decision seemed to violate federal law or the federal Constitution.[7]

The power of the federal government to regulate commerce among the states was also established. When New York gave to Robert Fulton—the inventor of the steamboat—the monopoly right to operate his steamboats on the rivers of that state, the Marshall Court overturned the license because the rivers connected New York and New Jersey and thus trade on those rivers would involve *inter*state commerce, and federal law in that area was supreme. Since there was a conflicting federal law on the books, the state law was void.[8]

All of this may sound rather obvious to us today, when the supremacy of the federal government is largely unquestioned. In the early 19th century, however, these were almost revolutionary decisions. The Jeffersonian Republicans were in power and had become increasingly devoted to states' rights; they were aghast at the Marshall decisions. President Andrew Jackson attacked the Court bitterly for defending the right of the federal government to create a national bank and for siding with the Cherokee Indians in a dispute with Georgia. In speaking of the latter case, Jackson is supposed to have remarked, "John Marshall has made his decision; now let him enforce it!"[9]

Though Marshall seemed to have secured the supremacy of the federal government over the state governments, another even more divisive issue had arisen; that, of course, was slavery. Roger B. Taney succeeded Marshall as chief justice in 1836. (See Table 12.3 on page 365 for a listing of all U.S. Chief Justices.) He was deliberately chosen by President Jackson because he was an advocate of states' rights, and he began to chip away at federal supremacy, upholding state claims that Marshall would have set aside. But the decision for which he is famous—or infamous—came in 1857 when, in the *Dred Scott* case, he wrote perhaps the most disastrous judicial opinion ever issued. A slave, Dred Scott, had been taken by his owner to a territory (near what is now St. Paul, Minnesota) where slavery was illegal under federal law. Scott claimed that since he had resided in a free territory, he was now a free man. Taney held that Negroes were not citizens of the United States and could not become so, and that the federal law—the Missouri Compromise—prohibiting slavery in Northern territories was unconstitutional.[10] The public outcry against this view was enormous, and the Court and Taney were discredited in the North, at least. The Civil War was ultimately fought over what the Court mistakenly had assumed was a purely legal question.

Government and the Economy

The supremacy of the federal government may have been established by John Marshall and the Civil War, but the scope of the powers of that government or even of the state governments was still to be defined. During the period from the end of the Civil War to the early years of the New Deal, the dominant issue the Supreme Court faced was deciding when the economy would be regulated by the states and when by the nation.

The Court revealed a strong though not inflexible attachment to private property. In fact, that attachment had always been there: the Founders thought political and property rights were inextricably linked, and Marshall certainly supported the sanctity of contracts. But now, with the muting of the federal supremacy issue and the rise of a national economy with important unanticipated effects, the property question became the dominant one. In general, the Court developed the view that the Fourteenth Amendment, adopted in 1868 primarily to protect African American claims to citizenship from hostile state action, also protected private property and the corporation from unreasonable state action. The crucial phrase was this: no state shall "deprive any person of life, liberty, or property, without due process of law." Once it became clear that a "person" could be a firm or a corporation as well as an individual, business and industry began to flood the courts with cases challenging various government regulations.

The Court quickly found itself in a thicket: it began ruling on the constitutionality of virtually every effort by any government to regulate any aspect of business or labor, and its workload rose sharply.

LANDMARK CASES

Marbury v. Madison

The story of *Marbury v. Madison* is often told, but it deserves another telling because it illustrates so many features of the role of the Supreme Court—how apparently small cases can have large results, how the power of the Court depends not simply on its constitutional authority, but also on its acting in ways that avoid a clear confrontation with other branches of government, and how the climate of opinion affects how the Court goes about its task.

When President John Adams lost his bid for re-election to Thomas Jefferson in 1800, he—and all members of his party, the Federalists—feared that Jefferson and the Republicans would weaken the federal government and turn its powers to what the Federalists believed were wrong ends (states' rights, an alliance with the French, hostility to business). Feverishly, as his hours in office came to an end, Adams worked to pack the judiciary with 59 loyal Federalists by giving them so-called midnight appointments before Jefferson took office.

John Marshall, as Adams's secretary of state, had the task of certifying and delivering these new judicial commissions. In the press of business, he delivered all but 17; these he left on his desk for the incoming secretary of state, James Madison, to send out. Jefferson and Madison, however, were furious at Adams's behavior and refused to deliver the 17. William Marbury and three other Federalists who had been promised these commissions hired a lawyer and brought suit against Madison to force him to produce the documents. The suit requested the Supreme Court to issue a writ of mandamus (from the Latin, "we command") ordering Madison to do his duty. The right to issue such writs had been given to the Court by the Judiciary Act of 1789.

Marshall, the man who had failed to deliver the commissions to Marbury and his friends in the first place, had become the chief justice and was now in a position to decide the case. These days, a justice who had been involved in an issue before it came to the Court would probably disqualify himself or herself, but Marshall had no intention of letting others decide this question. He faced, however, not simply a partisan dispute over jobs, but what was nearly a constitutional crisis. If he ordered the commission delivered, Madison might still refuse, and the Court had

(*continued*)

LANDMARK CASES (*Continued*)

no way—if Madison was determined to resist—to compel him. The Court had no police force, whereas Madison had the support of the president of the United States. And if the order were given, whether or not Madison complied, the Jeffersonian Republicans in Congress would probably try to impeach Marshall. On the other hand, if Marshall allowed Madison to do as he wished, the power of the Supreme Court would be seriously reduced.

Marshall's solution was ingenious. Speaking for a unanimous Court, he announced that Madison was wrong to withhold the commissions, that courts could issue writs to compel public officials to do their prescribed duty—*but* that the Supreme Court had no power to issue such writs in this case because the law (the Judiciary Act of 1789) giving it that power was unconstitutional. The law said the Supreme Court could issue such writs as part of its "original jurisdiction"—that is, persons seeking such writs could go *directly* to the Supreme Court with their request (rather than go first to a lower federal court and then, if dissatisfied, appeal to the Supreme Court). Article III of the Constitution, Marshall pointed out, spelled out precisely the Supreme Court's original jurisdiction; it did not mention issuing writs of this sort and plainly indicated that on all matters not mentioned in the Constitution, the Court would have only appellate jurisdiction. Congress may not change what the Constitution says; hence, the part of the Judiciary Act attempting to do this was null and void.

The result was that a showdown with the Jeffersonians was avoided—Madison was not ordered to deliver the commissions—but the power of the Supreme Court was unmistakably clarified and enlarged. As Marshall wrote, "It is emphatically the province and duty of the judicial department to say what the law is." Furthermore, "a law repugnant to the Constitution is void."

Judicial activism was born in the 1880s and 1890s as the Court set itself up as the arbiter of what kind of regulation was permissible. In the first 75 years of this country's history, only two federal laws were held to be unconstitutional; in the next 75 years, 71 were.[11] Of the roughly 1,300 state laws held to be in conflict with the federal Constitution since 1789, about 1,200 were overturned after 1870. In one decade alone—the 1880s—five federal and 48 state laws were declared unconstitutional.

Many of these decisions provided clear evidence of the Court's desire to protect private property: it upheld the use of injunctions to prevent labor strikes,[12] struck down the federal income tax,[13] sharply limited the reach of the antitrust law,[14] restricted the powers of the Interstate Commerce Commission to set railroad rates,[15] prohibited the federal government from eliminating child labor,[16] and prevented the states from setting maximum hours of work.[17] In 184 cases between 1899 and 1937, the Supreme Court struck down state laws for violating the Fourteenth Amendment, usually by economic regulation.[18]

But the Court also rendered decisions that authorized various kinds of regulation. It allowed states to regulate businesses "affected with a public interest,"[19] changed its mind about the Interstate Commerce Commission and allowed it to regulate railroad rates,[20] upheld rules requiring railroads to improve their safety,[21] approved state antiliquor laws,[22] approved state mine safety laws,[23] supported state workers' compensation laws,[24] allowed states to regulate fire-insurance rates,[25] and in time upheld a number of state laws regulating wages and hours. Indeed, between 1887 and 1910, in 558 cases involving the Fourteenth Amendment, the Supreme Court upheld state regulations over 80 percent of the time.[26]

To characterize the Court as pro-business or anti-regulation is both simplistic and inexact. More accurate, perhaps, is to characterize it as supportive of the rights of private property but unsure how to draw the lines that distinguish "reasonable" from "unreasonable" regulation. Nothing in the Constitution clearly differentiates reasonable from unreasonable regulation, and the Court has been able to invent no consistent principle of its own to make this determination. For example, what kinds of businesses are "affected with a public interest"? Grain elevators and railroads are, but are bakeries? Sugar refineries? Saloons? And how much of commerce is "interstate"—anything that moves? Or only something that actually crosses a state line? The Court found itself trying to make detailed judgments that it was not always competent to make and to invent legal rules where no clear legal rules were possible.

In one area, however, the Supreme Court's judgments were clear: the Fourteenth and Fifteenth Amendments were construed so narrowly as to give African Americans only the most limited benefits of their provisions. In a long series of decisions, the Court upheld segregation in schools and on railroad cars and permitted blacks to be excluded from voting in many states.

Government and Political Liberty

After 1936, the Supreme Court stopped imposing any serious restrictions on state or federal power to regulate the economy, leaving such matters in the hands of the legislatures. From 1937 to 1974, the Supreme Court did not overturn a single federal law designed to regulate business, but did overturn 36 congressional enactments that violated personal political liberties (see Figure 12.1 on page 372). It voided as unconstitutional laws that restricted freedom of speech,[27] denied passports to communists,[28] permitted the government to revoke a person's citizenship,[29] withheld a person's mail,[30] or restricted the availability of government benefits.[31]

This new direction began when one justice changed his mind, and it continued as the composition of the Court changed. At the outset of the New Deal, the Court was by a narrow margin dominated by justices who opposed the welfare state and federal regulation based on broad grants of discretionary authority to administrative agencies. President Franklin Roosevelt, who was determined to get just such legislation implemented, found himself powerless to alter the composition of the Court during his first term (1933–1937); because no justice died or retired, he had no vacancies to fill. After his overwhelming re-election in 1936, he moved to remedy this problem by "packing" the Court.

Roosevelt proposed a bill that would have allowed him to appoint one new justice for each one over the age of 70 who refused to retire, up to a total membership of 15. Since there were six men in this category then on the Supreme Court, he would have been able to appoint six new justices, enough to ensure a comfortable majority supportive of his economic policies. A bitter controversy ensued, but before the bill could be voted on, the Supreme Court, perhaps reacting to Roosevelt's big win in the 1936 election,

CONSTITUTIONAL CONNECTIONS

The "Exceptions" Clause

Article III, Section II of the Constitution provides that "the Supreme Court shall have appellate Jurisdiction, both as to Law and Fact, with such Exceptions, and under such Regulations as the Congress shall make." In the 1868 case of *Ex Parte McCardle*, the Court unanimously agreed that the "Exceptions" clause gives Congress the power to restrict the Court's appellate jurisdiction. Since then, many noted jurists and scholars have taken serious issue with that interpretation; but, the prevailing view is that, at least on an issue by issue basis, the

(continued)

CONSTITUTIONAL CONNECTIONS
(*Continued*)

exceptions clause gives Congress broad, if not unlimited, power to prohibit the federal courts, including the Supreme Court, from exercising judicial review.

Over the last several decades, each session of Congress has witnessed proposals to deny the federal courts appellate jurisdiction. There have been such proposals on abortion rights, busing to achieve racial balance in schools, school prayer, prisoners' rights, same-sex marriage, and many other issues. Some exception-clause proposals have become bills and made it into federal law; for example, the Illegal Immigration Reform and Immigrant Responsibility Act of 1996 prohibited the federal courts from hearing appeals regarding

certain decisions by the U.S. Immigration and Naturalization Service.

Typically, however, even exception-clause-related bills that come to a vote never make it into law. For example, in each of several post-2000 sessions, the House approved a bill prohibiting federal courts from exercising appellate jurisdiction in cases involving the invocation of "under God" in the Pledge of Allegiance. But none of these bills made it through the Senate. Likewise, in 2011, Rep. Ron Paul (R-TX) sponsored the Sanctity of Life Act, which would have stripped the federal courts of the authority to hear abortion cases; but that was just the latest in a series of such exception-clause bills on abortion that were much-debated but never enacted.

changed its mind. Whereas it had been striking down several New Deal measures by votes of 5 to 4, now it started approving them by the same vote (see Figure 12.1 on page 372). One justice, Owen Roberts, had switched his position. This was called the "switch in time that saved nine," but in fact Roberts had changed his mind *before* the FDR plan was announced.

The "Court-packing" bill was not passed, but it was no longer necessary. Justice Roberts had yielded before public opinion in a way that Chief Justice Taney a century earlier had not, thus forestalling an assault on the Court by the other branches of government. Shortly thereafter, several justices stepped down, and Roosevelt was able to make his own appointments (he filled seven seats during his four terms in office). From then on, the Court turned its attention to new issues—political liberties and, in time, civil rights.

With the arrival in office of Chief Justice Earl Warren in 1953, the Court began its most active period yet. Activism now arose to redefine the relationship of citizens to the government and

LANDMARK CASES

Power of the Supreme Court

- *Marbury v. Madison* (1803): Upheld judicial review of congressional acts.

- *Martin v. Hunter's Lessee* (1816): The Supreme Court can review the decisions of the highest state courts if they involve a federal law or the federal Constitution.

- *McCulloch v. Maryland* (1819): Ruled that creating a federal bank, though not mentioned in the Constitution, was a "necessary and proper" exercise of the government's right to borrow money.

- *Ex parte McCardle* (1869): Allowed Congress to change the appellate jurisdiction of the Supreme Court.

especially to protect the rights and liberties of citizens from governmental trespass. Although the Court has always seen itself as protecting citizens from arbitrary government, before 1937 that protection was of a sort that conservatives preferred; after 1937, it was of a kind that liberals preferred. Figure 12.1 traces the trends in Supreme Court rulings in the 20th century and into the 21st.

The Revival of State Sovereignty

For many decades, the Supreme Court allowed Congress to pass almost any law authorized by the Constitution, no matter how it affected the states. As we saw in Chapter 3, the Court had long held that Congress could regulate almost any activity if it affected interstate commerce, and in the Court's opinion virtually every activity did affect it. The states were left with few rights to challenge federal power. But since around 1992, the Court has backed away from this view. By narrow majorities, it has begun to restore the view that states have the right to resist some forms of federal action.

When Congress passed a bill that forbade anyone from carrying a gun near a school, the Court held that carrying guns did not affect interstate commerce, and so the law was invalid.[32] One year later, it

FIGURE 12.1 **Economics and Civil Liberties Laws Overturned by the U.S. Supreme Court, by Decade, 1900–2006**

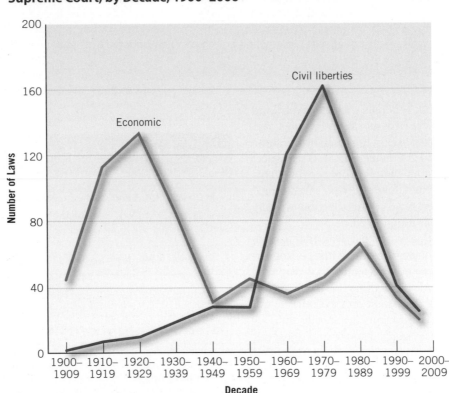

Note: Civil liberties category does not include laws supportive of civil liberties. Laws include federal, state, and local.

Source: Data adapted from Harold W. Stanley and Richard G. Niemi, *Vital Statistics on American Politics*, 2007–2008, 5th ed., p. 302 (Washington, D. C.: CQ Press, 2008).

struck down a law that allowed Indian tribes to sue the states in federal courts, arguing that Congress lacks the power to ignore the "sovereign immunity" of states—that is, the right, protected by the Eleventh Amendment, not to be sued in federal court. (It has since upheld that view in two more cases.) And the next year, it held that the Brady gun control law could not be used to require local law enforcement officers to do background checks on people trying to buy weapons.[33] These cases are all hints that there are some real limits to the supremacy of the federal government created by the existence and powers of the several states.

After the enactment of President Obama's health care plan in 2010, several states argued that its requirement that everyone purchase health insurance was unconstitutional. Some district courts agreed with the claims and others disagreed. The issue was whether Congress's authority to levy taxes or to regulate interstate commerce gave it the right to require citizens to purchase a product. In addition, some state officials questioned the constitutionality of provisions requiring state governments to expand health care coverage for low-income citizens via the federal–state Medicaid program or risk losing all existing federal funding for that program.

In *National Federation of Independent Business v. Sebelius* (2012), the Supreme Court decided these issues. It upheld the law's "individual mandate" to purchase "minimum essential" health insurance, ruling that the monetary "penalty" to be levied by the Internal Revenue Service on anyone that does not purchase insurance as required by the law is tantamount to a constitutionally permissible federal "tax."

But, in the same decision, the Court struck down the law's mandate that state governments expand Medicaid coverage by 2014, ruling that the provision "violates the Constitution" by impermissibly "threatening States with the loss of their existing" federal funding for the program. This part of the decision had important consequences for the law's implementation (see the "States and 'Health Exchanges'" feature on page 53), and it could in time have far-reaching implications for how the federal courts handle cases concerning intergovernmental programs (see Chapter 3):

> *Congress has no authority to order the States to regulate according to its instructions. Congress may offer the States grants and require the States to comply with accompanying conditions, but the States must have a genuine choice whether to comply.*

constitutional court A federal court authorized by Article III of the Constitution that keeps judges in office during good behavior and prevents their salaries from being reduced. They are the Supreme Court (created by the Constitution) and appellate and district courts created by Congress.

district courts The lowest federal courts; federal trials can be held only here.

courts of appeals Federal courts that hear appeals from district courts; no trials.

The Structure of the Federal Courts

The only federal court the Constitution requires is the Supreme Court, as specified in Article III. All other federal courts and their jurisdictions are creations of Congress. Nor does the Constitution indicate how many justices shall be on the Supreme Court (there were originally six, now there are nine) or what its appellate jurisdiction shall be.

Congress has created two kinds of lower federal courts to handle cases that need not be decided by the Supreme Court: constitutional and legislative courts. A **constitutional court** is one exercising the judicial powers found in Article III of the Constitution, and therefore its judges are given constitutional protection: they may not be fired (they serve during "good behavior"), nor may their salaries be reduced while they are in office. The most important of the constitutional courts are the **district courts** (a total of 94, with at least one in each state, the District of Columbia, and the commonwealth of Puerto Rico) and the **courts of appeals** (one in each of 11 regions, plus one in the District of Columbia and

> **Legislative courts** Courts created by Congress for specialized purposes whose judges do not enjoy the protections of Article III of the Constitution.

one federal circuit). There are also various specialized constitutional courts, such as the Court of International Trade.

Legislative courts are those set up by Congress for some specialized purpose and staffed with people who have fixed terms of office and can be removed or have their salaries reduced. Legislative courts include the Court of Military Appeals and the territorial courts.

Selecting Judges

Party background makes a difference in how judges behave. An analysis has been done of more than 80 studies of the link between party and either liberalism or conservatism among state and federal judges in cases involving civil liberties, criminal justice, and economic regulation. It shows that judges who are Democrats are more likely to make liberal decisions and Republican judges are more likely to make conservative ones.* The party effect is not small.[34] We should not be surprised by this, since we have

---

*A "liberal" decision is one that favors a civil right, a criminal defendant, or an economic regulation; a "conservative" one opposes the right or the regulation or supports the criminal prosecutor.

MAP 12.1   U.S. District and Appellate Courts

State boundaries
Circuit boundaries
District boundaries

Source: Administrative Office of the United States Courts (January 1983).

Note: Washington, D.C., is in a separate court. Puerto Rico is in the first circuit; the Virgin Islands are in the third; Guam and the Northern Mariana Islands are in the ninth. The Court of Appeals for the Federal Circuit, located in Washington, D.C., is a Title 3 court that hears appeals regarding patents, trademarks, international trade, government contracts, and from civil servants who claim they were unjustly discharged.

already seen that among political elites (and judges are certainly elites), party identification influences personal ideology.

But ideology does not entirely determine behavior. So many other things shape court decisions—the facts of the case, prior rulings by other courts, the arguments presented by lawyers—that there is no reliable way of predicting how judges will behave in all matters. Presidents sometimes make the mistake of thinking they know how their appointees will behave, only to be surprised by the facts. Theodore Roosevelt appointed Oliver Wendell Holmes to the Supreme Court, only to remark later, after Holmes had voted in a way that Roosevelt did not like, that "I could carve out of a banana a judge with more backbone than that!" Holmes, who had plenty of backbone, said he did not "give a damn" what Roosevelt thought. Richard Nixon, an ardent foe of court-ordered school busing, appointed Warren Burger chief justice. Burger promptly sat down and wrote the opinion upholding busing. Another Nixon appointee, Harry Blackmun, wrote the opinion declaring the right to an abortion to be constitutionally protected.

Federal judges tend to be white, male, and Protestant, and increasingly have been judges on some other court. There has been a decline in the proportion of Supreme Court justices who come directly from private law practice;

Louis Brandeis, creator of the "Brandeis Brief" that developed court cases based on economic and social arguments more than legal ones became the first Jewish Supreme Court justice. He served in the Court from 1916 until 1939.

almost all have been promoted from a lower-ranking judgeship. For example, of the nine justices chosen by President Franklin D. Roosevelt, only two had been judges, while of the 12 nominated by presidents Ronald Reagan, George H. W. Bush, Bill Clinton, George W. Bush, and Barack Obama, 10 had been judges. Sex, race, and ethnicity also have become important factors in selecting judges. (See Table 12.4 on page 384 for a listing of the Supreme Court justices in order of seniority.) As is evident in Figure 12.2, Democratic presidents since President Lyndon Johnson have appointed higher percentages of women, blacks, and Hispanics than Republican presidents have, including a record-shattering fraction of female appointees during President Obama's first term.

Senatorial Courtesy In theory, the president nominates a "qualified" person to be a judge, and the Senate approves or rejects the nomination based on those "qualifications." In fact, the tradition of *senatorial courtesy* gives heavy weight to the preferences of the senators from the state where a federal district judge is to serve. Ordinarily, the Senate will not confirm a district court judge if the senior senator from the state where the district is located objects (if he is of the president's party). The senator can exercise this veto power by means of the "blue slip"—a blue piece of paper on which the senator is asked to record his or her views on the nominee. A negative opinion, or even failure to return the blue slip, usually kills the nomination. This means that as a practical matter the president nominates only persons recommended to him by that key senator. Someone once suggested that, at least with respect to district judges, the Constitution has been turned on its head. To reflect reality, he said, Article II, section 2, ought to read: "The senators shall nominate, and by and with the consent of the President, shall appoint" federal judges.

The "Litmus Test" Of late, presidents have tried to exercise more influence on the selection of federal district and appellate court judges by getting the Justice Department to find candidates that not only are supported by their party's senators, but also reflect the political and judicial philosophy of the president. Presidents Carter and Clinton sought out liberal, activist judges; President Reagan sought out conservative, strict-constructionist ones. The party membership of federal judges makes a difference in how they vote.[35]

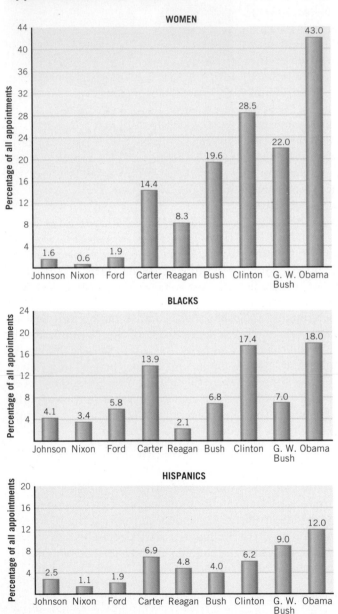

FIGURE 12.2 **Female and Minority Judicial Appointments, 1963–2013**

WOMEN

Source: Updated from Harold W. Stanley and Richard G. Niemi, *Vital Statistics on American Politics, 2005–2006* (Washington, D.C.: Congressional Quarterly, 2006), Table 7.5.

Because different courts of appeals have different combinations of judges, some will be more liberal than others. For example, there are more liberal judges in the court of appeals for the ninth circuit (which includes most of the far western states) and more conservative ones in the fifth circuit (Texas, Louisiana, and Mississippi). The ninth circuit takes liberal positions, the fifth more conservative ones. Since the Supreme Court does not have time to settle every disagreement among appeals courts, different interpretations of the law may exist in different circuits. In the fifth, for instance, it was for a while unconstitutional for state universities to have affirmative action programs, but in the ninth circuit that was permitted.

These differences make some people worry about the use of a political **litmus test**—a test of ideological purity—in selecting judges. When conservatives are out of power, they complain about how liberal presidents use such a test; when liberals are out of power, they complain about how conservative presidents use it. Many people would like to see judges picked on the basis of professional qualifications, without reference to ideology, but the courts are now so deeply involved in political issues that it is hard to imagine what an ideologically neutral set of professional qualifications might be.

A judicial nominee's view on abortion is the chief motive for using the litmus test. Since it is easy to mount a filibuster and it takes 60 votes to end one, the nominee usually must be assured of 60 Senate votes to be confirmed. In theory, the Senate could adopt a rule preventing filibusters of nominations—but it never has. In 2005, a group of 14 senators, half from each party, agreed they would vote to block a filibuster on court nominees unless there were "extraordinary circumstances." This group—called the Gang of Fourteen—made it possible for several nominees (including Samuel Alito) to be confirmed even though they had fewer than 60 votes (but still, of course, more than 50).

> **litmus test** An examination of the political ideology of a nominated judge.
>
> **federal-question cases** Cases concerning the Constitution, federal laws, or treaties.
>
> **diversity cases** Cases involving citizens of different states who can bring suit in federal courts.

The litmus test issue is of greatest importance in selecting Supreme Court justices. Here, there is no tradition of senatorial courtesy. The president takes a keen personal interest in the choices and, of late, has sought to find nominees who share his philosophy. In the Reagan administration, there were bruising fights in the Senate over the nomination of William Rehnquist to be chief justice (he won) and Robert Bork to be an associate justice (he lost), with liberals pitted against conservatives. When President George H. W. Bush nominated David Souter, there were lengthy hearings as liberal senators tried to pin down Souter's views on issues such as abortion. Souter refused to discuss matters on which he might later have to judge, however. Clarence Thomas, another Bush nominee, also tried to avoid the litmus test by saying he had not formed an opinion on prominent abortion cases. In his case, however, the litmus test issue was overshadowed by sensational allegations from a former employee, Anita Hill, that Thomas had sexually harassed her.

Of the 160 Supreme Court nominees presented to it, the Senate failed to confirm 36 of them. From the presidency of Harry Truman through the first term of President Barack Obama, 29 of 34 nominees have been confirmed. Of the five that were not confirmed, three (two nominated by President Richard Nixon, and one nominated by President Ronald Reagan) were voted on and rejected by a Senate majority, and two (one nominated by President Lyndon Johnson, and one nominated by President George W. Bush) withdrew before any Senate vote on the nomination. The reasons for rejecting a Supreme Court nominee are complex—each senator may have a different reason—but have involved such matters as the nominee's alleged hostility to civil rights, questionable personal financial dealings, a poor record as a lower-court judge, and Senate opposition to the nominee's political or legal philosophy. As we indicated earlier, nominations of district court judges are rarely defeated, because typically no nomination is made unless the key senators approve in advance.

The Jurisdiction of the Federal Courts

We have a dual court system—one state, one federal—and this complicates enormously the task of describing what kinds of cases federal courts may hear and how cases beginning in the state courts may end up before the Supreme Court. The Constitution lists the kinds of cases over which federal courts have jurisdiction (in Article III and the Eleventh Amendment) by implication; all other matters are left to state courts. Federal courts (see Figure 12.3) can hear all cases "arising under the Constitution, the laws of the United States, and treaties" (these are **federal-question cases**), and cases involving citizens of different states (called **diversity cases**).

Some kinds of cases can be heard in either federal or state courts. For example, if citizens of different states wish to sue one another and the matter involves more than $75,000, they can do so in either a federal or a state court. Similarly, if someone robs a federally insured bank, he or she has broken both state and federal law and thus can be prosecuted in state or federal courts, or both. Lawyers have become quite sophisticated in deciding whether, in a given civil case, their clients will get better treatment in a state or federal court. Prosecutors often send a person who has broken both federal and state law to whichever court system is likelier to give the toughest penalty.

FIGURE 12.3 The Jurisdiction of the Federal Courts

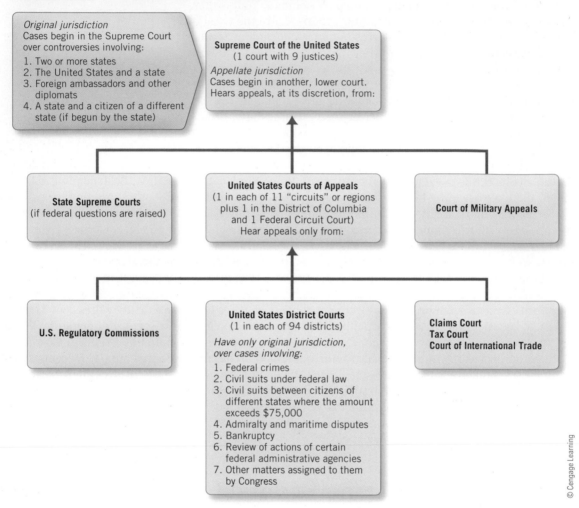

Original jurisdiction
Cases begin in the Supreme Court over controversies involving:

1. Two or more states
2. The United States and a state
3. Foreign ambassadors and other diplomats
4. A state and a citizen of a different state (if begun by the state)

Supreme Court of the United States
(1 court with 9 justices)
Appellate jurisdiction
Cases begin in another, lower court. Hears appeals, at its discretion, from:

State Supreme Courts
(if federal questions are raised)

United States Courts of Appeals
(1 in each of 11 "circuits" or regions plus 1 in the District of Columbia and 1 Federal Circuit Court)
Hear appeals only from:

Court of Military Appeals

U.S. Regulatory Commissions

United States District Courts
(1 in each of 94 districts)
Have only original jurisdiction, over cases involving:

1. Federal crimes
2. Civil suits under federal law
3. Civil suits between citizens of different states where the amount exceeds $75,000
4. Admiralty and maritime disputes
5. Bankruptcy
6. Review of actions of certain federal administrative agencies
7. Other matters assigned to them by Congress

Claims Court
Tax Court
Court of International Trade

© Cengage Learning

Sometimes defendants may be tried in both state and federal courts for the same offense. In 1992, four Los Angeles police officers accused of beating Rodney King were tried in a California state court and acquitted of assault charges. They were then prosecuted in federal court for violating King's civil rights. This time, two of the four were convicted. Under the dual sovereignty doctrine, state and federal authorities can prosecute the same person for the same conduct. The Supreme Court has upheld this doctrine on two grounds: first, each level of government has the right to enact laws serving its own purposes.[36] As a result, federal civil rights charges could have been brought against the officers even if they had already been convicted of assault in state court (though as a practical matter this would have been unlikely). Second, neither level of government wants the other to be able to block prosecution of an accused person who has the sympathy of the authorities at one level. For example, when certain Southern state courts were in sympathy with whites who had lynched blacks, the absence of the dual sovereignty doctrine would have meant that a trumped-up acquittal in state court would have barred federal prosecution.

Furthermore, a matter that is exclusively within the province of a state court—for example, a criminal case in which the defendant is charged with violating only a state law—can be appealed to the U.S. Supreme Court under certain circumstances (described below). Thus federal judges can overturn state court rulings even when they had no jurisdiction over the original matter. Under what circumstances this should occur has been the subject of long-standing controversy between the state and federal courts.

Sonia Sotomayor answers questions before a Senate committee after her nomination to be a Supreme Court justice, which the Senate approved, in 2009.

Some matters, however, are exclusively under the jurisdiction of federal courts. When a federal criminal law is broken—but not a state one—the case is heard in federal district court. If you wish to appeal the decision of a federal regulatory agency, such as the Federal Communications Commission, you can do so only before a federal court of appeals. And if you wish to declare bankruptcy, you do so in federal court. If there is a controversy between two state governments—say, California and Arizona sue each other over which state is to use how much water from the Colorado River—the case can be heard only by the Supreme Court.

The vast majority of all cases heard by federal courts begin in the district courts. The volume of business there is huge. In 2009, the 667 district court judges received 276,397 cases (more than 400 per judge). Most of the cases heard in federal courts involve rather straightforward applications of law; few lead to the making of new public policy. Cases that do affect how the law or the Constitution is interpreted can begin with seemingly minor events. For example, a major broadening of the Bill of Rights—requiring for the first time that all accused persons in *state* as well as federal criminal trials be supplied with a lawyer, free if necessary—began when impoverished Clarence Earl Gideon, imprisoned in Florida, wrote an appeal in pencil on prison stationery and sent it to the Supreme Court.[37]

The Supreme Court does not have to hear any appeal it does not want to hear. At one time, it was required to listen to certain appeals, but Congress has changed the law so that now the Court can pick the cases it wants to consider. It does this by issuing a **writ of certiorari**. *Certiorari* is a Latin word meaning, roughly, "made more certain"; lawyers and judges have abbreviated it to *cert*. It works this way: the Court considers all the petitions it receives to review lower-court decisions. If four justices agree to hear a case, cert is issued and the case is scheduled for a hearing.

In deciding whether to grant certiorari, the Court tries to reserve its time for cases decided by lower federal courts or by the highest state courts in which a significant federal or constitutional question has been raised. For example, the Court often will grant certiorari when one or both of the following is true:

Two or more federal circuit courts of appeals have decided the same issue in different ways.

The highest court in a state has held a federal or state law to be in violation of the Constitution or has upheld a state law against the claim that it is in violation of the Constitution.

writ of certiorari An order by a higher court directing a lower court to send up a case for review.

In a typical year, the Court may consider more than 7,000 petitions asking it to review decisions of lower or state courts. It rarely accepts more than about 100 of them for full review.

In exercising its discretion in granting certiorari, the Supreme Court is on the horns of a dilemma. If it grants it frequently, it will be inundated with cases. As it is, the Court's workload has quintupled in the last 50 years. If, on the other hand, the Court grants certiorari only rarely, then the federal courts of appeals have the last word on the interpretation of the Constitution and federal laws, and since there are 12 of these, staffed by about 167 judges, they may well be in disagreement. In fact this has already happened: because the Supreme Court reviews only about 1 or 2 percent of appeals court cases, applicable federal law may be different in different parts of the country.[38] One proposal to deal with this dilemma is to devote the Supreme Court's time entirely to major questions of constitutional interpretation and to create a national court of appeals that would ensure that the 12 circuit courts of appeals are producing uniform decisions.[39]

Because the Supreme Court has a heavy workload, the influence wielded by law clerks has grown. These clerks—recent graduates of law schools hired by the justices—play a big role in deciding which cases should be heard under a writ of certiorari. Indeed, some of the opinions written by the justices are drafted by the clerks. Since the reasons for a decision may be as important as the decision itself, and since these reasons are sometimes created by the clerks, the power of the clerks can be significant.

Getting to Court

In theory, the courts are the great equalizer in the federal government. To use the courts to settle a question, or even to fundamentally alter the accepted interpretation of the Constitution, one need not be elected to any office, have access to the mass media, be a member of an interest group, or be otherwise powerful or rich. Once the contending parties are before the courts, they are legally equal.

It is too easy to believe this theory uncritically or to dismiss it cynically. In fact, it is hard to get before the Supreme Court: it rejects over 96 percent of the applications for certiorari that it receives. And the costs involved in getting to the Court can be high. To apply for certiorari costs only $300 (plus 40 copies of the petition), but if certiorari is granted and the case is heard, the costs—for lawyers and for copies of the lower-court records in the case—can be very high. And by then one has already paid for the cost of the first hearing in the district court and probably one appeal to the circuit court of appeals. Furthermore, the time it takes to settle a matter in federal court can be quite long.

But there are ways to make these costs lower. If you are indigent—without funds—you can file and be heard as a pauper for nothing; about half the petitions arriving before the Supreme Court are **in forma pauperis** (such as the one from Gideon, described earlier). If your case began as a criminal trial in the district courts and you are poor, the government will supply you with a lawyer at no charge. If the matter is not a criminal case and you cannot afford to hire a lawyer, interest groups representing a wide spectrum of opinion sometimes are willing to take up the cause if the issue in the case seems sufficiently important. The American Civil Liberties Union (ACLU), a liberal group, represents some people who believe their freedom of speech has been abridged or their constitutional rights in criminal proceedings have been violated. The Center for Individual Rights, a conservative group, represents some people who feel that they have been victimized by racial quotas.

in forma pauperis A method whereby a poor person can have his or her case heard in federal court without charge.

But interest groups do much more than just help people pay their bills. Many of the most important cases decided by the Court got there because an interest group organized the case, found the plaintiffs, chose the legal strategy, and mobilized legal allies. The NAACP has brought many key civil rights cases on behalf of individuals. Although in the past most such cases were brought by liberal interest groups, of late conservative interest groups have entered the courtroom on behalf of individuals. One helped sue CBS for televising a program that allegedly libeled General William Westmoreland, once the American commander in Vietnam. (Westmoreland lost the case.) And many important issues are raised by attorneys representing state and local governments. Several price-fixing cases have been won by state attorneys general on behalf of consumers in their states.

fee shifting A rule that allows a plaintiff to recover costs from the defendant if the plaintiff wins.

plaintiff The party that initiates a lawsuit.

standing A legal rule stating who is authorized to start a lawsuit.

Fee Shifting

Unlike what happens in most of Europe, each party to a lawsuit in this country must pay its own way. (In England, by contrast, if you sue someone and lose, you pay the winner's costs as well as your own.) But various laws have made it easier to get someone else to pay. **Fee shifting** enables the **plaintiff** (the party that initiates the suit) to collect its costs from the defendant if the defendant loses, at least in certain kinds of cases. For example, if a corporation is found to have violated the antitrust laws, it must pay the legal fees of the winner. If an environmentalist group sues the Environmental Protection Agency and wins, it can get the EPA to pay the group's legal costs. Even more important to individuals, Section 1983 of Chapter 42 of the *United States Code* allows a citizen to sue a state or local government official—say, a police officer or a school superintendent—who has deprived the citizen of some constitutional right or withheld some benefit to which the citizen is entitled. If the citizen wins, he or she can collect money damages and lawyers' fees from the government. Citizens, more aware of their legal rights, have become more litigious, and a flood of such "Section 1983" suits has burdened the courts. The Supreme Court has restricted fee shifting to cases authorized by statute,[40] but it is clear that the drift of policy has made it cheaper to go to court—at least for some cases.

Standing

There is, in addition, a nonfinancial restriction on getting into federal court. To sue, one must have **standing**, a legal concept that refers to who is entitled to bring a case. It is especially important in determining who can challenge the laws or actions of the government itself. A complex and changing set of rules governs standings; some of the more important ones are these:

- There must be an actual controversy between real adversaries. (You cannot bring a "friendly" suit against someone, hoping to lose in order to prove your friend right. You cannot ask a federal court for an opinion on a hypothetical or imaginary case or ask it to render an advisory opinion.)

- You must show that you have been harmed by the law or practice about which you are complaining. (It is not enough to dislike what the government or a corporation or a labor union does; you must show that you were actually harmed by that action.)

- Merely being a taxpayer does not ordinarily entitle you to challenge the constitutionality of a federal governmental action. (You may not want your tax money to be spent in certain ways, but your remedy is to vote against the politicians doing the spending; the federal courts will generally require that you show some other personal harm before you can sue.)

Congress and the courts have recently made it easier to acquire standing. It has always been the rule that a citizen could ask the courts to order federal officials to carry out some act that they were under a legal

sovereign immunity The rule that a citizen cannot sue the government without the government's consent.

class-action suit A case brought by someone to help both himself or herself and all others who are similarly situated.

obligation to perform or to refrain from some action that was contrary to law. A citizen can also sue a government official personally to collect damages if the official acted contrary to law. For example, it was for long the case that if an FBI agent broke into your office without a search warrant, you could sue the agent and, if you won, collect money. However, you cannot sue the government itself without its consent. This is the doctrine of **sovereign immunity**. For instance, if the army accidentally kills your cow while testing a new cannon, you cannot sue the government to recover the cost of the cow unless the government agrees to be sued. (Since testing cannons is legal, you cannot sue the army officer who fired the cannon.) By statute, Congress has given its consent for the government to be sued in many cases involving a dispute over a contract or damage done as a result of negligence (for example, the dead cow). Over the years, these statutes have made it easier to take the government into court as a defendant.

Even some of the oldest rules defining standing have been liberalized. The rule that merely being a taxpayer does not entitle you to challenge in court a government decision has been relaxed where the citizen claims that a right guaranteed under the First Amendment is being violated. The Supreme Court allowed a taxpayer to challenge a federal law that would have given financial aid to parochial (or church-related) schools on the grounds that this aid violated the constitutional requirement of separation between church and state. On the other hand, another taxpayer suit to force the CIA to make public its budget failed because the Court decided that the taxpayer did not have standing in matters of this sort.[41]

Class-Action Suits

Under certain circumstances, a citizen can benefit directly from a court decision, even though the citizen himself or herself has not gone into court. This can happen by means of a **class-action suit**: a case brought into court by a person on behalf not only of himself or herself, but of all other persons in similar circumstances. Among the most famous of these was the 1954 case in which the Supreme Court found that Linda Brown, a black girl attending the fifth grade in the Topeka, Kansas, public schools, was denied the equal protection of the laws (guaranteed under the Fourteenth Amendment) because the schools in Topeka were segregated. The Court did not limit its decision to Linda Brown's right to attend an unsegregated school but extended it—as Brown's lawyers from the NAACP had asked—to cover all "others similarly situated."[42] It was not easy to design a court order that would eliminate segregation in the schools, but the principle was clearly established in this class action.

Since the *Brown* case, many other groups have been quick to take advantage of the opportunity created by class-action suits. By this means, the courts could be used to give relief not simply to a particular person but to all those represented in the suit. A landmark class-action case challenged the malapportionment of state legislative districts.[43] There are thousands of class-action suits in the federal courts involving civil rights, the rights of prisoners, antitrust suits against corporations, and other matters. These suits became more common partly because people were beginning to have new concerns that were not being met by Congress and partly because some class-action suits became quite profitable. The NAACP got no money from Linda Brown or from the Topeka Board of Education in compensation for its long and expensive labors, but, beginning in the 1960s, court rules were changed to make it financially attractive for lawyers to bring certain kinds of class-action suits.

Suppose, for example, that you think your telephone company overcharged you by $75. You could try to hire a lawyer to get a refund, but not many lawyers would take the case, because there would be no money in it. Even if you were to win, the lawyer would stand to earn no more than perhaps one-third of the settlement, or $25. Now suppose you bring a class action against the company on behalf of everybody who was overcharged. Millions of dollars might be at stake; lawyers would line up eagerly to take the case, because their share of the settlement, if they won, would be huge. The opportunity to win profitable class-action suits, combined with the possibility of having the loser pay the attorneys' fees, led to a proliferation of such cases.

In response to the increase in its workload, the Supreme Court decided in 1974 to drastically tighten the rules governing these suits. It held that it would no longer hear (except in certain cases defined by Congress, such as civil rights matters) class-action suits seeking monetary damages unless each and every ascertainable member of the class was individually notified of the case. To do this often is prohibitively expensive (imagine trying to find and send a letter to every customer that may have been overcharged by the telephone company!), and so the number of such cases declined and the number of lawyers seeking them out dropped.[44]

But it remains easy to bring a class-action suit in most state courts. State Farm automobile insurance company was told by a state judge in a small Illinois town that it must pay over $1 billion in damages on behalf of a "national" class, even though no one in this class had been notified. Big class-action suits powerfully affect how courts make public policy. Such suits have forced into bankruptcy companies making asbestos and silicone breast implants and have threatened to put out of business tobacco companies and gun manufacturers. (Ironically, in some of these cases, such as the one involving breast implants, there was no scientific evidence showing that the product was harmful.) Some class-action suits, such as the one ending school segregation, are good, but others are frivolous efforts to get companies to pay large fees to the lawyers who file the suits.

Linda Brown was refused admission to a white elementary school in Topeka, Kansas. On her behalf, the NAACP brought a class-action suit that resulted in the 1954 landmark Supreme Court decision Brown v. Board of Education.

Carl Iwasaki/Time Life Pictures/Getty Images

In sum, getting into court depends on having standing and having resources. The rules governing standing are complex and changing, but generally they have been broadened to make it easier to enter the federal courts, especially for the purpose of challenging the actions of the government. Obtaining the resources is not easy, but has become easier because laws in some cases now provide for fee shifting, private interest groups are willing to finance cases, and it is sometimes possible to bring a class-action suit that lawyers find lucrative.

The Supreme Court in Action

If your case should find its way to the Supreme Court—and of course the odds are that it will not—you will be able to participate in one of the more impressive, sometimes dramatic ceremonies of American public life. The Court is in session in its white marble building for 36 weeks out of each year, from early October until the end of June. The nine justices read briefs in their individual offices, hear oral arguments in the stately courtroom, and discuss their decisions with one another in a conference room where no outsider is ever allowed.

brief A written statement by an attorney that summarizes a case and the laws and rulings that support it.

amicus curiae A brief submitted by a "friend of the court."

Most cases, as we have seen, come to the Court on a writ of certiorari. The lawyers for each side may then submit their briefs. A **brief** is a document that sets forth the facts of the case, summarizes the lower-court decision, gives the arguments for the side represented by the lawyer who wrote the brief, and discusses the other cases that the Court has decided bear on the issue. Then the lawyers are allowed to present their oral arguments in open court. They usually summarize their briefs or emphasize particular points in them, and they are strictly limited in time—usually to no more than a half hour. (The lawyer speaks from a lectern that has two lights on it. When the white light goes on, the attorney has five minutes remaining; when the red flashes, he or she must stop—instantly.) The oral arguments give the justices a chance to question the lawyers, sometimes searchingly.

Since the federal government is a party—as either plaintiff or defendant—to about half the cases that the Supreme Court hears, the government's top trial lawyer, the solicitor general of the United States, appears frequently before the Court. The solicitor general is the third-ranking officer of the Department of Justice, right after the attorney general and deputy attorney general. The solicitor general decides what cases the government will appeal from lower courts and personally approves every case the government presents to the Supreme Court. In recent years, the solicitor general often has been selected from the ranks of distinguished law school professors.

In addition to the arguments made by lawyers for the two sides in a case, written briefs and even oral arguments may also be offered by "a friend of the court," or **amicus curiae**. An amicus brief is from an interested party not directly involved in the suit. For example, when Allan Bakke complained that he had been the victim of "reverse discrimination" when he was denied admission to a University of California medical school, 58 amicus briefs were filed supporting or opposing his position. Before such briefs can be filed, both parties must agree or the Court must grant permission. Though these briefs sometimes offer new arguments, they are really a kind of polite lobbying of the Court that declare which interest groups are on which side. The ACLU, the NAACP, the AFL-CIO, and the U.S. government itself have been among the leading sources of such briefs.

These briefs are not the only source of influence on the justices' views. Legal periodicals such as the *Harvard Law Review* and the *Yale Law Journal* are frequently consulted, and citations to them often

TABLE 12.4   Supreme Court Justices in Order of Seniority

Name (Birth Date)	Home State	Prior Experience	Appointed by (Year)
John G. Roberts, Jr., Chief Justice (1955)	Maryland	Federal judge	G. W. Bush (2005)
Antonin Scalia (1936)	Virginia	Federal judge	Reagan (1986)
Anthony Kennedy (1936)	California	Federal judge	Reagan (1988)
Clarence Thomas (1948)	Georgia	Federal judge	G. H. W. Bush (1991)
Ruth Bader Ginsburg (1933)	New York	Federal judge	Clinton (1993)
Stephen Breyer (1938)	Massachusetts	Federal judge	Clinton (1994)
Samuel Alito (1950)	New Jersey	Federal judge	G. W. Bush (2006)
Sonia Sotomayor (1954)	New York	Federal judge	Obama (2009)
Elena Kagan (1960)	New York	Law school dean	Obama (2010)

appear in the Court's decisions. Thus the outside world of lawyers and law professors can help shape, or at least supply arguments for, the conclusions of the justices.

The justices retire every Friday to their conference room, where in complete secrecy they debate the cases they have heard. The chief justice speaks first, followed by the other justices in order of seniority. After the arguments they vote, traditionally in reverse order of seniority: the newest justice votes first, the chief justice last. By this process an able chief justice can exercise considerable influence—in guiding or limiting debate, in setting forth the issues, and in handling sometimes temperamental personalities. In deciding a case, a majority of the justices must be in agreement: if there is a tie, the lower-court decision is left standing. (There can be a tie among nine justices if one is ill or disqualifies himself or herself because of prior involvement in the case.)

per curiam opinion A brief, unsigned court opinion.

opinion of the Court A signed opinion of a majority of the Supreme Court.

concurring opinion A signed opinion in which one or more members agree with the majority view but for different reasons.

dissenting opinion A signed opinion in which one or more justices disagree with the majority view.

Though the vote is what counts, by tradition the Court usually issues a written opinion explaining its decision. Sometimes the opinion is brief and unsigned (called a **per curiam opinion**); sometimes it is quite long and signed by the justices agreeing with it. If the chief justice is in the majority, he will either write the opinion or assign the task to a justice who agrees with him. If he is in the minority, the senior justice on the winning side will decide who writes the Court's opinion. There are three kinds of opinions—an **opinion of the Court** (reflecting the majority's view), a **concurring opinion** (an opinion by one or more justices who agree with the majority's conclusion but for different reasons that they wish to express), and a **dissenting opinion** (the opinion of the justices on the losing side). Each justice has three or four law clerks to help him or her review the many petitions the Court receives, study cases, and write opinions.

Many Supreme Court decisions, perhaps two-fifths of them, are decided unanimously. In these cases, the law is clear and no difficult questions of interpretation exist. But for the remaining ones, there appear to be two main blocs and one swing vote on today's Court:

* A conservative bloc of Samuel Alito, John Roberts, Antonin Scalia, and Clarence Thomas

* A liberal bloc of Stephen Breyer, Ruth Bader Ginsburg, Elena Kagan, and Sonia Sotomayor.

* A swing vote of Anthony Kennedy. He often votes with the conservatives on criminal law, but on some other cases (abortion, gay rights, and foreign combatants detained at Guantanamo Bay) votes with the liberals.

The Power of the Federal Courts

The great majority of the cases heard in the federal courts have little or nothing to do with changes in public policy: people accused of bank robbery are tried, disputes over contracts are settled, personal-injury cases are heard, and patent law is applied. In most instances, the courts are simply applying a relatively settled body of law to a specific controversy.

The Power to Make Policy

The courts make policy whenever they reinterpret the law or the Constitution in significant ways, extend the reach of existing laws to cover matters not previously thought to be covered by them, or design remedies for problems that involve the judges' acting in administrative or legislative ways. By any of these tests the courts have become exceptionally powerful.

The nine members of the U.S. Supreme Court are: Front row – Justices Clarence Thomas and Antonin Scalia, Chief Justice John Roberts, Justices Anthony Kennedy and Ruth Bader Ginsburg; second row – Justices Sonia Sotomayor, Stephen Breyer, Samuel Alito, and Elena Kagan.

One measure of that power is the fact that more than 160 federal laws have been declared unconstitutional. And as we shall see, on matters where Congress feels strongly, it can often get its way by passing slightly revised versions of a voided law.

Another measure, and perhaps a more revealing one, is the frequency with which the Supreme Court changes its mind. An informal rule of judicial decision making has been **stare decisis**, meaning "let the decision stand." It is the principle of precedent: a court case today should be settled in accordance with prior decisions on similar cases. (What constitutes a similar case is not always clear; lawyers are especially gifted at finding ways of showing that two cases are different in some relevant way.) There are two reasons why precedent is important. The practical reason should be obvious: if the meaning of the law continually changes, if the decisions of judges become wholly unpredictable, then human affairs affected by those laws and decisions become chaotic. A contract signed today might be invalid tomorrow. The other reason is at least as important: if the principle of equal justice means anything, it means that similar cases should be decided in a similar manner. On the other hand, times change, and the Court can make mistakes. As Justice Felix Frankfurter once said, "Wisdom too often never comes, and so one ought not to reject it merely because it comes late."[45]

However compelling the arguments for flexibility, the pace of change can become dizzying. By one count, the Court has overruled its own previous decisions in more than 260 cases since 1810.[46] In fact, it may have done it more often, because sometimes the Court does not say that it is abandoning a precedent, claiming instead that it is merely distinguishing the present case from a previous one.

A third measure of judicial power is the degree to which courts are willing to handle matters once left to the legislature. For example, the Court refused for a long time to hear a case about the size of congressional districts, no matter how unequal their populations.[47] The determination of congressional district boundaries was regarded as a **political question**—that is, as a matter that the Constitution left entirely to another branch of government (in this case, Congress) to decide for itself. Then in 1962, the Court decided that it was competent after all to handle this matter, and the notion of a "political question" became a much less important (but by no means absent) barrier to judicial power.[48]

By all odds the most powerful indicator of judicial power can be found in the kinds of remedies that the courts will impose. A **remedy** is a judicial order setting forth what must be done to correct a situation that a judge believes to be wrong. In ordinary cases, such as when one person sues another, the remedy is straightforward: the loser must pay the winner for some injury that he or she has caused, the loser must agree to abide by the terms of a contract he or she has broken, or the loser must promise not to do some unpleasant thing (such as dumping garbage on a neighbor's lawn).

stare decisis "Let the decision stand," or allowing prior rulings to control the current case.

political question An issue the Supreme Court will allow the executive and legislative branches to decide.

remedy A judicial order enforcing a right or redressing a wrong.

Today, however, judges design remedies that go far beyond what is required to do justice to the individual parties who actually appear in court. The remedies now imposed often apply to large groups and affect the circumstances under which thousands or even millions of people work, study, or live. For example, when a federal district judge in Alabama heard a case brought by a prison inmate in that state, he issued an order not simply to improve the lot of that prisoner but to revamp the administration of the entire prison system. The result was an improvement in the living conditions of many prisoners, at a cost to the state of an estimated $40 million a year. Similarly, a person who feels entitled to welfare payments that have been denied him or her may sue in court to get the money, and the court order will in all likelihood affect all welfare recipients. In one case certain court orders made an additional 100,000 people eligible for welfare.[49]

The basis for sweeping court orders can sometimes be found in the Constitution; the Alabama prison decision, for example, was based on the judge's interpretation of the Eighth Amendment, which prohibits "cruel and unusual punishments."[50] Others are based on court interpretations of federal laws. The Civil Rights Act of 1964 forbids discrimination on grounds of "race, color, or national origin" in any program receiving federal financial assistance. The Supreme Court interpreted that as meaning the San Francisco school system was obliged to teach English to Chinese students unable to speak it.[51] Since a Supreme Court decision is the law of the land, the impact of that ruling was not limited to San Francisco. Local courts and legislatures elsewhere decided that that decision meant that classes must be taught in Spanish for Hispanic children. What Congress meant by the Civil Rights Act is not clear; it may or may not have believed that teaching Hispanic children in English rather than Spanish was a form of discrimination. What is important is that it was the Court, not Congress, that decided what Congress meant.

Views of Judicial Activism

Judicial activism has, of course, been controversial. Those who support it argue that the federal courts must correct injustices when the other branches of the federal government, or the states, refuse to do so. The courts are the institution of last resort for those without the votes or the influence to obtain new laws, and especially for the poor and powerless. After all, Congress and the state legislatures tolerated segregated public schools for decades. If the Supreme Court had not declared segregation unconstitutional in 1954, it might still be law today.

Those who criticize judicial activism rejoin that judges usually have no special expertise in matters of school administration, prison management, environmental protection, and so on; they are lawyers, expert in defining rights and duties, but not in designing and managing complex institutions. Furthermore, however desirable court-declared rights and principles may be, implementing those principles means balancing the conflicting needs of various interest groups, raising and spending tax monies, and assessing the costs and benefits of complicated alternatives. Finally, federal judges are not elected; they are appointed and are thus immune to popular control. As a result, if they depart from their traditional role of making careful and cautious interpretations of what a law or the Constitution means and instead begin formulating wholly new policies, they become unelected legislators.

Checks on Judicial Power

No institution of government, including the courts, operates without restraint. The fact that judges are not elected does not make them immune to public opinion or to the views of the other branches of government. How important these restraints are varies from case to case, but in the broad course of history they have been significant.

One restraint exists because of the very nature of courts. A judge has no police force or army; decisions that he or she makes can sometimes be resisted or ignored, *if* the person or organization resisting is not highly visible and is willing to run the risk of being caught and charged with contempt of court. For example, long after the Supreme Court's controversial decisions that praying and Bible reading could not take place in public schools,[52] schools all over the country were still allowing prayers and Bible reading.[53] Years after the Court declared segregated schools to be unconstitutional, scores of school systems remained segregated. On the other hand, when a failure to comply is easily detected and punished, the courts' power is usually unchallenged. When the Supreme Court declared the income tax to be unconstitutional in 1895, income tax collections promptly ceased. When the Court in 1952 declared illegal President Truman's effort to seize the steel mills in order to stop a strike, the management of the mills was immediately returned to their owners.

Congress and the Courts

Congress has a number of ways of checking the judiciary. It can gradually alter the composition of the judiciary by the kinds of appointments the Senate is willing to confirm, or it can impeach judges it does not like. Fifteen federal judges have been the object of impeachment proceedings in our history, and nine others have resigned when such proceedings seemed likely. Of the 15 who were impeached, seven were acquitted, four were convicted, and one resigned. The most recent convictions were those of Alcee Hastings of Florida and Walter Nixon of Mississippi, both in 1989.[54] In practice, however, confirmation and impeachment proceedings do not make much of an impact on the federal courts because simple policy disagreements are not generally regarded as adequate grounds for voting against a judicial nominee or for starting an impeachment effort.

Congress can alter the number of judges, though, and by increasing the number sharply, it can give a president a chance to appoint judges to his liking. As described above, a "Court-packing" plan was proposed (unsuccessfully) by Franklin Roosevelt in 1937 specifically to change the political persuasion of the Supreme Court. In 1978, Congress passed a bill creating 152 new federal district and appellate judges to help ease the workload of the federal judiciary. This bill gave President Carter a chance to appoint over 40 percent of the federal bench. In 1984, an additional 84 judgeships were created; by 1988, President Reagan had appointed about half of all federal judges. In 1990, an additional 72 judges were authorized. During and after the Civil War, Congress may have been trying to influence Supreme Court decisions when it changed the size of the Court three times in six years (raising it from nine to 10 in 1863, lowering it again from 10 to seven in 1866, and raising it again from seven to nine in 1869).

Congress and the states can also undo a Supreme Court decision interpreting the Constitution by amending that document. This happens, but rarely: the Eleventh Amendment was ratified to prevent a citizen from suing a state in federal court; the Thirteenth, Fourteenth, and Fifteenth were ratified to undo the *Dred Scott* decision regarding slavery; the Sixteenth was added to make it constitutional for Congress to pass an income tax; and the Twenty-sixth was added to give the vote to 18-year-olds in state elections.

On more than 30 occasions, Congress has merely repassed a law that the Court has declared unconstitutional. In one case, a bill to aid farmers, voided in 1936, was accepted by the Court in slightly revised form three years later.[55] (In the meantime, of course, the Court had changed its collective mind about the New Deal.)

One of the most powerful potential sources of control over the federal courts, however, is the authority of Congress, given by the Constitution, to decide what the entire jurisdiction of the lower courts and the appellate jurisdiction of the Supreme Court shall be. In theory, Congress could prevent matters on which it did not want federal courts to act from ever coming before the courts. This happened

HOW WE COMPARE

Judicial Review in Canada and Europe

Courts outside the United States can declare laws to be unconstitutional, but most can do so in ways that are very different from those in the United States.

Canada: The highest court can declare a law unconstitutional, but not if the legislature has passed it with a special provision that says the law will survive judicial scrutiny notwithstanding the country's Charter of Rights. Such laws must be renewed every five years.

Europe: The European Court of Human Rights in Strasbourg can decide human rights cases that begin in any of the nations that make up the European Community.

France: Its Constitutional Council can declare a law unconstitutional, but only if asked to do so by government officials and only before (not after) the law goes into effect.

Germany: The Federal Constitutional Court can declare in an advisory opinion, before a case has emerged, that a law is unconstitutional, and it can judge the constitutionality of laws when asked to do so by a lower court (which itself cannot rule a law unconstitutional). The Federal Constitutional Court may hold an administrative or judicial action to be unjustified when a citizen, having exhausted all other remedies, files a petition.

in 1868. A Mississippi newspaper editor named McCardle was jailed by federal military authorities who occupied the defeated South. McCardle asked the federal district court for a writ of habeas corpus to get him out of custody; when the district court rejected his plea, he appealed to the Supreme Court. Congress at that time was fearful that the Court might find the laws on which its Reconstruction policy was based (and under which McCardle was in jail) unconstitutional. To prevent that from happening, it passed a bill withdrawing from the Supreme Court appellate jurisdiction in cases of this sort. The Court conceded that Congress could do this and thus dismissed the case because it no longer had jurisdiction.[56]

Congress has threatened to withdraw jurisdiction on other occasions, and the mere existence of the threat may have influenced the nature of Court decisions. In the 1950s, for example, congressional opinion was hostile to Court decisions in the field of civil liberties and civil rights, and legislation was proposed that would have curtailed the Court's jurisdiction in these areas. It did not pass, but the Court may have allowed the threat to temper its decisions.[57] On the other hand, as congressional resistance to the Roosevelt Court-packing plan shows, the Supreme Court enjoys a good deal of prestige in the nation, even among people who disagree with some of its decisions, and so passing laws that would frontally attack it would not be easy except perhaps in times of national crisis.

Furthermore, laws narrowing jurisdiction or restricting the kinds of remedies that a court can impose often are blunt instruments that might not achieve the purposes of their proponents. Suppose that you, as a member of Congress, would like to prevent the federal courts from ordering schoolchildren to be bused for the purpose of achieving racial balance in the schools. If you denied the Supreme Court appellate jurisdiction in this matter, you would leave the lower federal courts and all state courts free to do as they wished, and many of them would go on ordering busing. If you wanted to attack that problem, you could propose a law that would deny to all federal courts the right to order busing as a remedy for racial imbalance. But the courts would still be free to order busing (and of course a lot of busing goes on even without court orders), provided that they did not say that it was for the purpose of achieving racial balance. (It could be for the purpose of "facilitating desegregation" or making possible "redistricting.") Naturally, you could always make it illegal for children to enter a school bus for any reason, but then many children would not be able to get to school at all. Finally, the Supreme Court might well decide that if busing were essential to achieve a constitutional right, then any congressional law prohibiting such busing would itself be unconstitutional. Trying to think through how *that* dilemma would be resolved is like trying to visualize two kangaroos simultaneously jumping into each other's pouches.

Public Opinion and the Courts

Though they are not elected, judges read the same newspapers as members of Congress, and thus they, too, are aware of public opinion, especially elite opinion. Though it may be going too far to say the Supreme Court follows the election returns, it is nonetheless true that the Court is sensitive to certain bodies of opinion, especially of those elites—liberal or conservative—to which its members happen to be attuned. The justices will keep in mind historical cases in which their predecessors, by blatantly disregarding public opinion, very nearly destroyed the legitimacy of the Court itself. This was the case with the *Dred Scott* decision, which infuriated the North and was widely disobeyed. No such crisis exists today, but it is altogether possible that changing political moods affect the kinds of remedies that judges will think appropriate.

Opinion not only restrains the courts; it may also energize them. The most activist periods in Supreme Court history have coincided with times when the political system was undergoing profound and lasting changes. The assertion by the Supreme Court, under John Marshall's leadership, of the principles of national supremacy and judicial review occurred at the time when the Jeffersonian Republicans were coming to power and their opponents, the Federalists, were collapsing as an organized party. The pro-slavery decisions of the Taney Court came when the nation was so divided along sectional and ideological lines as to make almost any Court decision on this matter unpopular. Supreme Court review of economic regulation in the 1890s and 1900s came at a time when the political parties were realigning and the Republicans were acquiring dominance that would last for several decades. The Court decisions of the 1930s corresponded to another period of partisan realignment.

Pollsters have measured changes in public perceptions of how well the Supreme Court is handling its job. The results are shown in Figure 12.4. The percentage of people saying that they approve of how the Court is handling its job has fluctuated over the last 40 years. In the last half-decade, public approval of the Court's performance has been as high as 61 percent (in 2009) and as low as 46 percent (in 2011). These movements do not reflect any obvious swings in how the public perceives the Court's ideological tilt. Gallup polls and other opinion surveys indicate that, for most of the last decade, about four-fifths to half of the public thought the Court was neither too liberal nor too conservative, about a third thought the Court was too liberal, and about a fifth thought it was too conservative. Rather, the shifts in opinion seem to reflect the public's reaction not only to what the Court does but also to what the government as a whole is doing. The upturn in the early 1970s was probably caused by the Watergate scandal, an episode that simultaneously discredited the presidency and boosted the stock of those institutions (such as the courts) that seemed to be checking the abuses of the White House. The gradual upturn in the 1980s may have reflected a general restoration of public confidence in government during that decade.[58]

Though popular support for the Court sometimes declines, these drops have so far not resulted in any legal checks placed on it. As explained in this chapter's *Constitutional Connections* feature (see page 370–371), each Congress witnesses many proposals that restrict the jurisdiction of federal courts and prohibit them from exercising judicial review in relation to given issues, but these proposals almost never become bills that make their way into law. The changes that have occurred in the Court have been caused by changes in its personnel. Presidents Nixon and Reagan attempted to produce a less activist Court by appointing justices who were more inclined to be strict constructionists and conservatives. To some extent, they succeeded: Justices Kennedy, O'Connor, Rehnquist, and Scalia were certainly less inclined than Justice Thurgood Marshall to find new rights in the Constitution or to overturn the decisions of state legislatures. But as of yet, there has been no wholesale retreat from the positions staked out by the Warren Court. As noted above, a Nixon appointee, Justice Blackmun, wrote the decision making anti-abortion laws unconstitutional; and another Nixon appointee, Chief Justice Burger, wrote the opinion upholding court-ordered school busing to achieve racial integration. A Reagan appointee, Justice O'Connor, voted to uphold a right to an abortion. The Supreme Court has become somewhat less willing to impose restraints on police practices, and it has not blocked the use of the death penalty.

But in general, the major fea-tures of Court activism and liberalism during the Warren years—school integration, sharper limits on police practice, greater freedom of expression—have remained intact, as has the Court's deference to Congress and the presidency when they have established new agencies or expanded federal programs. The Warren E. Burger Court (1969–1986) was succeeded by Courts with conservative Chief Justices, namely William H. Rehnquist (1986–2005) and John G. Roberts (2005–present). The aforementioned 2012 Court decision upholding the constitutionality of all (save the Medicaid expansion provision) of the 2010 health care reform law was written by Chief Justice Roberts.

The reasons for the growth in court activism are clear. One is the sheer growth in the size and scope of the government as a whole. The courts have come to play a larger role in our lives because Congress, the bureaucracy, and the president have come to play larger ones. In 1890, hardly anybody would have thought of asking Congress—much less the courts—to make rules governing the participation of women in college sports or the district boundaries of state legislatures. Today such rules are commonplace, and the courts are inevitably drawn into interpreting them. And when the Court decided how the vote in Florida would be counted during the 2000 presidential election, it created an opportunity in the future for scores of new lawsuits challenging election results.

The other reason for increased activism is the acceptance by a large number of judges, conservative as well as liberal, of the activist view of the function of the courts. If courts once existed solely to "settle disputes," today they also exist in the eyes of their members to "solve problems."

FIGURE 12.4 **Public Approval of the Supreme Court's Performance, 1974–2011**

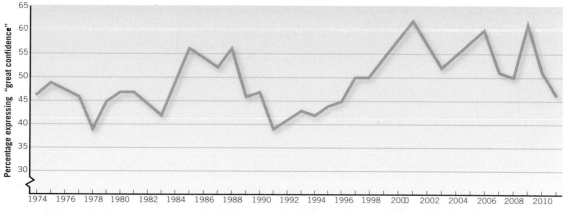

Source: Gallup polls

Bettmann/CORBIS

Thurgood Marshall became the first black Supreme Court justice. As chief counsel for the NAACP, Marshall argued the 1954 Brown v. Board of Education *case in front of the Supreme Court. He was appointed to the Court in 1967 and served until 1991.*

Though the Supreme Court is the pinnacle of the federal judiciary, most decisions, including many important ones, are made by the several courts of appeals and the 94 district courts. The Supreme Court can control its own workload by deciding when to grant certiorari. It has become easier for citizens and groups to gain access to the federal courts (through class-action suits, by amicus curiae briefs, and by laws that require government agencies to pay legal fees). At the same time, the courts have widened the reach of their decisions by issuing orders that cover whole classes of citizens or affect the management of major public and private institutions. However, the courts can overstep the bounds of their authority and bring upon themselves a counterattack from both the public and Congress. Congress has the right to control much of the courts' jurisdiction, but it rarely does so. As a result, the ability of judges to make law is only infrequently challenged directly.

LEARNING OBJECTIVES

LO 12.1 Where in the Constitution does it say that the Supreme Court has the power of judicial review?

Nowhere in the Constitution does it say that the Supreme Court has the power of judicial review. The Constitution is silent on this matter, but the Court has asserted, and almost every scholar has agreed, that our system of separated powers means that the Court must be able to defend the Constitution. Otherwise, Congress and the president would be free to ignore it.

LO 12.2 What is meant by an "Article III" federal judge?

An "Article III" federal judge is a federal judge who benefits from Article III of the Constitution, which guarantees judges that they can serve during good behavior. The Supreme Court, courts of appeal, and all district courts are all Title 3 courts. Congress has also established "legislative" courts whose members serve for fixed terms. Examples are the Tax Court and the Court of Appeals for the Armed Forces.

LO 12.3 What is the difference between original and appellate jurisdiction?

Original jurisdiction refers to a trial held before a court; appellate jurisdiction refers to an appeal a court hears from a trial in another court. Even the Supreme Court has original jurisdiction. For example, it will hear a trial involving ambassadors or a controversy between two or more states.

LO 12.4 Why should federal judges serve for life?

Strictly speaking, they serve during "good behavior," but that means they would have to be impeached and convicted in order to be removed. The reason for this protection is clear: the judiciary cannot be independent of the other two branches of government if judges could be easily removed by the president or Congress, and this independence ensures that they are a separate branch of government.

LO 12.5 Why should federal courts be able to declare laws unconstitutional?

Though the Constitution does not explicitly give them that power, they have acquired it on the reasonable assumption that the Constitution would become meaningless if the president and Congress could ignore its provisions. The Constitution, after all, states that it shall be the "supreme law of the land."

TO LEARN MORE

- Federal Judicial Center: **www.fjc.gov**
- Federal courts: **www.uscourts.gov**
- Supreme Court decisions: **www.law.cornell.edu**
- Finding laws and reports: **www.findlaw.com**
- Abraham, Henry J. *The Judicial Process*, 7th ed. New York: Oxford University Press, 1998. An excellent, comprehensive survey of how the federal courts are organized and function.
- Abraham, Henry J., and Barbara A. Perry. *Freedom and the Court*, 8th ed. Lawrence, KS: University of Kansas Press, 2003. Careful summary of civil liberties and civil rights cases.
- Cardozo, Benjamin N. *The Nature of the Judicial Process*. New Haven, CT: Yale University Press, 1921. Important statement of how judges make decisions, by a former Supreme Court justice.
- Ely, John Hart. *Democracy and Distrust*. Cambridge: Harvard University Press, 1980. Effort to create a theory of judicial review that is neither strict-constructionist nor activist.
- Greenburg, Jan Crawford. *Supreme Conflict*. New York: Penguin, 2007. A fascinating journalistic account of how the Supreme Court operates.
- Hall, Kermit L., and James W. Ely, Jr., eds. *The Oxford Guide to the United States Supreme Court Decisions*, 2nd ed. New York: Oxford University Press, 2009. Summarizes the 440 most important decisions of the Supreme Court and includes a comprehensive bibliography of books about the Court.
- Lasser, William. *The Limits of Judicial Power*. Chapel Hill: University of North Carolina Press, 1988. Shows how the Court through history has withstood the political storms created by its more controversial decisions.
- McCloskey, Robert G. *The American Supreme Court*, 4th ed. Edited by Sanford Levinson. Chicago: University of Chicago Press, 2005. Superb brief history of the Supreme Court, updated by one of McCloskey's former students who now teaches law at the University of Texas.
- Rabkin, Jeremy. *Judicial Compulsions*. New York: Basic Books, 1989. Explains (and argues against) the extensive Court intervention in the work of administrative agencies.
- Wolfe, Christopher. *The Rise of Modern Judicial Review*. New York: Basic Books, 1986. An excellent history of judicial review from 1787 to the present.

KRT/Newscom

13 | Domestic Policy

LEARNING OBJECTIVES

LO 13.1 What types of politics may matter to whether and how government acts on any given issue?

LO 13.2 Why are some social welfare policies and programs politically protected while others are politically imperiled?

LO 13.3 Why are environmental policies designed and enforced differently in America than in other industrialized nations?

LO 13.4 Does just one type of politics drive environmental policies and programs?

How do people come to believe that certain issues require governmental action? What explains why some issues are on the political agenda while others are not? Why are some issues more prominent on today's political agenda than they were either in previous historical periods or just a few years ago, and why are other issues less prominent than they once were? Why do elected officials sometimes suddenly shift attention away from some issues and toward others? What explains the timing and character of government action (or inaction) on any given issue?

The causes, contours, and consequences of government action or inaction on any given issue or any class of issues (domestic policy, economic policy, or foreign policy) are not easily explained. What at first glance may appear to be simple and stable policymaking patterns often turn out upon closer inspection to be more complex and dynamic than they seemed. For instance, consider what has happened in two domestic policy domains—social welfare policy and environmental protection policy.

Social Welfare Policy

THEN

Before the 1960s, neither most Washington lawmakers nor most citizens believed that the federal government should ensure that all retirees, whatever their work history, have enough money to live on; that all veterans of foreign wars have grants for college and subsidized medical care for life; that all poor children are guaranteed free or reduced price meals in schools and during summers; that all physically, mentally, or developmentally disabled people, like all people with life-threatening medical maladies, are insured for hospital stays and treatment including long-term nursing care; that all low-wage workers receive tax credits that effectively boost their wages; that all citizens who may need it have access to affordable housing; that all low-income children are able to attend preschools; that all special needs children receive special education; and that all full-time workers who lose their jobs receive unemployment benefits and (in many cases) job training. If they existed at all, national laws touching on these social welfare matters were few and thin, and federal departments, bureaus, or programs to fund or administer such social welfare benefits were virtually nonexistent.

NOW

Washington sets, funds, and implements policies on all these social welfare matters and others besides. By 2010, three giant programs—Social Security (established in 1935) plus Medicare and Medicaid (each established in 1965)—together accounted for over 40 percent of the federal budget (double what was spent on national defense). They were flanked by scores of smaller federal social welfare programs, most of them either established or expanded since 1965. The U.S. Department of Health and Human Services and the U.S. Department of Veterans Affairs are two of the main bureaucracies responsible for federal social welfare policies and programs, but benefits also emanate from several other federal departments. For instance, the U.S. Department of Justice has supported myriad programs for "at-risk youth" including ones that provide mentors to the children of prisoners and "second chance" job training to young adult ex-prisoners. But, in recent years, as policymakers have struggled with big annual budget deficits and a growing public debt, the future of many social welfare policies and programs, including the largest entitlement programs like Social Security and Medicare, has for the first time in more than a generation been placed in some serious doubt.

Environmental Policy

THEN

Environmental policies in the United States gained widespread public attention in the 1960s and 1970's, when reports of water and air pollution, pesticide use, and other threats to natural resources prompted the passage of legislation to control such activity. The Environmental Protection Agency was created in 1970 to set standards for environmental safety, track violations, and enforce compliance. Since then, the field has expanded to encompass concerns about broader national and international environmental issues such as global warming. In the 2008 presidential race, environmental politics was a major concern for the electorate, particularly young voters. A CBS News/MTV poll in the spring of 2008 found that 18 percent of voters aged 18–29 viewed environmental problems as the biggest challenge in the coming years, exceeded only by the economy, which was ranked first by 34 percent of voters in that age group. Both presidential candidates discussed the need to protect the environment for future generations: Barack Obama declared that the country faced a "defining moment in our history: Our nation is at war. The planet is in peril," while John McCain called for the need to "restore the health of our planet."[1]

NOW

Since the 2008 presidential race, and even after the disastrous oil spill in the Gulf of Mexico in May 2010, environmental issues have received less attention from federal policymakers. In the 2012 presidential race, environmental issues were less prominent than they were during the 2008 presidential race. Prior to 2008, Gallup polls stretching back to the 1980s found most Americans agreed that the environment should be given priority "even at the risk of curbing economic growth;" but, in 2013, for the fifth consecutive year, and "with the exception of a poll conducted shortly after" the aforementioned oil spill in the Gulf of Mexico, "support for the environment on this question ... remained the minority view."[2] Over the same period, however, the percentage of the public expressing a "great deal" of concern about various environmental issues fell only slightly. For example, from 2008 to 2013, the slight dips in deep public concern included pollution of rivers, lakes, and reservoirs (50 to 46 percent), air pollution (43 to 40 percent), loss of the tropical rain forests (40 to 36 percent), and global warming (37 to 33 percent).[3]

This chapter will elaborate and apply the theory of policymaking outlined in Chapter 1 to domestic policy dynamics on issues in social welfare policy and environmental policy. Each area of domestic policy has issues and policy dynamics all its own. But in social welfare and environmental policy, as in education, housing, homeland security, transportation, and other domestic policy domains, each of the four types of policymaking politics can be found. In Chapter 14, we will explore the politics of foreign and military policy.

Policymaking Politics Revisited

cost A burden that people believe they must bear if a policy is enacted.

benefit A satisfaction that people believe they will enjoy if a policy is adopted.

How are public policies proposed and then passed, rejected, or modified? Let us revisit our simple way of classifying the politics of policymaking. Once more, we begin by observing that each policy has a **cost** and a **benefit**. A cost is the burden of a program, whether it is financial or social, that is placed on people. It includes taxes, unpleasant regulations, or social stigma. A benefit is the gain, whether financial or social, that flows to people. This includes payments, subsidies, tax reductions, government contracts, or heightened prestige.

Remember, these are *perceived* costs and benefits. For example, some people may think the nation benefits by massive military and other defense spending. Others disagree and believe the country is better served by social spending. By the same token, some people may think that a government regulation is a cost, whereas others may think it is a benefit. It is also important to understand that people differ in their beliefs about who gets a benefit and who pays a cost. Those beliefs are about the **legitimacy** of various groups. For example, some people may think that public assistance to the needy is legitimate. Others believe that it is not legitimate for the needy to receive such benefits.

> ***legitimacy*** Political authority conferred by law or by a state or national constitution.
>
> ***majoritarian politics*** A policy in which almost everybody benefits and almost everybody pays.
>
> ***client politics*** A policy in which one small group benefits and almost everybody pays.

Perceived costs and benefits can be widely distributed or narrowly concentrated, giving us the by-now familiar (we hope!) four types of politics depicted by our four-box diagram (see Figure 13.1):

- Widely distributed benefits and widely distributed costs, or **majoritarian politics**. This means that all or most people benefit and all or most people pay.

- Narrowly concentrated benefits and widely distributed costs, or **client politics**. A few people, or some particular community or organization benefits, but most people pay for what they get.

- Narrowly concentrated benefits and narrowly concentrated costs, or **interest-group politics**. A few people, communities, or organizations benefit, and a few people, communities, or organizations pay.

- Widely distributed benefits and narrowly concentrated costs or **entrepreneurial politics**. Almost everybody benefits, but only a few people, communities, or organizations pay the costs.

Now, after in each case first learning some basic history and background facts about the policies and programs, let's try to apply our theory to domestic policy dynamics in two areas: social welfare and environmental policy. We begin with social welfare policy and consider each of four federal social welfare programs. As we shall see, Social Security and Medicare seem to exemplify majoritarian politics;

FIGURE 13.1   A Way of Classifying and Explaining the Politics of Different Policy Issues

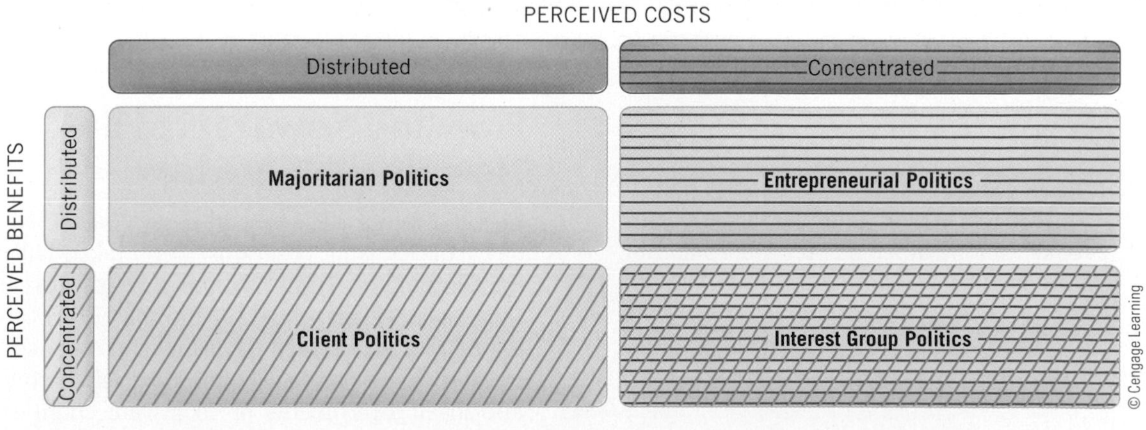

but Temporary Assistance to Needy Families (TANF), like the program that it succeeded, Aid to Families with Dependent Children (AFDC), has played out more as a client politics issue; and, finally, Medicaid, the large federal–state health care program, would seem to belong partly in the majoritarian politics box and partly in the client politics box.

Social Welfare Policy

Among the reasons given in the Preamble to the United States Constitution for establishing the national government is a desire to "promote the general Welfare." Article I, Section 8 of the Constitution states the power of Congress to "provide for the . . . general Welfare."

From the first, however, the Constitution's defenders disagreed about what the phrase was supposed to mean. Some, like James Madison, argued that it was meant to restrict Congress to taxing and spending only for things that the Constitution specifically empowered Congress to do (like regulating interstate commerce or maintaining the military). Others, like Alexander Hamilton, argued for a broader meaning that would allow Congress to tax and spend for things that it was not specifically empowered by the Constitution to do, but which might reasonably be expected to meet national needs and benefit some or all citizens.

In the 1930s, asserting a constitutional authority to advance the "general welfare," Congress enacted a host of new national policies and programs in response to the economic hardships wrought by the Great Depression. The biggest was the Social Security Act of 1935. Among other provisions, the law created a national system of old-age pensions and, to pay for it, imposed an income tax on workers that was deducted from their wages and paid by their employers. In 1937, in the case of *Helvering v. Davis*, the U.S. Supreme Court upheld the constitutionality of that provision, ruling that Congress has broad discretion to tax and spend "in aid of the 'general welfare,'" including policies and programs designed to ease the "plight of men and women" who lose their jobs and provide for others who are either temporarily or permanently "needy and dependent." Nobody, however, foresaw just how far Congress would go in exercising that power, or where doing so would lead.

LANDMARK CASES

Federal Laws About "General Welfare"

- *United States v. Butler* (1936): Found particular federal regulations on agricultural production to be unconstitutional, but proclaimed that Congress has wide power to tax and spend for whatever it deems to be for the "general welfare."

- *Helvering v. Davis* (1937): Upheld key provisions of the Social Security Act of 1935, and declared that Congress has broad discretion to tax and spend "in aid of the 'general welfare.'"

- *South Dakota v. Dole* (1987): Ruled that Washington could condition the receipt of federal highway funds on a state's compliance with a 21-year-old drinking age, and declared that Congress's power to define the "general welfare" and to spend in pursuit of it is virtually unlimited.

From the New Deal to the New Health Care Law

The first major steps toward today's social welfare policies and programs were taken after the election of 1932. At the time the Great Depression began in 1929, the job of providing relief (food, money, medicine, and other services) to needy people fell almost entirely to state and local governments or to private charities, and even these sources were primarily concerned with widows, orphans, and the elderly.[4] Hardly any state had a systematic program for supporting the unemployed, though many states provided some kind of help if it was clear that the person was out of work through no fault of his or her own. When the economy suddenly ground to a near standstill and the unemployment rate rose to include one-fourth of the workforce, private charities and city relief programs nearly went bankrupt. Americans sung the 1931 song "Brother, Can You Spare a Dime?" But, with families, neighbors, local churches, charities, and city agencies all unable to meet the economic crisis despite their best efforts, on the eve of the 1932 presidential election, ever more citizens had come to feel that it was time for Uncle Sam to lend a hand.

In 1932, unemployed workers line up at a soup kitchen during the Great Depression.

That election produced an overwhelming congressional majority for the Democrats and placed Franklin D. Roosevelt in the White House. Almost immediately, a number of emergency measures were adopted to cope with the depression by supplying federal cash to bail out state and local relief agencies and by creating public works jobs under federal auspices. These measures were recognized as temporary expedients, however, and were unsatisfactory to those who believed the federal government had a permanent and major responsibility for welfare.

Roosevelt created the Cabinet Committee on Economic Security to consider long-term policies. The committee drew heavily on the experience of European nations and on the ideas of various American scholars and social workers, but it understood that it would have to adapt these proposals to the realities of American politics. Chief among these was the widespread belief that any direct federal welfare program might be unconstitutional. The Constitution nowhere explicitly gave to Congress the authority to set up an unemployment compensation or old-age retirement program. And even if a welfare program were constitutional, many believed, it would be wrong because it violated the individualistic creed that people should help themselves unless they were physically unable to do so.

But failure by the Roosevelt administration to produce a comprehensive social security program, his supporters felt, might make the president vulnerable in the 1936 election to the leaders of various radical social movements. Huey Long of Louisiana was proposing a "Share Our Wealth" plan; Upton Sinclair was running for governor of California on a platform calling for programs to "End Poverty in California"; and Dr. Francis E. Townsend was leading an organization of hundreds of thousands of elderly people on whose behalf he demanded government pensions of $200 a month.

The plan that emerged from the Cabinet committee was carefully designed to meet popular demands within the framework of constitutional understandings. It called for two kinds of programs: (1) an **insurance program** for the unemployed and elderly, to which workers would contribute and from which they would benefit when they became unemployed or retired; and (2) an **assistance program** for

insurance program A self-financing government program based on contributions that provide benefits to unemployed or retired persons.

assistance program A government program financed by general income taxes that provides benefits to poor citizens without requiring contribution from them.

means test An income qualification program that determines whether one is eligible for benefits under government programs reserved for lower-income groups.

the blind, for dependent children, and for the aged. (Giving assistance as well as providing "insurance" for the aged was necessary because for the first few years the insurance program would not pay out any benefits.) The federal government would use its power to tax to provide the funds, but all of the programs (except for old-age insurance) would be administered by the states. Everybody, rich or poor, would be eligible for the insurance programs. Only the poor, as defined by a **means test** (a measure to determine that incomes are below a certain level), would be eligible for the assistance programs. Though bitterly opposed by some, the resulting Social Security Act passed swiftly and virtually unchanged through Congress. It was introduced in January 1935 and signed by President Roosevelt in August of that year.

The Social Security Act became a cornerstone of Roosevelt's New Deal. But many of the act's supporters also wanted Washington to guarantee all citizens including the elderly and the poor a certain minimum level of health care. The idea of having the government pay the medical and hospital bills of the elderly and the poor had been discussed in Washington since the drafting of the Social Security Act. President Roosevelt and his Committee on Economic Security sensed that medical care would be very controversial, and so health programs were left out of the 1935 bill in order not to jeopardize its chances of passage.[5] The proponents of the idea did not abandon it, however. Working mostly within the executive branch, they continued to press, sometimes publicly, sometimes behind the scenes, for a national health care plan. Democratic presidents, including Truman, Kennedy, and Johnson, favored it; Republican president Eisenhower opposed it; Congress was deeply divided on it. The American Medical Association attacked it as "socialized medicine." For 30 years, key policy entrepreneurs, such as Wilbur Cohen, worked to find a formula that would produce a congressional majority.

The first and highest hurdle to overcome, however, was not Congress as a whole but the House Ways and Means Committee, especially its powerful chairman from 1958 to 1975, Wilbur Mills of Arkansas. A majority of the committee members opposed a national health care program. Some members believed it wrong in principle; others feared that adding a costly health component to the Social Security system would jeopardize the financial solvency and administrative integrity of one of the most popular government programs. By the early 1960s, a majority of the House favored a health care plan, but without the approval of Ways and Means it would never reach the floor.

The 1964 elections changed all that. The Johnson landslide produced such large Democratic majorities in Congress that the composition of the committees changed. In particular, the membership of the Ways and Means Committee was altered. Whereas before it had three Democrats for every two Republicans, after 1964 it had two Democrats for every one Republican. The House leadership saw to it that the new Democrats on the committee were strongly committed to a health care program. Suddenly the committee had a majority favorable to such a plan, and Mills, realizing that a bill would pass and wanting to help shape its form, changed his position and became a supporter of what was to become Medicare.

Medicare became a cornerstone of Johnson's Great Society. The policy entrepreneurs in and out of the government who drafted the Medicare plan attempted to anticipate the major objections to it. First, the bill would apply only to the aged—those eligible for Social Security retirement benefits. This would reassure legislators worried about the cost of providing tax-supported health care for everybody. Second, the plan would cover only hospital expenses, not doctors' bills. Since doctors were not to be paid by the government, they would not be regulated by it; thus, presumably, the opposition of the American Medical Association would be blunted.

Unexpectedly, however, the Ways and Means Committee broadened the coverage of the plan beyond what the administration had thought was politically feasible. It added sections providing medical assistance, called Medicaid, for the poor (defined as those already getting public assistance payments) and payment of doctors' bills for the aged (a new part of Medicare). The new, much-enlarged bill passed both houses of Congress with ease. The key votes pitted a majority of the Democrats against a majority of the Republicans.

Johnson's Great Society programs and "war on poverty" went far beyond Roosevelt's New Deal programs. But neither the chief political architects of Social Security in 1935 nor the main political movers behind Medicare and Medicaid in 1965 ever envisioned scores of millions of Americans receiving food, money, medicine, and other benefits through programs funded largely by the federal government. And no one contemplated that middle-class and even upper-income citizens would one day become as likely to receive federally financed health care as the poorest of the poor.

But that day has long since arrived. In 2010, about 60 million Americans received Medicaid benefits, 54 million Americans received Social Security benefits, and 52 million Americans (45 million senior citizens and 7 million younger adults with permanent disabilities) received Medicare benefits.

The two largest federal social welfare programs, Social Security and Medicare, are bound for big increases in beneficiaries over the next several decades as the primary beneficiary population each program serves, persons age 65 and older, grows and grows. And Medicaid, for several decades now the largest program co-funded by the federal government and the states, is now being further expanded in most states in accordance with the latest federal health care law.

As discussed in several previous chapters, one of the most heated political controversies of recent years concerned social welfare policy, namely, the passage of the Patient Protection and Affordable Care Act of 2010. Dubbed by certain of its critics (and eventually called by President Obama himself) "Obamacare," the bill was passed by the House and Senate without a single Republican vote. Only 34 Democrats in the House and three in the Senate voted against it.[6] When it passed, public opinion polls indicated the plan was not popular. Its defenders argued that as the law took effect it would win over most people and that in time its cost would go down. Its critics claimed that it would stifle health care by heavy regulations and rapidly rising costs. In the November 2010 congressional elections, the law was not popular and may have contributed to large Republican gains in the House and Senate. A case challenging the law's constitutionality made it to the Supreme Court.

In 2012, the Supreme Court upheld the law's constitutionality, excepting its provisions requiring states to expand Medicaid coverage.[7] In 2013, a re-elected President Obama began his second term, public opinion on the law became more favorable, and the debate among federal policymakers shifted somewhat from disputes about the law's overall desirability to immediate concerns about its administrative workability and doubts about its long-term potential to contain costs.[8] Its major provisions are summarized in the *How Things Work* feature on the next page.

Two Kinds of Social Welfare Programs

Today, some eight decades after Social Security was first debated, two kinds of social welfare programs exist in this country: those that benefit most or all of the people and those that help only a small number of them. In the first category are Social Security and Medicare, programs that provide retirement benefits or medical assistance to almost every citizen who

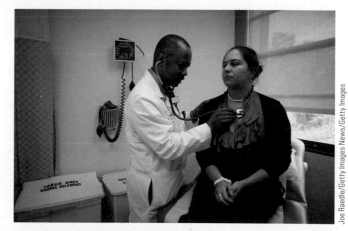

Joe Raedle/Getty Images News/Getty Images

The Affordable Care Act guarantees that all Americans will have access to health care.

HOW THINGS WORK

Patient Protection and Affordable Care Act of 2010, Major Provisions

- Extends health care insurance to some 32 million uninsured Americans
- Provides federal subsidies to people who have trouble paying
- Imposes a "tax" penalty on people who do not buy health insurance
- Dependent children under age 26 are covered by parent's insurance
- Adds more people to Medicaid
- Levies fees and taxes on medical devices, drugs, high-cost health insurance plans, health insurers

has reached a certain age. In the second are programs such as Temporary Assistance to Needy Children (TANF) and the Supplemental Nutrition Assistance Program (SNAP, which encompasses Food Stamps) that offer help only to people with low incomes. The *How Things Work* feature on page 403 briefly describes these and other major social welfare programs.

Legally, the difference between the two kinds of social welfare programs is that the first have no *means test* (they are available to everyone without regard to income) while the second are *means tested* (you must fall below a certain income level to enjoy them). Politically, the programs differ in how they get money from the government. The first kind of welfare program represents **majoritarian politics**: nearly everyone benefits, nearly everyone pays. The second kind represents **client politics**: a (relatively) low number of people benefit, but almost everyone pays. The biggest problem facing majoritarian welfare programs is their cost: who will pay, and how much will they pay? The biggest problem facing client-oriented programs is their legitimacy: who should benefit, and how should they be served?

This political difference between these programs has a huge impact on how the government acts in regard to them. Social Security and Medicare are sacrosanct. The thought of making any changes that might lower the benefits these programs pay is so politically risky that most politicians never even discuss them. As we will discuss in the next section, because of rising senior citizen populations, rising expenses, and rising demands for more benefits, Medicare is in deep financial trouble today, and Social Security will face high financial hurdles in a few decades. Federal policymakers are scrambling to look for ways of maintaining benefits while hiding the rising costs or postponing dealing with them. No politician wants to raise taxes or cut benefits, so they adopt a variety of halfhearted measures (like slowly increasing the age at which people can get these benefits) designed to postpone the tough decisions until they are out of office.

Client-based welfare programs—those that are means tested—are a very different matter. Like many other client-based programs, their political appeal changes as popular opinion about them changes. Take the old Aid to Families with Dependent Children (AFDC) program. When it was started in 1935, people thought of it as a way of helping poor women whose husbands had been killed in war or had died in mining accidents. The goal was to help these women support their children, who had been made fatherless by death or disaster. Most people thought of these women as the innocent victims of a tragedy. No one thought that they would take AFDC for very long. It was a program to help smooth things over for them until they could remarry. About 30 years later, however, the public's opinion of AFDC had begun to change. People started to think AFDC was paying money to women who had never married and had no intention of marrying. The government, according to this view, was subsidizing single-parent families, encouraging out-of-wedlock births, and creating social dependency. From the mid-1960s, through the mid-1990s, these views became stronger. AFDC had lost the legitimacy it needed, as a client program, to survive politically. As we shall discuss in more detail later in this chapter, even though it never accounted for as much as 1 percent of total federal spending, in 1996, AFDC suffered a fate that few decades-old federal programs of any type ever do, and that far more costly majoritarian social welfare programs never do: it was abolished.

Now, however, let's take a closer look at Washington's two biggest social welfare programs, Social Security and Medicare, and how the majoritarian politics surrounding each program helps to explain what federal policymakers are (or, more to the point, are not) doing as each program faces severe financial stresses.

HOW THINGS WORK

Major Social Welfare Programs

Insurance, or "Contributory," Programs

Old Age, Survivors, and Disability Insurance (OASDI) Monthly payments to retired or disabled people and to surviving members of their families. This program, popularly called Social Security, is paid for by a payroll tax on employers and employees. *No means test.*

Medicare Federal government pays for part of the cost of medical care for retired or disabled people covered by Social Security. Paid for by payroll taxes on employees and employers. *No means test.*

Assistance, or "Noncontributory," Programs

Unemployment Insurance (UI) Weekly payments to workers who have been laid off and cannot find work. Benefits and requirements determined by states. Paid for by taxes on employers. *No means test.*

Temporary Assistance for Needy Families (TANF) Payments to needy families with children. Replaced the old AFDC program. Partially paid for by block grants from the federal government to the states. *Means test.*

Supplemental Security Income (SSI) Cash payments to aged, blind, or disabled people whose income is below a certain amount. Paid for from general federal revenues. *Means test.*

Food Stamps (now part of the **Supplemental Nutrition Assistance Program, SNAP**) Vouchers, given to people whose income is below a certain level, that can be used to buy food at grocery stores. Paid for out of general federal revenues. *Means test.*

Medicaid Pays medical expenses of persons receiving TANF or SSI payments. *Means test.*

Earned Income Tax Credit Pays cash or tax credit to poor working families. *Means test.*

Social Security and Medicare: *Majoritarian Politics*

When Social Security began in 1935 and Medicare in 1965, many people benefited and the cost was small. In the late 1930s, an old-age check for a retired person on Social Security was paid for by taxes levied on 42 workers; today, only about 3 workers pay for each retired program beneficiary. The current Social Security tax is 12.4 percent of a person's earnings (half of this is paid by the employer). This money is used to make payments to current retirees, with the leftover funds invested in government bonds owned by the Treasury Department.

But that system is breaking down as millions more Americans retire and depend on Social Security for some or all of their income. By 2030, nearly one in five Americans will be 65 or older; each day, about 10,000 baby boomers (Americans born 1946 to 1964) turn 65. In 2012, Social Security paid benefits of about $775 billion to around 57 million people. In its 2013 report, the Social Security Board of Trustees projected that by 2033, if Congress does not act before then, Social Security will be able to pay only 77 percent of scheduled benefits.

Still, for at least three reasons, the program's prospects for remaining solvent are pretty good. First, Social Security is well run, costing less than 1 percent of total annual expenditures to administer. Second, the program remains highly popular with the public, and most people are aware that it faces a solvency problem. Third, and most importantly, Congress, as it has done in the past when the program's finances were faltering, will almost certainly act well before 2033 to increase future funding so that all scheduled benefits get paid.

Like Social Security, Medicare is a widely popular program. Medicare, however, poses a more formidable financial challenge than Social Security does. In 1965, supporters of Medicare said it would not cost more than $8 billion a year. Today, Medicare costs more than $550 billion a year. Even when adjusted for inflation (a dollar in 1965 bought what about $7.38 did in 2013), that is about 75 times what the program cost when it started. Medicare now has more than 50 million beneficiaries (about 45 million senior citizens and most of the rest younger citizens with disabilities). The number of Medicare beneficiaries is expected to grow by about 50 percent over the next 20 years, reaching about 80 million in the early 2030s.

As presently structured, Medicare allows beneficiaries to visit the doctor or go to the hospital pretty much whenever they feel they need to do so. The doctor or hospital is paid a fee for each visit. This creates

HOW WE COMPARE

Social Security

Most European democracies began social security systems earlier than the United States did. Even for its time, the U.S. Social Security program that began in 1935 was a relatively modest insurance-based retirement program.

Today, nearly eight decades later, the U.S. Social Security program has grown dramatically and covers more than "old age, disability, and survivors." Still, European nations not only started sooner but have developed far more comprehensive—and expensive—social security systems than America has yet known.

(continued)

HOW WE COMPARE (*Continued*)

In many European countries, social security programs extend well beyond retirement benefits or pensions to funding for work-related injury, sickness, maternity leave, and more; the retirement age for eligibility is lower than it is in the United States; and the benefits are, on average, greater.

For example, while the average American has received maybe half of his or her working-life income in benefits, a typical French or German worker has retired several years earlier and received as much as 70 percent of his or her working-life income in benefits. Social security benefits here are earnings-related, but many European nations (Ireland, Switzerland, and the United Kingdom, to name just three) provide a flat-rate pension independent of earnings.

Nothing is free: Europeans have paid two to three times as much as Americans in program-related taxes. And, unlike some European and other nations, the United States has avoided "dual Social Security taxation" via bilateral agreements and policies that do not require either foreign workers in America or Americans who work abroad to pay social security to both countries.

Source: US Social Security Administration, *Social Security Programs Throughout the World*, September 2008, and "U.S. International Social Security Agreements," 2009, accessed May 27, 2010 at www.ssa.gov/international/agreements_overview.html.

three problems: some people use medical services when they don't really need them; some doctors and hospitals overcharge the government for their services; and doctors and hospitals are paid on the basis of a government-approved payment plan that can change whenever the government wants to save money.

The health care reform law that was enacted in 2010 has scores of different provisions that affect Medicare. A number of these provisions are intended to make Medicare work better and cost less by instituting more sophisticated systems for tracking differences in pricing for given medical services. By 2013, it had already been discovered that for-profit hospitals billed Medicare at a 29 percent higher rate, on average, than nonprofit or government-owned hospitals.[9] To treat a Medicare patient with a simple case of pneumonia (no complications), Medicare paid $124,051 in Philadelphia, $5,093 in Water Valley, Mississippi, and, on average, $24,549 nationally.[10] Even within a given city, hospitals just blocks apart charged Medicare widely different prices for the same services (lower joint replacements, treating complicated cases of asthma or bronchitis, and many others).[11]

Whether efforts to make Medicare beneficiaries more cost-conscious and Medicare providers less prone to overbill will do much to contain costs or improve services remains to be seen. In its 2012 report, the Medicare Board of Trustees forecast that, even given favorable economic assumptions, including projected savings to be wrought by just such measures, the program's trust fund will run out of money in 2024.[12] Medicare's long-term liability is estimated to be more than $40 trillion. The program's administrative overhead costs are relatively low (about 5 percent of annual expenditures), but a 2011 report by the Government Accountability Office estimated that each year Medicare makes at least $48 billion in "improper payments" to doctors, hospitals, medical equipment companies, and other organizations and individuals that it pays or reimburses.

Federal policymakers at both ends of Pennsylvania Avenue and in both parties have struggled to solve each major social welfare program's problems. For instance, in 2001, the bipartisan Commission to Strengthen Social Security suggested, and President Bush proposed, modifying Social Security by allowing people to invest a portion of their tax contributions into private mutual funds that generate higher returns than what the government can pay. The commission provided this example: If the average worker paid 1 percent of his or her income, matched by 1 percent contributed by the government, into a mutual fund that held both stocks and bonds, and he or she worked from age 21 to 65, that person at age 65 would have more than $500,000, in addition to Social Security. If both husband and wife worked all of these years, they would have more than $1 million. Congress, however, did not agree, and since 2001 similar proposals have gone nowhere in Washington.

In 2003, a new Medicare bill was passed, designed in part to change the system by allowing people to save, tax free, money for medical expenses. But the gains this produced would be partially offset by a huge new benefit to retired persons that was the law's real centerpiece: payments for prescription drugs, or, as it became officially known, Medicare Part D (see the *How Things Work* feature on this page). In 2011, Senator Ron Wyden (D-OR) and Representative Paul Ryan (R-WI) introduced a Medicare reform plan. Among other provisions, the Wyden-Ryan plan reduced benefits for the wealthiest senior citizens. It featured a "premium support" (voucher-type) option under which beneficiaries could choose either a traditional Medicare plan or a Medicare-approved private plan. Total out-of-pocket Medicare costs

HOW THINGS WORK

Medicare ABCDs

Medicare is a federal health insurance program that covers most senior citizens 65 or older, some younger people with disabilities, and people with end-stage renal disease. Today, it covers more than 50 million elderly and disabled persons.

Part A: Hospital Insurance

It covers inpatient care in hospitals, and also helps cover skilled nursing facility care, hospice care, and home health care. Some people pay a monthly premium; others do not.

Part B: Medical Insurance

It covers doctors' services, hospital outpatient care, and some preventive services. The standard monthly premium in 2009 was $96.40. It gets deducted automatically from your Social Security check.

Part C: Medicare Advantage Plus

Basically, it sets the terms under which companies that contract with the Medicare program must provide benefits.

Part D: Prescription Drug Coverage

Participation is voluntary, and the monthly premium depends on how much coverage you have.

were to be capped at $6,000 per person, and low-income citizens who could not pay the cap would receive a subsidy from the government. The bipartisan proposal generated much election-year debate but resulted in no far-reaching Medicare reform legislation.

As we learned in Chapter 6, there are several significant inter-generational gaps in public opinion. "Millennial generation" Americans (ages 18 to 29) differ from senior citizens on issues ranging from same-sex marriage to immigration. There is a similar age gap in opinion on what to do about Social Security and Medicare. Unlike older Americans, most voters under age 30 favor putting Social Security taxes into private accounts and using Medicare benefits to purchase private health insurance (see Table 13.1).

But, as we learned in Chapter 8, older Americans vote at much higher rates than young Americans do, most especially in mid-term congressional elections. Besides, even after years of serious to dire public warnings by present and former lawmakers and blue-ribbon bodies of experts, in 2011, only 8 percent of the public was willing to entertain "major reductions in benefits" for either program, only a quarter (Social Security) and a third (Medicare) were willing to consider "minor reductions in benefits," and a majority in each case opposed increasing taxes to pay for benefits (see Table 13.2).

It may be tempting to see the politics of Social Security and Medicare as a species of client politics in which older citizens benefit and young and middle-aged citizens pay. But resist that temptation. It is true that older citizens vote at higher rates than young ones do. It is also true that interest groups like the AARP that advocate or lobby for the elderly and retirees have great influence in Washington. But most citizens, young and old alike, support the programs; and most oppose trimming benefits and tinkering too much with how the programs presently work. Each program is widely perceived as one into which all people pay and from which all people can and should benefit. The fact that many people receive more in benefits than they ever pay in, like the fact that the programs' massive unfunded liabilities do not fall equally on people of all ages (and will also be borne by citizens yet to be born), would seem to have little bearing on popular attitudes toward these highly popular programs.

Apparently, most federal policymakers also feel that way about the programs; regardless, even those that may feel differently know that they would court real re-election troubles if they publicly prescribed deep cuts in benefits or steep tax increases for either program. For instance, the first lines of the aforementioned Wyden-Ryan Medicare reform plan read like a majoritarian politics rhapsody: the goal was to "strengthen Medicare and health security for all," with "no changes for those in or near retirement," and guaranteeing that Americans age 56 and older "would see no changes to the structure of their benefits" save any changes they might voluntarily opt to make.

TABLE 13.1   **Opinion on Social Security and Medicare Proposals, By Generation**

	Millennial (18–29)	Gen X (30–43)	Boomer (45–63)	Silent (64–81)
	Percent Who Favor			
Changing Social Security to let younger workers put Social Security taxes into private accounts	86	69	58	52
Changing Medicare so people can use benefits toward purchasing private health insurance	74	60	61	48

Source: Adapted from Andrew Kohut, "Debt and Deficit: A Public Opinion Dilemma," Pew Research Center for the People & the Press, June 14, 2012.

TABLE 13.2 Public Opinion on Changing Medicare and Social Security

	Support (%)
Social Security	
Major Reduction in Benefits	8
Minor Reduction in Benefits	27
Raise Retirement Age from 67 to 68	42
Increase Program Tax Rates	35
Increase Benefits at a Slower Rate	45
Medicare	
Major Reduction in Benefits	8
Minor Reduction in Benefits	35
Raise Eligibility Age from 67 to 70	32
Increase Program Tax Rates	49
Replace Program with a Voucher System	35

Source: ABC News/Washington Post Poll, March 10–13, 2011; Kaiser Family Foundation/Harvard School of Public Health Poll, January 4–14, 2011; and School of Public Policy, University of Maryland and Center on Policy Attitudes, "How Americans Would Deal with the Budget Deficit," February 3, 2011, p. 49.

From AFDC to TANF: Client Politics

The Aid to Families with Dependent Children (AFDC) program began as part of the Social Security Act of 1935. It was scarcely noticed at the time. In response to the Great Depression, the federal government promised to provide aid to states that in many cases were already running programs to help poor children who lacked a father.

Because AFDC involved giving federal aid to existing state programs, it allowed the states to define what constituted "need," to set benefit levels, and to administer the program. Washington did set (and, over the years, continued to increase) a number of rules governing how the program would work, however. Washington told the states how to calculate applicants' incomes and, after 1965, required the states to give Medicaid to AFDC recipients (a fact that we will return to in the next section when we parse Medicaid's policy dynamics). The states had to establish mandatory job-training programs for many AFDC recipients and to provide child-care programs for working AFDC parents. Washington also required that women on AFDC identify their children's fathers. In addition to the growing list of requirements, Washington created new programs for which AFDC recipients were eligible, such as Food Stamps, the Earned Income Tax Credit (EITC—a cash grant to poor parents who were working), free school meals, various forms of housing assistance, and certain other benefits. But while all this was happening, public opinion moved against the AFDC program.

By the time that abolishing AFDC was being debated in Congress, opinion surveys found more than 70 percent of the public agreed that people "abuse the system by staying on too long," more than 60 percent agreed that the system "gives people benefits without requiring them to do work" and also permits people "to cheat and commit fraud to get welfare benefits," and about 60 percent agreed that the program encourages out-of-wedlock births.[13] The combination of souring public opinion, increasing federal regulations, and a growing roster of benefits produced a program that lost many one-time supporters. The states disliked having to conform to a growing list of federal regulations. The public disliked the program because over time it came to be viewed as weakening the family by encouraging out-of-wedlock births (since AFDC recipients received additional benefits for each new child). The public worried that AFDC recipients were working covertly on the side; the data proved that this was true of at least half of them in several large cities. AFDC recipients saw that the actual (inflation-adjusted) value of their AFDC checks was going down. Critics countered that if you added together all the benefits they were receiving (Food Stamps, Medicaid, housing assistance, and so on), benefit levels were actually going up. Politicians complained that healthy parents were living off AFDC instead of working. The AFDC law was revised many times, including in 1988 (just eight years before AFDC was abolished). But the program was never revised in a way that satisfied all, or even most, of its critics. Though AFDC recipients were only a small fraction of all Americans, they had become a large political problem.

What made the political problem worse was that the composition of the people in the program had changed. In 1970, about half of the mothers on AFDC were there because their husbands had died or divorced them; only a quarter had never been married. By 1994, the situation had changed dramatically: only about a quarter of AFDC mothers were widowed or divorced, and over half had never been married at all. And though most women on AFDC for the first time got off it after just a few years, almost two-thirds of the women on AFDC at any given moment had been on it for eight years or more.

These facts, combined with the increased proportion of out-of-wedlock births in the country as a whole, made it virtually impossible to sustain political support for what had begun as a noncontroversial client program. In 1996 AFDC was abolished. It was replaced by Temporary Assistance for Needy Families (TANF), a block grant program that set strict federal requirements about work and limited how long families can receive federally funded benefits. In 2002, during the largely consensual congressional debate over reauthorizing TANF, even many who had opposed these strategies in 1996 (when TANF replaced AFDC) now supported them. By 2006, a decade after abolishing AFDC, welfare caseloads nationally had declined by 62 percent. "Ending welfare as we know it," as in ending AFDC, was widely, albeit no means universally, viewed as a success.

During President Obama's first term, critics charged that the administration was weakening TANF's work requirements and permitting TANF recipients to receive benefits longer than the program's rules allowed. The facts, however, told a different tale: TANF recipients, like most Americans generally, were simply having ever greater trouble finding or keeping work amidst the nation's deep economic downturn. Similarly, the number of people receiving Food Stamps increased from about 28 million in 2008 to about 47 million in 2012. Even though most new Food Stamp recipients entered the program after losing jobs or having other financial problems that reduced their incomes, during the 2012 presidential campaign, a debate began over the estimated 2 million or so "able-bodied" Food Stamp recipients that did not meet all the usual program eligibility criteria, and over allegations concerning widespread "waste, fraud, and abuse" in the program. Again, the facts told a different tale: about 40 percent of all Food Stamps beneficiaries were children, about 8 percent were senior citizens, and nearly half of all persons receiving benefits lived in a household where someone worked for low wages.

In sum, although they may be quite controversial when they are first proposed and debated, social welfare programs like Social Security and Medicare that are perceived to benefit wide classes of citizens at a cost that is shared by most people (majoritarian politics) become politically sacrosanct even though, as is presently true for both Social Security and Medicare, they have huge costs, pose present and future financial burdens, make billions of dollars in improper payments, and pay out to most beneficiaries more than those beneficiaries ever pay in. In stark contrast, although they may stir little controversy or go virtually unnoticed when they are first proposed and debated, social welfare programs like the late AFDC that are perceived to benefit only certain groups of citizens at a cost that is shouldered by most people (client politics) will be established and remain politically protected only if the cost to the public at large is not perceived to be great *and* if the people receiving the benefit are widely deemed "deserving."

Medicaid: Client and Majoritarian

At first glance, Medicaid may seem closer to the old AFDC program and the present TANF program than it does to Social Security and Medicare. In 1965 Medicaid was enacted into law in the eleventh hour of Medicare's approval so that at least some low-income persons who were not Medicare-eligible senior citizens might receive some health care coverage. Today, Medicaid is still a means-tested program that pays the medical expenses of persons receiving TANF payments, mainly TANF-eligible low-income adults and their dependent children.

But now look closer. Medicaid also pays medical expenses of persons receiving Social Security benefits, including senior citizens that have spent down their life savings and require long-term medical care, people with permanent or total disabilities, and others, including certain Medi*care* enrollees. It is true that about two-thirds of all Medicaid beneficiaries are low-income children plus non-disabled low-income adults; the other third are non-elderly disabled adults plus low-income or disabled senior citizens. But it is also true that about two-thirds of Medicaid dollars are spent on the one-third of the Medicaid beneficiaries that are elderly or disabled. The other third or so of Medicaid dollars are spent on the roughly two-thirds of the Medicaid beneficiaries that are TANF-eligible non-disabled low-income adults or low-income children. The average annual per capita Medicaid expenditure for disabled and elderly beneficiaries has been more than four times the average annual per capita Medicaid expenditure for non-disabled adult or low-income child beneficiaries.

In the mid-1990s, when AFDC was being dismantled, more than five times as much public money was being spent on Medicaid as was being spent on AFDC, and a majority of Medicaid beneficiaries were also AFDC beneficiaries. But Medicaid has had, and continues to have, a beneficiary population that AFDC did not, namely, senior citizens and disabled persons. Today, just as it was some two decades ago when Congress was about the business of ending AFDC, Medicaid is the main source of public funding for long-term care, accounting for more than half of all government spending on nursing homes, intermediate-care facilities, and medical home-care services. In Congress, as well as in state legislatures, Medicaid has had political support from interest groups beyond those advocating directly for its various beneficiaries, namely, the for-profit firms and nonprofit organizations that receive billions of dollars each year to supply nursing home care and other services.

Thus it is that the policy dynamics surrounding Medicaid mix client politics with majoritarian politics. Over the last two decades, most proposals to "cut Medicaid" have actually been proposals to trim program benefits for the program's TANF-eligible adult, non-disabled populations. Almost nobody thinks of poor senior citizens, poor children, or disabled persons as "undeserving." Since the late 1990s, while Medicaid benefits for TANF-eligible adults have remained flat or been reduced in some states, Medicaid benefits for the program's youngest and oldest beneficiaries, as well for its disabled beneficiaries, have remained stable or grown just about everywhere, including through related policies and programs like the State Children's Health Insurance Program, known as S-CHIP.

In sum, because of its client politics components, Medicaid is not as politically sacrosanct as either Social Security or Medicare each are; but, because of its majoritarian politics components, Medicaid, unlike AFDC, has survived every major push for program-wide cuts while preserving most benefits for TANF-eligible non-disabled adults and expanding benefits for low-income children; and there is not now nor has there ever been any politically significant constituency for "ending Medicaid as we know it." Still, it is too soon to know how Medicaid's politics might change as the now roughly $400 billion a year federal–state program continues to expand, or whether the state-to-state differences in benefit levels for some or all of its beneficiary populations will shrink or widen as the new federal health care policy is implemented.

Environmental Policy

Since 1963, more than three dozen major federal environmental laws have been enacted. When an offshore well spewed thousands of gallons of oil onto the beaches of Santa Barbara, California, at the very time (January 1969) when protest politics was in the air, it became difficult or impossible for the government or business firms to resist the demand that threats to our natural surroundings be curtailed. The emerging environmental movement created an occasion—Earth Day, first celebrated on April 22, 1970—to celebrate its beginning.

The movement was hugely successful. In 1970, President Nixon created the Environmental Protection Agency (EPA) and Congress toughened the existing Clean Air Act and passed the Water Quality Improvement Act. Two years later, it passed laws designed to clean up the water; three years later, it adopted the Endangered Species Act. New laws were passed right into the 1990s. Existing environmental organizations grew in size, and new ones were formed. Public opinion rallied around environmental issues.

"Yeah, yeah, maybe it's cyclical but I don't feel any better."

The Politics of "Cap and Trade"

Of course, as on virtually all other issues, public sentiments on environmental policy are not perfectly stable. For instance, when the public is asked which should be more important, economic growth or environmental protection, they are today less prone to prefer environmental protection than they were just a half-decade ago. Still, overall, most Americans are now environmentalists first, including on the single most interesting and important environmental policy issue of our time, global warming.

Global warming occurs when gases, such as carbon dioxide, produced by people when they burn fossil fuels—wood, oil, or coal—get trapped in the atmosphere and cause the earth's temperature to rise. When the temperature goes up, bad things happen—floods on coastal areas as the polar ice caps melt, wilder weather as more storms are created, and the spread of tropical diseases. The policy dynamics of global warming have involved all four types of politics. The issue might be safely majoritarian by now were it not for partisan differences in how people understand it (see Table 13.3).

Despite the partisan divide, bipartisan efforts to address the issue have been made in each of the last several sessions of Congress. For example, the House of Representatives in mid-2009 passed the American Clean Energy and Security Act. The bill, however, did not make it through the Senate. It featured a "cap and trade" provision that would set maximum emissions of carbon dioxide for most large firms. The emissions allowed by these caps would

TABLE 13.3 Partisan Differences on Global Warming

	Percentage that Agree		
	Republicans	**Democrats**	**Independents**
There is solid evidence the earth is warming	38	79	56
Global warming is a "very serious" problem	14	50	30
The problem requires immediate action	24	68	44
The problem results from human activity	30	59	41

Source: Adapted from "Wide Partisan Differences on Global Warming," Pew Research Center, October 27, 2010.

decline as the years passed. If a firm produced less than the maximum emissions, it could sell part of its permit to another firm. The theory was that firms would take the least costly way to meet the standards: either lowering their emissions or, if that was too expensive, buying an additional permit from another firm. This strategy was used in the 1990s to reduce the emission of sulfur dioxide that people believed caused acid rain. This plan was similar to the cap-and-trade requirements imposed by the Kyoto Treaty of 1997, but the Senate had never ratified that bill in part because China, India, and other growing economies were not bound by it.

Some critics of the 2009 bill argued that it allowed firms to pay money in order to pollute and was not an efficient method to reduce pollution. Many of them argued that it should be replaced by a tax on carbon. Other critics said it would only work if the permits were auctioned off (instead, the plan allowed the government to give most away), that it required an unrealistically large decrease in carbon dioxide (85 percent by 2050), and that the decreased emissions would impose taxes on Americans and slow economic growth.

Despite the efforts of a small bipartisan group of senators, the bill did not come to a vote in their chamber. The White House was focused on passing health care reform, and the president's advisers were divided over how much the president should engage in the legislative negotiations about the environmental bill. Then the Senate majority leader, Democrat Harry Reid of Nevada, declared that immigration reform needed to pass before environmental reform, in an effort to win support from immigration activists in his home state, where he faced a tough (though ultimately successful) re-election campaign. Finally, the disastrous oil spill in the Gulf of Mexico doomed any prospects of passing legislation that had promised (with White House support) an expansion of offshore oil drilling in return for capping carbon emissions.[14]

After his failure to make headway on one of his signature campaign issues, President Obama, like his recent predecessors, has pursued environmental reforms through regulation instead of legislation. For example, the EPA has imposed stricter guidelines for coal mines to receive permits in compliance with the Clean Water Act. In 2011, the U.S. Fish and Wildlife Service debated whether a small desert lizard belonged on its endangered species list, which would mean prohibiting oil and gas production in the areas where the lizard resides. Interest group politics typically dominate regulatory efforts, while large-scale reform more often requires majoritarian support, which is more difficult for the administration to build in a time of economic turmoil.

Over the last four decades, the United States has constructed the most comprehensive and complicated body of environmental laws and regulations in the world. On such issues as endangered species (entrepreneurial), auto pollution (majoritarian), acid rain (interest group), and agricultural pesticides (client), environmental policies arose, persisted, and changed through one or more of the four types of politics we have been discussing. But before turning to explore each example, it is important to understand how environmental policy in America differs from environmental policy in many other modern democracies.

Environmental Policy in America: Three Distinctive Features

First, environmental policymaking in the United States is much more adversarial than it is in most European nations. In this country, there have been bitter and lasting conflicts over the contents of the Clean Air Act. Minimum auto emissions standards are uniform across the nation, regardless of local conditions (states can set higher standards if they wish). Many rules for improving air and water quality have strict deadlines and require expensive technology. Hundreds of inspectors enforce these rules, and hundreds of lawyers bring countless lawsuits to support or challenge this enforcement. Government and business leaders have frequently denounced each other for being unreasonable or insensitive. So antagonistic are the interests involved in environmental policy that it took 13 years, from 1977 to 1990, to agree on a congressional revision of the Clean Air Act.

In the United Kingdom, by contrast, rules designed to reduce air pollution were written by government and business leaders acting cooperatively. The rules are neither rigid nor nationally uniform; they are flexible and allow plenty of exceptions to deal with local variations in business needs. Compliance with the rules depends mostly on voluntary action, not formal enforcement. Lawsuits are rare. You might think all this sweetness and light were the result of having meaningless rules, but not so. As David Vogel has shown, by the early 1980s the British government had implemented an impressive and effective array of regulations intended to improve the nation's air and water quality.[15] Second, environmental policy here, as in so many other policy areas, depends heavily on the states. Though there are uniform national air quality standards, how those standards are achieved is left to the states (subject to certain federal controls). Though sewage treatment plants are in large measure paid for by Washington, they are designed, built, and operated by state and local governments.

Though the federal government decrees that radioactive waste must be properly disposed of somewhere, the states have a big voice in where that is. Federalism reinforces adversarial politics: one of the reasons environmental issues are so contentious in this country is that cities and states fight over what standards should apply where.

Third, the separation of powers guarantees that almost anybody who wants to wield influence over environmental policy will have an opportunity to do so. In the United Kingdom and in most European

HOW THINGS WORK

Major Environmental Laws

Smog Clean Air Act (passed in 1970; amended in 1977 and 1990)

- **Stationary sources:** EPA sets national air quality standards; states must develop plans to attain them. If the state plan is inadequate, EPA sets a federal plan. Local sources that emit more than a certain amount of pollutants must install pollution control equipment.

- **Gasoline-powered vehicles:** Between 1970 and 1990, pollution from cars was cut by between 60 and 80 percent. Between 1991 and 1998 there was another 30 percent reduction. All states must have an auto pollution inspection system.

- **Cities:** Classifies cities in terms of how severe their smog problem is and sets deadlines for meeting federal standards.

Water Clean Water Acts of various years state that there is to be no discharge of wastewater into lakes and streams without a federal permit; to get a permit, cities and factories must meet federal discharge standards.

Toxic wastes EPA is to clean up abandoned dump sites with money raised by a tax on the chemical and petroleum industries and from general revenues. (Many thousands of such sites exist.)

Environmental impact statements Since 1969, any federal agency planning a project that would significantly affect the human environment must prepare in advance an environmental impact statement (EIS).

Acid rain The Clean Air Act of 1990 requires a reduction of 10 million tons of sulphur dioxide (mostly from electric-generating plants that burn coal) by 1995. The biggest sources must acquire government allowances (which can be traded among firms) setting emission limits.

An EPA environmental scientist surveys a Superfund site in Houston, TX, where bacteria is used to clean up toxic industrial waste.

nations, the centralized, parliamentary form of government means that the opponents of a policy have less leverage. Here, environmental pressures are brought by interest groups; in Europe, where such groups have less influence, environmentalists form political parties, such as the Green party, so as to be represented in the legislature.

The distinctive features of environmental policy in America are evident in the policy dynamics history of each of four different issues: endangered species, pollution from automobiles, acid rain, and agricultural pesticides.

Endangered Species: Entrepreneurial Politics

Passed in 1973, the Endangered Species Act (ESA) forbids buying or selling a bird, fish, animal, or plant the government regards as "endangered"—that is, likely to become extinct unless it receives special protection—or engaging in any economic activity (such as building a dam or running a farm) that would harm an endangered species. There have been more than 600 species on the protected list; about half are plants. The regulations forbid not only killing a protected species but also adversely affecting its habitat.

The ESA is run by the Fish and Wildlife Service and the National Oceanic and Atmospheric Administration. They can add species to the endangered or threatened list on their own accord or in response to a private petition. Trafficking in an endangered species can lead to criminal penalties; fines may be imposed for managing private land in ways that might harm a species. Several species (such as bald eagles, grizzly bears, gray wolves, and sea otters) have increased in number since being listed and a few (such as bald eagles and gray wolves) have been taken off the list.

Firms and government agencies that wish to build a dam, bridge, factory, or farm in an area where an endangered species lives must comply with federal regulations. The complaints of such clients about these regulations are outweighed by the public support for the law. Sometimes the law preserves a creature, such as the bald eagle, that almost everyone admires; sometimes it protects a creature, such as the snail darter, that almost no one has ever heard of.

Wood product companies and loggers want access to forests under the control of the U.S. Forest Service. Though only a small fraction of all cut timber comes from these forests and most of the U.S. forest system is already off-limits to logging, environmentalists want further restrictions, especially to prevent clear-cutting (cutting down all the trees in a given area) and to prevent harvesting trees from the old-growth forests of Oregon and Washington. But Congress has generally supported the timber industry, ordering the Forest Service to sell harvesting rights at below-market prices, in effect subsidizing the industry. Some activists have worked to convert this client politics into entrepreneurial politics by demanding that clear-cutting in certain forests be stopped in order to protect endangered species, such as the spotted owl.

Pollution from Automobiles: Majoritarian Politics

The Clean Air Act of 1970 imposed tough restrictions on the amount of pollutants that could come out of automobile tailpipes. Indeed, most of the debate over that bill centered on this issue.

Initially, the auto emissions control rules followed the pattern of entrepreneurial politics: an aroused public with media support demanded that automobile companies be required to make their cars less polluting. It seemed to be "the public" against "the interests," and the public won: by 1975, new cars would have to produce 90 percent less of two pollutants (hydrocarbons and carbon monoxide), and by 1976 achieve a 90 percent reduction in another (nitrous oxides). This was a tall order. There was no time to redesign automobile engines or to find an alternative to the internal combustion engine; it would be necessary to install devices (called catalytic converters) on exhaust pipes that would transform pollutants into harmless gases.

> **environmental impact statement** A report required by federal law that assesses the possible effect of a project on the environment if the project is subsidized in whole or part by federal funds.

But a little-noticed provision in the 1970 law soon shoved the battle over automobile pollution into the arena of majoritarian politics. That provision required states to develop land-use and transportation rules to help attain air quality standards. What that meant in practice was that in any area where smog was still a problem, even after emission controls had been placed on new cars, there would have to be rules restricting the public's use of cars. There was no way for cities such as Denver, Los Angeles, and New York to get rid of smog just by requiring people to buy less-polluting cars—the increase in the number of cars or in the number of miles driven in those places outweighed the gain from making the average car less polluting. That meant the government would have to impose such unpopular measures as bans on downtown parking, mandatory use of buses and carpools, and even gasoline rationing. But efforts to do this failed. Popular opposition to such rules was too great, and the few such rules put into place didn't work. Congress reacted by postponing the deadlines by which air quality standards in cities would have to be met; the EPA reacted by abandoning any serious effort to tell people when and where they could drive.[16]

Even the effort to clean up the exhausts of new cars ran into opposition. Some people didn't like the higher cost of cars with catalytic converters; others didn't like the loss in horsepower these converters caused (many people disconnected them). The United Auto Workers union began to worry that antismog rules would hurt the U.S. auto industry and cost them their jobs. Congress took note of these complaints and decided that despite a lot of effort, new cars could not meet the 90 percent emission reduction standard by 1975–1976, and so in 1977 it amended the Clean Air Act to extend these deadlines by up to six years.

The Clean Air Act, when revised again in 1990, set new, tougher auto emission control standards—but it pushed back the deadline for compliance. It reiterated the need for getting rid of smog in the smoggiest cities and proposed a number of ways to do it—but it set the deadline for compliance in the worst area (Los Angeles) at 20 years in the future.

Most clean-air laws passed since 1990 have targeted particular industries. For example, in 2004 the Bush administration approved a new measure to dramatically reduce emissions from heavy-use diesel engines used in construction, agricultural, and other industrial machinery. The public will support such tough environmental laws when somebody else pays or when the costs are hidden (as in the price of a car); it will not give as much support when it believes it is paying, especially when the payment takes the form of changing how and when it uses the family car. Here are more examples of each kind of majoritarian politics.

Majoritarian Politics When People Believe the Costs Are Low The National Environmental Policy Act (NEPA), passed in 1969, contained a provision requiring that an **environmental impact statement** (EIS) be written before any federal agency undertakes an activity that will "significantly" affect the quality of the human environment. (Similar laws have been passed in many states, affecting not only what government does but also what private developers do.) Because it required only a "statement" rather than some specific action and because it was a pro-environment law, NEPA passed by overwhelming majorities.

As it turned out, the EIS provision was hardly innocuous. Opponents of virtually any government-sponsored project have used the EIS as a way of blocking, changing, or delaying the project. Hundreds of lawsuits have been filed to challenge this or that provision of an EIS or to claim that a project was not supported by a satisfactory EIS. In this way, environmental activists have challenged the Alaska pipeline, a Florida canal, and several nuclear power plants, as well as countless dams, bridges, highways, and office buildings. Usually the agency's plan is upheld, but this does not mean the EIS is unimportant: the EIS induces the agency to think through what it is doing, and it gives critics a chance to examine, and often to negotiate, the content of those plans.

Despite the grumbling of many people adversely affected by fights over an EIS (someone once complained that Moses would never have been able to part the Red Sea if he had had to file an EIS first), popular support for it remains strong because the public at large does not believe it is paying a high price and does believe it is gaining a significant benefit.

Majoritarian Politics When People Believe the Costs Are High From time to time, someone proposes that gasoline taxes be raised sharply. Such taxes would discourage driving, and this not only would conserve fuel but also would reduce smog. Almost everyone would pay, but almost everyone would benefit. However, it is only with great difficulty that the public can be persuaded to support such taxes. The reason is that the people pay the tax first, and the benefit, if any, comes later, and may be a general, rather than individual, result. Unlike Social Security, where the taxes we pay now support cash benefits we get later, gasoline taxes support noncash benefits (cleaner air, less congestion) that many people doubt will ever appear or, if they do, may not be meaningful to them.[17]

When gasoline taxes have been raised, it has usually been because the politicians did not push the tax hike as an environmental measure. Instead, they promised that in return for paying higher taxes the public would receive some concrete benefits—more highways, more buses, or a reduction in the federal deficit (as happened with the gas tax hike of 1990 and again in 1993).

Since it cannot easily cut gasoline use by raising taxes, the government has turned to other approaches. One is to provide tax breaks and other incentives to companies that seek to develop alternative energy sources. Another is to offer incentives to car manufacturers to build vehicles that consume less fuel by relying in whole or in part on electricity.

Acid Rain: Interest Group Politics

Sometimes the rain, snow, or dust particles that fall onto the land are acidic. This is called *acid rain*. In the 1970s, policymakers began to debate policies to deal with it. As everyone acknowledged, one source of acid precipitation is burning fuel such as certain types of coal that contain a lot of sulfur. Some of the sulfur (along with nitrogen) will turn into sulfuric (or nitric) acid as it comes to earth. Steel mills and electric power plants that burn high-sulfur coal are concentrated in the Midwest and Great Lakes regions of the United States. The prevailing winds tend to carry those sulfurous fumes eastward, where some fall to the ground.

That much was certain. Everything else about the issue, however, was surrounded by controversy. Many lakes and rivers in the eastern United States and in Canada had become more acidic, and some forests in these areas had died back. Some part of this was the result of acid rain from industrial smokestacks, but some part of it was also the result of naturally occurring acids in the soils and rainfall. How much of the acidification is man-made and how much is a result of the actions of Mother Nature was a matter of dispute. Some lakes were not affected by acid rain; some were. Why were some affected more than others? Each side in the debate mustered its favorite experts. They provided some support for each side in what became a fierce interest group battle. Residents of Canada and New England have complained bitterly of the loss of forests and the acidification of lakes, blaming it on Midwestern smokestacks. Midwestern businesses, labor unions, and politicians denied that their smokestacks were the major cause of the problem (if, indeed, there was a problem) and argued that, even if they were the cause, they shouldn't have to pay the cost of cleaning up the problem.

An attempt to deal with the issue in 1977 reflected the kind of bizarre compromises that sometimes result when politically opposed forces have to be reconciled. There were essentially two alternatives. One was to require power plants to burn low-sulfur coal. This would undoubtedly cut back on sulfur emissions, but it would cost money, because low-sulfur coal is mined mostly in the West, hundreds of miles away from the Midwestern coal-burning industries. The other way would be to require power plants to install scrubbers—complicated and very expensive devices that would take sulfurous fumes out of the gas before it came out of the smokestack. In addition to their cost, the trouble with scrubbers was that they didn't always work and that they generated a lot of unpleasant sludge that would

LANDMARK CASES

Government and the Environment

- *Union Electric Co. v. Environmental Protection Agency* (1976): EPA rules must be observed without regard to their cost or technological feasibility.

- *Chevron v. National Resources Defense Council* (1984): States should comply with EPA decisions, even if not explicitly authorized by statute, provided they are reasonable efforts to attain the goal of the law.

- *Whitman v. American Trucking Associations* (2001): Allows Congress to delegate broad authority to regulatory agencies.

- *Massachusetts v. Environmental Protection Agency* (2007): The EPA must hear a petition asking it to regulate greenhouse gases.

have to be hauled away and buried somewhere. Their great advantage, however, was that they would allow Midwestern utilities to continue their practice of using cheap, high-sulfur coal.

Congress voted for the scrubbers for all new coal-burning plants, even if they burned low-sulfur coal. In the opinion of most economists, this was the wrong decision,[18] but it had four great political advantages. First, the jobs of miners in high-sulfur coal mines would be protected. They had powerful allies in Congress. Second, environmentalists liked scrubbers, which they seemed to regard as a definitive, technological "solution" to the problem, an approach far preferable to relying on incentives to induce power plants to buy low-sulfur coal. Third, scrubber manufacturers liked the idea, for obvious reasons. Finally, some eastern governors liked scrubbers because if all new plants had to have them, it would be more costly, and thus less likely, for existing factories in their states to close down and move into the West.

The 1977 law in effect required scrubbers on all new coal-burning plants—even ones located right next to mines where they could get low-sulfur coal. As two scholars later described the law, it seemed to produce "clean coal and dirty air."[19] The 1977 bill did not solve much. Many of the scrubbers, as predicted, didn't work very well. And there remained the question of what to do about existing power plants and factories.

When a solution was finally agreed upon, it was a compromise. President Bush the elder proposed a two-step regulation. In the first phase, 111 power plants would be required to reduce their emission of sulfur by a fixed amount. They could decide for themselves how to do it: buy low-sulfur coal, install scrubbers, or use some other technology. This would be done by 1995. In the second phase, with a deadline in the year 2000, there would be sharper emission reductions for many more plants, and this would probably require the use of scrubbers. To create some flexibility in how much each utility must cut its emissions, a system of sulfur dioxide allowances that could be bought and sold was established. This compromise became part of the Clean Air Act of 1990.

In the mid-2000s, interest groups, advocates, and experts on all sides of the issue were once again poised to battle each other over new and proposed changes to the relevant parts of several different environmental laws. They did, but by 2010, the groups arguing for maintaining the policies were supported by longitudinal data from the national program that monitors the composition of precipitation. The data indicated that, though the problem was still far from solved, since 1994 there had been a dramatic decrease in acid rain falling in the parts of the country where the problem had been most severe, and that decrease was achieved largely without the adverse economic and other impacts that the critics had been predicting since the 1977 law took effect.[20] Still, the interest group politics of the issue continued just the same, including but not limited to political battles in 2011 over efforts by the EPA to bolster anti-acid rain regulatory enforcement.

Agricultural Pesticides: Client Politics

Some client groups have so far escaped this momentum. One such group is organized farmers, who have more or less successfully resisted efforts to restrict the use of pesticides or to control the runoff of pesticides from farmlands.

For a while, it seemed as though farmers would also fall before the assaults of policy entrepreneurs. When Rachel Carson published *Silent Spring* in 1962,[21] she set off a public outcry about the harm to wildlife caused by the indiscriminate use of DDT, a common pesticide. In 1972, the EPA banned the use of DDT.

That same year, Congress directed the EPA to evaluate the safety of *all* pesticides (herbicides, insecticides, fungicides, and others) on the market; unsafe ones were to be removed. However, that was easier said than done. By the late 1970s, there were more than 50,000 pesticides in use, with 5,000 new ones introduced every year.[22] Testing all of these chemicals proved to be a huge, vastly expensive, and very time-consuming job, especially since any health effects on people could not be observed for several years. Pesticides have many beneficial uses; therefore, the EPA had to balance the gains and the risks of using a given pesticide and compare the relative gains and risks of two similar pesticides.

In 2004, Congress directed the EPA to expand and improve its pesticides regulation. Again, that would be a tall order. As summarized in a 2011 EPA report, today in America there are some 112 pesticides producers and about 13,000 pesticides distributors; and about $12 billion a year is spent on pesticides by about 78 million households and 1.2 million farms.[23]

The client politics of the issue makes the EPA's huge regulatory task even harder. American farmers are the most productive in the world, and most of them believe they cannot achieve that output (and thus their present incomes) without using pesticides. These farmers are well organized to express their interests and well represented in Congress (especially on the House and Senate Agricultural Committees). Complicating matters is the fact that the subsidies the taxpayers give to farmers often encourage them to produce more food than they can sell and thus to use more pesticides than they really need. Though many of these chemicals do not remain in the crops harvested, large amounts sink into the soil, contaminating water supplies. But these problems are largely invisible to the public and are much harder to dramatize than the discovery of a toxic waste dump like that at Love Canal, New York.

Though opposed by environmental organizations, farm groups have been generally successful at practicing client politics. Even with the aforementioned 2004 mandate to expand and improve pesticides regulation, now, as when the effort began, the EPA's budget for reviewing pesticides has been kept small. Very few pesticides have been taken off the market, and those that have been removed have tended to be ones that, because they were involved in some incident receiving heavy media coverage (such as the effect of DDT on birds), were decided through entrepreneurial politics.

Beyond Domestic Policy

Challenge yourself to learn more about some or all of the various domestic issues, policies, and programs discussed in this chapter. In each case, ask yourself how, if at all, what you have learned tells you about the type (or types) of policymaking politics that is (or was) most important to whether, when, and how government acted (or failed to act). The next chapter explores foreign and military policy and examines which type of politics has mattered most on such issues as international trade and decisions to commit troops abroad.

LEARNING OBJECTIVES

LO 13.1 What types of politics may matter to whether and how government acts on any given issue?

Four types of politics matter, each based on how most people perceive the distribution of monetary and other costs and benefits associated with the policy or program: majoritarian (everybody benefits, everybody pays), interest group (one small group pays, another small group benefits), client (almost everybody pays, one small group benefits), and entrepreneurial (almost everybody benefits, one small group pays).

LO 13.2 Why are some social welfare policies and programs politically protected while others are politically imperiled?

The answer relates mainly to who benefits directly, or who is perceived to benefit directly, from given social welfare policies and programs. For example, Social Security and Medicare benefit almost all people who have reached a certain age, while the Food Stamps program, like the old AFDC program's successor, TANF, benefits only people with low incomes. The first type of social welfare program has no means test (they are available to everyone without regard to income), while the second type is means-tested (only people who fall below a certain income level are eligible). The first type represents majoritarian politics and is almost always politically protected; the second type represents client politics and is often politically imperiled. Medicaid, the federal–state health program, is means-tested, but it has as beneficiaries not only low-income persons but also the aged and the disabled. It mixes majoritarian and client politics, making it less politically sacrosanct than Social Security or Medicare, but more so than the Food Stamps program, TANF, and other means-tested programs.

LO 13.3 Why are environmental policies designed and enforced differently in America than in other industrialized nations?

The adversarial nature of American politics, as well as the system of federalism, complicates policymaking in America, as illustrated by efforts to pass and enforce legislation on automobile emissions, clean air and water, and other environmental issues.

LO 13.4 Does just one type of politics drive environmental policies and programs?

No. While entrepreneurial politics figure prominently in environmental policy dynamics, including on an issue like protecting endangered species, there are environmental issues in each "box," like pollution from automobiles (majoritarian), acid rain (interest group), and agricultural pesticides (client politics). The same can be said for social welfare, business regulation, and other domestic policies and programs.

TO LEARN MORE

Nonpartisan reviews of public policy issues
- www.publicagenda.org
- www.people-press.org

Selected social welfare programs
- Social Security: www.ssa.gov
- Medicare and Medicaid: www.cms.gov
- TANF: www.acf.hhs.gov/programs/ofa

Selected federal agencies
- Environmental Protection Agency: www.epa.gov
- National Labor Relations Board: www.nlrb.gov
- Occupational Safety and Health Administration: www.osha.gov

- Allen, Will. *The Good Food Revolution: Growing Healthy Food, People, and Communities.* New York: Gotham, 2012. Account by a former professional basketball player and fast-food executive who built an "urban farm" program that employs sustainable food cultivation strategies, creates local jobs, promotes healthier eating habits, and has been replicated in many cities all across the country.
- Derthick, Martha. *Policymaking for Social Security.* Washington, D.C.: Brookings Institution, 1979. A detailed analysis of how the Social Security program grew during its first four decades.
- Gore, Al. *Earth in the Balance.* Boston: Houghton Mifflin, 2000. Revised edition of the book on the environment first written when Gore was a senator.
- Heclo, Hugh. *Modern Social Politics in Britain and Sweden.* New Haven, CT: Yale University Press, 1974. Classic comparative analysis of how social welfare programs came to Britain and Sweden.
- Kingdon, John W. *Agendas, Alternatives, and Public Policies.* Boston: Little, Brown, 1984. An insightful account of how domestic issues, especially those involving health and transportation, get on (or drop off) Washington's political agenda.
- Mead, Lawrence M. *From Prophecy to Charity: How to Help the Poor.* Washington, D.C.: American Enterprise Institute, 2011. Argues that the work-based welfare reform programs that succeeded AFDC have been largely successful and prescribes more "paternalistic programs" plus a wider role for charities in administering anti-poverty policies.
- Monsma, Stephen V. *Putting Faith in Partnerships: Welfare-to-Work in Four Cities.* Ann Arbor: University of Michigan Press, 2004. Careful study of the six different types of organizations that administer welfare-to-work programs in big cities.
- Rosenbaum, Walter A. *Environmental Politics and Policy*, 8th ed. Washington, D.C.: Congressional Quarterly Press, 2010. Analyses of the politics of air and water pollution, the use of chemicals, and other environmental issues.
- Vogel, David. *National Style of Regulation: Environmental Policy in Great Britain and the United States.* Ithaca, NY: Cornell University Press, 1986. An explanation of why environmental politics in America tends to be adversarial.
- Washington Post Staff. *Landmark: The Inside Story of America's New Health Care Law and What It Means for All of Us.* New York: Public Affairs, 2010. A lively journalistic account of the politics that produced the Patient Protection and Affordable Care Act of 2010.
- Wilson, James Q., ed. *The Politics of Regulation.* New York: Basic Books, 1980. Analyzes regulatory politics in nine agencies and provides a more detailed statement of the theory of policymaking politics presented in the text.

US Army Photo / Alamy

Foreign and Military Policy

14

LEARNING OBJECTIVES

LO 14.1   Is American foreign policy set by public opinion or elite views?

LO 14.2   If only Congress can declare war, why has the president become so powerful in military affairs?

LO 14.3   Should our foreign policy be based on American interests or some conception of human rights?

Every American knows we struggle against terrorists—that is, against private groups that attack unarmed civilians. But this is not a recent development.

THEN

Between 1801 and 1805 President Thomas Jefferson sent our navy to fight the Barbary Pirates who operated out of various North African countries against merchant shipping in the Mediterranean. They were sponsored by the Ottoman Empire, a Muslim organization based in Turkey. In the 19th century, American warships did battle with pirates in the Caribbean and along our Atlantic coast. Some terrorists operated inside the country. John Brown fought against slavery by raiding the supplies of the American military at Harper's Ferry. One might sympathize with his antislavery views, but he and his followers killed innocent civilians. He was caught and hanged.

After the Civil War, the Ku Klux Klan (KKK) was formed to block the emancipation of blacks by lynching them and shooting into their homes, as well as those of sympathetic whites. The first KKK, created in the 19th century, was replaced by a second one created in the 20th; each of them enrolled several million members and continued the policy of harassment and murder. Although a KKK still exists, it only has a few thousand members and rarely commits an illegal act. To defeat the Klan, in 1871 Congress passed the "Klan Act" that gave the president the power to suspend the writ of habeas corpus in any state where ordinary law enforcement procedures were unavailable and afforded people the right to sue officials who violated their rights.

In the 1960s and 1970s, the Weather Underground, a radical leftist organization, bombed police stations, the Pentagon, and a townhouse; threw Molotov cocktails through a judge's window; and robbed a Brink's armored car. Though several of its leaders have abandoned radical action and taken respectable jobs, they denounce conservatives in and out of government in the strongest language.

NOW

The 9/11 attacks by hijacked aircraft against the World Trade Center and the Pentagon ushered in a new phase and represented a much more deadly form of terrorism than what we have encountered in the past. The evidence suggests that this attack, as well as the bombing of two American embassies and the suicide attack on the USS *Cole*, were carried out by al Qaeda, a radical Islamic group founded by Osama bin Laden and his colleagues. ("Al Qaeda" means "the base.") But these attacks were different from that on Pearl Harbor: the latter attack had, so to speak, a return address—we knew who did it and where they lived. But 9/11 had no return address: it was a terrorist attack waged by small groups that could be located anywhere.

In response, the United States launched an attack on Afghanistan, where the ruling party, the Taliban, had supported and helped train al Qaeda, and passed the Patriot Act, which improved cooperation among intelligence and law enforcement agencies. The federal government amended the Foreign Intelligence Surveillance Act (FISA) that makes it possible for the government to eavesdrop on communications that cross our national borders. In 2011, Osama bin Laden, the founder of al Qaeda, was found in Pakistan and killed by American special forces operatives.

Such choices must be made in a democracy, and some observers think democratic politics makes managing foreign and military policy harder. Tocqueville said the conduct of foreign affairs requires precisely those qualities most lacking in a democratic nation: "A democracy can only with great difficulty regulate the details of an important undertaking, persevere in a fixed design, and work out

Aamir Qureshi/AFP/Getty Images

In May 2011 Osama bin Laden was killed by U.S. special forces in the house behind this wall, located in Abbottabad, Pakistan.

its execution in spite of serious obstacles. It cannot combine its measures with secrecy or await their consequences with patience."[1] In plain language, a democracy is forced to play foreign policy poker with its cards turned up. As a result, aggressors from Hitler to Saddam Hussein can bluff a democracy, but the reverse is far more difficult.

But other writers disagree with Tocqueville. To them, the strength of democracy is that, though it rarely if ever wages an unjustified war on another country, its people, when mobilized by the president, will support our overseas engagements even when many deaths occur.[2]

Kinds of Foreign Policy

The majoritarian component of foreign policy includes those decisions (and non-decisions) perceived to confer widely distributed benefits and impose widely distributed costs. The decision to go to war is an obvious example of this. So, too, are the establishment of military alliances with Western Europe, the negotiation of a nuclear test ban treaty or a strategic arms limitation agreement, the response to the placement of Soviet offensive missiles in Cuba, and the opening up of diplomatic relations with the People's Republic of China. These may be good or bad policies, but the benefits and costs accrue to the nation generally.

Some argue that the costs of many of these policies are in fact highly concentrated—for example, soldiers bear the burden of a military operation—but that turns out, on closer inspection, not to shape the positions that people take on issues of war and peace. Though soldiers and their immediate families may feel the costs of war to an especially high degree, public opinion surveys taken during the Vietnam War showed that having a family member in the armed forces did not significantly affect how people evaluated the war.[3] There is a sense that, during wartime, we are all in this together.

Foreign policy decisions may also reflect interest group politics. Tariff decisions confer benefits on certain business firms and labor unions and impose costs on other firms and unions. If the price of Japanese steel imported into this country is increased by tariffs, quotas, or other devices, this helps the American steel industry and the United Steel Workers of America. On the other hand, it hurts those firms (and associated unions) that had been purchasing the once-cheap Japanese steel.

Examples of client politics also occur in foreign affairs. Washington often provides aid to American corporations doing business abroad because the aid helps those firms directly without imposing any apparent costs on an equally distinct group in society. Americans support Israel partly because Jewish organizations back her and partly because they admire that embattled democracy. Arab Americans have begun to organize and to press concerns on the government that are very different from the pro-Israel arguments.

Who has power in foreign policy depends very much on what kind of foreign policy we have in mind. Where it is of a majoritarian nature, the president is clearly the dominant figure, and much, if not everything, depends on his beliefs and skills and on those of his chief advisers. Public opinion will ordinarily support this presidential leadership, but it will not guide it. Woe to the president who by his actions forfeits that trust.

When interest group or client politics is involved, Congress plays a much larger role. Although Congress has a subsidiary role in the conduct of foreign diplomacy, the decision to send troops overseas, or the direction of intelligence operations, it has a large one in decisions involving foreign economic aid, the structure of the tariff system, the shipment of weapons to foreign allies, the creation of new weapons systems, and the support of Israel.

And Congress is the central political arena on those occasions when entrepreneurial politics shapes foreign policy. If a multinational corporation is caught in a scandal, congressional investigations shake the usual indifference of politicians to the foreign conduct of such corporations. If presidential policies abroad lead to reversals, as when in 1986 presidential aides sought to trade arms for U.S. hostages in Iran and then use some profits from the arms sales to support the anti-Marxist contras fighting in Nicaragua, Congress becomes the forum for investigations and criticism. At such moments Congress often seeks to expand its power over foreign affairs.

In this chapter, we will be chiefly concerned with foreign policy insofar as it displays the characteristics of majoritarian politics. Limiting the discussion in this way permits us to focus on the grand issues of foreign affairs—war, peace, and global diplomacy. It allows us to see how choices are made in a situation in which public majorities support but do not direct policy, in which opinion tends to react to events, and in which interest groups are relatively unimportant.

The Constitutional and Legal Context

The Constitution defines the authority of the president and of Congress in foreign affairs in a way that, as Edward Corwin put it, is an "invitation to struggle."[4] The president is commander-in-chief of the armed forces, but Congress must authorize and appropriate money for those forces. The president appoints ambassadors, but they must be confirmed by the Senate. The president may negotiate treaties, but the Senate must ratify these by a two-thirds vote. Only Congress may regulate commerce with other nations and "declare" war. (In an early draft of the Constitution, the Framers gave Congress the power to "make" war, but changed this to "declare" so that the president, acting without Congress, could take military measures to repel a sudden attack.) Because power over foreign affairs is shared by the president and Congress, conflict between them is to be expected.

Yet almost every American thinks instinctively that the president is in charge of foreign affairs, and what popular opinion supposes, the historical record confirms. Presidents have asserted the right to send troops abroad on their own authority in more than 125 instances. Only five of the 11 major wars that this country has fought have followed a formal declaration of war by Congress.[5] The State Department, the Central Intelligence Agency, and the National Security Agency are almost entirely "presidential" agencies, with only modest congressional control. The Defense Department, though keenly sensitive to congressional views on weapons procurement and the location of military bases, is very much under the control of the president on matters of military strategy. While the Senate has, since 1789, ratified well over 1,000 treaties signed by the president, the president during this period also has signed around 7,000 executive agreements with other countries that did not require Senate ratification and yet have the force of law.[6]

Evaluating the Power of the President

Whether one thinks the president is too strong or too weak in foreign affairs depends not only on whether one holds a domestic or international point of view but also on whether one agrees or disagrees with his policies. Historian Arthur M. Schlesinger, Jr., thought that President Kennedy exercised commendable presidential vigor when he made a unilateral decision to impose a naval blockade on Cuba to induce the Soviets to remove missiles installed there. However, he viewed President Nixon's decision to extend U.S. military action in Vietnam into neighboring Cambodia as a deplorable example of the "imperial presidency."[7] To be sure, there were important differences between these two actions, but that is precisely the point: an office strong enough to do something that one thinks proper is also strong enough to do something that one finds wrong.

The Supreme Court has fairly consistently supported the view that the federal government has powers in the conduct of foreign and military policy beyond those specifically mentioned in the Constitution.

Moreover, the Supreme Court has been reluctant to intervene in disputes over the conduct of foreign affairs. When various members of Congress brought suit challenging the right of President Nixon to enlarge the war in Vietnam without congressional approval, the court of appeals handled the issue, as one scholar was later to describe it, with all the care of porcupines making love. The Court said it was a matter for the president and Congress to decide and that if Congress was unwilling to cut off the money to pay for the war, it should not expect the courts to do the job for it.[8]

The Supreme Court upheld the extraordinary measures taken by President Lincoln during the Civil War and refused to interfere with the conduct of the Vietnam War by Presidents Johnson and Nixon.[9] After Iran seized American hostages in 1979, President Carter froze Iranian assets in this country. To win the hostages' freedom the president later agreed to return some of these assets and to nullify claims on them by American companies. The Court upheld the nullification because it was necessary for the resolution of a foreign policy dispute.[10]

How great the deference to presidential power may be is vividly illustrated by the actions of President Franklin Roosevelt in ordering the army to move more than 100,000 Japanese Americans—the great majority of them born in this country and citizens of the United States—from their homes on the West Coast to inland "relocation centers" for the duration of World War II. Though this action was a wholesale violation of the constitutional rights of U.S. citizens and was unprecedented in American history, the Supreme Court decided that with the West Coast vulnerable to attack by Japan, the president was within his rights to declare that people of Japanese ancestry might pose a threat to internal security; thus the relocation order was upheld.[11] (No Japanese American was ever found guilty of espionage or sabotage.) One of the few cases in which the Court denied the president broad wartime powers occurred in 1952, when by a 5-to-4 vote it reversed President Truman's seizure of the steel mills—a move that he had made in order to avert a strike that, in his view, would have imperiled the war effort in Korea.[12]

Checks on Presidential Power

If there is a check on the powers of the federal government or the president in foreign affairs, it is chiefly political rather than constitutional. The most important check is Congress's control of the purse strings. In addition, Congress has imposed three important kinds of restrictions on the president's freedom of action, all since Vietnam.

Limitations on the President's Ability to Give Military or Economic Aid to Other Countries
For example, between 1974 and 1978 the president could not sell arms to Turkey because of a dispute between Turkey and Greece over control of the island of Cyprus. The pressure on Congress from groups supporting Greece was much stronger than that from groups supporting Turkey. In 1976, Congress prevented President Ford from giving aid to the pro-Western faction in the Angolan civil war. Until the method was declared unconstitutional, Congress for many years could use a legislative veto, a resolution disapproving of an executive decision (see Chapter 11), to block the sale by the president of arms worth more than $25 million to another country.

The War Powers Act Passed in 1973 over a presidential veto, this law placed the following restrictions on the president's ability to use military force:

- He must report in writing to Congress within 48 hours after he introduces U.S. troops into areas where hostilities have occurred or are imminent.

- Within 60 days after troops are sent into hostile situations, Congress must, by declaration of war or other specific statutory authorization, provide for the continuation of hostile action by U.S. troops.

- If Congress fails to provide such authorization, the president must withdraw the troops (unless Congress has been prevented from meeting as a result of an armed attack).

- If Congress passes a concurrent resolution (which the president may not veto) directing the removal of U.S. troops, the president must comply.

Until recently the War Powers Act has had very little influence on American military actions. Since its passage every president—Ford, Carter, Reagan, Bush the elder, Clinton, Bush the younger, and Obama—has sent American forces abroad without any explicit congressional authorization. (Bush the elder asked for that support when he attacked Iraq and, by a narrow margin, received it.) No president has acknowledged that the War Powers Act is constitutional. In its 1983 decision in the *Chadha* case, the Supreme Court struck down the legislative veto, which means that this section of the act is already in constitutional trouble.[13]

Even if the act is constitutional politically, it is all but impossible to use. Few members of Congress would challenge a president who carried out a successful military operation (for example, those in Grenada, Panama, and Afghanistan). More might challenge the president if, after a while, the military action were in trouble, but the most direct way to do that would be to cut off funding for the operation, which could pose grave risks on the battlefront.

National Archives and Records Administration

Following the attack on Pearl Harbor on December 7, 1941, President Franklin D. Roosevelt in 1942 ordered that all Japanese Americans living on the West Coast be relocated to internment camps.

Intelligence Oversight Owing to the low political stock of President Nixon during the Watergate scandal and the revelations of illegal operations by the Central Intelligence Agency (CIA) within the United States, Congress required that the CIA notify appropriate congressional committees about any proposed covert action (between 1974 and 1980 it had to notify *eight* different committees). Today it must keep two groups, the House and the Senate Intelligence Committees, "fully and currently informed" of all intelligence activities, including covert actions. The committees do not have the authority to disapprove such actions.

However, from time to time Congress will pass a bill blocking particular covert actions. This happened when the Boland Amendment (named after its sponsor, Representative Edward Boland) was passed on several occasions between 1982 and 1985. Each version of the amendment prevented, for specifically stated periods, intelligence agencies from supplying military aid to the Nicaraguan contras.

The 9/11 terrorist attacks left everyone wondering why our intelligence agencies had not foreseen them. After the attacks, there was an investigation to find out why the CIA had not warned the country of this risk. In an effort to improve matters, Congress passed and President Bush signed a law creating the Office of the Director of National Intelligence (DNI). It was designed to coordinate the work of the CIA, the FBI, the Defense Intelligence Agency (DIA), and the intelligence units of several other government agencies. The DNI replaced the director of the CIA as the president's chief adviser. It is too early to tell how much real coordination will occur; the DNI's office is another large bureaucracy placed on top of other big ones.

The Machinery of Foreign Policy

From the time that Thomas Jefferson took the job in Washington's first administration until well into the 20th century, foreign policy was often made and almost always carried out by the secretary of state. No more. When America became a major world power during and after World War II, our commitments overseas expanded dramatically. With that expansion two things happened. First, the president began to put foreign policy at the top of his agenda and to play a larger role in directing it. Second, that policy was shaped by the scores of agencies (some brand-new) that had acquired overseas activities.

Today Washington, D.C., has not one State Department but many. Every new secretary of state bravely announces he or she is going to "coordinate" and "direct" this enormous foreign policy establishment. He or she never does. The reason is partly that the job is too big for any one person and partly that most of these agencies owe no political or bureaucratic loyalty to the secretary of state. If anyone is to coordinate them, it will have to be the president. But the president cannot keep track of what all these organizations are doing in the more than 190 nations and 50 international organizations where we have representatives, or in the more than 800 international conferences that we attend each year.

So he has hired a staff to do the coordinating for him. That staff is part of the National Security Council (NSC), a committee created by statute and chaired by the president, whose members include by law the vice president and the secretaries of state and defense, by custom the director of national intelligence (DNI), the chairman of the Joint Chiefs of Staff, and often the attorney general. Depending on the president, the NSC can be an important body in which to hammer out foreign policy. Attached to it is a staff headed by the national security adviser. That staff, which usually numbers a few dozen men and women, can be (again, depending on the president) an enormously powerful instrument for formulating and directing foreign policy.

The way in which the machinery of foreign policymaking operates has two major consequences for the substance of that policy. First, as former secretary of state George Shultz asserted, "It's never over." Foreign policy issues are endlessly agitated, rarely settled. The reason is that the rivalries *within* the executive branch intensify the rivalries *between* that branch and Congress. In ways already described, Congress has steadily increased its influence over the conduct of foreign policy. Anybody in the executive branch who loses out in a struggle over foreign policy can take his or her case (usually by means of a well-timed leak) to a sympathetic member of Congress, who then can make a speech, hold a hearing, or introduce a bill.

Second, the interests of the various organizations making up the foreign policy establishment profoundly affect the positions that

LANDMARK CASES

Foreign Affairs

- *Curtiss-Wright Export Corp. v. United States* (1936): American foreign policy is vested entirely in the federal government where the president has plenary power.

- *Korematsu v. United States* (1944): Sending Japanese Americans to relocation centers during World War II was based on an acceptable military justification.

- *Youngstown Sheet & Tube Co. v. Sawyer* (1952): The president may not seize factories during wartime without explicit congressional authority even when they are threatened by a strike.

- *Hamdi v. Rumsfeld* (2004): An American citizen in jail because he allegedly joined the Taliban extremist group should have access to a "neutral decision maker."

- *Rasul v. Bush* (2004): Foreign nationals held at Guantanamo Bay because they are believed to be terrorists have a right to bring their cases before an American court.

they take. Because the State Department has a stake in diplomacy, it tends to resist bold or controversial new policies that might upset established relationships with other countries. Part of the CIA has a stake in gathering and analyzing information; that part tends to be skeptical of the claims of other agencies that their overseas operations are succeeding. Another part of the CIA conducts covert operations abroad; it tends to resent or ignore the skepticism of the intelligence analysts. The Air Force flies airplanes and so tends to be optimistic about what can be accomplished through the use of air power in particular and military power in general; the Army, on the other hand, which must fight in the trenches, is often dubious about the prospects for military success. During the American war in Iraq, the conflict between the CIA and the Defense Department was great, with each side leaking information to the press.

Foreign Policy and Public Opinion

These organizational conflicts shape the details of foreign policy, but its broad outlines are shaped by public and elite opinion.

World War II was the great watershed event in American foreign policy. Before that time, a clear majority of the American public opposed active involvement in world affairs. The public saw the costs of such involvement as being substantially in excess of the benefits, and only determined, skillful leaders were able—as was President Roosevelt during 1939–1940—to affect in even a limited fashion the diplomatic and military struggles then convulsing Europe and Asia.

In 1939, after World War II had begun in Europe but before Pearl Harbor was attacked, only 13 percent of Americans polled thought that we should enter the war against Germany. Just a month before Pearl Harbor, only 19 percent felt that the United States should take steps, at the risk of war, to prevent Japan from becoming too powerful.[14] Congress reflected the noninterventionist mood of the country: in the summer of 1941, with war breaking out almost everywhere, the proposal to continue the draft passed the House of Representatives by only one vote.

The Japanese attack on Pearl Harbor on December 7 changed all that. Not only was the American war effort supported almost unanimously, not only did Congress approve the declaration of war with only one dissenting vote, but World War II—unlike World War I—produced popular support for an active assumption of international responsibilities that continued after the war had ended.[15] Whereas after World War I a majority opposed U.S. entry into the League of Nations, after World War II a clear majority favored our entry into the United Nations.[16]

This willingness to see the United States remain a world force persisted. Even during the Vietnam War, the number of people thinking that we should "keep independent" in world affairs as opposed to "working closely with other nations" rose from 10 percent in 1963 to only 22 percent in 1969.[17] In 1967, after more than two years of war in Vietnam, 44 percent of Americans believed that this country had an obligation to "defend other Vietnams if they are threatened by communism."[18]

Before 9/11, hardly any American thought we should fight a war in Afghanistan, but after that attack we fought exactly that war in order to get rid of the Taliban regime. The Taliban, a group of radical young Muslims, had taken control of that country and allowed Osama bin Laden, the head of al Qaeda, to use the nation as a place to train and direct terrorists. Though al Qaeda designed and carried out the 9/11 attacks on America, it is not a single organization located in one place and thus easily defeated. It is instead a network of terrorist cells found all over the world that is allied with other terrorist groups.

But the support for an internationalist American foreign policy was, and is, highly general and heavily dependent on the phrasing of poll questions, the opinions expressed by popular leaders, and the impact of world events. Public opinion, while more internationalist than once was the case, is both mushy and volatile. Just prior to President Nixon's decision to send troops into Cambodia, only 7 percent of the people said they supported such a move. After the troops were sent and Nixon made a speech explaining his move, 50 percent of the public said they supported it.[19] Similarly, only 49 percent of the people favored halting the American bombing of North Vietnam before President Johnson ordered such a halt in 1968; afterward 60 percent of the people said they supported such a policy.[20]

Backing the President

Much of this volatility in specific opinions (as opposed to general mood) reflects the already-mentioned deference to the "commander-in-chief" and a desire to support the United States when it confronts other nations. Table 14.1 shows the proportion of people who said that they approved of the way the president was doing his job before and after various major foreign policy events. Almost every foreign crisis increased the level of public approval of the president, often dramatically. The most vivid illustration of this was the Bay of Pigs fiasco: an American-supported, American-directed invasion of Cuba by anti-Castro Cuban émigrés was driven back into the sea. President Kennedy accepted responsibility for the aborted project. His popularity *rose*. (Comparable data for domestic crises tend to show no similar effect.)

This tendency to "rally round the flag" operates for some but not all foreign military crises.[21] The rally not only helped Kennedy after the Bay of Pigs, but it also helped Ronald Reagan when he invaded Grenada and George Bush the elder when he sent troops to fight Iraq. But it did not help Bill Clinton when he sent forces to Bosnia or launched bombing attacks on Iraq. If there is an attack on America,

TABLE 14.1   **Popular Reactions to Foreign Policy Crises**

Percentage of public saying that they approve of the way the president is handling his job

Foreign Policy Crisis		Before	After
1960	American U-2 spy plane shot down over Soviet Union	62%	68%
1961	Abortive landing at Bay of Pigs in Cuba	73	83
1962	Cuban missile crisis	61	74
1975	President Ford sends forces to rescue the American ship	40	51
1979	American embassy in Tehran seized by Iranians	32	61
1980	Failure of military effort to rescue hostages in Iran	39	43
1983	U.S. invasion of Grenada	43	53
1989	U.S. invasion of Panama	71	80
1990	U.S. troops to Persian Gulf	60	75
1995	U.S. troops to Bosnia	59	54
1999	U.S. troops to Kosovo	55	51
2001	U.S. combat in Afghanistan	51	86
2003	U.S. invasion of Iraq	58	71
2011	U.S. kills Osama bin Laden	46	52
2011	NATO intervention in Libya; Muammar Gaddafi killed	48	45

Sources: Updated from Theodore J. Lowi, *The End of Liberalism* (New York: Norton, 1969), p. 184. Poll data are from Gallup poll and realclearpolitics.com. Time lapse between "before" and "after" samplings of opinion was in no case more than one month.

then the public typically unites in support of the president. Just before September 11, 2001, George Bush's favorability rating was 51 percent; just after the attack, it was 86 percent.

In sum, people tend to be leery of overseas military expeditions by the United States—until they start. Then they support them and want to win, even if it means more intense fighting. When Americans began to dislike our involvement in Korea and Vietnam,[22] they did not conclude that we should pull out; they concluded instead that we should do whatever was necessary to win. The invasion of Iraq did not raise large questions for many Americans until terrorist attacks on the American military continued after the Iraqi army had been defeated.

Despite the tendency for most Americans to rally round the flag, there has been for many decades some public opposition to almost any war in which the United States participates. About one-fifth of Americans opposed our invading Iraq, about the same level of opposition to our wars in Korea and Vietnam. Opposition has generally been highest among Democrats, African Americans, and people with a postgraduate degree.[23] For the U.S. intervention in Libya in 2011, just 47 percent of Americans approved of this military action, with 37 percent in opposition.[24]

Mass versus Elite Opinion

The public is poorly informed about foreign affairs. It probably has only a vague idea where Kosovo is, how far it is from Baghdad to Kuwait, or why the Palestinians and the Jews disagree about the future of Israel. But that is to be expected. Foreign affairs are, well, foreign. They do not have much to do with the daily lives of American citizens, except during wartime. But the public, since World War II, has consistently felt that the United States should play an important international role.[25] And if our troops go abroad, it is a foolish politician who will try to talk the public out of supporting them.

Political elites, however, have a different perspective. They are better informed about foreign policy issues, but their opinions are more likely to change rapidly. Initially, college-educated people gave *more* support to the war in Vietnam than those without college training; by the end of the war, however, that support had decreased dramatically. Whereas the average citizen was upset when the United States seemed to be on the *defensive* in Vietnam, college-educated voters tended to be more upset when the United States was on the *offensive*.[26]

Though the average citizen did not want our military in Vietnam in the first place, he or she felt that we should support our troops once they were there. The average person also was deeply opposed to the antiwar protests taking place on college campuses. When the Chicago police roughed up antiwar demonstrators at the 1968 Democratic convention, public sentiment was overwhelmingly on the side of the police.[27] Contrary to myths much accepted at the time, younger people were *not* more opposed to the war than older ones. There was no "generation gap."

By contrast, college-educated citizens, thinking at first that troops should be involved, soon changed their minds, decided that the war was wrong, and grew increasingly upset when the United States seemed to be enlarging the war (by invading Cambodia, for example). College students protested against the war largely on moral grounds, and their protests received more support from college-educated adults than from other citizens.

Elite opinion changes more rapidly than public opinion. During the Vietnam War, upper-middle-class people who regularly read several magazines and newspapers underwent a dramatic change in opinion between 1964 (when they supported the war) and 1968 (when they opposed it). But the views of blue-collar workers scarcely changed at all.[28]

The cleavage between mass and elite opinion is even wider if you restrict the definition of *elite* to only those involved in making foreign policy rather than including all college-educated people. In Figure 14.1, we see the differences in foreign policy views of a cross section of American citizens and

FIGURE 14.1   **Public's View of America as World Leader**

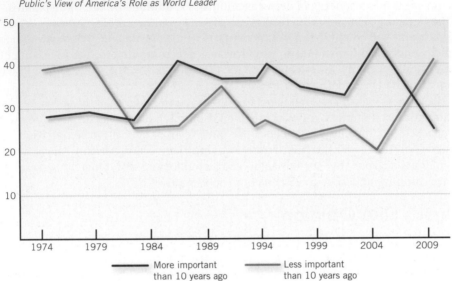

Public's View of America's Role as World Leader

More important than 10 years ago

Less important than 10 years ago

Source: Pew Research Center for the People & the Press, "U.S. Seen As Less Important, China as More Powerful: Isolationist Sentiment Surges to Four-Decade High," 3 December 2009.

a group of 450 leaders active in government, academia, the mass media, and various organizations concerned with foreign affairs.[29]

In general the leaders have a more liberal and internationalist outlook than the public: they are more likely to favor giving economic aid to other countries and defending our allies. The public, on the other hand, wants the United States to be less active overseas and worries about protecting the jobs of American workers. Accordingly, it wants the United States to protect American jobs from foreign competition and give less economic aid to other nations.

Cleavages among Foreign Policy Elites

As we have seen, public opinion on foreign policy is permissive and a bit mushy: it supports presidential action without giving it much direction. Elite opinion therefore acquires extraordinary importance. Of course events and world realities are also important, but since events have no meaning except as they are perceived and interpreted by people who must react to them, the attitudes and beliefs of those people in and out of government who are actively involved in shaping foreign policy often assume decisive importance.

Contrary to the views of people who think that some shadowy, conspiratorial group of insiders runs our foreign policy, the foreign policy elite in this country is deeply divided. That elite consists not only of those people with administrative positions in the foreign policy field—the senior officials of the State Department and the staff of the National Security Council—but also the members and staffs of the key congressional committees concerned with foreign affairs (chiefly the Senate Foreign Relations Committee and the House International Relations Committee) and various private organizations that help shape elite opinion, such as the members of the Council on Foreign Relations and the editors of two important publications, *Foreign Affairs* and *Foreign Policy.* To these must be added influential columnists and editorial writers whose work appears regularly in the national press. One could extend the list by adding ever-wider circles of people with some influence (lobbyists, professors, leaders of veterans' organizations); this would complicate without changing the central point: elite beliefs are probably more important in explaining foreign policy than in accounting for decisions in other policy areas.

How a Worldview Shapes Foreign Policy

These beliefs can be described in simplified terms as **worldviews** (or, as some social scientists put it, as paradigms)—more or less comprehensive mental pictures of the critical problems facing the United States in the world and of the appropriate and inappropriate ways of responding to these problems. The clearest, most concise, and perhaps most influential statement of one worldview that held sway for many years was in an article published in 1947 in *Foreign Affairs,* titled "The Sources of Soviet Conduct."[30] Written by a "Mr. X" (later revealed to be George F. Kennan, director of the Policy Planning Staff of the State Department and thereafter ambassador to Moscow), the article argued that the Russians were pursuing a policy of expansion that could only be met by the United States' applying "unalterable counterforce at every point where they show signs of encroaching upon the interests of a peaceful and stable world." This he called the strategy of "containment," and it became the governing principle of American foreign policy for at least two decades.

There were critics of the containment policy at the time—Walter Lippmann, in his book *The Cold War,* argued against it in 1947[31]—but the criticisms were less influential than the doctrine. A dominant worldview is important precisely because it prevails over alternative views. One reason why it prevails is that it is broadly consistent with the public's mood. In 1947, when Kennan wrote, popular attitudes toward the Soviet Union—favorable during World War II when Russia and America were allies—had turned quite hostile. In 1946, less than one-fourth of the American people believed Russia could be trusted to cooperate with this country,[32] and by 1948 over three-fourths were convinced the Soviet Union was trying not simply to defend itself, but to become the dominant world power.[33]

Such a worldview was also influential because it was consistent with events at the time: Russia had occupied most of the previously independent countries of Eastern Europe and was turning them into puppet regimes. When governments independent of both the United States and the Soviet Union attempted to rule in Hungary and Czechoslovakia, they were overthrown by Soviet-backed coups. A worldview also becomes dominant when it is consistent with the prior experiences of the people holding it.

Four Worldviews Every generation of political leaders comes to power with a foreign policy worldview shaped, in large measure, by the real or apparent mistakes of the previous generation.[34] This pattern can be traced back, some have argued, to the very beginnings of the nation. Frank L. Klingberg traces the alteration since 1776 between two national "moods" that favored first "extroversion" (or an active, internationalist policy) and then "introversion" (a less active, even isolationist posture).[35]

Since the 1920s, American elite opinion has moved through four dominant worldviews: isolationism, containment (or anti-appeasement), disengagement, and human rights. **Isolationism** was the view adopted as a result of our unhappy experience in World War I. Our efforts to help European allies had turned sour: thousands of American troops had been killed in a war that had seemed to accomplish little and certainly had not made the world, in Woodrow Wilson's words, "safe for democracy." As a result, in the 1920s and 1930s elite opinion (and popular opinion) opposed U.S. involvement in European wars.

worldviews A comprehensive opinion of how the United States should respond to world problems.

isolationism The opinion that the United States should withdraw from world affairs.

containment The belief that the United States should resist the expansion of aggressive nations, especially the former Soviet Union.

disengagement The belief that the United States was harmed by its war in Vietnam and so should avoid supposedly similar events.

The **containment** (or anti-appeasement) paradigm was the result of World War II. Pearl Harbor was the death knell for isolationism. Senator Arthur H. Vandenberg of Michigan, a staunch isolationist before the attack, became an ardent internationalist not only during but after the war. He later wrote of the Japanese attack on Pearl Harbor on December 7, 1941, "that day ended isolationism for any realist."[36] At a conference in Munich, efforts of British and French leaders to satisfy Hitler's territorial demands in Europe had led not to "peace in our time," as British Prime Minister Neville Chamberlain had claimed, but to ever-greater territorial demands and ultimately to world war. This crisis brought to power men determined not to repeat their predecessors' mistakes: "Munich" became a synonym for weakness, and leaders such as Winston Churchill made anti-appeasement the basis of their postwar policy of resisting Soviet expansionism. Churchill summed up the worldview that he had acquired from the Munich era in a famous speech delivered in 1946 in Fulton, Missouri, in which he coined the term *iron curtain* to describe Soviet policy in Eastern Europe.

The events leading up to World War II were the formative experiences of those leaders who came to power in the 1940s, 1950s, and 1960s. What they took to be the lessons of Pearl Harbor and Munich were applied repeatedly—in building a network of defensive alliances in Europe and Asia during the late 1940s and 1950s, in operating an airlift to aid West Berlin when road access to it was cut off by the Russians, in coming to the aid of South Korea, and finally in intervening in Vietnam. Most of these applications of the containment worldview were successful in the sense that they did not harm American interests, they proved welcome to allies, or they prevented a military conquest.

The **disengagement** (or "Vietnam") view resulted from the experience of the younger foreign policy elite that came to power in the 1970s. Unlike previous applications of the anti-appeasement view, our entry into Vietnam had led to a military defeat and a domestic political disaster. There were three ways of interpreting that crisis: (1) we applied the correct worldview in the right place but did not try hard enough; (2) we had the correct worldview but tried to apply it in the wrong place under the wrong circumstances; (3) the worldview itself was wrong. By and large, the critics of our Vietnam policy tended toward the third conclusion, and thus when they supplanted in office the architects of our Vietnam policy, they inclined toward a worldview based on the slogan "no more Vietnams." Critics of this view called it the "new isolationism," arguing that it would encourage Soviet expansion.

The debates over the Vietnam War colored many subsequent discussions of foreign policy. Almost every military initiative since then has been debated in terms of whether it would lead us into "another Vietnam": sending the Marines to Lebanon, invading Grenada, dispatching military advisers to El Salvador, supporting the contras in Nicaragua, helping South American countries fight drug producers, and sending troops to invade Iraq.

How elites thought about Vietnam affected their foreign policy views for many years. If they thought the war was "immoral," they were reluctant to see American military involvement elsewhere. These elites played a large role in the Carter administration, but were replaced by rival elites—those more inclined to a containment view—during the Reagan presidency.[37] When George H. W. Bush sought to expel Iraqi troops from Kuwait, the congressional debate pitted those committed to containment against those who believed in disengagement. The Senate vote on Bush's request for permission to use troops was narrowly carried by containment advocates.

When Clinton became president in 1992, he brought to office a lack of interest in foreign policy coupled with advisers who were drawn from the ranks of those who believed in disengagement. His strongest congressional supporters were those who had argued against the Gulf War. But then a remarkable change occurred. When Slobodan Milosevic, the Serbian leader, sent troops into neighboring

Kosovo to suppress the ethnic Albanians living there, the strongest voices for American military intervention came from those who once advocated disengagement. During the Gulf War, 47 Senate Democrats voted to oppose U.S. participation. A few years later, 42 Senate Democrats voted to support our role in Kosovo.

human rights The view that we should try to improve the lives of people in other countries.

What had happened? The change was inspired by the view that helping the Albanians was required by the doctrine of **human rights**. Liberal supporters of U.S. air attacks on Serbian forces believed that we were helping Albanians escape mass killing. By contrast, many conservative members of Congress who had followed a containment policy in the Gulf War now felt that disengagement ought to be followed in Kosovo. Of course, politics also mattered. Clinton was a Democratic president; Bush had been a Republican one.

But politics was not the whole story. Advocates of intervention declared that the attack in Kosovo resembled the genocide—that is, the mass murder of people because of their race or ethnicity—that the Jews had suffered in Nazi Germany. They held that we must "never again" permit a whole people to be killed. Anti-interventionists said if American foreign policy were guided by human rights, then the United States would have to send troops to many places. How would military action resolve a conflict that had gone on for centuries?

In the aftermath of 9/11, a new issue has arisen that may divide foreign policy elites in the future. Should the United States "go it alone" against its enemies abroad, or do so only on the basis of a broad coalition of supporting nations? President Bush the elder assembled just such a coalition to force Iraq out of Kuwait, but President Bush the younger acted without UN support in invading Afghanistan and later Iraq, though he received crucial support from the United Kingdom, Australia, and Poland.

Political Polarization

For as long as we have records, public opinion has been slow to favor our military actions overseas in the abstract but quick to support them once they occur. However, that pattern ended with our invasion of Iraq in 2003. Public opinion became deeply divided about that war, with most Democrats strongly opposing it and most Republicans favoring it.

That was not how things worked out during our wars in Korea and Vietnam. The war in Korea produced angry divisions in Congress, especially after General Douglas MacArthur, the allied commander in Korea, was fired in 1951 for having disobeyed the president. He received a hero's welcome when he returned to this country and gave an emotional speech to a joint session of Congress. Many Republicans demanded that President Truman be impeached. Despite this public support for MacArthur and these angry congressional words, the country was not split along partisan lines. Slightly more Republicans than Democrats said the war was a mistake (roughly half of each party), but the differences between these voters was not great.

The war in Vietnam split American political elites even more deeply. Journalists and members of Congress took sharply opposing sides, and some Americans traveled to North Vietnam to express their support for the Communist cause. When the North Vietnamese launched a major offensive to destroy American and South Vietnamese troops during the Tet holidays in 1968, it failed, but the American press reported it as a Communist victory, and demands to bring our troops home were heard during the presidential campaign that year. But public opinion did not divide along party lines; in 1968, Democratic and Republican voters had just about the same views (a little over half thought the war was a mistake, about a third thought it wasn't).

Our invasion of Iraq was a different story. From the very first, Democratic voters strongly opposed it and Republican ones favored it. By 2006, 76 percent of Democrats said we should have stayed out of Iraq, while 71 percent of Republicans said that the invasion was the right thing to do.[38]

TABLE 14.2 Foreign Policy Goals

Percentage who think each of the following is a "very important" foreign policy goal of the United States.

	Republican	Democrat	Independent
Protecting the jobs of American workers	84	84	82
Reducing U.S. dependence on foreign oil	78	77	73
Preventing the spread of nuclear weapons	76	74	67
Combating international terrorism	73	64	57
Maintaining superior military power worldwide	68	48	46
Controlling and reducing illegal immigration	70	43	48
Combating world hunger	31	54	40
Strengthening the United Nations	28	46	29
Limiting climate change	16	46	33
Helping to bring a democratic form of government to other nations	11	21	10

Sources: Chicago Council on Global Affairs, "Foreign Policy in the New Millennium: Results of the 2012 Chicago Council Survey of American Public Opinion and U.S. Foreign Policy," Table 5.2, "Foreign Policy Goals," p. 43.

American public opinion has become more polarized by our foreign policy. **Polarization** means a deep and wide conflict, usually along party lines, over some government policy. It has replaced the bipartisan foreign policy of the Second World War and the modest differences in public opinion during Korea and Vietnam.[39]

It is clear from Table 14.2 that what political party we belong to is strongly linked to our views on foreign policy. The public is deeply divided about these matters, and so, we think, will be the people for whom they vote.

The Use of Military Force

Foreign policy takes many forms—discussions are held, treaties are signed, organizations are joined—but in many cases it depends on the ability to use military force. Troops, ships, and aircraft are not the only ways of influencing other countries; international trade and foreign aid are also useful. But in modern times, as in the past, the nations of the world know the difference between a "great power" (that is, a heavily armed one) and a weak nation.

With the collapse of the Soviet Union and the end of the cold war, one might think that military power has become less important. But in fact it remains as important as ever. Since the Soviet Union was dissolved and the Berlin Wall came down in 1989, the United States has used military force to attack Iraq, maintain order in Bosnia, defend Kosovo, and go to war in Afghanistan. Various rogue nations, such as Iran and North Korea, have acquired or are about to acquire long-range rockets and weapons of mass destruction (that is, nuclear, chemical, and biological arms). Many nations that feel threatened by their neighbors, such as China, India, Pakistan, and Israel, have nuclear bombs. And Russia still has many of the nuclear

polarization A deep and wide conflict over some government policy.

weapons that the old Soviet Union built. It would be foolish to assume that the end of the cold war means the end of war.

There are two views about the role of the military in American life. One is majoritarian: the military exists to defend the country or to help other nations defend themselves. When troops are used, almost all Americans benefit and almost all pay the bill. (Some Americans, such as those who lose a loved one in war, pay much more than the rest of us.) The president is the commander-in-chief, and Congress plays a largely supportive role.

military-industrial complex
An alleged alliance between military leaders and corporate leaders.

Although the other view does not deny that the armed forces are useful, it focuses on the extent to which the military is a large and powerful client. The real beneficiaries of military spending are the generals and admirals, as well as the big corporations and members of Congress whose districts get fat defense contracts. Everyone pays, but these clients get most of the benefits. What we spend on defense is shaped by the **military-industrial complex**, a supposedly unified bloc of Defense Department leaders and military manufacturers.

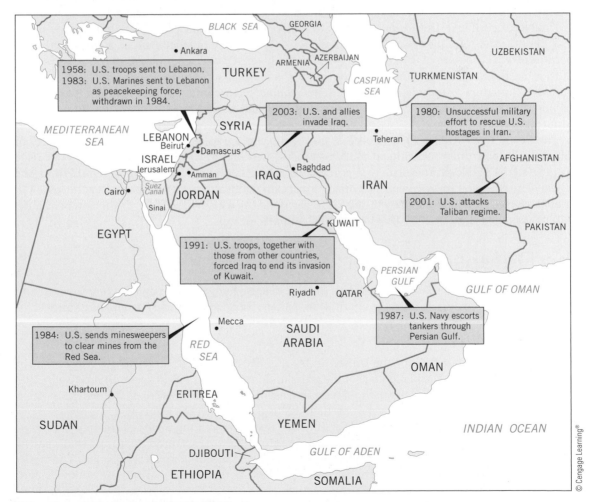

U.S. military intervention in the Middle East.

© Cengage Learning®

War in Iraq

After the Iraqi army under Saddam Hussein had invaded neighboring Kuwait in 1990, the United Nations passed a resolution demanding that Iraq withdraw and authorizing force to expel it. In January 1991, the United States led a coalition of forces from several nations that attacked Iraq; within 100 days, the Iraqi army had retreated from Kuwait and fled home. The U.S.-led military forces ended their attack, allowing Saddam to remain in power in Baghdad, the Iraqi capital.

After the war, a no-fly zone was established under which Iraqi flights in certain areas were prohibited. This ban was enforced for 12 years by U.S., British, and French planes that shot down Iraqi aircraft violating the rule.

Throughout this time, United Nations (UN) inspectors were sent to Iraq to look for weapons of mass destruction (WMDs): chemical, biological, and nuclear materials that could be used to attack others. There was no doubt such weapons existed, as Saddam had dropped chemical weapons on people living in his own country. The UN inspectors found evidence of such a program, but in 1997 Saddam expelled them from his country, only to allow them to return a few years later. Saddam's misleading statements led American and British leaders to conclude that his regime was a threat to peace.

Unable to convince the United Nations to support a war, America, the United Kingdom, and other countries decided to act alone. On March 30, 2003, they invaded Iraq in a campaign called Operation Iraqi Freedom; within about six weeks, the Iraqi army was defeated and the American-led coalition occupied all of the country. After the war, a large group of inspectors toured Iraq looking for WMDs, but they found virtually none. Later, a bipartisan commission concluded that Saddam had apparently cancelled his WMD program, but had told hardly any of his own military leaders about this.[40]

The newly freed Iraqi people voted first for an interim parliament, then for a new constitution, and finally for a regular government. But this process was offset by the terrorist activities of various insurgents, first aimed at American troops and later at Iraqi civilians, killing several tens of thousands of them. The situation in Iraq became a major American political issue, contributing to the loss of the Republican congressional majority in the 2006 elections. As we shall see later in this chapter, a new military strategy began in 2007 that improved conditions in Iraq.

The Defense Budget

There are two key issues to understand with the U.S. defense budget: how much money we spend and how it is divided up. The first reflects majoritarian politics, the second, interest group bargaining.

Total Spending

Throughout most of our history the United States has not maintained large military forces during peacetime. For instance, the percentage of the gross national product (GNP) spent on defense in 1935, on the eve of World War II, was about the same as it was in 1870, when we were on the eve of nothing in particular. We armed when a war broke out, then we disarmed when the war ended.

But all of that changed after World War II, when defense spending declined sharply but did not return to its prewar levels. And in 1950, our defense expenditures soared again. In that year, we rearmed to fight a war in Korea, but when it was over, we did not completely disarm. The reason was our containment policy toward the Soviet Union. For about 40 years—from the outbreak of the Korean War in 1950 to the collapse of the Soviet Union in 1991—American military spending was driven by our desire to contain the Soviet Union and its allies. The Soviet Union had brought under

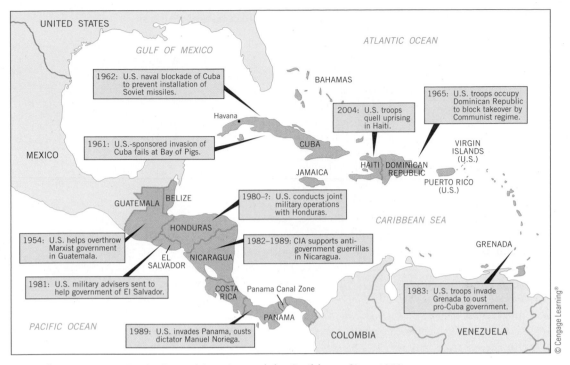

U.S. military intervention in Central America and the Caribbean Since 1950.

its control most of Eastern Europe; would it also invade Western Europe? Russia had always wanted access to the oil and warm-water ports of the Middle East; would the Soviets someday invade or subvert Iran or Turkey? The Soviet Union was willing to help North Korea invade South Korea and North Vietnam to invade South Vietnam; would it next use an ally to threaten the United States? Soviet leaders supported "wars of national liberation" in Africa and Latin America; would they succeed in turning more and more nations against the United States?

To meet these threats, the United States built up a military system designed to repel a Soviet invasion of Western Europe and at the same time help allies resist smaller-scale invasions or domestic uprisings. Figure 14.2 depicts the dramatic increase in military spending in 1950. It also shows that even after we decided to have a large military force, there were many ups and downs in the actual level of spending. After the Korean War was over, we spent less; when we became involved in Vietnam, we spent more; when the Soviet Union invaded Afghanistan and we invaded Iraq, we spent more again. These changes in spending tended to reflect changes in public opinion about the defense budget.

As Figure 14.3 shows, a majority of Americans have said that our defense program is either "about right" or "not strong enough," but other studies show that popular support for spending more money on defense changes from year to year.

After the collapse of the Soviet Union, there has been a debate about defense strategy. Liberals demanded sharp cuts in defense spending, weapons procurement, and military personnel, arguing that with the Soviet threat ended, it was time to collect our "peace dividend" and divert funds from the military to domestic social programs. Conservatives agreed that some military cuts were in order, but they argued that the world was still a dangerous place and therefore that a strong (and well-funded) military remained essential to the nation's defense. This disagreement reflected different predictions

FIGURE 14.2 **Trends in Military Spending (outlays in constant dollars)**

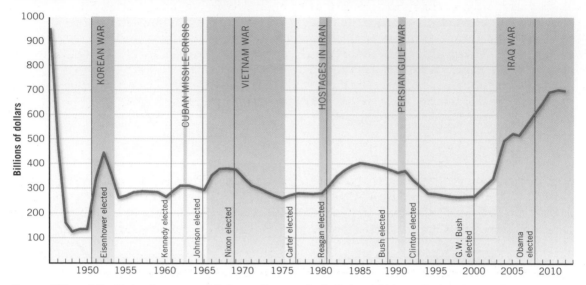

Source: Office of the Under Secretary of Defense (Comptroller), National Defense Budget Annual Estimates and Reports."

FIGURE 14.3 **Most Americans Think National Defense Is Either "About Right" or "Not Strong Enough"**

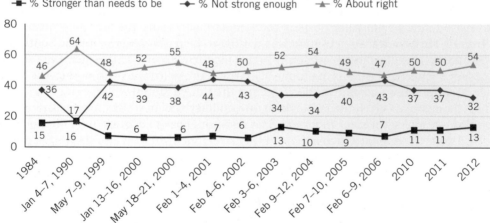

Source: Gallup Poll.

about what the future would be like. Many liberals (and some conservatives, such as Pat Buchanan, who believed that America should "stay at home") argued that we could not afford to be the "world's policeman." Many conservatives (and some liberals) responded by saying that Russia was still a military powerhouse that might once again fall under the control of ruthless leaders and that many other nations hostile to the United States (such as North Korea, Iran, and Iraq) were becoming potential adversaries as they tried to build or acquire nuclear weapons and missile systems.

American campaigns in Afghanistan and Iraq made clear that whether or not the United States was the "world's police officer," there was no escaping its need to use military force. They also made clear that the United States had reduced its armed forces so sharply since Desert Storm (there were half a million fewer people in the military in 1996 than in 1991) that it was hard-pressed to carry out any sustained military campaign. When the national budget deficit was eliminated in 1999, both President Clinton and the Republican Congress called for more military spending.

But that increase did not pay for what the military had been authorized to buy, and did little to get us ready for the war in Afghanistan against Osama bin Laden. Once the battle began, however, the federal purse strings loosened and the defense budget grew.

What Do We Get with Our Money?

We get people, of course—soldiers, sailors, airmen, and airwomen. They are the most expensive part of the defense budget. Then we get hardware of roughly two kinds—big-ticket items, like aircraft carriers and bombers, and small-ticket items, like hammers and screwdrivers. Each of these kinds of hardware has its own politics. Finally, we get "readiness"—training, supplies, munitions, fuel, and food.

Personnel Efforts to develop our military forces before World War II reflected the considerable American discomfort with a strong central government. The United States did not institute a peacetime draft until 1940, when the rest of the world was already at war, and the draft was renewed the following year (only a few months before Pearl Harbor) by only a one-vote margin in the House. Until 1973, the United States relied on the draft to obtain military personnel. Then, at the end of the Vietnam War, it replaced the draft with the all-volunteer force (AVF). After getting off to a rocky start, the AVF began to improve, thanks to increases in military pay and rising civilian unemployment. Abolishing the draft had been politically popular: nobody likes being drafted, and even in congressional districts that otherwise are staunch supporters of a strong defense, voters tell their representatives that they do not want to return to the draft (and many military leaders agree).

There has been a steady increase in the percentage of women in the military (in 2011, they constituted 14.5 percent of the total). For a long time, however, women were barred by law from serving in combat roles. (What constitutes a "combat role" is a bit difficult to say, since even personnel far from the main fighting can be hit by an enemy bomb or artillery shell.) In 1993 Congress ended the legal ban on assigning women to Navy combat ships and Air Force fighter jets, and soon women were serving on three aircraft carriers. Twenty years later, the Pentagon lifted its official ban on women serving in combat. The military's rules on sexual orientation and military service also have changed significantly in the past two decades. Until 1993, it was the long-standing policy of the U.S. armed forces to bar gay and lesbian soldiers from entering the military and to discharge them if they were discovered when serving. Gay and lesbian rights organizations had long protested this exclusion. In 1993, a gay soldier won a lawsuit against the Army for having discharged him; he settled for back pay and retirement benefits in exchange for a promise not to re-enlist. In 1993, a judge ordered the Navy to reinstate a discharged sailor who had revealed on national television that he was gay. In response to the growing controversy, presidential candidate Bill Clinton promised to lift the official ban on gays and lesbians serving in the military if he were elected to office.

Once in office, he discovered that it was not that easy. Many members of the armed forces believed that knowingly serving alongside and living in close quarters with gays and lesbians would create unnecessary tension and harm military morale and troop solidarity. The Joint Chiefs of Staff opposed lifting the ban, and several key members of Congress said they would try to pass a law reaffirming it. President Clinton was forced to settle for a compromise: "don't ask, don't tell." Under this policy, persons

cost overruns When the money actually paid to military suppliers exceeds the estimated costs.

gold plating The tendency of Pentagon officials to ask weapons contractors to meet excessively high requirements.

entering or serving in the military would not be asked to reveal their sexual orientation and would be allowed to serve, provided they did not engage in homosexual conduct. If a person stated that he or she was gay, that would not have been automatic grounds for discharge, but it may have been grounds for launching an investigation to determine whether rules against homosexual conduct had been violated.

In 1994, the new Pentagon rules designed to implement "don't ask, don't tell" went into effect, but the challenges of implementation soon prompted calls for ending altogether the prohibition on soldiers revealing their sexual orientation. President Obama signed a law repealing "don't ask, don't tell" in 2010 with the strong support of his secretary of defense and chairman of the Joint Chiefs, who said this would not harm military readiness.

Big-Ticket Items Whenever the Pentagon buys a new submarine, airplane, or missile, we hear about **cost overruns**. In the 1950s, actual costs were three times greater than estimated costs; by the 1960s, things were only slightly better—actual costs were twice estimated costs.

There are five main reasons for these overruns. First, it is hard to know in advance what something that has never existed before will cost once you build it. People who have remodeled their homes know this all too well. So do government officials who build new subways or congressional office buildings. It is no different with a B-2 bomber.

Second, people who want to persuade Congress to appropriate money for a new airplane or submarine have an incentive to underestimate the cost. To get the weapon approved, its sponsors tell Congress how little it will cost; once the weapon is under construction, the sponsors go back to Congress for additional money to cover "unexpected" cost increases.

Third, the Pentagon officials who decide what kind of new aircraft they want are drawn from the ranks of those who will fly it. These officers naturally want the best airplane (or ship or tank) that money can buy. As Air Force General Carl "Tooey" Spaatz once put it, "A second-best aircraft is like a second-best poker hand. No damn good."[41] But what exactly is the "best" airplane? Is it the fastest one? Or the most maneuverable one? Or the most reliable one? Or the one with the longest range? Pentagon officials have a tendency to answer, "All of the above." Of course, trying to produce all of the above is incredibly expensive (and sometimes impossible). But asking for the expensive (or the impossible) is understandable, given that the air force officers who buy it will also fly it. This tendency to ask for everything at once is called **gold plating**.

Fourth, many new weapons are purchased from a single contractor. This is called sole-sourcing. A contractor is hired to design, develop, and build an airplane. As a result there is no competition, and so the manufacturer has no strong incentive to control costs. And if the sole manufacturer gets into financial trouble, the government, seeking to avoid a shutdown of all production, has an incentive to bail the company out.

Fifth, when Congress wants to cut the military budget, it often does so not by canceling a new weapons system but by stretching out the number of years during which it is purchased. Say that Congress wants to buy 100 F-22s, 25 a year for four years. To give the appearance of cutting the budget, it will decide to buy only 15 the first year and take five years to buy the rest. Or it will authorize the construction of 20 now and then ask again next year for the authority to build more. But start-and-stop production decisions and stretching out production over more years drives up the cost of building each unit. If Toyota built cars this way, it would go broke.

There are ways to cope with four of these five problems. You cannot do much about the first, ignorance, but you can do something about low estimates, gold plating, sole-sourcing, and stretch-outs.

If the Pentagon would give realistic cost estimates initially (perhaps verified by another agency); if it would ask for weapons that meet a few critical performance requirements instead of every requirement that can be thought of; if two or more manufacturers were to compete in designing, developing, and manufacturing new weapons; and if Congress were to stop trying to "cut" the budget using the smoke-and-mirrors technique of stretch-outs, then we would hear a lot less about cost overruns.

Some of these things are being done. There is more competition and less sole-sourcing in weapons procurement today than once was the case. But the political incentives to avoid other changes are very powerful. Pentagon officers will always want "the best." They will always have an incentive to understate costs. Congress will always be tempted to use stretch-outs as a way of avoiding hard budget choices.

Readiness Presumably, we have a peacetime military so that we will be ready for wartime. Presumably, therefore, the peacetime forces will devote a lot of their time and money to improving their readiness.

A U.S. Marine goes on patrol in Afghanistan.

ADEK BERRY/AFP/Getty Images

Not necessarily. The politics of defense spending is such that readiness often is given a very low priority. Here is why.

Client politics influences the decision. In 1990, Congress was willing to cut almost anything, provided it wasn't built or stationed in some member's district. That doesn't leave much. Plans to stop producing F-14 fighters for the Navy were opposed by members from Long Island, where the Grumman manufacturing plant was located. Plans to kill the Osprey aircraft for the Marines were opposed by members from the places where it was to be built. Plans to close bases were opposed by every member with a base in his or her district.

That leaves training and readiness. These things, essential to military effectiveness, have no constituencies and hence few congressional defenders. When forced to choose, the services themselves often prefer to allocate scarce dollars to developing and buying new weapons than to spending for readiness. Moreover, the savings from buying less fuel or having fewer exercises shows up right away, while the savings from canceling an aircraft carrier may not show up for years. Not surprisingly, training and readiness are usually what get the ax.

Retired Navy commander Zoe Dunning (2nd from left) and her friends celebrate the end of "Don't Ask, Don't Tell" in San Francisco.

Paul Chinn/San Francisco Chronicle/Corbis

Bases At one time, the opening and closing of military bases was pure client politics, which meant that a lot of bases were opened and hardly any were closed. Almost every member of Congress fought to get a base in his or her district, and *every* member fought to keep an existing base open. Even the biggest congressional critics of the U.S. military, people who would vote to take a gun out of a soldier's hand, would fight hard to keep bases in their districts open and operating.

In 1988, Congress finally concluded that no base would ever be closed unless the system for making decisions was changed. It created a Commission on Base Realignment and Closure (BRAC), consisting of private citizens (originally 12, later 8) who would consider recommendations from the secretary of defense. By law Congress would have to vote within 45 days for or against the commission's list as a whole, without having a chance to amend it. Since 1988, there have been five BRAC reports. Congress approved each one, resulting in the closing of more than 350 bases.

Congress, it appears, has finally figured out how to make some decisions that most members know are right, but that each member individually finds it politically necessary to oppose.

The Structure of Defense Decision Making

The formal structure within which decisions about national defense are made was in large part created after World War II, but it reflects concerns that go back at least to the time of the Founding. Chief among these is the persistent desire by citizens to ensure civilian control over the military.

The National Security Act of 1947 and its subsequent amendments created the Department of Defense. It is headed by the secretary of defense, under whom serve the secretaries of the Army, the Air Force, and the Navy, as well as the Joint Chiefs of Staff. The secretary of defense, who must be a civilian (though one former general, George C. Marshall, was allowed by Congress to be the secretary), exercises, on behalf of the president, command authority over the defense establishment. The secretary of the Army, the secretary of the Navy,* and the secretary of the Air Force also are civilians and are subordinate to the secretary of defense. Unlike him, they do not attend Cabinet meetings or sit on the National Security Council. In essence, they manage the "housekeeping" functions of the various armed services, under the general direction of the secretary of defense and his deputy and assistant secretaries of defense.

The four armed services are separate entities; by law, they cannot be merged or commanded by a single military officer, and each has the right to communicate directly with Congress. There are two reasons for having separate uniformed services functioning within a single department: the fear of many citizens that a unified military force might become too powerful politically, and the desire of each service to preserve its traditional independence and autonomy. The result, of course, is a good deal of interservice rivalry and bickering, but this is precisely what Congress intended when it created the Department of Defense. Rivalry and bickering, it was felt, would ensure that Congress would receive the maximum amount of information about military affairs and would enjoy the largest opportunity to affect military decisions.

Since the end of World War II, Congress has aimed both to retain a significant measure of control over the military's decision making and to ensure the adequacy of the nation's defenses. Congress does not want a single military command headed by an all-powerful general or admiral, but neither does it want the services to be so autonomous or their heads so equal that coordination and efficiency suffer. In 1986, Congress passed and the president signed a defense reorganization plan known as the Goldwater-Nichols Act, which increased the power of the officers who coordinate the activities of the different services. The 1947 structure was left in place, but with revised procedures.

---

*The secretary of the Navy manages two services, the Navy and the Marine Corps.

Joint Chiefs of Staff

The Joint Chiefs of Staff (JCS) is a committee consisting of the uniformed heads of each of the military services (the Army, Navy, Air Force, and Marine Corps), plus a chairman and a (nonvoting) vice chairman, also military officers, who are appointed by the president and confirmed by the Senate. The JCS does not have command authority over troops, but it plays a key role in national defense planning. Since 1986, the chairman of the joint chiefs has been designated the president's principal military adviser, in an effort to give him more influence over the JCS.

Assisting the JCS is the Joint Staff, consisting of several hundred officers from each of the four services. The staff draws up plans for various military contingencies. Before 1986, each staff member was loyal to the service whose uniform he or she wore. As a result, the staff was often "joint" in name only, since few members were willing to take a position opposed by their service for fear of being passed over for promotion. The 1986 law changed this in two ways: first, it gave the chairman of the JCS control over the Joint Staff; now it works for the chairman, not for the JCS as a group. Second, it required the secretary of defense to establish guidelines to ensure that officers assigned to the Joint Staff (or to other interservice bodies) are promoted at the same rate as officers whose careers are spent entirely with their own services.

The Services

Each military service is headed by a civilian secretary—one for the Army, the Navy (including the Marine Corps), and the Air Force—plus a senior military officer: the chief of staff of the Army, the chief of naval operations, the commandant of the Marine Corps, and the chief of staff of the Air Force. The civilian secretaries are in charge of purchasing, auditing, congressional relations, and public affairs. The military chiefs oversee the discipline and training of their uniformed forces and in addition represent their services on the JCS.

The Chain of Command

Under the Constitution the president is the commander-in-chief of the armed forces. The chain of command runs from him to the secretary of defense (also a civilian), and from him to the various unified and specified commands. These orders may be transmitted through the JCS or its chairman, but by law the chairman of the JCS does not have command authority over the combat forces. Civilians are in charge at the top to protect against excessive concentration of power.

The New Problem of Terrorism

Since 9/11, both our foreign policy and our military policy have had to focus on terrorism and what to do with nations we have conquered that harbored terrorists. During the cold war, this was easy. For a half century, each president, operating through the National Security Council, made it clear that our chief goal was to prevent the Soviet Union from overrunning Western Europe, bombing the United States, or invading other nations.

But the Soviet Union has disappeared and no other nation has acquired the power to take its place. During the cold war, we lived in a **bipolar world** made up of two superpowers. Now we live in a **unipolar world** made up of the United States as the only superpower. But our superpower status, though it means no other

bipolar world A political landscape with two superpowers.

unipolar world A political landscape with one superpower.

country can challenge us militarily, still leaves us vulnerable here and abroad to terrorist attacks, as 9/11 amply confirms.

To respond, President George W. Bush, in September 2002, issued a document that emphasized a new view of our policies. Instead of waiting to be attacked, the president said that America "will act against such emerging threats before they are fully formed" because we "cannot defend America and our friends by hoping for the best." We will identify and destroy a terrorist threat "before it reaches our borders" and "we will not hesitate to act alone."[42] In the case of Iraq, this meant a commitment to "regime change"; that is, getting rid of a hostile government, even if the United Nations did not support us.

This has been called a doctrine of preemption; that is, of attacking a determined enemy before it can launch an attack against us or an ally. In fact, it is not really new. President Bill Clinton launched cruise missile strikes against training camps that followers of Osama bin Laden were using in the aftermath of their bombing of American embassies in Kenya and Tanzania in 1998. President Bush elevated the policy of preemption into a clearly stated national doctrine.

Supporters of this view hailed it as a positive step to defeat terrorists abroad before they could attack us at home. Critics attacked the argument as justifying preemptive and possibly unjust wars and abandoning the United Nations. This debate has divided Congress in a way that puts an end to the old adage that partisanship ends at the water's edge.

Since the end of the cold war, we have not had a common enemy that, in the opinion of critics of our overseas efforts, should justify a nonpartisan view. Most liberal Democrats opposed both our effort to get Iraq out of Kuwait in 1991 and our invasion of Iraq in 2003; most Republicans supported both efforts.[43] But when President Clinton launched attacks on hostile forces in Kosovo, he was supported by many liberal Democrats and opposed by many conservative Republicans.[44] Party differences and political ideology now make a big difference in foreign policy.

Sometimes we have sought and obtained United Nations support, as we did when going to war in Korea (1950) and in launching our effort to force Iraqi troops out of Kuwait (1991). We did not seek it in fighting against North Vietnam (in the 1960s), in occupying Haiti (1994), or in going to the assistance of friendly forces in Bosnia (1994) or Kosovo (1999). When we invaded Iraq in 2003, we asked for but did not get UN support; we went anyway, aided by allies such as the United Kingdom and Australia.

After we conquered Afghanistan and Iraq, we faced the problem of rebuilding these nations. The United States has had a lot of experience, some good and some bad, with this problem. We helped put Germany and Japan back on their feet after World War II. From 1992 to 1994, we tried to bring peace among warring factions to Somalia. From 1994 to 1996, we worked to install a democratically elected president and rebuild the local police force in the Caribbean country Haiti. Starting in 1995, we worked with European allies to restore order to Bosnia and Kosovo, located in what used to be Yugoslavia. In 2001, we began helping Afghans create a new government and economy, and in 2003 we started doing the same thing in Iraq.

We succeeded in Germany and Japan, failed in Somalia and Haiti, and made progress in Bosnia and Kosovo.[45]

Iraq and Afghanistan

After easily defeating the Iraqi army in 2003, we tried to bring stability and democracy to the country in mistaken ways. We abolished the Iraqi army (and so had no native defense force), relied on too few American troops (and so could not pacify the country), and kept these troops when they were not fighting in American compounds (thus leaving Iraqi civilians unprotected). Iran funneled arms and terrorists into the country to help attack American soldiers. Public opinion in this country, though deeply divided along party lines, became hostile to our efforts there.

To deal with this problem, President Bush (over the objections of many subordinates) announced a new strategy. We would send another 30,000 troops to Iraq (the "surge") and instruct these troops to work in Iraqi neighborhoods and build alliances with local groups. He assigned General David Petraeus to be our military leader.

The surge worked. Deaths of American forces and Iraqi civilians fell dramatically, an elected Iraqi government began to function effectively, and new Iraqi elections in 2009 were held peacefully. The American government negotiated an agreement with Iraqi leaders that called for withdrawing most American troops from the country by 2011. Because of this progress and because our economy went into a recession, American public opinion began to lose interest in Iraq.

Afghanistan is a more difficult problem. Unlike Iraq, it has never been a unified nation and lacks a large middle class or many populous cities. We easily defeated the Taliban regime and managed to put in office a moderate leader. Troops from other nations arrived to help out. But creating an effective central government in a country that has rarely had one and ending terrorist attacks has proved to be a difficult assignment. During the 2008 presidential campaign, Barack Obama promised to send more forces to that country, and beginning in 2009 he did so. By the middle of the year we had 60,000 troops there, but they were not enough. In 2009, the general leading our forces there asked President Obama for another 40,000 troops; the president sent 30,000. In 2011, the Obama administration began to draw down its "surge" in Afghanistan, with plans for withdrawal of most troops by 2014, but the prospects for long-term stability there remained uncertain.

LEARNING OBJECTIVES

LO 14.1 Is American foreign policy set by public opinion or elite views?

Elite views matter greatly because most Americans pay little attention to foreign affairs most of the time. And on many key issues, the public disagrees with the elite. But when the president sends troops overseas to fight, the public will rally around him.

LO 14.2 If only Congress can declare war, why has the president become so powerful in military affairs?

The Constitution makes him the commander-in-chief of the military, and the Supreme Court has made it clear that he has great powers on foreign affairs. The president often has sent troops to fight without a declaration of war, but Congress has invariably supported him. Technically, he should get Congress's approval under the War Powers Act, but if Americans are already fighting it would be very hard for Congress to say no.

LO 14.3 Should our foreign policy be based on American interests or some conception of human rights?

Sometimes this is not a problem because in a few cases a threat to our interests and a violation of human rights coincide. But at other times, they do not. This is a continuing issue that divides American foreign policy elites. In Congress, liberal members supported and conservative ones opposed our intervention in Bosnia and Kosovo even though neither country threatened us; in Iraq, conservative ones supported and many liberal ones opposed our intervention.

TO LEARN MORE

- U.S. Army: **www.army.mil**

- U.S. Air Force: **www.af.mil**

- U.S. Navy: **www.navy.mil**

- Central Intelligence Agency: **www.cia.gov**

- Department of State: **www.state.gov**

- Allison, Graham T. *Essence of Decision: Explaining the Cuban Missile Crisis.* Boston: Little, Brown, 1971. Shows how the decision made by a president during a major crisis was shaped by bureaucratic and organizational factors.

- Barnett, Thomas P. M. *The Pentagon's New Map: War and Peace in the Twenty-First Century.* New York: Berkley Books, 2004. Discusses what America's foreign and military policy should be in the global war against terror.

- Commission on the Intelligence Capabilities of the United States Regarding Weapons of Mass Destruction. *Report to the President of the United States.* Washington, D.C.: Government Printing Office, 2005. Thorough examination by a bipartisan group of why American intelligence agencies did not understand Iraq's WMD efforts.

- Kissinger, Henry. *White House Years.* Boston: Little, Brown, 1979. A brilliant insider's account of the politics and tactics of "high diplomacy" during the Nixon administration.

- Mead, Walter Russell. *Special Providence.* New York: Knopf, 2001. Argues that American foreign policy, though often criticized, has been remarkably successful.

- Mueller, John E. *War, Presidents, and Public Opinion.* New York: Wiley, 1973. Best summary of the relationship between presidential foreign policy decisions and public opinion.

Robyn Beck/AFP/Getty Images

American Democracy, Then and Now

LEARNING OBJECTIVES

LO 15.1   Name three things that for many years kept the agenda of the federal government short.

LO 15.2   Name three things that have expanded the agenda of the federal government.

LO 15.3   Contrast three features of the Old System versus the New System of American government.

LO 15.4   How has the challenge of political leadership changed since the days of the Constitutional Convention?

Like most Americans, you probably worry about some social problems. These might include abortion, crime, drug abuse, civil rights, gun control, homelessness, or school quality. Maybe you have argued about these matters with your friends, discussing what Washington should do about these things. While you argue, remember this: until the mid-20th century all of this talk would have been nonsense. None of these things were matters that people believed the federal government could or should do anything about.

THEN: Restraints on the Growth of Government

When Dwight Eisenhower was president, none of these issues except civil rights was even thought to be a matter for federal policy, and on civil rights Congress didn't do very much. Our national political agenda was very short. During the Eisenhower administration, we decided to build an interstate highway system, admit Alaska and Hawaii into the union, and fight over the power of labor unions. For *eight years*, these were about the only major domestic political issues. The rest of the time, Washington worried about foreign affairs.

This was about what the Founders had expected, though many of them would have objected to some things that were done in the Eisenhower administration. Some would have thought Washington shouldn't build any highways because the Constitution did not authorize Congress to make laws about such matters. The federal government, in their view, should limit itself to war, peace, interstate commerce, establishing a national currency, and delivering the mail. And for a long time, the prevailing interpretation of the Constitution sharply limited what policies the federal government could adopt. The Supreme Court restricted the authority of the government to regulate business and prevented it from levying an income tax. Most important, the Supreme Court refused, with some exceptions, to allow the delegation of broad discretionary power to administrative agencies.

The Supreme Court could not have maintained this position for as long as it did if it had acted in the teeth of popular opposition. But popular opinion was also against the growth of government. It was not thought legitimate for the federal government to intervene deeply in the economy (even the American Federation of Labor, led by Samuel Gompers, resisted federal involvement in labor-management issues). It was certainly not thought proper for Washington to upset racial segregation as it was practiced in both the North and the South. It took constitutional amendments to persuade Congress that it had the authority to levy an income tax or to prohibit the sale of alcoholic beverages. Even in the 1930s, public opinion polls showed that as many as half the voters were skeptical of a federal unemployment compensation program.

That was the Old System. Today, under the New System, federal politics is not about some small list of problems thought to be truly national; it is about practically everything. It is almost impossible to think of a problem about which Washington has no policy at all or around which it does not carry on intense debates. Listen to radio talk shows, and you will hear discussions about why Washington has a good or bad policy on almost any issue you can imagine.

What is puzzling about this change from the Old System to the New System is that the Constitution is filled with arrangements designed to make it hard, not easy, for the federal government to act. The separation of powers permits the president, Congress, and the courts to check one another; federalism guarantees that states will have an important role to play; and the division of legislative authority between the House and the Senate ensures that each body will be inclined to block the other. To get a new law passed, you have to please a large number of political actors; to get a new one blocked, you only have to convince one congressional committee.

That system made the national government relatively unimportant for many decades. Until well into the 20th century, governors and mayors were more important than the president. Most members of Congress did not serve more than one or two terms in Washington; there didn't seem to be much point in becoming a career legislator because Congress didn't do much, didn't pay much, and wasn't in session for very long.

NOW: Relaxing the Restraints

As we have said, the constraints on federal action have now weakened or disappeared altogether. First, the courts have altered their interpretation of the Constitution in ways that have not only permitted but sometimes even required government action. The Bill of Rights has been extended so that almost all its important provisions are now regarded as applying to the states (by having been incorporated into the due process clause of the Fourteenth Amendment). This means that a citizen can use the federal courts to alter state policy to a greater degree than ever before. (Overturning state laws that ban abortions or require racially separate schools are two important examples of this change.) The special protection the courts once granted property rights has been substantially reduced so that business can be regulated to a greater degree than previously. The Court has permitted Congress to give broad discretionary powers to administrative agencies, allowing bureaucrats to make decisions that once only Congress could make.

Second, public opinion has changed in ways that support an expanded role for the federal government. The public demanded action to deal with the Great Depression (the programs that resulted, such as Social Security, survived in part because the Supreme Court changed its mind about the permissible scope of federal action). Political elites changed their minds faster than the average citizen. Well-educated, politically active people began demanding federal policies regarding civil rights, public welfare, environmental protection, consumer safety, and foreign aid well before the average citizen became concerned with such things.

Once in place, most of these programs proved popular, so their continuance was supported by mass as well as elite opinion. The cumulative effect of this process was to blur, if not erase altogether, the line that once defined what the government had the authority to do. At one time, a new proposal was debated in terms of whether it was *legitimate* for the federal government to do it all. Federal aid to education, for example, usually was opposed because many people feared it would lead to federal control of local schools. But after so many programs (including federal aid to education) had been passed, people stopped arguing about whether a certain policy was legitimate and argued instead about whether it was *effective*.

Third, political resources have become more widely distributed. The number and variety of interest groups have increased enormously. The funds available from foundations for organizations pursuing specific causes have grown. It is now easier to get access to the federal courts than formerly was the case, and once in the courts the plaintiffs are more likely to encounter judges who believe that the law and the Constitution should be interpreted broadly to permit particular goals (for example, prison reform) to be attained by legal rather than legislative means. Hundreds of magazines, newsletters, and websites have arisen to provide policy information to specialized segments of opinion. The techniques of mass protest, linked to the desire of television to show visually interesting accounts of social conflict, have been perfected in ways that convey the beliefs of a few into the living rooms of millions.

Campaign finance laws and court rulings have given legal status and constitutional protection to thousands of political action committees (PACs) that raise and spend tens of millions of dollars from millions of small-time contributors. College education, once the privilege of a tiny minority, has become the common experience of millions of people, so that the effects of college—in encouraging political participation and in shaping political beliefs (usually in a liberal direction)—are now widely shared. The ability of candidates to win nomination for office no longer depends on their ability to curry favor with a few powerful bosses; it now reflects their skill at raising money, mobilizing friends and activists, cultivating a media image, and winning a primary election.

TABLE 15.1 **How American Politics Has Changed**

Old System	Congress	New System
Chairs relatively strong		Chairs relatively weak
Small staffs		Large staffs
Few subcommittees		Many subcommittees
	Interest Groups	
A few large blocs (farmers, business, labor)		Many diverse interests that form ad hoc coalitions
Rely on "insider" lobbying		Mobilize grassroots
	Presidency	
Small staff		Large staff
Reaches public via press conferences		Reaches public via radio, television, and internet
	Courts	
Allow government to exercise few economic powers		Allow government to exercise broad economic power
Take narrow view of individual freedoms		Take broad view of individual freedoms
	Political Parties	
Dominated by state and local party leaders meeting in conventions		Dominated by activists chosen in primaries and caucuses
	Policy Agenda	
Brief		Long
	Key Question	
Should the federal government enter a new policy area?		How can we fix and pay for an existing policy?
	Key Issue	
Would a new federal program abridge states' rights?		Would a new federal program prove popular?

© Cengage Learning

So great have been the changes in the politics of policymaking in this country starting in the 1930s that we can refer, with only slight exaggeration, to one policymaking system having been replaced by another (see Table 15.1).

The Old System

The Old System had a small agenda. Though people voted at a high rate and often took part in torchlight parades and other mass political events, political leadership was professionalized in the sense that the leadership circle was small, access to it was difficult, and the activists in social movements generally were kept out. Only a few major issues were under discussion at any time. A member of Congress had a small staff (if any at all), dealt with his or her colleagues on a personal basis, deferred to the prestige of House and Senate leaders, and tended to become part of some stable coalition (the farm bloc, the labor bloc, the Southern bloc) that persisted across many issues.

When someone proposed adding a new issue to the public agenda, a major debate often arose over whether it was legitimate for the federal government to take action at all on the matter. A dominant theme in this debate was the importance of "states' rights." Except in wartime, or during a very brief period when the nation expressed interest in acquiring colonies, the focus of policy debate was on domestic affairs.

Food products now contain health warnings, such as one for nuts in this package of cookies.

Members of Congress saw these domestic issues largely in terms of their effect on local constituencies. The presidency was small and somewhat personal; there was only a rudimentary White House staff. The president would cultivate the press, but there was a clear understanding that what he said in a press conference was never to be quoted directly.

For the government to take bold action under this system, the nation usually had to be facing a crisis. War presented such crisis, and so the federal government during the Civil War and World Wars I and II acquired extraordinary powers to conscript soldiers, control industrial production, regulate the flow of information to citizens, and restrict the scope of personal liberty. Each succeeding crisis left the government bureaucracy somewhat larger than it had been before, but when the crisis ended, the exercise of extraordinary powers ended. Once again, the agenda of political issues became small, and legislators argued about whether it was legitimate for the government to enter some new policy area, such as civil rights or industrial regulation.

The New System

The New System began in the 1930s, but did not take its present form until the 1970s. It is characterized by a large policy agenda, the end of the debate over the legitimacy of government action (except in the area of First Amendment freedoms), the diffusion and decentralization of power in Congress, and the multiplication of interest groups. The government has grown so large that it has a policy on almost every conceivable subject, and so the debate in Washington is less often about whether it is right and prudent to take some bold new step and more often about how the government can best cope with the strains and problems that arise from implementing existing policies. As someone once said, the federal government is now more concerned with managing than with ruling.

For example, in 1935 Congress debated whether the nation should have a Social Security system at all; in the 1980s, it debated whether the system could best be kept solvent by raising taxes or by cutting benefits; in 2004 and 2005, it debated whether some part of each person's Social Security payments could be invested in the stock market. In the 1960s, Congress argued over whether there should be any federal civil rights laws at all; by the 1980s and 1990s, it was arguing over whether those laws should be administered in a way that simply eliminated legal barriers to equal opportunity for racial minorities or in a way (by affirmative action) that made up for the disadvantages that burdened such minorities in the past. As late as the 1950s, the president and Congress argued over whether it was right to adopt a new program if it meant the government had to borrow money to pay for it. As late as the 1960s, many members of Congress believed the federal government had no business paying for the health care of its citizens; today, hardly anyone argues against having Medicare, but many worry about how best to control its rising cost.

The differences between the Old and New Systems should not be exaggerated. The Constitution still makes it easier for Congress to block the proposals of the president, or for some committee of Congress to defeat the preferences of the majority of Congress, than in almost any other democratic government. The system of checks and balances operates as before. The essential differences between the Old and the New Systems are these:

1. Under the Old System, the checks and balances made it difficult for the federal government to *start* a new program, and so the government remained relatively small. Under the New System, these checks and balances have made it hard to *change* what the government is already doing, and so the government has remained large.

2. Under the Old System, power was *somewhat centralized* in the hands of party and congressional leaders. There was still plenty of conflict, but the number of people who had to agree before something could be done was not large. Under the New System, power is much more *decentralized*, and so it is harder to resolve conflict because so many more people—party activists, interest group leaders, individual members of Congress, heads of government agencies—must agree.

The transition from the Old to the New System occurred chiefly during two periods in American politics. The first was in the early 1930s, when a catastrophic depression led the government to explore new ways of helping the needy, regulating business, and preventing a recurrence of the disaster. Franklin Roosevelt's New Deal was the result. The huge majorities enjoyed by the Democrats in Congress, coupled with popular demands to solve the problem, led to a vast outpouring of new legislation and the creation of dozens of new government agencies. Though initially the Supreme Court struck down some of these measures as unconstitutional, a key member of the Court changed his mind and others retired from the bench; by the late 1930s, the Court had virtually ceased opposing any economic legislation.

The second period was in the mid-1960s, a time of prosperity. There was no crisis akin to the Great Depression or World War II, but two events helped change the face of American politics. One was an intellectual and popular ferment that we now refer to as the spirit of "the sixties"—a militant civil rights movement, student activism on college campuses aimed at resisting the Vietnam War, growing concern about threats to the environment, the popular appeal of Ralph Nader and his consumer protection movement, and an optimism among many political and intellectual leaders that the government could solve whatever problems it was willing to address. The other was the 1964 election that returned Lyndon Johnson to the presidency with a larger share of the popular vote than any other president in modern times. Johnson swept into office, and with him came liberal Democratic majorities in both the House and Senate.

The combination of organized demands for new policies, elite optimism about the likely success of those policies, and extraordinary majorities in Congress meant that President Johnson was able, for a few years, to get almost any program he wanted enacted into law. So large were his majorities in Congress that the conservative coalition of Republicans and Southern Democrats was no longer large enough to block action; Northern Democratic liberals were sufficiently numerous in the House and Senate to take control of both bodies. Consequently, much of Johnson's "Great Society" legislation became law. This included the passage of Medicare (to help pay the medical bills of retired people) and Medicaid (to help pay the medical bills of people on welfare); greatly expanded federal aid to the states (to assist them in fighting crime, rebuilding slums, and running transit systems); the enactment of major civil rights laws and of a

The federal government bailed out the U.S. automobile industry in 2009 to help companies avoid bankruptcy.

program to provide federal aid to local schools; the creation of a "War on Poverty" that included various job-training and community-action agencies; and the enactment of a variety of laws regulating business for the purpose of reducing auto fatalities, improving the safety and health of industrial workers, cutting back on pollutants entering the atmosphere, and safeguarding consumers from harmful products.

These two periods—the early 1930s and the mid-1960s—changed the political landscape in America. Of the two, the latter was perhaps the more important, for not only did it witness the passage of so much unprecedented legislation, but also it saw major changes in the pattern of political leadership. It was during this time that the great majority of the members of the House of Representatives came to enjoy relatively secure seats, the primary elections came to supplant party conventions as the decisive means of selecting presidential candidates, interest groups increased greatly in number, and television began to play an important role in shaping the political agenda and perhaps influencing the kinds of candidates nominated.

Consequences of Government Growth

One way of describing the New System is to call it an "activist" government. It is tempting to make a sweeping judgment about such a government, either praising it because it serves a variety of popular needs, or condemning it because it is a bureaucratic affliction. Such generalizations are not entirely empty, but neither are they very helpful. The worth of any given program, or of any collection of programs, can be assessed only by a careful consideration of its costs and benefits, of its effects and side effects. But we may discover some general political consequences of the enlarged scope of government activity.

First, as the government gets bigger, its members must spend more time managing the consequences—intended and unintended—of existing programs and less time debating at length new ideas. As a result, all parts of the government, not just the executive agencies, become more bureaucratized. The White House Office and the Office of Management and Budget (OMB) grow in size and influence, as do the staffs of Congress. At the same time, private organizations (corporations, unions, universities) that deal with the government must also become more bureaucratic. The government hires more people when it is running 80 programs concerned with employment than when it is running two. By the same token, a private employer will hire (and give power to) more people when it is complying with 80 sets of regulations than when it is complying with two.

Second, the more government does, the more it will appear to be acting in inconsistent, uncoordinated, and cumbersome ways. When people complain of red tape, bureaucracy, stalemates, and confusion, they often assume these irritants are caused by incompetent or self-seeking public officials. There is incompetence and self-interest in government just as in every other part of society, but these character traits are not the chief cause of the problem. As citizens, we want many different and often conflicting things. The result is the rise of competing policies, the division of labor among separate administrative agencies, the diffusion of accountability and control, and the multiplication of paperwork. And because Americans are especially energetic about asserting their rights, we must add to the above list of problems the regular use of the courts to challenge policies that we do not like.

Third, an activist government is less susceptible to control by electoral activity than a passive one. When the people in Washington did little, elections made a larger difference in policy than when they began to do a lot. We have pointed out in this book the extent to which both political parties and voter turnout have declined. There are many reasons for this, but an important one often is forgotten. If elections make less of a difference—because the few people for whom one votes can do little to alter the ongoing programs of government—then it may make sense for people to spend less time on party or electoral activities and more on interest group activities aimed at specific agencies and programs.

The rapid increase in the number and variety of interest groups and their enlarged role in government are not pathological. They are a rational response to the fact that elected officials can tend to only a few things, and therefore we must direct our energies at the appointed officials (and judges) who tend to all other government matters. Every president tries to accomplish more, usually by trying to reorganize the executive branch. But no president and no reorganization plan can affect more than a tiny fraction of the millions of federal employees and thousands of government programs. "Coordination" from the top can at best occur selectively, for a few issues of exceptional importance.

Ronald Reagan learned this when he took office in 1981 after promising to reduce the size of government. He did persuade Congress to cut taxes and increase defense spending, but his plans to cut domestic spending resulted in only small declines in some programs and actual increases in many others. Though some programs, such as public housing, were hard hit, most were not, and agricultural subsidies increased dramatically.

When George W. Bush became president in 2001, his philosophy was summarized by the phrase "compassionate conservatism," words that implied that, though he was a conservative, he was not much interested in simply cutting the size of the federal government. And while in office, he proposed policies that would increase spending on many programs. His actions suggest a fact: cutting down on what Washington does is virtually impossible because the people want so much of what it does.

Finally, the more government tries to do, the more things it will be held responsible for and the greater the risk of failure. From time to time in the 19th century, the business cycle made many people unhappy with the federal government—recall the rise of various protest parties—though then the government did very little. If federal officials were lucky, popular support would rise as soon as economic conditions improved. If they were unlucky and a depression lasted into the election campaign, they would be thrown out of office. Today, however, the government—and the president in particular—is held responsible for crime, drug abuse, abortion, civil rights, the environment, the elderly, the status of women, the decay of central cities, the price of gasoline, and international tensions in half a dozen places around the globe.

No government and no president can do well on all or even most of these matters most of the time. Indeed, most of these problems, such as crime, may be totally beyond the reach of the federal government, no matter what its policy. It should not be surprising, therefore, that opinion surveys taken since the early 1960s have shown a steep decline in public confidence in government. There is no reason to believe that this represents a loss of faith in our form of government or even in the design of its institutions, but it clearly reflects a disappointment in, and even cynicism about, the performance of government.

It is too soon to know how, if at all, public sentiments about the performance of government will change as Washington (in response to the 2008–2009 economic crisis) has expanded government activity faster than it has grown in any periods since the late 1930s and the mid-1960s. President Barack Obama proposed a budget for Fiscal Year 2012 that contemplated a deficit of $1.645 trillion. Congressional Republicans, who won control of the House in 2010, objected. After long negotiations with the White House, the two sides agreed on a compromise that made some cuts in spending, thereby avoiding a shutdown of the federal government until November 2011. The large spending increases, however, are only half the story. The other half concerns the federal government taking on new responsibilities and challenges: It has become the majority stockholder in what was once the world's largest automotive company, General Motors; it has more closely controlled dozens of other companies and diverse financial markets; and it has enacted a large, new government-regulated health care system.

University of Maryland political scientist Donald F. Kettl has argued that the "financial meltdown accelerated our expectations that government will keep us safe. ... We've gone from debates over privatizing the public sector to big steps toward governmentalizing the private sector."[1] The far-reaching changes include "more public money in the private economy, more rules to shape how the private sector behaves, and more citizen expectations that government will manage the risks we face."[2]

We cannot yet say whether multi-trillion-dollar budget deficits and policies that betoken government-guaranteed corporate capitalism will persist for years to come. But it seems a fair bet that the New System is entering a new era which, not unlike the expansion that began in the late 1930s, has been fueled by economic problems that have afflicted or threatened most Americans.

It also seems likely that, if anything, public disenchantment with government performance will continue to grow along with government's role in people's lives. Such disenchantment is hardly unique to the United States; it appears to be a feature of almost every democratic political system. The disenchantment is in fact probably greater elsewhere. Americans who complain of high taxes might feel somewhat differently if they lived in Sweden, where taxes are nearly twice as high as here. Those who grouse about bureaucrats in this country probably have never dealt with the massive, centralized bureaucracies of Italy or France. People who are annoyed by congestion, pollution, and inflation ought to arrange a trip to Beijing, Mexico City, or Tokyo. However frustrating private life and public affairs may be in this country, every year thousands living in other nations immigrate to this country. Few Americans choose to migrate to other places.

The 2009 stimulus bill allowed people to get money if they traded in an old car that burned a lot of gas.

The enormous expansion of the scope and goals of the federal government has not been random or unguided. The government has tended to enlarge its powers more in some directions than in others; certain kinds of goals have been served more frequently than others. Though many factors shape this process of selection, two are of special importance. One is our constitutional structure, and the other our political culture.

The Influence of Structure

To see the influence of structure, it is necessary to perform a mental experiment. Suppose the Founders had adopted a centralized, parliamentary regime instead of a decentralized, congressional one. They had the British model right before their eyes. Every other European democracy adopted it. What difference would it have made had we followed the British example?

No one can be certain, of course, because the United States and the United Kingdom differ in many ways, and not just in their political forms. At best, our mental experiment will be an educated guess. But the following possibilities seem plausible.

A parliamentary regime of the British sort centralizes power in the hands of an elected prime minister with a disciplined partisan majority in the legislature and frees him or her from most of the constraints created by independent congressional committees or independent, activist courts. Had the Framers adopted a parliamentary system, we might see these features in the political life of the United States today:

- *Quicker adoption of majoritarian policies, such as those in the area of social welfare.* Broad popular desires would be translated sooner into national policy when they are highly salient and conform to the views of party leaders.

- *More centralization of bureaucratic authority—more national planning, and less local autonomy.* More decisions would be made bureaucratically, both because bureaucracies would be proportionately larger and because they would have wider discretionary authority delegated to them. (If the prime minister heads *both* the executive branch and the legislature, he or she sees no reason why decisions cannot be made as easily in one place as the other.) Local authorities would not have been able to prevent groups of citizens (such as African Americans) from voting or otherwise participating in public life by maintaining segregated facilities at the local level.

- *Fewer opportunities for citizens to challenge or block government policies of which they disapprove.* Without independent and activist courts, without local centers (state and city) of autonomous power, U.S. citizens would have less of a chance to organize to stop a highway or an urban-renewal project, for example, and hence fewer citizen organizations with these and similar purposes would exist.

- *Greater executive control of government.* If a situation like Watergate occurred, we would never know about it. No legislative investigating committees would be sufficiently independent of executive control to be able to investigate claims of executive wrongdoing.

- *Similar foreign policy.* We probably would have fought in about the same number of wars and under pretty much the same circumstances.

- *Higher and more centralized taxation.* Taxes would be higher, and a larger share of our tax money would be collected at the national level. Thus we would find it harder to wage a "tax revolt" (since it is easier to block local spending decisions than national ones).

If this list of guesses is even approximately correct, it means that you would get more of some things that you want and less of others. In general, it would be easier for temporary majorities to govern and harder for individuals and groups to protect their interests.

The Founders would probably not be surprised at this list of differences. Though they could not have foreseen all the events and issues that would have led to these outcomes, they would have understood them, because they thought they were creating a system designed to keep central power weak and to enhance local and citizen power. They would have been amazed, of course, at the extent to which central power has been enhanced and local power weakened in the United States, but if they visited Europe, they would learn that, by comparison, American politics remains far more sensitive to local concerns than does politics abroad.

The Influence of Ideas

The broadly shared political culture of Americans has also influenced the policies adopted by the U.S. government. Paramount among these attitudes is the preoccupation with rights. More than the citizens of perhaps any other nation, Americans define their relations with one another and with political authority in terms of rights. The civil liberties protected by the Bill of Rights have been assiduously defended and their interpretation significantly broadened even while the power of government has been growing.

For example, we expect that the groups affected by any government program will have a right to play a role in shaping and administering that program. In consequence, interest groups have proliferated. We think citizens should have the right to select the nominees of political parties as well as to choose between the parties; hence primary elections have largely replaced party conventions in selecting candidates. Individual members of Congress assert their rights, and thus the power of congressional leaders and committee chairs has steadily diminished. We probably use the courts more frequently than the citizens of any other nation to make or change public policy; in doing so, we are asserting one set of rights against a competing set. The procedural rules that set forth how government is to act—the Freedom of Information Act, the Privacy Act, the Administrative Procedure Act—are more complex and demanding than the rules under which any other democratic government must operate. Each rule exists because it embodies what somebody has claimed to be a right: the right to know information, to maintain one's privacy, to participate in making decisions, and to bring suit against rival parties.

The more vigorously we assert our rights, the harder it is to make government decisions or to manage large institutions. We recognize this when we grumble about red tape and bureaucratic confusion, but we rarely give much support to proposals to centralize authority or simplify decision making. We seem to accept whatever it costs in efficiency or effectiveness in order to maintain the capacity for asserting our rights.

We do not always agree on which rights are most important, however. In addition to the influence of the widely shared commitment to rights generally, government is also shaped by the views that certain political elites have about which rights ought to be given the highest priority. Elite opinion tends to favor freedom of expression over freedom to manage or dispose of property. Mass opinion, though it has changed a good deal in the last few decades, is less committed to the preferred position of freedom of expression. Rank-and-file citizens often complain that what the elite calls essential liberty should instead be regarded as excessive permissiveness. People who own or manage property often lament the extent to which the rights governing its use have declined.

The changes in the relative security of personal and property freedom are linked to a fundamental and enduring tension in American thought. Tocqueville said it best: Americans, he wrote, "are far more ardently and tenaciously attached to equality than to freedom." Though democratic communities have a "natural taste for freedom," that freedom is hard to preserve, because its excesses are immediate and obvious and its advantages are remote and uncertain. The advantages of equality, on the other hand, are readily apparent, and its costs are obscure and deferred.[3] For example, Americans believe in free speech, but most of us rarely take advantage of that right and notice the problem only when somebody says something we don't like. We have to remind ourselves that freedom has to be protected even when it does not help us directly. By contrast, we notice equality immediately, as when everybody of a certain age gets Social Security even when they are already rich. Equality makes us feel comfortable even if a few people don't need the benefits they are getting.

Tocqueville, however, may have underestimated the extent to which political liberties would endure, because he did not foresee the determination of the courts to resist, in the long run if not the short, the passions of temporary majorities seeking to curtail such liberties. But he did not underestimate the extent to which in the economic and social realms Americans would decide that improving the conditions of life would justify restrictions on the right to dispose of property and to manage private institutions. At first, the conflict was between liberty and equality of opportunity; more recently it has become a conflict—among political elites, if not within the citizenry itself—between equality of opportunity and equality of results.

The fact that decisions can be influenced by opinions about rights indicates that decisions can be influenced by opinions generally. As the political system has become more fragmented and more individualized as a result of our collective assertion of rights, it has come more under the sway of ideas. When political parties were strong and congressional leadership was centralized (as in the latter part of the 19th and the early part of the 20th centuries), gaining access to the decision-making process in Washington was difficult, and the number of new ideas that stood a chance of adoption was small. However, those proposals that could command leadership support were more easily adopted: though there were powerful organizations that could say no, those same organizations could also say yes.

Today, these and other institutions are fragmented and in disarray. Individual members of Congress are far more important than congressional leaders. Political parties no longer control nominations for office. The media have given candidates direct access to the voters; campaign finance laws have restricted, but not eliminated, the influence that interest groups can wield by spending money. Forming new, issue-oriented lobbying groups is much easier today than formerly, thanks to the capability of computers and direct-mail advertising.

HOW WE COMPARE

Deficit Spending in America and Europe

From 1800 to 1932, the federal government had an annual budget deficit about one-third of the time. In that 132-year stretch, the federal government had large and consecutive annual budget deficits only during the Civil War and again during World War I. From the dawn of the New Deal in 1933 to the eve of the Great Society in 1964, the federal government had an annual budget deficit about five-sixths of the time. Deficit spending soared during World War II, and it was only in each of five subsequent pre-1965 years (1947, 1948, 1956, 1957, and 1960) that the federal budget was in surplus. From 1965 to 2013, a 49-year period, the federal government had an annual budget surplus in each of only two years (1999 and 2000).

(continued)

HOW WE COMPARE (*Continued*)

America is not the only modern democracy to have settled into a persistent pattern of annual deficit spending, or to run annual deficits that are large relative to the nation's economy. For instance, in 2010, the federal deficit was about 10.7 percent of U.S. Gross Domestic Product. Here are that year's comparable figures for a host of European democracies:

Nation	Deficit as a percentage of Gross Domestic Product
Ireland	32.4%
Greece	10.5
United Kingdom	10.5
Spain	9.2
Portugal	9.1
Poland	7.9
France	7.0
Denmark	2.7
Finland	2.4
Sweden	0.0

Source: Office of Management and Budget, *Historical Tables: Fiscal Year 2011*, Table 1.1, pp. 21–23; "EU States with the Biggest Deficits and Debts," *Telegraph*, April 26, 2011, reporting data from Eurostat.

These idea-based changes in institutions affect how policy is made. When there is widespread enthusiasm for an idea—especially among political elites, but also in the public at large—new programs can be formulated and adopted with great speed. This happened when Lyndon Johnson's Great Society legislation was proposed, when the environmental and consumer protection laws first arrived on the public agenda, and when campaign finance reform was proposed in the wake of Watergate. So long as such symbols have a powerful appeal, so long as a consensus persists, change is possible. But when these ideas lose their appeal—or are challenged by new ideas—the competing pressures make change extremely difficult. Environmentalism today is challenged by concerns about creating jobs and economic growth; social legislation is challenged by skepticism about its effectiveness and concern over its cost; campaign finance reforms are, to some critics, merely devices for protecting incumbents.

This may all seem obvious to a reader raised in the world of contemporary politics. But it is different in degree, if not in kind, from the way in which politics was once carried out. In the 1920s, the 1930s, the 1940s, and even the 1950s, people described politics as a process of bargaining among organized interests, or "blocs," representing business, farming, labor, ethnic, and professional groups. With the expansion of the scope of government policy, there are no longer a few major blocs that sit astride the policy process. Instead, thousands of highly specialized interests and constituencies seek above all to protect whatever benefits, intangible as well as tangible, they get from government.

American Democracy—Then, Now, and Next

We have a large government—and large expectations about what it can achieve. But the government finds it increasingly difficult to satisfy those expectations. The public's acceptance of a larger and larger role for government has been accompanied by a decline in public confidence in those who lead and manage that government. We expect more and more from government, but are less and less certain that we will get it, or get it in a form and at a cost that we find acceptable. This perhaps constitutes the greatest challenge to political leadership in the years ahead: to find a way to serve the true interests of the people while restoring and retaining their confidence in the legitimacy of government itself. We might begin by challenging the increasingly popular notion that present-day American democracy's problems are so deep because its political leaders are so shallow, not least by comparison to the nation's first leaders.

THEN

When the Constitution was created and ratified, national leaders beholden only to their own consciences could meet in secret to debate and decide even the most controversial and consequential questions about government. They could belittle, berate, or battle each other one day, and beseech, bargain, or broker deals with each other the next day, all without their words or deeds (or misdeeds) being a matter of public record, or widely known at all.

NOW

In stark contrast, the political leaders that today hold office under the terms of that same Constitution, amended only 27 times in more than 220 years, must deliberate and legislate while the whole world—friend and foe alike—is listening and watching. Contemporary presidents and congresspersons face the challenge of leading a large and diverse population, coping with an all-pervasive mass communications media, and steering a federal government that is far bigger, and administered in a way that is far more complicated, than any of the Constitution's authors ever envisioned.

As a class, today's elected officials at both ends of Pennsylvania Avenue and in both parties are often much-maligned, not only, at times, by each other and by their other respective partisan and ideological opponents, but by the public at large, with majorities disparaging the "politicians" about as readily as they denounce the "bureaucrats." But now reflect seriously on questions like the following:

- How do you suppose James Madison, George Washington, or the other authors of the Constitution would have fared if they had led, not a slave-holding society of barely 4 million people, but a demographically diverse and free society of more than 300 million people?

- How do you think the nation's early political leaders, bitterly divided over the Constitution as they were (see Chapter 2), would have held up had they faced anything like the incessant public stare and media glare that Democratic President Barack Obama and Republican President George W. Bush, Republican House Speaker John Boehner and Democratic House Speaker Nancy Pelosi, and other present-day national political leaders now routinely face even when not battling with each other?

- Do you believe that American democracy's first generation of leaders would in our present-day context come any closer than today's leaders have come to forging a national consensus and getting decisive action on difficult issues like the federal government's annual budget deficits and the growing national debt?

- As contentious and complicated as the debates over federalism (see Chapter 3) were when the republic was founded, do you think that those who forged the compromises that then defined federal–state relations would be significantly more effective than today's federal, state, and local public officials are when it comes to ensuring that the more than $600 billion a year that Washington now spends on grants to state and local governments for social welfare (see Chapter 13) and other public purposes is all money well spent?

- And do you suppose that earlier generations of leaders would be any more adept than today's leaders are when it comes to ensuring that the private, for-profit firms and nonprofit organizations that are a big part of today's proxy-government system of public administration (see Chapter 11) serve the public well?

We suspect that Madison himself, if he were returned to our political moment in time, might conclude that exercising effective leadership now is even harder than it was then.

Regardless, the next chapters in the still-unfolding story of American democracy remain to be written by the nation's next generation of leaders including, we hope, some students whose interest in politics, government, and public policy was stirred in part by this book.

- At each level of government, whatever one's party or policy preferences, to be a public-spirited "politician" that wins elected office and participates in the democratic legislative process, or to be a judge responsible for interpreting and applying laws including in cases that involve civil liberties (see Chapter 4) and civil rights (see Chapter 5), is to live a truly noble calling.

- To be a "bureaucrat"—a career public servant—that serves the public by responsibly translating democratically enacted laws on health, housing, trade, transportation, education, environmental protection, nuclear energy, or any other policy area into administrative action is a truly noble calling, too.

- And, for those who, like most people, are called instead to careers in business, the arts, or other fields, to yet be an engaged citizen of American democracy, to seek to know ever more about American government, political institutions, and public policies, is a most worthy intellectual and civic pastime.

So, we end with words from *Federalist* No. 51 that should remind us all why the subject you have been studying with the aid of this book is so important:

> *Justice is the end of government. It is the end of civil society. It ever has been and ever will be pursued until it be obtained, or until liberty be lost in the pursuit.*

LEARNING OBJECTIVES

LO 15.1 Name three things that for many years kept the agenda of the federal government short.

The Supreme Court restricted the ability of Congress to delegate broad discretionary powers to administrative agencies.
Public opinion supported the idea of a limited federal government.
Washington could not levy an income tax.

LO 15.2 Name three things that have expanded the agenda of the federal government.

The Supreme Court has allowed the delegation of broad discretionary powers to top administrative agencies.
Public opinion has supported a more activist government.
The Constitution has been amended to allow for an income tax.

LO 15.3 Contrast three features of the Old System versus the New System of American government.

Old: Congress had strong committee chairpersons, small staffs, and few subcommittees.
New: Congress has weak committee chairpersons, large staffs, and many subcommittees.
Old: The courts allowed government to exercise few economic powers and took a narrow view of individual freedoms. New: The courts allow the government many economic powers and take a broad view of individual freedoms.
Old: Political parties were dominated by local party leaders meeting in conventions. New: Political parties are dominated by activists chosen in primaries and caucuses.

LO 15.4 How has the challenge of political leadership changed since the days of the Constitutional Convention?

In at least some respects, it has become harder. Unlike the authors of the Constitution and most other previous generations of political leaders, today's presidents and members of Congress make important decisions under intense public scrutiny. They lead a demographically diverse and free society of more than 300 million citizens, with a government that constitutes a much larger share of the nation's economy than any of the Framers ever envisioned and that touches virtually every facet of contemporary economic, social, and civic life.

Appendix

The Declaration of Independence

In Congress, July 4, 1776

The Unanimous Declaration of the Thirteen United States of America

When, in the course of human events, it becomes necessary for one people to dissolve the political bands which have connected them with another, and to assume, among the powers of the earth, the separate and equal station to which the laws of nature and of nature's God entitle them, a decent respect to the opinions of mankind requires that they should declare the causes which impel them to the separation.

We hold these truths to be self-evident: That all men are created equal; that they are endowed by their Creator with certain unalienable rights; that among these are life, liberty, and the pursuit of happiness; that, to secure these rights, governments are instituted among men, deriving their just powers from the consent of the governed; that whenever any form of government becomes destructive of these ends, it is the right of the people to alter or to abolish it, and to institute new government, laying its foundation on such principles, and organizing its powers in such form, as to them shall seem most likely to effect their safety and happiness. Prudence, indeed, will dictate that governments long established should not be changed for light and transient causes; and accordingly all experience hath shown that mankind are more disposed to suffer, while evils are sufferable, than to right themselves by abolishing the forms to which they are accustomed. But when a long train of abuses and usurpations, pursuing invariably the same object, evinces a design to reduce them under absolute despotism, it is their right, it is their duty, to throw off such government, and to provide new guards for their future security. Such has been the patient sufferance of these colonies; and such is now the necessity which constrains them to alter their former systems of government. The history of the present King of Great Britain is a history of repeated injuries and usurpations, all having in direct object the establishment of an absolute tyranny over these states. To prove this, let facts be submitted to a candid world.

He has refused to assent to laws, the most wholesome and necessary for the public good.

He has forbidden his governors to pass laws of immediate and pressing importance, unless suspended in their operation till his assent should be obtained; and, when so suspended, he has utterly neglected to attend to them.

He has refused to pass other laws for the accommodation of large districts of people, unless those people would relinquish the right of representation in the legislature, a right inestimable to them, and formidable to tyrants only.

He has called together legislative bodies at places unusual, uncomfortable, and distant from the depository of their public records, for the sole purpose of fatiguing them into compliance with his measures.

He has dissolved representative houses repeatedly, for opposing, with manly firmness, his invasions on the rights of the people.

He has refused for a long time, after such dissolutions, to cause others to be elected; whereby the legislative powers, incapable of annihilation, have returned to the people at large for their exercise; the state remaining, in the mean time, exposed to all dangers of invasions from without and convulsions within.

He has endeavored to prevent the population of these states; for that purpose obstructing the laws for naturalization of foreigners; refusing to pass others to encourage their migration hither, and raising the conditions of new appropriations of lands.

He has obstructed the administration of justice, by refusing his assent to laws for establishing judiciary powers.

He has made judges dependent on his will alone, for the tenure of their offices, and the amount and payment of their salaries.

He has erected a multitude of new offices, and sent hither swarms of officers to harass our people and eat out their substance.

He has kept among us, in times of peace, standing armies, without the consent of our legislatures.

He has affected to render the military independent of, and superior to, the civil power.

He has combined with others to subject us to a jurisdiction foreign to our constitution, and unacknowledged by our laws, giving his assent to their acts of pretended legislation:

For quartering large bodies of armed troops among us:

For protecting them, by a mock trial, from punishment for any murders which they should commit on the inhabitants of these states;

For cutting off our trade with all parts of the world;

For imposing taxes on us without our consent;

For depriving us, in many cases, of the benefits of trial by jury;

For transporting us beyond seas, to be tried for pretended offenses;

For abolishing the free system of English laws in a neighboring province, establishing therein an arbitrary government, and enlarging its boundaries, so as to render it at once an example and fit instrument for introducing the same absolute rule into these colonies;

For taking away our charters, abolishing our more valuable laws, and altering fundamentally the forms of our governments;

For suspending our own legislatures, and declaring themselves invested with power to legislate for us in all cases whatsoever.

He has abdicated government here, by declaring us out of his protection and waging war against us.

He has plundered our seas, ravaged our coasts, burned our towns, and des-troyed the lives of our people.

He is at this time transporting large armies of foreign mercenaries to complete the works of death, desolation, and tyranny already begun with circumstances of cruelty and perfidy scarcely paralleled in the most barbarous ages, and totally unworthy the head of a civilized nation.

He has constrained our fellow-citizens, taken captive on the high seas, to bear arms against their country, to become the executioners of their friends and brethren, or to fall themselves by their hands.

He has excited domestic insurrections among us, and has endeavored to bring on the inhabitants of our frontiers the merciless Indian savages, whose known rule of warfare is an undistinguished destruction of all ages, sexes, and conditions.

In every stage of these oppressions we have petitioned for redress in the most humble terms; our repeated petitions have been answered only by repeated injury. A prince, whose character is thus marked by every act which may define a tyrant, is unfit to be the ruler of a free people.

Nor have we been wanting in our attentions to our British brethren. We have warned them, from time to time, of attempts by their legislature to extend an unwarrantable jurisdiction over us. We have reminded them of the circumstances of our emigration and settlement here. We have appealed to their native justice and magnanimity; and we have conjured them, by the ties of our common kindred, to disavow these usurpations, which would inevitably interrupt our connections and correspondence. They, too, have been deaf to the voice of justice and of consanguinity. We must, therefore, acquiesce in the necessity which denounces our separation, and hold them, as we hold the rest of mankind, enemies in war, in peace friends.

We, therefore, the representatives of the United States of America, in General Congress assembled, appealing to the Supreme Judge of the world for the rectitude of our intentions, do, in the name and by the authority of the good people of these colonies, solemnly publish and declare, that these United Colonies are, and of right ought to be, FREE AND INDEPENDENT STATES; that they are absolved from all allegiance to the British crown, and that all political connection between them and the state of Great Britain is, and ought to be, totally dissolved; and that, as free and independent states, they have full power to levy war, conclude peace, contract alliances, establish commerce, and do all other acts and things which independent states may of right do. And for the support of this declaration, with a firm reliance on the protection of Divine Providence, we mutually pledge to each other our lives, our fortunes, and our sacred honor.

JOHN HANCOCK [*President*]
[*and fifty-five others*]

The Constitution of the United States

We the People of the United States, in Order to form a more perfect Union, establish Justice, insure domestic Tranquility, provide for the common defence, promote the general Welfare, and secure the Blessings of Liberty to ourselves and our Posterity, do ordain and establish this Constitution for the United States of America.

ARTICLE I.

Section 1.   All legislative Powers herein granted shall be vested in a Congress of the United States, which shall consist of a Senate and House of Representatives.

Section 2.   The House of Representatives shall be composed of Members chosen every second Year by the People of the several States, and the Electors in each State shall have the Qualifications requisite for Electors of the most numerous Branch of the State Legislature.

No Person shall be a Representative who shall not have attained to the age of twenty five Years, and been seven Years a Citizen of the United States, and who shall not, when elected, be an Inhabitant of that State in which he shall be chosen.

Representatives and direct Taxes shall be apportioned among the several States which may be included within this Union, according to their respective Numbers, which shall be determined by adding to the whole Number of free Persons, including those bound to Service for a Term of Years, and excluding Indians not taxed, three fifths of all other Persons.[1] The actual Enumeration shall be made within three Years after the first Meeting of the Congress of the United States, and within every subsequent Term of ten Years, in such Manner as they shall by Law direct. The Number of Representatives shall not exceed one for every thirty Thousand, but each State shall have at Least one Representative; and until such enumeration shall be made, the State of New Hampshire shall be entitled to chuse three, Massachusetts eight, Rhode-Island and Providence Plantations one, Connecticut five, New-York six, New Jersey four, Pennsylvania eight, Delaware one, Maryland six, Virginia ten, North Carolina five, South Carolina five, and Georgia three.

When vacancies happen in the Representation from any State, the Executive Authority thereof shall issue Writs of Election to fill such Vacancies.

The House of Representatives shall chuse their Speaker and other Officers; and shall have the sole Power of Impeachment.

Section 3.   The Senate of the United States shall be composed of two Senators from each State, *chosen by the Legislature thereof,*[2] for six Years; and each Senator shall have one Vote.

Immediately after they shall be assembled in Consequence of the first Election, they shall be divided as equally as may be into three Classes. The Seats of the Senators of the first class shall be vacated at the Expiration of the second Year, of the second Class at the Expiration of the fourth Year, and of the third Class at the Expiration of the sixth Year, so that one third may be chosen every second Year; *and if Vacancies happen by Resignation, or otherwise, during the Recess of the Legislature of any State, the Executive thereof may make temporary Appointments until the next Meeting of the Legislature, which shall then fill such Vacancies.*[3]

No Person shall be a Senator who shall not have attained to the Age of thirty Years, and been nine Years a Citizen of the United States, and who shall not, when elected, be an Inhabitant of that State for which he shall be chosen.

The Vice President of the United States shall be President of the Senate, but shall have no Vote, unless they be equally divided.

---

[1] Changed by the Fourteenth Amendment, Section 2.

Note: Excluding the Preamble and Closing, those portions set in italic type have been superseded or changed by later amendments.

[2] Changed by the Seventeenth Amendment.

[3] Changed by the Seventeenth Amendment.

The Senate shall chuse their other Officers, and also a President pro tempore, in the Absence of the Vice President, or when he shall exercise the Office of President of the United States.

The Senate shall have the sole Power to try all Impeachments. When sitting for that Purpose, they shall be on Oath or Affirmation. When the President of the United States is tried the Chief Justice shall preside: And no Person shall be convicted without the Concurrence of two thirds of the Members present.

Judgment in Cases of Impeachment shall not exceed further than to removal from Office, and disqualification to hold and enjoy any Office of honor, Trust or Profit under the United States: but the Party convicted shall nevertheless be liable and subject to Indictment, Trial, Judgment and Punishment, according to Law.

Section 4.   The Times, Places and Manner of holding Elections for Senators and Representatives, shall be prescribed in each State by the Legislature thereof; but the Congress may at any time by Law make or alter such Regulations, except as to the Places of chusing Senators.

The Congress shall assemble at least once in every Year, and such Meeting shall be on the *first Monday in December, unless they shall by Law appoint a different Day.*[4]

Section 5.   Each House shall be the Judge of the Elections, Returns and Qualifications of its own Members, and a Majority of each shall constitute a Quorum to do Business; but a smaller number may adjourn from day to day, and may be authorized to compel the Attendance of absent Members, in such Manner, and under such Penalties as each House may provide.

Each House may determine the Rules of its Proceedings, punish its Members for disorderly Behaviour, and, with the Concurrence of two thirds, expel a Member.

Each House shall keep a Journal of its Proceedings, and from time to time publish the same, excepting such Parts as may in their Judgment require Secrecy; and the Yeas and Nays of the Members of either House on any question shall, at the Desire of one fifth of those Present, be entered on the Journal.

Neither House, during the Session of Congress, shall, without the Consent of the other, adjourn for more than three days, nor to any other Place than that in which the two Houses shall be sitting.

Section 6.   The Senators and Representatives shall receive a Compensation for their Services, to be ascertained by Law, and paid out of the Treasury of the United States. They shall in all Cases, except Treason, Felony and Breach of the Peace, be privileged from Arrest during their Attendance at the Session of their respective Houses, and in going to and returning from the same; and for any Speech or Debate in either House, they shall not be questioned in any other Place.

No Senator or Representative shall, during the Time for which he was elected, be appointed to any civil Office under the Authority of the United States, which shall have been created, or the Emoluments whereof shall have been encreased during such time; and no Person holding any Office under the United States, shall be a Member of either House during his Continuance in Office.

Section 7.   All Bills for raising Revenue shall originate in the House of Representatives; but the Senate may propose or concur with Amendments as on other Bills.

Every Bill which shall have passed the House of Representatives and the Senate, shall, before it become a Law, be presented to the President of the United States; If he approve he shall assign it, but if not he shall return it, with his Objections to that House in which it shall have originated, who shall enter the Objections at large on their Journal, and proceed to reconsider it. If after such Reconsideration two thirds of that House shall agree to pass the Bill, it shall be sent, together with the Objections, to the other House, by which it shall likewise be reconsidered, and if approved by two thirds of that House, it shall become a Law. But in all such Cases the Votes of both Houses shall be determined by yeas and Nays, and the Names of the Persons voting for and against the Bill shall be entered on the Journal of each House respectively. If any Bill shall not be returned by the President within ten Days (Sundays excepted) after it shall have been presented to him, the Same shall be a Law, in like Manner, as if he had signed it, unless the Congress by their Adjournment prevent its Return, in which Case it shall not be a Law.

Every Order, Resolution, or Vote to which the Concurrence of the Senate and House of Representatives may be necessary (except on a question of Adjournment) shall be presented to the President of the United States; and before

[4]Changed by the Twentieth Amendment, Section 2.

the Same shall take Effect, shall be approved by him, or being disapproved by him, shall be repassed by two thirds of the Senate and House of Representatives, according to the Rules and Limitations prescribed in the Case of a Bill.

Section 8.   The Congress shall have Power To lay and Collect Taxes, Duties, Imposts and Excises, to pay the Debts and provide for the common Defence and general Welfare of the United States; but all Duties, Imposts and Excises shall be uniform throughout the United States.

To borrow Money on the credit of the United States;

To regulate Commerce with foreign Nations, and among the several States, and with the Indian Tribes;

To establish an uniform Rule of Naturalization, and uniform Laws on the subject of Bankruptcies throughout the United States;

To coin Money, regulate the Value thereof, and of foreign Coin, and fix the Standard of Weights and Measures;

To provide for the Punishment of counterfeiting the Securities and current Coin of the United States;

To establish Post Offices and post Roads;

To promote the Progress of Science and useful Arts, by securing for limited Times to Authors and Inventors the exclusive Right to their respective Writings and Discoveries;

To constitute Tribunals inferior to the Supreme Court;

To define and punish Piracies and Felonies committed on the high Seas, and Offences against the Law of Nations;

To declare War, grant Letters of Marque and Reprisal, and make Rules concerning Captures on Land and Water;

To raise and support Armies, but no Appropriation of Money to that Use shall be for a longer Term than two Years;

To provide and maintain a Navy;

To make Rules for the Government and Regulation of the land and naval Forces;

To provide for calling forth the Militia to execute the Laws of the Union, suppress Insurrections and repel Invasions;

To provide for organizing, arming, and disciplining, the Militia, and for governing such Part of them as may be employed in the Service of the United States, reserving to the States respectively, the Appointment of the Officers, and the Authority of training the Militia according to the discipline prescribed by Congress;

To exercise exclusive Legislation in all Cases whatsoever, over such District (not exceeding ten Miles square) as may, by Cession of Particular States, and the Acceptance of Congress, become the Seat of the Government of the United States, and to exercise like Authority over all Places purchased by the Consent of the Legislature of the State in which the Same shall be, for the Erection of Forts, Magazines, Arsenals, dock-Yards and other needful Buildings;—And

To make all Laws which shall be necessary and proper for carrying into Execution the foregoing Powers, and all other Powers vested by this Constitution in the Government of the United States, or in any Department or Officer thereof.

Section 9.   The Migration or Importation of such Persons as any of the States now existing shall think proper to admit, shall not be prohibited by the Congress prior to the Year one thousand eight hundred and eight, but a Tax or duty may be imposed on such Importation, not exceeding ten dollars for each Person.

The Privilege of the Writ of Habeas Corpus shall not be suspended, unless when in Cases of Rebellion or Invasion the public Safety may require it.

No bill of Attainder or ex post facto Law shall be passed.

No Capitation, or other direct, Tax shall be laid, *unless in Proportion to the Census or Enumeration herein before directed to be taken.*[5]

No Tax or Duty shall be laid on Articles exported from any State.

No Preference shall be given by any Regulation of Commerce or Revenue to the Ports of one State over those of another; nor shall Vessels bound to, or from, one State, be obliged to enter, clear or pay Duties in another.

No Money shall be drawn from the Treasury, but in Consequence of Appropriations made by Law; and a regular Statement and Account of the Receipts and Expenditures of all public Money shall be published from time to time.

---

[5]Changed by the Sixteenth Amendment.

No Title of Nobility shall be granted by the United States: And no Person holding any Office of Profit or Trust under them, shall, without the Consent of the Congress, accept of any present, Emolument, Office, or Title, of any kind whatever, from any King, Prince, or foreign State.

Section 10. No State shall enter into any Treaty, Alliance, or Confederation; grant Letters of Marque and Reprisal; coin Money; emit Bills of Credit; make any Thing but gold and silver Coin a Tender in Payment of Debts; pass any Bill of Attainder, ex post facto Law, or Law impairing the Obligation of Contracts, or grant any Title of Nobility.

No State shall, without the Consent of the Congress, lay any Imposts or Duties on Imports or Exports, except what may be absolutely necessary for executing its inspection Laws; and the net Produce of all Duties and Imposts, laid by any State on Imports or Exports, shall be for the Use of the Treasury of the United States; and all such Laws shall be subject to the Revision and Controul of the Congress.

No State shall, without the Consent of Congress, lay any Duty of Tonnage, keep Troops, or Ships of War in time of Peace, enter into any Agreement or Compact with another State, or with a foreign Power, or engage in War, unless actually invaded, or in such imminent Danger as will not admit of delay.

ARTICLE II.

Section 1. The executive Power shall be vested in a President of the United States of America. He shall hold his Office during the term of four Years, and, together with the Vice President, chosen for the same Term, be elected, as follows

Each State shall appoint, in such Manner as the Legislature thereof may direct, a Number of Electors, equal to the whole Number of Senators and Representatives to which the State may be entitled in the Congress: but no Senator or Representative, or Person holding an Office of Trust or Profit under the United States, shall be appointed an Elector.

The Electors shall meet in their respective States, and vote by Ballot for two Persons, of whom one at least shall not be an Inhabitant of the same State with them-selves. And they shall make a List of all the Persons voted for, and of the Number of Votes for each; which List they shall sign and certify, and transmit sealed to the Seat of the Government of the United States, directed to the President of the Senate. The President of the Senate shall, in the Presence of the Senate and House of Representatives, open all the Certificates, and the Votes shall then be counted. The Person having the greatest Number of Votes shall be the President, if such Number be a Majority of the whole Number of Electors appointed; and if there be more than one who have such Majority, and have an equal Number of Votes, then the House of Representatives shall immediately chuse by Ballot one of them for President; and if no Person have a Majority, then from the five highest on the List the said House shall in like Manner chuse the President. But in chusing the President, the Votes shall be taken by States, the Representation from each State having one Vote; a quorum for this Purpose shall consist of a Member or Members from two thirds of the States, and a Majority of all the States shall be necessary to a Choice. In every Case, after the Choice of the President, the Person having the greatest Number of Votes of the Electors shall be the Vice President. But if there should remain two or more who have equal Votes, the Senate shall chuse from them by Ballot the Vice President.[6]

The Congress may determine the Time of chusing the Electors, and the Day on which they shall give their Votes, which Day shall be the same throughout the United States.

No Person except a natural born Citizen, or a Citizen of the United States, at the time of the Adoption of this Constitution, shall be eligible to the Office of President; neither shall any person be eligible to that Office who shall not have attained to the Age of thirty five Years, and been fourteen Years a Resident within the United States.

In Case of the Removal of the President from Office, or of his Death, Resignation, or Inability to discharge the Powers and Duties of the said Office, the Same shall devolve on the Vice President, and the Congress may by Law provide for the Case of Removal, Death, Resignation or Inability, both of the President and Vice President, declaring what Officer shall then act as President, and such Officer shall act accordingly, until the Disability be removed, or a President shall be elected.[7]

---

[6]Superseded by the Twelfth Amendment.

[7]Modified by the Twenty-Fifth Amendment.

The President shall, at stated Times, receive for his Services, a Compensation, which shall neither be encreased nor diminished during the Period for which he shall have been elected, and he shall not receive within that Period any other Emolument from the United States, or any of them.

Before he enter on the Execution of his Office, he shall take the following Oath or Affirmation:—"I do solemnly swear (or affirm) that I will faithfully execute the Office of President of the United States, and will to the best of my Ability, preserve, protect and defend the Constitution of the United States."

Section 2. The President shall be Commander in Chief of the Army and Navy of the United States, and of the Militia of the several States, when called into the actual Service of the United States; he may require the Opinion, in writing, of the principal Officer in each of the executive Departments, upon any Subject relating to the Duties of their respective Offices, and he shall have Power to grant Reprieves and Pardons for Offences against the United States, except in Cases of Impeachment.

He shall have Power, by and with the Advice and Consent of the Senate, to make Treaties, provided two thirds of the Senators present concur; and he shall nominate, and by and with the Advice and Consent of the Senate, shall appoint Ambassadors, other public Ministers and Consuls, Judges of the supreme Court, and all other Officers of the United States, whose Appointments are not herein otherwise provided for, and which shall be established by Law: but the Congress may by Law vest the Appointment of such inferior Officers, as they think proper, in the President alone, in the Courts of Law, or in the Heads of Departments.

The President shall have Power to fill up all Vacancies that may happen during the Recess of the Senate, by granting Commissions which shall expire at the End of their next Session.

Section 3. He shall from time to time give to the Congress Information of the State of the Union, and recommend to their Consideration such Measures as he shall judge necessary and expedient; he may, on extraordinary Occasions, convene both Houses, or either of them, and in Case of Disagreement between them, with Respect to the Time of Adjournment, he may adjourn them to such Time as he shall think proper; he shall receive Ambassadors and other public Ministers; he shall take Care that the Laws be faithfully executed, and shall Commission all the Officers of the United States.

Section 4. The President, Vice President and all civil Officers of the United States, shall be removed from Office on Impeachment for, and Conviction of, Treason, Bribery, or other high Crimes and Misdemeanors.

ARTICLE III.

Section 1. The judicial Power of the United States, shall be vested in one supreme Court, and in such inferior Courts as the Congress may from time to time ordain and establish. The Judges, both of the supreme and inferior Courts, shall hold their Offices during good Behaviour, and shall, at stated Times, receive for their Services, a Compensation, which shall not be diminished during their Continuance in Office.

Section 2. The judicial Power shall extend to all Cases, in Law and Equity, arising under this Constitution, the Laws of the United States, and Treaties made, or which shall be made, under their Authority;—to all Cases affecting Ambassadors, other public Ministers and Consuls;—to all Cases of admiralty and maritime Jurisdiction;—to Controversies to which the United States shall be a Party;—to Controversies between two or more States;—*between a State and Citizens of another State;*[8]—between Citizens of different States;—between Citizens of the same State claiming Lands under Grants of different States, and between a State, or the Citizens thereof, and foreign States, Citizens or Subjects.

In all Cases affecting Ambassadors, other public Ministers and Consuls, and those in which a State shall be Party, the supreme Court shall have original Jurisdiction. In all the other Cases before mentioned, the supreme Court shall have appellate Jurisdiction, both as to Law and Fact, with such Exceptions, and under such Regulations as the Congress shall make.

[8]Modified by the Eleventh Amendment.

The Trial of all Crimes, except in Cases of Impeachment, shall be by Jury; and such Trial shall be held in the State where the said Crimes shall have been committed; but when not committed within any State, the Trial shall be at such Place or Places as the Congress may by Law have directed.

Section 3.   Treason against the United States, shall consist only in levying War against them, or in adhering to their Enemies, giving them Aid and Comfort. No Person shall be convicted of Treason unless on the Testimony of two Witnesses to the same overt Act, or on Confession in open Court.

The Congress shall have Power to declare the Punishment of Treason, but no Attainder of Treason shall work Corruption of Blood, or Forfeiture except during the Life of the Person attainted.

ARTICLE IV.

Section 1.   Full Faith and Credit shall be given in each State to the public Acts, Records, and judicial Proceedings of every other State. And the Congress may by general Laws prescribe the Manner in which such Acts, Records and Proceedings shall be proved, and the Effect thereof.

Section 2.   The Citizens of each State shall be entitled to all Privileges and Immunities of Citizens in the several States.

A person charged in any State with Treason, Felony, or other Crime, who shall flee from Justice, and be found in another State, shall on Demand of the executive Authority of the State from which he fled, be delivered up, to be removed to the State having Jurisdiction of the Crime.

No Person held to Service or Labour in one State, under the Laws thereof, escaping into another, shall, in Consequence of any Law or Regulation therein, be discharged from such Service or Labour, but shall be delivered up on Claim of the Party to whom such Service or Labour may be due.[9]

Section 3.   New States may be admitted by the Congress into this Union; but no new State shall be formed or erected within the Jurisdiction of any other State; nor any State be formed by the Junction of two or more States, or Parts of States, without the Consent of the Legislatures of the States concerned as well as of the Congress.

The Congress shall have Power to dispose of and make all needful Rules and Regulations respecting the Territory or other Property belonging to the United States; and nothing in this Constitution shall be so construed as to Prejudice any Claims of the United States, or of any particular State.

Section 4.   The United States shall guarantee to every State in this Union a Republican Form of Government, and shall protect each of them against Invasion; and on Application of the Legislature, or of the Executive (when the Legislature cannot be convened) against domestic Violence.

ARTICLE V.

The Congress, whenever two thirds of both Houses shall deem it necessary, shall propose Amendments to this Constitution, or, on the Application of the Legislatures of two thirds of the several States, shall call a Convention for proposing Amendments, which, in either Case, shall be valid to all Intents and Purposes, as Part of this Constitution, when ratified by the Legislatures of three fourths of the several States, or by Conventions in three fourths thereof, as the one or the other Mode of Ratification may be proposed by the Congress; Provided that no Amendment which may be made prior to the Year One thousand eight hundred and eight shall in any Manner after the first and fourth Clauses in the Ninth Section of the first Article; and that no State, without its Consent, shall be deprived of its equal Suffrage in the Senate.

ARTICLE VI.

All Debts contracted and Engagements entered into, before the Adoption of this Constitution, shall be as valid against the United States under this Constitution, as under the Confederation.

---

[9]Changed by the Thirteenth Amendment.

This Constitution, and the Laws of the United States which shall be made in Pursuance thereof; and all Treaties made, or which shall be made, under the Authority of the United States, shall be the Supreme Law of the Land; and the Judges in every State shall be bound thereby, any Thing in the Constitution or Laws of any State to the Contrary notwithstanding.

The Senators and Representatives before mentioned, and the Members of the several State Legislatures, and all executive and judicial Officers, both of the United States and of the several States, shall be bound by Oath or Affirmation, to support this Constitution; but no religious Test shall ever be required as a Qualification to any Office or public Trust under the United States.

ARTICLE VII.

The Ratification of the Conventions of nine States, shall be sufficient for the Establishment of this Constitution between the States so ratifying the Same.

Done in Convention by the Unanimous Consent of the States present the Seventeenth Day of September in the Year of our Lord one thousand seven hundred and Eighty seven and of the Independence of the United States of America the Twelfth In witness whereof We have hereunto subscribed our Names,

GO. WASHINGTON–*Presidt.*
and deputy from Virginia

AMENDMENT I

Congress shall make no law respecting an establishment of religion, or prohibiting the free exercise thereof; or abridging the freedom of speech, or of the press; or the right of the people peaceably to assemble, and to petition the Government for a redress of grievances.

AMENDMENT II

A well regulated Militia, being necessary to the security of a free State, the right of the people to keep and bear Arms, shall not be infringed.

New Hampshire { JOHN LANGDON / NICHOLAS GILMAN

Massachusetts { NATHANIEL GORHAM / RUFUS KING

Connecticut { WM. SAML. JOHNSON ROGER / SHERMAN

New York { ALEXANDER HAMILTON

New Jersey { WIL. LIVINGSTON / DAVID BREARLEY / WM. PATERSON / JONA. DAYTON

Pennsylvania { B FRANKLIN / THOMAS MIFFLIN / ROBT. MORRIS / GEO. CLYMER / THOS. FITZSIMONS / JARED INGERSOLL / JAMES WILSON / GOUV MORRIS

Delaware { GEO. READ / GUNNING BEDFORD JUN / JOHN DICKINSON / RICHARD BASSETT / JACO. BROOM

Maryland { JAMES MCHENRY / DAN OF ST. THOS. JENIFER / DANL. CARROLL

Virginia { JOHN BLAIR— / JAMES MADISON JR.

North Carolina { WM. BLOUNT / RICH D. DOBBS SPAIGHT / HU WILLIAMSON

South Carolina { J. RUTLEDGE / CHARLES COTESWORTH PINCKNEY / CHARLES PINCKNEY / PIERCE BUTLER

Georgia { WILLIAM FEW / ABR BALDWIN

[The first ten amendments, known as the "Bill of Rights," were ratified in 1791.]

AMENDMENT III

No Soldier shall, in time of peace be quartered in any house, without the consent of the Owner, nor in time of war, but in a manner prescribed by law.

AMENDMENT IV

The right of the people to be secure in their persons, houses, papers, and effects, against unreasonable searches and seizures, shall not be violated, and no Warrants shall issue, but upon probable cause, supported by Oath or affirmation, and particularly describing the place to be searched, and the persons or things to be seized.

AMENDMENT V

No person shall be held to answer for a capital, or otherwise infamous crime, unless on a presentment or indictment of a Grand Jury, except in cases arising in the land or naval forces, or in the Militia, when in actual service in time of War or public danger; nor shall any person be subject for the same offence to be twice put in jeopardy of life or limb; nor shall be compelled in any criminal case to be a witness against himself, nor be deprived of life, liberty, or property, without due process of law, nor shall private property be taken for public use, without just compensation.

AMENDMENT VI

In all criminal prosecutions, the accused shall enjoy the right to a speedy and public trial, by an impartial jury of the State and district wherein the crime shall have been committed, which district shall have been previously ascertained by law, and to be informed of the nature and cause of the accusation; to be confronted with the witnesses against him; to have compulsory process for obtaining witnesses in his favor, and to have Assistance of Counsel for his defence.

AMENDMENT VII

In Suits at common law, where the value in controversy shall exceed twenty dollars, the right of trial by jury shall be preserved, and no fact tried by a jury, shall be otherwise reexamined in any Court of the United States, than according to the rules of the common law.

AMENDMENT VIII

Excessive bail shall not be required, nor excessive fines imposed, nor cruel and unusual punishments inflicted.

AMENDMENT IX

The enumeration in the Constitution, of certain rights, shall not be construed to deny or disparage others retained by the people.

AMENDMENT X

The powers not delegated to the United States by the Constitution, nor prohibited by it to the States, are reserved to the States respectively, or to the people.

AMENDMENT XI [*RATIFIED IN 1795.*]

The Judicial power of the United States shall not be construed to extend to any suit in law or equity, commenced or prosecuted against one of the United States by Citizens of another State, or by Citizens or Subjects of any Foreign State.

The Constitution of the United States   A11

AMENDMENT XII [*RATIFIED IN 1804.*]

The Electors shall meet in their respective states and vote by ballot for President and Vice President, one of whom, at least, shall not be an inhabitant of the same state with themselves; they shall name in their ballots the person voted for as President, and in distinct ballots the person voted for as Vice President, and they shall make distinct lists of all persons voted for as President, and of all persons voted for as Vice President, and of the number of votes for each, which lists they shall sign and certify, and transmit sealed to the seat of the government of the United States, directed to the President of the Senate;—The President of the Senate shall, in the presence of the Senate and House of Representatives, open all the certificates and the votes shall then be counted;—The person having the greatest number of votes for President, shall be the President, if such number be a majority of the whole number of Electors appointed; and if no person have such majority, then from the persons having the highest numbers not exceeding three on the list of those voted for as President, the House of Representatives shall choose immediately, by ballot, the President. But in choosing the President, the votes shall be taken by states, the representation from each state having one vote; a quorum for this purpose shall consist of a member or members from two-thirds of the states, and a majority of all the states shall be necessary to a choice. *And if the House of Representatives shall not choose a President whenever the right of choice shall devolve upon them, before the fourth day of March next following, then the Vice President shall act as President, as in the case of the death or other constitutional disability of the President.*—[10] The person having the greatest number of votes as Vice President, shall be the Vice President, if such number be a majority of the whole number of Electors appointed, and if no person have a majority, then from the two highest numbers on the list, the Senate shall choose the Vice President; a quorum for the purpose shall consist of two-thirds of the whole number of Senators, and a majority of the whole number shall be necessary to a choice. But no person constitutionally ineligible to the office of President shall be eligible to that of Vice President of the United States.

AMENDMENT XIII [*RATIFIED IN 1865.*]

Section 1.   Neither slavery nor involuntary servitude, except as a punishment for crime whereof the party shall have been duly convicted, shall exist within the United States, or any place subject to their jurisdiction.

Section 2.   Congress shall have power to enforce this article by appropriate legislation.

AMENDMENT XIV [*RATIFIED IN 1868.*]

Section 1.   All persons born or naturalized in the United States and subject to the jurisdiction thereof, are citizens of the United States and of the State wherein they reside. No State shall make or enforce any law which shall abridge the privileges or immunities of citizens of the United States; nor shall any State deprive any person of life, liberty, or property, without due process of law; nor deny to any person within its jurisdiction the equal protection of the laws.

Section 2.   Representatives shall be apportioned among the several States according to their respective numbers, counting the whole number of persons in each State, excluding Indians not taxed. But when the right to vote at any election for the choice of electors for President and Vice President of the United States, Representatives in Congress, the Executive and Judicial officers of a State, or the members of the Legislature thereof, is denied to any of the *male* inhabitants of such State, being *twenty-one*[11] years of age, and citizens of the United States, or in any way abridged, except for participation in rebellion, or other crime, the basis of representation therein shall be reduced in the proportion which the number of such male citizens shall bear to the whole number of male citizens twenty-one years of age in such State.

Section 3.   No person shall be a Senator or Representative in Congress, or elector of President and Vice President, or hold any office, civil or military, under the United States, or under any State, who, having previously taken an oath, as a member of Congress, or as an officer of the United States, or as a member of any State legislature, or as an executive or judicial officer of any State, to support the Constitution of the United States, shall have engaged in

---

[10]Changed by the Twentieth Amendment, Section 3.

[11]Changed by the Twenty-Sixth Amendment; the reference to "male inhabitants" may also have been by the Nineteenth Amendment.

insurrection or rebellion against the same, or given aid or comfort to the enemies thereof. But Congress may by a vote of two-thirds of each House, remove such disability.

Section 4.   The validity of the public debt of the United States, authorized by law, including debts incurred for payment of pensions and bounties for services in suppressing insurrection or rebellion, shall not be questioned. But neither the United States nor any State shall assume or pay any debt or obligation incurred in aid of insurrection or rebellion against the United States, or any claim for the loss or emancipation of any slave; but all such debts, obligations and claims shall be held illegal and void.

Section 5.   The Congress shall have power to enforce, by appropriate legislation, the provisions of this article.

AMENDMENT XV [*RATIFIED IN 1870.*]

Section 1.   The right of citizens of the United States to vote shall not be denied or abridged by the United States or by any State on account of race, color, or previous condition of servitude.

Section 2.   The Congress shall have power to enforce this article by appropriate legislation.

AMENDMENT XVI [*RATIFIED IN 1913.*]

The Congress shall have power to lay and collect taxes on incomes, from whatever source derived, without apportionment among the several States, and without regard to any census or enumeration.

AMENDMENT XVII [*RATIFIED IN 1913.*]

The Senate of the United States shall be composed of two Senators from each State, elected by the people thereof, for six years; and each Senator shall have one vote. The electors in each State shall have the qualifications requisite for electors of the most numerous branch of the State legislatures.

When vacancies happen in the representation of any State in the Senate, the executive authority of such State shall issue writs of election to fill such vacancies: *Provided,* That the legislature of any State may empower the executive thereof to make temporary appointments until the people fill the vacancies by election as the legislature may direct.

This amendment shall not be so construed as to affect the election or term of any Senator chosen before it becomes valid as part of the Constitution.

AMENDMENT XVIII [*RATIFIED IN 1919.*]

Section 1.   *After one year from the ratification of this article the manufacture, sale, or transportation of intoxicating liquors within, the importation thereof into, or the exportation thereof from the United States and all territory subject to the jurisdiction thereof for beverage purposes is hereby prohibited.*

Section 2.   *The Congress and the several States shall have concurrent power to enforce this article by appropriate legislation.*

Section 3.   *This article shall be inoperative unless it shall have been ratified as an amendment to the Constitution by the legislatures of the several States, as provided in the Constitution, within seven years from the date of the submission hereof to the States by the Congress.*[12]

AMENDMENT XIX [*RATIFIED IN 1920.*]

The right of citizens of the United States to vote shall not be denied or abridged by the United States or by any State on account of sex.

Congress shall have power to enforce this article by appropriate legislation.

---

[12]Repealed by the Twenty-First Amendment.

AMENDMENT XX [*RATIFIED IN 1933.*]

Section 1.   The terms of the President and Vice President shall end at noon on the 20th day of January, and the terms of Senators and Representatives at noon on the 3d day of January, of the years in which such terms would have ended if this article had not been ratified; and the terms of their successors shall then begin.

Section 2.   The Congress shall assemble at least once in every year, and such meeting shall begin at noon on the 3d day of January, unless they shall by law appoint a different day.

Section 3.   If, at the time fixed for the beginning of the term of the President, the President elect shall have died, the Vice President elect shall become President. If a President shall not have been chosen before the time fixed for the beginning of his term, or if the President elect shall have failed to qualify, then the Vice President elect shall act as President until a President shall have qualified; and the Congress may by law provide for the case wherein neither a President elect nor a Vice President elect shall have qualified, declaring who shall then act as President, or the manner in which one who is to act shall be selected, and such person shall act accordingly until a President or Vice President shall have qualified.

Section 4.   The Congress may by law provide for the case of the death of any of the persons from whom the House of Representatives may choose a President whenever the right of choice shall have developed upon them, and for the case of the death of any of the persons from whom the Senate may choose a Vice President whenever the right of choice shall have devolved upon them.

Section 5.   Sections 1 and 2 shall take effect on the 15th day of October following the ratification of this article.

Section 6.   This article shall be inoperative unless it shall have been ratified as an amendment to the Constitution by the legislatures of three-fourths of the several States within seven years from the date of its submission.

AMENDMENT XXI [*RATIFIED IN 1933.*]

Section 1.   The eighteenth article of amendment to the Constitution of the United States is hereby repealed.

Section 2.   The transportation or importation into any State, Territory, or possession of the United States for delivery or use therein of intoxicating liquors, in violation of the laws thereof, is hereby prohibited.

Section 3.   This article shall be inoperative unless it shall have been ratified as an amendment to the Constitution by conventions in the several States, as provided in the Constitution, within seven years from the date of the submission hereof to the States by the Congress.

AMENDMENT XXII [*RATIFIED IN 1951.*]

Section 1.   No person shall be elected to the office of the President more than twice, and no person who has held the office of President, or acted as President, for more than two years of a term to which some other person was elected President shall be elected to the office of the President more than once. But this Article shall not apply to any person holding the office of President when this Article was proposed by the Congress, and shall not prevent any person who may be holding the office of President, or acting as President, during the term within which this Article becomes operative from holding the office of President or acting as President during the remainder of such term.

Section 2.   This Article shall be inoperative unless it shall have been ratified as an amendment to the Constitution by the legislatures of three-fourths of the several States within seven years from the date of its submission to the States by the Congress.

AMENDMENT XXIII [*RATIFIED IN 1961.*]

Section 1.   The District constituting the seat of Government of the United States shall appoint in such manner as the Congress may direct:

A number of electors of President and Vice President equal to the whole number of Senators and Representatives in Congress to which the District would be entitled if it were a State, but in no event more than the least populous State; they shall be in addition to those appointed by the States, but they shall be considered, for the purposes of the election of President and Vice President, to be electors appointed by a State; and they shall meet in the District and perform such duties as provided by the twelfth article of amendment.

Section 2.   The Congress shall have power to enforce this article by appropriate legislation.

AMENDMENT XXIV [*RATIFIED IN 1964.*]

Section 1.   The right of citizens of the United States to vote in any primary or other election for President or Vice President, for electors for President or Vice President, or for Senator or Representative in Congress, shall not be denied or abridged by the United States or any State by reason of failure to pay any poll tax or other tax.

Section 2.   Congress shall have power to enforce this article by appropriate legislation.

AMENDMENT XXV [*RATIFIED IN 1967.*]

Section 1.   In case of the removal of the President from office or of his death or resignation, the Vice President shall become President.

Section 2.   Whenever there is a vacancy in the office of the Vice President, the President shall nominate a Vice President who shall take office upon confirmation by a majority vote of both Houses of Congress.

Section 3.   Whenever the President transmits to the President pro tempore of the Senate and the Speaker of the House of Representatives his written declaration that he is unable to discharge the powers and duties of his office, and until he transmits to them a written declaration to the contrary, such powers and duties shall be discharged by the Vice President as Acting President.

Section 4.   Whenever the Vice President and a majority of either the principal officers of the executive departments or of such other body as Congress may by law provide, transmit to the President pro tempore of the Senate and the Speaker of the House of Representatives their written declaration that the President is unable to discharge the powers and duties of his office, the Vice President shall immediately assume the powers and duties of the office as Acting President.

Thereafter, when the President transmits to the President pro tempore of the Senate and the Speaker of the House of Representatives his written declaration that no inability exists, he shall resume the powers and duties of his office unless the Vice President and a majority of either the principal officers of the executive department[s] or of such other body as Congress may by law provide, transmit within four days to the President pro tempore of the Senate and the Speaker of the House of Representatives their written declaration that the President is unable to discharge the powers and duties of his office. Thereupon Congress shall decide the issue, assembling within forty-eight hours for that purpose if not in session. If the Congress, within twenty-one days after receipt of the latter written declaration, or, if Congress is not in session, within twenty-one days after Congress is required to assemble, determines by two-thirds vote of both Houses that the President is unable to discharge the powers and duties of his office, the Vice President shall continue to discharge the same as Acting President; otherwise, the President shall resume the powers and duties of his office.

AMENDMENT XXVI [*RATIFIED IN 1971.*]

Section 1.   The right of citizens of the United States, who are eighteen years of age or older, to vote shall not be denied or abridged by the United States or by any State on account of age.

Section 2.   The Congress shall have power to enforce this article by appropriate legislation.

AMENDMENT XXVII [*RATIFIED IN 1992.*]

No law varying the compensation for the services of the Senators and Representatives shall take effect, until an election of Representatives shall have intervened.

The Federalist No. 10

James Madison

November 22, 1787

TO THE PEOPLE OF THE STATE OF NEW YORK

Among the numerous advantages promised by a well constructed Union, none deserves to be more accurately developed than its tendency to break and control the violence of faction. The friend of popular governments, never finds himself so much alarmed for their character and fate, as when he contemplates their propensity to this dangerous vice. He will not fail therefore to set a due value on any plan which, without violating the principles to which he is attached, provides a proper cure for it. The instability, injustice and confusion introduced into the public councils, have in truth been the mortal diseases under which popular governments have every where perished; as they continue to be the favorite and fruitful topics from which the adversaries to liberty derive their most specious declamations. The valuable improvements made by the American Constitutions on the popular models, both ancient and modern, cannot certainly be too much admired; but it would be an unwarrantable partiality, to contend that they have as effectually obviated the danger on this side as was wished and expected. Complaints are every where heard from our most considerate and virtuous citizens, equally the friends of public and private faith, and of public and personal liberty; that our governments are too unstable; that the public good is disregarded in the conflicts of rival parties; and that measures are too often decided, not according to the rules of justice, and the rights of the minor party; but by the superior force of an interested and over-bearing majority. However anxiously we may wish that these complaints had no foundation, the evidence of known facts will not permit us to deny that they are in some degree true. It will be found indeed, on a candid review of our situation, that some of the distresses under which we labor, have been erroneously charged on the operation of our governments; but it will be found, at the same time, that other causes will not alone account for many of our heaviest misfortunes; and particularly, for that prevailing and increasing distrust of public engagements, and alarm for private rights, which are echoed from one end of the continent to the other. These must be chiefly, if not wholly, effects of the unsteadiness and injustice, with which a factious spirit has tainted our public administrations.

By a faction I understand a number of citizens, whether amounting to a majority or minority of the whole, who are united and actuated by some common impulse of passion, or of interest, adverse to the rights of other citizens, or to the permanent and aggregate interests of the community.

There are two methods of curing the mischiefs of faction: the one, by removing its causes; the other, by controlling its effects.

There are again two methods of removing the causes of faction: the one by destroying the liberty which is essential to its existence; the other, by giving to every citizen the same opinions, the same passions, and the same interests.

It could never be more truly said than of the first remedy, that it is worse than the disease. Liberty is to faction, what air is to fire, an aliment without which it instantly expires. But it could not be a less folly to abolish liberty, which is essential to political life, because it nourishes faction, than it would be to wish the annihilation of air, which is essential to animal life, because it imparts to fire its destructive agency.

The second expedient is as impracticable, as the first would be unwise. As long as the reason of man continues fallible, and he is at liberty to exercise it, different opinions will be formed. As long as the connection subsists between his reason and his self-love, his opinions and his passions will have a reciprocal influence on each other; and the former will be objects to which the latter will attach themselves. The diversity in the faculties of men from which the rights of property originate, is not less an insuperable obstacle to a uniformity of interests. The protection of these faculties is the first object of Government. From the protection of different and unequal faculties of acquiring property, the possession of different degrees and kinds of property immediately results: and from the influence of these on the sentiments and views of the respective proprietors, ensues a division of the society into different interests and parties.

The latent causes of faction are thus sown in the nature of man; and we see them every where brought into different degrees of activity, according to the different circumstances of civil society. A zeal for different opinions concerning religion, concerning Government and many other points, as well of speculation as of practice; an attachment to different leaders ambitiously contending for pre-eminence and power; or to persons of other descriptions whose fortunes have been interesting to the human passions, have in turn divided mankind into parties, inflamed them with mutual animosity, and rendered them much more disposed to vex and oppress each other, than to co-operate for their common good. So strong is this propensity of mankind to fall into mutual animosities, that where no substantial occasion presents itself, the most frivolous and fanciful distinctions have been sufficient to kindle their unfriendly passions, and excite their most violent conflicts. But the most common and durable source of factions, has been the various and unequal distribution of property. Those who hold, and those who are without property, have ever formed distinct interests in society. Those who are creditors, and those who are debtors, fall under a like discrimination. A landed interest, a manufacturing interest, a mercantile interest, a monied interest, with many lesser interests, grow up of necessity in civilized nations, and divide them into different classes, actuated by different sentiments and views. The regulation of these various and interfering interests forms the principal task of modern Legislation, and involves the spirit of party and faction in the necessary and ordinary operations of Government.

No man is allowed to be a judge in his own cause; because his interest would certainly bias his judgment, and, not improbably, corrupt his integrity. With equal, nay with greater reason, a body of men, are unfit to be both judges and parties, at the same time; yet, what are many of the most important acts of legislation, but so many judicial determinations, not indeed concerning the rights of single persons, but concerning the rights of large bodies of citizens; and what are the different classes of legislators, but advocates and parties to the causes which they determine? Is a law proposed concerning private debts? It is a question to which the creditors are parties on one side, and the debtors on the other. Justice ought to hold the balance between them. Yet the parties are and must be themselves the judges; and the most numerous party, or, in other words, the most powerful faction must be expected to prevail. Shall domestic manufactures be encouraged, and in what degree, by restrictions on foreign manufactures? are questions which would be differently decided by the landed and the manufacturing classes; and probably by neither, with a sole regard to justice and the public good. The apportionment of taxes on the various descriptions of property, is an act which seems to require the most exact impartiality; yet, there is perhaps no legislative act in which greater opportunity and temptation are given to a predominant party, to trample on the rules of justice. Every shilling with which they over-burden the inferior number, is a shilling saved to their own pockets.

It is in vain to say, that enlightened statesmen will be able to adjust these clashing interests, and render them all subservient to the public good. Enlightened statesmen will not always be at the helm: Nor, in many cases, can such an adjustment be made at all, without taking into view indirect and remote considerations, which will rarely prevail over the immediate interest which one party may find in disregarding the rights of another, or the good of the whole.

The inference to which we are brought, is, that the *causes* of faction cannot be removed; and that relief is only to be sought in the means of controlling its *effects*.

If a faction consists of less than a majority, relief is supplied by the republican principle, which enables the majority to defeat its sinister views by regular vote: It may clog the administration, it may convulse the society; but it will be unable to execute and mask its violence under the forms of the Constitution. When a majority is included in a faction, the form of popular government on the other hand enables it to sacrifice to its ruling passion or interest, both the public good and the rights of other citizens. To secure the public good, and private rights, against the danger of such a faction, and at the same time to preserve the spirit and the form of popular government, is then the great object to which our enquiries are directed: Let me add that it is the great desideratum, by which alone this form of government can be rescued from the opprobrium under which it has so long labored, and be recommended to the esteem and adoption of mankind.

By what means is this object attainable? Evidently by one of two only. Either the existence of the same passion or interest in a majority at the same time, must be prevented; or the majority, having such co-existent passion or interest, must be rendered, by their number and local situation, unable to concert and carry into effect schemes of oppression. If the impulse and the opportunity be suffered to coincide, we well know that neither moral nor religious motives can be relied on as an adequate control. They are not found to be such on the injustice and violence of individuals, and lose their efficacy in proportion to the number combined together; that is, in proportion as their efficacy becomes needful.

From this view of the subject, it may be concluded, that a pure Democracy, by which I mean, a Society, consisting of a small number of citizens, who assemble and administer the Government in person, can admit of no cure for the mischiefs of faction. A common passion or interest will, in almost every case, be felt by a majority of the whole; a communication and concert results from the form of Government itself; and there is nothing to check the inducements to sacrifice the weaker party, or an obnoxious individual. Hence it is, that such Democracies have ever been spectacles of turbulence and contention; have ever been found incompatible with personal security, or the rights of property; and have in general been as short in their lives, as they have been violent in their deaths. Theoretic politicians, who have patronized this species of Government, have erroneously supposed, that by reducing mankind to a perfect equality in their political rights, they would, at the same time, be perfectly equalized and assimilated in their possessions, their opinions, and their passions.

A republic, by which I mean a government in which the scheme of representation takes place, opens a different prospect, and promises the cure for which we are seeking. Let us examine the points in which it varies from pure democracy, and we shall comprehend both the nature of the cure and the efficacy which it must derive from the union.

The two great points of difference, between a democracy and a republic, are, first, the delegation of the government, in the latter, to a small number of citizens, elected by the rest; secondly, the greater number of citizens, and greater sphere of country, over which the latter may be extended.

The effect of the first difference is, on the one hand, to refine and enlarge the public views, by passing them through the medium of a chosen body of citizens, whose wisdom may best discern the true interest of their country, and whose patriotism and love of justice, will be least likely to sacrifice it to temporary or partial considerations. Under such a regulation, it may well happen, that the public voice, pronounced by the representatives of the people, will be more consonant to the public good, than if pronounced by the people themselves, convened for the purpose. On the other hand the effect may be inverted. Men of factious tempers, of local prejudices, or of sinister designs, may by intrigue, by corruption, or by other means, first obtain the suffrages, and then betray the interest of the people. The question resulting is, whether small or extensive republics are most favorable to the election of proper guardians of the public weal, and it is clearly decided in favor of the latter by two obvious considerations.

In the first place, it is to be remarked that, however small the republic may be, the representatives must be raised to a certain number, in order to guard against the cabals of a few; and that however large it may be, they must be limited to a certain number, in order to guard against the confusion of a multitude. Hence, the number of representatives in the two cases not being in proportion to that of the constituents, and being proportionally greatest in the small republic, it follows, that if the proportion of fit characters be not less in the large than in the small republic, the former will present a greater option, and consequently a greater probability of a fit choice.

In the next place, as each Representative will be chosen by a greater number of citizens in the large than in the small Republic, it will be more difficult for unworthy candidates to practise with success the vicious arts, by which elections are too often carried; and the suffrages of the people being more free, will be more likely to center on men who possess the most attractive merit, and the most diffusive and established characters.

It must be confessed, that in this, as in most other cases, there is a mean, on both sides of which inconveniences will be found to lie. By enlarging too much the number of electors, you render the representatives too little acquainted with all their local circumstances and lesser interests; as by reducing it too much, you render him unduly attached to these, and too little fit to comprehend and pursue great and national objects. The Federal Constitution forms a happy combination in this respect; the great and aggregate interests being referred to the national, the local and particular, to the state legislatures.

The other point of difference is, the greater number of citizens and extent of territory which may be brought within the compass of Republican, than of Democratic Government; and it is this circumstance principally which renders factious combinations less to be dreaded in the former, than in the latter. The smaller the society, the fewer probably will be the distinct parties and interests composing it; the fewer the distinct parties and interests, the more frequently will a majority be found of the same party; and the smaller the number of individuals composing a majority, and the smaller the compass within which they are placed, the more easily will they concert and execute their plans of oppression. Extend the sphere, and you take in a greater variety of parties and interests; you make it less probable that a majority of the whole will have a common motive to invade the rights of other citizens; or if such a common motive exists, it will be more difficult for all who feel it to discover their own strength, and to act in unison with each other. Besides other impediments, it may be remarked, that where there is a consciousness of unjust or dishonorable purposes, communication is always checked by distrust, in proportion to the number whose concurrence is necessary.

Hence it clearly appears, that the same advantage, which a Republic has over a Democracy, in controlling the effects of factions, is enjoyed by a large over a small Republic—is enjoyed by the Union over the States composing it. Does this advantage consist in the substitution of Representatives, whose enlightened views and virtuous sentiments render them superior to local prejudices, and to schemes of injustice? It will not be denied, that the Representation of the Union will be most likely to possess these requisite endowments. Does it consist in the greater security afforded by a greater variety of parties, against the event of any one party being able to outnumber and oppress the rest? In an equal degree does the increased variety of parties, comprised within the Union, increase this security? Does it, in fine, consist in the greater obstacles opposed to the concert and accomplishment of the secret wishes of an unjust and interested majority? Here, again, the extent of the Union gives it the most palpable advantage.

The influence of factious leaders may kindle a flame within their particular States, but will be unable to spread a general conflagration through the other States: a religious sect, may degenerate into a political faction in a part of the Confederacy but the variety of sects dispersed over the entire face of it, must secure the national Councils against any danger from that source: a rage for paper money, for an abolition of debts, for an equal division of property, or for any other improper or wicked project, will be less apt to pervade the whole body of the Union, than a particular member of it; in the same proportion as such a malady is more likely to taint a particular county or district, than an entire State.

In the extent and proper structure of the Union, therefore, we behold a Republican remedy for the diseases most incident to Republican Government. And according to the degree of pleasure and pride, we feel in being Republicans, ought to be our zeal in cherishing the spirit, and supporting the character of Federalists.

PUBLIUS

The Federalist No. 51

James Madison

February 6, 1788

TO THE PEOPLE OF THE STATE OF NEW YORK

To what expedient then shall we finally resort for maintaining in practice the necessary partition of power among the several departments, as laid down in the constitution? The only answer that can be given is, that as all these exterior provisions are found to be inadequate, the defect must be supplied, by so contriving the interior structure of the government, as that its several constituent parts may, by their mutual relations, be the means of keeping each other in their proper places. Without presuming to undertake a full development of this important idea, I will hazard a few general observations, which may perhaps place it in a clearer light, and enable us to form a more correct judgment of the principles and structure of the government planned by the convention.

In order to lay a due foundation for that separate and distinct exercise of the different powers of government, which to a certain extent, is admitted on all hands to be essential to the preservation of liberty, it is evident that each department should have a will of its own; and consequently should be so constituted, that the members of each should have as little agency as possible in the appointment of the members of the others. Were this principle rigorously adhered to, it would require that all the appointments for the supreme executive, legislative, and judiciary magistracies, should be drawn from the same fountain of authority, the people, through channels, having no communication whatever with one another. Perhaps such a plan of constructing the several departments would be less difficult in practice than it may in contemplation appear. Some difficulties however, and some additional expense, would attend the execution of it. Some deviations therefore from the principle must be admitted. In the constitution of the judiciary department in particular, it might be inexpedient to insist rigorously on the principle; first, because peculiar qualifications being essential in the members, the primary consideration ought to be to select that mode of choice, which best secures these qualifications; secondly, because the permanent tenure by which the appointments are held in that department, must soon destroy all sense of dependence on the authority conferring them.

It is equally evident that the members of each department should be as little dependent as possible on those of the others, for the emoluments annexed to their offices. Were the executive magistrate, or the judges, not independent of the legislature in this particular, their independence in every other would be merely nominal.

But the great security against a gradual concentration of the several powers in the same department, consists in giving to those who administer each department, the necessary constitutional means, and personal motives, to resist encroachments of the others. The provision for defense must in this, as in all other cases, be made commensurate to the danger of attack. Ambition must be made to counteract ambition. The interest of the man must be connected with the constitutional rights of the place. It may be a reflection on human nature, that such devices should be necessary to control the abuses of government. But what is government itself but the greatest of all reflections on human nature? If men were angels, no government would be necessary. If angels were to govern men, neither external nor internal controls on government would be necessary. In framing a government which is to be administered by men over men, the great difficulty lies in this: You must first enable the government to control the governed; and in the next place, oblige it to control itself. A dependence on the people is no doubt the primary control on the government; but experience has taught mankind the necessity of auxiliary precautions.

This policy of supplying by opposite and rival interests, the defect of better motives, might be traced through the whole system of human affairs, private as well as public. We see it particularly displayed in all the subordinate distributions of power; where the constant aim is to divide and arrange the several offices in such a manner as that each may be a check on the other; that the private interest of every individual, may be a sentinel over the public rights. These inventions of prudence cannot be less requisite in the distribution of the supreme powers of the state.

But it is not possible to give each department an equal power of self defense. In republican government the legislative authority, necessarily, predominates. The remedy for this inconveniency is, to divide the legislature into different branches; and to render them by different modes of election, and different principles of action, as little connected with each other, as the nature of their common functions, and their common dependence on the society, will admit. It may even be necessary to guard against dangerous encroachments by still further precautions. As the weight of the legislative authority requires that it should be thus divided, the weakness of the executive may require, on the other hand, that it should be fortified. An absolute negative, on the legislature, appears at first view to be the natural defense with which the executive magistrate should be armed. But perhaps it would be neither altogether safe, nor alone sufficient. On ordinary occasions, it might not be exerted with the requisite firmness; and on extraordinary occasions, it might be prefidiously abused. May not this defect of an absolute negative be supplied, by some qualified connection between this weaker department, and the weaker branch of the stronger department, by which the latter may be led to support the constitutional rights of the former, without being too much detached from the rights of its own department?

If the principles on which these observations are founded be just, as I persuade myself they are, and they be applied as a criterion, to the several state constitutions, and to the federal constitution, it will be found, that if the latter does not perfectly correspond with them, the former are infinitely less able to bear such a test.

There are moreover two considerations particularly applicable to the federal system of America, which place that system in a very interesting point of view.

First. In a single republic, all the power surrendered by the people, is submitted to the administration of a single government; and usurpations are guarded against by a division of the government into distinct and separate departments. In the compound republic of America, the power surrendered by the people, is first divided between two distinct governments, and then the portion allotted to each, subdivided among distinct and separate departments. Hence a double security arises to the rights of the people. The different governments will control each other; at the same time that each will be controlled by itself.

Second. It is of great importance in a republic, not only to guard the society against the oppression of its rulers; but to guard one part of the society against the injustice of the other part. Different interests necessarily exist in different classes of citizens. If a majority be united by a common interest, the rights of the minority will be insecure. There are but two methods of providing against this evil: The one by creating a will in the community independent of the majority, that is, of the society itself, the other by comprehending in the society so many separate descriptions of citizens, as will render an unjust combination of a majority of the whole, very improbable, if not impracticable. The first method prevails in all governments possessing an hereditary or self appointed authority. This at best is but a precarious security; because a power independent of the society may as well espouse the unjust views of the major, as the rightful interests, of the minor party, and may possibly be turned against both parties. The second method will be exemplified in the federal republic of the United States. While all authority in it will be derived from and dependent on the society, the society itself will be broken into so many parts, interests and classes of citizens, that the rights of individuals or of the minority, will be in little danger from interested combinations of the majority. In a free government, the security for civil rights must be the same as for religious rights. It consists in the one case in the multiplicity of interests, and in the other, in the multiplicity of sects. The degree of security in both cases will depend on the number of interests and sects; and this may be presumed to depend on the extent of country and number of people comprehended under the same government. This view of the subject must particularly recommend a proper federal system to all the sincere and considerate friends of republican government: Since it shows that in exact proportion as the territory of the union may be formed into more circumscribed confederacies or states, oppressive combinations of a majority will be facilitated, the best security under the republican form, for the rights of every class of citizens, will be diminished; and consequently, the stability and independence of some member of the government, the only other security, must be proportionally increased. Justice is the end of government. It is the end of civil society. It ever has been, and ever will be pursued, until it be obtained, or until liberty be lost in the pursuit. In a society under the forms of which the stronger faction can readily unite and oppress the weaker, anarchy may as truly be said to reign, as in a state of nature where the weaker individual is not secured against the violence of the stronger: And as in the latter state even the stronger individuals are prompted by the uncertainty of their condition, to submit to a government which may protect the weak as well as themselves: So in the former state, will the more powerful factions or parties be gradually induced by a like motive, to wish for a government which will protect all parties, the weaker as well as the more powerful. It can be little doubted, that if the state of Rhode Island was separated from the confederacy, and left to itself, the insecurity of rights under the popular form of government within such narrow limits, would be displayed by such reiterated oppressions of factious majorities, that some power altogether independent of the people would soon be called for by the voice of the very factions whose misrule had proved the necessity of it. In the extended republic of the United States, and among the great variety of interests, parties and sects which it embraces, a coalition of a majority of the whole society could seldom take place on any other principles than those of justice and the general good; and there being thus less danger to a minor from the will of the major party, there must be less pretext also, to provide for the security of the former, by introducing into the government a will not dependent on the latter; or in other words, a will independent of the society itself. It is no less certain than it is important, notwithstanding the contrary opinions which have been entertained, that the larger the society, provided it lie within a practicable sphere, the more duly capable will be of self government. And happily for the *republican cause*, the practicable sphere may be carried to a very great extent, by a judicious modification and mixture of the *federal principle*.

PUBLIUS

Rev. Dr. Martin Luther King, Jr.'s Speech:"I Have a Dream"

Aug. 28, 1963

I am happy to join with you today in what will go down in history as the greatest demonstration for freedom in the history of our nation.

Five score years ago a great American in whose symbolic shadow we stand today signed the Emancipation Proclamation. This momentous decree came as a great beacon light of hope to millions of Negro slaves who had been seared in the flames of withering injustice. It came as a joyous daybreak to end the long night of their captivity. But one hundred years later, the Negro still is not free. One hundred years later, the life of the Negro is still sadly crippled by the manacles of segregation and the chains of discrimination. One hundred years later, the Negro lives on a lonely island of poverty in the midst of a vast ocean of material prosperity. One hundred years later, the Negro is still languished in the corners of American society and finds himself an exile in his own land. So we've come here today to dramatize a shameful condition.

In a sense we've come to our nation's capital to cash a check. When the architects of our republic wrote the magnificent words of the Constitution and the Declaration of Independence, they were signing a promissory note to which every American was to fall heir. This note was a promise that all men—yes, black men as well as white men—would be guaranteed the unalienable rights of life, liberty, and the pursuit of happiness. It is obvious today that America has defaulted on this promissory note insofar as her citizens of color are concerned. Instead of honoring this sacred obligation, America has given the Negro people a bad check, a check which has come back marked "insufficient funds."

But we refuse to believe that the bank of justice is bankrupt. We refuse to believe that there are insufficient funds in the great vaults of opportunity of this nation. So we have come to cash this check, a check that will give us upon demand the riches of freedom and the security of justice.

We have also come to this hallowed spot to remind America of the fierce urgency of now. This is no time to engage in the luxury of cooling off or to take the tranquilizing drug of gradualism. Now is the time to make real the promises of democracy. Now is the time to rise from the dark and desolate valley of segregation to the sunlit path of racial justice. Now is the time to lift our nation from the quicksands of racial injustice to the solid rock of brotherhood.

Now is the time to make justice a reality for all of God's children. It would be fatal for the nation to overlook the urgency of the moment. This sweltering summer of the Negro's legitimate discontent will not pass until there is an invigorating autumn of freedom and equality. 1963 is not an end, but a beginning. Those who hope that the Negro needed to blow off steam and will now be content will have a rude awakening if the nation returns to business as usual.

There will be neither rest nor tranquility in America until the Negro is granted his citizenship rights. The whirlwinds of revolt will continue to shake the foundations of our nation until the bright day of justice emerges. But there is something that I must say to my people who stand on the warm threshold which leads into the palace of justice. In the process of gaining our rightful place we must not be guilty of wrongful deeds. Let us not seek to satisfy our thirst for freedom by drinking from the cup of bitterness and hatred.

We must forever conduct our struggle on the high plane of dignity and discipline. We must not allow our creative protest to degenerate into physical violence. Again and again we must rise to the majestic heights of meeting physical force with soul force. The marvelous new militancy which has engulfed the Negro community must not lead us to distrust of all white people, for many of our white brothers, as evidenced by their presence here today, have come to realize that their destiny is tied up with our destiny.

And they have come to realize that their freedom is inextricably bound to our freedom. We cannot walk alone. And as we walk, we must make the pledge that we shall always march ahead. We cannot turn back. There are those who are asking the devotees of civil rights, "When will you be satisfied?" We can never be satisfied as long as the Negro is the victim of the unspeakable horrors of police brutality.

We can never be satisfied as long as our bodies, heavy with the fatigue of travel, cannot gain lodging in the motels of the highways and the hotels of the cities.

We cannot be satisfied as long as the Negro's basic mobility is from a smaller ghetto to a larger one. We can never be satisfied as long as our children are stripped of their selfhood and robbed of their dignity by signs stating "For Whites Only."

We cannot be satisfied as long as a Negro in Mississippi cannot vote and a Negro in New York believes he has nothing for which to vote.

No, no, we are not satisfied, and we will not be satisfied until justice rolls down like waters and righteousness like a mighty stream.

I am not unmindful that some of you have come here out of great trials and tribulations. Some of you have come fresh from narrow jail cells. Some of you have come from areas where your quest for freedom left you battered by the storms of persecution and staggered by the winds of police brutality. You have been the veterans of creative suffering.

Continue to work with the faith that unearned suffering is redemptive. Go back to Mississippi, go back to Alabama, go back to South Carolina, go back to Georgia, go back to Louisiana, go back to the slums and ghettos of our northern cities, knowing that somehow this situation can and will be changed. Let us not wallow in the valley of despair.

I say to you today, my friends, though, even though we face the difficulties of today and tomorrow, I still have a dream. It is a dream deeply rooted in the American dream. I have a dream that one day this nation will rise up and live out the true meaning of its creed: "We hold these truths to be self-evident, that all men are created equal."

I have a dream that one day on the red hills of Georgia the sons of former slaves and the sons of former slave owners will be able to sit down together at a table of brotherhood. I have a dream that one day even the state of Mississippi, a state sweltering with the heat of injustice, sweltering with the heat of oppression, will be transformed into an oasis of freedom and justice.

I have a dream that my four little children will one day live in a nation where they will not be judged by the color of their skin but by the content of their character. I have a dream today. I have a dream that one day down in Alabama, with its vicious racists, with its governor having his lips dripping with the words of interposition and nullification, one day right there in Alabama little black boys and black girls will be able to join hands with little white boys and white girls as sisters and brothers.

I have a dream today.

I have a dream that one day every valley shall be exalted, every hill and mountain shall be made low. The rough places will be made plain, and the crooked places will be made straight. And the glory of the Lord shall be revealed, and all flesh shall see it together. This is our hope. This is the faith that I go back to the South with. With this faith we will be able to hew out of the mountain of despair a stone of hope. With this faith we will be able to transform the jangling discords of our nation into a beautiful symphony of brotherhood. With this faith we will be able to work together, to pray together, to struggle together, to go to jail together, to stand up for freedom together, knowing that we will be free one day.

This will be the day when all of God's children will be able to sing with new meaning, "My country, 'tis of thee, sweet land of liberty, of thee I sing. Land where my fathers died, land of the pilgrim's pride, from every mountainside, let freedom ring." And if America is to be a great nation, this must become true. So let freedom ring from the prodigious hilltops of New Hampshire. Let freedom ring from the mighty mountains of New York. Let freedom ring from the heightening Alleghenies of Pennsylvania. Let freedom ring from the snowcapped Rockies of Colorado. Let freedom ring from the curvaceous slopes of California.

But not only that. Let freedom ring from Stone Mountain of Georgia. Let freedom ring from Lookout Mountain of Tennessee. Let freedom ring from every hill and molehill of Mississippi. From every mountainside, let freedom ring...

And when this happens, when we allow freedom to ring—when we let it ring from every village and every hamlet, from every state and every city, we will be able to speed up that day when all of God's children, black men and white men, Jews and Gentiles, Protestants and Catholics, will be able to join hands and sing in the words of the old Negro spiritual, "Free at last! Free at last! Thank God Almighty, we are free at last!"

References

Chapter 1

1. *Federalist*, No. 45.
2. Patrick Henry, Virginia Convention, June 12, 1788, in Bernard Bailyn, ed., *The Debate on the Constitution*, Part Two (New York: The Library of America, 1993), p. 683.
3. Rockefeller Institute of Government and Pew Center on the States, *States' Revenue Estimating: Cracks in the Crystal Ball*, March 2011.
4. Martin Meyerson and Edward C. Banfield, *Politics, Planning, and the Public Interest* (New York: Free Press, 1955), p. 304.
5. Ibid.
6. Henry Milner, *The Internet Generation: Engaged Citizens or Political Dropouts* (Medford, MA: Tufts University Press, 2010).
7. Jane Eisner, *Taking Back the Vote: Getting American Youth Involved in Our Democracy* (Boston, MA: Beacon Press, 2004).
8. Martin P. Wattenberg, *Is Voting for Young People?* 3ᵈ ed. (Boston, MA: Pearson, 2012), which prescribes compulsory voting.
9. David E. Campbell, *Why We Vote: How Schools and Communities Shape Our Civic Life* (Princeton, NJ: Princeton University Press, 2006), which prescribes enhanced civic education in high schools.
10. Aristotle, *Politics*, iv.4.
11. Joseph A. Schumpeter, *Capitalism, Socialism, and Democracy*, 3ᵈ ed. (New York: Harper Torchbooks, 1950), p. 269. First published in 1942.
12. Samuel P. Huntington, *The Third Wave: Democratization in the Late Twentieth Century* (Norman, OK: University of Oklahoma Press, 1993), p. 7.
13. Ibid.
14. Ibid., pp. 12–13.
15. Karl Marx and Friedrich Engels, "The Manifesto of the Communist Party," in *The Marx-Engels Reader*, 2ᵈ ed. Robert C. Tucker (New York: Norton, 1978), pp. 469–500.
16. C. Wright Mills, *The Power Elite* (New York: Oxford University Press, 1956).
17. H. H. Gerth and C. Wright Mills, eds. *From Max Weber: Essays in Sociology* (London: Routledge and Kegan Paul, 1948), pp. 232–235.
18. David B. Truman, *The Governmental Process: Political Interests and Public Opinion* (New York: Knopf, 1951).
19. Samuel P. Huntington, *American Politics: The Promise of Disharmony* (Cambridge, MA: Harvard University Press, 1981).
20. James Q. Wilson, *Political Organizations* (New York: Basic Books, 1973), Chapter 16, and *The Politics of Regulation* (Basic Books, 1980), pp. 367–372. There are other ways of classifying public policies, notably that of Theodore J. Lowi, "American Business, Public Policy, Case Studies, and Theory," *World Politics* 16 (July 1964).
21. Aristotle, The Niomachean Ethics, I.3.

Chapter 2

1. Quoted in Bernard Bailyn, *The Ideological Origins of the American Revolution* (Cambridge: Harvard University Press, 1967), p. 61, n. 6.
2. Quoted in Bailyn, ibid., pp. 135–137.
3. Quoted in Bailyn, ibid., p. 77.
4. Quoted in Bailyn, ibid., p. 160.
5. *Federalist* No. 37.
6. Gordon S. Wood, *The Creation of the American Republic* (Chapel Hill: University of North Carolina Press, 1969). See also *Federalist* No. 49.
7. Letter of George Washington to Henry Lee (October 31, 1787), in *Writings of George Washington*, vol. 29, ed. John C. Fitzpatrick (Washington, D.C.: Government Printing Office, 1939), p. 34.
8. Letters of Thomas Jefferson to James Madison (January 30, 1787) and to Colonel William S. Smith (November 13, 1787), in *Jefferson Himself*, ed. Bernard Mayo (Boston: Houghton Mifflin, 1942), p. 145.
9. Thomas Hobbes, *Leviathan* (Oxford: Basil Blackwell, 1957). First published in 1651; John Locke, *Second Treatise of Civil Government* (New York: Hafner Publishing Co., 1956). First published in 1690.
10. *Federalist* No. 51.
11. *Federalist* No. 48.
12. *Federalist* No. 51.
13. Ibid.
14. Ibid.
15. "The Address and Reasons of Dissent of the Minority of the State of Pennsylvania to Their Constituents," in *The Anti-Federalist*, ed. Cecelia Kenyon (Indianapolis: Bobbs-Merrill, 1966), p. 39.
16. Max Farrand, *The Framing of the Constitution of the United States* (New Haven, CT: Yale University Press, 1913), p. 185.
17. See, for example, John Hope Franklin, *Racial Equality in America* (Chicago: University of Chicago Press, 1976), ch. 1, esp. pp. 12–20.
18. Max Farrand, *The Records of the Federal Convention of 1787*, 4 vols. (New Haven, CT: Yale University Press), pp. 1911–1937.
19. Theodore J. Lowi, *American Government: Incomplete Conquest* (Hinsdale, IL: Dryden Press, 1976), p. 97.
20. Article I, section 2, para. 3.
21. Gary Wills, *"Negro President": Jefferson and the Slave Power* (Boston: Houghton Mifflin, 2003).
22. Article I, section 9, para. 1.
23. Article IV, section 2, para. 3

24. Charles A. Beard, *An Economic Interpretation of the Constitution* (New York: Macmillan, 1913), esp. pp. 26–51, 149–151, 324–325.
25. Forrest McDonald, *We the People* (Chicago: University of Chicago Press, 1958); Robert E. Brown, *Charles Beard and the Constitution* (Princeton: Princeton University Press, 1956).
26. Robert A. McGuire, "Constitution Making: A Rational Choice Model of the Federal Convention of 1787," *American Journal of Political Science* 32 (May 1988): pp. 483–522. See also Forrest McDonald, *Novus Ordo Seclorum* (Lawrence: University of Kansas Press, 1985), p. 221.
27. McDonald, *Novus Ordo Seclorum*, pp. 202–221.
28. Robert A. McGuire and Robert L. Ohsfeldt, "Economic Interests and the American Constitution: A Quantitative Rehabilitation of Charles A. Beard," *Journal of Economic History* 44 (June 1984): pp. 509–519.
29. Lloyd N. Cutler, "To Form a Government," *Foreign Affairs* (Fall 1980): pp. 126–143.

Chapter 3

1. Woodrow Wilson, *Constitutional Government in the United States* (New York: Columbia University Press, 1961), p. 173. First published in 1908.
2. Martin Diamond, "The Federalists' View of Federalism," in *Essays in Federalism*, ed. George C. S. Benson (Claremont, Calif.: Institute for Studies in Federalism, 1961), pp. 21–64; Samuel H. Beer, "Federalism, Nationalism, and Democracy in America," *American Political Science Review* 72 (March 1978): pp. 9–21.
3. *United States v. Sprague*, 282 U.S. 716 (1931).
4. *Garcia v. San Antonio Metropolitan Transit Authority*, 105 S. Ct. 1005 (1985), overruling *National League of Cities v. Usery*, 426 U.S. 833 (1976).
5. *McCulloch v. Maryland*, 4 Wheat. 316 (1819).
6. *Pollock v. Farmers' Loan & Trust Co.*, 157 U.S. 429 (1895); *South Carolina v. Baker*, No. 94 (1988).
7. *Texas v. White*, 7 Wall. 700 (1869).
8. *Champion v. Ames*, 188 U.S. 321 (1903).
9. *Hoke v. United States*, 227 U.S. 308 (1913).
10. *Clark Distilling Co. v. W. Md. Ry.*, 242 U.S. 311 (1917).
11. *Hipolite Egg Co. v. United States*, 220 U.S. 45 (1911).
12. *United States v. E. C. Knight Co.*, 156 U.S. 1 (1895).
13. *Paul v. Virginia*, 8 Wall. 168 (1869).
14. *Veazie Bank v. Fenno*, 8 Wall. 533 (1869).
15. *Brown v. Maryland*, 12 Wheat. 419 (1827).
16. *Wickard v. Filburn*, 317 U.S. 111 (1942); *NLRB v. Jones & Laughlin Steel Corp.*, 301 U.S. 58 (1937).
17. *Kirschbaum Co. v. Walling*, 316 U.S. 517 (1942).

18. *Goldfarb v. Virginia State Bar*, 421 U.S. 773 (1975); *Flood v. Kuhn*, 407 U.S. 258 (1972); *Gonzales v. Raich*, No. 03-1454 (2005).
19. David B. Truman, "Federalism and the Party System," in *Federalism: Mature and Emergent*, ed. Arthur McMahon (Garden City, N.Y.: Doubleday, 1955), p. 123.
20. Harold J. Laski, "The Obsolescence of Federalism," *New Republic* (May 3, 1939): pp. 367–369.
21. William H. Riker, *Federalism: Origin, Operation, Significance* (Boston: Little Brown, 1964), p. 154.
22. Daniel J. Elazar, *American Federalism: A View from the States* (New York: Crowell, 1966), p. 216.
23. Martha Derthick, *Keeping the Compound Republic: Essays on American Federalism* (Washington, D.C.: Brookings Institution, 2001), p. 140.
24. Donald F. Kettl, ed., *The Department of Homeland Security's First Year: A Report Card* (New York: Century Foundation Report, 2004), pp. 18, 102.
25. Samuel H. Beer, "The Modernization of American Federalism," *Publius* 3 (Fall 1973): esp. pp. 74–79; and Beer, "Federalism," pp. 18–19.
26. Congressional Budget Office, *Federal Constraints on State and Local Government Actions* (Washington, D.C.: Government Printing Office, 1979).
27. William T. Gormley, Jr., "Money and Mandates: The Politics of Intergovernmental Conflict," *Publius: The Journal of Federalism* 36(4): p. 527.
28. Ibid., pp. 535–537.
29. U.S. Advisory Commission on Intergovernmental Relations, *Federally Induced Costs Affecting State and Local Governments*, September 1994.

Chapter 4

1. P. Ford, ed., *Works of Thomas Jefferson*, 1905, vol. 9, p. 449.
2. *Snyder v. Phelps*, 131 S. Ct. 1207 (2011); *New York Times Co. v. United States*, 403 U.S. 713 (1971); *Kunz v. New York*, 340 U.S. 290 (1951).
3. *Barron v. Baltimore*, 7 Pet. 243 (1833).
4. *Chicago, Burlington, and Quincy Railroad Co. v. Chicago*, 166 U.S. 226 (1987); *Gitlow v. New York*, 268 U.S. 652 (1925); *Palko v. Connecticut*, 302 U.S. 319 (1937).
5. *District of Columbia v. Heller*, 554 U.S. 570 (2008); *McDonald v. Chicago*, 130 S. Ct. 3020 (2010).
6. William Blackstone, *Commentaries*, vol. 4 (1765), pp. 151–152.
7. Jefferson's remarks are from a letter to Abigail Adams (quoted in Walter Berns, *The First Amendment and the Future of American Democracy*, New York: Basic Books, 1976, p. 82), and from a letter to Thomas McKean, governor of Pennsylvania, February 19, 1803 (Paul L. Ford, ed., *The Writings of Thomas Jefferson: 1801–1806*, vol. 8, New York: Putnam, 1897, p. 218).
8. *Schenck v. United States*, 249 U.S. 47 (1919), p. 52.

9. *Gitlow v. New York*, 268 U.S. 652 (1925), p. 666.
10. *Fiske v. Kansas*, 274 U.S. 380 (1927); *Stromberg v. California*, 283 U.S. 359 (1931); *Near v. Minnesota*, 283 U.S. 697 (1931); *De Jonge v. Oregon*, 299 U.S. 353 (1937).
11. *Dennis v. United States*, 341 U.S. 494 (1951), 510ff. The test was first formulated by Judge Learned Hand of the court of appeals: see *Dennis v. United States*, 183 F.2d 201 (1950), p. 212.
12. *Yates v. United States*, 354 U.S. 298 (1957).
13. *Brandenburg v. Ohio*, 395 U.S. 444 (1969).
14. *Village of Skokie v. National Socialist Party*, 432 U.S. 43 (1977); 366 N.E.2d 349 (1977); and 373 N.E.2d 21 (1978).
15. *R.A.V. v. City of St. Paul*, 112 S. Ct. 2538 (1992).
16. *Wisconsin v. Mitchell*, No. 92–515 (1993).
17. C. Herman Pritchett, *Constitutional Civil Liberties* (Englewood Cliffs, NJ: Prentice-Hall, 1984), p. 100.
18. *New York Times v. Sullivan*, 376 U.S. 254 (1964); but compare *Time, Inc. v. Firestone*, 424 U.S. 448 (1976).
19. Henry J. Abraham, *Freedom and the Court*, 4th ed. (New York: Oxford University Press, 1982), 193, fn 189.
20. Justice Stewart's famous remark was made in his concurring opinion in *Jacobellis v. Ohio*, 378 U.S. 184 (1964), p. 197.
21. *Miller v. California*, 413 U.S. 15 (1973).
22. *Jenkins v. Georgia*, 418 U.S. 153 (1974).
23. *Schad v. Borough of Mt. Ephraim*, 452 U.S. 61 (1981).
24. *Barnes v. Glen Theatre*, 111 S. Ct. 2456 (1991).
25. *American Booksellers Association v. Hudnut*, 771 F.2d 323 (1985), affirmed at 475 U.S. 1001 (1986).
26. *Renton v. Playtime Theatres*, 475 U.S. 41 (1986). See also *Young v. American Mini-Theatres, Inc.*, 427 U.S. 50 (1976).
27. *Reno v. American Civil Liberties Union*, 521 U.S. 844 (1997); *Ashcroft v. Free Speech Coalition*, 122 S. Ct. 1389 (2002).
28. *United States v. O'Brien*, 391 U.S. 367 (1968).
29. *Texas v. Johnson*, 109 S. Ct. 2533 (1989).
30. *United States v. Eichman*, 496 U.S. 310 (1990).
31. *First National Bank of Boston v. Bellotti*, 435 U.S. 765 (1978); *Federal Election Commission v. Massachusetts Citizens for Life, Inc.*, 479 U.S. 238 (1986).
32. *44 Liquormart v. Rhode Island*, 517 U.S. 484 (1996); *Greater New Orleans Broadcasting Association v. United States*, 527 U.S. 173 (1999).
33. *Pacific Gas and Electric Co. v. Public Utilities Commission*, 475 U.S. 1 (1986). Some limitations on corporate speech have been upheld, including a state law prohibiting a firm from spending money on candidates for elective office. *Austin v. Michigan Chamber of Commerce*, 100 S. Ct. 1391 (1990).
34. *Board of Trustees of the State University of New York v. Fox*, 492 U.S. 469 (1989).
35. *Bates v. State Bar of Arizona*, 433 U.S. 350 (1977); *Edenfield v. Bane*, 113 S. Ct. 1792 (1993).

36. *McConnell v. Federal Election Commission*, 124 S. Ct. 619 (2003); *Federal Election Commission v. Wisconsin Right to Life*, No. 06-969 (2007).
37. *Hazelwood School District v. Kuhlmeier et al.*, 484 U.S. 260 (1988).
38. *Murdock v. Pennsylvania*, 319 U.S. 105 (1943).
39. *Church of the Lukumi Babalu Aye v. City of Hialeah*, 508 U.S. 520 (1993).
40. *Reynolds v. United States*, 98 U.S. 145 (1878).
41. *Jacobson v. Massachusetts*, 197 U.S. 11 (1905).
42. *Employment Division, Department of Human Resources of Oregon v. Smith*, 110 S. Ct. 1595 (1990).
43. *Society for Krishna Consciousness v. Lee*, 112 S. Ct. 2701 (1992).
44. *Welsh v. United States*, 398 U.S. 333 (1970); Pritchett, *Constitutional Civil Liberties*, pp. 140–141.
45. *Sherbert v. Verner*, 374 U.S. 398 (1963); *Wisconsin v. Yoder*, 406 U.S. 205 (1972); *Hobbie v. Unemployment Appeals Commission of Florida*, 480 U.S. 136 (1987); *Estate of Thornton v. Caldor, Inc.*, 472 U.S. 703 (1985).
46. Berns, *The First Amendment*.
47. Pritchett, *Constitutional Civil Liberties*, pp. 145–147.
48. *Everson v. Board of Education*, 330 U.S. 1 (1947).
49. *Engel v. Vitale*, 370 U.S. 421 (1962).
50. *Lubbock Independent School District v. Lubbock Civil Liberties Union*, 669 F.2d 1038.
51. *School District of Abington Township v. Schempp*, 374 U.S. 203 (1963).
52. *Lee v. Weisman*, 112 S. Ct. 2649 (1992); *Santa Fe Independent School District v. Jane Doe*, 530 U.S. 290 (2000).
53. *Epperson v. Arkansas*, 393 U.S. 97 (1968); *McLean v. Arkansas Board of Education*, 529 F. Supp. 1255 (1982).
54. *McCollum v. Board of Education*, 333 U.S. 203 (1948); *Zorach v. Clauson*, 343 U.S. 306 (1952).
55. *Tilton v. Richardson*, 403 U.S. 672 (1971).
56. *Board of Education v. Allen*, 392 U.S. 236 (1968).
57. *Walz v. Tax Commission*, 397 U.S. 664 (1970).
58. *Mueller v. Allen*, 463 U.S. 388 (1983).
59. *Zobrest v. Catalina Foothills School District*, 509 U.S. 1 (1993); *Mitchell v. Helms*, 2000 Lexis 4485.
60. *Lemon v. Kurtzman*, 403 U.S. 602 (1971).
61. *Committee for Public Education v. Nyquist*, 413 U.S. 756 (1973).
62. *Meek v. Pittenger*, 421 U.S. 349 (1975); *Wolman v. Walter*, 433 U.S. 229 (1977).
63. *Edwards v. Aguillard*, 482 U.S. 578 (1987); *Board of Education of Kiryas Joel Village School v. Louis Grumet*, 114 S. Ct. 2481 (1994).
64. *Agostini v. Felton*, 521 U.S. 203 (1997), overruled *Aguilar v. Felton*, 473 U.S. 402 (1985).
65. *Zelman v. Simmons-Harris*, 536 U.S. 639 (2002).
66. *Lemon v. Kurtzman*, 403 U.S. 602 (1971).

67. *Lynch v. Donelly*, 465 U.S. 668 (1984); *Allegheny v. ACLU*, 109 S. Ct. 3086 (1989); *McCreary County, Kentucky, v. ACLU*, 125 S. Ct. 2722 (2005); *Van Orden v. Perry*, 125 S. Ct. 2854 (2005).
68. *Marsh v. Chambers*, 492 U.S. 573 (1983).
69. *Ex parte Quirin*, 317 U.S. 1 (1942).
70. *Rasul v. Bush*, 542 U.S. 466 (2004).
71. *Hamdi v. Rumsfeld*, 542 U.S. 507 (2004).
72. Military Commissions Act, Public Law 109-366 (2006).
73. Public Law 109-13 (2005).
74. *In re Sealed Case*, Foreign Intelligence Review Court, No. 02-001 (2001).

Chapter 5

1. *United States v. Carolene Products Co.*, 304 U.S. 144 (1938); *San Antonio Independent School District v. Rodriguez*, 411 U.S. 1 (1973).
2. Gunnar Myrdal, *An American Dilemma* (New York: Harper, 1944), ch. 27.
3. Richard Kluger, *Simple Justice* (New York: Random House/Vintage Books, 1977), pp. 89–90.
4. Paul B. Sheatsley, "White Attitudes Toward the Negro," in *The Negro American*, ed. Talcott Parsons and Kenneth B. Clark (Boston: Houghton Mifflin, 1966), pp. 305, 308, 317.
5. *Strauder v. West Virginia*, 100 U.S. 303 (1880).
6. *Civil Rights Cases*, 109 U.S. 3 (1883).
7. *Plessy v. Ferguson*, 163 U.S. 537 (1896).
8. *Cumming v. Richmond County Board of Education*, 175 U.S. 528 (1899).
9. *Missouri ex rel. Gaines v. Canada*, 305 U.S. 337 (1938).
10. *Sipuel v. Board of Regents of the University of Oklahoma*, 332 U.S. 631 (1948).
11. *Sweatt v. Painter*, 339 U.S. 629 (1950); *McLaurin v. Oklahoma State Regents for Higher Education*, 339 U.S. 637 (1950).
12. *Brown v. Board of Education of Topeka*, 347 U.S. 483 (1954).
13. *Brown v. Board of Education of Topeka*, 349 U.S. 294 (1955). This case is often referred to as "Brown II."
14. Frederick S. Mosteller and Daniel P. Moynihan, eds., *On Equality of Educational Opportunity* (New York: Random House, 1972), pp. 60–62.
15. *Brown v. Board of Education of Topeka*, 347 U.S. 483 (1954).
16. C. Herman Pritchett, *Constitutional Civil Liberties* (Englewood Cliffs, NJ: Prentice-Hall, 1984), pp. 250–251, 261.
17. *Green et al. v. County School Board of New Kent County*, 391 U.S. 430 (1968).
18. *Swann v. Charlotte-Mecklenburg Board of Education*, 402 U.S. 1 (1971).
19. Busing *within* the central city was upheld in *Armour v. Nix*, 446 U.S. 930 (1980); *Keyes v. School District No. 1*, Denver, 413 U.S. 189 (1973); *Milliken v. Bradley*, 418 U.S. 717 (1974); *Board of School Commissioners of Indianapolis v. Buckley*, 429 U.S. 1068 (1977); and *School Board of Richmond v. State Board of Education*, 412 U.S. 92 (1972). Busing *across* city lines was upheld in *Evans v. Buchanan*, 423 U.S. 963 (1975), and *Board of Education v. Newburg Area Council*, 421 U.S. 931 (1975).
20. *Pasadena City Board of Education v. Spangler*, 427 U.S. 424 (1976).
21. See, for example, Herbert McClosky and John Zaller, *The American Ethos* (Cambridge: Harvard University Press, 1984), pp. 92, 100; and data reported in Chapter 5 of this text.
22. NES, *1952–1990 Cumulative Data File, 1992 NES Pre/Post Election Study* (1992).
23. *Freeman v. Pitts*, 112 S. Ct. 1430 (1992); *Parents v. Seattle School District*, No. 05-908 (2007).
24. Robert S. Erikson and Norman R. Luttbeg, *American Public Opinion* (New York: Wiley, 1973), 49; Hazel Erskine, "The Polls: Demonstrations and Race Riots," *Public Opinion Quarterly* 31 (Winter 1967–1968): pp. 654–677.
25. Howard Schuman, Charlotte Steeh, and Lawrence Bobo, *Racial Attitudes in America* (Cambridge: Harvard University Press, 1985), pp. 69, 78–79.
26. Ibid., pp. 102, 110, 127–135.
27. *Grove City College v. Bell*, 465 U.S. 555 (1984).
28. *Mueller v. Oregon*, 208 U.S. 412 (1908).
29. Equal Pay Act of 1963; Civil Rights Act of 1964, Title VII, and 1978 amendments thereto; Education Amendments of 1972, Title IX.
30. *Reed v. Reed*, 404 U.S. 71 (1971).
31. *Frontiero v. Richardson*, 411 U.S. 677 (1973).
32. *Stanton v. Stanton*, 421 U.S. 7 (1975).
33. *Craig v. Boren*, 429 U.S. 190 (1976).
34. *Dothard v. Rawlinson*, 433 U.S. 321 (1977).
35. *Cleveland Board of Education v. LaFleur*, 414 U.S. 632 (1974).
36. *Fortin v. Darlington Little League*, 514 F.2d 344 (1975).
37. *Roberts v. United States Jaycees*, 468 U.S. 609 (1984); *Board of Directors Rotary International v. Rotary Club of Duarte*, 481 U.S. 537 (1987).
38. *Arizona Governing Committee for Tax Deferred Annuity and Deferred Compensation Plans v. Norris*, 463 U.S. 1073 (1983).
39. *EEOC v. Madison Community Unit School District No. 12*, 818 F.2d 577 (1987).
40. *Michael M. v. Superior Court*, 450 U.S. 464 (1981).
41. *Vorchheimer v. School District of Philadelphia*, 430 U.S. 703 (1977).
42. *Kahn v. Shevin*, 416 U.S. 351 (1974).
43. *Schlesinger v. Ballard*, 419 U.S. 498 (1975).
44. *Bennett v. Dyer's Chop House*, 350 F. Supp. 153 (1972); *Morris v. Michigan State Board of Education*, 472 F.2d 1207 (1973); *Fitzgerald v. Porter Memorial Hospital*, 523 F.2d 716 (1975); *Kruzel v. Podell*, 226 N.W.2d 458 (1975).
45. *United States v. Virginia*, 116 S. Ct. 2264 (1996).
46. *Rostker v. Goldberg*, 453 U.S. 57 (1981).
47. *Gebser v. Lago Vista School District*, 118 S. Ct. 1989 (1998); *Faragher v. Boca Raton*, 118 S. Ct. 2275 (1998); *Burlington Industries v. Ellerth*, 118 S. Ct. 2257 (1998).
48. *Griswold v. Connecticut*, 381 U.S. 479 (1965).
49. *Roe v. Wade*, 410 U.S. 113 (1973).
50. Though the constitutionality of the Hyde Amendment was upheld in *Harris v. McRae*, 448 U.S. 297 (1980), other limitations on access to abortions were struck down in *Planned Parenthood Federation of Central Missouri v. Danforth*, 428 U.S. 52 (1976); *Akron v. Akron Center for Reproductive Health*, 462 U.S. 416 (1983); and *Thornburgh v. American College of Obstetricians and Gynecologists*, 476 U.S. 747 (1986).
51. *Planned Parenthood v. Casey*, 112 S. Ct. 2791 (1992).
52. *Gonzales v. Carhart*, No. 05-380 (2007).
53. For an argument in support of a color-blind Constitution, see Andrew Kull, *The Color-Blind Constitution* (Cambridge: Harvard University Press, 1992).
54. *Regents of the University of California v. Bakke*, 438 U.S. 265 (1978).
55. *Fullilove v. Klutznick*, 448 U.S. 448 (1980).
56. *City of Richmond v. J.A. Croson Co.*, 488 U.S. 469 (1989).
57. *Metro Broadcasting v. FCC*, 497 U.S. 547 (1990).
58. *Northeastern Florida Contractors v. Jacksonville*, 508 U.S. 656 (1993).
59. *Firefighters Local Union No. 1784 v. Stotts*, 467 U.S. 561 (1984); *Wygant v. Jackson Board of Education*, 476 U.S. 267 (1986); *City of Richmond v. J.A. Croson Co.*, 488 U.S. 469 (1989).
60. *Local No. 28 of the Sheet Metal Workers' International Association v. Equal Employment Opportunity Commission*, 478 U.S. 421 (1986); *Wards Cove Packing Co. v. Atonio*, 490 U.S. 642 (1989); *Price Waterhouse v. Hopkins*, 490 U.S. 228 (1989). (Note: *Wards Cove* and *Price* were both superseded in part by the Civil Rights Act of 1991.)
61. *Fullilove v. Klutznick*, 448 U.S. 448 (1980); *Metro Broadcasting v. FCC*, 497 U.S. 547 (1990).
62. *United Steelworkers of America v. Weber*, 443 U.S. 193 (1979); *Johnson v. Santa Clara County Transportation Agency*, 480 U.S. 616 (1987).
63. *Wygant v. Jackson Board of Education*, 476 U.S. 267 (1986); *United States v. Paradise*, 480 U.S. 149 (1987).
64. Seymour Martin Lipset and William Schneider, "An Emerging National Consensus," *The New Republic* (October 15, 1977): pp. 8–9.
65. John R. Bunzel, "Affirmative Re-Actions," *Public Opinion* (February/March 1986): pp. 45–49; *The New York Times* (December 14, 1997).
66. *Adarand Constructors v. Pena*, 515 U.S. 200 (1995).
67. *Hopwood v. Texas*, 78 F.3d 932 (1996).
68. *Gratz v. Bollinger*, 539 U.S. 244 (2003).
69. *Grutter v. Bollinger*, 539 U.S. 306 (2003).
70. *Bowers v. Hardwick*, 478 U.S. 186 (1986).
71. *Romer v. Evans*, 517 U.S. 620 (1996).
72. *Lawrence v. Texas*, 539 U.S. 558 (2003).
73. *Goodridge v. Department of Public Health*, 440 Mass. 309 (2003) and 440 Mass. 1201 (2004).
74. *Boy Scouts of America v. Dale*, 530 U.S. 640 (2000).

Chapter 6

1. Shanto Iyengar, Media Politics: A Citizen's Guide, 2nd edition (New York: W.W. Norton and Company, 2011), p. 13.
2. See "The Watergate Story," The Washington Post, available at http://www.washingtonpost .com/wp-srv/politics/special/watergate/.
3. Coverage of the Iran-Contra affair by selected news networks is available through the Vanderbilt University Television News Archive.
4. Mayhill Fowler, "Obama: No Surprise That Hard-Pressed Pennsylvanians Turn Bitter," Huffington Post, 11 April 2008.
5. Pew Research Center for the People & the Press, "In Changing News Landscape, Even Television Is Vulnerable," September 27, 2012. Available at http://www.people-press. org/2012/09/27/in-changing-news-landscape-even-television-is-vulnerable/.
6. For example, see Bernard Berelson, et al., Voting: A Study of Opinion Formation in a Presidential Campaign (Chicago: University of Chicago Press, 1954), and Phillip E. Converse, "The Nature of Belief Systems in Mass Publics," in Ideology and Discontent, ed. David E. Apter (New York: Free Press, 1964).
7. For example, see V. O. Key, The Responsible Electorate (Cambridge: Harvard University Press, 1966); Samuel Popkin, The Reasoning Voter: Communication and Persuasion in Presidential Campaigns (Chicago: University of Chicago Press, 1991); Benjamin I. Page and Robert Y. Shapiro, The Rational Public: Fifty Years of Trends in Americans' Policy Preferences (Chicago: University of Chicago Press, 1991).
8. Terry M. Moe, Schools, Vouchers, and the American Public (Washington, D.C.: Brookings Institution, 2001), p. 253.
9. James Q. Wilson, "The Press at War," City Journal (Autumn 2006): pp. 54–63.
10. M. Kent Jennings and Richard G. Niemi, "The Transmission of Political Values from Parent to Child," American Political Science Review 62 (March 1968): 173; Robert D. Hess and Judith V. Torney, The Development of Political Attitudes in Children (Chicago: Aldine, 1967), p. 90.
11. John R. Alford, Carolyn L. Funk, and John R. Hibbing, "Are Political Orientations Genetically Transmitted?" American Political Science Review, 99 (May 2005): pp. 153–167; James Q. Wilson, "The DNA of Politics," City Journal (Winter 2009): pp. 83–87; Thomas J. Bouchard, et al., "Evidence for the Construct Validity and Heritability of the Wilson-Patterson Conservatism Scale," Personality and Individual Differences, 24 (2003): pp. 959–969.
12. Several studies of child-parent agreement on party preference are summarized in David O. Sears, "Political Behavior," in The Handbook of Social Psychology, 2d ed., ed. Gardner Lindzey and Elliot Aronson (Reading, MA: Addison-Wesley, 1969), vol. 5, p. 376.
13. Norman H. Nie, Sidney Verba, and John R. Petrocik, The Changing American Voter (Cambridge: Harvard University Press, 1976), ch. 4.
14. Richard Niemi and M. Kent Jennings, "Issues and Inheritance in the Formation of Party Identification," American Journal of Political Science (November 1991): pp. 970–988.
15. Pew Forum on Religion and Public Life, "Support for Same-Sex Marriage Edges Upward," October 6, 2010.
16. Elizabeth Humel, et. al., "Younger Voters," Public Perspective (May/June 2003): p. 11.
17. Pew Forum on Religion and Public Life, Survey: More Americans Question Religion's Role in Politics, August 21, 2008.
18. Pew Forum on Religion and Public Life, Survey: Religious Groups Agree—Fixing the Nation's Economy Is Job One, March 4, 2009.
19. V. O. Key, Jr., Public Opinion and American Democracy (New York: Knopf, 1961), pp. 122–138.
20. Richard E. Dawson, Public Opinion and Contemporary Disarray (New York: Harper & Row, 1973), ch. 4.
21. David Bositis, Public Opinion 1998: Political Attitudes (Washington, D.C.: Joint Center for Political and Economic Studies, 1998), table 18A.
22. "The Black and White of Public Opinion," Pew Research Center for the People & the Press (October 31, 2005).
23. Ibid.
24. Lisa J. Montoya, et al., "Latina Politics: Gender, Participation, and Leadership," PS: Political Science and Politics 33 (September 2000): p. 557.
25. Bruce Cain and Roderick Kiewit, "California's Coming Minority Majority," Public Opinion (February/March 1986): pp. 50–52.
26. Ibid.
27. Pew Hispanic Center, Survey of Latino Attitudes on the War in Iraq, Pew Research Center, February 7, 2005.
28. Richard Frey, et al., Hispanics and the Social Security Debate, Pew Research Center, March 16, 2005.
29. Ibid.
30. Lydia Saad, "Conservatives Maintain Edge as Top Ideological Group," Gallup Organization, October 26, 2009.
31. Adam J. Berinsky, Silent Voices: Public Opinion and Political Participation in America (Princeton, NJ: Princeton University Press, 2004); Berinsky, "Two Faces of Public Opinion," American Journal of Political Science (October 1999): pp. 1209–1230.
32. Ibid.
33. John Zaller, The Nature and Origins of Mass Opinion (Cambridge: Cambridge University Press, 1992).
34. David E. Butler, "Why America's Political Reporting Is Better than England's," Harper's (May 1963): pp. 15–25.
35. Gerard Alexander, "Illiberal Europe," Weekly Standard, April 10, 2006.
36. Quoted in F. L. Mort, American Journalism, 1690–1960, 3rd ed. (New York: Macmillan, 1962), p. 529.
37. Center for Media and Public Affairs, "The Incredible Shrinking Sound Bite," press release, Washington, D.C., September 28, 2000.
38. Pew Internet & American Life Project, "The Internet and Campaign 2010," March 2011.
39. Updated from Times Mirror Center for the People and the Press, June 28, 1990.
40. Edward J. Epstein, News from Nowhere: Television and the News (New York: Random House, 1973), p. 37.
41. Near v. Minnesota, 283 U.S. 697 (1931).
42. New York Times v. United States, 403 U.S. 713 (1971).
43. New York Times v. Sullivan, 376 U.S. 254 (1964).
44. Miami Herald Publishing Co. v. Tornillo, 418 U.S. 241 (1974).
45. Yates v. United States, 354 U.S. 298 (1957).
46. David O. Sears and Richard E. Whitney, "Political Persuasion," in Pool, Handbook of Communication, pp. 253–289.
47. Robert S. Erickson, "The Influence of Newspaper Endorsements in Presidential Elections: The Case of 1964," American Journal of Political Science 20 (May 1976): pp. 207–233.
48. Kim Fridkin Kahn and Patrick J. Kenney, "The Slant of the News: How Editorial Endorsements Influence Campaign Coverage and Citizens' Views of Candidates," American Political Science Review 96 (2002): pp. 381–394; James N. Druckman and Michael Parkin, "The Impact of Media Bias," Journal of Politics 67 (2005): pp. 1030–1049.
49. Stefano Della Vigna and Ethan Kaplan, "The Fox News Effect: Media Bias and Voting," Working paper 12160 (Cambridge, MA: National Bureau of Economic Research, 2006).
50. Alan Gerber, Dean Karlan, and Daniel Bergan, "Does the Media Matter? A Field Experiment." Unpub. paper, Department of Political Science, Yale University, January 2006. See also Gerber, et al., "How Large and How Long-lasting Are the Persuasive Effects of Televised Ads?" American Political Science Review 105 (2011): pp. 135–150.
51. Maxwell E. McCombs and Donald R. Shaw, "The Agenda Setting Function of the Mass Media," Public Opinion Quarterly 36 (Summer 1972): pp. 176–187; Shanto Iyengar and Donald R. Kinder, News That Matters (Chicago: University of Chicago Press, 1987).
52. G. Ray Funkhouser, "The Issues of the Sixties," Public Opinion Quarterly 37 (Spring 1973): pp. 62–75.
53. Benjamin I. Page, Robert Y. Shapiro, and Glenn R. Dempsey, "What Moves Public Opinion?" American Political Science Review 81 (March 1987): pp. 23–43; Benjamin I. Page, "The Media as Political Actors," PS: Political Science and Politics (March 1996): p. 21.

Chapter 7

1. Leon D. Epstein, "Political Parties," in Handbook of Political Science, ed. Fred I. Greenstein and Nelson W. Polsby (Reading, MA: Addison-Wesley, 1975), vol. 4, p. 230.

2. Quoted in Henry Adams, *History of the United States of America during the Administrations of Jefferson and Madison*, ed. Ernest Samuels, abridged ed. (Chicago: University of Chicago Press, 1967), p. 147.

3. Walter Dean Burnham, *Critical Elections and the Mainsprings of American Politics* (New York: Norton, 1970), p. 10.

4. James L. Sundquist, *Dynamics of the Party System* (Washington, D.C.: Brookings Institution, 1973), ch. 7.

5. Edward G. Carmines and James A. Stimson, "Issue Evolution, Population Replacement, and Normal Partisan Change," *American Political Science Review* 75 (March 1981): pp. 107–118; and Gregory Markus, "Political Attitudes in an Election Year," *American Political Science Review* 76 (September 1982): pp. 538–560.

6. Ray Wolfinger and Michael G. Hagen, "Republican Prospects: Southern Comfort," *Public Opinion* (October/November 1985): pp. 8–13. But compare Richard Scammon and James A. Barnes, "Republican Prospects: Southern Discomfort," *Public Opinion* (October/November 1985): pp. 14–17.

7. Jerold G. Rusk, "The Effect of the Australian Ballot Reform on Split-Ticket Voting: 1876–1908," *American Political Science Review* 64 (December 1970): pp. 1220–1238.

8. Morton Keller, *Affairs of State* (Cambridge: Harvard University Press, 1977), p. 239.

9. Quoted in Keller, ibid., p. 256.

10. Martin Shefter, "Parties, Bureaucracy, and Political Change in the United States," in *The Development of Political Parties*, Sage Electoral Studies Yearbook, vol. 4, ed. Louis Maisel and Joseph Cooper (Beverly Hills, CA: Sage, 1978).

11. James Q. Wilson, *The Amateur Democrat: Club Politics in Three Cities* (Chicago: University of Chicago Press, 1962).

12. Samuel J. Eldersveld, *Political Parties: A Behavioral Analysis* (Chicago: Rand McNally, 1964), pp. 278, 287.

13. Robert H. Salisbury, "The Urban Party Organization Member," *Public Opinion Quarterly* 29 (Winter 1965–1966): pp. 550–564.

14. Ibid., pp. 557, 559

15. Eldersveld, *Political Parties*; and J. David Greenstone, *Labor in American Politics* (New York: Knopf, 1969), p. 187.

16. David R. Mayhew, *Placing Parties in American Politics* (Princeton, NJ: Princeton University Press, 1986), chs. 2, 3.

17. *Boston Globe* (July 9, 1984): p. 1.

18. Congressional Quarterly. "Browse by Party System." Political Handbook of the World. Last modified 2012. Accessed May 31, 2013.

19. American National Election Studies, August 5, 2010, table 2B.4; reporting data for the period 1952–2008.

20. For example, see *The Public Perspective* (April/May 1998).

21. American National Election Survey, November 27, 2005, table 2B.3; reporting data for the period 1972–2000.

22. *Williams v. Rhodes*, 393 U.S. 23 (1968).

23. Lee Jared Drutman, *The Business of America Is Lobbying: The Expansion of Corporate Activity and the Future of American Pluralism*, Ph.D. Dissertation, University of California, Berkeley, Fall 2010; Kay Lehrman Schlozman, et al., "Who Sings in the Heavenly Chorus? The Shape of Organized Interest Group Activity," paper presented at the annual meeting of the American Political Science Association, Boston, MA, August 2008.

24. Ibid.

25. The use of injunctions in labor disputes was restricted by the Norris-LaGuardia Act of 1932; the rights to collective bargaining and to the union shop were guaranteed by the Wagner Act of 1935.

26. *Historical Abstract of the United States, Colonial Times to 1970*, vol. 1, p. 386.

27. Dana Priest and William M. Arkin, "A Hidden World, Growing Beyond Control" and "National Security Inc," *The Washington Post*, July 19–21, 2010.

28. Timothy P. Carney, "The TSA and the Full-Body Scanner Lobby," *The Washington Examiner*, December 29, 2009; Kimberly Kindy, "Ex-Homeland Security Chief Head Said to Abuse Public Trust by Touting Body Scanners," *The Washington Post*, January 1, 2010.

29. Mancur Olson, Jr., *The Logic of Collective Action* (Cambridge: Harvard University Press, 1965), pp. 153–157.

30. J. Scott Applewhite, "What Is the 'Tea Party' and How Is It Shaking Up American Politics?" *Christian Science Monitor*, September 15, 2010.

31. Walter A. Rosenbaum, *Environmental Politics and Policy*, 8th ed. (Washington, D.C.: Congressional Quarterly College Press, 2010).

32. Jane Mansbridge, *Why We Lost the ERA* (Chicago: University of Chicago Press, 1986), ch. 10.

33. Ibid.

34. Drutman, *The Business of America*, p. 5.

35. Federal Election Commission data compiled on Center for Responsive Politics website, opensecrets.org.

36. Robert O'Harrow and Scott Higham, "Report Finds DHS Lax on Contracting Procedures," *The Washington Post*, November 22, 2006.

37. *United States v. Harris*, 347 U.S. 612 (1954).

38. *United States Code*, Title 26, section 501(c)(3).

Chapter 8

1. Michael McDonald and Samuel L. Popkin, "The Myth of the Vanishing Voter," *American Political Science Review* 95 (December 2001).

2. U.S. Bureau of the Census, *Current Population Survey*, "Reasons for Not Voting," June 2008, table 6.

3. Matthew R. Knee and Donald P. Green, "The Effects of Registration Laws on Voter Turnout: An Updated Assessment," in Paul M. Sniderman and Benjamin Highton, eds., *Facing the Challenges of Democracy*

(Princeton, NJ: Princeton University Press, 2011): p. 326; and John P. DiIulio, "The Liberalization of Absentee and Mail-In Voting, 1996–2008," unpublished paper, November 2008.

4. Raymond E. Wolfinger and Jonathan Hoffman, "Registering and Voting with Motor Voter," *PS: Political Science and Politics* 34 (March 2001): p. 90.

5. Donald P. Green and Alan S. Gerber, *Get Out the Vote: How to Increase Voter Turnout* (Washington, D.C. : The Brookings Institution Press, 2008).

6. Alan S. Gerber, et al., "Social Pressure and Voter Turnout: Evidence from a Large-Scale Field Experiment," *American Political Science Review* 102 (February 2008).

7. Morton Keller, *Affairs of State* (Cambridge, MA: Harvard University Press, 1977), p. 523.

8. *United States v. Reese*, 92 U.S. 214 (1876); *United States v. Cruikshank*, 92 U.S. 556 (1876); and *Ex Parte Yarbrough*, 110 U.S. 651 (1884).

9. *Guinn and Beall v.* United States, 238 U.S. 347 (1915).

10. *Smith v. Allright*, 321 U.S. 649 (1944).

11. *Schnell v. Davis*, 336 U.S. 993 (1949).

12. *Historical Statistics of the United States: Colonial Times to 1970*, part 2, pp. 1071–1072.

13. Walter Dean Burnham, "The Changing Shape of the American Political Universe," *American Political Science Review* 59 (March 1965): p. 11; and William H. Flanigan and Nancy H. Zingale, *Political Behavior of the American Electorate*, 3d ed. (Boston, MA: Allyn and Bacon, 1975), p. 15.

14. Burnham, "The Changing Shape;" and E. E. Schattschneider, *The Semi-Sovereign People* (New York: Holt, Rinehart & Winston, 1960), chs. 5, 6.

15. Philip E. Converse, "Change in the American Electorate," in *The Human Meaning of Social Change*, ed. Angus Campbell and Philip E. Converse (New York: Russell Sage Foundation, 1972), pp. 263–338.

16. Raymond Wolfinger and Benjamen Highton, "What If They Gave an Election and Everyone Came?," Public Affairs Report, University of California at Berkeley, June 1999, pp. 11–13; Stephen Ansolabehere and Eitan Hersh, "Who *Really* Votes?," in Sniderman and Highton, *Facing the Challenge of Democracy*, op. cit.: p. 290.

17. The Center for Public Integrity, *Campaign Consultants*, Georgetown University, Washington, D.C., September 26, 2006, p. 1.

18. Ted Bader, *Campaigning for Hearts and Minds: How Emotional Appeals Work in Political Ads* (Chicago: University of Chicago Press, 2006).

19. Ibid., pp. 140–143.

20. *Wesberry v. Sanders*, 376 U.S. 1 (1964).

21. Richard F. Fenno, Jr., "U.S. House Members and Their Constituencies: An Exploration," *American Political Science Review* 71 (September 1977): pp. 883–917, esp. 914.

22. John A. Ferejohn, *Pork Barrel Politics* (Stanford, CA: Stanford University Press, 1974).

23. Douglas Arnold, *Congress and the Bureaucracy* (New Haven, CT: Yale University Press, 1979).

24. Arthur H. Miller, et al., "A Majority Party in Disarray: Policy Polarization in the 1972 Election," *American Political Science Review* 70 (1976): p. 757.

25. Angus Campbell, Philip E. Converse, Warren E. Miller, and Donald E. Stokes, *The American Voter* (New York: Wiley, 1960), ch. 8.

26. V. O. Key, Jr., *The Responsible Electorate* (Cambridge: Harvard University Press, 1966).

27. Morris P. Fiorina, *Retrospective Voting in American National Elections* (New Haven, CT: Yale University Press, 1981).

28. Jay P. Greene, "Forewarned before Forecast: Presidential Election Forecasting Models and the 1992 Election," *P.S.: Political Science and Politics* (March 1993): p. 20.

29. Paul Freedman and Ken Goldstein, "Measuring Media Exposure and the Effects of Negative Campaign Ads," *American Journal of Political Science* 43 (October 1999): pp. 1189–1208.

30. Robert Axelrod, "Where the Votes Come From: An Analysis of Electoral Coalitions, 1952–1968," *American Political Science Review* 66 (1972): pp. 11–20; and Axelrod, "Communication," *American Political Science Review* 68 (1974): pp. 718–719.

Chapter 9

1. Thomas E. Mann and Norman J. Ornstein, *The Broken Branch: How Congress Is Failing America and How to Get It Back on Track*, 2nd ed. (New York: Oxford University Press, 2008). Also see Richard F. Fenno, "If as Ralph Nader Says Congress Is the 'Broken Branch,' How Come We Love Our Congressmen So Much More than Our Congress?" in *Congress in Change: Evolution and Reform*, ed. Norman J. Ornstein (New York: Praeger Publishers, 1975).

2. Fenno, "If as Ralph Nader Says," p. 286.

3. Norman J. Ornstein and Thomas E. Mann, *Vital Statistics on Congress, 1995–1996* (Washington, D.C.: Congressional Quarterly Press, 1996), pp. 199–200.

4. "A Polarized Congress," *National Journal* (January 21, 2006): p. 21, reporting data compiled by David Rhode and John Aldrich.

5. Ibid.

6. "Vicious or Virtuous? America's Political System May Have Become Too Polarized to Produce Compromise," *The Economist* (April 16, 2011): p. 38.

7. Tim Alberts, "The Cabal that Quietly Took Over the House," *National Journal*, May 26, 2013.

8. H. Douglas Price, "Careers and Committees in the American Congress," in *The History of Parliamentary Behavior*, ed. William O. Aydelotte (Princeton: Princeton University Press, 1977); John F. Bibby, et al., *Vital Statistics on Congress, 1980* (Washington,

D.C.: American Enterprise Institute, 1980), pp. 53–54.

9. David Mayhew, *Congress: The Electoral Connection* (New Haven: Yale University Press, 1974).

10. Harold W. Stanley and Richard G. Niemi, *Vital Statistics on American Politics, 1999–2000* (Washington, D.C.: Congressional Quarterly Press, 2000), table 1-18, and post-2000 data updated by Marc Siegel.

11. Mayhew, *Congress*; Morris P. Fiorina, *Congress: Keystone of the Washington Establishment* (New Haven: Yale University Press, 1977).

12. Rhodes Cook, "House Republicans Scored a Quiet Victory in '92," *Congressional Quarterly* (April 17, 1993): p. 966.

13. Bruce E. Cain and David Butler, "Redrawing District Lines: What's Going On and What's At Stake," *The American Enterprise* (July/August 1991): p. 37.

14. "Redistricting Rows: Not So Easy," *The Economist* (May 7, 2011): p. 27.

15. Richard F. Fenno, *Congressmen in Committees* (Boston: Little, Brown, 1973).

16. Bibby, et al., *Vital Statistics*, pp. 65–74.

17. Fiorina, *Congress*.

18. Bibby, et al., *Vital Statistics*, p. 60.

19. Michael J. Malbin, "Delegation, Deliberation, and the New Role of Congressional Staff," in *The New Congress*, eds. Thomas E. Mann and Norman J. Ornstein (Washington, D.C.: American Enterprise Institute, 1981), pp. 134–177, esp. 170–171.

20. Malcolm E. Jewell and Samuel C. Patterson, *The Legislative Process in the United States*, 3rd ed. (New York: Random House, 1977), p. 349.

21. Mann and Ornstein, *Broken Branch*; Joshua D. Clinton and John S. Lapinski, "Measuring Legislative Accomplishment," *American Journal of Political Science* 56 (2006): pp. 232–249; J. Tobin Grant and Nathan J. Kelly, "Legislative Productivity of the U.S. Congress," *Political Analysis* 16 (2008): pp. 303–323.

22. Mann and Ornstein, *Broken Branch*.

23. David Mayhew, *Divided We Govern: Party Control, Lawmaking, and Investigations* (New Haven: Yale University Press, 1991); Grant and Kelly, "Legislative Productivity."

24. Tom Coburn, "The Spending Process Is Broken," *Extensions: Journal of the Carl Albert Research and Studies Center* (Spring 2007): p. 16, reporting data from the Congressional Research Service and the Congressional Budget Office.

25. Diana Evans, "Appropriations in the Republican Era," *Extensions: Journal of the Carl Albert Congressional Research and Studies Center* (Spring 2007): p. 13.

Chapter 10

1. Nicholas Confessore and Jo Craven McGinty, "Obama, Romney, and Their Parties on Track to Raise $2 Billion," *The New York Times*, 25 October 2012.

2. Jean Blondel, *An Introduction to Comparative Government* (New York: Praeger, 1969), as cited in Nelson W. Polsby, "Legislatures,"

in *Handbook of Political Science*, ed. Fred I. Greenstein and Nelson W. Polsby (Reading, MA: Addison-Wesley, 1975), vol. 5, p. 275.

3. Donald F. Kettl, *Deficit Politics: Public Budgeting in Its Institutional and Historical Context* (New York: Macmillan, 1992), p. 13.

4. Morris P. Fiorina, *Divided Government* (New York: Macmillan, 1992), pp. 86–111.

5. David Mayhew, *Divided We Govern: Party Control, Lawmaking, and Investigations, 1946–1990* (New Haven, CT: Yale University Press, 1991), p. 76.

6. Woodrow Wilson, *Congressional Government* (New York: Meridian Books, 1956), pp. 167–168, 170. First published in 1885.

7. Richard E. Neustadt, *Presidential Power and the Modern Presidents: The Politics of Leadership from Roosevelt to Reagan* (New York: The Free Press, 1990), ch. 4.

8. Walter D. Burnham, "Insulation and Responsiveness in Congressional Elections," *Political Science Quarterly* 90 (Fall 1975): pp. 412–413; George C. Edwards III, *Presidential Influence in Congress* (San Francisco: Freeman, 1980), pp. 70–78; Warren E. Miller, "Presidential Coattails: A Study in Political Myth and Methodology," *Public Opinion Quarterly* 19 (Winter 1955–1956): p. 368; and Miller, "The Motivational Basis for Straight and Split Ticket Voting," *American Political Science Review* 51 (June 1957): pp. 293–312.

9. *Clinton v. City of New York*, 118 S. Ct. 2091 (1998).

10. *Marbury v. Madison*, 1 Cranch 137 (1803).

11. *United States v. Nixon*, 418 U.S. 683 (1974).

12. *Clinton v. Jones*, 520 U.S. 681 (1997); *In re Grand Jury Subpoena Duces Tecum*, 112 F.3d 910 (1997); *In re Sealed Case*, 121 F.3d 729 (1997).

13. Christopher S. Kelley, "A Comparative Look at the Constitutional Signing Statement," paper presented at the Midwest Political Science Association meeting, April 2003; Kelley, "To Be (Unitarian) or Not to Be (Unitarian): Presidential Power in the George W. Bush Administration," *White House Studies* 10, no. 2 (2010): pp. 115–129.

14. Data available through the University of California, Santa Barbara, American Presidency Project at http://www.presidency.ucsb.edu/.

15. Walter Dellinger, "Memorandum for Bernard N. Nussbaum, Counsel to the President," Office of Legal Counsel, U.S. Department of Justice, November 3, 1993.

16. *Chevron v. NRDC*, 467 U.S. 837 (1984).

17. Edwin S. Corwin, *The Presidency: Office and Powers* (New York: New York University Press, 1957), p. 171.

18. Stephen Hess, *Organizing the Presidency* (Washington, D.C.: Brookings Institution, 1976), p. 3; R. W. Apple, "Clinton's Refocusing," *The New York Times*, May 6, 1993, A22; Michael K. Frisby, "Power Switch," *The Wall Street Journal*, March 26, 1993, A1, A7.

19. David T. Stanley, et al., *Men Who Govern* (Washington, D.C.: Brookings Institution, 1967), pp. 41–42, 50.
20. Adapted from Paul C. Light, *The President's Agenda* (Baltimore, MD: Johns Hopkins University Press, 1982), pp. 217–225.

Chapter 11

1. Charles E. Lindblom, *Politics and Markets* (New York: Basic Books, 1977), p. 114.
2. Donald F. Kettl, *Government by Proxy: (Mis?) Managing Federal Programs* (Washington, D.C.: Congressional Quarterly Press, 1988); John J. DiIulio, Jr., "Government by Proxy: A Faithful Overview," *Harvard Law Review* (March 2003): pp. 1272–1284.
3. Mark Hemmingway, "Warriors for Hire," *Weekly Standard*, December 18, 2006, p. 25.
4. Ibid., p. 26.
5. Martha Derthick, *Keeping the Compound Republic: Essays on American Federalism* (Washington, D.C.: Brookings Institution, 2001), p. 63.
6. Donald F. Kettl, *The Next Government of the United States: Why Our Institutions Fail Us and How to Fix Them* (New York: W.W. Norton, 2008), pp. 1–14.
7. Article II, section 2, para. 2.
8. Article II, section 3.
9. Calculated from data in *Historical Statistics of the United States: Colonial Times to 1970* (Washington, D.C.: Government Printing Office, 1975), vol. 2, pp. 1102–1103.
10. *Panama Refining Co. v. Ryan*, 293 U.S. 388 (1935).
11. *Hampton Jr. & Co. v. United States*, 276 U.S. 394 (1928).
12. Edward S. Corwin, *The Constitution and What It Means Today*, 13th ed. (Princeton, NJ: Princeton University Press, 1973), p. 151.
13. Bruce D. Porter, "Parkinson's Law Revisited: War and the Growth of American Government," *Public Interest* (Summer 1980): pp. 50–68.
14. See the cases cited in Corwin, *The Constitution*, p. 8.
15. *U.S. Statutes*, vol. 84, sec. 799 (1970).
16. *Historical Statistics of the United States*, vol. 2, p. 1107.
17. Department of Homeland Security, Hearings Before the Subcommittee on Oversight and Management Efficiency, Committee on Homeland Security, U.S. House of Representatives, 113th, 1st Sess. (2013); U.S. Government Accountability Office, *Key Issues: DHS Implementation and Transformation*, 2013; also see Kettl, *The Next Government*, op. cit., p. 52.
18. Heclo, "Issue Networks and the Executive Establishment," pp. 87–124.
19. David H. Rosenbloom, "Reevaluating Executive-Centered Public Administrative Theory," in *The Oxford Handbook of American Bureaucracy*, ed. Robert F. Durant. Oxford University Press, 2010, p. 114.
20. Ibid., pp. 121–122.
21. Richard F. Fenno, Jr., *The Power of the Purse* (Boston: Little, Brown, 1966), pp. 450, 597.

22. John E. Schwartz and L. Earl Shaw, *The United States Congress in Comparative Perspective* (Hinsdale, IL.: Dryden Press, 1976), 262–263; *National Journal* (July 4, 1981): pp. 1211–1214.
23. *Immigration and Naturalization Service v. Chadha*, 462 U.S. 919 (1983); *Maine v. Thiboutot*, 448 U.S. 1 (1980).
24. See cases cited in Corwin, *The Constitution*, 22.
25. William Safire, *Safire's Political Dictionary* (Random House, 1978).
26. Steven Kelman, "The Grace Commission: How Much Waste in Government?" *Public Interest* (Winter 1985): pp. 62–87.
27. Daniel Katz, et al., *Bureaucratic Encounters* (Ann Arbor: Survey Research Center, University of Michigan, 1975), pp. 63–69, 118–120, 184–188.
28. U.S. Government Accountability Office, *Government Performance Lessons Learned*, GAO Report, July 24, 2008, as cited in Kettl, *The Next Government*, op. cit., 173, p. 255.
29. Ibid.

Chapter 12

1. Russell Wheeler, *Judicial Nominations and Confirmations in Obama's First Term*, Governance Studies, Brookings Institution, December 13, 2012, p.1.
2. Ibid.
3. Ibid.
4. Henry J. Abraham, *The Judicial Process*, 3d ed. (New York: Oxford University Press, 1975), pp. 279–280.
5. Robert G. McCloskey, *The American Supreme Court* (Chicago: University of Chicago Press, 1960), p. 27.
6. *Marbury v. Madison*, 5 U.S. 137 (1803); and *McCulloch v. Maryland*, 17 U.S. 316 (1819).
7. *Martin v. Hunter's Lessee*, 14 U.S. 304 (1816) and *Cohens v. Virginia*, 19 U.S. (1821).
8. *Gibbons v. Ogden*, 22 U.S. (1824).
9. Quoted in Albert J. Beveridge, *The Life of John Marshall* (Boston: Houghton Mifflin, 1919), vol. 4, p. 551.
10. *Dred Scott v. Sandford*, 60 U.S. 393 (1857).
11. Abraham, *The Judicial Process*, p. 286.
12. *In re Debs*, 158 U.S. 564 (1895).
13. *Pollock v. Farmers' Loan & Trust Co.*, 157 U.S. 429 (1895).
14. *United States v. Knight*, 156 U.S. 1 (1895).
15. *Cincinnati, N.O. & T.P. Railway Co. v. Interstate Commerce Commission*, 162 U.S. 184 (1896).
16. *Hammer v. Dagenhart*, 247 U.S. 251 (1918).
17. *Lochner v. New York*, 198 U.S. 45 (1905).
18. McCloskey, *The American Supreme Court*, p. 151.
19. *Munn v. Illinois*, 94 U.S. 113 (1877).
20. *Dayton-Goose Creek Railway Co. v. United States*, 263 U.S. 456 (1924).
21. *Atchison, Topeka, and Santa Fe Railroad Co. v. Matthews*, 174 U.S. 96 (1899).
22. *Mugler v. Kansas*, 123 U.S. 623 (1887).
23. *St. Louis Consolidated Coal Co. v. Illinois*, 185 U.S. 203 (1902).
24. *New York Central Railroad Co. v. White*, 243 U.S. 188 (1917).

25. *German Alliance Insurance Co. v. Lewis*, 233 U.S. 389 (1914).
26. Morton Keller, *Affairs of State* (Cambridge: Harvard University Press, 1977), p. 369. See also Mary Cornelia Porter, "That Commerce Shall Be Free: A New Look at the Old Laissez-Faire Court," in *The Supreme Court Review*, ed. Philip B. Kurland (Chicago: University of Chicago Press, 1976), pp. 135–159.
27. *Chief of Capitol Police v. Jeannette Rankin Brigade*, 409 U.S. 972 (1972).
28. *Aptheker v. Secretary of State*, 378 U.S. 500 (1964).
29. *Trop v. Dulles*, 356 U.S. 86 (1958); *Afroyim v. Rusk*, 387 U.S. 253 (1967); and *Schneider v. Rusk*, 377 U.S. 163 (1964).
30. *Lamont v. Postmaster General*, 381 U.S. 301 (1965); and *Blount v. Rizzi*, 400 U.S. 410 (1971).
31. *Richardson v. Davis*, 409 U.S. 1069 (1972); *U.S. Department of Agriculture v. Murry*, 413 U.S. 508 (1973); *Jimenez v. Weinberger*, 417 U.S. 628 (1974); and *Washington v. Legrant*, 394 U.S. 618 (1969).
32. *United States v. Lopez*, 514 U.S. 549 (1995).
33. *Seminole Tribe of Florida v. Florida*, 517 U.S. 44 (1996); *Alden v. Maine*, 527 U.S. 706 (1999); *Florida v. College Savings Bank*, 527 U.S. 627 (1999).
34. Daniel R. Pinello, "Linking Party to Judicial Ideology in American Courts: A Meta-Analysis," *Justice System Journal* 20 (1999): pp. 219–254.
35. An opinion survey of federal judges shows how party affects ideology: see Althea K. Nagai, Stanley Rothman, and S. Robert Lichter, "The Verdict of Federal Judges," *Public Opinion* (November/December 1987): pp. 52–56.
36. *United States v. Lanza*, 260 U.S. 377 (1922). Cf. *Abbate v. United States*, 359 U.S. 187 (1959), and *Bartkus v. Illinois*, 359 U.S. 121 (1989).
37. *Gideon v. Wainwright*, 372 U.S. 335 (1963). The story is told in Anthony Lewis, *Gideon's Trumpet* (New York: Random House, 1964).
38. Erwin Griswold, "Rationing Justice: The Supreme Court's Case Load and What the Court Does Not Do," *Cornell Law Review* 60 (1975): pp. 335–354.
39. Joseph Weis, Jr., "Disconnecting the Overloaded Circuits—A Plan for a Unified Court of Appeals," *St. Louis University Law Journal* 39 (1995): p. 455.
40. *Alyeska Pipeline Service Co. v. Wilderness Society*, 421 U.S. 240 (1975).
41. *Flast v. Cohen*, 392 U.S. 83 (1968), which modified the earlier *Frothingham v. Mellon*, 262 U.S. 447 (1923); *United States v. Richardson*, 418 U.S. 166 (1947).
42. *Brown v. Board of Education of Topeka*, 347 U.S. 483 (1954).
43. *Baker v. Carr*, 369 U.S. 186 (1962).
44. See Louise Weinberg, "A New Judicial Federalism?" *Daedalus* (Winter 1978): pp. 129–141.
45. Quoted in Abraham, *The Judicial Process*, p. 330.

46. Carolyn D. Richmond, "The Rehnquist Court: What Is in Store for Constitutional Precedent?" *New York Law Review* 39 (1994): p. 511.
47. *Colegrove v. Green*, 328 U.S. 549 (1946).
48. The Court abandoned the "political question" doctrine in *Baker v. Carr*, 369 U.S. 186 (1962), and began to change congressional-district apportionment in *Wesberry v. Sanders*, 376 U.S. 1 (1964).
49. Donald L. Horowitz, *The Courts and Social Policy* (Washington, D.C.: Brookings Institution, 1977), p. 6.
50. *Gates v. Collier*, 349 F. Supp. 881 (1972).
51. *Lau v. Nichols*, 414 U.S. 563 (1974).
52. *Abington School District v. Schempp*, 374 U.S. 203 (1963).
53. Robert H. Birkby, "The Supreme Court and the Bible Belt," *Midwest Journal of Political Science* (1966): p. 3.
54. Cass R. Sunstein, "Impeaching the President," *University of Pennsylvania Law Review* 147 (1998): p. 279.
55. *United States v. Butler*, 297 U.S. (1936).
56. *Ex parte McCardle*, 74 U.S. 506 (1869)
57. Walter F. Murphy, *Congress and the Court* (Chicago: University of Chicago Press, 1962); and C. Herman Pritchett, *Congress Versus the Supreme Court* (Minneapolis: University of Minnesota Press,1961).
58. Gregory A. Caldeira, "Neither the Purse nor the Sword: Dynamics of Public Confidence in the U.S. Supreme Court," *American Political Science Review* 80 (1986): pp. 1209–1226. See also Joseph T. Tannenhaus and Walter F. Murphy, "Patterns of Public Support for the Supreme Court: A Panel Study," *Journal of Politics* 43 (1981): pp. 24–39.

Chapter 13

1. Barack Obama, speech at Jefferson-Jackson dinner, Des Moines, Iowa, November 10, 2007, available at www.washingtonpost.com/wp-dyn/content/article/2008/12/17/AR2008121703661.html; John McCain, speech at Republican National Convention, Minneapolis, Minnesota, September 4, 2008, available at http://elections.nytimes.com/2008/president/conventions/videos/20080904_MCCAIN_SPEECH.html.
2. Lydia Saad, "More Americans Still Prioritize Economy Over Environment," Princeton, NJ, Gallup, April 3, 2013.
3. Environment: Gallup Historical Trends, available at www.gallup.com/poll/1615/Environment/aspx
4. Edwin E. Witte, *The Development of the Social Security Act* (Madison: University of Wisconsin Press, 1962); Martha Derthick, *Policymaking for Social Security* (Washington, D.C.: Brookings Institution Press, 1979).
5. Theodore Marmor, "Doctors, Politics, and Health Insurance for the Aged: The Enactment of Medicare," in *Cases in Contemporary American Government*, ed. Allan Sindler (Boston: Little, Brown, 1969).
6. Washington Post Staff, *Landmark: The Inside Story of America's New Health Care Law*

and *What It Means for All of Us* (New York: Public Affairs, 2010).
7. *National Federation of Independent Business Et Al v. Sebelius, Secretary of Health and Human Services, Et Al.*, 576 U.S. (2012).
8. Richard P. Nathan, "America's Health Care Cost Crisis and What to Do About It," Rockefeller Institute, March 2013, available at www.rockinst.org.
9. Sarah Kliff and Dan Keating, "One Hospital Charges $8,000—Another $38,000," *The Washington Post*, May 8, 2013.
10. Ibid.
11. Ibid.
12. *2012 Annual Report of the Boards of Trustees of the Federal Hospital Insurance and Federal Supplementary Medical Insurance Trust Funds*: 28, available at www.cms.gov.
13. *The Values We Live By: What Americans Want from Welfare Reform* (New York: Public Agenda Foundation, 1996): p. 42.
14. Ryan Lizza, "As the World Burns," *New Yorker*, October 22, 2010.
15. David Vogel, *National Styles of Regulation* (Ithaca, NY: Cornell University Press, 1986): pp. 19–30.
16. R. Shep Melnick, *Regulation and the Courts: The Case of the Clean Air Act* (Washington, D.C.: Brookings Institution Press, 1983), ch. 9.
17. Pietro S. Nivola, *The Politics of Energy Conservation* (Washington, D.C.: Brookings Institution Press, 1986): pp. 11–12, 244–247.
18. Robert W. Crandall, "Pollution, Environmentalists, and the Coal Lobby," in *The Political Economy of Deregulation*, ed. Roger G. Noll and Bruce M. Own (Washington, D.C.: American Enterprise Institute, 1983): pp. 83–84; Crandall, *Controlling Industrial Pollution* (Washington, D.C.: American Enterprise Institute, 1983).
19. Bruce A. Ackerman and William T. Hassler, *Clear Coal/Dirty Air* (New Haven, CT.: Yale University Press, 1981).
20. Bill Chalmeides, "U.S. Acid Rain Regulations: Did They Work?," Huffington Post, May 5, 2012, available at http://www.huffingtonpost.com/bill-chameides/us-acid-rain-regulations_b_1507392.html
21. Rachel Carson, *Silent Spring* (New York: Houghton Mifflin, 1962).
22. Robert Dorfman, "Lessons from Pesticide Regulation," in *Reform of Environmental Regulation*, ed. Wesley A. Magat (Cambridge, MA: Ballinger, 1982): pp. 13–30.
23. Arthur Grube et al, *Pesticide Industry Sales and Usage 2006 and 2007: Market Estimates* (Washington, D.C.: U.S. Environmental Protection Agency, February 2011).

Chapter 14

1. Alexis de Tocqueville, *Democracy in America*, vol. 1, ed. Phillips Bradley (New York: Knopf, 1951), p. 235.
2. See Victor Davis Hanson, *Carnage and Culture* (New York: Anchor Books, 2002); and Hanson, *The Soul of Battle* (New York: Free Press, 1999).
3. Richard Lau, Thad A. Brown, and David O. Sears, "Self-Interest and Civilians'

Attitudes Toward the Vietnam War," *Public Opinion Quarterly* 42 (1978): pp. 464–481.
4. Edward S. Corwin, *The President: Office and Powers* (New York: New York University Press, 1940), p. 200.
5. Louis W. Koenig, *The Chief Executive*, 6th ed. (Fort Worth, TX: Harcourt Brace, 1992), p. 216.
6. Louis Fisher, *President and Congress* (New York: Free Press, 1972), p. 45; *United States v. Belmont*, 301 U.S. 324 (1937).
7. Arthur M. Schlesinger, Jr., *A Thousand Days: John F. Kennedy in the White House* (Boston: Houghton Mifflin, 1965), chs. 30, 31. Schlesinger, at p. 841, described Kennedy's actions as a "brilliantly controlled," "matchlessly calibrated" combination of "nerve and wisdom." His view of Nixon's actions was a good deal less charitable in *The Imperial Presidency* (Boston: Houghton Mifflin, 1974), ch. 7.
8. *Mitchell v. Laird*, 488 F.2d 611 (1973).
9. *Prize Cases*, 67 U.S. 635 (1863); *Mora v. McNamara*, 389 U.S. 934 (1964); *Massachusetts v. Laird*, 400 U.S. 886 (1970).
10. *Dames and Moore v. Regan*, 435 U.S. 654 (1981).
11. *Korematsu v. United States*, 323 U.S. 214 (1944).
12. *Youngstown Sheet & Tube Co. v. Sawyer*, 343 U.S. 579 (1952).
13. *Immigration and Naturalization Service v. Chadha*, 103 S. Ct. 2764 (1983).
14. Robert S. Erikson and Norman R. Luttbeg, *American Public Opinion* (New York: Wiley, 1973), pp. 50–51.
15. William R. Caspary, "The 'Mood Theory': A Study of Public Opinion and Foreign Policy," *American Political Science Review* 64 (June 1970): pp. 536–547.
16. Erikson and Luttbeg, *American Public Opinion*, p. 52.
17. John E. Mueller, *War, Presidents, and Public Opinion* (New York: Wiley, 1973), p. 110.
18. Ibid., p. 112.
19. Milton J. Rosenberg, Sidney Verba, and Philip E. Converse, *Vietnam and the Silent Majority* (New York: Harper and Row, 1970), pp. 26–27.
20. Erikson and Luttbeg, *American Public Opinion*, p. 155.
21. John R. Oneal and Brad Lian, "Presidents, the Use of Military Force, and Public Opinion," Working Papers in International Security I–92–8, Hoover Institution, Stanford, CA (July 1992).
22. Mueller, *War, Presidents, and Public Opinion*, 45–47, p. 169.
23. James Q. Wilson and Karlyn Bowman, "Defining the Peace Party," *The Public Interest* (Fall 2003): p. 69–78.
24. Jones, Jeffrey M. "Americans Approve of Military Action Against Libya, 47% to 37%." *Gallup Politics*. Last modified March 22, 2011.
25. Everett Carll Ladd, "Since World War II, Americans Have Persistently Looked Outward," *The Public Perspective* (August/September 1997): pp. 5–34.

26. Howard Schuman, "Two Sources of Antiwar Sentiment in America," *American Journal of Sociology* 78 (1973): pp. 513–536.

27. Philip E. Converse, Warren E. Miller, Jerrold G. Rusk, and Arthur C. Wolfe, "Continuity and Change in American Politics," *American Political Science Review* 63 (December 1969): pp. 1083–1105; John P. Robinson, "Public Reaction to Political Protest: Chicago, 1968," *Public Opinion Quarterly* 34 (Spring 1970): pp. 1–9.

28. James D. Wright, "Life, Time, and the Fortunes of War," *Transaction* 9 (January 1972).

29. John E. Rielly, *American Public Opinion and U.S. Foreign Policy, 1999* (Chicago: Chicago Council on Foreign Relations, 1999).

30. X, "The Sources of Soviet Conduct," *Foreign Affairs* 25 (July 1947): p. 566.

31. Walter Lippmann, *The Cold War* (New York: Harper Brothers, 1947).

32. Erikson and Luttbeg, *American Public Opinion*, p. 52.

33. Mueller, *War, Presidents, and Public Opinion*, p. 40.

34. Michael Roskin, "From Pearl Harbor to Vietnam: Shifting Generational Paradigms and Foreign Policy," *Political Science Quarterly* 89 (Fall 1974): p. 567.

35. Frank L. Klingberg, "The Historical Alternation of Moods in American Foreign Policy," *World Politics* 4 (1952): pp. 239–273.

36. Roskin, "From Pearl Harbor," p. 567.

37. *American Public Opinion and U.S. Foreign Policy, 1987* (Chicago: Chicago Council on Foreign Relations, 1987), p. 33.

38. Carl M. Cannon, "Comment," in Pietro S. Nivola and David W. Brady, eds., *Red and Blue Nation?* (Washington, D.C.: Brookings Institution, 2006), p. 168; and Cannon, "Administration: A New Era of Partisan War," *National Journal*, March 18, 2006.

39. For a lively debate over the extent of political polarization, see Morris Fiorina and Matthew S. Levendusky, "Disconnected: The Political Class Versus the People"; Alan I. Abramowitz, "Comment"; and Gary C. Jacobson, "Comment,"—all in Nivola and Brady, op. cit.

40. Commission on the Intelligence Capabilities of the United States Regarding Weapons of Mass Destruction, *Report to the President* (Washington, D.C.: Government Printing Office, 2005), pp. 243–249.

41. Quoted in Robert J. Art, *The TFX Decision* (Boston: Little, Brown, 1968), p. 126.

42. *The National Security Strategy of the United States of America*, September 2002, cover letter and p. 6.

43. The vote on the Persian Gulf War as reported in *Congress and the Nation*, vol. 8 (Washington, D.C.: Congressional Quarterly Press, 1993), p. 310; the vote on the war in Iraq as reported in *The New York Times*, October 12, 2002, A11.

44. There were no congressional votes on our military efforts in Bosnia and Kosovo, but speeches supporting them were made by (among others) Democratic Senators Barbara Boxer, Carl Levin, and Paul Wellstone and Representative David Bonior; speeches opposing them were made by (among others) Republican Senators Don Nickles and John Warner and by Representatives Robert Barr and Dan Burton. In the vote on the invasion of Iraq, each group took the opposite position.

45. James Dobbins, et al., *America's Role in Nation Building* (Santa Monica, CA: RAND, 2003).

Chapter 15

1. Donald F. Kettl, "Heading for Disaster, "*Government Executive*, February 1, 2009.

2. Ibid.

3. Alexis de Tocqueville, *Democracy in America*, vol. 2, ed. Phillips Bradley (New York: Knopf, 1951), book 2, ch. 1.

Glossary

Activist An individual, usually outside government, who actively promotes a political party, philosophy, or issue he or she cares about.

Activist approach (judicial) The view that judges should discern the general principles underlying the Constitution and its often vague language and assess how best to apply them in contemporary circumstances, in some cases with the guidance of moral or economic philosophy.

Affirmative action The requirement, imposed by law or administrative regulation, that an organization (business firm, government agency, labor union, school, or college) take positive steps to increase the number or proportion of women, blacks, or other minorities in its membership.

Amicus curiae A Latin term meaning "a friend of the court." Refers to interested groups or individuals, not directly involved in a suit, who may file legal briefs or make oral arguments in support of one side.

Antifederalists Opponents of a strong central government who campaigned against ratification of the Constitution in favor of a confederation of largely independent states. Antifederalists successfully marshaled public support for a federal bill of rights. After ratification, they formed a political party to support states' rights. *See also* Federalists.

Appropriation A legislative grant of money to finance a government program. *See also* Authorization legislation.

Articles of Confederation A constitution drafted by the newly independent states in 1777 and ratified in 1781. It created a weak national government that could not levy taxes or regulate commerce. In 1789, it was replaced by our current constitution to create a stronger national government.

Australian ballot A government-printed ballot of uniform size and shape to be cast in secret that was adopted by many states around 1890 to reduce the voting fraud associated with party-printed ballots cast in public.

Authorization legislation Legislative permission to begin or continue a government program or agency. An authorization bill may grant permission to spend a certain sum of money, but that money does not ordinarily become available unless it is also appropriated. Authorizations may be annual, multiyear, or permanent. *See also* Appropriation.

Benefit Any satisfaction, monetary or nonmonetary, that people believe they will enjoy if a policy is adopted.

Bicameral legislature A lawmaking body made up of two chambers or parts. The U.S. Congress is a bicameral legislature composed of a Senate and a House of Representatives.

Bill of Rights The first ten amendments to the U.S. Constitution, containing a list of individual rights and liberties, such as freedom of speech, religion, and the press.

Blanket primary A primary election that permits all voters, regardless of party, to choose candidates. A Democratic voter, for example, can vote in a blanket primary for both Democratic and Republican candidates for nomination.

Block grant Grant of money from the federal government to states for programs in certain general areas rather than for specific kinds of programs. *See also* Categorical grant; Grants-in-aid.

Brief A legal document prepared by an attorney representing a party before a court. The document sets forth the facts of the case, summarizes the law, gives the arguments for its side, and discusses other relevant cases.

Budget deficit A situation in which the government spends more money than it takes in from taxes and fees.

Budget resolution A proposal submitted by the House and Senate budget committees to their respective chambers recommending a total budget ceiling and a ceiling for each of several spending areas (such as health or defense) for the current fiscal year. These budget resolutions are intended to guide the work of each legislative committee as it decides what to spend in its area.

Budget surplus A situation in which the government takes in more money than it spends.

Bureaucracy A large, complex organization composed of appointed officials. The departments and agencies of the US government make up the federal bureaucracy.

Cabinet By custom, the cabinet includes the heads of the 15 major executive departments.

Categorical grant A federal grant for a specific purpose defined by federal law: to build an airport, for example, or to make welfare payments to low-income mothers. Such grants usually require that the state or locality put up money to "match" some part of the federal grant, though the amount of matching funds can be quite small. *See also* Block grants; Grants-in-aid.

Caucus (congressional) An association of members of Congress created to advocate a political ideology or a regional, ethnic, or economic interest.

Checks and balances The power of the legislative, executive, and judicial branches of government to block some acts by the other two branches. *See also* Separation of powers.

Circular structure A method of organizing a president's staff whereby several presidential assistants report directly to the president.

Civil liberties Rights—chiefly, rights to be free of government interference—accorded to an individual by the Constitution: free speech, free press, and so on.

Civil rights The rights of citizens to vote, to receive equal treatment before the law, and to share equally with other citizens the benefits of public facilities (such as schools).

Class-action suit A case brought into court by a person on behalf of not only himself or herself but all other persons in the country under similar circumstances. For example, in *Brown v. Board of Education of Topeka*, the Court decided that not only Linda Brown but all others similarly situated had the right to attend a local public school of their choice without regard to race.

Client politics A policy under which some small group receives the benefits and the public at large endures the costs.

Closed primary A primary election limited to registered party members. Prevents members of other parties from crossing over to influence the nomination of an opposing party's candidate. *See also* Open primary; Primary election.

Closed rule An order from the House Rules Committee in the House of Representatives that sets a time limit on debate and forbids a particular bill from being amended on the legislative floor.

Cloture resolution A rule used by the Senate to end or limit debate. Designed to prevent "talking a bill to death" by filibuster. To pass in the Senate, three-fifths of the entire Senate membership (or 60 senators) must vote for it. *See also* Filibuster.

Cluster structure A system for organizing the White House in which a group of subordinates and committees all report to the president directly.

Coalition An alliance among different interest groups (factions) or parties to achieve some political goal. An example is the coalition sometimes formed between Republicans and conservative Democrats.

Committee clearance The ability of a congressional committee to review and approve certain agency decisions in advance and without passing a law. Such approval is not legally binding on the agency, but few agency heads will ignore the expressed wishes of committees.

Competitive service The government offices to which people are appointed on grounds of merit as ascertained by a written examination or by having met certain selection criteria (such as training, educational attainments, or prior experience). *See also* Excepted service.

Concurrent resolution An expression of congressional opinion without the force of law that requires the approval of both the House and Senate but not of the president. Used to settle housekeeping and procedural matters that affect both houses. *See also* Joint resolution; Simple resolution.

Concurring opinion A Supreme Court opinion by one or more justices who agree with the majority's conclusion but for different reasons. *See also* Opinion of the Court; Dissenting opinion.

Conditions of aid Federal rules attached to the grants that states receive. States must agree to abide by these rules to receive the grant.

Confederation or confederal system A political system in which states or regional governments retain ultimate authority except for those powers that they expressly delegate to a central government. The United States was a confederation from 1776 to 1787 under the Articles of Confederation. *See also* Federal system; Federalism; Unitary system, p.85.

Conference committees *See* Joint committees.

Congress A national legislature composed of elected representatives who do not choose the chief executive (typically, a president).

Congressional campaign committee A party committee in Congress that provides funds to members who are running for reelection or to would-be members running for an open seat or challenging a candidate from the opposition party.

Conservative In general, a person who favors more limited and local government, less government regulation of markets, more social conformity to traditional norms and values, and tougher policies toward criminals. *See also* Liberal.

Constitutional court A federal court exercising the judicial powers found in Article III of the Constitution and whose judges are given constitutional protection: they may not be fired (they serve during "good behavior"), nor may their salaries be reduced while they are in office. The most important constitutional courts are the Supreme Court, the 94 district courts, and the courts of appeals (1 in each of 11 regions plus 1 in the District of Columbia).

Continuing resolution A congressional enactment that provides funds to continue government operations in the absence of an agreed-upon budget.

Cost Any burden, monetary or nonmonetary, that some people must bear, or think they must bear, if a policy is adopted.

Courts of appeals The federal courts with authority to review decisions by federal district courts, regulatory commissions, and certain other federal courts. Such courts have no original jurisdiction; they can hear only appeals. There are a total of 12 courts of appeals in the United States and its territories plus 1 for a nationwide circuit. *See also* Constitutional court; District courts; Federal-question cases.

Critical or realigning periods Periods during which a sharp, lasting shift occurs in the popular coalition supporting one or both parties. The issues that separate the two parties change, and so the kinds of voters supporting each party change.

Cue (political) A signal telling a congressional representative what values (for example, liberal or conservative) are at stake in a vote—who is for and who is against a proposal—and how that issue fits into his or her own set of political beliefs or party agenda.

Deficit The annual excess of government spending over government revenue.

Democracy Political system where the people rule.

Direct democracy Political system in which most citizens make policy, as in a town meeting.

Discharge petition A device by which any member of the House, after a committee has had a bill for 30 days, may petition to have it brought to the floor. If a majority of the members agree, the bill is discharged from the committee. The discharge petition was designed to prevent a committee from killing a bill by delaying it for too long.

Discretionary authority The extent to which appointed bureaucrats can choose courses of action and make policies that are not spelled out in advance by laws.

Dissenting opinion A Supreme Court opinion by one or more justices in the minority to explain the minority's disagreement with the Court's ruling. *See also* Opinion of the Court; Concurring opinion.

District courts The lowest federal courts where federal cases begin. They are the only federal courts where trials are held. There are a total of 94 district courts in the United States and its territories. *See also* Courts of appeals; Constitutional court; Federal-question cases.

Diversity cases Cases involving citizens of different states over which the federal courts have jurisdiction because at least $75,000 is at stake. *See also* Federal-question cases.

Division vote A congressional voting procedure in which members stand and are counted. *See also* Voice vote; Teller vote; Roll call.

Double tracking Setting aside a bill against which one or more senators are filibustering so that other legislation can be voted on.

Dual federalism A constitutional theory that the national government and the state governments each have defined areas of authority, especially over commerce.

Due-process clause Protection against arbitrary deprivation of life, liberty, or property as guaranteed in the Fifth and Fourteenth Amendments.

Elite (political) An identifiable group of persons who possess a disproportionate share of some valued resource—such as money or political power.

Entrepreneurial politics A policy under which society as a whole benefits while some small group pays the costs. *See also* Policy entrepreneur.

Equality of opportunities A view that it is wrong to use race or sex either to discriminate against or give preferential treatment to blacks or women. *See also* Reverse discrimination.

Equal protection clause The provision in the Fourteenth Amendment to the Constitution guaranteeing that no state shall "deny to any person" the "equal protection of the laws."

Establishment clause A clause in the First Amendment to the Constitution stating that Congress shall make no law "respecting an establishment of religion."

Excepted service Provision for appointing federal offices without going through the competitive service. *See also* Competitive service.

Exclusionary rule A rule that holds that evidence gathered in violation of the Constitution cannot be used in a trial. The rule has been used to implement two provisions of the Bill of Rights—the right to be free from unreasonable searches or seizures (Fourth Amendment) and the right not to be compelled to give evidence against oneself (Fifth Amendment). *See also* Good-faith exception.

Executive privilege A presidential claim that he may withhold certain information from Congress.

Faction According to James Madison, a group of people who seek to influence public policy in ways contrary to the public good.

Federalism A political system in which ultimate authority is shared between a central government and state or regional governments. *See also* Confederation; Federal system; Unitary system, p.85.

Federalist Papers A series of 85 essays written by Alexander Hamilton, James Madison, and John Jay (all using the name "Publius") that were published in New York newspapers in 1787–1788 to convince New Yorkers to adopt the newly proposed Constitution. They are classics of American constitutional and political thought.

Federalists Supporters of a stronger central government who advocated ratification of the Constitution. After ratification, they founded a political party supporting a strong executive and Alexander Hamilton's economic policies. *See also* Antifederalists.

Federal money Money raised to support the campaign of a candidate for federal office. Amounts regulated by federal law.

Federal-question cases Cases concerning the Constitution, federal law, or treaties over which the federal courts have jurisdiction as described in the Constitution. *See also* Diversity cases.

Fee shifting A law or rule that allows the plaintiff (the party that initiates the lawsuit) to collect its legal costs from the defendant if the defendant loses.

Filibuster An attempt to defeat a bill in the Senate by talking indefinitely, thus preventing the Senate from taking action on it. From the Spanish *filibustero*, which means a "freebooter," a military adventurer.

Fiscal policy The taxing and spending system of the government.

527s Organizations that raise money for political campaigns that are not (yet) regulated by campaign finance laws.

Franking privilege The ability of members of Congress to mail letters to their constituents free of charge by substituting their facsimile signature (frank) for postage.

Free-exercise clause A clause in the First Amendment to the Constitution stating that Congress shall make no law prohibiting the "free exercise" of religion.

Gender gap Differences in the political views and voting behavior of men and women.

General election An election used to fill an elective office. *See also* Primary election.

Good-faith exception Admission at a trial of evidence that is gathered in violation of the Constitution if the violation results from a technical or minor error. *See also* Exclusionary rule.

Government The institution that, with a monopoly on the lawful use of power, can make decisions binding the whole society.

Grants-in-aid Federal funds provided to states and localities. Grants-in-aid are typically provided for airports, highways, education, and major welfare services. *See also* Categorical grant; Block grants.

Great or Connecticut Compromise A compromise at the Constitutional Convention in 1787 that reconciled the interests of small and large states by allowing the former to predominate in the Senate and the latter in the House. Under the agreement, each state received two representatives in the Senate, regardless of size, but was allotted representatives on the basis of population in the House.

Gross domestic product The total amount of goods and services produced in a country.

Ideological party A party that values principled stands on issues above all else, including winning. It claims to have a comprehensive view of American society and government radically different from that of the established parties.

Impeachment An accusation against a high federal official charging him or her with "treason, bribery, or other high crimes and misdemeanors." An impeachment requires a majority vote in the House of Representatives. To be removed from office, the impeached official must be tried before the Senate and convicted by a vote of two-thirds of the members present.

Incorporation A doctrine whereby the Supreme Court incorporates—that is, includes—many parts of the Bill of Rights into restrictions on state government actions.

Independent expenditures Political money raised and spent by an organization on behalf of a candidate done without direction of or coordination with the candidate.

In forma pauperis A procedure whereby a poor person can file and be heard in court as a pauper, free of charge.

Interest group An organization of people, or a "letterhead" organization, sharing a common interest or goal that seeks to influence the making of public policy.

Interest group politics A policy under which one small group bears the costs and another small group receives the benefits. *See also* Majoritarian politics.

Iron triangle A close relationship between an agency, a congressional committee, and an interest group that often becomes a mutually advantageous alliance. *See also* Client politics.

Issue network A loose collection of leaders, interest groups, bureaucratic agencies, and congressional committees interested in some public policy.

Joint committees Committees on which both representatives and senators serve. An especially important kind of joint committee is the *conference committee* made up of representatives and senators appointed to resolve differences in the Senate and House versions of the same piece of legislation before final passage. *See also* Select committees; Standing committees.

Joint resolution A formal expression of congressional opinion that must be approved by both houses of Congress and by the president. Joint resolutions proposing a constitutional amendment are not signed by the president. *See also* Concurrent resolution; Simple resolution.

Judicial activism The view that the federal courts must correct injustices when the other branches of the federal government, or the states, refuse to do so.

Judicial review The power of the courts to declare acts of the legislature and of the executive to be unconstitutional and, hence, null and void.

Legislative court A court that is created by Congress for some specialized purpose and staffed with judges who do not enjoy the protection of Article III of the Constitution. Legislative courts include the Court of Military Appeals and the territorial courts.

Legislative veto The rejection of a presidential or administrative-agency action by a vote of one or both houses of Congress without the consent of the president. In 1983, the Supreme Court declared the legislative veto to be unconstitutional.

Legitimate Political authority conferred by public opinion.

Libel Injurious written statements about another person.

Liberal In general, a person who favors a more active federal government for regulating business, supporting social welfare, and protecting minority rights, but who prefers less regulation of private social conduct. *See also* Conservative.

Line-item veto The power of an executive to veto some provisions in an appropriations bill while approving others. The president does not have the right to exercise a line-item veto and must approve or reject an entire appropriations bill. *See also* Pocket veto; Veto message.

Lobbyists Persons who try to influence legislation on behalf of an interest group.

Majoritarian politics A policy from which almost everybody benefits (or thinks they benefit) and for which almost everybody pays. *See also* Interest group politics.

Majority leader The legislative leader elected by party members holding the majority of seats in the House of Representatives or the Senate. *See also* Minority leader.

Mandates Rules imposed by the federal government on the states to require that the states pay the costs of certain nationally defined programs.

Matching funds In presidential elections, money given by the national government to match, under certain conditions, money raised by each candidate.

Material incentives Benefits that have monetary value, including money, gifts, services, or discounts received as a result of one's membership in an organization.

Minority leader The legislative leader elected by party members holding a minority of seats in the House of Representatives or the Senate. *See also* Majority leader.

Motor-voter law A bill passed by Congress in 1993 to make it easier for Americans to register to vote. The law, which went into effect in 1995, requires states to allow voter registration by mail, when one applies for a driver's license, and at state offices that serve the disabled or poor.

Name-request job A job to be filled by a person whom a government agency has identified by name.

National chairman A paid, full-time manager of a party's day-to-day work who is elected by the national committee.

National committee A committee of delegates from each state and territory that runs party affairs between national conventions.

National convention A meeting of party delegates elected in state primaries, caucuses, or conventions that is held every four years. Its primary purpose is to nominate presidential and vice-presidential candidates and to ratify a campaign platform.

National debt The total amount of money that the government has spent over its history that exceeds the total amount of money that it has taken in through taxes.

Necessary-and-proper clause or elastic clause The final paragraph of Article 1, section 8, of the Constitution, which authorizes Congress to pass all laws "necessary and proper" to carry out the enumerated powers. Sometimes called the "elastic clause" because of the flexibility that it provides to Congress.

New class That part of the middle class that has college and postgraduate degrees and works in occupations that involve using symbols (such as writers and teachers). It tends to have liberal views.

New Deal coalition The different, sometimes opposed voters—southern whites, urban blacks, union workers, and intellectuals—whom Franklin D. Roosevelt made part of the Democratic party in the 1930s and 1940s.

Nullification A theory first advanced by James Madison and Thomas Jefferson that the states had the right to "nullify" (that is, declare null and void) a federal law that, in the states' opinion, violated the Constitution. The theory was revived by John C. Calhoun of South Carolina in opposition to federal efforts to restrict slavery. The North's victory in the Civil War determined once and for all that the federal union is indissoluble and that states cannot declare acts of Congress unconstitutional, a view later confirmed by the Supreme Court.

Office-bloc ballot A ballot listing all candidates for a given office under the name of that office; also called a "Massachusetts" ballot. *See also* Party-column ballot.

Open primary A primary election that permits voters to choose on election day the party primary in which they wish to vote. They may vote for candidates of only one party. *See also* Blanket primary; Closed primary; Primary election.

Open rule An order from the House Rules Committee in the House of Representatives that permits a bill to be amended on the legislative floor. *See also* Closed rule; Restrictive rule.

Opinion of the Court A Supreme Court opinion written by one or more justices in the majority to explain the decision in a case. *See also* Concurring opinion; Dissenting opinion.

Parliament A national legislature composed of elected representatives who choose the chief executive (typically, the prime minister).

Parliamentary system A government that vests power in an elected legislature that chooses the chief executive.

Party-column ballot A ballot listing all candidates of a given party together under the name of that party; also called an "Indiana" ballot. *See also* Office-bloc ballot.

Party polarization A vote in which a majority of Democratic legislators oppose a majority of Republican legislators and vice versa.

Party vote There are two measures of such voting. By the stricter measure, a party vote occurs when 90 percent or more of the Democrats in either house of Congress vote together against 90 percent or more of the Republicans. A looser measure counts as a party vote any case in which at least 50 percent of the Democrats vote together against at least 50 percent of the Republicans.

Per curiam opinion A brief, unsigned opinion issued by the Supreme Court to explain its ruling. *See also* Opinion of the Court.

Personal following The political support provided to a candidate on the basis of personal popularity and networks.

Pluralist theory (politics) A theory that competition among all affected interests shapes public policy.

Plurality system An electoral system, used in almost all American elections, in which the winner is the person who gets the most votes, even if he or she does not receive a majority of the votes.

Pocket veto One of two ways for a president to disapprove a bill sent to him by Congress. If the president does not sign the bill within 10 days of his receiving it, and Congress has adjourned within that time, the bill does not become law. *See also* Veto message; Line-item veto.

Police powers The authority of a government to safeguard and promote public order, safety, and morals.

Policy entrepreneur A political leader who has the ability to mobilize an otherwise uninterested majority into supporting a policy opposed by a well-organized group. *See also* Entrepreneurial politics.

Political action committee (PAC) A committee set up by and representing a corporation, labor union, or special interest group that raises and spends campaign contributions on behalf of one or more candidates or causes.

Political efficacy A citizen's sense that he or she can understand and influence politics.

Political ideology A coherent and consistent set of attitudes about who ought to rule and what policies ought to be adopted.

Political machine A party organization that recruits its members by dispensing *patronage*—tangible incentives such as money, political jobs, an opportunity to get favors from government—and that is characterized by a high degree of leadership control over member activity.

Political party A group that seeks to elect candidates to public office by supplying them with a label—a "party identification"—by which they are known to the electorate.

Political question An issue that the Supreme Court refuses to consider because it believes the Constitution has left it entirely to another branch to decide. Its view of such issues may change over time, however. For example, until the 1960s, the Court refused to hear cases about the size of congressional districts, no matter how unequal their populations. In 1962, however, it decided that it was authorized to review the constitutional implications of this issue.

Politics The management of conflict over who shall rule and what policies shall be made.

Poll A survey of public opinion. *See also* Random sample.

Power The ability to give or withhold support for a course of action.

Precedent A judicial rule that permits the court ruling settling an old case to settle a similar new one.

Presidential primary A special kind of primary used to pick delegates to the presidential nominating conventions of the major parties.

Presidential system A government that vests power in a separately elected president and legislature.

Primary election An election prior to the general election in which voters select the candidates who will run on each party's ticket. *See also* Closed primary; Open primary.

Prior restraint The traditional view of the press's free speech rights as expressed by William Blackstone, the great English jurist. According to this view, the press is guaranteed freedom from censorship—that is, rules telling it in advance what it can publish. After publication, however, the government can punish the press for material that is judged libelous or obscene.

Probable cause *See* Search warrant.

Proportional representation A voting system in which representatives in a legislature are chosen by the proportion of all votes each candidate (or each candidate's party) gets.

Prospective voters Voters who vote for a candidate because they favor his or her ideas for addressing issues after the election. (Prospective means "forward-looking.") *See also* Retrospective voters.

Public interest lobby A political organization, the stated goals of which will principally benefit nonmembers.

Public opinion How people think or feel about particular things.

Purposive incentive The benefit that comes from serving a cause or principle from which one does not personally benefit.

Pyramid structure A method of organizing a president's staff in which most presidential assistants report through a hierarchy to the president's chief of staff.

Random sample A sample selected in such a way that any member of the population being surveyed (for example, all adults or voters) has an equal chance of being interviewed. *See also* Poll.

Red tape Complex bureaucratic rules and procedures that must be followed to get something done.

Registered voters People who are registered to vote. Although almost all adult American citizens are theoretically eligible to vote, only those who have completed a registration form by the required date may do so.

Remedy A judicial order preventing or redressing a wrong or enforcing a right.

Representative democracy Political system in which policy is made by officials elected by the people.

Republic A form of democracy in which power is vested in representatives selected by means of popular competitive elections. *See also* Representative democracy.

Restrictive rule An order from the House Rules Committee in the House of Representatives that permits certain kinds of amendments but not others to be made to a bill on the legislative floor. *See also* Closed rule; Open rule.

Retrospective voters Voters who vote for or against the candidate or party in office because they like or dislike how things have gone in the recent past. (Retrospective means "backward-looking.") *See also* Prospective voters.

Reverse discrimination Using race or sex as a basis to give preferential treatment to some individuals. *See also* Equality of opportunities.

Riders Amendments on matters unrelated to a bill that are added to an important bill so that they will "ride" to passage through the Congress. When a bill has many riders, it is called a Christmas-tree bill.

Roll call vote A congressional voting procedure that consists of members answering "yea" or "nay" to their names. When roll calls were handled orally, it was a time-consuming process in the House. Since 1973, an electronic voting system permits each House member to record his or her vote and learn the total automatically. *See also* Voice vote; Division vote; Teller vote.

Runoff primary A second primary election held in some states when no candidate receives a majority of the votes in the first primary; the runoff is between the two candidates with the most votes. Runoff primaries are common in the South.

Sampling error The difference between the results of two surveys or samples. For example, if one random sample shows that 60 percent of all Americans like cats and another random sample taken at the same time shows that 65 percent do, the sampling error is 5 percent.

Search warrant An order from a judge authorizing the search of a place; the order must describe what is to be searched and seized, and the judge can issue it only if he or she is persuaded by the police that good reason (probable cause) exists that a crime has been committed and that the evidence bearing on the crime will be found at a certain location.

Selective attention Paying attention only to those parts of a newspaper or broadcast story with which one agrees. Studies suggest that this is how people view political ads on television.

Senatorial courtesy A tradition that makes it impossible to confirm a presidential nominee for office if a senator files a personal objection.

Separate-but-equal doctrine The doctrine, established in *Plessy v. Fergusson* (1896), in which the Supreme Court ruled that a state could provide "separate but equal" facilities for blacks.

Separation of powers A principle of American government whereby constitutional authority is shared by three separate branches of government—the legislative, the executive, and the judicial. *See also* Checks and balances.

Shays's Rebellion A rebellion in 1787 led by Daniel Shays and other ex–Revolutionary War soldiers and officers to prevent foreclosures of farms as a result of high interest rates and taxes. The revolt highlighted the weaknesses of the Confederation and bolstered support for a stronger national government.

Signing statements Written comments by the president about a bill he has just signed. Those that raise constitutional questions are controversial.

Simple resolution An expression of opinion either in the House of Representatives or the Senate to settle housekeeping or procedural matters in either body. Such expressions are not signed by the president and do not have the force of law. *See also* Concurrent resolution; Joint resolution.

Single-member districts Legislative districts from which one representative is chosen.

Soft money Money raised by political parties for activities other than directly supporting a federal candidate.

Solidarity An incentive that relies on friendship or sociability.

Solidary incentives The social rewards that lead people to join local or state political organizations. People who find politics fun and want to meet others who share their interests are said to respond to solidary incentives.

Sovereign immunity A doctrine that a citizen cannot sue the government without its consent. By statute Congress has given its consent for the government to be sued in many cases involving a dispute over a contract or damage done as a result of negligence.

Sovereignty A governmental unit that has supreme authority and is accountable to no higher institution.

Speaker The presiding officer of the House of Representatives and the leader of his party in the House.

Split-tickets Voting for candidates of different parties for various offices in the same election. For example, voting for a Republican for senator and a Democrat for president. *See also* Straight-ticket voting.

Spots (campaign) Short television advertisements used to promote a candidate for government office.

Standing A legal concept establishing who is entitled to bring a lawsuit to court. For example, an individual must ordinarily show personal harm in order to acquire standing and be heard in court.

Standing committees Permanently established legislative committees that consider and are responsible for legislation within certain subject areas. Examples are the House Ways and Means Committee and the Senate Judiciary Committee. *See also* Select committees; Joint committees.

Stare decisis A Latin term meaning "let the decision stand." The practice of basing judicial decisions on precedents established in similar cases decided in the past.

Straight-ticket voting Voting for candidates who are all of the same party. For example, voting for Republican candidates for senator, representative, and president. *See also* Split-ticket voting.

Strict constructionist approach (judicial) The view that judges should decide cases on the basis of the language of the Constitution.

Strict scrutiny The standard by which the Supreme Court judges classifications based on race. To be accepted, such a classification must be closely related to a "compelling" public purpose.

Suspect classification Classifications of people on the basis of their race and ethnicity. The courts have ruled that laws classifying people on these grounds will be subject to "strict scrutiny."

Symbolic speech An act that conveys a political message, such as burning a draft card to protest the draft.

Traditional middle class That part of the middle class that has jobs in business or farming and tends to have conservative views.

Trial balloon Information provided to the media by an anonymous public official as a way of testing the public reaction to a possible policy or appointment.

Trust funds Funds for government programs that are collected and spent outside the regular government budget; the amounts are determined by preexisting law rather than by annual appropriations. The Social Security trust fund is the largest of these. *See also* Appropriation.

Unicameral legislature A lawmaking body with only one chamber, as in Nebraska.

Veto Literally, "I forbid"; it refers to the power of a president to disapprove a bill. It may be overriden by a two-thirds vote of each house of Congress.

Veto message One of two ways for a president to disapprove a bill sent to him by Congress. The veto message must be sent to Congress within 10 days after the president receives it. *See also* Pocket veto; Line-item veto.

Visual (campaign) A campaign activity that appears on a television news broadcast. *See also* Spots.

Voting-age population (VAP) The citizens who are eligible to vote after reaching a minimum age requirement. In the United States, a citizen must be at least 18 years old in order to vote.

Voting-eligible population (VEP) The VAP less aliens and felons.

Wall of separation A Supreme Court interpretation of the Establishment clause in the First Amendment that prevents government involvement with religion, even on a nonpreferential basis.

Whip A senator or representative who helps the party leader stay informed about what party members are thinking, rounds up members when important votes are to be taken, and attempts to keep a nose count on how the voting on controversial issues is likely to go.

Writ of certiorari A Latin term meaning "made more certain." An order issued by a higher court to a lower court to send up the record of a case for review. Most cases reach the Supreme Court through the writ of certiorari, issued when at least four of the nine justices feel that the case should be reviewed.

Index